MENACHEM
BEGIN

MENACHEM BEGIN

A Life

AVI SHILON

Translated from the Hebrew by
Danielle Zilberberg & Yoram Sharett

Yale
UNIVERSITY PRESS
NEW HAVEN & LONDON

Published with assistance from the foundation established in memory of Amasa Stone Mather of the Class of 1907, Yale College.

Originally published in Hebrew as *Begin, 1913–1992* by Am Oved Publishers Ltd 2007. Copyright © by Avi Shilon and Am Oved Publishers Ltd 2007. English translation copyright © 2012 by Avi Shilon and Am Oved Publishers Ltd. Published by arrangement with the Proprietors.
All rights reserved.
This book may not be reproduced, in whole or in part, including illustrations, in any form (beyond that copying permitted by Sections 107 and 108 of the U.S. Copyright Law and except by reviewers for the public press), without written permission from the publishers.

Yale University Press books may be purchased in quantity for educational, business, or promotional use. For information, please e-mail sales.press@yale.edu (U.S. office) or sales@yaleup.co.uk (U.K. office).

Designed by Lindsey Voskowsky.
Set in Janson type by Westchester Book Group.

Library of Congress Cataloging-in-Publication Data

Shilon, Avi.
  [Begin. English]
  Menachem Begin : a life / Avi Shilon ; translated from the Hebrew by Danielle Zilberberg and Yoram Sharett.
      p. cm.
  Includes bibliographical references and index.
  ISBN 978-0-300-16235-6 (clothbound : alk. paper)
  1. Begin, Menachem, 1913–1992. 2. Revisionist Zionists—Israel—Biography.
  3. Prime ministers—Israel—Biography. 4. Israel—Politics and government—
  20th century. I. Title.
  DS126.6.B33S5413 2012
  956.9405'4092—dc23
  [B]   2012012189

A catalogue record for this book is available from the British Library.

CONTENTS

PREFACE vii

ACKNOWLEDGMENTS xi

ONE Political Talent 1

TWO A Commander's Getaway 25

THREE Going Underground 39

FOUR Declaration of Rebellion 48

FIVE A Bomb in the Heart of the Empire 81

SIX Jubilation and Disappointment 106

SEVEN Rejected and Outcast 146

EIGHT Be Killed but Do Not Transgress 166

NINE Buds of Legitimacy 184

TEN The Breakthrough 199

ELEVEN Once More a Rebel 220

TWELVE	Against Expectations	233
THIRTEEN	God, You Have Chosen Us to Rule	248
FOURTEEN	No More War	259
FIFTEEN	Deterioration	314
SIXTEEN	The Begin Doctrine	335
SEVENTEEN	King of Israel	348
EIGHTEEN	"There Will Be Not a Single Katyusha"	363
NINETEEN	The Downfall	408
TWENTY	Self-Flagellation	424
TWENTY-ONE	"Sharon Was Afraid of Me"	436

EPILOGUE 447

NOTES 453

BIBLIOGRAPHY 521

INDEX 529

PREFACE

The power of the Menachem Begin name became apparent to me during a visit to the family home of my best friend from high school. On television Yitzhak Shamir, then prime minister, was being interviewed as part of a report on the preparations for the general elections of 1988. I remember the interviewer asking him if he consulted with Begin.

"Say yes, say yes!" my friend's father shouted excitedly at the small screen. "Admit that you regularly confer with Begin!"

I could not understand why it was so important to hear that Begin—the same Menachem Begin who had withdrawn from the world and shut himself up in his apartment—was still active behind the scenes. What was the meaning of the passionate feelings that the present-yet-absent leader still elicited from many Israelis?

From then on, my curiosity over his seemingly magical impact continued to grow.

While pursuing my Master's studies in Jewish history, I realized that no one had yet written a comprehensive biography about Begin in Hebrew. The reasons for this varied; they could be social or political or owing to rules relating to research and the use of government archives. I therefore decided to rise to the challenge, with the help of Am Oved Publishing.

This book is the result of five years' worth of research and writing. I have tried to portray Begin and his work within the context of the historical developments described in all the sources to which I had access. When I first embarked upon my research, I was entirely free of any preconceptions—willing to accept or rule out certain data and to study Begin's admirers and enemies alike through a transparent, emotionless screen. Only when I had immersed myself in the archival documents, read testimonies, and met with his acquaintances did I understand just how very much the subject was still emotionally charged.

Writing a biography is hard work. The biographer must rummage and sift through masses of data and decide how best to provide the reader with tools with which to decipher the secrets of the subject's personality, views, feelings, and decisions. The temptation to present hard and fast conclusions is considerable. But Begin's personality was complex and the story of his life ill-suited to unequivocal conclusions. Throughout his life he appears to have borne the hallmarks of manic depression—or bipolar disorder, as it is now known—and some experts have indeed argued that he suffered from that condition. But I have resisted such speculation, and the psychological aspect is not the central motif of this book for two reasons: Begin was never diagnosed as suffering from bipolar disorder, and in my view, a person's deeds are a far better testimony of his character than any psychological analysis. In order to understand why he abruptly withdrew from public life the way he did—an action that piqued the curiosity of many, myself included—we cannot be content with the motives set out in the final chapter of this book but must delve more deeply into his life story from its very beginnings.

Above all, I have tried to describe Begin the person, to trace the roots of his hates, fanaticisms, and loves, to understand how he could be both petty and noble—all within the context of historical developments. To this end I consulted many testimonies, which by their very nature are subjective. At times, within an account that was intended to be complimentary, I saw criticism; on other occasions, I found compliments hidden within the criticism hurled at him by opponents. In the final chapters—dealing with the period of his second term in office as prime minister—I relied more upon the testimonies of close associates than on documents and transcripts, one of which, in any event, is still classified. This approach had both advantages and disadvantages: oral stories are often better at describing a person and his motives and feelings, but it meant relying on secondary sources.

Begin and his actions still invoke controversy and strong feelings. He was, and remains, a legend—a fact that has had an impact upon the testimonies of those involved and has made the task of deciphering the man and his enterprise all the more difficult. I hope that distancing myself emotionally and ideologically has helped me to cast an appropriate and true light upon the personal history of Menachem Begin, who was undoubtedly one of the most fascinating leaders of modern Israel.

ACKNOWLEDGMENTS

Over the years of my research and writing I have enjoyed working with some professionals who have contributed significantly to this book. I wish to thank, first and foremost, Professor Eli Shaltiel for his insights and remarks; Bina Pe'er, my meticulous language editor; Am Oved editor Nir Baram, who gave helpful advice from his experience as a writer; Yaron Sadan, the CEO of Am Oved Publishing, who supported me in the process of writing and translating; and my PhD mentor, Professor Giora Goldberg, who instilled confidence in me as to the final outcome of the text.

Thanks to Professor Yaakov Shavit for his advice on the first chapters; to minister Dan Meridor, who spent many hours in conversations with me; and to Shlomo Lev-Ami, who passed away in 2011 but had the chance to share his experiences with me as the last of the surviving figures who were part of the Etzel headquarters.

The translation process would not have been successful without the dedicated work of Danielle Zilberberg and Yoram Sharett, whose vast knowledge and expertise improved the English version. I also wish to thank my agent, Linda Langton, who believed in this book, and the editors at Yale University Press—Sarah Miller, Christina Tucker, and Bojana Ristich.

Finally, thanks to my devoted and beloved family.

This book is dedicated to my wife, Lior, the love of my life; without her all this would mean nothing.

ONE

POLITICAL TALENT

Ze'ev-Dov, a forty-four-year-old Zionist, froze as he gazed at his twenty-seven-year-old wife, Chasia, who was lying in a hospital bed staring at their newborn baby girl. It was the summer of 1909, at a hospital in Brisk (Brest-Litovsk). Ze'ev-Dov turned away from the young mother, attempting to hide his disappointment. After a silent moment he pulled himself together: "Let's do it anyway? Let's name her Herzliya?"

Chasia, her face pale and her hair tightly pulled back, refused. Despite her apparent weakness, her eyes were adamant. "We will wait for the next time," she said. Ze'ev-Dov relented, and the eldest daughter was named after her grandmother, Rachel. The local Zionist's dream to name his eldest son after the admired Jewish leader Theodor Herzl had dissipated.[1] Two years later, in 1911, when his second child was born, Ze'ev-Dov fulfilled his dream and named their son Herzl. The youngest child, born two years later, was Menachem, a name taken from the Haftarah (selections from the books of Prophets in the Old Testament), which Ze'ev-Dov and Chasia had read in synagogue a week before he was born.

Menachem's character was shaped within the confines of a home that blended Jewish tradition with the early buds of Zionism. For his father, Zionism was not merely an ideology; Ze'ev-Dov, who was fluent in four languages, earned his living from it, mostly by writing letters on behalf of the Jewish community in Brisk in an attempt to lobby local authorities. Supporting the community and promoting Zionist activities provided his daily bread as well as food for his soul. It was almost inevitable that Menachem's life developed along the single track it did. His dominant father's Zionist activities stood out in Brisk, a town that at the time had not been penetrated by modern secular and educated currents and whose main authority was still the famous rabbi Chaim Soloveitchik.[2] Soloveitchik feared the destruction of Jewish tradition and therefore opposed the stirrings of Jewish nationalism that had started to appear among the town's Jews.

Brest-Litovsk, known by the Jews as Brisk, was founded in the late ninth century. During the fourteenth and fifteenth centuries the town was a center for Lithuanian Jews.[3] In 1388 Witold, son of Kiaistot, the prince of Lithuania, granted the town's Jews autonomy over their own community and the right to purchase land. Until Prince Alexander Kazimierz ordered their deportation in 1495, the Jews of Brisk, who were mostly merchants, ruled the town's economy. Upon their expulsion the property they had accumulated was seized by the local authorities. Eight years later Jan Olbrecht, king of Poland, and his brother Alexander, prince of Lithuania, permitted the Jews to return to Brisk, and their property was returned to them, mainly because they were familiar with local business practices. In 1516 tax collector Michael Yosefovich was appointed head of the Lithuanian Jewish community.

Brisk, which was geographically situated between Russia and Poland, constantly changed hands between the two countries. In 1569 it was declared the capital of Lithuania. In 1595, during a division of Poland, the town was annexed to Russia. During the Chmelnitski Uprising, Ukrainian Cossacks who rebelled against the Polish authorities murdered thousands of Jews from the community and its surroundings, but the Poles did nothing to protect them.[4]

During the seventeenth century many new cities were built in Brisk's vicinity, so it slowly lost its standing as the region's commercial capital. In 1648 the local synagogue was shut down because it was unable to pay its taxes, an event that testifies to the difficulties with which the Jewish community struggled at the time.

During the second half of the eighteenth century the situation of the Brisk Jews took another turn for the worse, this time owing to the policies of King Stanislaus Poniatowski of Poland, who implemented the laws of the Russian empire during the reign of Catherine the Great in the Polish communities.

According to a population census conducted in Brisk in 1897, the town had a population of some forty thousand, among which were about thirty thousand Jews. In 1865, when Ze'ev-Dov was born (the eldest of nine children born to David-Eliezer, a wood merchant who had come to Brisk from Polsia in Belarus), most of the Jews earned a humble living in retail. At the time of the census the town ran a Jewish hospital and several Jewish schools. In 1921 the town was annexed to Poland; in 1940 the Soviet Union gained sovereignty over the area; a year later the Nazis occupied it; and in 1943 it was liberated by the Red Army.

Before his seventeenth birthday Ze'ev-Dov left home to discover the vast and tempting world outside his home town. He dreamt of studying medicine in Berlin, but his father did not support this endeavor, mostly because he had chosen him to inherit the family business. Ze'ev-Dov succumbed to his dominant father's wishes, and immediately upon his return to Brisk he began to learn his father's wood trade business. While working with his father, Ze'ev-Dov also studied at the yeshiva headed by Rabbi Chaim Soloveitchik.

Although he had come to terms with the fact that he would not study medicine, Ze'ev-Dov persisted in his attempts to discover his life's calling, and as a result he experienced many emotional upheavals. His first marriage ended months after his wedding—an uncommon occurrence in those days. The short-lived marriage was never fully discussed in his second marriage to Chasia Kossovski (who was referred to in Russian as "Raskashchicha," the storyteller). Chasia, who was seventeen years his junior, was also from a family of wood merchants from the rural region of Wolyn. Unlike her husband, she had never attempted to fulfill her dream of becoming an actress. Her main desire had been to play the role of Bar-Kokhba, a great historical military leader, but instead she settled into the role of wife and mother.[5]

Ze'ev-Dov struggled to adjust to the wood trade business but regularly joined his close friends, Ben Zion Neumark and Mordechai Scheinermann (Ariel Sharon's grandfather), at Zionist meetings.[6] His choice to go to such meetings was not made lightly, as Rabbi Soloveitchik, who still served as Brisk's supreme authority, opposed the Zionist movement. However, Ze'ev-Dov was not deterred by the rabbi's hostile comments about his newfound activity, and he even founded a self-defense organization whose weapons inventory, used only in sporadic training sessions, was stored in his house.

Until World War I Begin's family was considered wealthy. They lived in a spacious four-bedroom apartment run by two maids, one Polish and one Jewish. The Jewish maid was permitted to eat with the family at the dining room table, but the Polish maid had to dine in the kitchen.

The children saw nothing wrong with this custom, as they were taught to distinguish between Jews and Gentiles.[7]

After Ze'ev-Dov's younger brothers had grown up, his father yielded to his repeated requests to leave the wood trade business; in any case he did not excel in it. Ze'ev-Dov started to work as a clerk, particularly taking jobs in which he drafted official letters to institutions. Because he knew several languages, he was elected the town secretary. From this position he began to promote the Zionist network in Brisk, which he had jointly initiated, while also founding the people's synagogue, The Revival (Hatechiya), and the Hebrew gymnasium, Culture.

Brisk, with a large Hasidic population living among the many who joined the Zionist movement (which was considered a threat to the religious way of life), was often affected by raging violence. In early 1904, when Rabbi Soloveitchik refused to open the main synagogue so that a memorial service could be held for Theodor Herzl, Ze'ev-Dov broke the lock with an axe, and the memorial service was held. When Menachem was growing up, Ze'ev-Dov told this story time and again, as he saw it as a model of Jewish persistence.[8]

During the 1920s Ze'ev-Dov was a journalist for the daily Jewish newspaper *Haynt*. In 1922 he regularly visited the new branch of Keren Hayesod (the Palestine Foundation Fund), which opened on Tofolova Street. In 1923 he became chairman of Hashomer Hatzair (Young Guards), a left-wing Socialist-Zionist youth movement and the only active Zionist movement operating in Brisk at the time.

In 1924, when the Jewish Affairs Ministry and other state institutions shut down and a gradual violation of rights that had been granted to the Brisk Jews began, the financial position of Begin's family's took a turn for the worse.[9] Adding insult to injury, the family also struggled with the community's prevailing sense of isolation. Just before World War II broke out, anti-Jewish propaganda increased throughout Lithuania and Poland, and many Jews were attacked.[10] As a response to the events in Europe, Ze'ev-Dov stressed the need to emigrate to Palestine,[11] while he continued to engage in public activities. (Ze'ev-Dov garnered a reputation as a man who was strict regarding ceremonies—all ceremonies, not necessarily Jewish ones. When the U.S. ambassador to Turkey, Henry Morgenthau, made an official visit to Brisk, Ze'ev-Dov greeted him, kneeled down, and vigorously brushed the dust from his shoes.)[12]

During World War I, when Polish army units led by Marshal Józef Piłsudski entered Brisk and emancipated it, they ordered the arrest of the community's Jewish leaders on the suspicion that they were connected to the Bolsheviks. Ze'ev-Dov insisted that they show him an official arrest warrant; upon his request, the embarrassed soldiers withdrew their demand. Menachem was asleep when his father argued with the soldiers, but the story was told so many times that it seemed as though he had actually witnessed the event.

The Polish soldiers went on a rampage, attacking Jews throughout Brisk, and in one of these incidents a soldier aimed his rifle at Ze'ev-Dov's head. As usual, Ze'ev-Dov tried to calm things down. The soldier fired and missed, but the rumor that Ze'ev-Dov was dead spread rapidly. Begin was just eight years old when, for a few hours, he felt what it would be like to be an orphan.[13] In 1977, when he became prime minister, Begin referred to this incident when he said that his father was "the bravest man I ever met."[14]

When the Germans entered Brisk on September 15, 1939, Ze'ev-Dov presented a certificate proving that he had been a translator for the German Army during World War I and demanded information regarding the fate of his fellow Jews who had been arrested. The Germans considered his demand to be insolent and were angered by his arrogance but chose to ignore him. A week later, the Soviet Army entered Brisk, drove the Nazis from the town, and remained there until July 1941.

Menachem's mother, Chasia Kossovski, was rarely seen in public during those days. She preferred to rule within the walls of her home and to raise her children. Later, when Begin was asked to describe her, he depicted her as a passive woman who preferred to worry rather than to advise and guide: "Mother always suffered without complaining and in this respect she was a model of virtue for us; she was not bossy, did not interfere, and asked no awkward questions. We felt very free at home. She was dependable, not controlling; comforting, not teasing."[15]

On July 22, 1941, the Germans captured Brisk.[16] Chasia became ill and was hospitalized with pneumonia. Two weeks after the Germans invaded Brisk, his mother was murdered, together with the other hospitalized patients. A few months later the Nazis thwarted Ze'ev-Dov's plan to emigrate to Palestine. Begin would later recall how his father and his brother Herzl, as well as five thousand Jews from Brisk, were shot and thrown into the river and that his father's last words were "A day of retribution will come upon you too."[17]

Begin's sister, Rachel Halperin, told a different version of the story: Some time before the mass murders, her father decided to sneak out without approval from the area where the Jews had been gathered in order to properly bury one of the town's most prominent Jews, who had died a natural death. When Ze'ev-Dov was approached by a Nazi officer who questioned him, he answered, "This is what I have to do." In response, the officer shot him.[18]

What remains clear, however, is that Menachem's parents and brother were murdered by the Nazis. After Menachem's release from a Soviet prison at the end of 1941, where he was sent for Zionist activities, he served in the Polish Anders Army; he could only assume, having heard the rumors surrounding the fate of his Jewish community, that his family was among the victims of the Nazis.

Menachem never returned to Brisk. In 1954 he stated that he had wiped his hometown from his memory: "I will never again stand at the gates of the city where I was born, in which I dreamed, suffered, and was happy, for it is gone. No, I will not follow the shadows within myself."[19]

Begin never overcame his obsession with Germany and the Germans, although he had not been educated toward such an obsession at home. Before World War II his father had instilled in his children an appreciation for German culture and subscribed to the German magazine *Berliner Tagbilt*.[20] He told his daughter in great detail how much he admired the German culture and that he could not believe that the Nazis would commit the crimes attributed to them, and he had even been eager for their arrival because he anticipated that it would bring the high culture he so admired. Ze'ev-Dov trusted the German nobility even after the Nazis rose to power and even tried to persuade German soldiers to treat Jewish prisoners of war better. To his last day he believed he could appease the Nazis, but he was not entirely naive: he hated the Poles and cursed them at every opportunity.[21]

Unlike her brother Menachem, who tuned out such details, Rachel admitted that "my father loved the Germans, and he would tell me on our walks to 'Wait, the Germans will come.' To this day, the Nazis do not represent what is German for me."[22] Begin would not forget until the end of his life that the people his father admired the most were eventually those who murdered his family.

Menachem Begin was born on August 16, 1913, into an era of world wars.[23] When just two and a half years old, he already lay beneath his cradle while his mother protected him from the German bombardments of World War I. During the heavy battles his family was relocated to the town of Kobrin, where they huddled together in a tiny kitchen. The family returned to Brisk only after Germany and Russia signed the Treaty of Brest-Litovsk in 1918. Menachem's brother Herzl was sent to study at the Cheder (the Room), the traditional European Jewish primary school for boys where the basics of Judaism and Hebrew were taught, while his sister Rachel was sent to a nonreligious Jewish school.

When it came to Menachem's education, his father vacillated. At the age of three and a half, Menachem was sent to the Cheder like his brother, and a year later he was transferred to the Jewish school Tachkemoni, which was somewhat of a compromise between the Cheder and the secular Hebrew school Culture. This type of compromise was not uncommon during those days in Brisk, which incorporated a mixture of Hasidic beliefs, secularism, and new and revolutionary social ideologies.

As noted, Begin grew up in a nationalistic Zionist home that kept Jewish traditions as well. Every Saturday Menachem prayed in the synagogue, and at home they recited the Kiddush (the blessing over wine on Shabbat Eve), but the high school to which he was sent was a state school, and Begin, who was short, was an easy target for pranks and teasing by the Polish teenagers, who were influenced by the nationalistic atmosphere that was prevalent under the rule of Marshal Piłsudski. "We were simply beaten up," he said of his youth.[24] It is likely that the small and thin body of the boy, who spent most his time reading books with his thick spectacles, provoked the harassment, but he took advantage of his meager stature to develop his escape reflexes.[25] For Begin, the harassment was a result of one thing only: mere anti-Semitism, an easier solution than soul-searching and an understanding of differences between him and the other children.

Suspicion of Gentiles was part and parcel of the strict education Ze'ev-Dov gave his children. For Begin, his father's teachings were a haven from the regular assaults he experienced at school. Ze'ev-Dov never spoke to his children about women or about youthful fooling around. He even put limits to love. "At home I was taught that if one person in a relationship wants to emigrate to Palestine and the other does not, that person is entitled to ask for a divorce, as Judaism comes before love," Rachel recalled.[26] Ze'ev-Dov's vocabulary was always proper and formal; even when he sent a note to a friend congratulating him on his marriage, he incorporated nationalist values in his blessing.[27] His pride about his good Hebrew was apparent when he spoke, as in those days Yiddish was still the predominant language among the town's Jews. Financially, however, the Begins had no reason to brag anymore. The family lived in a two-bedroom apartment. Because of

Ze'ev-Dov's social position, they regularly had many visitors, so the children were used to blending into the background rather than receiving attention.

The family's financial distress, accompanied by feelings of nationalistic weakness, forged Begin's worldview around three main issues: "to love Jews, to not be afraid of Gentiles, and [to feel] that it is good for a man to bear a burden in his youth."[28] At home, a tension "between two worlds" existed.[29] Rachel, who had grown up in a town that had changed hands several times, idolized characters from Chekhov's novels. Her classmates, however, preferred characters from Polish literature. Ze'ev-Dov refused to learn Polish and made a great effort to speak Hebrew at all times. The name "Begin" comes from the Russian word *begun*, which means "to run," and Ze'ev-Dov changed it to "Begin," as the Germans pronounce it, in order to stress his admiration for the German culture.

Ze'ev-Dov taught his family to be proud of their Judaism during times when they were forced to conceal it, a stance that highlighted his tendency to be defiant;[30] such defiance was characteristic of Begin as a leader. During meals he occasionally asked his children, "Who knows why Laban, who aimed to bring about the destruction of the Jews, did not go down in history as a villain?" (This is one of the passages in the Passover Haggadah.) The children learned to answer, "Because when you aim to destroy an entire family, an entire people, and they are united, you cannot do it."[31] It is not surprising that when Begin was prime minister he said that the most important decision he made in his adult life was "to deter the outbreak of a civil war during the Saison."[32] (The Saison—*la saison de chasse* in French, or the hunting season—refers to the actions committed by the Haganah, the paramilitary organization of the mainstream Jewish community in Palestine, intended to sabotage the Etzel and Lehi insurgencies against the British. "Etzel" is the Hebrew acronym for Irgun Tzvai Leumi [National Military Organization], a.k.a. the Irgun; "Lehi" stands for Lochamei Herut Israel [Fighters for the Freedom of Israel]).

Ze'ev-Dov often spoke of the Jewish people's solidarity and adamantly opposed and was even vicious toward those who disagreed with him. His resolute attitude, full of pathos, was expressed in an angry letter he wrote to the town's rabbis and to the non-Zionist wheeler-dealers, calling them "flies of death, bacterial poison."[33] In this atmosphere, Menachem, who never disobeyed his father, formed his worldview. Ze'ev-Dov made sure his children received a strict education, eliciting awe even among his opponents, but when he was ten years old, Menachem learned that there was a disparity between his father's honorable and rigid position as the Jewish community secretary and the treatment he received from Polish soldiers. When a Polish soldier attempted to cut off his beard in order to humiliate him, Ze'ev-Dov hit him with his walking stick. But by the end of the encounter, Ze'ev-Dov was battered and bruised. His children found it difficult to see their father in this shameful state. "We were worried," Begin admitted years later but emphasized that his father maintained his "good spirits" and noted that his reaction was a symbol of dignity.[34] Begin preferred not to elaborate on the effect it had on him to witness his father in such a humiliating position.

In 1925, all three of Ze'ev-Dov's children joined the Shomer Hatzair, the only Zionist youth movement in Brisk at the time. Thus, ironically, Begin's political activity started in this left-wing youth group.

Menachem lived in the shadow of his siblings Rachel and Herzl, not only because of his age. Rachel was very close to their father and was considered the dominant sibling; Herzl was considered a mathematical genius. Menachem spent his time reading books while his companions participated in social activities. Due to his poor vision, Menachem began wearing glasses when he was eight years old. He was not particularly good-looking. He had protruding teeth with a wide frontal gap. Because he had been thin and pale in his youth, some people believed that he had tuberculosis. Such circumstances only increased his ambition.[35] Unlike his siblings, Begin drew strength from his faith in God and always volunteered to accompany his father to the synagogue. After his bar mitzvah Menachem continued to lay tefillin, and in his adult life, when he became a heavy smoker, he used to refrain from smoking on the Sabbath. He also kept kosher outside the home and was often heard saying "God willing."

Among Menachem's peers the common tendency was to turn away from a religious education, but Begin saw tradition, and especially its external frills, as a way of life. The tension between Zionism and religious values was strange to him, and he did not turn his back on a religious education, in part because his father, unlike other Zionists in his time, merged nationalism with Zionism.[36]

In 1926, the Shomer Hatzair youth group joined the Trumpeldor Scouts, a movement that had been established two months earlier; it was a natural consolidation at the time but became very unusual not long afterward. (Yosef Trumpeldor, an early Zionist, had established the Zion Mule Corps of the British Army in World War I with Ze'ev Jabotinsky; he fell in the defense of Tel Chai in 1921, where he famously said, "It is good to die for our country.") A year later, the youth movement fell apart due to political disagreements. When the movement made the decision to emphasize the socialist struggle over the Zionist struggle, Ze'ev-Dov instructed his children to withdraw from the group. The children then joined a new branch in Brisk of the Beitar movement (Beitar, the Hebrew acronym of Brit [covenant] Yosef Trumpeldor, emanated from the Trumpeldor Scouts), which was established in 1929, six years after the first branch was established in Riga.[37] The ideas emphasized in the articles by Ze'ev Jabotinsky, head of the global Beitar movement, which were distributed in pamphlets and published in newspapers, were close to the heart of the pale and bespectacled boy; they stressed the need for Jews to hold their heads high, shelve socialist notions, and focus on nationalistic issues and their demise and were opposite to the ideas pushed by the heads of the World Zionist Organization (WZO).[38]

In 1929 Begin also had his first political experience. Jabotinsky was scheduled to speak at the theater in Brisk, but despite the fact that the lecture had been sold out, Begin decided he had to see the revered leader at any cost and managed to sneak in under the stage, where the orchestra usually sat. Jabotinsky was already what his wheeler-dealer father aspired to be: well-spoken, well-dressed, and stern. The Jews who listened to his speeches were fascinated by his promises of a future for them in Israel, but Begin experienced a personal transformation listening to him. The power of the Jewish people, to which Jabotinsky referred, provided Begin with the personal confidence that he greatly lacked. He compared the connection he felt with Jabotinsky to that of holy matrimony.[39] After listening to Jabotinsky, he decided that his future lay with the Beitar movement.

On June 12, 1931, Begin received his high school diploma, which stated that he had "completed his schooling in the humanities and [was] worthy of a higher education." He did not excel in his studies—his average grades were "good"—but in history and religious studies he received "very good," and fortunately for him these two subjects interested his father the most. He received only a "satisfactory" grade in mathematics, but he nevertheless enrolled in the Warsaw Law School when he turned eighteen.[40]

During Begin's university years, his family's financial situation was at its worst. Ever since giving up the wood trade business, his father had supported his family only on a welfare pension, which was not always paid on time and often did not even reach him; on several occasions he was forced to apply for a postponement of tuition payments.[41] On February 15, 1932, Ze'ev Dov personally asked his son's dean to postpone the payment of fifty-three zlotys.[42] In the evenings Begin earned a living giving private lessons in law and Jewish history.

Throughout his university years Begin lived in the student dormitories run by the Jewish community. He became well known in the community due to his regular participation in the public academic debates conducted by the students. He had no girlfriend, nor did he express interest in any university activities that did not relate to the Zionist-Jewish cause. Begin focused mainly on Beitar-related issues and adhered to the field in which he was most likely to succeed—Zionist activism. No one remembers him excelling in sports or in any social activity. He drew his self-confidence mostly from a stubborn determination to achieve his goals, and he used his metallic-sounding voice to express his views.[43] On days when people paid to listen to lectures as though they were a form of entertainment, Begin's rhetoric became a subject of its own.

Thanks to his Polish friends at university, Begin was introduced to Polish culture. He confessed to Yitzhak Shamir, one of the Beitar youth at the time, that he admired the romantic valor expressed by the Polish poets in their opposition to their country's enslavement—a confession that he did not dare make to his father, who despised Polish culture. He especially admired "Pan Tadeusz," written by Adam Mitskevich, who wrote mainly about Poland's struggle against its conquerors. Begin felt that such poems were relevant to the Zionist movement, as they signified to him both the personal and general struggle for existence. On many occasions Begin would refer to Mitskevich's poem about the fall of the fort in Granada and about Almanzor's revenge against the Spanish occupiers:

> They shattered the night of the Moors, and they gave them
> A burden of iron, without pity
> But there in Granada the fortress still rallies.[44]

Unlike Jabotinsky, who drew his inspiration from European liberal nationalism and from Western democracies, Begin and his contemporaries in the Polish Beitar group, all of whom were born in the years 1910–1920, were profoundly influenced by the Polish national movement, led by Marshal Piłsudski, which was gaining power throughout the country and seemed incredibly appealing to the Beitar members. Among other things, the movement viewed the cult of the leader and military measures as a means of removing obstacles in the nation's path to victory. Beitar's major objective was to provide its members with a military education so that they could serve their country as professional soldiers. Its militant attitude was also expressed in the status of its leader—Ze'ev Jabotinsky—against which it was almost impossible to appeal. When Beitar members disagreed with him, almost no one dared to contemplate the possibility of replacing him.[45]

To understand the rigid, intolerant core of Polish nationalism, we should note the prolonged oppression of the Poles by their neighbors. Moreover, there was a high proportion of foreigners living in Poland—about 30 percent—a factor that accentuated Marshal Piłsudski's stance against foreigners. In 1914 the marshal established the Polish Military Organization. The expansion of Poland was his paramount goal so that Poland could return to being a sovereign state. Between 1920 and 1921 he managed to expand Poland's territory by military force beyond the borders agreed by the European powers, and his success proved to the influential Beitar members that military force was the way to achieve their nation's liberation. It is hard to ignore the similarity between the Polish organization's name and the name selected for the underground set up by the Beitar youth in Palestine, Etzel (National Military Organization). In some respects, Begin applied the Polish nationalistic concepts to his perception of Jewish nationalism—especially regarding the importance of using military means to expand territory—and to this notion he added the spiritual nationalistic anchor—Jewish tradition.

When Begin became the prime minister of Israel, he refrained from elaborating on the effects that the Polish nationalism of his youth had had on his concepts of Jewish nationalism. Nevertheless, despite the fact that he was influenced—as he liked to mention—by Herzl's letters, where he identified the core of Jabotinsky's ideas,[46] it is obvious that the national life for which Begin yearned was more characterized by Mitskevich's poems, which expressed a romantic, perhaps even a messianic, spirit.[47]

What characterized Begin was the fact that he blended nationalism with law; with such a combination he justified the conflicting desire to receive international approval for the establishment of the state of Israel while expressing sentimental fervor for such an occurrence.[48] However, it is clear that Begin's national aspirations also sprung from his private wish to escape the loneliness and material distress characteristic of his life in Europe.

Following his graduation Begin received the title of Magister of Law. In 1933 Beitar promoted him to officer, and thus he became one of the nine commission members of Beitar in the Polish headquarters. "We must shoot," he explained after his appointment regarding his ideas of how to establish a Jewish state. "We have to shoot, even if it gets us imprisoned and sentenced to death."[49]

The young Begin was influenced not only by romantic Polish nationalism, but also by the Italian figure Giuseppe Garibaldi, who combined the traits of both an intellectual and a military strategist.[50] Begin was particularly impressed by Garibaldi's ability to liberate his country in the midst of war. Begin, whose timidity made it difficult for him to enter into relationships with women and whose Jewishness came between him and Polish students, was impressed by a man who, despite being a republican, agreed to establish a monarchy in order to unite Italy—a man who understood the need to forgo his party's fundamental positions in favor of the nation's needs.

Meanwhile, new young people had joined the Beitar group in Brisk, and two years after its establishment, it had grown from 150 to 800 members.[51] The members declared their intention to emigrate to Palestine, but only a few managed to obtain the necessary certificates (authorizations by the British Mandate for those who wanted to emigrate).

When Begin became a Beitar officer in Poland, his first order was to organize a parade in which Beitar members marched through town in uniform, equipped with firearms. (Later, when he was elected prime minister, one of his first steps was to reinstate the military parade on Independence Day.) Despite his fondness for extravagant parades and the ostentatious display of weapons (which he saw as a means of expressing Jewish power), he focused rather on propaganda. His quill pen was always at hand. He wrote articles in Hebrew, Yiddish, and Polish. Simultaneously he traveled throughout Poland, lecturing Jewish communities on Zionism. During his trips he often found himself sleeping on park benches, as he refused to stay with strangers without paying, despite its being an acceptable custom.[52] Word of Begin's rhetorical skills spread throughout Poland, and his lectures, which combined a strict argumentative structure with legal and emotional enthusiasm, were in high demand.[53]

Like his father, Begin maintained a strict and precise approach toward rituals, hierarchy, and official procedures. During a Beitar commanders' meeting in Warsaw in March 1933 he was adamant about the formulation of clear structural definitions within the organization. "In Danzig we accepted the notion of regiments, which should include all three ranks.... This decision did not materialize," he scolded his colleagues.[54] Later that year he ignited a heated debate about a different procedure: he insisted that everyone should stand at attention in the presence of Beitar commanders. His proposal was indeed accepted, but other members began to feel that his fondness for ceremonies was exaggerated.[55]

In a pamphlet published in 1934 Begin introduced a principle that became the foundation of his famous rhetoric: the denigration of his rivals in the face of controversy. Any social perception or notion contrary to his own he dubbed "red poison," and he called for a stop to the artificial war of classes and a focus on the national struggle of the Jews.[56] Such verbal aggression was Begin's way of distinguishing Beitar from other left-wing parties; at times it was reminiscent of his father's statements against his opponents, and many assumed Begin used this approach to draw attention away from his physical flaws.

Over time Begin exaggerated his claims. During Beitar's second world conference in Krakow in January 1935, he rejected an agreement Jabotinsky had signed with David Ben Gurion, secretary general of the Histadrut (the General Workers' Federation), regarding the recognition of the National Labor Federation (the Revisionist workers' federation) and its commitment to avoid the unnecessary use of violence when legitimate political debate was still an option. Jabotinsky requested that Hatzohar, his party, approve the agreement he had signed with Ben Gurion to ease the tensions between two groups within the Zionist movement—the Revisionists and the labor camp—following the murder of Chaim Arlosoroff, head of the Jewish Agency's political department and a leader in Mapai (the Party of the Workers of Eretz Israel, a socialist Zionist party and the dominant political party in the Yishuv since 1930) and after violent brawls had broken out between the two groups in the Land of Israel. Begin arrived at the conference with a suitcase full of books and explained that he intended to utilize every moment to study history. His colleagues were very impressed, a fact that did not go unnoticed by Begin himself,[57] but in the end most of the delegates supported Jabotinsky.

However, in March the Histadrut rejected the agreement, and the Revisionists reconvened to discuss it in the spring of 1935. Begin drew the Revisionist members' attention to the animosity between Jabotinsky and Ben Gurion and said, "Perhaps Mr. Jabotinsky has forgotten that Ben Gurion called him Vladimir Hitler, but our memory hasn't betrayed us." Jabotinsky was quick to scold Begin: "I will never forget that men like Ben Gurion, Ben Tzvi, Golomb, wore the uniform of the regiment and fought beside me, and I'm sure that if Zionism demands it of them, they will not hesitate to wear that uniform again and fight." Begin's firm position, a twenty-two-year-old's defiant and radical means of expression, began to show the deepening gap between the teacher and his student. Jabotinsky already years before had been alarmed by the growing personality cult in the right-wing movement and even wrote to his wife Johanna, in typical reflective irony, to prepare another suit, larger than his usual size, for his upcoming trip to the United States, so it would fit the enormous and legendary stature with which he was attributed.[58]

Begin did not possess that kind of sarcastic sense of humor. He sought to intensify the myth surrounding the leader; later, when heading the Herut (Freedom) movement in Israel, he was as sensitive of his own honor as he was of Jabotinsky's when he headed Beitar.

Due to Histadrut's opposition to the agreement, the decision of the Zionist Executive Committee to prohibit all Zionist parties from taking part in any independent political activity, and the rejection of his proposal to declare that the Zionist goal was a Jewish state, Jabotinsky decided to withdraw from the Zionist organization and to hold a conference in Vienna founding the New Zionist Organization (NZO).[59]

As he took his first steps into politics, Begin was also taking his first steps as a young man seeking to find his way in life. He still had no girlfriend, and he was not surrounded by many friends. As noted, he saw his future with Beitar, and after the 1935 conference he was confident that he had chosen the correct path. But he managed to impress only the junior Beitar members; many of the senior commission members were disappointed in him because Begin was considered quick to talk and slow to act. His position of authority was undefined, and he never attempted to clarify it but rather focused on the enthusiastic responses to his speeches. Isaac Ramba, the deputy of Aaron Propes, the commissioner of Beitar in Poland, stressed in a report that Begin was in charge of activities that had not yet been ascertained. "There is little action in this office," noted Ramba, and he tried not to blame Begin directly for this.[60]

This "little action" may be the reason Begin was transferred in 1935 to become deputy commissioner of Beitar in Czechoslovakia. Ostensibly this was a promotion, but in fact the organization there was less active than in Poland. Begin decided to personally escort Jewish emigrants to ports from which ships would get them into Palestine illegally during the time of the British Mandate, and later he told his son Benny that doing so was the most important thing he did during his time in Beitar. Beyond that, in Czechoslovakia he mainly gave lectures, this time in the provincial areas, as he realized that certain promises that came with his new position were not going to be fulfilled. He acted as a martyr but not like before, when he had sanctified his pain as part of the job. During his tour he chose once again to sleep in public parks and sometimes even skipped meals. But he could not conceal his indignation with Beitar: he refused to attend the founding conference of Jabotinsky's New Zionist Organization in Vienna.[61]

In 1937 Begin returned to serve as the Beitar Commission officer in Poland, and during one of the party events in Łodź, he quoted with pathos—a characteristic trait of his—a song in Polish by the poet Maria Konofnitzka: "We will not throw to waste this land that is the core of our creation, so help us God."[62] Yet, like in his first year in a position of responsibility, a considerable gap between his words and his actions was becoming clear. In a report submitted to Jabotinsky, Beitar member Shalom Rosenfeld noted, just like Ramba had done several years earlier, that Begin, like the other commissioners, was a better talker than a doer and that the commissioners needed to be "shocked" into action. The feeling was that the post of commissioner was prestigious and comfortable and that the officers were not collapsing under the weight of pressure. Rosenfeld dryly described Begin's contribution: "Officer Begin roams the fields."[63]

Begin lacked the capacity for organization, and it was his rhetorical skills that had gained him his elevated position. Not only could he talk, but Begin loved to talk and almost never missed any opportunity to do so. One Sunday in winter Begin walked slowly through Łodź on his way to the Philharmonic Hall, where weekly lectures were given to Jews. At the time Łodź was a socialist workers' city, and Begin knew this. But he insisted on going to the hall when he heard that a replacement lecturer was being sought. The mediators between the lecturers and the hall were a group called the General Zionists, and they did not bother to update the audience about changes in the lineup. When the announcer declared, "Magister Begin, please," the entire hall erupted, and the members of the audience, who had expected a socialist speaker, rose to their feet shouting, "Fraud! Cheat! Give us our money back!"[64]

Begin's frail body, submerged in his worn and faded suit, only intensified the crowd's disappointment. But to his advantage he was blessed with impressive oratorical abilities. The hostility stimulated Begin, who used to motivate himself by throwing arrows at imaginary enemies. The longer he spoke, the more the audience's agitation subsided, and his dramatic gestures—rhetorical questions, methodical pauses just as he reached a point, hand gestures, and a commanding tone (among others)—slowly captivated the crowd.[65]

Begin never wrote his text in advance but rather prepared headlines on small notes and made sure to speak to mass logic—that is, to the emotions—so much so that by the end of his lecture opinions started to spread that he was a "better speaker than Jabotinsky."[66]

Begin's ability to stir up his audience also gained him a sojourn in prison. In 1937, after a somewhat truthful rumor had broken out that the Jewish Agency was delaying certificates to Palestine for Beitar members, Begin headed a demonstration during which he spoke in front of the British Embassy in Warsaw, and some of his listeners began to throw stones at the building. Begin was arrested in the middle of his speech, charged with incitement, and sent to jail for six weeks.

While his new friends in prison were not his intended audience, Begin found a common language with the criminals. His stubbornness and persistence were well received among the prisoners—after all, their language was also unique, with codes that only they could understand. But Begin tended to clash with the political prisoners, especially the Communists, and made sure to patronize them because of "their low cultural level."[67] Later this prison term was labeled a victory because he had been undeterred from doing time for his beliefs. Rumors circulating about him suggested that he was due to become the next leader of the Beitar movement,[68] and the story about his imprisonment confirmed what had been said about him in 1935—"Here is a man who is not afraid to argue even with Jabotinsky."[69]

Begin also drew resolution from the activities of the underground Etzel, founded in Palestine in 1931. Despite the ideological affinity between Etzel and the Revisionist movement, they did not grow from the same roots.[70] Etzel was founded when several people from the Haganah, headed by Avraham Tehomi, left the movement and formed the Haganah B, which in time became a separate organization called the National Military Organization, or Etzel. Tehomi appointed

Jabotinsky as commander in chief of Etzel, but his role was largely symbolic.

In 1937 Tehomi became discouraged by the Haganah B's lack of means and returned to the Haganah. Less than a year later, David Raziel was appointed the commander of the Haganah B. By that time only extreme activists were left in the Haganah B, including Avraham (Yair) Stern, Hillel Kook, and Jonathan Ratosh, and they drafted a new underground proclamation. Etzel's activities made waves as far as the Beitar youth in Poland. Hillel Kook, a commander at the time, traveled to Poland to recruit local youth to join the organization in Palestine, and Jabotinsky began to realize that the Revisionist leadership in Israel did not attach great importance to his moderate position—he persisted in the belief that ties with Britain could help establish the desired Jewish state and thought that a mutiny was impractical and unviable.

Begin was enthusiastic about Etzel's activities. Moreover, he saw the way the wind was blowing among the Beitar youth, and it motivated his most significant confrontation with Jabotinsky in September 1938, during the third Beitar world conference in Warsaw.

World War II was just about to begin, and the Arabs in Palestine began to express an intense nationalism, which manifested itself in terrorist attacks throughout 1936–1939. The Jews called these attacks "the Arab Events," while the Arabs called them "the Great Arab Revolt." Beitar was struggling through a growing internal dispute. Some Revisionists supported a policy of restraint while dealing with Arab terrorism, but many started to express the need to fight back.

Meanwhile, Etzel intensified its actions against the Arabs. In April 1938 it decided to place a bomb in the Arab vegetable market in the Old City of Jerusalem. The number of casualties was much larger than planned due to a miscalculation in the quantity of explosives; ten people were killed and over thirty were wounded.[71]

Shortly after the bombing, Shlomo Ben Yosef, an Etzel member, opened fire on an Arab bus near Safed, in the north, on his own accord and was subsequently executed by hanging. Beitar called him the First Martyr (after the Ten Martyrs of the Talmud), and despite his having acted without the organization's approval, his execution angered the Beitar youth both in Palestine and in Poland. Jabotinsky sided with those who called for restraint in order to garner British support and international understanding, which the Jewish community needed to be protected. Begin opposed acts of revenge but found himself trapped in an ideological vise: on the one hand, he continued to believe that the solution lay in applying diplomatic pressure on Britain and opposed the indiscriminate murder of Arabs (Jabotinsky's position); on the other hand, he was a supporter of the Etzel spirit, but most Etzel members in Palestine did not feel committed to Jabotinsky's and the Revisionist leadership's position on this issue.

The spirit of militancy that characterized Etzel in Palestine began to penetrate Beitar in Poland, and Begin, who found it difficult to separate himself from Beitar and join Etzel, preferred his own solution. He suggested that Beitar take more extreme measures and support military operations. Begin erected a buffer between himself and Jabotinsky, as the leader of a legitimate party could not afford to publicly side with the underground resistance.

Begin presented a bleak worldview in his speech at Beitar's third world conference in Warsaw in 1938, a result of the crisis in Europe and the situation in Palestine. He said that Zionism was "standing on the brink of destruction" and demanded that Beitar transfer all the money it had collected to the fighters in Palestine.[72] The speech symbolized the generational struggle within Beitar: Begin challenged Jabotinsky's leadership, which he saw as too compromising, while the Beitar leader often thrashed Begin in his own speeches.

However, Begin insisted, "The question is not what, but how? What means will achieve the goal? Do we want to fight, to die, or to win?" As in the Italian fight for liberation, Begin identified the strategy in three stages: "We started with practical Zionism, then moved on to political Zionism, and we are now on the threshold of a militant Zionism. A combination of militant Zionism and political Zionism will follow later."

Jabotinsky was aware of the erosion of his authority through this ongoing ideological confrontation.[73] He ridiculed Begin on the distance between his words and his actions and stressed the differences between the national movement in Italy and the Jewish national movement, even in terms of the proportion of Jews in Palestine compared to the Italians in Italy: "I urge you, sir, to remember the percentage of Italians vs. non-Italians in Italy." Begin replied: "I'll try to give an example of a different war of liberation, in Ireland. One cannot fight for his homeland in another country."

> *Jabotinsky:* "Explain to me, sir, how you plan to station Beitar soldiers in Palestine without the grace of support of the international community."

Begin: "If a force is created, help from the Diaspora will follow."
Jabotinsky: "Have you noticed, sir, the amount of Jewish military force in Israel as opposed to Arab power?"
Begin: "We will win on moral grounds."[74]

Begin concluded his speech by saying that "the world's conscience has ceased to respond" and by so doing expressed his opposition to Jabotinsky's reliance on Britain and the international powers to help establish a Jewish state. He even sought to change the words in Section D of the Beitar oath from "I will lift my arm to use my strength for defense" to "We will fight to defend our people and to conquer the homeland."

Begin's attempt to change the oath and the fervent support he garnered threatened Jabotinsky. In a speech in response, Jabotinsky claimed that Begin was detached from reality and that only diplomatic pressure on Britain would lead to the establishment of a Hebrew state.[75] Moreover, he characterized Begin's speech as the raspy "noise of a creaking door." He also rebuked Begin by saying that "each of us may, of course, express our opinion, but there are limits. Conscience rules the world. I respect that, and this should not be disrespected nor be treated as a joke."[76] He concluded by saying, semi-sarcastically and semi-disgustedly, that if Begin refused to believe in the world's conscience, he had no choice but to drown himself in the Vistula River. The conflict between the student and his teacher was now a visible rift.

The argument between the two highlighted two characteristics of Begin's that would become dominant in his political career: courage (in this case, to stand up against his leader), and a remarkable ability to discern the public mood (in this case, that of the Beitar youth, who were in favor of military action).

Begin's proposal to change the Beitar oath passed, and he found himself in a strange situation: the conflict within Beitar had subsided, but he realized that his victory had been premature and that he had been influenced by Etzel's activities without properly assessing his own position. He was alarmed by the storm he had stirred up in the conference and hurried to approve Jabotinsky's appointment as the head of Beitar, despite the fact that it was no longer necessary, and even exclaimed joyfully, "We are all at your command!" Begin's supporters felt that Jabotinsky could no longer ignore the power that he had demonstrated during the conference. But Begin's hopes of replacing Aaron Propes (the Beitar commissioner who identified himself with Jabotinsky) and to take over the Beitar leadership in Poland were shattered.[77]

Jabotinsky was impressed by Begin's fervor and his rhetoric, but he disapproved of his position; he preferred to hamper his student's enthusiasm and delayed his promotion. Begin did not dare publicly complain about his status, and he meanwhile strengthened his position through his activities and speeches. Only in March 1939, when it had become clear that Beitar in Poland preferred Begin as its leader did Jabotinsky support his appointment to head the Polish headquarters—a very powerful role, as the organization in Poland had seventy thousand members. Begin's great achievement—appointment as commissioner of Beitar Poland—was the result of a political compromise. Despite Jabotinsky's discomfort with Begin's position, Propes was viewed as too mild, and Begin was aware of the importance in bridging the gap between Etzel and Beitar.[78]

In his new role Begin focused on raising the level of reporting in Beitar's official newspaper, *Hamedina* (The State). But he knew that the power of his speeches was undoubtedly greater than the written word, despite the fact that he disliked human contact. He was friendly toward a large audience but not always to the individuals in it, and no Beitar members recall him as a warm person. His eyes were cold, distant from his addressee, and due to his timidity he shared no personal details or hardships, even with his closest friends, preferring to concentrate on matters relating to the organization. Most conversations revolved around ideological issues, and he never expressed enthusiasm for the theater, ballgames, or the like, and he never went out dancing or drinking. His mannerisms cast the twenty-six-year-old as a vigorous old man.[79] Perhaps interaction with thousands of people was his way of having a relationship. At the end of every speech he noted his thoughts about the event. He measured a speech's success by the extent to which it was accepted, not by its content.[80] His pockets were always full of little notes that he wrote for his speeches.

During the time Begin served as the commissioner of Beitar in Poland, he was regularly escorted by two commission members—his closest friends, David Yotan and Israel Epstein. In the view of Israel Eldad, who was then a member of Beitar and who considered Begin a rival for the leadership (and later bore him a grudge, in part because Begin refused to elect him to the Knesset on behalf of Herut), the friendship among the three friends, who were unequal in the party's hierarchy, highlighted another of Begin's traits: he preferred to surround himself with disciples, like a rabbi, and usually kept his distance from powerful people with independent opinions.[81]

After he was appointed commander of Beitar, Begin immediately started reorganizing, despite the fact that many members were extremely fearful of an impending war and its possible impact on the Jews. One night in the summer of 1939 Begin asked Eldad to implement the recommendations for an education program. "I cannot work on an education program at this late hour," Eldad responded, and Begin, who was not used to being criticized or refused, did not know what to say. "I understand, I understand," Begin muttered and remained silent.[82] During the preparations for Purim celebrations that year Begin asked Eldad to verify whether everything was in order. Again Eldad was astounded that at a time when everyone was concerned about an impending war, Begin was interested in trivialities.[83]

Begin's gestures and excessive interest in ceremonies, while he ignored urgent questions, raised concerns.[84] One morning a Beitar member decided it was time to ask Begin how he planned to implement his grandiose scheme to send forty thousand Jews to Palestine to fight the British and establish a Jewish state. Begin was dumbfounded by the question. He looked at the questioner with disappointment that he had even needed to ask and answered, "We'll leave it to the experts."[85] This was one of the first instances where Begin's tendency to disengage from practical solutions and hold onto nebulous ideas became evident.[86]

In his ideological conflict with the leftist movements Begin was intolerant toward intellectuals. In courses held by Etzel, the intellectual, a person of culture, was ridiculed, as part of a general criticism of the hated Left. [87] Begin was more comfortable among commoners, as his rhetoric excited them and was not subjected to profound analysis. Jews from the lower social classes who felt personally and nationally deprived were his audience.[88]

Begin constantly attempted to justify the contradiction between his position in favor of individual liberty and his conviction that the nation came before the individual.[89] His central argument was that in order to construct a nation all its members had to have equal opportunities—though he did not believe in enforced economic equality—thus maintaining the individual's uniqueness as it related to the nation.[90]

The year 1939 was important in the young politician's life. After he had fulfilled his dream of being appointed Beitar commissioner in Poland, Begin—surprisingly, since he was obsessive regarding everything in Beitar—wanted to take a break from politics. He wanted to become more professional as a lawyer in the Drohobych court. His change of interest was a direct response to his encounter with his first and last girlfriend—Aliza Arnold.[91] The love that sparked between them provided him, for the first time, with another perspective—the romantic. Suddenly his future involved his ability to support a family and not just to establish a nation. Thus at the age of twenty-six he almost gave up politics for a different career.[92]

It was love at first sight—rare and noble. When they first met, Begin, who had absolutely no experience with women, did not dare utter a word. The following day he sent Aliza a note: "I saw you, miss, for the first time, but I feel as though I've known you all my life."[93]

The Arnold family had settled in Galicia at the beginning of the twentieth century. Herman Tzvi Arnold's and his wife Fredericka's attitude toward Jewish tradition was expressed in the untraditional names of their four daughters: Gisela, Henrietta, and the twins Leonia and Aliza (cheerful). The wealthy family's source of income was Herman Tzvi's oil company.[94]

Begin was introduced to the family over dinner during a campaign to raise money for Beitar. Herman Tzvi, who had connections with the Revisionist party in his town and whose daughter Aliza had already begun to learn Hebrew when she was seven, was sympathetic to Zionism but not to religion. Begin was captivated by Aliza and was especially impressed with her silence throughout the dinner, which he saw as a sign of modesty and exemplary education.

During the meal Begin and Herman Tzvi talked about politics, and Begin did his best to demonstrate good table manners. He did not talk to Aliza but sporadically looked at her longingly. The next day, after he handed her the note, which won her affections, he hastened to ask her father for her hand in marriage. Her father thought Begin was an example of a successful scholar, and because he considered Henrietta's husband incompetent, Herman Tzvi quickly consented to the young man with the impressive political potential.[95] Begin and Aliza remained faithful to each other to the end and had a youthful and loving relationship throughout their life together.

Aliza was nineteen when they got married in Drohobych. The young couple spent hours on end together, and despite the fact that Aliza was characterized by verbal and emotional restraint—unlike her husband, who was known at times to speak with great pathos—she had a profound influence on him.[96] Ze'ev Jabotinsky honored them with his presence at their wedding, and when Aliza, who was nearsighted, lost her wedding ring, Beitar's world chairman crawled under the table with her to search for it.[97]

In addition to her myopia Aliza also suffered from asthma, a psychosomatic illness, which made it difficult for her to join her husband on his lecture tours, but they almost never parted. Over time her love for Menachem made her identify with everything he said and did, and she was the one who remembered and never forgave those who criticized her husband. Both Aliza and Menachem had the desire to express power. Aliza, like Begin, never talked about personal adversity even with her closest friends, who pointed out that her asthma attacks would occur at times of great distress, especially after a repression of personal problems.[98] When they eventually emigrated to Palestine, she was furious at Israel Eldad's criticisms of Begin in his articles. Despite her close friendship with Eldad's wife Batya, she did not hesitate to send Batya invitations that stated, "The invitation does not include your husband." When Begin became the head of Etzel, she held heated debates with anyone who opposed his views and often said, "What about Lehi? There is only Etzel."[99]

TWO

A COMMANDER'S GETAWAY

When World War II broke out, Begin proposed in Beitar headquarters in Poland that a Hebrew youth brigade be established with the help of the Polish Army. The Polish leadership had sympathy for Etzel's and Beitar's nationalistic ideas, which had a positive effect on relations between them and the government. However, such positive relations did not influence the Polish leadership in favor of Begin's proposal. It avoided the issue.[1]

Begin and Aliza, as well as several other members of the Polish Beitar commission, fled Warsaw shortly after this episode for fear of the Nazis. Since then people have claimed that Begin's hatred of the Germans sprung from his guilt that he had chosen to escape.[2] But this was the only way to survive. Natan Yellin Mor (who later became one of the three commanders of Lehi) obtained exit permits for them. There were no seats on the train out of Warsaw, so Begin and Aliza sat on the carriage floor. During the ride planes flying above the train suddenly dropped bombs over the area, and the train was forced to stop. Begin and his wife, along with two other passengers, jumped off the train and hid among the bushes. Eventually they arrived in Lvov.

In October 1939 Menachem and his wife boarded another train in Lvov. This time they were destined for Vilnius (Vilna), where Moshe Sneh (from the General Zionists) was staying, along with many members of Beitar who had managed to escape Warsaw. Avraham Amper, Avraham Stern's assistant, gave Begin and several other Beitar members a crash course in weapons, but they never discussed the option of defending themselves if they encountered the Nazis. This was the first and only instance that Begin touched a firearm.

In Vilna Begin was distressed by a matter that did not concern his comrades: boredom. Most commission members spent their time playing chess and drinking coffee. Begin visited the Café de la Paix on a daily basis, but unlike his friends he had business on his mind, as he managed the members' salaries, the money for which he had withdrawn before they had fled Warsaw.

During that time Begin feared for his family. He did not know exactly where they were, had lost touch with them, and had trouble getting information about them, but he never stopped trying. A tall, well-dressed Pole who spent time in the café in what seemed to be secret conversations with people and in exchanging money attracted Begin's attention. They had made eye contact on several occasions, and one night the man initiated a conversation. "If you're interested, I can save your family," the Pole assured Begin. Startled, Begin asked for an explanation. "Give me a thousand dollars," continued the Pole, "and I'll get them out." It was a huge amount of money in those days, and Begin did not possess such a sum, but he adamantly wanted to seize the opportunity to save his family. He had been hearing alarming rumors, and he immediately told Yaakov Banai (a member of Beitar and later the head of Lehi's operational department), about the offer. "He seems shady," Banai exclaimed; "besides, where are you going to get that kind of money?" Begin did not answer. "He promised me that he would rescue them," he said, "and he seems serious." They did not continue the conversation. Banai was convinced that Begin had given up on the idea until he met him one day in the café, sullen and gloomy. "He took the money and disappeared," Begin lamented. Banai never asked Begin where he had gotten the money.[3]

In Vilna Begin was publicly humiliated for the first time since becoming a leader. Shimshon Yunichman, a Beitar commissioner in Palestine, had exchanged letters with Begin while in Europe about the necessity of fighting the Nazis. He believed that Beitar members should express their ideals in actions, not words. Begin disagreed: "This war is not our war.... We will not fight for the homeland as individuals in various foreign units."[4] Begin was not alone in this belief; the Zionist parties were focusing on the war that was thought would take place in Palestine.[5] In a letter to Begin, Yunichman deviated from the fundamental argument and attacked him personally. "Why did you leave Warsaw? It is common knowledge that when the ship is sinking, the captain is the last to leave," he wrote, despite there being no point in staying in Warsaw after the bombings began.[6] Batya and Israel Eldad said that when Begin received Yunichman's letter, he fell into a depression, but at the time no one attached any importance to his state of mind. The correspondence testifies to the fact that the Jews in Palestine did not understand the situation in Europe at the beginning of the war. However, Begin viewed Yunichman's letter as a blow to his image. Yunichman's hinting that Begin had fled the battle humiliated him, and no one was better than Begin at internalizing insults.

Begin summoned all Beitar members from Warsaw to an "emergency session." Everyone reported immediately, fearing bad news. To their surprise, Begin suggested that they all "swiftly return to Warsaw." Dozens of members were shocked at this proposal to change plans and forgo the only opportunity they would have to obtain certificates. In response Begin read them the letter he had received from Yunichman and suggested that the proposal be put to a vote. The commission members remained silent and rejected the proposal by an absolute majority. Behind Begin's back the members discussed his distorted reasoning in light of the blow to his honor, and they even suggested that the meeting had been a sham, aimed at supporting his desire to stay in Vilna.[7]

Begin expressed his impressive theatricality when he visited the Polish-Lithuanian University in Vilna, where he was invited to speak at a conference marking the school's fifteenth anniversary. In the middle of his lecture, just when he began urging the students to emigrate to Eretz Israel, a frightened young boy burst into the hall holding a crumpled note. The message was unequivocal: Soviet tanks had occupied the city. The conference moderator was alarmed and asked that the ceremony end and the hall be evacuated. The attendees understood that something dramatic was taking place and began whispering among themselves. But Begin put a stop to the commotion and called for them all to sing "Hatikva" (the Zionist national anthem, which would later become that of Israel) before dispersing. Some remained in the hall and sang, while many made a run for it.[8]

On August 4, 1940, Ze'ev Jabotinsky died from a heart attack in New York while visiting a Beitar youth summer camp. Suddenly, without a higher authority to lean on, even one with whom Begin had battled, his power was diminished. Due to the uncertainties regarding the movement's political future, Begin overcame his love of public speaking and settled for a simple Kaddish prayer for "our father and teacher," as he called him, during the memorial ceremony at the end of the shivah (the seven days of mourning after a death).

Naturally, Begin felt somewhat like an orphan and did not give much thought to the legacy that Jabotinsky had left him. The first time he had seen the Beitar leader, when he was sixteen years old, he saw in him a combination of power and romance, and over time his initial enchantment became profound identification. Begin felt that he was like Stalin in the power triangle of Marx-Lenin-Stalin (with Herzl as Marx and Jabotinsky as Lenin), and he believed that a continuous line connected Herzl, Jabotinsky, and himself. But in fact the line was not continuous. It was no coincidence that the student had fought with his teacher during the Beitar conference. From Jabotinsky Begin had inherited a maximalist Revisionist program, contempt for the official Zionist leadership, hostility toward leftist parties, and dramatic gestures in public speaking, but he did not internalize Jabotinsky's liberalism and European spirit. This was true not only because in some ways Begin strived to be more like Jabotinsky than Jabotinsky himself, but also because their entire outlooks had radically different starting points.

Jabotinsky came from a secular family in Odessa; he had studied in Italy and wrote liberal humorous skits unrelated to his political ideology. He was like the Italian intellectual Giuseppe Mazzini, who saw no contradiction between the universal ideal of human progress and his nationalistic ideas. In Jabotinsky's novel *Shimshon* (Samson), the hero is a man endowed with humor who admires the Philistines and mocks his own people.

In contrast, Begin grew up in a traditional family that lived under foreign anti-Semitic rule, and he drew his ideas from radical Polish nationalism. He never publicly questioned the truth of his ways and refrained from gaining any profound understanding of his political opponents' motivations. Throughout his life Jabotinsky supported an alliance with the British, and when the British expressed hostility, he continued to believe that eventually the "good" British would prevail, while Begin saw the British as another link in Jewry's chain of oppressors. Begin's conservative outlook was accentuated in comparison to Jabotinsky's liberal one; Jabotinsky was fond of cafés and hard liquor, and he settled in Paris after the British forbade him from moving to Palestine. In an article he published in *Maariv* in 1973 entitled "Leftism, Nationalism, and Nationality," Begin claimed that "leftism and lenience were created together, as the Left allows itself whatever it wants." Begin used to say that his meeting with Jabotinsky could not be compared to any other encounter.[9] It appears that their differences only added to Begin's growing admiration for the head of the movement.

During the days of mourning for Jabotinsky, Begin became increasingly fearful of the NKVD (the Soviet secret police) operating in Vilna, and after consulting with Aliza, they decided that they would join Israel and Batya Eldad in a small Catholic village five miles away. They stayed there with Aliza's brother in-law.

The September weather in a village that progress had bypassed was Begin's only consolation while chopping down trees with Eldad. During their constant sawing, they would play chess, while Aliza gathered strawberries to make jam. His fear of the future and his break from political activity took their toll on Begin. He rarely spoke and tended to retreat into himself, using physical work as his only escape from mental distress. "Let me be," he would say when the others tried to get him to talk, as though he was a victim.[10]

Begin did not know what to do. He had to hide from the NKVD detectives and struggled to accept the total uncertainty regarding his future. He was frustrated by the inability to control his own life, so he insisted on spending his days running the household as though it was a self-sustained farm, which it was not.[11]

Meanwhile, Begin had scant knowledge about Etzel and the fact that it had split in Palestine. Following David Raziel's decision to cease all military actions against the British while they were fighting the Nazis, a number of Etzel members sided with Avraham Stern, who argued that they should continue to fight. Nor did Begin know that before his death Jabotinsky had said that he preferred Raziel to Stern.

NKVD detectives continued to follow him. Sensing that he was in danger, Begin refused the request of one of his friends to return to Vilna, as he feared that he would be arrested there.

Part of his prediction was fulfilled: at noon on September 20, 1940, Begin was arrested, not in Vilna but in the village where he was staying. When the detectives knocked on the door and asked Begin to join them for "errands at the municipality," Batya Eldad burst into tears, as she understood that they would not see him again for a long time. But Aliza, standing beside her in the doorway, remained composed and invited the detectives to join them for a meal. They politely refused. Out of pride Begin asked that he be allowed to polish his shoes before they left. Just before departing with the detectives, he told Eldad to wait for the next round because it seemed that he had been losing the chess match that they had been playing before the detectives arrived.[12]

Aliza and the Eldads later learned that Begin had received an immigration certificate several days before his arrest but had decided that this time the captain would not be the first to abandon the sinking ship.[13] But why had he not used the certificate since he had in any case fled from the NKVD in Vilna? The answer rests in his character. Perhaps he recalled Yunichman's accusations, and it is possible that his conscience tormented him for having left Warsaw before the other Beitar members were able to escape. Eldad thought that his decision to wait for his arrest was also related to his inability to make decisions under pressure and his dependence on fate during stressful times.[14]

Frozen on the spot, Aliza looked on as her husband's silhouette slowly vanished into the distance. Right there and then she swore to the Eldads that she would never leave Lithuania without him and that she would leave no stone unturned in her quest for his release. Only months later, when rumors of Nazi atrocities reached their ears and the wait for her husband's return proved futile, did Aliza agree to flee from Lithuania using a passport prepared for her by the American Jewish Joint Distribution Committee (JDC, or Joint).[15]

Upon arriving in Palestine, Aliza was immediately arrested, as she was holding an expired passport. She was sent to Atlit detention camp, where she had a severe asthma attack. After her release she did not know where to go or to whom to turn for help, as she had no relatives in Palestine. Because she was the wife of the Beitar commander in Poland, Yosef Klarman, the NZO representative in Israel, wrote a letter on her behalf to the Committee for the Jews of Poland with a request for financial support.[16] With the money she received Aliza rented a small apartment on Ovadya Street in Kerem Avraham, near Camp Schneller in Jerusalem. The new immigrant had few friends and spent most of her time alone in her apartment.[17] She enrolled in archaeology studies in the university in Jerusalem, the department headed by Professor Eleazar Sukenik, the father of Yigael Yadin, who later became chief of staff of the Israel Defense Forces. But she did not persevere with her studies and took a nursing course at the Red Cross. In late 1941, she learned that her husband had been sentenced to eight years of imprisonment with hard labor in Vorkuta in the northern Soviet Union.

"And do not forget to tell Scheib [Eldad] that he won the last game," Begin managed to yell to Aliza before being carried away by the NKVD. September 20, 1940, was not a very rainy day. Begin let out a sigh of relief, despite knowing that he would spend a long time in prison.

Nevertheless, he felt that the nightmare was finally over—the fear of the future, of the unknown, the futile hiding, the stagnant situation that had prevented his emigration to Palestine even though he had already received the certificates.

Begin had known for a long time that he was being followed.[18] Already at their wedding he had told Aliza that their lives would not be easy. "There will be arrests," he said.[19] Thus in a whirlwind of fatalism, Begin entered the interrogation cells in Lokiski Prison in Vilna. In his memoirs he claimed that he took the Bible with him upon his departure,[20] but in the prison protocols it states that he arrived with Andre Maurois's biography of Disraeli and a German-English dictionary. He did not complete the reading of either of them, as the NKVD detectives burned them during his investigation.[21]

Begin was imprisoned in a wooden cell. He could always hear the squeaking of the door with a peephole in it, through which he and his two cellmates were watched. Living conditions in the little village had not been much better, but there at least he was not constantly afraid of a beating. After his incarceration, the thing he feared most was physical injury. He was troubled by rumors of injections designed to hypnotize prisoners into disclosing information, and he was relieved when other prisoners told him that the abuse would be less sophisticated.[22] And Begin was lucky; in all his time in prison he was not beaten even once.[23]

Begin had never had a healthy appetite. However, he had a difficult time adjusting to three meals of porridge a day. During his first days in prison, the anticipation of three meals a day and a bucket for his toilet needs were the center of his daily routine.[24] The prison food also helped him fast on Yom Kippur every year, thus gaining him the respect of his fellow inmates, who were impressed by his determination to stick to his principles.[25]

Begin's time in prison can be reconstructed almost entirely from his memoir, *White Nights: The Story of a Prisoner in Russia*, which he wrote more than a decade after the events. It should be noted that in 1992, after the collapse of the Soviet Union, his investigation protocols were discovered in the KGB archives under file number 782783, and there were no significant discrepancies between the memoir and the file. (The file was transferred to the Jabotinsky Archives.)

According to Begin, he spent much time talking to the other detainees about Zionism, capitalism, communism, and Eretz Israel (Land of Israel, the Hebrew term for Palestine) and almost anticipated his interrogations so that he could lecture the interrogators.[26] During the interrogations, he spoke as if in front of an audience of hundreds; he was thus referred to as a *chudak* (eccentric).²⁷ The head interrogator—a handsome and relatively kind man in his thirties—introduced himself as Kianchenko. He asked Begin to call him "citizen-judge-interrogator" and added that his rank was that of sub-lieutenant.²⁸

Begin's reasoning amused the interrogators. "It's Talmudism," they would say of his answers. But sometimes they lost patience with his ramblings. "Like the other prisoners, you think out of your ass and sleep on your head, instead of vice versa," they would tell him. But Begin insisted in lengthy and precise responses. On at least one occasion his legal education came to his aid: he asked to be released under the terms of Article 129 of Stalin's constitution, which stipulated that "the Soviet Union would grant rights to persecuted foreign citizens in order to protect their scientific work or the workers' interests or their struggle for national liberation." Begin claimed that he had acted on Polish territory. The detectives responded, "Your legal doctrine is funny. You're a *chudak*. You are actually accused under Section 58, which applies to every person in the world. The question is only when [every person] will come to us or when we will get to him."²⁹

Often, when they were in good spirits, the interrogators conducted fascinating ideological arguments with Begin. Kianchenko argued that Zionism was a comedy, a coverup for imperialism, and that one was either an imperialist agent or wrong and misled. In response Begin claimed that a comedy could not last for two thousand years, and Kianchenko answered in return that imperialism had taken advantage of his emotions, as the Jews would not emigrate en masse to Palestine.

Kianchenko's claims were founded on early Zionism. "You force doctors and engineers to work the land; where is the logic? I heard from a Jewish prisoner that you set up *kolkhozy*. How can you in honesty build *kolkhozy* if they are financed by American millionaires? The Bolshevik revolution needs the Jews," he said. "But the youngsters among you are trying, under British influence, to rescue their Jewish comrades from the commitment to a revolution in favor of fostering Zionism." Kianchenko also commented on Beitar and called it a bourgeois-nationalistic party striking out against global social classes.³⁰

Begin was forced to side with the socialism of his opponents from the Zionist movements and referred to Birobidzhan, a region where the Soviets sought to create an autonomous Jewish state to prove that they too recognized the Jewish nation. The interrogator claimed that Zionism was colonialism, and Begin in return claimed that there was room for millions of Arabs in Palestine and that they too would be granted sufficient land.[31] Begin was excited by such discussions, as he was especially irritated by the anonymity imposed on him after having gained recognition as a good public speaker. "It's not easy to live knowing that your words will most likely never reach anyone," he wrote in his memoirs.[32]

Due to the fact that Beitar's activities in Poland were out in the open, from a review of the protocols it is difficult to estimate how capable Begin was of keeping a secret. He gave his interrogators the names of every Beitar member but withheld the information that he was the Beitar commissioner in Czechoslovakia and also said that he did not remember the names of the members who had participated in the last Beitar meeting. It remains unclear why he chose to withhold the names of participants in the last meeting or information about his activities in Czechoslovakia. One possibility is that he may have believed that these activities were in defiance of the Soviets, but there is no doubt that he did not want to provide them with all the information he had. He took full responsibility for the distribution of certificates to Palestine, though he made sure to emphasize that the certificates were already addressed to people who had received permission to enter Palestine.[33] During one interrogation Kianchenko threatened, "Tell us the truth about your activities against the Soviet regime. It will be a shame if you don't; your wife is still young." After the first interrogation Begin was required to write out his resume. When he had finished, one of the guards gave him his first punishment: Begin had to stare at the wall for sixty consecutive hours.[34]

Upon returning to his cell, Begin discovered that one of his cellmates had been replaced by an elderly man who had an impeccable sense of order and cleanliness. The moment he entered, his new neighbor ordered him to scrub the floor clean. When he completed his task, Begin discovered that he had absentmindedly left a wooden spoon out of place. He immediately apologized to his cellmate, and the incident was forgotten. Begin got along with the third cellmate, who repeatedly told graphic sex stories about nuns and priests.

The interrogators started to focus on trivial details. When asked about his role as head of Beitar in Poland, Begin said he was just a lecturer and Hebrew teacher.[35] Though his words were all documented in the protocols, he reiterated that "this [idea that Jews should have nationalistic aspirations] is [only] my opinion. I did not run any counterpropaganda regarding this."[36] His fear and worry were obvious—unlike during his ideological arguments. He also claimed that he met Jabotinsky only six or seven times, an account completely different from the way their relationship was presented after he became the leader of Herut. He said that the instructions he had received from the leader of the Beitar movement were guidelines focused on strengthening the party and nothing else.[37] Yet he continued to get into trouble.

One day Begin's Jewish guard overheard him laughing with his two cellmates, and he was sure that they were mocking him.[38] His punishment—a week in solitary—had long-term effects: he was allowed to take eight steps only, and this march inside the solitary cell became a habit. When he became prime minister, he would walk around his office while contemplating important issues.[39]

When he returned to his cell from the week's confinement, Begin found that the bag with all his belongings had been stolen. A young Jewish boy who had been falsely charged with theft and jailed by mistake with the political detainees hurried to share Begin's belongings with his co-criminal detainees. "He is thin and weak; he probably won't return from solitary confinement," he said in justification. Begin was saddened by the loss of his possessions but preferred not to confront the thief.

Begin also made some extraordinary changes upon his return. Because he could not remove the dirt clinging to him, his cellmates washed him with homemade soap. Now the previously majestic man stopped changing his clothes, became ridden with lice, and ceased to wash his hands before meals. Most difficult of all, he decided to stop smoking. Cigarettes in prison were rare, and Begin never knew how powerful the decision to "acclimatize" could be.[40]

Begin made only one true friend in prison, a Jew named Garin who was suspected of supporting Trotsky. In the evenings, Garin would lie on his hard bunk and try to persuade Begin that Zionism was the Jewish nationalism, equivalent to German nationalism. "Palestine belongs to the Arabs, and the Jews are stealing it from them under the pretext of imperialism," he would say. Begin wanted to avoid confrontations with Garin and preferred to see him as an "enchanted baby."[41]

The interrogations were drawing to a close, and Begin held steadfastly to his central argument of legality. He stuck by his assertions that his activities in Poland had all been legal and often, as noted, described them in semantic detail.[42] When asked whether he was the Beitar commissioner in Poland, he spent over five hours (from eight o'clock in the evening until one thirty in the morning) admitting to the facts but insisting that he was not guilty.[43] The interrogators lost their temper over his persistence, demanded that he immediately stop talking nonsense, and said that if he did not sign a confession they would send the document to the prosecutor without his signature. Begin shrunk down in his seat. His interrogators started to treat him as a man who had lost his mind. "Look, he's talking to himself now," they said laughingly.[44] But Begin would not relent and signed that he admitted to the facts but pled not guilty.

One November night before his sentence came through, Begin was told that a family member had come to visit him. He believed it was his wife. He was especially worried about her asthma attacks and kept remembering their beautiful moments together.[45] But the "relative" turned out to be another prisoner, Yaakov Schechter, a Revisionist leader from Krakow who had been summoned to finger Begin as the one responsible for the distribution of the certificates (an act that was against Soviet policy). Schechter accepted responsibility, but Begin denied that Schechter had had any hand in it and took all the responsibility upon himself. Neither of them blamed the other, and the confrontation ended without any other charges being made.[46]

On December 18, the interrogations ended. Begin had often enjoyed them, if only because they disrupted the monotonous prison routine. Now he had to wait for his sentencing.

On March 8, 1941, Begin was sentenced to eight years of imprisonment at a labor camp: "The special advisory committee for the Internal Affairs Commission has determined that Menachem Ben Ze'ev Begin is a dangerous element to society and has decided to imprison him in a work camp for eight years."[47] Without trial and without his presence at the committee meeting where his verdict was announced, the investigators, as "a special commission for the security of the state of the Soviet Union," convicted Begin on the count of "joining the anti-revolutionary, Revisionist-Zionist organization Beitar in Brisk and Warsaw" under section 58 of the Criminal Law of the Russian Soviet Federative Socialist Republic.[48] One of the prison guards read the sentence to Begin three weeks after the verdict was issued. He was also told that he would be transferred to a work camp in Kotlas, Siberia. He stood and listened. The punishment was what he had expected.

Meanwhile, Begin received a package from his friends at Beitar containing white linen with the letters "Ola" embroidered on it. He was sure it was a message from Aliza. But he did not understand why they had written "Ola" when her nickname was "Ela." One of the prisoners, a Jewish member of the Bund, solved the riddle: it meant "Ola" in Hebrew, the term for immigrating to Palestine. The things that console people in prison are often strange, and the knowledge that Aliza was far away provided Begin with great comfort.

Although Begin was pleased that Aliza had been saved from extermination, he was grief-stricken about his own fate. He even considered getting a divorce so that she could move on with her life. Nobility of character was a source of strength for him, a means of regaining power to help overcome life's hazards. He shared his thoughts with many prisoners but soon realized it was a mistake to do so. They grew angry at his stories as they invoked nostalgic memories that made their time in prison unbearable.[49] He apologized. Over time he became an optimist, but he also grew jealous of his loved one and changed his mind about divorce. Only if he was not released within three years would he grant Aliza a divorce. In any event, he never sent word to her.

Shortly before leaving for the work camp, Begin learned that he was entitled to one visit, and he was asked to choose whom he would like to see. Despite knowing that Aliza had emigrated to Palestine, he asked to see his wife.[50]

As he approached the visitors' cell, he almost believed it was Aliza: the girl who came to see him was similar to her. She was skinny, she wore glasses, and her black hair was tightly pulled back. It was Paula Deichs, a Beitar member. Begin was excited, despite the disappointment. "Yes, I understand, I understand," he rushed her along as she talked of her experiences in Beitar so that he could begin to ask her questions. "And how are you, how's the family, the friends, what's the situation, what is going to happen?" He wanted to hear as many details as possible. Deichs told him that his siblings and parents were still in Brisk and that they were well; she told him that Aliza had arrived in Israel. When the guard urged them to finish their conversation, Begin asked her to tell Aliza that he was well, strong, and proud and that he promised to return to her. The idea of a divorce was completely forgotten. Before parting, Deichs handed him a bag containing a piece of soap, undergarments, and food, but these were immediately confiscated. The guard even unwrapped the soap to make sure that no codes had been inscribed on it, but he missed a letter sent to him by Natan Yellin Mor. The letter said that Aaron Propes, a Revisionist leader in the United States and the Beitar commissioner Begin had replaced, was working to get him released.[51] The plan was to get the Americans to apply pressure for his release or to obtain the citizenship for him in one of the South American countries,[52] but a few days later, in early June, he was sent to the labor camp.

On the way to the labor camp, about two hundred miles north of Fitchura, two thousand prisoners, with Begin in their midst, were ordered to be strip-searched. One of the prisoners suffered from an upset stomach, and the sounds that he made broke the silence. Begin later wrote in his memoirs that he and his colleagues found it difficult to hide their smiles.[53] Following the search, the prisoners boarded freight trains and were transported to the camp, where a doctor examined them. During his inspection Begin realized that if he bribed the doctor, he could be sent to the hospital for more tests, where he would certainly have a much easier time. He gave the doctor his nightshirt and was sent on "vacation" for two weeks.[54]

On his arrival at the work camp Begin quickly had to adjust to hard and tedious physical work—loading timber destined for the building of railroad bridges. Despite the hard work Begin felt a sense of stability in his daily routine, and this saved him from emotional distress. When winter came, about six months after his arrival at the work camp, the Polish prisoners as well as Begin—to his surprise—were ordered to pack up their belongings and were moved to a reeducation camp.

Begin was still wary of hoping that his release was near, but a few days later he learned that by an agreement signed between the Polish Army and the Soviet Army all Polish prisoners were to be recruited into the Polish Army to fight against the Nazis. Meanwhile, the prisoners were to prepare for a trip to the port of Krasnovodsk on the Caspian Sea.

Begin suffered intensely at the reeducation camp. One night he had alternating hot and cold spells, and for the first time since he had arrived, he allowed himself to show self-pity in public. The self-pity frightened him as much as his disease, as he knew that it would break his spirit. He begged for a day of rest, but the guards refused.[55]

At the camp he befriended a strange man who was known to everyone as "Toilet" because he had lost control over his bladder. What aroused the other prisoners' laughter evoked Begin's mercy. The two spent many nights together, and Begin even gave him the cigarettes he received.[56]

One morning a Russian officer asked him if he was a Polak (that is, Polish). "I am a Jew," Begin said, "but yes, a Polish citizen as well." "I do not understand," the officer wondered, "Polish or not?" Begin understood that there was no point in arguing about the relationship between religion and nationality and muttered, "Yes, a Polish citizen."

"So you're among those who are going to be released." That was how Begin learned about his upcoming liberation.

Begin's name was first on the list of newly liberated men, and when one of the criminal prisoners shouted, "He's a Yid, not a Pole," Begin did not even argue with him as he would usually have done. When the prisoners began to talk about their plans, Begin focused on his work so as not to forfeit the opportunity he had been granted. But a rumor started that some of the prisoners who were to join the Polish Army would first be transferred to a different work camp, and at this point Begin took a stand. Because of his legal training, many prisoners asked him to represent them in front of an emissary who had come to the camp from Moscow, requesting that they be allowed to stay where they were. But Begin feared such a task, not wishing to stand out, and this was the first time that he refused to lecture, preach, or lead.[57] But while in prison he had learned (among other things) that it was best not to oppose the will of the majority, so he asked the Russian emissary why they were being moved to another camp if they were in any event going to join the army. The officer was courteous, to his surprise, and replied briefly that as long as the date of recruitment was not set, they were to continue their tasks. Begin was among the prisoners sent to the new work camp, but their ship sailed southward, toward a new future. When the ship anchored, Begin ran toward the gangway to get off, but someone shouted yet again, "He is a Yid, not a Pole." A long arm stopped Begin in his stride. Begin managed to get away without a word and jumped into a waiting boat.

The new camp was in Tashkent. When Begin arrived, he attempted to find out what had happened to his family. The terrible fate of Europe's Jews had slowly begun to be apparent. "The worst day of my life," he wrote in his memoirs about the moment he learned that his entire family had perished except for his sister Rachel.[58] Later, when he emigrated, he met with the Eldads and told them about the crises in his life. "Providence has helped me," he noted, adding, "I was not just saved. I have a purpose."[59] His sense of purpose—which destined him for a role in the history of Israel—accompanied him to his last day.

At the camp Begin joined hundreds of Polish Jews awaiting recruitment. After a brief medical examination (which almost disqualified him due to a heart defect), he was ranked a corporal. He was twenty-nine years old and just about to enter a new chapter in his life.

THREE

GOING UNDERGROUND

The Anders Army was established in the Soviet Union in July 1941 after the country was attacked by Germany.[1] In an agreement signed in London between General Władysław Sikorski, the exiled Polish prime minister, and Ivan Mayski, Soviet ambassador to the United Kingdom, it was agreed that a Polish force would be created within the Red Army. This force was named after its commander, General Władysław Anders. The Anders Army had seventy thousand soldiers, including five thousand Jews, most of whom were volunteers. In January 1942, Begin was recruited into one of its four brigades.

In late 1942 the Anders Army left its bases in the Soviet Union, joined the British forces in the Middle East, and headed toward the Western Desert. On the way it passed through Iran, Iraq, and Palestine. From the Western Desert it invaded Sicily with the British forces and then continued to Italy and joined the Allied forces in the battle of Monte Cassino and other battles on the Adriatic coast. Thousands of soldiers were killed, among them several hundred Jews.

Many Jews regarded the Anders Army as a means to fight the Nazis, but many looked for another purpose. When the army started moving toward the Middle East, families of Jewish soldiers, as well as orphaned Jewish children, joined the troops. Upon reaching Tehran, the children were placed in the care of messengers who brought them to Palestine on a mission known as the Tehran Children Aliyah (Aliyah [literally "going up"] means immigration to Palestine and later to Israel). When the Anders Army arrived in Israel, most of its Jewish soldiers deserted and assimilated into the local population. This mass desertion was known by the Jews as the Anders Aliyah, while the Poles called it treason and therefore refused to recruit any more Jews.²

The Revisionist activists in Israel utilized the Anders Army initially to free Begin from prison and then to bring him to Israel. Meir Kahn, a lawyer from Warsaw who had represented Jabotinsky in Poland before the war broke out; Miron Sheskin, a civilian adviser; and Yochanan Bader, a senior Beitar official from Krakow, sought to benefit from the good relations between the Polish government and the Revisionists—relations that were influenced by the ideological similarity between militant Polish nationalism and Beitar's militant nationalism—to create a separate Jewish brigade within the Anders Army that would fulfill the goal of resettling Palestine in the future. The army assigned Begin the role of military clerk; as such he would be neither a simple soldier nor a combat officer but rather "something in between."³

As expected, Begin made it very difficult to enlist him. Despite being released from prison because of his Polish nationality, he refused to have this nationality written on his identification card. "I'm not Polish," he said. Bader, who had gone to great lengths to have Begin recruited and even to secure him a comfortable position, could not contain his anger. "You idiot! If you had a chance to emigrate as a Muslim, wouldn't you take it?"⁴ Begin insisted that he did not want to lie. Three days later he changed his mind, offering no explanation. His longing to be reunited with Aliza, the desire to take the opportunity that had come his way, and the offer to return to Warsaw, which had already been bombed to the ground, convinced him to "lie," despite the fact that as a Zionist his goals were not the same as those of the Polish Army. When they set off, Begin suggested to one of his friends among the Jewish soldiers, Yitzhak Hochman, that they organize a separate group of Jews,⁵ and on his own accord, he updated the other soldiers on the political situation in Palestine.

In April 1942 the Anders Army arrived in Palestine by truck. The first stop was at Gedera. Begin looked out of the window mesmerized, and when they passed by a group of children, he yelled out to them "Hello, children, hello, children," as well as, "I am the Beitar commissioner."⁶

When the truck arrived at Gedera, Begin heard a distant shouting, "Menachem, Menachem, are you there?" It was Aliza! Begin, excited, asked the driver to stop and jumped from the truck. Upon their meeting Begin learned that Moshe Zak, a young journalist who used to work for the Revisionist newspaper *Hamashkif* (the Observer), had informed her that he would be arriving in Palestine as part of his service in the Anders Army. Zak did not know exactly when and where,[7] but Aliza found out, after a comprehensive investigation, that he would be passing through Gedera on his way to his base in Ashdod. In the evening the couple met in Ashdod and caught up on "other things," as Yitzhak Hochman demurely expressed it.[8]

Begin had not been recruited so that he could reunite with his wife; shortly after meeting with her, he had to adapt quickly to the military environment. The first thing he did after reporting to base was to receive a medical exemption from physical training because of his visual impairments and heart murmur. During the training sessions Begin kept busy by hosting visitors; the soldiers were so impressed by Begin's work that they soon insisted he should become the leader of the army's Jewish platoon.

When the company prepared to make its way to the Italian theater of battle, the Haganah tried to persuade the Jewish soldiers to defect and join the fighters in Palestine, maintaining that the Jewish communities in Europe were already a lost cause. The Haganah's efforts instigated arguments and fights among the Jewish soldiers, but when Begin was asked what to do, he could not decide. Ever since enlisting in Poland, he had considered the struggle against the British Mandate more important than the war against the Nazis (because he thought that the Jews alone could not defeat the Nazis anyway), but he would not encourage defection. "There is a global enemy, and to leave would be running away," he said. But he was not at peace with himself, perhaps because he had not joined the Anders Army in order to fight the Nazis. "You know what? Each man should choose according to his own conscience," he declared.[9]

Begin struggled to cope with military discipline, particularly with the need to fold his sheets precisely. His commanding officers told him that his behavior was a stain on the entire unit, but because they thought him detached from reality, they helped him with his chores rather than reprimanding him. A red and white tag that he punctiliously displayed on his uniform lapel marked him as a counselor, indicating that he was one of the intelligent soldiers in the company, and it helped him make a favorable impression.[10]

When the company left for Syria on the way to Italy, Begin was reassigned to serve as a clerk at the Jaffa Street headquarters of the Anders Army in Jerusalem, where he was put in charge of translations. With Aliza he rented a studio apartment, and all in all he seemed satisfied.

Meanwhile, he started to strengthen his ties with Beitar in Palestine. He often visited the Jabotinsky Institute in Tel Aviv. After Israel Eldad introduced him to the poet Uri Tzvi Greenberg, the poet noted that he was impressed with Begin but added that "he thinks he is Jabotinsky."[11] Begin started to write articles for the Beitar newspaper *Hamadrich* under the pseudonym "M. Ben Ze'ev." In his articles he called for Palestine's youth to wake up and fight the British.[12] When Begin's friends suggested that he should desert the Polish Army and join Etzel in its struggle against the British, Begin refused, saying, "I am not a deserter." In late 1942 he was appointed as the Beitar commissioner in Palestine, and he asked David Lotan and Israel Epstein, his friends from Beitar in Poland, to assist him in his new position.[13]

Meanwhile, speculations were being raised about what Begin would do when he was discharged from the Polish Army. Natan Yellin-Mor, at the time one of the three Lehi commanders—the other two were Yitzhak Shamir (original family name: Yazernitski) and Israel Eldad (Shayeb)—adamantly insisted that Begin should join Lehi. Eldad, who was aware of the large gap between Begin's verbal aggression and his actions, thought Begin would join Etzel. He was not mistaken.[14]

Little is known about the seventeen months between Begin's arrival in Palestine and his appointment as commander of Etzel, as Begin himself was not inclined to elaborate on that time. These months of adjustment to the land that Begin had learned to love from a distance were not easy for him. He traveled all over the country, first to the Western Wall (the Wailing Wall) in the Old City of Jerusalem. He mostly befriended acquaintances from Beitar in Poland who had immigrated to Palestine,[15] such as Menachem Bocwitz, his partner from the Polish Aliyah organization. When Bocwitz was invited to visit Begin at his home, he was surprised to find that Begin recited the Kiddush and avoided traveling on the Sabbath.[16]

In March 1943, ten months after Begin had reunited with Aliza, the couple's first son, Binyamin Ze'ev (named after Begin's father, not after Jabotinsky as presumed), was born. Begin announced the Brit Milah in *Hamashkif*; the ceremony was held at Hadassah Hospital.[17]

In December, British intelligence reported to the Polish Army about Begin's activity in Beitar, and he was forced to resign his position ahead of schedule. Begin was disappointed but realized that holding his Beitar post while serving in the army was a waste of time.

During 1942–1943, Etzel was at its ebb. On May 20, 1941, Etzel commander David Raziel was killed in Iraq during a British military mission whose importance was controversial.[18] His replacement, Yaakov Meridor, an engineer, struggled to lead the underground organization. Meridor was too deeply involved in the dispute that had split Etzel in 1939, which had arisen when Avraham Stern had demanded that Etzel continue fighting the British despite the fight against the Nazis—a dispute that even led to information being leaked to the British Crime Investigation Department (CID). Because his demand was rejected, Stern quit and formed Lehi with his followers. Etzel headquarters suspected that Stern had contacts with British intelligence double agents, as they had become too close.[19]

During 1943 Etzel was in fact paralyzed and carried out only sporadic operations, most of them conducted by frustrated members acting on their own. Many members thought that the organization needed a different kind of leader. "We need a political figure, a counselor and an educator. Not a leader who has only military knowledge; in fact, [military knowledge] is not even necessarily a requirement," said Eliyahu Lankin, a member of Etzel headquarters.[20] (Etzel headquarters was composed of five to nine members, depending on the period and the situation.)

Begin, who was in Vilnius when the split occurred, was not directly involved in the internal rivalry, and for this reason he became one of the major candidates for the organization's leadership. Fate had created a once-in-a-lifetime opportunity for the man who had never fired a gun in his life. "There was nobody else for the job," said Yitzhak Shamir later.[21] At first, Begin, who had already learned to use the local slang, refused the suggestion and with his close friends used the term "laughter aside" (meaning "as funny as it is, this is a serious matter"). "I am a soldier in the Polish Army," he clarified; "I cannot desert; I have to be legally discharged."[22]

One stormy night in January 1943, Meir Kahn, who had orchestrated Begin's recruitment, decided to convince him to defect. Kahn was excited about his upcoming meeting with Begin, at last in Palestine, in Begin's apartment in Jerusalem. When he entered the apartment, he found Begin lying on the sofa covered with his army coat, cold and grumpy. "What do you want from me?" Begin scowled at Kahn as if he already knew the answer to his question. Kahn ignored this strange hospitality and went straight to the point: "Menachem, look, whether we like it or not, the birds of heaven are passing the word that you should be the Etzel commander. We should do everything to get you out of the army." Begin looked at Kahn with a blank expression. Kahn continued: "I have an idea, but I cannot disclose any more ideas without your consent." After their conversation, Begin was less determined than before to stay in the army and merely stated, "You can do beautiful things; if possible, a blessing will come on to you."[23]

Kahn was certain he had convinced Begin. But Begin stubbornly held to his position against desertion and was not enthusiastic about taking on the leadership role. While his resistance was admirable, Begin started to appear hesitant, almost cowardly. Was this the way a man meant to lead a terrorist organization should act? Was Begin unable to distinguish between the end and the means, between the wheat and the chaff? Was it personal integrity or the conservative views of a man afraid to break the rules through illegal activity?[24]

Begin was reluctant not only because he objected to desertion, but also because he secretly hoped to be appointed leader of Hatzohar (the Hebrew acronym for Revisionist Zionist Party), headed after Jabotinsky's death by Arie Altman; he knew that if he deserted the army now, he would not be able to engage openly in politics.

Eventually Arie Ben Eliezer and Meir Kahn pressured the Polish government into releasing Begin, and he was temporarily discharged for a year.[25] The argument that led to his release was the need to add Begin to a delegation of Jewish soldiers, all members of the Revisionist movement, who were about to leave for the United States on a publicity campaign on behalf of the exiled Polish government; the delegation was intended to convince American Jews to influence public opinion so as to get the United States involved on behalf of the exiled Polish government.[26] The delegation never left, however, because of objections from the British Mandate authorities, thus leaving Begin free to join Etzel in Palestine.

Begin's refusal to defect is still seen today as an example of his characteristic honesty,[27] although from a formal aspect, emphasized by Begin, it is unclear whether his next step was legal because when the year of temporary discharge was up, Begin neglected to find out what the Polish Army wanted and justified not returning by the fact that he was not called back to the ranks.[28] Now he started planning his future.

After his temporary discharge, Begin asked for two months off in order to settle his personal affairs; during this time Shlomo Lev Ami served as the head of Etzel. While waiting, Begin strategized about his first moves as Etzel commander, and in a typical manner, he decided to declare a rebellion against British rule: "Yes, we will cripple them; we will crush the head of the British serpent. We will take action; we will strike them down and continue in the path of the Maccabees."[29] But how was this to be accomplished? He left this part of the plan to the experts and concentrated on ideals.

An hour before he was scheduled to depart for his first meeting at Etzel headquarters as commander of the organization on October 17, 1943, on Hess Street in Tel Aviv, Begin had prepared for everything but one minor detail—his clothes. Until that moment he had worn the Polish uniform, and he realized he had nothing to wear. Kahn waited patiently for him while he prepared, and Aliza asked, "Exactly how are you planning to go? You have to return the uniform to the quartermaster. Are you going out in your underwear?" She suggested that Kahn choose clothes appropriate to his new position, and Begin did not part from the gray suit Kahn chose for him at a Jerusalem tailor's until his last day with Etzel.[30] Kahn was not surprised that Begin had nothing to wear, as during his previous visits to the Begin household he had become aware of Begin's helplessness regarding daily functions. Every time he saw Begin trying to feed his son Benny, he knew that by the end of it both father and son would need to be cleaned up.[31] Perhaps this is why Aliza told Kahn before they departed for the meeting, "I would prefer he did not roam around alone, so please escort him all the way to the meeting and back."[32]

Not all Etzel members welcomed Begin's appointment as commander. Regardless of their agreement on the need to appoint a political leader from the outside, many questioned his military capabilities.[33] Key members, such as Dov Rubinstein, the top official from the Tel Aviv headquarters, threatened to resign. They claimed that Begin lacked any military knowledge and had only recently immigrated to Palestine.[34] One member, Yerachmiel Ben Dov Halevi, referred to him as "a stranger, a new immigrant," and at the end of the first meeting he told his friends that Begin had made "no impression."[35]

Even his manners were strange. Etzel commanders used to include a pretty young woman to escort them to meetings so as to provide them with a romantic camouflage, and Begin used to kiss his escort's hand every time they crossed the street.[36] "What's wrong with him? Is he sick?" one member asked Shlomo Lev Ami, trying to understand the commander's behavior.[37] Lev Ami felt that "this was a time of confusion for Begin, who did not seem to understand what was happening around him. He had no knowledge about leading an underground or commanding operations; his strong point was that Etzel considered him a man of the world who had come to Palestine from Europe and knew languages."[38]

Some members had wanted to appoint Arie Ben Eliezer to the leadership; he had come to Palestine in order to strengthen the organization, but because he was known to the British, the idea was shelved.[39] When Begin learned about this, he turned to his friend Yochanan Bader, who had recently immigrated himself, and divulged his feelings: "The reform plan for Etzel is my idea! Mine! It has nothing to do with America."[40] Bader tried to calm him down. But the fear that the organization might split again or miss the opportunity to fulfill its purpose if it did not become stronger, as well as pressure from members in the field—three junior members planned to assassinate the British high commissioner at the beginning of October 1943 of their own accord (an event that, had it taken place, would have had disastrous consequences for the Yishuv, the Jewish community in Palestine prior to establishment of the state)[41]—forced the headquarters members to agree to Begin's appointment as the new commander despite their doubts and despite the fact that he had been only a corporal in the Polish Army and had never participated in a real battle. During the first meeting it was decided to call him "Ben David," and they never discussed the nickname's connection to the name of the Messiah (the Hebrew expression is "Messiah Ben David"—the Messiah, son of David).

During his early days in the organization Begin still lived on the ground floor at 25 Alfasi Street in Jerusalem. Every Sunday morning he traveled to Tel Aviv, returning to Jerusalem for the weekends. In Tel Aviv he focused on getting acquainted with the organization and formulating a strategy for the opening of the rebellion. Not long afterward, when Aliza realized that their house was being watched, Begin decided to move.[42] His selection for their new residence was both strange and brilliant: the Hotel Savoy, a small hotel on Geula Street in Tel Aviv. The owner was a veteran Revisionist, a man who could be trusted, yet Kahn did not trust him enough to tell him about Begin's position in the organization and instead introduced him as a relative and lawyer from Jerusalem who was in Tel Aviv to open a practice.

Begin lived alone at the hotel for the first two months, after which Aliza and Benny were smuggled into the Savoy, to room 17. But even there Begin knew no peace. The British police conducted routine searches in the hotel's vicinity, convincing Begin once again to relocate.[43] Etzel members hastily put the family up in a small house at the edge of the Yemenite neighborhood near Petach Tikva, though they overlooked the possibly suspicious fact that the Begins were the only Ashkenazi family in the neighborhood. A month later the family moved again, this time to the Hasidof neighborhood, near Kfar Sirkin, where Begin pretended to be a lawyer called Israel Halperin.

The danger that the Germans would enter the Middle East had passed, and the British tried to appease the Arabs in the Middle East in general and in Palestine in particular, mostly because they wanted the area to be peaceful enough to prevent the United States and the Soviet Union from interfering in the region. In light of the ending war in Europe, they recognized the importance of the Middle East and its oil reserves; a document published by the British Foreign Office in January 1944 stated that the solution to the problems in Palestine should not focus solely on global sympathy for the suffering of the Jews.[44]

The leaders of the Yishuv discussed the ramifications of the end of the war on the British Mandate and agreed that an important change was about to take place, but they did not agree on the form it would take.[45] David Ben Gurion, chairman of the Jewish Agency, waited for the realization of Winston Churchill's promise that "after the war the Jews will receive the biggest plum in the cake" (according to the Biltmore Program of May 1942)[46] and hoped that because of the suffering of displaced Jews who remained homeless they would garner international support for the idea of a Jewish country.

Begin saw the British refusal to allow the Jewish refugees of the Holocaust entrance into Palestine as a reason for intensifying the struggle against them. Unlike Lehi, which saw the struggle against the British in Palestine as a battle against British imperialism in general, and like his teacher Ze'ev Jabotinsky, Begin persisted in his belief that there was room for future collaboration with the British, but as long as there was no official Jewish state, for him Britain was the enemy. The notion that the end of the war lessened the need for solidarity with the British, mainly because of the emerging change of stance in America—President Roosevelt had declared in May, "Full justice will be done to those who seek a Jewish national home"[47]—convinced Begin that the British government was the main obstacle in the way of establishing a Jewish state. As Etzel commander he could not influence diplomatic decisions, and in light of the political direction that seemed to be developing among Jewish leaders, Begin thought that terrorist activities against the British Mandate in Palestine were warranted in order to pressure them to leave the region and to arouse public opinion in the United States regarding the distress of the Jews in Eretz Israel.

FOUR

DECLARATION OF REBELLION

In January 1944, when Begin decided—after serving only three months as Etzel commander, aware of the doubts surrounding his ability to lead the organization—to announce to Etzel headquarters members that he would declare the beginning of a military revolt against the British, it was pouring rain. When he entered the conference room in which the members were waiting, wearing his gray suit, they stood to attention. Military discipline still appealed to him, and even his close associates at Etzel headquarters were instructed to refer to him as "sir."[1] His face revealed his distress, like someone who had not left himself an escape route, as he strode to and fro across the room.

As in all the meetings Begin had attended during the prior three months, everyone remained standing until he had shaken the hand of every single member. The gap between the standing to attention and the personal handshake was characteristic of Begin, whose actions involved something of ritual and sentiment. He also decided that Etzel decisions would not be voted upon but rather that no decision would be accepted until every last member had been convinced to support it. Since Begin was an adamant man, his overbearing insistence was imposed on the members, to the point that they were convinced to accept.

The importance Begin attached to ceremony and the historical perspective that was evident in all Etzel activities were reflected in his very first decision as a leader—the dictation of protocols. Until January 1944 Etzel protocols had been written irregularly, mainly due to the assumption that a documentation of events might damage the organization during the game of hide-and-seek it was playing with the British. But Begin thought about the future and convinced his friend and headquarters member Eliyahu Lankin to suggest to fellow members that they start keeping orderly protocols of every conference.[2]

Transcription was momentarily halted when Begin stated that the revolt against the British must be explicitly announced. Looking at the faces of those around him, he found they all looked shocked and hesitant. "Maybe we should start in action," suggested Chief of Staff Shlomo Lev Ami. "We're tired of making announcements," added Lankin. Most members supported them. Lev Ami also stressed that Etzel had only 1,200 members, of which only 350 were trained fighters. The weapons count was also discouraging: one machine gun, five submachine guns, ninety pistols, sixty rifles, one hundred hand grenades, and five tons of explosives.[3] Begin was convinced that this stockpile was enough to start driving the British out of the land of Israel.

Begin's confidence of victory did not stem from military strategy alone. The call for revolt was characteristic of Begin not only because of his demand to open it with a public announcement—like his days in the Polish Beitar, he first voiced his ideology and only then began thinking about its practical execution—but also because he believed that a public announcement calling for a general strike would carry the masses. As expected, his prediction was not fulfilled.[4]

Begin needed a great deal of confidence to suggest a rebellion so decisively; he was aware of the talk in many circles, as well as articles in the Haganah's magazine, that emphasized the impertinence of a recent arrival in Palestine who had not participated in the building of the Yishuv and who had not tried to obtain the support of the majority and yet was daring to create mayhem, thereby endangering what had been achieved. Begin knew that the Etzel members would find it difficult to ignore the criticism aimed at him. But his suggestion was important on the political level as well: with his announcement he had taken upon himself political responsibility for the entire Revisionist movement, despite the fact that Hatzohar still believed that the Yishuv and the British Mandate had common interests.[5]

Etzel had never been Hatzohar's operational arm, even though Jabotinsky had been its high commander, and the fact that many members of the underground were Revisionists and Beitarists did not oblige Begin to adhere to the guidelines of the party, which was headed by Arie Altman, who opposed the use of firearms. As noted, even before Begin's appointment as Etzel commander, party member Arie Ben Eliezer had been sent from the United States to Palestine in order to strengthen the organization.[6] Unlike Hatzohar members, Etzel leaders did not oppose military action against the British, but most of them did not understand the logic behind a public announcement promoting military action, especially as they feared that a military operation would fail.

Begin was determined not to give up. He believed that there would be difficulties and disappointments, which is precisely why he thought they should define how long a revolt would take.[7] In fact, Begin counted on the fighting spirit of the younger members when he declared the rebellion. He recognized their frustration at the lack of military action, which was manifested in the plan to assassinate the British high commissioner, and with this recognition he showed the traits of a gifted politician.

During the January meeting Begin laid out the political considerations guiding his decision to declare a rebellion: the fear that the Arabs would start another revolt, as they had during the notorious 1936–1939 riots; the importance of preempting them so that British appeasement of the Arabs would not hurt Jewish interests; the belief that a revolt would gain international sympathy and increase British citizens' objection to their government's presence in the region; the extra burden on the British budget and the damage to Britain's prestige; and the buttressing of the Yishuv's self-confidence. In general, Begin believed that the younger members' spirit of nationalism would be enough for the rebellion to succeed.[8]

Begin did not share one other consideration with the members during the meeting, but he confided it to Moshe Sneh, head of the Haganah national headquarters. He understood that Etzel, which he had joined when it was almost completely paralyzed, had no right to exist if it did not maintain an active resistance. "If not for our military operations, the Jewish Agency would not have paid us any attention," Begin said.[9]

Begin did not find it easy to convince the members. He pledged that "our war will come after the announcement," and by so doing, he addressed their feelings. "Give me credit," he half requested, half demanded.[10] Begin was convinced that the members of the headquarters, who knew that bringing him into the organization had been intended to inspire new action, would not resist his offer,[11] and eventually his adherence to the idea of revolt bore fruit.

On January 28, 1944, after the meeting, Begin began to write the announcement in terms of the ideas he had formulated before the discussion. David Yotan copied what he had written and took it to the printer. Begin waited for the printed version at the apartment on Mazeh Street in Tel Aviv, and when it arrived, he felt as though he had seen Moses's Burning Bush: his dreams had been materialized. He held the manifesto and shouted, "It's colossal, it's huge."[12] Years later he recalled how he had come up with the plan to rebel during his days in the Polish Army, before knowing whether Etzel could pull it off.[13] He thought there was an ideological link between the revolt and the ideas of Jabotinsky, who had called for the establishment of a Jewish Legion in the 1920s, although Jabotinsky saw the legion's actions as an alternative to illegal activities and adamantly opposed terrorism.

Confidence, innocence, and pride were all present in Begin's personality, and his belief that destiny had led him to this moment lifted his spirits.[14]

The manifesto expressed the style and principles Begin would instill in Etzel in almost every dimension: pathos, a passionate belief in the righteousness of the organization's path, a gap between ambition and political realism, and inflammatory talk:

> We are nearing the final stage of the war. We are facing a decision that will change the fate of generations to come. The cease-fire announced at the beginning of World War II has been broken by the British. The rulers of our land did not take loyalty, concessions, or sacrifices into account; they have fulfilled and are still moving forward with their plan: the elimination of national Zionism.... We shall draw our conclusions fearlessly.... No more cease-fire in the land of Israel between the people and the Hebrew youth and the British administration, which hands over our brothers to Hitler.... The leadership will be placed immediately in the hands of a temporary Jewish government.... The establishment of a Jewish government that will achieve its goals is the only way to save our people, to save our lives and our honor.... Hebrews! The fighting youth will not be deterred by the victims of war and pain, blood, and suffering. They shall not surrender and they shall not rest as long as they are unable to bring back a time when our people had a land of their own, freedom, dignity, bread, justice, and law.[15]

The declaration of rebellion was also broadcast on the underground radio station Kol Zion Halochemet (the Voice of Fighting Zion). Begin preferred to refer to the announcement as La Palabra (Spanish: the

Word), and only in the 1950s did he understand why people used to mock him by calling it "Begin's Palabra."[16] He learned that in slang *palabra* means "arrogance without content."

Begin's announcement of a rebellion was indeed defiant and daring, but it was devoid of content in terms of Etzel's military capabilities. Yet Begin's emotion-laden manifesto should be understood as an attempt to alter the image of the Jews in exile. Therefore, despite the ridicule of his opponents, he persisted. Later, during the War of Independence, when his words were translated from Hebrew into English during a press conference following the battle over Jaffa, journalist Shalom Rosenfeld plaintively told the translator on behalf of Begin, "You have translated well but excluded all the pathos."[17]

The manifesto was accompanied by a demand to establish a Jewish state. It heightened Ben Gurion's fears that Begin's will to lead the Jewish state was real and strengthened his resolve to bring down Etzel, even though he did not believe it had any real military capabilities.

The Yishuv's position on Begin's announcement changed on March 22, 1944, when Etzel simultaneously struck British intelligence facilities in Jerusalem, Jaffa, and Haifa, and the Yishuv realized that Etzel could not only threaten but also act. Begin would have preferred a more complicated symbolic act—for example, kidnapping the high commissioner from his palace in Talpiot in Jerusalem in order either to expel him from the country or to execute him—but Etzel members preferred actions that would not arouse a strong British reaction that would endanger the entire organization.[18] Prior to the attack, Begin would ask Eitan Livni, the head of the Etzel operations staff, on an almost daily basis, "When will we be ready?"[19] Livni persuaded him to attack three targets at once in order to intensify the effect. Begin agreed, thinking that "at least one will be successful."[20] But all three targets were hit, so Begin, excited about his ability to make a decision and act upon it, pressured Etzel also to execute a mission code-named "The Wall," which was planned in order to enable the Jews to blow the Shofar at the Western Wall on Yom Kippur—despite a British ruling that no religious ceremonies would be held at the Western Wall because they feared riots by the Arabs. The Etzel members supported the plan, but it remained a low priority from an operational perspective. Nevertheless, at every meeting Begin reminded the members of the "disgrace of the repression imposed on the last vestige of the Jewish people's heritage."[21]

In 1944 before Yom Kippur, Etzel published a warning saying, "Any British policeman who interferes with the blowing of the Shofar will be deemed a criminal." Toward the end of Yom Kippur, Etzel had still made no appearance at the Western Wall as it had warned, but the British officers in the area preferred to avoid conflict with the worshipers and turned a blind eye. Thus prayers were not obstructed, and Begin felt like he had won the game, even though the British returned to the site immediately after to signal that they were still in charge.

Operation Wall was not the most important in the history of Etzel, but it emphasized Begin's main approach in the organization's initial operations: symbolic declarative acts, not necessarily with any real military content. Toward the end of that day, March 22, Etzel attacked four police stations—ostensibly in response to the British presence at the Western Wall during prayer time, but in actual fact the operation had been preplanned under the assumption that the British would still be occupied at the Western Wall.[22] The police station attacks were of more interest to other Etzel members than to Begin, who announced the following day that the blowing of the Shofar was a "historic victory." In any event, the British and Ben Gurion were now no longer willing to let Begin dictate the national agenda.

Since Etzel's founding, members had argued that military pressure would affect British policy more than diplomacy,[23] but only after the declaration of revolt, which put an end to the post–World War II peaceful relations with the British, did the organization embark on its important military chapter. Ben Gurion believed that Etzel's actions were dangerous, both because they went against his strategy to withhold resistance against the British forces and because they threatened the legitimacy of the institutions currently in place.

Two weeks after the attacks on the British facilities, the executive members of the Jewish Agency held the first hearing on the actions that should be taken against Begin. Golda Meir could not restrain herself and demanded that the dissidents be physically eliminated. Ben Gurion responded, partly sarcastically and partly concerned, and asked in a typical manner, "What if they retaliate?" They adjourned undecided but knew they were nearing the day of reckoning. In April, Eliyahu Golomb, commander of the Haganah, convened a press conference in which he said, among other things, that "the Yishuv has a moral obligation to put an end to the terrorist phenomenon of two wayward groups.... Our interest should be to avoid civil war, though we should not assume that they will not drag us into it."[24] During the discussion held before the press conference, the Jewish Agency was told that the government of the British Mandate was not satisfied with its condemnations and demanded cooperation that entailed the Agency's giving the British information about Etzel and Lehi members. Most members of the Jewish Agency rejected this demand, in part because they objected to handing over Jews to the British, but also because of a growing opinion that they should take independent action. In the discussion Ben Gurion declared, "With Jewish force and Jewish means, we must prevent the gangs' actions."[25]

At the beginning of 1945 Begin moved to a two-bedroom apartment on Yehoshua Bin Nun Street (now Bashan Street) in Tel Aviv and changed his name to Israel Sasover. He also changed his physical appearance: he grew a beard along with the mustache he had grown during his time in the Polish Army. He also attached the title "Rabbi" to his name, so he made sure to keep a prayer book and teffilin at arm's reach. But he found it difficult to cope with the withdrawal from society and the forced loneliness and endangered the compartmentalization that was practiced in the underground. When Eitan Livni asked Shraga Alis from the Etzel planning division to prepare a hiding place in the commander's apartment, the latter did not suspect a thing. Alis was told that Rabbi Sasover's family was willing, when necessary, to host a family fleeing the fighting; he did not inquire about the other rooms, as he was told that there was a dying grandmother in one of them and he had better not open any doors. Two hours later Begin came out of the room with a cup of tea. Alis, who had known Begin from the Anders Army, did not even need to guess. Begin told him who he was (since he was undercover), and Alis, astounded at the revelation, said, "Yes, sir," ignoring all the rules of secrecy. What if they arrest me and I give him up? he found himself thinking. But Begin could not let pass an opportunity to converse with a member of the organization, and he mentioned that he wanted a new radio with shortwave reception that would "open up my space."[26] "Had there been telephones back then, Begin would never have survived his time in the underground," Yechiel Kadishai, his personal aide since 1964, recalled.[27]

The first to suspect Begin were his neighbors, not the British. One of them approached him, and Begin, startled, did not hesitate to raise the subject of the Holocaust and use his theatrical skills to fool him. He stammered a bit and made it clear that since he had fled the Nazis, he remained in a state of shock and all he could do was pray.[28] Ironically, the more the British and the Haganah searched for Etzel members, the more the lines blurred between Begin's cover identity and his real life: the commander of the underground avoided making eye contact with other members, and in order to get some exercise, he often went to the synagogue to pray.

Usually, after his meetings in Tel Aviv, Begin tried to return to his own apartment on Yehoshua Bin Nun Street, where Aliza and Benny were waiting. But sometimes, fearing the British, Begin would stay with his friend Yaakov Tabin, the Etzel head of intelligence whose apartment at 71 Kishon Street served as a hideout. Tabin, his wife Miryam, and Begin all slept in the same narrow bed, with Tabin between his wife and Begin. "We don't have a decent place to spend the night hours, while others our age are happily lounging in cafes," said Begin. "Jewish complacency. But do not be angry. They will learn. By our way. By the way of the rifle. What happened in Europe will not happen here."[29] Tabin listened. He knew his commander well, and he was used to hearing him make associations between the Holocaust and the current situation in Palestine.

Aliza was used to such alterations in plans and did not complain. She reminded Begin of his mother. Sometimes Begin forgot to give her the household allowance and pocket money—25–30 pounds a month,[30] granted by Etzel—since he himself would skip meals.[31] It seemed that the only way the commander could demonstrate some sort of physical prowess was by overcoming his hunger, as he spent many days doing nothing.[32] In those days he would read, listen to the radio, and think.[33]

Although Begin served as Etzel's political commander, he gleaned most of his information from the newspapers, especially the *Times*, but also the Hagana journal *Eshnav* (Hebrew: small window) and newspapers of the other parties; also he obsessively listened to the radio. He could only dream about holding meetings on political matters.

Every morning his contact woman would come to his hideout with all the daily newspapers. When he did not go to headquarters meetings, he would stay in his room and analyze the various reports and political opinions. Despite being unable to interfere with diplomatic proceedings, he reiterated that it was not necessary to meet with diplomats in order to formulate policies, as in this day and age one could learn everything about British policies from the *Times*. He also listened regularly to the BBC news and thus created his own private intelligence network.[34] Cigarettes, newspapers, and radio—with them he spent his days in the underground.

Begin relied on the media not only because of the reality imposed on him, but also because he internalized their influence to a high degree. During a meeting of headquarters members that convened in October

1944 Begin claimed that the reports about Etzel indicated that it was a success: "The newspapers have proved to the English people that the situation is serious. The *Times* has remarked that if the situation were to continue along these lines, it could lead to anarchy." Upon realizing that not all members believed there was such a strong connection between what was printed and what was actually happening, he clarified that "[media reports] make an impression on the reader, and the public is already showing signs of demanding a change in the situation." As an example of the media's efficiency he referred to *The Economist* and the left-wing British newspaper *New Statesman*, adding that after a meeting of a member of Etzel headquarters with a journalist from a Yiddish newspaper in America, "We learned that we have gained tremendous public opinion in our favor."[35] Begin saw the media themselves as a political factor; later his extensive knowledge of and acquaintance with various publications became part of his personal power.

In 1978, when he was prime minister, Begin invited Chanan Porat, a leader of the right-wing group Gush Emunim, to update him on the talks conducted in Washington about the Palestinian plan for autonomy. Old copies of the *New York Times* were strewn on the floor of the Prime Minister's Residence, and Begin told the astonished Porat, "Look what they wrote about me when I came to power. I'll show them that the one who they said would bring about Israel's destruction is the one who will bring peace!"[36]

As noted above, Begin's obsession with newspapers developed because of the reality of his situation. The headquarters members met less and less frequently, as the need to take precautions became imminent when the British promised a 10,000-pound reward for anyone who could hand Begin over to the authorities. Begin, in his thirties, missed human contact and often clashed with members of the headquarters in his efforts to convince them to loosen the security precautions.[37] Even his facial hair, which he had grown as a disguise, started to irritate him.[38] But he had no choice. He laughed when he heard that "the British claim that two SS skinheads are assigned to my security twenty-four hours a day," while his security precautions were so poor.[39]

During Begin's days in the underground, Moshe Dayan, at the time a senior commander in the Haganah, was one of the few people with whom Begin met who was not in Etzel. They met after both Etzel and Lehi had had resounding operational successes. On May 17, 1944, Etzel attacked and seized the central broadcasting station in Ramallah, and in July it blew up the CID district headquarters building in Jerusalem; a month later Lehi unsuccessfully tried to assassinate High Commissioner Harold MacMichael, and the mere bravado of executing an action that could sabotage relations with the British Mandate startled Jewish Agency leaders.

Begin and Dayan agreed to meet in August at the apartment on Kishon Street in Tel Aviv. Begin was mainly impressed with Dayan's "quiet tone of voice. He had lost his eye in Syria, but he certainly had not lost his courage."[40] Dayan, for his part, was surprised when he saw Begin so smartly dressed. In the report he sent to the Haganah's Information Service, Shai (Hebrew: Sherut Yediot), after their meeting, he noted that he was particularly impressed with the commander's appearance: "He has large and parted front teeth and is well dressed."[41]

Indeed, despite the fact that he was in hiding, Begin utilized his free time quite well, cultivating his stylish mustache and wearing fashionable sunglasses. He was not an attractive man and often ridiculed his own appearance. The British circulated a photo of him with a shaved head and a beard that made him look dangerous; Begin said that the photo was a mistake and remarked, "In my usual appearance I am much uglier."[42]

Dayan was one of the Haganah activists. He did not rule out rebellion, but unlike Begin, he believed that Etzel should accept the authority of the institutions representing the people. "You have no right to act without coordination and approval," he stated. Begin claimed that the British would leave only once their interests in the land had been damaged and added that he would accept Ben Gurion's leadership only if he would head a unified military unit. "Since Jabotinsky's death, we have had no ambitions to lead the Yishuv," he stressed, hinting at Ben Gurion's suspicions about him. Dayan expressed his respect for Etzel because it had taught that Jews were able to react, but he added that it was not the right time for it, in part because they were not yet permitted to do so. The two men respected each other: Begin admired any Jew who agreed to carry arms, and Dayan's eye-patch symbolized courage to him, while the young Dayan thought Begin's policies were consistent with his belief that the battle for a Jewish state would lead to a show of arms. However, in meeting with Begin he took a stance representing the Yishuv leaders, who preferred to hold onto Winston Churchill's promise that the British would help establish a Jewish brigade, which both Ben Gurion and the Jewish Agency saw as a basis for the establishment of a Jewish army. As noted, the Yishuv and the

Jewish Agency saw the activities of Begin, who was still a new immigrant, as provocative and insolent and feared that he was threatening their hopes of a Jewish brigade, whether he was conscious or unconscious of the fact. Their hostility toward him was fiercer than the hostility they felt toward Lehi, many of whose members were working class, led a lifestyle similar to that of the members of the Palmach (Hebrew acronym for "shock companies," the Haganah's elite fighting force, comprised mainly of kibbutzniks), and carried out their underground activities in a way similar to that of the partisans.[43] Because of the warnings against Etzel published in various newspapers by the Jewish Agency, Begin asked Dayan at the end of their meeting, "Are you also in favor of violence against us?" Dayan said no. But before they parted, Dayan reminded him that he was first and foremost a soldier, and therefore, "If I receive an order to [use violence against Etzel], I will."[44] A month later Begin held a meeting with Moshe Sneh, head of the Haganah national staff, during which he understood the actual meaning of Dayan's statement.

The initiative to hold the conference with Sneh arose during a meeting between Eliyahu Lankin from Etzel headquarters and Eliezer Livneh, editor of *Eshnav*, who proposed to bring Begin and Ben Gurion together. Etzel headquarters decided to accept the suggestion. Begin refused to intervene in the decision and let Lankin deal with the other members. "It's important for the consolidation of the Yishuv and for Etzel's status," Lankin said. Begin listened, smiled, and said the proposal was "enthusiastic."[45] Begin was actually the one who was most excited about meeting with Ben Gurion but was too proud to bring it up himself. Lankin's energetic support for the joint conference made it easier for Begin to "surrender" to the proposal.[46] Begin needed this meeting to obtain certain information, but he also had another agenda: he believed that the meeting would not only even out the status of the two organizations—or would at least acknowledge Etzel's significance—but would also even the playing field between Ben Gurion and himself. This was precisely why Ben Gurion did not want to meet with him. When Etzel decided to hold the meeting, Yaakov Tabin was assigned to make the preparations. Despite the plan, Ben Gurion refused to meet with Begin, claiming that "In any case I won't find any common language with him,"[47] and he asked Sneh to take his place.

The first meeting was held on Sunday, September 8, 1944, six months after the revolt began. Etzel was in charge of security measures. Tabin met Sneh at his apartment, and the two walked along Sheinkin Street in Tel Aviv. When they reached Magen David Square, Tabin stopped a taxi and ordered the driver to go to northern Tel Aviv. Half an hour later the taxi arrived back at Sheinkin Street. Surprised, Sneh asked why they had driven around in circles. Tabin explained that he wanted to make sure that they were not being followed. They made their way to 74 Yonah Hanavi Street. Tabin and Sneh met Lankin on the staircase, and then Tabin departed. Sneh and Lankin then went up to the apartment of Luca and Israel Wax. Sneh was surprised that there was no security at the meeting place.

Begin greeted his guests wearing his grey suit, pacing back and forth as was his habit. This was a crucial meeting for him as Etzel commander, and the very possibility of associating with one of the most influential people in the Yishuv raised his spirits immensely. Up until the moment Sneh entered the apartment, Begin had hoped that Ben Gurion would come to the meeting, and his disappointment was apparent on learning that Sneh had been asked to replace his great rival.

Begin invited Sneh to join him and the others at a round table laid out with fruit and cigarettes in a corner of the living room. But Sneh surprised him and requested that they meet tête-à-tête. Lankin quickly left the living room before Begin could even respond to the request and joined Mr. and Mrs. Wax in the kitchen. Lankin was aware of his commander's tendency to be pedantic about matters pertaining to honor and wished to avoid any conflict at the beginning of the meeting.

Begin had first met Sneh in 1939, when the two had tried to escape from Vilna. They did not cultivate a strong friendship. Sneh was born in Rodzin, where a combination of ultra-Orthodox Jews alongside a large community of secular Jews provoked civil unrest, both culturally and ideologically.[48] Begin respected Sneh because he had strong views and because he was a Zionist with a developed social consciousness. Both were brilliant orators, though their styles were different; Sneh spoke clearly, adamantly, and precisely and without melodrama. Despite their stylistic differences, once they were alone, Begin approached to embrace him. Sneh, who was not accustomed to such gestures, drew back. "He is too theatrical," Sneh wrote in disapproval of Begin in his report to Ben Gurion following their meeting.[49] Unlike Etzel members, Sneh thought that Begin's grand gestures were irritating at best and devoid of content at worst. "I know him from Poland—a pathetic man," he reported to his friends.[50] Their different styles were not the only gap between the two. They were both young, and their political activities were the result not only of their ideologies, but also because they were men. (Despite the fact that Begin was only thirty-two years old, not much older than the Etzel members [most of whom were in their mid-twenties], he liked the nickname "the Old Man,"[51] which they had attached to him. Eventually they stopped using this nickname because it was also the popular nickname of his political rival, Ben Gurion.)

The meeting between Begin and Sneh lasted three hours, most of it in the guise of a friendly and professional get-together, but their mutual distrust was apparent. Sneh's distrust of Begin was so great that in his report to Ben Gurion he wrote it was possible that Begin was an American spy. "I only suggest it, without any proof, but by the confidence and enthusiasm he expressed when speaking about American support [for the establishment of a Jewish state] it is possible that he is actually in contact with . . . them."[52]

Begin spoke the first words at the meeting, as he did at Etzel meetings. Despite being aware that this time he would mainly have to listen to Sneh, he gave a lengthy overview of the political situation, of which he was well informed.[53] Because he spent most of his time in seclusion, no one escaped such summaries whenever he had the chance to talk with someone. (Even the Etzel manifestos he published—which were mainly written by him in a style quite foreign to the spirit of the youth surrounding him—were a form of conversation with the outside world.)

Sneh was not impressed with Begin's overview and was in fact particularly unimpressed by the way he spoke, a thought he expressed in his concluding report, which noted that Begin was boring, tedious, and tended to speak in a florid style.[54] To detract from the importance Begin attached to his role, Sneh asked, "But how do you allow yourself to wage a war without any military assistance from intelligence sources?" It was as if he were saying, "You only head an underground unit, and you set policies based on information you receive from the radio, nothing more." Sneh asked the question in a subdued manner because unlike Ben Gurion or Chaim Weizmann, president of the World Zionist Organization, he himself already believed that the upcoming battle against the British would entail the use of firearms. He also believed that at the end of World War II the British might call for arrangements that would not be in the Yishuv's interest, but because the Jewish Agency was making an effort to obtain approval for the establishment of a Jewish brigade (which was granted only in December 1944), he concluded that he should remove any doubts that could influence the British decision.[55] Sneh tried to draw Begin's attention to the damage his decisions could cause regarding the fulfillment of the optimal goal—the establishment of a Jewish state—and believed that the problem was not in the struggle but in the timing.[56] In his elaborate response Begin detailed his political worldview.

While the Yishuv leaders still had high hopes regarding the British, Begin thought, correctly, that the United States would inherit the influential stronghold in the Middle East.[57] He believed that Etzel's actions, oriented toward gaining acknowledgment from the West, would draw the world's attention to Palestine and would force the United States to apply pressure on the British to remove their troops out of the country faster. (After the new state was founded, Begin credited Etzel for the British departure,[58] although he was not as pretentious in his meeting with Sneh.) Begin saw Etzel's military approach as a continuation of the Jewish Agency's diplomatic endeavors.

At the end of his opening remarks Begin made it clear that he understood the weight of the task at hand, but in those modern times, he felt the information he obtained from the radio and newspapers was enough to accurately analyze the situation. Later, when he was prime minister, he relied on his past experience as a one-man intelligence organization and refused for a whole week to meet with Major General Shlomo Gazit, head of military intelligence, as he knew the latter would give him an assessment conflicting with his quest for negotiations with President Anwar Sadat of Egypt.[59]

When the issue of the Yishuv's authority was raised, Sneh said that since Etzel had no chance of being in the leadership, it should obey the current legal authority; otherwise they would "clash."[60] Begin tried to refute Sneh's suspicions about his own political ambitions. If he decided to go to war, "We [would] have no problem fighting under Ben Gurion's command," he said.[61]

But Begin did have political ambitions. The man who had defeated Jabotinsky at the Beitar convention and had taken charge of Etzel did not plan to settle for the leadership of the underground resistance. In a confidential report, he hinted at his aspirations, although he did not intend to fulfill his goals immediately: "Although I informed the leaders of the Left that I did not intend to seize power, they understand that objective developments could lead to that."[62]

Begin understood that Etzel was not ready to lead the Yishuv, and in internal conversations with members of his headquarters he repeated his willingness to accept Ben Gurion's leadership—if Ben Gurion decided to fight the British. But Ben Gurion, whose greatness was also apparent in his ability to grasp the wider picture, understood that Begin's influence must be immediately controlled.

Toward midnight Begin grew tired of Sneh's apparent contempt. "We are men who have paid their debts in life. I experienced Siberia and the NKVD. Nothing can scare me anymore.... You should know that we will not be the ones to raise a gun at you—but if you raise your gun, we will not hesitate to respond."[63]

The intensity of Begin's response only strengthened Sneh's distrust. Sneh ignored Begin's comments and appealed instead to his logic: "If the national institutions take a passive approach to the violent actions of Etzel and Lehi, it would appear as tacit approval and support for them. This means that the Yishuv's institutions [would] become politically responsible for their outcome, against their will and ideology." But Begin rejected Sneh's request for a temporary truce and declared once again that the whip of revolt was a moral obligation because the British had shut the gates of the country to the Jews both during and after the Holocaust. He stressed once again that he would bow to the authority of the Zionist administration as soon as it decided to escalate the struggle, but Sneh answered impatiently, "Listen, I do not ask if they [the British] are worth this whip but whether it is justified and purposeful. What are you, a judge on behalf of Providence? Do you want to execute justice?"[64] It was hard to bridge the gap between Sneh's focused attitude and Begin's judgmental, moral, and almost religious perceptions. A brief handshake signaled the end of the conversation.

After the meeting, Begin updated Lankin and Mr. and Mrs. Wax about it. He expressed his frustration and ridiculed Sneh's "devout enthusiasm" regarding Ben Gurion.[65] It was late, so Begin and Lankin decided to stay in the apartment until morning.

Even before the Jewish Agency made any decision, the Palmach started to prepare for an attack. On October 16, 1944, a week after Begin's meeting with Sneh, Etzel members met to discuss their being followed by the Palmach, which was planning to kidnap several of the top ones.

During those days Begin often suffered from mood swings, sometimes for no apparent reason. Lankin noticed these changes. The two had planned to meet one day at noon, but Begin had been unable to finish an article for the *Herut* newspaper and did not even lift his head to greet him as he entered the room. He complained about proofreading errors, threw the pages down, and started to run nervously around the room. Lankin felt superfluous. As he was leaving, Begin suddenly offered to play a game of chess with him. Lankin asked no questions. He had become used to his commander's moods.[66]

During a meeting with the Etzel headquarters staff Begin expressed his anger at the situation and hinted that he was planning a confrontation: "There were implied threats by Sneh to eliminate the 'Maamad' [Status, the code name for Etzel members]. We decided to be careful and to avoid responding to provocations, to do everything to prevent an internal battle. However, if there is no choice, we will defend ourselves. We will retaliate against any acts of aggression against us."[67] The members present did not protest. On the contrary, the general feeling was that they should be prepared for conflict, but that Etzel should not fire the first shot.

Most Etzel members advocated the Revisionist ideology but were not committed to the Zionist Revisionist Party. Nonetheless, Ben Gurion did not overlook the ties between the party and Etzel. He recognized the danger inherent in the underground organization precisely because of its political backing, although from 1931 onward the Revisionist Party had little influence on Etzel. Ben Gurion respected Lehi more than Etzel because its members, though fanatics, were fearless and without political aspirations, whereas he mistrusted Etzel for its political aspirations. He expressed his views in a Jewish Agency board meeting: "There are two groups. [The first is] the Stern Group [Lehi], which is small and backed by no party. They are fanatics who are currently running a war on the outside only and plan to expel the 'occupier' and leave the country for the Jews and the Arabs. On the other hand, [the second group] Etzel is backed by a party. Members of this group are not just idealistic. The sad fact is that Etzel has many supporters, not only because of its political backing, but also due to its social ideas, as it is considered a weapon against the 'Left.' It has connections in political circles. It gets exit permits from Palestine, etc., because the British government wants to strengthen the forces against us."[68]

It was not by chance that Ben Gurion mentioned the ties between Etzel and the British; rumors had spread in the Yishuv that Begin was a British agent. But this was not the only rumor about him. His release from a Russian prison after only one year, even though he had been sentenced to eight, spurred rumors that he was an NKVD agent. (This rumor subsided only after the collapse of the Soviet Union, when Begin's file could be opened.) Begin was not indifferent to these rumors, and his sensitivity to public opinion was what eventually shaped his political career. "'Unrestrained' incitement is being promoted so that they will hate me," he said and cringed when he reminded his fellow members of the rumors that he was being supported by the British CID. He estimated, sarcastically, that there would be many more rumors in the future.[69]

Meanwhile, leaders of the Jewish Agency had spoken with Revisionist Party officials and asked them to convince Etzel not to attack the British. These talks resulted in a meeting between Begin and the Revisionist Party leader Arie Altman, who ignored the fact that the declaration of revolt had damaged the relations between the party and Etzel.[70] Altman, a pleasant man, told Begin about the pressure applied on him to try to influence Etzel but did not ask the commander to put an end to Etzel's military operations. He knew Begin well and therefore knew that it would do no good to argue with him, but he emphasized that "the diplomatic route has not been sufficiently used." The essence of his approach was to "act little and do it slowly." Begin summarized the situation for him and concluded that there was no other choice but to fight the British until their withdrawal. He concluded by offering that the Revisionist leaders join him in the underground battle against the British.[71] This was a strange offer, and it is hard to believe that Begin genuinely thought that the Revisionist Party, a legitimate organization, would accept such a proposal. But the proposal characterized his approach throughout his life: he believed in his ability to convince the other side as he seemingly managed to convince himself. The meeting with Altman was not fruitful, and Altman informed the Jewish Agency that his organization was cutting all ties with Etzel;[72] then on October 31, 1944, Sneh was sent to hold his most important meeting with Begin.

"Perhaps you could help make it more pleasant," Begin said to Lankin in persuading him to join the meeting,[73] and this time Sneh also arrived with a partner, Eliyahu Golomb, commander of the Haganah. On their way to the apartment on Yonah Hanavi Street, Ben Gurion's envoys laughed at Etzel's careless security measures. "Perhaps they have especially arranged for the light in the stairwell to turn off when we climb up," said Golomb.[74]

The meeting took place with the feeling that the Haganah was about to attack Etzel. A dim light filtered into the second-floor apartment through the closed shutters. Some cold drinks and a cake were intended to ease the tension, but it was clear to everyone that this time the meeting would have immediate consequences. Surprisingly, Begin did not give an overview of the geopolitical situation. The testimonies of the meeting—Sneh's report to the Shai and Begin's account in *The Revolt*—matched.

During the meeting, Begin raised a new argument in favor of a revolt against the British—the need to shake up the complacent Yishuv: "What did the Yishuv sacrifice during the Massacre [the Holocaust]? It was a little shocked, it donated some money, it closed stores for two hours on a day of mourning.... But the cafés are still open, the Jews are engrossed in their businesses.... We must show them that the fight is necessary."[75] Begin saw the Holocaust as an associative sequence related to the battle against the British rather than an exceptional event, and it served to establish his lifelong suspicion of Gentiles.[76] The weight Begin attached to the Holocaust in terms of its importance in Jewish history is reflected in a much more impressive historic perspective than that of the Yishuv leaders, whose attitude to the murder of the Jews of Europe was still vague at the time.

Golomb had a more practical outlook on the military concepts and claimed that Begin's attitude was too simplistic—that the military operations Etzel was capable of executing were marginal at most. For five hours both sides held to their positions, and finally Golomb said, "We do not want to start a civil war, but we will if we have to. We don't think the British police can eliminate you, but the Yishuv can. Obviously we are not talking about physical elimination, but this development [revolt] could lead to that—to your complete destruction. And then it won't matter who started it." Sneh quickly added his reservations: "I reject the phrase 'elimination,'" but he added, "We cannot accept independent military activities that we believe to be harmful and that will destroy all our hopes."[77]

Begin raised his voice and made it clear that Etzel operations aroused the Yishuv's sympathy, as well as global respect, while simultaneously encouraging the British to vacate the region earlier because of the financial burden created by its actions. He added, "It was not necessary to get together for this meeting in order to listen to your threats. We don't believe you can eliminate us. We are not afraid of destruction. And let me say it straightforwardly—we will not stop our war." Golomb stressed that Etzel operations harmed the entire community's ability to act because the British, under the excuse of looking for terrorists, were searching for hidden weapons caches in the kibbutzim. He added that the day was drawing near when all the organizations would work together, but for now they needed to accept the rule of the majority.

Begin, who seemed to have been waiting for some sign of reconciliation, made it clear that he wanted to avoid stretching the boundaries too far. His concern for Etzel's fate, the consequences of civil war, and

Golomb's aura of authority led him to propose a compromise: "We have not committed to carrying out operations every twenty-four hours. There are breaks. We may find it necessary to execute the next one in six months' time, but it may also be tomorrow. In any case we will not announce a cease-fire because that is what the British are waiting for." But for Golomb, a temporary cease-fire was a matter of too little, too late. "We will not stand aside on this matter," he said, arose from his chair, and started walking toward the door. "The war is between us and the British—don't get caught in the middle," Begin managed to say before his guests departed grimly, and then he asked Lankin for another cigarette.

The next day, November 1, 1944, just before ten o'clock in the morning, Etzel headquarters members met on Mazeh Street in Tel Aviv. They already knew what the results of the meeting were likely to be, even without being updated with the details. When he entered the room, Begin asked whether anyone had anything to discuss before he spoke.[78] As expected, they all waited for his summary. "They threatened to start an actual fight against us and said that they would use any necessary measures to end our war. A serious situation is likely to arise if this is so, and if we are not prepared to handle this correctly, we could end up in a civil war," he said, and it was apparent that he had already made up his mind. He spoke lightly and calmly, like someone who had already accepted his fate. He ordered his men to publicize his decision not to respond to "provocations" by the Left or to the Haganah's attacks so as to gain favorable public opinion. He knew that it would be difficult to convince the junior Etzel members to refrain from retaliating and therefore demanded that his edict be presented to them as a show of restraint, a sign of power. Finally he added, knowing that explanations would not necessarily be enough to restrain his men, that at this crucial time it was necessary to be disciplined and to obey orders.[79]

Begin's decision to show restraint immortalized him in history as a man who refused to surrender to the Yishuv's dictates while simultaneously preventing civil war. But in actual fact he had surrendered. He informed Etzel headquarters to cease all operations on the pretext that the organization needed to stock up on new weapons, not because he "feared the threats," as he had noted.[80] In retrospect, this unknown fact is amazing: despite having told Sneh and Golomb that he would not halt Etzel operations, he ordered his men to cease all military action. It is a plausible assumption that had he been willing to forgo his organization's honor, Begin might have been able to reach a compromise with the Haganah. Nevertheless, his decision to restrain Etzel independently indicates that he valued its sovereignty just as much as he wanted to avoid civil war.

Personally Begin found it more difficult to decide on restraint than to announce a revolt. In January 1944 he reprimanded his subordinates for their hesitation and by so doing reestablished his image as a fighter, appropriate to the new type of commander. In the previous November his decision on restraint risked his position as leader of the resistance, as it could have been misconstrued as a sign of weakness and too compromising.

While relations between the Jewish Agency and Etzel took a turn for the worse, the two so-called "gangs"—Etzel and Lehi—began to strengthen their ties. Ever since the souring of relations between David Raziel and Avraham Stern, animosity had prevailed between the two organizations, and they regularly turned in each other's members. But when Begin became Etzel commander, the distinctions between the two organizations blurred, although Etzel objected to assassinating British leaders and did not rule out the establishing of ties with Britain after the Mandate fell. In mid-July 1944 Begin attended a meeting with Yitzhak Shamir, one of Lehi's three leaders. Shamir, like Begin, had a long "rabbinical" beard.

The two young "rabbis" talked about possible cooperation so that the two organizations would at least not sabotage each other's activities. Begin wanted to combine Etzel with Lehi, and on July 23, 1944, he reported that he had notified Lehi that "its political slogans are faulty" but that in his opinion "there is significant progress toward a full understanding."[81] But Begin had overestimated his persuasive skills; Lehi had been negotiating with him only in order to defuse the hostility between the two organizations and nothing more. A week later he realized that his efforts had failed and reported to his headquarters that Lehi still refused to acknowledge his authority. Nevertheless, the heads of the two organizations decided not to interfere with each other's activities, and they started to hold regular friendly meetings. Ironically, the trigger for the Haganah's attacks against Etzel was the Lehi operation that broke this unofficial agreement.

November 6, 1944, was a hot day in the Middle East. Cairo was bustling. Lord Moyne, a tall, well-dressed man who was the British resident minister of state in the Middle East, did not forgo his daily siesta. Moyne was responsible in part for the execution of the White Paper (also known as the MacDonald White Paper) policies that limited the immigration quota. Lehi, which held him personally responsible for turning away immigrant ships from the shores of Palestine, published pamphlets against him throughout 1944 calling him a murderer. Lehi, known by the British as the "Stern Gang," did not settle for mere talk. Two of its members—Eliyahu Hakim and Eliyahu Beit Zuri—were dispatched to Cairo to assassinate Moyne. Their youthful enthusiasm to undertake the task gave them an opportunity to break the monotony of their idle lives. In the letters they left behind they noted how angered they had been by their friends' inaction during British rule.[82]

On the morning of November 6, after a month in Egypt, the two men ambushed the minister while he was on his way to his home in one of Cairo's suburbs. With him in the car were his driver, his secretary, and his aide-de-camp (ADC). When the minister's car stopped in front of the house and the ADC stepped out to open the door for him, Hakim and Beit Zuri jumped out from their hiding place near the fence. Hakim slowly neared the car and calmly fired three shots into the minister's head. Beit Zuri stayed behind to cover for Hakim. The driver jumped on Hakim, but Beit Zuri shot him, and they quickly mounted bicycles and merged into the busy traffic. To their misfortune, a motorcycle policeman happened to hear the driver's cries and started to chase the fugitives. The policeman opened fire and hit Beit Zuri in the ribs. Hakim hurried to his aid, despite Beit Zuri's pleas to leave him and escape. When the police captured them, they gave false names, and only after a few days did they admit that they were members of Lehi.

Lord Moyne's assassination rattled the entire Yishuv and brought on global waves of condemnation. Chaim Weizmann was afraid it would destroy any chance of achieving the Zionist goals. Winston Churchill, who was Moyne's friend, asked whether "our dreams for Zionism are to end in the smoke of an assassin's pistol."[83]

Begin too was outraged. He immediately understood the trouble all the dissidents would face. In his typical dramatic fashion he referred to the Lehi decision as a "Jewish tragedy." Yellin Mor retorted that Begin's reaction was just "infantile rage" and attacked his weak points: his tendency to be sentimental and bombastic.[84] Begin was upset that he had not been informed in advance, even though, despite their preapproval, the Lehi leaders themselves were surprised that the mission had been executed; owing to limited means of communication they had not stayed in continuous contact with the assassins and had not known when exactly the mission would take place.[85]

Three days later, after he had calmed down, Begin said during an Etzel headquarters meeting, "A deed has been done in untimely fashion, and it will perhaps lead to serious political consequences, but no fatal disaster has occurred, and we have nothing to apologize for." Despite his objection to the assassinations in Cairo—"So thirty or forty British will be killed; they will be replaced," Begin said, berating Lehi's pattern of assassinations—the members decided not to publish a statement of condemnation. They also reinforced their precautions: among other things, they reduced the number of meetings they held and frequently used codes to guard against harassment by the Haganah or the CID. "If they catch me—carry on without me," Begin stressed.[86] Did he say that because he suspected something specific, or was it simply another melodramatic gesture? The most likely answer is a combination of the two.

The consequences of Lord Moyne's assassination were irreversible in regard to relations between the Yishuv and the dissidents. "After the murder, even those who weren't convinced that the inherent nature of these terrorist groups would bring on tragedy were horrified," Israel Galili wrote later.[87] British pressure on the Jewish Agency became unbearable, especially after Sir Bernard Paget, the commander-in-chief of the Middle East Command, said that serious collaboration between the British and the Agency would now be required, including the Agency's providing the British with information that might in turn lead to the complete destruction of the underground. On November 11, 1944, the Jewish Agency convened for a special meeting regarding the measures to be taken against the dissidents.

Ben Gurion was concise, as usual: "We must uproot this mistake as if there really is a prohibition against assisting the [British] government, as if there really is a secret Jewish conspiracy to cover up the murder. This is why we have found it necessary to request help in preventing such acts of terrorism and dismantling the organizations.... It would be no disaster were some of the men to sit in prison for some time. It would be much better than having Jews hanged, and Jews, Arabs, and the British would not be murdered in the name of the Jewish people."[88]

While everyone was still in shock about Lord Moyne's assassination and feared British retaliation, Ben Gurion managed to recruit the Palmach against Etzel and also succeeded in uniting Hashomer Hatzair (which opposed Ben Gurion and supported the idea of a bi-national country) with Hakibbutz Hameuchad (United Kibbutz Movement), whose members even opposed the 1947 Partition Proposal.[89] He proved to the British that the Jewish Agency could act on their statements against terrorism, but not less important, he found employment for Palmach members who refused to join the British Army.

On November 20, following approval by the Jewish Agency to commence unrestrained action against the underground organizations, the decision was approved by a large majority of the Histadrut executive committee. "We are faced with two inevitable choices," Ben Gurion declared. "The first: terrorism or a Zionist political struggle.... The second: terrorist organizations or an organized community, an organized people, an organized labor movement. Again—it's one or the other."

It was also decided that Palmach members would be recruited for each mission as needed. This decision raised reservations even among the Far Left circles of the Yishuv. Hugo Bergman, a member of the left-wing movement Brit Shalom who was in favor of a bi-national Jewish-Arab state, called the situation about to be created "a regime of terror."[90] Moshe Sharett, head of the Jewish Agency's political department, stated in response that "a civil war already exists. So the question is—are you with us or against us?" The aim was, as Ben Gurion put it, "to expel Etzel members and supporters from their workplaces; to ban the provision of shelter to Etzel members out of 'fake Jewish compassion'; to resist blackmail attempts; to cooperate with the British police."[91]

The major reason for Ben Gurion's attitude toward Etzel was his quest for political gain. He was also motivated by a desire to prevent Begin from gaining more power in the Yishuv, as he was aware of the growing sympathy for Begin's actions among the youth.[92]

In November talk moved to action. Palmach members, who had been trained only in fieldcraft, were sent to special training courses in urban warfare, mainly in the kibbutzim.[93] One hundred and seventy-one Palmach members participated in this training, which focused mainly on hand-to-hand combat and surveillance. The Jewish department of the Haganah's Shai gathered considerable intelligence—meeting places as well as the names of underground supporters and other personal information. Due to a fear of exposure of the whole of the Shai, only a few officers were selected to communicate with the British. This connection was kept secret, as legitimacy for the operation was based on public approval, not on the law.

Yaakov Dori, one of the high commanders of the Haganah, headed the operation, named the Saison. The main contact between the Jewish

Agency and the British was Teddy Kollek. Yigal Allon, deputy commander of the Palmach, proposed to capture hundreds of senior Etzel members and imprison them all at once. Later on he denied the fact that when he was speaking of St. Bartholomew's Night,[94] he intended to have Etzel members executed.[95] When he learned that the British would participate in the operation, he wished to resign from his position. He was not alone, as many junior Haganah members did not want to take action against Jews. Several of them were punished, but they were permitted to remain members.[96] Ben Gurion knew that they could not forcefully impose action on anyone in this matter among Jews.[97]

The Saison's focus was undoubtedly Etzel. When Ben Gurion was asked why Lehi was not persecuted as much as Etzel, he answered that "Lehi is an organization which innocently believes that it can bring redemption by murdering the British. Etzel does not want to lead us to salvation as it claims, but rather seeks to gain political power in the Yishuv."[98] But it seems that similar perceptions were also factored into the decision to ignore Lehi while persecuting the other dissidents. At the time, Lehi tried to distance itself from Revisionist ideology and adhered to more socialist terms.[99]

Despite the fact that Lehi ridiculed Begin for the restraint he imposed on Etzel members and called them "hopeless patriots," Begin declared that his organization would also protect Lehi members. This statement angered Lehi, who saw it as patronization. "We do not need Etzel's mercy," it stressed and reminded its members that during Avraham Stern's leadership he had highlighted individualism, preferring "unique persons" over "good human material."[100]

The Saison was designed to break Etzel's spirit. Its members were beaten up, some were handed over to the British, and most were jailed in detention rooms prepared in advance in several kibbutzim. One detention room was prepared in Ein Harod.[101] At the edge of the farm, near the cowshed, was a large barn, inside of which an elongated hut was built and hidden beneath the hay. The hut was sealed so that light would not penetrate it, and the entrance, through a small door, was also hidden behind bales of hay. The abductees were kept in the dark around the clock and could not distinguish day from night; for good measure, they were tied to their beds.

The kidnappers' reasoning was not always clear. Two senior Etzel commanders, Yaakov Meridor and Eliyahu Lankin, were given up to the British before the Shai interrogated them. While in hiding, Meridor had been overwhelmed by a longing for his family, and when he visited them, he was ambushed and seized;[102] he was handed over to the British, and on February 22, 1945, they deported him to East Africa. In contrast, Tabin, commander of Delek, the Etzel intelligence branch, was not handed over to the British but rather was kept imprisoned in a cave in Kibbutz Givat Hashlosh. His kidnappers pretended they were going to execute him so that he would disclose information. Tabin was chained to his bed for over six months. There is no evidence that the British demanded that Etzel members be imprisoned, but it seems in this case that the Palmach went beyond what it was required to do. When Eliyahu Ravid, who was in charge of the Etzel arsenals, was arrested, his wife Miryam tried to use her family ties with Moshe Dayan to release him. Dayan agreed to pass her letters to him. When she vented her anger at him, saying that she was jealous of her friends who needed only to ask the British CID for information about their detained husbands while she had to beg a Jew for information, he replied, "If that's what you want, it can be arranged." Later she said she would never forget his condescending smile.[103]

In December 1944 the Palmach discovered Etzel's intelligence and financial headquarters on Herzl Street in Tel Aviv, and thousands of index cards containing the names of activists and donors were confiscated.[104]

The Saison policy was to punish the sons and daughters of Etzel members as well. A new committee established for this purpose, the Committee for Students, had over thirty students expelled from schools throughout the country. Geula Cohen was studying at the time in the Tel Aviv Teachers' College, and she was blocked from entering the class in which she was about to take her final accreditation test.

When the Saison began, many Etzel members assumed that Begin would retract his decision to show restraint. In a meeting between Yellin Mor and Golomb, a month after the beginning of the Saison, Yellin Mor estimated that Etzel would respond even without authorization from the supreme command. Indeed, the junior members prepared to violate Begin's directive. Their friends' arrests and rumors that Begin had imposed his viewpoint on headquarters members aroused their fury.[105]

Begin's position remained steadfast, however: absolute restraint. The restraint he imposed upon his men, who were eager for action, surprised even the Haganah leaders, who were prepared for a response; one of the Palmach's first tasks was to guard the homes of the Yishuv leaders. Begin was required to display his own restraint and patience as well, but these were not foreign to him, as he was used to an austere lifestyle. It appears that his inability to violate the rule by which he had lived since childhood—never a fraternal war—as well as a fear of failure if he indeed entered into a conflict within the Yishuv—contributed to his determination. (The term "fraternal war," which he repeatedly used, blurred the fact that it was not a confrontation between equal forces but between the majority and a dissident minority.) His national outlook—which was based on concepts such as "All parts of Israel are responsible for one another" (a Jewish value from the Talmud) and "A Jew who sins is still a Jew"—also contributed to his decision, as did the perception that he had escaped the Nazis owing to divine providence, which had destined him to a leadership role.[106] Begin was accustomed to abusing his political rivals with words, but heading a struggle among Jews went against his basic principles.[107] Had he not stayed true to his principles, he would have lost his moral strength. But political considerations were not strange to him either. Begin understood that with most members of the headquarters arrested, if he backed down from his decision at this point, it would be equivalent to an admission of failure, and his ability to command the organization would be questioned.

It seems that Begin had no choice but to adhere to his decision once it was executed. "We must act wisely in order to avoid entering a fraternal war. The choice is between our own private disaster and a national disaster. We know how a civil war starts, but we never know when it will end," he warned his headquarters members.[108] "A strict order must be issued to all our people: we will not respond to any provocation by the Left. We will publicize all their actions. But our people will have to exercise caution and not be dragged into a conflict among Jews."[109] "Our restraint will serve us in the future," he proclaimed in a manifesto during the Saison.[110] As Etzel commander, he believed that the organization's restraint would have political benefits, as it would win it public opinion after its recovery.

Yet one of the Saison's major goals was, of course, to capture Begin, whose photographs were hung throughout the Yishuv. It seemed at the time that the efforts had borne fruit, and even Haganah members were surprised at the pace at which their goals were being achieved. One of the guards of the National Institutions in Jerusalem claimed that he saw Begin walking down Keren Kayemet Street. The British CID immediately received word that Begin had been spotted in the Rehavia neighborhood and that his place of residence had been revealed. The police dispatched heavy forces to the area, but the man who was captured was Yosef Leizerovich, a junior Etzel activist who lived with his aunt in a building in front of the National Institutions. Although the man claimed to be Yosef Leizerovich, the interrogators would not let him go, as they were loath to give up the hope that they had caught a big fish. Only when Moshe Sneh was asked to identify the man and verified that a mistake had been made was Leizerovich released; he continued to be active in Etzel without further fear of being caught.

Begin chose to continue to hide with his family in their regular hiding place on Bashan Street, disguised as Rabbi Sasover. Because of the heightened danger of capture, he had to decrease the number of meals he had a day. Tzippora Kessel, his contact, would bring his few groceries in the morning with the newspapers, including Haganah publications, and every evening he would pass on messages to headquarters members and the radio station through her. The apartment curtains were always drawn. When in good spirits, Begin would play his favorite game, chess, with Eitan Livni. The few times he left home, he dared to go only as far as the staff apartment on Bialik Street in Tel Aviv, where he dined with Chaim Landau. They mainly ate bread, herring, and onions.[111]

Aliza and Benny suffered from the enhanced safety measures. Benny knew nothing about his father's activities but was apparently affected by the atmosphere at home because he used to tell people by mistake that his father was a member of Lehi. Begin was cautious now even about going to the synagogue. One time, when he was getting some fresh air with some of the other worshippers, one of them asked how come a Jewish queen had been given the foreign name of Helena. Begin was unable to stop himself, and despite the risk of exposure he explained that although Helena was a Greek name, it was customary to use it at the time. The rabbi was amazed at Begin's extensive knowledge. Such behavior was an uncalculated risk; until then Begin had made sure to cultivate the impression of being a useless fellow. The neighbors had even pitied Aliza for her problematic match.[112] On another occasion the worshippers found out that Begin had an annotated prayer book, considered improper by religious people, but once again he avoided exposure by mumbling incomprehensible utterings that quickly restored his image as an eccentric. The Haganah never found his hideaway during the Saison.

As the arrests continued, Etzel members grew increasingly restless. Many were forced to leave their jobs because of the need to hide, some had to cut ties with their families, and Begin was informed of rumors that the members in the field were close to breaching the commander's orders. In late January 1945, Begin decided to leave his apartment for a meeting with the field commanders, "the battle force department," as they were called in Etzel. The arrests, extraditions, and rumors of torture had paralyzed the organization, and the field commanders had formulated a decision before the meeting: they wanted to respond.

When Begin arrived at the meeting place in Ramat Gan (a packing house in an orchard in front of the former Café Oasis), he was hidden behind a prepared curtain.[113] This was not only for security reasons, but also to enhance the importance of a meeting with the commander. A dozen field commanders waited nervously. They too were endangered by the meeting, which in those days was considered a mass gathering.

This meeting was a significant test of Begin's leadership. Before the Saison he had managed to quickly consolidate his authority in the organization despite the difficulties. The opposition to his appointment due to his lack of military skills had not been forgotten,[114] and since Etzel was not an organized military organization, his fears increased.

In many conflicts between Begin and the headquarters members he was often decisive—for example, when they had discussed Operation Wall. But it was not unusual for his proposals to be rejected, and he did not fight such decisions; he even accepted the members' praise that he was a "friendly" leader.[115] He found it reasonable to accept the headquarters members' decisions, as they took both political and diplomatic aspects into consideration. Now he was facing fighters, who were less patient and more eager to take action. He especially had to confront Amichai Paglin, a charismatic twenty-three-year-old commander.

Paglin (nicknamed Gidi), the son of one of the established bourgeois merchant families in the Yishuv, had never had much patience. In fact, he had even acted on his own accord two weeks before the declaration of rebellion, sabotaging a British economic office in Jaffa. A year before the Saison he had been a member of the Haganah. He had become frustrated with the Haganah's inaction, especially in light of his eldest brother's death in a controversial Palmach operation known as the Kaf-Gimel [Hebrew: twenty-three] Seamen, in which twenty-three members had been sent in 1941 on a mission to destroy an oil refinery in Tripoli in Lebanon and had disappeared without a trace; the operation had increased Paglin's hostility toward the Haganah and pushed him into joining Etzel.

Paglin the Sabra (a native-born "New Jew") was tall and slim, with a small mustache and black hair—an almost ascetic look—and the fighters adored him. His appearance and his qualities were in distinct contrast to the European qualities of Etzel's commander. Unlike Begin with his rhetorical skills, Paglin was mainly known for his daring attitude, in addition to his impressive battle planning and his technical inventions (later on he designed the furnace in which the body of Adolf Eichmann was cremated). Paglin was not accustomed to showing restraint—he had not abandoned the Haganah for that. A combination of the skills of the two men was ideal for the underground organization, but it inadvertently spawned confrontation.

When Begin left for the meeting with his field commanders, he knew the young fighters wanted to strike back. He also knew that if he lost them, Etzel would become an organization devoid of content once the Saison ended. Since Begin understood the mood around him and even profited from it (he had suggested the rebellion in part because he had realized the frustration caused by inaction), he felt that this was the most important meeting during the Saison.

This time Begin was not certain that he would manage to convince his young commanders to forsake their demands, but he knew how to give a speech. "Friends," he started, "who are we fighting against? Of course, we're fighting against the British enslavers. And what do the British wish to do? Their answer is short—to destroy us. For this purpose they are using the Haganah forces. Of course, their plan is to achieve three goals. First, to divert us from our goal—the rebellion. Second, to drag us into a fraternal war. And when the British think that they have eliminated Etzel and the Haganah is exhausted by this fraternal war, they will engage the Haganah forces and eliminate them as well. When the Haganah realizes its persecutors' plan, it will stop chasing after us, and the way will be open for a joint battle against the British forces of evil. Gentlemen, there will be no fraternal war. There will never, never be a fraternal war. And never will a Jew raise his hand to another Jew." Then he pulled a blank sheet of paper out of his briefcase and added, "The boundary between purity and contamination is as thin as this sheet of paper. Be careful not to cross it."[116]

Begin knew that he was walking an extremely thin line by insisting on maintaining restraint. But the line held: the fighters were convinced that they should maintain restraint, and his leadership was not undermined. But the young activists in the organization were still frustrated and confused. In his pocket Paglin habitually carried a matchbox filled with dynamite, and he defiantly announced that he would accept the policy of restraint but would blow himself up if he was approached by the British.[117] Leaflets were distributed in the Yishuv with the slogan "We'll repay you, Cain,"[118] but they continued to exercise restraint.

During the entire Saison, Livni hid in Begin's house. In February 1945, almost four months after the Saison had begun, he told Begin that Etzel members were planning to kidnap Ephraim Krasner, one of the heads of the Shai, as well as Moshe Sharett. Livni also said that they had decided to begin following the two.

Before Begin had time to respond, Livni added that the advantage of kidnapping was that it did not involve bloodshed: "We've suffered enough; the members cannot stand it anymore."[119] Begin was surprised, as he had not been aware that his men were planning a surveillance, but putting the personal insult aside, he started to explain the ideological arguments for restraint. When Livni insisted, Begin turned to an emotional appeal.[120] "This will end badly. It would be crazy," he said. "After this we won't be able to put an end to the zeal and the cruelty. And we will be in a disadvantageous position, as the Haganah will only focus on the Saison, and we will also have to fight the British. What did we unite for? It will be our blood that will be shed, not that of the others."[121]

Livni knew that he would not be able to change Begin's mind, but he decided to order the surveillance of the senior Jewish Agency members nonetheless. A week later he made another attempt to convince Begin: "If we don't decide on an action, someone will do something independently. The result will be the same, but at least under our supervision nothing irreparable will occur."[122]

Little by little Begin started to lose his confidence. Although he hardly left his house, he was aware of everything going on in the organization. He realized it would be difficult to enforce restraint with mere words and decided on a compromise: in late February, in an unusual move, he decided to hold a headquarters vote regarding Livni's proposal. The headquarters had only five members, only two of which had been there since before the Saison. Livni and David Groseberg supported the plan to kidnap Krasner and Sharett. Begin, Betzalel Amitsur, and Chaim Landau objected, so the proposal fell through. The headquarters members gathered at the home of one of the junior members, where Begin and Livni stayed for the night. "Don't take it to heart, sometimes you're in the minority," Begin muttered before they fell asleep.[123]

Despite the Etzel decision to make no effort to ask for a truce, Begin sent Sneh a letter requesting an end to the Saison policy and expressed

DECLARATION OF REBELLION 77

the hope "that one day we will all serve in the same Jewish army." Sneh did not respond. Begin never talked about this letter, but Sneh mentioned it during a joint interview in 1966. Begin pretended he was surprised and asked, "Have you got the letter?" Sneh replied that he vividly remembered the last line, which expressed the hope of establishing a unified army. Begin noted dryly, "I'm proud of my suggestion to serve in a unified army," and said no more.[124]

Begin finally succumbed—Livni's efforts to persuade him toward action had worked, and his wall had finally cracked—but his proposal was different from what his operations officer had hoped for. During a conversation with Livni one day, Begin suddenly froze, as if he had drifted off in thought. Livni was concerned and asked if he was all right. "Eitan, we cannot execute actions. We have no weapons. People are arrested every day," said Begin. "I propose we gather a hundred people to take over an area in Old Jerusalem and hoist a flag over it. We will hold to the last man—but no one will be able to say that Etzel did not fulfill its mission. There is no knowing how long the Saison will last and what irreversible damage will be caused."[125]

Livni was horrified. Suicide? Was this Begin's decision once he was bound to respond to the requests for action? He could hardly speak; he looked at his commander in silence and thought what he dared not utter: the loneliness and sorrow caused by the arrests of his close friends had undermined the sangfroid required of a resistance commander. When Begin asked for his opinion, Livni replied that he would refuse such an order and did not even bother to explain why. Now it was Begin's turn to be astonished. He expected at least an expression of gratitude for his proposal.

"Eitan, you would disobey me? You would refuse an order?"

"It's not a simple thing to do so, but you wouldn't manage to recruit a hundred people anyway," Livni snapped at Begin. "You see, most of the combat fighters are Sabras; they were born here. They are willing to risk their lives to destroy enemy installations, but they will not participate in such a dramatic act. We won't manage to recruit even ten. Furthermore, even if we were to succeed, we might be noted as a heroic chapter of Jewish history, but that would be the end of Etzel." Begin realized that Livni was hinting that he, Begin, was a foreigner, but he focused on one thing: the personal insult of having his subordinate, who had been living in his house for two months, defy him. "Eitan, would you really disobey me?" he asked. "My considerations are more correct," said Livni.[126]

At that point the two men drifted apart. Livni was disappointed when he realized that his commander's mental anguish had caused him to blur the distinction between reality and the historical mythical world that was often the world in which he lived. He left Begin's apartment for a new hiding place and never spoke about the incident again.[127]

Etzel also began to suffer from financial difficulties; the coffers were emptied as most members had been forced to quit their jobs and go into hiding. The organization's efforts focused on so-called "fund-raising activities"—robberies and acts of extortion that were intended to replenish the cash reserves.[128] During one of these events, in February 1945, Etzel stole two bagfulls of diamonds with the assistance of Arie Schwartzberg, a post office clerk. The bags' contents were worth forty thousand lira (Israeli pounds), a fortune in those days. This action, which took place during the Saison, was the only activity in which Begin participated during that time. Because his house was one of the few that the Haganah had not yet discovered, that was where the diamonds were hidden. Begin and Livni burned the packaging in the water heater in the bathroom. Excited by the action, Begin exulted: "My God, who would have believed that there would ever be so much money in my house?"[129] The money was for Etzel of course, but it was the only time that Begin ever expressed enthusiasm about money. (When he resigned the premiership, his relatives were astonishment to learn that he did not have enough savings to buy an apartment.) He ordered another operation of that sort, but this time it was foiled by the British.

No exact figures exist regarding the number of activists arrested during the Saison. In his memoirs, Begin claimed that several hundred Etzel members had been arrested by March 1945, most of whom were activists from the Revisionist Party. The *History Book of the Haganah* records that the Haganah gave over seven hundred names to the British and that three hundred of those named were imprisoned in jails and fifty in the kibbutzim. British Member of Parliament Richard Crossman argued that over a thousand activists were handed in.[130]

The Saison policy ended in March 1945, even though the termination was opposed by Yitzhak Sadeh, the first commander of the Palmach (1941–1945), because he believed that Etzel's total destruction was close.[131] At Kibbutz Yagur, Moshe Sneh had to struggle to convince Palmach members that the Saison policy had run its course.[132] Golomb supported him and stressed that terrorism had been destroyed—and surprisingly claimed that this had only helped the British. It seems that

Ben Gurion's conclusion that the Saison had not gained anything contributed to its end. "It was in vain," he testified before the Anglo-American committee that questioned him about it in March 1946.

The Saison drastically harmed Etzel's activities but increased the youth's sympathy toward this small organization, a fact that the Haganah took into consideration in its decision to end it. Members of the Palmach proudly noted, "We have damaged the myth of the underground," but the myth that Begin sought to instill was completely different.[133] Etzel had prevented a fraternal war—that was what its followers would stress later. The organization had almost been eliminated, but Begin himself grew stronger. He stuck to his opinions and rebuffed the pressures applied on him in a way that impressed even those who were opposed to the restraint he enforced. It became clear that those who believed that his background in politics might bring about positive changes in the organization had been right.

Begin never regretted his decision for restraint. During a cabinet meeting on February 8, 1982, regarding the approval of compensation for evacuees from the Yamit settlements, Begin suddenly declared, "During my days in the underground I wrote an article entitled 'Fraternal War—Never.' After my death I hope, above all, to be remembered as the man who prevented a fraternal war. This is more important to me than the command of the underground, than being prime minister, than the peace treaty, and than the Golan Heights annexation."[134]

FIVE

A BOMB IN THE HEART OF THE EMPIRE

The fact that Begin was a political leader greatly affected the underground from a military aspect. Unlike the commander of Lehi, Begin prohibited Etzel members from carrying weapons outside the framework of their operations, claiming that the benefits of carrying a gun were outweighed by the likelihood that a British police officer would open fire on an armed Etzel member.[1] Similarly, he stuck to the principle of the "open underground": most Etzel members continued to provide for their families while being active in the organization. It seems that due to this principle many Etzel members were spared incarceration; upon being detained for a check by the British, they would present legal identification documents and would be immediately released.

Even in his private life Begin differed from the Lehi commander. He continued to maintain his family life under a false identity, either because he had had enough of forced separation from his wife during his imprisonment or because he found it so utterly unbearable to live in seclusion. But his family paid the price for being part of the underground organization. Batya Eldad, Aliza's friend, did not dare tell her that her son Benny might be harmed by this kind of life.[2] The mysterious aura surrounding his father prevented Benny from connecting with children his age. He was considered a stranger, weird and peculiar, and he spent most of his time secluded in his room. He longed for social interaction and would pounce on any visitors to their hideout, calling them "uncle." Betzalel Amitzur, one of the Etzel headquarters officials, never visited Begin's house without a gift for Benny, giving the boy great joy.[3] The members' nicknames confused Benny; Livni, who was known as Yerucham, was introduced to Benny as Uncle Moshe, and Benny would naively call him "Uncle Moshe, whose name is Yerucham."[4] In 1947, when Begin's family moved to 1 Rosenbaum Street and Begin changed his name yet again (this time to Dr. Jona Konigshofer), Benny was teased by the other children and called "Benny Konig-bluffer," as he apparently appeared unreliable.

Etzel officials assisted the Begin family financially, as their life in the two-bedroom apartment was not easy. Tzippora Kessel (nicknamed "Yael" by the underground), who was Begin's communications link with headquarters, deciphered his impossible handwriting, typed his letters, and helped Aliza with shopping and babysitting.[5] Begin was responsible for cleaning the apartment, and often when his subordinates visited him, he was busy dusting and sweeping. This activity was of great value to him, serving both as a form of exercise and a means of relieving his boredom, and Aliza believed that it was psychologically important for him since keeping busy protected him from mood swings.

Begin often burst into stories and enthusiastically reiterated to Aliza how far he had come from his childhood in Brisk, raised by a Zionist father, to become commander of an organization that was often mentioned in British newspapers. He would tell his stories while sitting on the couch and smoking a cigarette. "Aliza, can you believe that we did all that?" "Did you read what was written about us in the newspaper?" Aliza would interrupt him and say, "Menachem, someone has to clean the house."[6] She preferred to cool his enthusiasm, as she was also aware of the lows that followed the highs. Aliza also helped regulate the household finances.[7] These had never interested him, and even when he needed additional funding, he left it to others to get it for him.[8]

In all his years in the underground Begin never left his apartment armed. Hiding was the only security measure he took, even though it meant being separated from the men in the field. Begin did not know how to buy bread at the grocery store; even the cigarettes that he smoked at a rapid pace were purchased for him. In winter, when leaving the hideout to attend meetings, he would wear a long black coat, making him look like a rabbi. When a meeting was scheduled far from his apartment, he would take a taxi and discuss only matters of the Torah with the driver.[9] Later on, when he stopped hiding, he would ride on a bus with a friend who would pay his fare. He spent his own money only on tips to waiters.[10]

In February 1948, when Aliza went into labor with their daughter Chasia, they were alone in the apartment. "Menachem, I need a doctor," Aliza moaned, and Begin, who was both excited and scared, tried to calm her down and said, "Soon, Ala; we'll get organized immediately." But Begin feared being exposed if he left the apartment late at night and waited until dawn to leave the house, when he went to Kessel's house, knocked on her window, and asked her to call the doctor.[11] For some reason, precisely when Aliza needed him to rush out and call a doctor, he decided to remain secretive, although sometimes his desire to have human contact sabotaged efforts to remain in hiding. Perhaps in this case he was overly excited.

Begin's yearning for human contact often angered the members. One morning, while sitting in a café, Kahn saw Kessel rushing toward him. "The commander wants to see you, immediately," she panted. "But what about you? It's broad daylight—what if you've been followed?" he responded, irritated. Before he could vent his anger he noticed Livni coming toward them with the very same message: "Come, the commander has called for us." When he noticed yet another member nearing them, he remarked "At least let's not go together as if we were in a demonstration."[12] None of them remember that there was an urgent reason justifying the abrupt appointment.

Other than writing leaflets, reading newspapers, and listening to the radio, Begin spent hundreds of hours directing the organization's affairs from his home, assigning people to certain positions. He slowly strengthened his understanding of his managerial duties, despite the fact that he had never met most of the people he was managing.[13] When he grew bored, he would analyze political developments in the Middle East. He spent many hours doing this by himself but often with friends as well. He had a habit of proudly showing his friends the first drafts of his articles before final proofing. Even the most disapproving members never dared to share with him their impressions of his writing; like Shmuel Katz, who helped him write on several occasions, they thought it was too bombastic. They were cautious with him not only because they respected their commander, but also because of a simple humane consideration: his most active role at the time was to write the leaflets and letters, and insulting this work would have hurt his feelings. In addition to the leaflets and letters, Begin also wrote articles for the *Herut* newspaper. He did not always sign his name. Sometimes he signed as Ben David.[14]

While Begin kept himself busy by analyzing the international situation, most of Etzel's military actions were initiated by the commanders in the field.[15] When considering whether to approve an operation,

Begin focused mainly on general issues such as conditions for withdrawal and the avoidance of casualties. His comrades believed that his grasp of what could or would happen was brilliant and that he predicted outcomes they would not have considered. For example, he rejected a proposal to destroy Iraq's oil pipeline in 1944 on the grounds that it might harm the British in their war against the Nazis, but he suggested that the topic be revisited toward the end of the war. The Etzel members considered this politically wise.[16] It is hard not to admire the fact that Begin had an understanding of complex issues, such as his prediction, made already in the late 1940s, that after Stalin's death, the Soviet Union would begin to fall apart.[17] The only question is whether he predicted the collapse of the Soviet Union through cold political analysis or because of his resentment toward the regime that had tormented him in prison.

Meanwhile, after the end of World War II, the terrible sight of tens of thousands of displaced Jews in the transition camps in Europe shocked the Yishuv and strengthened Begin's anti-British stance. In June 1945, the Jewish Agency sent a memorandum to the British government, pleading that one hundred thousand Jews be allowed to immigrate to Palestine immediately.[18] The British refused. The surprising results of the British elections on July 5, 1945—the Labor Party, headed by Clement Attlee, replaced Winston Churchill's party—also affected the mood in Palestine. Attlee's election was good news for the Jewish community, but disappointment was not far away. Ernest Bevin, who was appointed as foreign minister by Attlee, hastened to call upon the nations of the world to open their doors to Holocaust survivors because "the Land of Israel cannot be the solution." Earl G. Harrison, who researched the situation of the Jews in the transition camps in Germany at the request of U.S. president Harry Truman, tried to persuade the president to propose the immediate immigration of one hundred thousand displaced Jews to Palestine, but the Yishuv's hopes faded when Attlee stipulated that immigration would be approved only if the United States assisted Britain in overcoming Arab resistance to the idea.[19]

The deeper the Yishuv's disappointment, the more radical Begin's leaflets became: "the Occupation Government" was slowly turning into a "Nazo-British enemy."[20] The Holocaust had become a personal wound for him; it was not the Jewish people who had been harmed but "my people."[21]

When in September 1945 the Jews were finally disillusioned with the Labor government, negotiations began, encouraged by Ben Gurion,[22] among the Haganah, Etzel, and Lehi for the establishment of a common resistance movement. Moshe Sneh first contacted Lehi with the proposal, and Begin was shocked to hear about it. Since becoming Etzel commander, he had preached the unification of forces, and now Lehi and the Haganah were making unification plans without him, despite the fact that he was the one who had ordered restraint during the Saison. In a letter to Sneh, Begin stressed that after the Saison it should have been expected that the other underground groups would reach out to Etzel, but he was careful not to write anything that could ruin the chances of unity.[23] This time, unlike his usual stance, Begin gave up the pathos and his trappings of honor and wrote directly and simply: "Tell your friends—especially Mr. Galili, whose movement advocates this school of thought—to forget about this nonsense about 'fascism' and the 'abyss.' There is no abyss."[24] His appeal was fruitful and accelerated the unification process.

Begin refused to merge Etzel with the Haganah, both because of the residual feelings of ill will following the Saison and because he did not want to undermine his position as a leader with a different point of view. "It is not the right time for it," he explained; "we cannot commit to accepting the [National] Institutions' authority as long as there is no guarantee that the fighting will not suddenly stop in favor of a different policy."[25]

In the joint discussions, an ad hoc unity was decided upon for the purpose of undefined fighting. Etzel, the Haganah, and Lehi became the Jewish Resistance Movement, headed by an operational headquarters—Begin represented Etzel, Yellin Mor Lehi, and Moshe Sneh and Israel Galili the Haganah. It was also decided that a political committee, named Committee X, would approve the missions, without the approval being detailed or dated. Six committee members were appointed, and only Peretz Bernstein from the General Zionists was considered sympathetic to the dissenters.[26] Begin and the Lehi commanders pledged to withhold unauthorized actions, except for "acquisitions" actions, meaning the theft of money and weapons.

At the time an agreement was reached among the organizations, Ben Gurion was in London. He supported the agreement but did not sign the draft approval sent to him by Sneh. The agreement was meant to take effect on November 1, 1945. However, on October 12, Etzel attacked the British demobilization camp in Rehovot and robbed its weapons bunker. This mission jeopardized cooperation because it had not been approved, and the Haganah saw it as a typical Etzel act of deceit. Sneh was furious with Begin but did not know how loose Begin's control was over the organization he commanded; the action was an initiative of local commanders who had decided to forgo headquarters approval. This was not an unusual occurrence, and the initiators even expected Begin's retroactive approval; after all, the operation had been a success. But this time Begin decided that the breach of discipline required a response. "This is not the way an army functions, and we cannot continue like this," he shouted during a meeting convened in one of the headquarters' hideouts, this time in Ramat Gan.[27] Because of this action, and especially because he felt the need to explain his men's motives to Sneh, Begin found himself in a tricky situation that was almost impossible to escape without humiliation. He could either appear as a caricature to the Haganah or he could confront his men. He decided to appoint Meir Kahn (the man who had him freed from the Polish Army) as investigative judge, as if he hoped that Kahn would find that it was not his subordinates who had attacked the camp.

When Begin received the report that it was indeed his men who had initiated the attack, he was faced with a serious dilemma: should he reprimand them? What if they ridiculed him? Would he expel them? Who would replace them? And what would Sneh think? "Well, what do you advise, what should I tell them?" urged Kahn. Finally they decided to reenact exactly the meeting Begin had held with the field commanders during the Saison. Begin would reprimand them late at night, in one of the orchards, while hiding behind a large cloth screen. Begin was enthralled after the night talk with his men, as if he had discovered the magic of the underground game. The fighters accepted his authority and apologized. "Listen, this was something special," Begin told Kahn while they folded the screen.[28] It was now easier to explain to Sneh what had happened, and the Jewish Resistance Movement could continue.

Because of the necessity to remain undetected, the heads of the underground found it difficult to organize meetings, and even the missions they agreed to execute often lacked coordination. This was the case during a mission to blow up the railroad tracks in Lod (also known as Lydda) on November 1.[29] Etzel did not know that the Haganah was also supposed to operate in the area. Hearing the explosions, the British deployed troops, and the operation ended with many Etzel members wounded. Such occurrences increased the organizations' suspicions of one another. Begin had to deal with his subordinates' complaints that the Haganah was deliberately limiting Etzel's role and restricting its involvement in larger missions.

When Begin asked for permission to attack a British police station, Israel Galili refused to authorize the plan without providing an explanation. Begin believed that the reason was that the Haganah had a munitions warehouse nearby, and he ordered his men to shelve the idea. A few days later he learned that Galili had refused him authorization because he had already approved the same plan from the Haganah several days earlier. Begin's image was once more undermined, as his fighters could not understand his naivety.

Begin was not naive, but his emotions often clouded his judgment. Cooperating with the Haganah gave him enormous satisfaction. He saw the mere establishment of the Jewish Resistance Movement as a personal achievement, both because the Haganah was drawn into combat operations according to the Etzel theory of revolt and because it finally legitimized his leadership. He also did not consider actions such as the attack on the police station important because the union of the undergrounds overshadowed such trifles. These were his days of greatness; the legitimacy granted to his leadership lifted his spirits, and he always ended the exchange of notes among the underground leaders (which were placed in a mailbox on Dizengoff Street) with a ceremonious "right-hand shake."[30]

But the internal frictions intensified. In February 1946, in a mission led by Amichai Paglin, Etzel fighters destroyed twenty-eight bombers on the ground at Kastina airfield. The attackers fled to Moshav Ezra and Bitzaron, where they asked for shelter and assistance for one of the fighters who was critically wounded. But members of the *moshav* disliked Etzel and chased the fighters out of the settlement. The injured man was abandoned in the field and died of his wounds. In this event the Haganah acknowledged that Etzel had suffered too much, and the fighter was buried near Be'er Tuvia with full military honors. Begin passed on an urgent request to Sneh that the Haganah should also express its participation in the mourning.[31]

The missions intensified too, while at the same time the illegal immigration activities (such as the Ha'apala, or Aliyah Bet) were also stepped up. Not all operations achieved their goals and some exposed Etzel's incompetence in complex operations, but they made waves among the public. Meanwhile, citizens of the United Kingdom struggled with the austerity regime implemented by the government after five exhausting years of war, making it even more difficult for the public to accept the burden of transferring more military forces to Palestine. The British also suffered from Arab pressure, which continued to intensify. On November 2, 1945, the day of the Balfour Declaration (which had been adopted twenty-eight years before), anti-Zionist demonstrations were held in Syria, Lebanon, Egypt, and Iraq.

In Palestine, however, it seemed as if the roles had been reversed. Following the suppression of the Great Arab Revolt of 1936, the Arabs began demanding their rights through demonstrations and diplomatic pressure, while the Jews took a violent and rebellious approach. For this reason, until the U.N. resolution of November 29, 1947, that decided on the partition of Palestine into two states, Begin refrained from making any significant statements regarding future Arab-Jewish relations. From the little he published in the Etzel pamphlets regarding the Palestinian Arabs, it appears that Begin believed the tensions between Jews and Arabs would be relieved only after the Arabs realized that the Jews were too powerful to be subdued and that they would have to be satisfied with equal rights and control of their holy sites.[32] In fact, Begin referred to the Arabs as a religious community and did not take their nationalistic aspirations too seriously, unlike Jabotinsky, who already in 1923 had written in his essay "The Iron Wall" that the buildup of Jewish power was crucial because the Arabs would not easily give up their nationalistic aspirations regarding Palestine.[33]

In Etzel's internal manuals Begin expanded on the attitude that should be taken toward the Arabs and promised they would be better off under Jewish rule. Another option that Begin did not rule out was a voluntary transfer: "If the Arabs choose to live with their brothers in Iraq and go there of their own free will, we will not stand in their way."[34] In fact, between the declaration of revolt in 1944 and the U.N. declaration of November 1947, which provoked civil war, Etzel focused on fighting the British and was therefore unprepared to fight the Arabs during the War of Independence. By 1946 Ben Gurion had already understood the need to prepare for a struggle against the Arabs and had worked to turn the Haganah into an army based on British military concepts.[35]

In the midst of the activities of the Jewish Resistance Movement, Attlee's government decided—partly in order to distract the attention of the international community, which was increasing its pressure to resolve the issue of displaced Jews in Europe—to establish another Anglo-American inquiry committee to investigate Arab allegations and Jewish actions in Palestine. Simultaneously, the British force in Palestine, under General Evelyn Barker's command, stepped up the fight against the Jewish underground. During February and March 1946, before coming to Palestine, the committee members spent a month touring the camps of displaced Jews in Europe. Representatives of the Jewish Agency prepared the Jews in the camps for interviews and made sure that committee members met only with Jews favoring the Zionist solution. The Jewish Agency also made thorough preparations in Palestine, composing a thousand-page book presenting Arab backwardness and Jewish enlightenment and progress.[36]

The committee published its conclusions on May 1, 1946. One of them stated that one hundred thousand visas should be granted immediately to the displaced Jews, as most of them wanted to settle in Palestine. But the joy following this announcement was marred by the solution proposed by the committee: the establishment of one country for the two peoples, with this country remaining under the British Mandate for the time being. Ernest Bevin too was disappointed with the committee's conclusions and demanded the dismantling of the undergrounds as a precondition for the issuance of visas.[37] Chaim Weizmann, president of the WZO, pressured the Yishuv leaders to dismantle the Jewish Resistance Movement on the grounds that the committee's conclusions should be fully implemented.

The headquarters of the Jewish Resistance Movement was not unanimous about ceasing operations during the committee's stay in Palestine. The Haganah refrained from attacks, while Etzel and Lehi continued them.[38] When the committee members left the country, the Haganah resumed military operations; on June 16, 1946, it destroyed the eleven bridges connecting Palestine and its neighboring countries in the Night of the Bridges operation.

A harsh reaction shortly followed. On June 29, in what became known as the Black Sabbath, dozens of settlements where the Haganah had members or bases were taken under siege. The British discovered the organization's main arsenal at Kibbutz Yagur in the north and arrested over three thousand persons, including most of the management of the Jewish Agency (Ben Gurion was in Paris at the time; Moshe Sharett was the most senior member arrested). This paralyzed all political activity, and the Jewish Agency concluded that the Jewish Resistance Movement was not helpful to the Yishuv. Ben Gurion sent Sneh a message to halt all cooperation with the dissidents and to avoid independent military operations.

But Begin continued to demand more military actions. He ignored international considerations, explaining that his men demanded that operations should continue and that it would be difficult to stop them.[39] Sneh preferred to maintain the cooperative framework and found himself in the middle, between Ben Gurion, on the one hand, and Begin on the other. Weizmann threatened to resign if the Jewish Resistance Movement was not dismantled, and the political committee in charge of Committee X agreed to his demand. In response, Sneh resigned his position and went to Paris in July to persuade Ben Gurion to countermand his harsh decree. Meanwhile, he ordered the Haganah to terminate all operations, but Begin and Yellin Mor were only told to suspend actions.[40] Torn between his support for cooperative actions and his devotion to the Zionist Federation, Sneh had a simple strategy: to delay responding to Begin. He was aware of Begin's mood swings and feared that if he was told that operations were completely prohibited, he would sink into a deep despair and order an escalation of operations, which without Haganah supervision would then be impossible to restrain.

On July 22, 1946, while Sneh was on board a ship on his way to France, Jerusalem was experiencing a heat wave. At 12:37 p.m. a huge explosion startled the entire city, and a thick cloud covered the skies. An entire wing of the King David Hotel had collapsed. The plan—Etzel's—had been to blow up the British military and administrative wing of the hotel after issuing a warning, but something had gone wrong and the explosion killed 91 people, leaving 476 wounded.[41] After this operation, the Jewish Resistance Movement was permanently dismantled.

The hotel had begun operating in January 1931. In October 1938 the British Mandate expropriated several floors, which became its military and administrative center, while one-third of the rooms remained a hotel. Etzel had come up with the plan to blow up the hotel in 1945, before the establishment of the Jewish Resistance Movement. After its establishment, Begin urged his men to carry out the operation. Yellin Mor supported him, Galili had reservations, and Begin was sure Sneh would eventually approve.[42] On July 1, Begin's contact woman went to his mailbox on Ben Yehuda Street and extracted the order, signed by Sneh, to go through with the destruction of the hotel. The first section categorically stated: "You must immediately execute Malonchik (Little Hotel, the code name given to the hotel). . . . Let me know the date. . . . The executing body must not take credit for the attack—neither directly nor implicitly."[43]

Begin felt as though he had hit the jackpot. The hotel bombing was of the highest priority in his opinion, mainly because of the symbolism of sabotaging the British Mandate's center and the dramatic destruction of the most advanced hotel in the region. He ordered Paglin to prepare the mission and appointed Israel Levy, who was not yet twenty years old, as commander of the operation. He hardly considered the risks in attacking a hotel crowded with civilians because Paglin assured him that Etzel would alert the civilians ahead of time and that no one would be hurt.

As Paglin was filling milk cans with explosives, Sneh's doubts about the necessity of such an operation increased. On July 19, two days after Begin met with Galili, who demanded that the mission be stopped, Sneh sent another note to Begin: "I have heard from a friend about the recent conversation you held with Galili. If you still respect my opinion, I urge you to postpone the planned actions for a few more days." This was the second request for a postponement, and since the execution of such an intricate operation demanded a large task force, Begin feared that information would be leaked. He did not answer Sneh's appeal, and on the morning of the operation, while Sneh waited at Haifa Port for the ship that was about to smuggle him to France, he sent Begin another message: "Shalom! You must momentarily delay the Jerusalem operation." At the time the explosion occurred, Sneh was already asleep on board the ship.[44]

The correspondence between Sneh and Begin became the focus of the debate that arose after the operation. Had the Haganah supported the operation, or had Begin ignored the last-minute attempts to prevent him from following through with it? Because the results were so devastating, a debate also arose regarding the amount of time the British had been given to evacuate the hotel after the warning was issued. Over the years, Paglin and Galili, who had met covertly before the mission to discuss it off the record, developed different versions of what had happened.[45] Nevertheless, even if the British were warned in time, they did not hurry to evacuate the premises.[46] Following the event a rumor spread that, according to Etzel historians, overshadowed any other version of the event: upon hearing the warning, the British commander shouted, "I am here to give orders to the Jews, not to take orders from them!"[47]

While the operation was being carried out, Begin sat in his usual place next to the radio in his apartment in Tel Aviv with Chaim Landau. He did not intervene with the technical aspects of the operation and expected to be updated over the radio. He remained silent as they waited. When the BBC reported on the many casualties and Begin realized that the building had not been evacuated before the explosion, he was shocked. He went closer to the radio to make sure he was hearing correctly, and when the station started playing a funeral march, he sagged into his armchair. The mournful tune increased his agitation. Begin muttered to himself, ignoring Landau, "What happened, what the hell happened?"[48] When he learned that among those killed was a deputy secretary of the British government, Richard Jacobs, an Englishman of Jewish descent, he burst out at Landau, "Was it not possible to warn him?" Landau was more practical. Without Begin's noticing, he fiddled with the radio wiring, and as the radio fell silent, his commander calmed down.

The first response by the Haganah to the attack was restrained and did not point any accusatory fingers. Etzel was subdued; it did not boast about the operation. But it took only a few hours before the Jewish Agency denounced the attack, and tensions between the Haganah and Etzel intensified. Begin was not surprised by the condemnation. He saw the Jewish Agency's hostility as an edict of fate, a deterministic hostility, apparently part of the burden every Jew was forced to carry. "These are the same people who hated Jabotinsky, and their hatred toward us is just an extension of that same hostility," he explained.[49]

To Begin's disappointment, shortly after his organization had finally been accepted and considered legitimate, it was tagged once again as dissident and impulsive, even though he possessed a document proving the Haganah's involvement in the operation. The next day Begin met with Galili, to whom he complained that the Haganah had forgotten that the Jewish Resistance Movement had approved the attack. This complaint expressed his ambiguous attitude: on one hand, he chose to rebel against authority and formal institutions, while on the other he wanted their recognition.

Galili tried to soften the blow and clarified confidentially that his organization was also having difficulties; moreover, simply because Jewish Agency leaders had still been held in detention after Black Sabbath, a misunderstanding had arisen that ended in a denunciation of the attack. But Galili added a reservation that would eventually become a historical debate: "You were not supposed to execute the attack at noon, when the hotel was fully occupied."[50] Begin denied it. From his point of view Galili was trying to shirk his responsibility. The debate, which grew as thunderous as the explosions on that day, centered on responsibility for the mistakes; the debate continued after Israel declared independence, in part because Etzel assumed that the attack on the hotel had also served the Haganah commanders, who thought that documents captured on Black Sabbath, linking the Jewish Agency with the Haganah, were stored in the hotel. The arguments were the final chord of the Jewish Resistance Movement. On August 5, 1946, Jewish Agency executives convened in Paris and decided to abandon the use of force in the struggle against the British.[51]

The Jewish Resistance Movement was dismantled, but an unplanned collaboration began: the Haganah continued to work to bring Jews into the country (from August 1945 until May 14, 1948, over seventy thousand illegal immigrants arrived in Palestine),[52] while Etzel and Lehi continued to fight the British. Despite the Yishuv's opposition to the dissidents' activities, the Saison policies could not be reapplied. Moshe Sharett even stated, "Eradicating evil by using external forces is out of the question."[53]

Etzel resumed its activities in September. During one of the operations, a raid on a bank in Jaffa, Binyamin Kimchi, a young member of the organization, was captured and on December 12 was sentenced to eighteen years in prison and eighteen lashes. "Such a thing cannot happen!" Begin declared in a headquarters meeting; he was not referring to the eighteen-year-old's sentence but rather to the flogging." "This is humiliation," he ruled; "it is not his posterior that will be injured but our national dignity."[54]

When Begin said, "We will respond to the flogging punishment," he referred to the image of the Jew as a victim and thought of his childhood memories of fleeing the anti-Semitic children who had beaten him in Brisk, his father after a Polish soldier tried to cut off his beard, and Jabotinsky's concept of a proud and erect Jew that he had worked so hard to instill in Jewish society.[55] That same evening he wrote a leaflet (also distributed in English) in which he pledged that Etzel would react to the flogging by flogging and instructed the members to prepare a mission to flog British officers.

Etzel squads armed with whips were sent to Petach Tikva, Kfar Saba, Netanya, and Rishon Letzion to kidnap British officers. In a Kfar Saba café they saw a British officer, but the place was too crowded for kidnapping. At Café Theresa in Rishon Letzion they captured a British sergeant-major dancing the tango with a local girl and administered eighteen lashes to his behind. In Netanya, they entered the Tripoli Hotel, separated a British major from his wife, read the verdict out loud that "flogging an Etzel member as is done in primitive barbaric tribes has no place in a cultured society," and flogged him eighteen times too. Every member administered two lashes, and only after the celebratory count was completed was the major sent back to the hotel. His trousers were confiscated on the grounds that "Etzel might need them."[56]

Begin's speech following the mission surprised many of the organization's members. He discussed the relationship between the British and the whip, even the activities in which they used it for fun, and said, with a smile, that one of the posters that stated that the response to the flogging of an Etzel member would be the flogging of a British soldier said, "Please don't forget my sergeant-major."[57]

This case lifted Begin's spirits, as he supposedly had finally gotten his revenge against the neighborhood bully and had succeeded simultaneously in administering his rough justice and thumbing his nose at the British. Later, when he wrote *The Revolt*, he was still delighted with the operation, dedicating an entire chapter to it. "We managed to damage the British Empire's prestige," he noted.[58] Moreover, the mission improved his image, especially among the youth in Palestine, who were also amused. But the consequences for Etzel were tragic. One of the squads participating in the operation was captured while trying to seize a British officer, and its members were severely beaten by the officer's comrades. Avraham Mizrachi died of his wounds, and three others—Yechiel Dresner, Eliezer Kashani, and Mordechai Alkachi—were sentenced to death for bearing arms. In the disgraced eyes of the British, the whip the squad members carried was a pretext for their severe sentence.

In general, Etzel had both impressive successes and embarrassing defeats. For example, in late 1946, while attacking a prison in Jerusalem, one of the squad commanders fled from the scene upon hearing shots fired—the first shots he had ever heard. Events such as this increased both the Etzel members' frustration and internal pressures to unite with Lehi. Paglin's deputy, Shraga Alis, decided to express the members' desire to Begin: "Why aren't we united? We're doing the same kinds of operations."[59] Begin used his favorite tactic: he pretended that he was secretly confiding especially in Alis, and told him that "we almost reached an agreement. But," he added sadly, "Lehi rejected it, as the new joint organization would define Jabotinsky as its founder." Alis fell silent and suddenly said, "Jabotinsky himself would turn in his grave if he heard of this. What difference does it make?"

Begin in his turn fell silent. He finally decided to remind Alis about who made the decisions and who executed them: "Oh, I see you know how to lecture and not just to fight."[60]

Alis wanted to hear the Lehi leader's version of the story as he could not accept Begin's version, and he discovered that Begin's was not only a matter of semantics. Although many Lehi members had started out as Beitar members, the movement's strength seemed to be that it attracted people with different opinions, joined together by their mutual opposition to the British. Begin's demand that Jabotinsky be named as the founder of a joint organization would have violated Lehi's basic structure and would have extremely reduced its power. (Following the establishment of the state, its members scattered into various ideological groups of thought.)[61] Meanwhile, as during the negotiations for the establishment of the Jewish Resistance Movement, it became clear that Begin's desire for unity was not stronger than his will to lead a united organization under his own ideological terms.[62]

Begin's contacts with Lehi in 1946 shed light on another aspect of his character. During one of the conversations between Etzel and Lehi, when Yellin Mor wondered what would happen if they did unite and conflicting ideas afterward broke out, Begin pulled out a ready answer: "An objective arbitrator will decide." When Yellin Mor asked who that person would be, Begin replied without hesitation: "Me."[63] In this exchange he revealed not only his wit and his faith in the righteousness of his way, but also his quest for power. But there was another reason for the union's failure. The Lehi members noticed that it was not difficult to influence Begin's mood, even though an underground leader was supposed to be calm and collected. "Bad news worsened his mood, and good news thrilled him, perhaps even more than it did others," Yitzhak Shamir said.[64] The two organizations continued on their separate paths.

By 1947, three years after the declaration of revolt against the British, Etzel was exhausted. Since the commencement of military operations, hundreds of its members had been arrested, its arms supplies were dwindling, and it had become increasingly difficult to raise money for the continuation of operations. It was also a decisive year for the Yishuv's relationship with the British. Due to the underground's activities, the British had fenced off their military bases with barbed wire, gathered inside areas that were scornfully known by the Jews as "Bevingrads" (named for Foreign Minister Bevin, with reference to

Stalingrad), stepped up security measures, and imposed a curfew on Tel Aviv and its environs. The curfew achieved its goal: Etzel members were caught, and Yishuv hostility toward the dissident group sabotaged its activities.

Etzel members grew increasingly depressed, and Begin decided to meet with leading members in one of their hiding places near the Tel Aviv central bus station. Begin's optimism, although often detached from reality, was valuable during these times. His ability to break away from the physical and the mental raised his friends' morale during these stressful times. The atmosphere during the meeting was mournful, but Begin was both astonished and delighted at the number of people who had come.[65] He promised, "One hundred thousand British soldiers will not break us. . . . Britain will leave because it has no choice. . . . Its economic situation, new considerations in its imperialist policy, and relations with other world powers will force it to vacate the region."[66] In the end he announced that within two to three years, five at most, a Jewish state would be established. His words were interesting not because his predictions were optimistic but because he chose to use Ben Gurion's assessments of the British departure for his own analysis in this closed gathering—that is, it would not be Etzel that would force the British out but the political situation. In any event, his speech raised the members' hopes.[67] His ability to raise his comrades' spirits was unmatched.

Being in hiding also gave Begin one important advantage. Because he met with very few people during his time in the underground, his image became more threatening (whereas his tiny, thin body and strict manners belied his position as the head of a terrorist organization).[68] All who met him during those days were surprised at the gap between their expectations—a tough warrior, a manly man—and the reality—a conspicuously pale and strangely polite man with dwindling hair (he began to go bald in his thirties) who looked like a courteous clerk.[69] But this very gap seemed to increase people's admiration for him.

In any case, Begin's main activity did not change. He focused mainly on drafting Etzel's leaflets and dictating radio announcements.[70] He held most of his meetings in his home, especially with the contact woman who reported to him every day and with Landau.[71] Even in intimate situations he acted as if he was being watched—the result of growing up with a father whose Zionist activities had integrated the private and the public. He would even ask for a cup of tea with sentimental pathos: "Our Scotta [his nickname for Luca Wax], give us a cup of hot tea, strong and sweet, like love."[72] It seems that the writings of Jabotinsky were not only the source of his etiquette, but also an "iron wall" for him.[73] Like a religious person holding onto his faith, Begin held onto his own unique patterns of behavior, creating a world of his own that, according to his rules, would never be defeated.

But Begin's sense of etiquette also exposed the alienation he felt in conversations about everyday matters. He always treated his contact woman with the utmost respect but never expressed any personal opinions or feelings to her.[74] The man who addressed crowds as though he were talking to a lover found it difficult to listen to the feelings of others. Begin was too shy, withdrawn, and suspicious to discuss personal matters.[75] His conversations dealt with the needs of the hour. Those around him noticed that when he happened upon a conversation about personal distress, he tended to grow bored quickly and withdraw into himself.[76] Aliza was no different. She loved to entertain and to converse with guests but never expressed weakness publicly and, like her husband, preferred to focus on matters of state, on the "Way," and on the "fighting family."[77]

At the time, Begin's relationship with his sister Rachel, who was still in Europe, was not close. Even after she immigrated to Israel (in 1962) their interaction was characterized by emotional compartmentalization. She was opinionated, and in her eyes Begin was still her little brother, the youngest child. She used to pester him with questions, and since he knew her well, he treated her with patience and respect, despite the fact that she often embarrassed him.[78]

Begin knew that he was no military genius and made sure to always emphasize this fact after being appointed commander of Etzel, mainly as a defense against any possible criticism. He often expressed firm political opinions, but regarding operations he tended to consult with others and was not interested in every detail. One autumn morning he held a meeting in his apartment to discuss recruitment procedures and officer training. One of the commanders, Yitzhak Avinoam, read from notes he had prepared for the meeting and was thrilled that his commander appeared satisfied. But Begin interrupted him and said, "Come, let me show you something good." Avinoam followed him into the next room, expecting a surprise related to their activities. Begin showed him little Chasia. "Little doll Kachka," he said; "isn't she cute?" An embarrassed Avinoam agreed, understanding the hint: Begin was not interested in the minute details of the plan he was presenting.[79]

Due to the British watchfulness Etzel found it difficult to convene meetings, and because Begin was forced more and more to restrict his movements, he decided to permit his district commanders to prepare operations without bringing them to him for his approval, although in any case they had not always done so in the past. In response to the "Bevingrads," in 1947 Paglin improved what Etzel historians refer to as "barrel bombs"—barrels that after being tossed off trucks rolled around fences until they exploded. Etzel continued to warn the British before assaults but continued to hit important targets, such as Camp Schneller in Jerusalem on Shabbat. By doing so, Begin deviated from his principle of withholding all operations on Shabbat out of respect for the Jewish religion. Simultaneously, the Jewish Agency spread photographs of the illegal Jewish immigrants being expelled from the land of Israel to criticize British policy.

The logistical difficulties suffered by the British Army, weakened after World War II, as well as the rise of anti-imperialist movements in Britain itself, led Bevin to propose a new solution for the Palestine problem: the Morrison-Grady Plan.[80] The plan proposed to divide Palestine into four cantons—a Jewish autonomy, an Arab autonomy, and two areas (including Jerusalem and the Negev Desert) under British rule, with the British continuing to set foreign policy and all matters of defense and economics. The plan also proposed the immediate immigration of one hundred thousand displaced Jews from Europe and stressed that the regional problem would be resolved in the distant future by the establishment of a bi-national state.

The Arabs rejected the offer; nor was the Jewish Agency satisfied with it. On February 18, 1947, Bevin announced to the British Parliament that he intended to raise the issue of Palestine in the United Nations because "we cannot accept the plans suggested by either the Jews or the Arabs, and we cannot forcefully impose a solution on them."[81]

Historians still disagree about the reasons behind the British evacuation from Palestine, but it was clear that they were fed up with Etzel's continuous actions. It is also clear that both the British opposition to allowing Holocaust survivors to immigrate and their battle against the Haganah, which nevertheless continued to bring immigrants in illegally, damaged the British image. These factors, as well as Palmach operations and increasingly negative public opinion in Britain, decisively influenced the British decision to relinquish the Mandate. After all, almost one hundred thousand British soldiers then stationed in the country (five times the number of troops that had suppressed the Arab revolt in 1936–1939) had been unable to impose order in Palestine. Yet the most influential issue seemed to be the postwar lack of sufficient financial means. U.S. President Harry Truman's announcement on October 4, 1946, that he supported the establishment of a Jewish state came at a time when Britain desperately needed U.S. assistance, leaving it with no other choice but to leave the decision about Palestine's future up to the United Nations.[82]

Meanwhile, the strict discipline of the British troops stationed in Palestine slowly eroded. On July 30, after the "affair of the hanged sergeants" (discussed below), British soldiers went on a rampage in Tel Aviv, destroying shops and firing shots indiscriminately. Five Jewish civilians were killed, and the British authorities became increasingly anxious about their soldiers' loss of control. Begin still doubted that the British intended to give up the Mandate. He ordered that the attacks be stepped up and even approved a Saturday attack on a British officers' club, convinced that the choice of day would diminish the chances of harming innocent bystanders. By so doing, he again deviated from his principle of withholding all operations on Shabbat out of respect for the Jewish religion. Seventeen British soldiers were killed in the attack, twelve of them officers.[83]

While the United Nations debated whether to allow Jewish Agency members into the discussions regarding the future of Israel, the news of the Acre Prison Break was announced.[84] This was one of Etzel's boldest operations. It was planned by Paglin, who became the organization's operations officer after Eitan Livni was arrested. Twenty-four Etzel members were broken out of prison, including Livni, and two hundred Arabs took advantage of the commotion and escaped as well. The prison break carried a heavy price: nine Etzel members were killed and eight were captured. Three of the captured were sentenced to death.

When Begin saw the newspaper headlines from around the world, he said, "London is frightened."[85] He gave Paglin a copy of the *New York Times* and told him to read it.[86] The little mistakes in the article—such as an assertion that the Etzel members had been partisans in World War II—did not bother him. Even a reference to them as "terrorists" did not bother him. After all, during his days in the underground, he mainly had an ongoing dialogue with headlines; reading them gave him so much pleasure that he started referring to current events in analogies to his favorite historical images: slaves, free men, Napoleon, the gallows. "This is the beginning of the end," he told Paglin in May 1947. Four months later the United Nations fulfilled his prophecy.[87]

The U.N. inquiry commission, also known as the United Nations Special Committee on Palestine (UNSCOP), was headed by Swedish judge Emil Sandstroem, who was sympathetic to the Zionist idea. The Arabs decided to boycott the committee, while the Jewish Agency hosted its members in the Yishuv industrial enterprises, which were presented as an antithesis to the enterprises of the primitive Arabs.[88] In the summer of 1947, when the committee members arrived in Palestine, two events shook up the local community: the hanging of two British sergeants and the expulsion of the SS *Exodus*.

On July 12, 1947, after three Etzel members were sentenced to death for breaking into Acre Prison,[89] Etzel kidnapped two British sergeants from a Netanya café: Clifford Martin (probably of Jewish origin) and Mervyn Paice. Begin said he would release them if his men were not hanged. Netanya was placed under a curfew, and the British sent troops on extensive searches in the area. But Etzel hid the sergeants in a well-protected location: they were held for seventeen days in a cellar under an abandoned building equipped with a ventilation system, toilets, and a refrigerator.

Two weeks after the kidnappings the British stopped the searches. On July 27, at 2 a.m., all three Etzel members were hanged, and Begin, who had already threatened to retaliate for the British hangings with Etzel hangings, was thrown into great distress. He was convinced that his threat would deter the British from executing their sentence, and when he had to respond as promised, he felt anger, pain, and fear. He knew that if he did not hang the British sergeants, his credibility would be damaged. But talk is one thing and actions are another; the man who commanded operations in which dozens of British and Jews were killed could not instruct his men to kill in cold blood. Begin was good at talking and threatening, but he would become squeamish at the sight of blood even at a Brit Milah, and when he served as a godfather, he would turn his head away from the circumcised baby.[90]

When he tried to convince Paglin not to hang the two sergeants, he did not admit that he found it too difficult to order his men to murder. Rather he explained that he feared for the fate of the executioners, mainly because Netanya was still crawling with British soldiers who might catch them in the act. But Paglin insisted: "Trust me; they will not get caught." Begin walked back and forth across his room as Paglin waited for a ruling: to hang or not hang?

"Fine, go to Netanya," decided Begin, "and decide for yourself."[91]

That same evening the two sergeants were hanged and their bodies were wired with explosives. A British captain was injured when he tried to remove them from the noose. "The Nazis could not have gone further than that with their inhumanity," the *Times* of London stated.[92]

Begin's aversion to this action is apparent in the last interview he ever gave, in which he said that hanging the sergeants was the harshest and cruelest action he ever ordered in his life.[93] A week after they were hanged, Begin published a leaflet titled "A Response to a British Father's Grief," which suggested that the bereaved parents should turn their criticism to 10 Downing Street (the residence of the British prime minister) and pointed a finger of blame at Attlee for his policy, but it was apparent that he was still battling with his guilty conscience.

The hangings undermined the Yishuv's relations with Etzel once again. A month earlier, on June 18, 1947, the Haganah had revealed a tunnel Etzel had dug under the Hadar Building in Tel Aviv, where a British headquarters was located. Begin planned to blow up the headquarters once the U.N. delegates had left the region, but one of the Haganah members discovered the tunnel, ignored the sign "Danger, Mines," stepped on one, and was killed. During his funeral, threats against Etzel were voiced, and Ben Gurion declared again, "There aren't, and there will not be, negotiations with dissidents."[94]

The Yishuv's hostility toward Etzel did not stem entirely from its military activities or from Ben Gurion's fears of the organization's political power but was also due to Begin's style of leadership. The man who was considered the number one terrorist in the Yishuv, with a reward on his head of 10,000 Palestinian pounds, cultivated military etiquette in his organization.[95] His left-wing opponents saw Etzel's rituals—such as awarding medals and promotions and holding parades[96]—as fascist characteristics.

Begin's leadership style was inspired by Jabotinsky, who wanted to put an end to the image of the "detached Jew" by educating toward order and discipline. This was the essence of Jewish *hadar* (glory, splendor) in his view.[97] During the years of the rebellion Begin was punctilious in cultivating this type of military etiquette. In 1944 he even refused to forgo a military parade on the anniversary of Jabotinsky's death; the parade was attended by many Etzel members at the risk of exposure. The ceremony opened with three minutes of silence, followed by Begin's speech about "our father and teacher's" legacy. The speech was followed by a promotion ceremony, and prior to each recipient's promotion Begin called out, "On the day of the death of our high commander I promote you with headquarters' approval to the rank of. . . ."[98]

For some of the reasons alluded to above—the ceremonial and ritual spirit prevalent in Etzel, the spirit of informal camaraderie characterizing the Haganah, and the Yishuv's contempt toward formalities and the bourgeoisie—Haganah and Lehi members created alliances in prisons in which the members of the different underground groups met, despite the fact that Lehi was even more extreme than Etzel. Etzel members were derisively known in the Yishuv as "dandies," the same nickname that elite soldiers scornfully applied to policemen.

Begin's attempts to incorporate *hadar* and terrorism into the Jewish community's policy were also ridiculed in the Yishuv. After the first operation in which a British soldier was killed, Begin wrote an obituary for the soldier at the bottom of an Etzel leaflet justifying the action. Lehi found this duplicity hilarious.[99] It is no wonder that when the Jewish Resistance Movement was dismantled and Golda Meir asked Lehi leaders to cease all their military actions, she also specified, "We distinguish between Lehi, real patriots, and Etzel, who wants to control not the Commissioner's Palace, but the entire Jewish people."[100] This was the paradox of Menachem Begin. Despite having prevented civil war and continuously talking about Jewish solidarity, he was considered an eccentric, an impostor, both because people found it difficult to believe that he really preferred unity over power and because he always conveyed his opinions in a grandiose style.

The Saison resumed in the fall of 1947 but on a limited scale. The trauma caused by the hangings of the British sergeants and the rage sparked by the "confiscations" or "donations" (as Etzel referred to them)—that is, the robbery of businessmen and bankers[101]—increased the hostility toward Etzel, and Ben Gurion took this opportunity to weaken his opponents. Due to Etzel's dire financial situation, it adopted methods that, excluding ideological differences, seemed very similar to the methods of the underworld, and Begin authorized some of them.[102] At the same time, Natan Alterman, the famous Jewish poet, published the poem "I Will Not Fight My Brother," which ridiculed the argument that the dissidents should not be opposed to one another because of Jewish solidarity.[103]

In October matters had deteriorated to hijackings and violent clashes, mainly in Tel Aviv and Rishon Letzion. This time Begin did not call for restraint and allowed Etzel members to kidnap Haganah members in response.[104] But the reason that the Saison did not develop to the dimensions of the previous Saison was surprisingly similar to Begin's reason not to call for restraint: as the time for the British withdrawal from the region approached, the atmosphere began to change. In August, Yitzhak Greenbaum of the General Zionists said, "I will never allow an alliance between Bevin and Ben Gurion against Begin," a notion backed by most of the Yishuv.[105]

The atmosphere in the Yishuv was also affected by the traumatic deportation of the SS *Exodus* on September 8, 1947, forcing the return of thousands of Jewish immigrants to the port of Hamburg, Germany. A return to the country that had led the worst Jewish massacre ever known inflamed spirits both in the Yishuv and abroad, promoting international recognition of the need to find a solution for the Jews—a country of their own. There also ensued a change in the Soviet position: Andrei Gromyko, Soviet ambassador to the United Nations, announced his support for the establishment of a Jewish state.[106]

UNSCOP was the first international institution to request a meeting with Begin, who had not yet recuperated from the affair of the two sergeants and was managing the little Saison at the time. The request gave him the international legitimacy he had longed for ever since being appointed Etzel commander. UNSCOP had requested a meeting with representatives from all the organizations, even those with minimal influence—including one with Dr. Yehuda Leib Magnes from Brit Shalom (the Jewish-Palestinian Peace Alliance), who met with the committee despite Ben Gurion's objections—but the very fact that UNSCOP saw Etzel as a force to reckon with encouraged Begin, who had not been so excited since the time he had argued with his interrogators in prison.[107]

The meeting with UNSCOP, which lasted three hours, took place in the apartment of the poet Yaakov Cohen, an Etzel supporter, in the center of Tel Aviv. Begin was accompanied by Chaim Landau and Shmuel Katz, the officer in charge of foreign publications. When Begin spoke about the death penalties Etzel members had received, he raised his voice and waved his arms in the air. The UNSCOP members told him it would be better if he did not yell because his shouts could expose their location.[108] It is not certain whether they were just being spiteful or were really worried that they would end up in a gunfight. In any event, Begin relaxed.

The conversation revolved around the rights of the Jews and how Begin could be incorporated into the establishment of a Jewish state. Begin reiterated that Jewish rights were anchored in history, not in the

U.N. resolution, and although he guaranteed that once the state was established he would dismantle the underground, he declared that his organization would object to the partition plan. This statement was surprising because it sabotaged the international legitimacy he had hoped for, although it should be noted that not long afterward he urged Ben Gurion to declare independence within the limited borders of the proposed partition.

UNSCOP's final report was submitted to the United Nations on September 1, 1947. The committee recommended a division of the country into two states—Jewish and Arab—and the enforcement of an international trusteeship over Jerusalem and Bethlehem. It also suggested that over two years, until the establishment of the two states, the British would maintain their mandate and allow 150,000 Jews to immigrate to Palestine. The British government decided to expedite the process: on November 13, it announced that it would withdraw its forces no later than August 1, 1948. The lot had been cast: the Jewish state had become a fact.[109]

Before the U.N. conference to approve the partition plan, military actions were toned down and political activity was accelerated. Even before the proposal's approval Britain announced that it would advance the departure of its forces to May 15 and that until then it would maintain the White Paper policies. Thirty-three countries voted for the partition plan, including the United States and the Soviet Union. Thirteen countries voted against it. On November 29, 1947, when the results of the vote became known, most of the Jews in Palestine poured into the streets in celebration. Begin and his men were not among them.

In a leaflet Begin published the following day, he wrote, "Much more blood will be spilled for the country we have worked for" and declared, "I will not recognize the partition plan." A suspicion haunted him that the British would try to provoke a dispute between the Jews and the Arabs and cause chaos so that they would be requested to instill peace and order once again. When Paglin said, "This is a turning point. We must turn against the Arabs and completely forget our activity against the British," Begin objected and said that there was no use attacking the Arabs. Paglin persisted, and eventually Begin ruled—as usual, his decision was sweetened with words of praise—"Forget it; no Arab in the [Middle] East will raise a hand against a Jew. After the barrels you threw and all the incredible actions we executed, no one will raise a hand against Jews."[110] In all his time in the underground, Begin objected to harming Arabs, although he often supported such operations in retrospect.¹¹¹ He opposed Paglin's proposition not only because he knew that fighting the Arabs according to Paglin's methods would harm many innocent bystanders but also because he was still concentrating on the British.

Paglin summarized the conversation with the word "disappointment." He felt that only those who had not been in Palestine during the Great Arab Revolt did not understand that the real conflict was between the Jews and the Arabs. He also felt that a satisfaction with British vulnerability had blinded Begin to the reality: he could not see that he had failed to gain political power in the Yishuv, and he was unable to recognize the main goal that would follow after the British withdrawal.¹¹²

SIX

JUBILATION AND DISAPPOINTMENT

Following the U.N. partition plan for Palestine, the first phase of the War of Independence began—a civil war between the Arabs and the Jews of Palestine. In fighting on a new front against the Arab countries and the Palestinian Arabs, who opposed the partition, Etzel needed capabilities that it had not yet developed, and its two major military operations—seizing Deir Yassin and Jaffa—sparked great controversy.

In 1948, Deir Yassin was a relatively small Arab village west of Jerusalem, and its residents maintained peaceful neighborly relations with the nearby Jewish communities—despite the occasional times they opened fire in their direction. The village symbolized the historic relations between Jews and Arabs throughout the twentieth century, and though it had no strategic value, it was considered important mainly because it was one link in the chain of villages through which Arab reinforcements made their way from Hebron and Bethlehem to the battles in Jerusalem. The Jews valued the location because next to the village was a flat spread of land that was intended for the establishment of an airfield.

In early April, Ben Gurion ordered Operation Nachshon—the breach of the siege of Jerusalem—despite the opposition of many commanders, who feared defeat. During the operation the Palmach fighters seized Qastel Hill, but the Arabs recaptured it. At the height of the battle the Haganah asked Etzel and Lehi for assistance (that April an agreement of operational cooperation had been signed among Etzel, Lehi, and the Haganah), but Mordechai Raanan, Etzel's Jerusalem commander, said that his forces were not ready. When he announced that his forces were prepared, it was too late—the Haganah had already seized Qastel Hill for the second time, after the Arabs had abandoned the hill in order to bury their revered commander Abed al-Qader Husseini, who was killed in the battle.

Raanan was disappointed about the idleness forced upon his men and suggested that they move on Deir Yassin. David Shaltiel, Haganah's Jerusalem regional commander, authorized the action provided that it would be "a seize operation, not a hit-and-run mission." Etzel soldiers were dispatched with Lehi on April 9 for the mission; their high motivation compensated for the flawed planning. They were sent into battle without any means of communication or coordination; due to technical problems with the machine guns, hastily manufactured in Etzel's facilities in Tel Aviv, the fighters could not employ automatic fire; and the truck with a loudspeaker intended to warn the inhabitants to leave the village got stuck in a ditch the villagers had dug to prevent vehicles from entering the village.[1]

This last, seemingly insignificant, problem became, in retrospect, the focus of a historical debate about the morality of Etzel, which argued that had the truck functioned, the villagers would have heard the warnings. When Iraqi volunteers opened fire on the Etzel positions, most of the platoon and squad leaders were hit. The junior fighters, startled at the turn of events, returned a stream of random gunfire. A Palmach force that arrived on the scene shortly after the fighting began was ordered to withdraw, and the Etzel soldiers, who were untrained for house-to-house combat, started to throw hand grenades into the village homes until the shooting stopped. The operation ended at four o'clock in the afternoon. Five Etzel and Lehi members were killed and thirty-one were injured—one-third of the soldiers there. And then the horror was unveiled: as the village was searched, it was found that almost every house that had been attacked was piled with dead bodies.

Etzel's attempt to seize the village carried a heavy toll. Begin was accused, of course, of having planned the massacre, but in fact he did not dwell on the details when he was updated on the situation. Due to the primitive means of radio communication, the Jerusalem commander in charge of the operation had sent Begin a message about the attack but with no details and no exact date and time.[2] Begin rarely spoke about his incidental involvement with the operation, even when he was severely attacked about it, in part because he was ashamed of his lack of control over his organization. Etzel members believed that Begin acted correctly in accepting responsibility for the action.[3]

Rumors of a terrible massacre in Deir Yassin spread like wildfire, partly because such rumors served all the groups involved. The Haganah used them to stain the dissenters' reputation; Etzel used them to frighten the Arabs; and the Arabs used them to disgrace the Jews. Either way, the rumors caused panic among the country's Arabs, and many of them abandoned their homes. As it turned out, investigations of the massacre found that descriptions of the atrocity had been exaggerated, as was the specified number of casualties. Immediately after the battle it was reported that over 250 Arabs had been killed, including the elderly, women, and children; however, historians who have studied the incident are unanimous in assessing the number of casualties at one hundred.[4]

Begin responded by publishing Shaltiel's letter to Raanan approving the attack, while Ben Gurion took advantage of this opportunity, as a cunning leader would, and sent King Abdullah of Jordan a letter of apology condemning the dissidents' actions.[5] In this manner he damaged Etzel's prestige in the Yishuv and made a decisive contribution to the decision not to include the Revisionist Party in the first government. A few weeks after the Deir Yassin massacre, Ben Gurion ordered the paving of a landing strip on the land adjacent to the village.

In late April Etzel forces deployed once more for a large operation—the conquering of Jaffa, which, according to the partition plan, was supposed to remain an Arab enclave alongside the Jewish city of Tel Aviv. The location of such an Arab enclave disturbed the Yishuv leaders, but they believed that a military operation of such proportions before the British evacuation could jeopardize the international community's support of the partition plan. Etzel, however, sought to challenge the plan. Basing his analysis on media reports, Begin became worried that the Egyptian Army would invade the country via the port of Jaffa and therefore believed that it was urgent to invade the town.[6] He ordered Paglin to prepare an operational plan.

At this stage Etzel headquarters was located in Freud Hospital on Yehuda Halevi Street, which was relatively close to Jaffa, but during the organization's headquarters meeting, Begin hesitated to give the operation his final authorization, as he feared it would involve many casualties. Only after Paglin's appeals and the Haganah victories in battles against the Arabs did he say to Paglin, "You are right; we're taking Jaffa."[7]

It was the largest operation in Etzel history, demanding the mobilization of six hundred soldiers. Begin ordered his men to make black armbands inscribed with the words "Rak Kach" (Hebrew: Only this way). "In two weeks, Ben Gurion is likely to declare independence, and the residents of Tel Aviv should know which army came to their rescue," Begin said.[8] The operation began with a military parade; Begin was scheduled to address the soldiers, but he had not made such a public appearance for a long time. Concerned about his ability to sweep away his listeners, Begin considered simply hugging each and every soldier. Eventually, he decided on an option that indicated how worried he was about a colossal defeat—he briefly wished the soldiers good luck, and in a rare gesture he asked Paglin to brief them for battle.[9] Before taking his leave of them, he made sure that his officers knew the alternatives for secure withdrawal.[10] Paglin was confident of his plan and ordered the six Etzel companies to proceed on foot toward the Manshiyya neighborhood north of Jaffa after a march through the streets of Tel Aviv. Some residents gathered in the streets to cheer the soldiers, while others cursed them.

On April 25, 1948, at sunrise, Etzel troops bombarded Jaffa with 81-mm. mortars that they had stolen three weeks earlier during a raid on a British military train near Pardes Hanna.[11] Yet the Etzel soldiers' meager experience in battles of this sort, together with the low quality of the mortars and the Arabs' stubborn resistance, halted the operation by its second day. The British, who initially thought that these were Haganah troops, were quick to respond upon uncovering their true identity, and they stationed a tank battalion and artillery on the outskirts of the battlefield. During the first two days of fighting eleven Etzel soldiers were killed, and Begin, apprehensive that the British would carry out their threats to bomb Tel Aviv from the air if the fighting continued, ordered his soldiers to retreat.[12] Begin was alarmed not only by the reports of numerous victims and the fear of British reaction. He also had to cope with increasing ridicule in the Yishuv, which viewed the action as unnecessary and extravagant. *Haaretz* wrote, "If Etzel is having difficulties in seizing Jaffa, it can always console itself with the conquest of Tel Aviv," and *Davar* dubbed the operation the "National Military Fabrication."[13]

But the soldiers did not obey Begin's orders to retreat. When Paglin arrived in the battle area, he refused to retreat. In his memoirs, Begin admitted that this was "the first time my soldiers revolted against orders. They simply refused to retreat."[14] His declaration was inaccurate (it was not the first time the soldiers had acted against orders), but it clearly described the chaotic atmosphere among the soldiers, now under Paglin's command.

Begin did not easily give up his authority, even though he knew it was rapidly slipping through his fingers. There was a distinct contrast between Paglin, a man of action and few words, and Begin, the leader. Working with Paglin was like walking a tightrope,[15] and Begin had excelled at it up to this moment. "Fate favored me," he confided to his comrades at headquarters, "when it introduced me to a military genius like Amichai."[16] But there were undercurrents of tension between the officer and the gentleman during their entire time together—mostly due to Paglin's demands for an Etzel response during the Saison and his aspirations of taking control of the Yishuv after the establishment of the state; these differed from Begin's vision of the democratic-political path he aimed to take until he became, in due time, the head of the state. "He is too complacent," Paglin used to say about Begin.[17] Yet despite their differences, they were wise enough not to exacerbate them to a point of conflict. In the battle over Jaffa, the Etzel commander was the one who backed down, and the soldiers continued to fight despite the order to retreat.

Meanwhile, a compromise was reached with the British, whose Spitfire planes circled over the battle. The Haganah would occupy Etzel positions in Manshiyya while British tanks would patrol the area to prevent clashes. The compromise was never realized because before their retreat, Etzel members blew up buildings lining the streets, blocking the tanks' way. The British could not defend Manshiyya, which was eventually overrun by Etzel forces, who frightened the fleeing Arabs. The horrible rumors of the massacre at Deir Yassin and the looting by Etzel soldiers discouraged the people of Jaffa, who assumed that the British would not protect them.[18]

The blowing up of buildings—the decisive act of the battle—was initiated by Paglin but confirmed by Begin. Although he had already given his forces the order to retreat, Begin realized that it was no longer relevant and went to the battle scene to see for himself. This time Begin the leader triumphed over Begin the commander; he chose to support his men, who wanted to fight.[19] When the town's prominent leaders raised the white flag, only 4,000–5,000 residents remained out of a previous population of 80,000.[20]

Just before the Declaration of Independence, it seemed as though everything was becoming intricately complicated. The first volunteers from Arab countries—the Yarmuk Army—arrived in Palestine; Arab leaders threatened an invasion; alarming rumors spread that Washington was considering opposing the partition plan and supporting a U.N. trusteeship instead; and several Jewish Agency executives also opposed the partition plan and sought other solutions. All of these possibilities changed Etzel's standpoint, and although Begin continued to object to the principle of partition, he announced his support for a declaration of independence. He later claimed that Ben Gurion had sent Eliezer Livneh to ask Begin to publicly threaten that if the Provisional State Council did not declare the establishment of the state, Etzel would.[21] In early May, Begin published a resolute pamphlet: "The Hebrew government will be established. There is no maybe—it will rise. If the official leadership establishes a government, we will back it. But if the government gives in to threats, our forces and the majority of the land's youth will back the free government that will grow from the underground."[22]

On May 12, the Provisional Government of Israel decided to declare independence by a majority of six to four. Two days later, after a meeting lasting only half an hour, Ben Gurion declared the establishment of the state. "The State of Israel has been established. This meeting is adjourned," he uttered dryly, knowing that a heavy battle against the neighboring Arab armies was imminent.[23] Simultaneously, negotiations were accelerated between Begin and Galili to integrate Etzel into the Israel Defense Forces (IDF), the new national army. The announcement of the Declaration of Independence, set for Friday noon, disrupted Begin's plan to follow up with his own victory speech. So as not to desecrate the Shabbat, Begin decided to wait until Saturday evening. Meanwhile, he worked on his speech. When a messenger sent by Ben Gurion asked to read it, Begin agreed, in a gesture of cooperation in honor of the historical moment, but when his friends claimed that it was an admission of surrender, he retracted his decision.

On Saturday evening Begin stood excitedly in front of a microphone in the Etzel radio station in Metzudat Ze'ev (Ze'ev Fortress, named after Jabotinsky and also known as Beit Jabotinsky—Etzel headquarters on King George Street in Tel Aviv, later the headquarters of Herut and nowadays the Likud headquarters). Unlike in the days of the British Mandate, when he rushed through his speeches during meetings for fear of being caught,[24] he took pleasure in the new status: "Blessed are we who have lived to see this day . . . the first Jewish revolt that has triumphed since the Hasmonean revolt. . . . We must humbly praise Tzur Israel [the Creator of Israel/Rock of Israel] and his redeemer." The words "Tzur Israel" were the only ones in Begin's speech that Ben

Gurion had used in the Declaration of Independence. Begin said that the state of Israel could be established "only this way" (the Etzel slogan). Begin also requested an end to all "empty talk about immigration capacity" and proposed to bring in all the Jews who sought to immigrate, "even if they have to sleep under the open skies." In regard to interior policy, Begin reiterated the importance of relations with foreign converts as mentioned in the Bible, which was "a supreme decree for our neighbors." Regarding foreign policy, he recommended that Israel maintain a neutral stance in its relations with both the United States and the Soviet Union.[25]

Begin spoke for over an hour. When dusk turned into night, he stepped out into the deserted street, and now—unlike less than five years earlier, when he had been a soldier in Poland—he was a free man, a citizen of the state, a leader who knew perfectly well that the most memorable sentence in his pathos-filled speech was the one stating his decision to dismantle Etzel. The new movement he founded, Herut, revealed a recognizable character trait of Begin the man, drawing him closer to the man who had once been the Beitar commander in Poland and distancing him from the man he had become as leader of Etzel—as if his political skill had lain dormant while he commanded Etzel.

Begin began preparing for the establishment of a political party even before the Declaration of Independence, when he realized that Etzel had completed its historical role. One hundred and fifty Etzel members, including Begin, were exempt from conscription into the IDF so that they could establish the party. When he completed a list of party members who he thought should serve in the first Assembly of Representatives, he did not include several Etzel members, as he thought that they might harm the image he hoped to portray for Herut or that they were unfit for politics. Begin hoped to create a party based mostly on former Etzel members but not only on them. He assigned the Etzel staff in the United States—also known as the Hebrew Committee for National Liberation (a group of radical revisionists who had been operating in the United States since the 1940s, when Begin was commanding the underground)—an important role in the new party, despite ideological and personal differences. The group, considered Etzel's intellectual elite, included Hillel Kook (known in the United States as Peter Bergson); Eri, Jabotinsky's son; Arie Ben Eliezer; and Shmuel Merlin.[26]

Begin assigned the task of writing Herut's party platform to Yochanan Bader, an Etzel member, and Begin himself focused on writing a chapter about the party's foreign relations.[27] In any event, Begin had planned to base the party's policies on a speech he delivered on May 15 and not on the official party platform.[28] Indeed, it was his most important political speech to date, as it outlined for the first time the views and aspirations of the man who intended to lead the country. The Revisionist columnist Kalman Katznelson wrote after the speech, "It was not an orator who spoke, nor a military commander; it was a leader who spoke."[29] However, Begin continued to run Etzel as a fighting underground in Jerusalem, so his rush to establish himself as a political leader was taken with a grain of salt, as he held a pen in one hand while the other was still on the trigger. He positioned Herut in the gray area between straightforward politics and revolutionary activities, a position from which he struggled to escape for many years following the establishment of Israel.[30]

Begin was not guided solely by political considerations. Although both his children were born in Israel, deep down inside he did not fully consider the country his own. Ever since he had arrived in the land of Israel, he had behaved like an outsider. His distancing from the new state is indicated in the fact that the term "the state of Israel" is mentioned only twice in Herut's official principles. Begin never shared his sense of estrangement with anyone, as it both contradicted the melting pot ideology he advocated and exposed his personal vulnerability. But when he announced that he was disbanding Etzel and agreed to participate in the democratic game, he succeed in shifting Etzel members, including several extremists and activists, onto a democratic political track despite the difficulties in doing so. In this way he made an important contribution to the new democracy.

There was no doubt that Begin's highest hurdle was the strict line drawn by Etzel headquarters in Paris, where the senior members demanded that Etzel become the political body representing the people and refused to recognize the newly elected government.[31] But Begin saw the political path, which was more natural to him than the military one, as the only means to power in the new country and often used motifs from mysticism to convince his friends of this position. "The establishment of the state is a miracle, a supernatural event," he stressed, "and therefore we should renounce any military action that could divide the nation."[32] He preferred to think of parliamentary activity as the arena from which he could replace the government, although he still did not fully believe in Israeli democracy under Ben Gurion's control.

Herut was formed in haste, lacking a prior agreement by all its members about its elementary principles. While Begin commanded Etzel, the uniting principle was obvious: the removal of the British. It was supported by all the members. Disagreements about operations were settled quite easily due to Begin's willingness to be flexible. But he soon learned that he would find it difficult to be flexible on ideological issues, and his attempts to skim over details so as to clear away insignificant factors merely damaged his position in the party.

Herut's first ideological conflict occurred when an Etzel delegation headed by Kook was preparing to travel to the United States and the party members could not agree on whether to include the concept of a Hebrew nation in the party's policy. Kook noted the difference between a Hebrew nation—which was meant to be formed upon the establishment of Israel—and the Jewish people, whom he thought of as a religious community that would become redundant and outdated upon its gathering in Israel. Kook wanted Hebrew youth to disaffiliate themselves from Judaism and argued that Judaism was not a nation but a religion, and as such one could be Jewish anywhere. For a nation to genuinely arise in Palestine, its Jewish inhabitants must uncouple themselves from Judaism and form a Hebrew nation with its own unique identity. For Begin, the term "Hebrew" had been associated with the Zionist aspiration of creating a strong, self-confident "New Jew," but he did not want to abandon Jewish tradition.

When Bader wrote the party's platform, he preferred to use the word "Hebrew" rather than "Jew," as he had partly internalized Kook's notion that Jews' interests changed according to the country in which they lived. The Jews in the Diaspora in the 1940s, Kook maintained, were not a united force, as they did not share common aspirations. Jews in the United States, for example, would be afraid to help the Jews of Poland, where anti-Semitism was prevalent, so as not to create a visible distinction between themselves and other U.S. citizens. Kook's conclusion was that a Hebrew republic should be established in Israel that would distinguish between state and religion. One of the main goals of his push to separate state and religion was a partnership with the local non-Jewish population in Israel, whom he saw as Hebrew Arabs. He estimated that some Arabs would support this goal while others would choose the alternative of being foreign residents. In the eyes of the Etzel delegation to the United States, "Jews" were a "faint constellation," with religion being the only thing linking the people of different nationalities.[33]

Kook was in a sense the first post-Zionist of his kind, with something of a Canaanite leaning. (The Canaanites, a small group, mostly influential intellectuals and artists, hoped to revive what they believed to be a Hebrew-speaking civilization in antiquity, creating a "Hebrew nation" disconnected from the Jewish past and embracing the Arab population as well.) In his first speech upon his arrival in the United States, he demanded that the Jewish Agency be disbanded, that Arabs be incorporated into the government, and that religion be separated from the state.[34]

Begin often used the word "Hebrew" but did not go as far with his ideas as Kook. He thought of "Hebrew" as a rhetorical substitute for "Jew," and it had nothing to do with his concept that the Jews were a nation in every respect, that they had originated from the same ancestor, that they based their traditions on Jewish law, and that therefore nation and religion overlapped.[35] Moreover, he saw religion as a unifying element for the Jewish people. His national concept was based on the assumption that nationalism stemmed from the Jewish people in its biblical version. In a 1958 Knesset speech about nationality and citizenship he clarified that there was no need to explain why nation and religion were intertwined. "The answer for the reasons not to separate state and religion with regard to the Jewish people is—that's just the way it is," he began; then he stressed, "I believe what I'm about to say with all my heart and soul and with the complete faith on which I was raised by my father and mother and which I will believe until my last day on earth"; then he concluded, "The God of Israel decided who is Jewish. This is how the history of our people began."[36]

This fundamental difference of opinion among Etzel members could be bridged as long as the organization's goal was the expulsion of the British and the establishment of the state. When Etzel members were incorporated into Herut, the state versus religion issue became the source of many internal and personal battles.

Begin, like Moshe Sneh (who had abandoned the General Zionists and joined Mapam) drew confidence from the popular assumption that in the elections for the Constituent Assembly, the young radicals who had advocated fighting would be a critical group of voters.[37] "Herut is not a party of wheeler-dealers," he stressed, and reiterated its reputation as a group of men of action, adding that its opposition to the boundaries assigned to the state by the partition plan would not be expressed only in words. "Etzel," he said, "will continue to operate in Jerusalem until it is included in the country's boundaries." Moreover, he added, "Our plows will plow the fields of Gilead."[38] His claim that Jews had the right to establish a land within the boundaries of a biblical version of their homeland—more precisely, he referred to the boundaries set by the League of Nations Council as the borders of the British Mandate—not only echoed Jabotinsky's slogan, "Both banks of the Jordan River," but was also meant to distinguish between Herut and the Revisionist Zionist Party, the original revisionists.[39] Unlike for the Revisionists, who also swore by Jabotinsky's slogan, this was more than just a statement for Herut, which added the Etzel symbol—a hand grasping a rifle above the slogan "Only this way"—to its map of the country. The message was clear: Begin saw the military path as a legitimate means to the desired end.

Begin assumed that the reputation of Etzel fighters would appeal to many Revisionist supporters,[40] irrevocably severing the historical ties between Etzel and Hatzohar, and he even went so far as to turn the underground newspaper into a political paper to rival the Revisionist newspaper *Hamashkif*.[41] With his sharp political instincts, Begin noticed that he could distinguish his party from Hatzohar by "fostering friendly relations with the Soviet Union," as opposed to the general alignment with Western countries (the United States in particular), while simultaneously adhering to a neutral stance relating to the struggle between the two blocs. His new approach suggested that he was willing to foster ties with new audiences in order to achieve power. He admitted that "In the past, there were hostile relations between the revolutionaries and the Hebrew liberation movement," but argued, "The Soviet Union has recognized our right to sovereignty and independence . . . and we will never forget the fact that the Russian Army saved hundreds of thousands of Jews from the grasp of the Nazi predators."[42] With the new stance he pleased both former Mapam members and some ex-Lehi activists, who espoused a pro-Soviet ideology. The question Begin had often asked himself—What would Ze'ev Jabotinsky have done, he who advocated Western democracy and the man to whom Begin referred as "the Immortal"?[43]—became of marginal importance to him.

Begin attributed great importance to propaganda. He ordered the founding of a political newspaper and turned the underground's radio station, Kol Zion Halochemet, into a political station called Kol Haherut (the Voice of Freedom). In addition, he lectured to the junior Etzel members to try and convince them to support the new party, proving over and over again that he was still a devout supporter of revolutionary concepts. On June 14, 1948, he addressed more than 1,200

Etzel members in Ramat Gan, where he noted that the underground would continue to operate in Jerusalem for the sole purpose of "accumulating power and weapons for the right time to storm the land and conquer the entire country."[44] The crowd rose to cheer their leader, who raised his fist in the air, momentarily forgetting that the point of the gathering was to discuss the transition from resistance to politics. Begin, who had not fought for power before the establishment of the state, had no intention of fighting for it afterward, but he still found it difficult to let go of old rhetorical patterns.

Begin gave his supporters the sense that Etzel's role was over but not completed, a fact that Ben Gurion could not ignore, mostly because Begin went on to add exaggerations into his speeches, such as his remarks at Be'er Yaakov the following day when he threatened, "If the enemy continues to bomb our holy sites in Jerusalem, we will bomb their holy sites abroad. They should not for a second think that we don't have forces there."[45] When Begin lectured, he was simultaneously a speaker and his own most enthusiastic listener. He rarely wrote his speeches in advance; he usually satisfied himself with chapter headings, but he maintained a distinct style. During his speeches he often shook his fists, paused methodically for dramatic emphasis, and utilized rhetorical questions. In his speech in Be'er Yaakov he added another element of visual innovation—fashionable sunglasses, part of his unique style, which distinguished him from the unkempt Mapai leaders. In the middle of his speech he suddenly stopped without warning and asked the crowd to stand for three minutes in memory of those executed on the gallows, while he added, "We swear to God that we will fulfill the role imposed on us: not to rest until we have liberated the entire Hebrew homeland."[46] Ten Etzel members fainted from the heat, congestion, and excitement.

The strong impression Begin left on his followers increased Ben Gurion's fears that he was not only a charismatic political rival who could rise to power by democratic means, but also a radical who would not hesitate to use the underground to seize power. This was the psychopolitical background of the *Altalena* affair, which highlighted Begin's advantages and disadvantages under conditions of stress; despite his attempts to translate the turn of events into public sympathy, he ended up harming Herut's chances in the elections.

When statehood was declared, Begin was still unaccustomed to his new political position. Only three weeks earlier, he had signed an agreement under which Etzel would be integrated into the IDF and announced that as a politician, he planned to focus on establishing Herut, but his actions contradicted his decision to put an end to the underground activities and brought about the *Altalena* crisis. Begin believed his actions matched his decisions. It was clear to him that in order to make his way into politics he would have to get rid of his image as a dissident and a rebellious terrorist who lacked political discretion. However, he was well aware that he would have to fortify his political platform by reliance on the Etzel reserves, and therefore he tended to maneuver between the two alternatives.

To understand what happened between June 21 and June 24, 1948, during which a small-scale civil war broke out on Kfar Vitkin Beach and the streets of Tel Aviv, it is essential to return to Begin's decision to establish Herut immediately after the United Nations had adopted the partition plan.

Begin struggled to convince some Etzel members that the resistance should be dismantled. Etzel headquarters abroad believed that it must not accept a partitioned state and demanded a continuation of the fighting until the enemy was pushed back behind the historical borders.[47] Begin emphatically opposed underground activity alongside official military activity, and he made his unilateral position clear in a letter to Eliyahu Lankin in which he wrote that he consistently opposed a bloody internal war.

From the beginning of negotiations with the Haganah in December 1947 for the establishment of a unified military force, Begin had sought to attain equality among all the underground armies, at least in principle. Galili, one of the top Haganah commanders (who was appointed assistant secretary of defense with the establishment of the state), insisted that Etzel be dismantled and that every member be individually recruited into the new unified army; Begin wanted his men to be enlisted as a separate brigade into the IDF.[48] The negotiations lasted several months, initially without a formal mandate by the Jewish Agency board, which confirmed the negotiations only in mid-January 1948.[49] For his part, Ben Gurion insisted that Begin dismantle Etzel and accept the National Institutions' authority with no preconditions. "We do not negotiate with dissidents. They must first commit to cease all separate actions—including blackmail and any form of threats," he wrote in his diary.[50]

Only in March 1948 did they agree on a "union of fighting forces in the land of Israel."[51] The agreement noted that Etzel would be dismantled after the founding of the IDF, and until then it would be subject to the Haganah commanders.[52] This was an important agreement in Begin's eyes, as it recognized Etzel as a separate fighting force, even if temporarily.[53] The agreement was adopted by the Acting Zionist Committee (part of the World Zionist Organization) in April, though it triggered complaints because of Begin's involvement in the operation at Deir Yassin. Moshe Erem, a member of Mapam, cried out at the approval of the agreement, "This is an agreement with murderers, the heroes of Deir Yassin."[54]

Begin announced the agreement two weeks after the Declaration of Independence, but he still found it difficult to say the army's official name, calling it the "United Forces."[55] On June 1, Begin and Galili signed the official agreement. Begin's demand to induct his men as a separate brigade was rejected, and the Haganah withdrew its demand for personal enlistments. The agreement stated that Etzel soldiers would be enlisted in regimental formations if they so wanted.[56]

At this stage it was clear that Begin was maneuvering between his new role as a political leader and his old role as an underground commander. He publicly announced that the agreement, an example of good statehood, enforced Etzel's disbandment, but in private conversations with his commanders—who were obviously displeased with the agreement, which stripped them of their positions—he spoke of the need for money: Etzel had to be integrated into the army, he explained, "because we could not afford to maintain thousands of troops and to provide for their families."[57] Ben Gurion, on the other side of the fence, found it difficult to hide his disdain for Etzel and its commanders, saying dryly, "If the agreement passes—I say good riddance."[58]

The main barrier to the deal—Etzel's demand that as long as Jerusalem was not annexed to the country, it would continue to operate there—was not removed but overridden. Eventually, a compromise was reached: "Etzel will cease to operate as a military brigade in Israel and in the government's area of jurisdiction."[59] Galili concluded that "the government domain" included Jerusalem, in which the IDF remained active despite the fact that it was not under Israeli jurisdiction, while Begin's legal mind saw in this a punctiliousness concealing a totally different meaning: Etzel did not commit itself to act outside the government's official jurisdiction only to cease to operate within its borders. The forthcoming events in Jerusalem, which ultimately led to the destruction of Etzel, were preceded by the *Altalena* affair, illustrating how far off Begin was in his assessment that the middle path—between the underground and politics—was possible.

In the summer of 1947, the Hebrew Committee for National Liberation bought a former LST (Landing Ship, Tank) displacing 4,500 tons. The deal was led by Avraham Stavsky, who had been acquitted of the murder of Chaim Arlosoroff owing to a lack of evidence and had left Palestine after the trial.[60] Stavsky also suggested the name for the ship—*Altalena* (Italian: swing), Jabotinsky's pen name, thus indicating the ship's connection to the Revisionists. In March 1948, the ship docked in Italy, where the plan was to load on board weapons and Jewish immigrants.

While the British were speeding up their evacuation, a war broke out between the Jews and the Arabs of Palestine—the first act of war between the IDF, hastily founded on the base of the Haganah, and the Arab armies. Early in 1948 Begin sent a telegram to Lankin, at the time head of Etzel headquarters in Paris, in which he made clear that Etzel was the only organization that could win the war to "impose the nation's rule on the entire land."[61] In order to execute his plan he would require military equipment and ten thousand warriors. Lankin immediately began to raise money and recruit fighters.

Now that his plan to rebel against the British had been achieved, Begin was left either to argue for recognition of the organization's contribution to the establishment of Israel or to continue harassing the British with insignificant actions, as his fighters found it difficult to operate within the framework of an organized army.[62] With his sharp political senses Begin realized that Etzel must participate in the war against the Arabs, and he therefore pressured headquarters to build up the organization's fighting forces.[63] But the quality and quantity of volunteers were disappointing. The Paris headquarters reported that most of them were not suitable for combat and that the focus should be on purchasing arms.[64]

An arms deal contradicted Etzel's signed agreement, which stated that the Haganah had to approve any purchase of weapons. Ben Gurion was briefed on Etzel's activities but saw these as a minor problem.[65] His main concern regarding Etzel at the time was French foreign minister Georges Bidault's sympathy for it (owing to his opposition to Britain, for diplomatic reasons, and because of his objection to Israel)[66] and the minister's official comparison of the status of Etzel to that of the Jewish Agency.[67]

On May 16, at midnight—the second night of the Arab armies' invasion of Israel—Begin, encouraged by his dramatic speech after the Declaration of Independence and concerned about the difficulty of raising money to purchase arms, summoned Haganah representatives to an emergency consultation at Etzel headquarters, whose location was overt since the battle over Jaffa.[68] Begin suggested an enticing deal to Galili, Levi Eshkol, and David Cohen, now representatives of the newly established Ministry of Defense who were concerned about the situation at the borders: the Haganah would give Etzel $250,000 to complete the arms acquisition, and in return Etzel would put the ship, including the passengers and weapons on board, at its disposal.[69] Begin called *Altalena* the "Ship of Salvation" and said that if it reached Israel's shores, it would determine the fate of the country's battles. But Ben Gurion's representatives, exhausted and surprised, were less enthusiastic about the idea. Two days later Galili returned to Begin with a negative answer.[70] One of the reasons for the rejection of the offer was the Haganah's assumption that the media had already received word of the ship and that its existence could not be hidden from the British, who had not yet left the country. At around the same time, Etzel's man in Paris, Shmuel Ariel, was informed that the French would give him, free of charge, weapons originally intended for the French Army, including 5,000 rifles, 250 machine guns, and 5 million rounds of ammunition.[71] The only condition was that the weapons arrive in Israel after the evacuation of the last British soldier.

While Etzel was concerned with *Altalena*, the battles along Israel's borders had become heavier. By June 10, only four weeks after the war erupted, the IDF had suffered heavy casualties, although the casualties in the four armies fighting against Israel were much greater. Israel succeeded in maintaining control over most of the territories designated by the United Nations, excluding the unpopulated areas of the Negev, and the initiative was now in the hands of the IDF, which blocked most of the attacks. But it had come to a point where it needed a break to reorganize its forces, as did the Arabs.[72]

Meanwhile, a mediator appointed by the United Nations, Count Folke Bernadotte—a Swede who had helped save Jews during World War II—increased his efforts to achieve a cease-fire. On June 10, all parties agreed to a truce, accepting the prohibition of inserting soldiers or weapons into the theater of battle. That night Ben Gurion officially announced the cease-fire on the radio, explaining the IDF's consent as a "fundamental principle of mutual understanding and compliance with the United Nations," and adding that "the government will not tolerate anyone's attempts to violate the truce. . . . Those who do so will be considered enemies of Israel."[73] *Altalena*, now anchored in Marseilles, set sail the next day.

Upon hearing Ben Gurion's speech, Begin feared that *Altalena*'s arrival in Israel would be considered a breach of the truce. That same night he summoned the Etzel radio operator and asked her to contact the ship to tell it to delay its approach. Half an hour later, after realizing that there was a communications problem, he gave up. He did not realize that the ship was already under way and did not verify that it had received his message.

Lankin, the ship's commander, and Monroe Fein, a Zionist Jew from Chicago who was appointed the ship's captain, knew about the ceasefire and understood that Etzel was trying to transmit an urgent message, but they feared that the ship would be seen as suspicious in a port city teeming with Muslims, so they decided to set sail, assuming that they would manage to evade the U.N. inspectors.[74] They were also apprehensive that radio surveillance would expose their relations with the French government.[75] In any case they were anxious to set sail and trusted that a satisfactory arrangement would have been reached by the time they made landfall in Israel. The *Altalena* approached Israel's shores unbeknownst to Begin.[76]

June 12, two days after the cease-fire went into effect, was the Jewish holiday Shavuot (the Pentecost); it was the first time since coming to Palestine, four years earlier, that Begin felt he could celebrate without fearing the British. He invited Paglin and several other friends for a festive dinner at his home. Aliza was in charge of the culinary part of the evening; Begin told tales of the past and spoke of the future to be. At 11 p.m. he asked his guests to quiet down so that he could listen, as usual, to the BBC news report. That is when he first found out that the *Altalena* was nearing Israel's shores. (Ironically, history repeated itself when he was prime minister: he first heard of the Sabra and Shatila massacres while listening to the BBC.)

Begin was seized by a fear of the unknown, and anxiety spread across his face.[77] He understood that he now had to choose between his agreement to a cease-fire and his support of Etzel. He ordered the radio operator to send the *Altalena* a message to reverse course. The operator did indeed transmit the message—"Stay back and wait for instructions"—but keyed in the wrong code. Meanwhile, Begin's visitors dispersed, and because Begin believed that the message had been transmitted, he went to bed without making sure his message had been received—as he had done several days before. But this time he was awakened by the sound of knocking on his door. The frightened operator reported that she might have tapped in the wrong code. "This is very serious," he said, but in the face of her fear, he tried to control his anger. "Transmit it again," he said. She toiled for hours, transmitting the message for the ship to reverse course and to wait for instructions, but this time she felt that the problem was not technical difficulties but that someone on board was not doing his utmost to decipher the message.[78] Lankin later admitted that because he did not understand the message, he chose to treat it as an order to increase speed.[79] The ship continued to approach the coast.[80]

Only three days later was contact established with the ship. The next day, Begin met with Galili and Eshkol for instructions on how to proceed: to keep the ship at sea or to have it sail into shore.[81] Eshkol asked how much money Etzel was asking for, and Begin replied proudly, "Not a penny."[82] He did not tell them that Etzel had received the weapons gratis and did not admit that a dispute had arisen with the headquarters members in Paris so as not to harm his status in the eyes of the government representatives and his authority toward his people. This was probably the seed of destruction: Ben Gurion saw Begin as an underground leader scheming against the provisional government, although he was only a mediator.

After Ben Gurion was notified of the ship's approach, he told his men to inform Begin that the ship must anchor off Kfar Vitkin Beach.[83] The official reason was that the Moshav Kfar Vitkin settlement was surrounded by Jews, while Tel Aviv was overexposed to U.N. inspectors supervising the cease-fire.[84] Begin was not pleased with the decision, yet upon reporting it to his headquarters, it appeared to the members that they were finally dictating the diplomatic moves. He told them that the government had promised him help in unloading the ship but forgot one detail: Moshav Kfar Vitkin was a Mapai settlement. "Menachem," Paglin hastened to quell his enthusiasm, "it's a trap"; he demanded that they adhere to the original plan and that the ship sail toward the shores of Tel Aviv.[85] Begin looked at him mercifully, as at a man who had lost his political instincts. "We've been promised, Amichai," he whispered. "The Palyam [the Palmach naval force] will help us unload." If not in Tel Aviv, suggested Paglin and his deputy, we could unload the ship at Bat Yam, just not at Kfar Vitkin. But Begin hinted that he did not intend to back off. "This will end badly," stressed Paglin again, but Captain Fein was notified to approach Kfar Vitkin.[86]

This time Begin was decisive: he preferred to confront Paglin and the operations staff rather than Ben Gurion, but he did not dare to place entire responsibility on the government or accept its authority. Instead, he swung between cooperating with the government and ensuring that Etzel remain responsible for managing the situation. But in fact Begin lost control over the sequence of events.

A dispute broke out regarding the distribution of the weapons on the *Altalena*. Although Begin agreed that the weapons would be distributed to IDF soldiers according to the decisions of the operations echelon, he also demanded that 20 percent of them be earmarked for Jerusalem—that is, for the Etzel troops in the city. Galili agreed but insisted that this 20 percent be distributed among all the units in Jerusalem, including those of the Haganah. Begin considered Galili's insistence ungrateful and saw in it an attempt to belittle Etzel's part in the War of Independence. Ben Gurion saw the distribution issue as evidence of Begin's intentions: to arm his troops in order to sustain a separate military body within the IDF. Because no accurate records were kept regarding the distribution of equipment to IDF soldiers, it is difficult to say with certainty that the Etzel soldiers who had already joined the army felt deprived because they received outdated weapons. It is most likely that resentments and remnants of past disagreements had not subsided and that the issue was not merely technical, but also fraught with emotion.[87]

The conflict between Begin and Galili continued while they scrambled along the beach. Begin, wearing a sweat-stained white shirt, asked urgently for a phone line. His initial enthusiasm for the ship's arrival had been replaced with fear of what was to come. As they continued to argue, Begin insisted on one more condition, influenced by Paglin: that at least one Etzel soldier be assigned to guard the 80 percent of the weapons intended for the IDF.[88] Galili requested time to review the matter. Meanwhile, Ben Gurion received word that Begin had posed another obstacle. He had demanded that an Etzel representative explain how the weapons had been obtained to each and every IDF unit about to receive them. In this way, a simple technical issue became a complicated affair. Galili announced that due to Begin's last demand, he had decided to retract his offer to assist with the unloading of the ship's cargo.

At this point, Begin should have realized that he was losing control of the situation, yet he maintained the belief that he could regain it.

On June 20, when the *Altalena* cast anchor off Kfar Vitkin Beach, dozens of enthusiastic spectators gathered in the area, and the roads to Netanya and its surroundings were filled with Etzel soldiers who had deserted their military units after they had already been inducted. The government saw this as an ominous sign: Etzel was rebelling. The next day Ben Gurion sent a telegram to Galili: "Either they take orders and obey them or we shoot."[89]

Why did Ben Gurion choose such an aggressive approach? It is reasonable to assume that it was not because he wanted to obtain the weapons since if that had been his goal, he would have achieved it through negotiations. It seems that beyond his belief that Begin wished to rebel, he viewed Etzel's action, even if it was not meant to be so, as a flaunting of authority. At the same time, as his main goal was the consolidation of a new army at a time of war, the situation with the *Altalena* was a chance to prove to all wayward citizens that in the new sovereign country there was only one army and one rule. But Begin, even though he truly believed that the weapons would make an important contribution to the war, did not intend to allow his organization to be pushed aside in the developing country.

"Come on, let the people be happy," Begin hissed through his smile at Paglin, who was troubled by the dozens of people gathering around the ship.[90] The unloading started while, unbeknownst to Begin, the government had decided to consider his refusal to hand over all the weapons as a "serious development" since a sovereign state at war cannot abide a violation of its authority. In a cabinet meeting on the next day the members decided, "We unanimously agree to give the IDF authority to counteract [Begin's demand]. The commander in place must attempt to prevent [the event] without force but shall use force if his word is not obeyed."[91] Dan Even, commander of the Alexandroni Brigade, was sent to take over the ship.

Meanwhile, a junior IDF officer arrived at the beach and requested that Begin meet with Galili, but Paglin answered on behalf of his commander, "If Galili wants to meet with Begin, he should come here," and the unloading continued. "Forget it, Amichai, you're tired," Begin tried to alleviate Paglin's fears. "They will not shoot at us, and there is no need to sail for Tel Aviv." Paglin was insulted and asked to be dismissed from the task, and as Begin was already tired of arguing with him, he agreed and appointed Yaakov Meridor to take charge of the unloading operation.[92] When the Alexandroni troops arrived on the beach, they found dozens of Etzel soldiers who had deserted their base in order to help their friends unload.[93] Begin was later astonished at the claims of desertion and said that the Etzel soldiers' response was the only one that could have been humanly expected.[94] But the massive desertion proved that the state of Israel did not yet have a unified army. In a letter that Ben Gurion' wrote to Interior Minister Yitzhak Greenbaum, who sought to formulate a compromise, he explicitly clarified that this was not a time for negotiations, and in any case he concluded, "I doubt whether it is advisable for any government member to meet with an Etzel official under such circumstances."[95]

On the morning of Tuesday, June 22, Begin was in a terrible mood. The feeling that a confrontation with the IDF troops was imminent and Paglin's departure made Etzel members question his judgment. He is too naive, people said on the beach; he believes the wrong people at the wrong time.[96] Now that he was alone and realizing that his people were doubting his command, Begin felt that he had to keep his dignity and reject an ultimatum that Even sent him in a crumpled note: Surrender "within ten minutes."[97] Most of the eight hundred volunteers who had traveled on the *Altalena* had already dispersed throughout the country. Yaakov Meridor, who took the ultimatum seriously, proposed to Begin that they board the ship and redeploy to another beach. Begin had an idea: "We shall arrange an on-the-spot parade; we'll outline the chronology of the negotiations, and then we'll speed up the unloading."[98]

Begin promised, "We will board the ship, sail to Tel Aviv, and from there I will summon all the inhabitants of the country."[99] At that moment the first shots were heard, a turn of events for which the *Altalena* affair is remembered as one of the most tragic episodes in Israel's history. Etzel members swear to this day that the shots were fired without warning.[100] According to witnesses, the shots were intended primarily as a deterrent.[101] Following a quick consultation, during which some of his people demanded to fight to the last man, Begin boarded the ship and ordered the captain to move out of range.[102] The plan was to sail to the shores of Tel Aviv, where thousands of his supporters would gather, making it difficult for the IDF to oppose the unloading of the weapons.

As the *Altalena* made its way to the coast of Tel Aviv, the riots spread, in part because rumors that Begin himself had been killed enflamed the Etzel members' anger.[103] Meridor was appalled at the developments and decided to accept his deputy's advice to agree to the Alexandroni Brigade commander's call for surrender.[104] The next day Ben Gurion sent a letter to all members of the government expressing his satisfaction with Etzel's surrender and justified the use of force.[105] Ben Gurion's rigidity surprised even several members of the government. "Will he order the navy to subdue the ship even if it leaves Israel's territorial waters?" the interior minister wondered. "Absolutely," concluded Ben Gurion.[106]

Begin stayed on deck; his words became sharper as he spoke to more than one hundred shocked Etzel members gathered in the dining room who were adamant about continuing to fight. He described the history of the betrayal against Etzel over the background sounds of the men's singing and harmonica playing, which were heard over the loudspeaker and increased the doomsday atmosphere on board.[107]

After midnight on June 22, just as they reached their destination—Frishman Beach—the *Altalena* ran aground. Soldiers from the Kiryati Brigade were lined up facing them, under orders to halt the unloading of the ship.[108] Begin had selected Frishman Beach because he thought its proximity to U.N. headquarters would make it a safe choice. He was convinced that the IDF would refrain from firing so as not to endanger the U.N. forces. He did not, however, place much importance on the fact that the navy and air force headquarters were situated on Hayarkon Street, adjacent to the beachfront.[109]

In the morning an announcement was made over the loudspeaker to the men on the *Altalena* that an emissary of the IDF wanted to board the ship in order to reach an agreement.[110] Using the ship's own speaker, the men responded that they would first like permission for Etzel headquarters members to board the ship for consultations.[111] When word was sent to Ben Gurion, he hastened to declare to the government, "They have announced that they would not allow a government official on board before the Etzel commanders board the ship for consultations. We have refused. I have now ordered: gather forces for subduing the ship."[112]

For a moment, Begin considered going ashore, but Lankin forbade him to do it, fearing that he would be stepping into a trap.[113] Begin was left with no other option than to engage in propaganda. They played underground and traditional homeland songs over the loudspeaker, accompanied by calls such as, "Hello, Tel Aviv, from the Hebrew arms ship," and "Our Tel Aviv, in blue and white." Begin himself addressed the soldiers on land over the loudspeaker, saying, "We have come to fight with you, not against you—do not open fire."[114] But *Davar* stated, "They broadcast slogans, including slanderous remarks about the Israeli government, and called for its citizens to revolt."[115]

When hundreds of Etzel members and their supporters approached the shore, Begin ordered them to start unloading.[116] The IDF called in reinforcements—the Har'el Brigade—and Yitzhak Rabin, the brigade commander who happened to be in the area, took over command of the Palmach headquarters.[117] The streets of Tel Aviv became enflamed, and only calls from both sides saying that "Jews do not shoot at Jews" prevented a conflagration.[118]

At around four in the afternoon, while the men on the *Altalena* were unloading the remaining arms, the thundering sound of field guns was heard. The first two shells landed near the ship. The captain waved a white flag, fearing that the ammunition stored in the ship would explode. But then five more rounds were fired, and one of them hit the deck.[119] Some of the Etzel members returned fire, and most of them jumped into the water and swam to shore.

Begin could not swim. He froze on deck and found it hard to hide his consternation at the sight of blood on the clothes of the wounded, while Lankin urged him repeatedly, "Get into the lifeboat." After the cries had increased, Begin replied that he wanted everyone to get off before him.[120] Lankin struggled to understand why Begin was risking his life. "Menachem, go down immediately into the lifeboat," he cried. "I'm in command now—go down!" Begin, wearing a khaki cap, looked down at Lankin and finally muttered, "All right, calm down; I'll come."[121] After being strapped into a life jacket, he sat silently in the boat, which made its way to shore.

Begin disappeared once the lifeboat was beached. Etzel command ceased to function, its members acting independently. He turned away, alone, and walked through the streets, with the cries of the wounded and the commotion echoing in his ears. He did not yet know the price of the incident: three killed and fifteen wounded from the IDF and sixteen killed and over forty wounded among the Etzel forces.[122] On his way to Yehuda Halevi Street, without his glasses (which had been lost at sea), barefoot, wet, and with ruffled hair, he met David Tahori, an Etzel soldier who could not believe that the person walking slumped over and tattered before him was in fact his commander, and he was afraid to approach him. After a few steps, with Begin still withdrawn into silence, Tahori told him that he had decided to accompany him. Begin nodded and went to headquarters, where he waited for his friends. Meanwhile, Tahori ran to Begin's home on Rosenbaum Street to gather clean clothes for him. Aliza was lying in bed with a fever. "Something terrible has happened," she said on seeing him. Tahori told her the news, took a white shirt and Begin's gray suit, and not forgetting a tie, ran back to headquarters. Begin sat silently in his room. Nobody dared approach him until he emerged and hissed, imbued with a fighting spirit, "I thought that we should all go our separate ways, but after what the government has done to us, we will establish a movement to fight it."[123]

Etzel members who were starting to arrive at headquarters reported that the military police had begun to make widespread arrests and had even broken into Metzudat Ze'ev. Israel Eldad, a Lehi member who came to the Etzel headquarters too, estimated that the government would now seek to destroy Begin and urged him to escape. "It's not heroic to stay here at headquarters," he told Begin. "Even Lenin led the revolution from the forest he was hiding in." "I am not Lenin," Begin exclaimed and continued to make threats against the "regime."[124] In this time of heightened emotions, the Etzel members forgot that Ben Gurion had actually refrained from taking the decisive step of eliminating Etzel; the IDF did not approach Etzel headquarters, even though its location was known.

Begin's first decision after the incident was typical: he would deliver a fiery speech so that all would understand that a despicable act had been perpetrated in Israel. Without any notes and without consulting anyone, he went to one of the underground radio stations in Tel Aviv and delivered a speech that eventually came to be known as the "crying speech" and provoked much criticism. He made dramatic claims and spoke of the feelings of the persecuted victim. As he spoke, bloody images flashed again before his eyes, and overwhelmed, his voice broke and he burst into tears.[125] He opened the speech by saying, "I come to tell you, my brothers and sisters, of one of the worst events to occur in the history of our people and perhaps in the history of all nations across the globe. But also of one of the most spectacular acts of heroism displayed by individuals in the face of mortal danger." He spoke of the "magnificent ship" that carried "wonderful equipment" and exaggerated that it had "10,000 anti-aircraft bombs," adding that if we had them, "we would be standing today on the shores of the Jordan River and possibly beyond." At the end of the two-hour speech Begin demanded that his men show restraint. Although he was disconcerted, he did not deviate from his iron rule: "I call on my brothers not to open fire. . . . There will be no fraternal war. . . . The enemy is at the gate."[126]

Only years later, when the *Altalena* myth had grown, was Begin praised for preventing a violent conflict, though at the time his speech shocked many Etzel members, who were disappointed at their leader's weakness.[127] "Crybaby," Shmuel Katz hissed angrily.[128] "He has destroyed our image as winners after our triumph in the occupation of Jaffa," others maintained. "Begin is too emotional, and the mental stress and the long days have overwhelmed him."[129] Nevertheless, Begin saw nothing wrong with his tears and later wrote the following in his memoirs: "There are some tears that no man should be ashamed of; there are tears that every man can be proud of. . . . Sometimes the choice is between tears or blood."[130] Ben Gurion followed the events with equanimity. "The Etzel day," he wrote in his diary. "What happened today was destined to finally happen."[131]

After the attack on the *Altalena*, five Etzel leaders were arrested for disobeying orders, and Begin, before preparing for his next step—the political stage of his career—had to calm down his men, some of whom wanted to fight back.[132] "There will be no use of weapons under any circumstances," he announced at a press conference after realizing the extent of the damage to the nation and to the political party he intended to lead.[133] He even went to the home of one of the Etzel members who had declared that he intended to assassinate Ben Gurion and told him, "If you want to kill Jews, you had better shoot me first."[134]

In light of the events, Ben Gurion retracted the agreement signed on June 1 regarding the integration of Etzel into the IDF. Etzel was outlawed and its storage facilities were confiscated. During a State Council meeting, Ben Gurion said, "Blessed is the gun that bombarded the ship. This gun deserves to stand close to the temple, if it is built."[135]

The Etzel members were helpless; the leader they had trusted had led them to a dead end. Despite his decision to expedite the establishment of the new party, Begin now struggled to function. When he visited Katz's wife after his arrest, he hardly uttered a word, as if admitting his failure; the silence was broken only by slight sips from his cup of tea.[136] His followers were split. Some wanted to rebel openly against the government, while others demanded to be integrated into the IDF and that an end be put to the battle once and for all since Herut was in any case meant to replace the underground.[137] Yet most were in agreement that their leader had failed. "We should have given in to Ben Gurion and at least gotten public sympathy," said Katz, "and in any case, not have delivered such a speech." His friends agreed.[138] Now that it was apparent to all that the *Altalena* affair had turned sour, Begin's political wisdom was being questioned—and most Etzel members had regarded that as his most important attribute when he was commanding the resistance against the British.[139] Tired and weary, Begin was aware of his colleagues' complaints; he decided to put an end to the *Altalena* story and gathered two hundred Etzel officers who had not yet been recruited and asked them to join the IDF and to pass the message to join on to all Etzel soldiers.[140]

Over the next two weeks Ben Gurion decided to release all of the arrested Etzel members except the five senior officers, who remained in administrative detention.[141] By September 1948 Etzel had been permanently disbanded, and only the Jerusalem branch continued to function.

In late June 1948, while most of his comrades believed that Begin would still be struggling to recover from the *Altalena* affair, he returned vigorously to work in the political field. He invited nine former Etzel members to his office on Tchernichovsky Street and joyfully announced that they had been selected to be "the provisional administration of the Herut party."[142] The aftermath of the *Altalena* affair was now translated into a political demand: Begin declared that Herut would fight for the release of the five senior members who remained in state custody, as part of its struggle "for democracy and against emergency regulations." He compared the terms of their incarceration to methods used in the concentration camps: "Holding hostages is a proven method. The Nazis in Germany used it against the resistance fighters in Europe."[143] The five were released in August, and at the party organized to celebrate their return at Café Bustan in Tel Aviv, Begin toasted the "end of the concentration camp regime."[144] This time he made sure to take advantage of the situation and to garner political clout on his favorite terms. By turning the spotlight on the five prisoners, he established Herut as a party standing not only for security matters, but also for personal issues such as human rights.

The political activity brought vitality back into Begin's life. After his many years in the exhausting role of Etzel commander, it was clear that he felt more comfortable in the guise of a politician. He saw himself as Jabotinsky's heir, despite the ideological differences between them; they both believed in the power of words and in the power of statements to shape reality and consciousness. In line with the sanctity Ben Gurion attached to the gun that had fired at the *Altalena*, Begin coined his own new phrase: "the sacred ballot." Many of the underground members expressed surprise upon his shift from advocating the bomb to advocating the ballot. It was a drastic change for them.

Years later, in the Rightist paper *Sulam* (Ladder) Eldad slammed Begin for sanctifying the ballot, as he argued that there was a difference between "important" and "holy" and he ridiculed Begin, saying that his entrance into politics had made him forget his original concepts.[145]

However, Begin's biggest political problem was not the extreme rightists in *Sulam* but rather Etzel headquarters in the United States, which saw itself as the organization's political body during the struggle for the establishment of the state—unlike Begin, who thought of the U.S. headquarters as more of a public relations and fund-raising branch of the organization—and now wanted to determine Herut's political path. A dispute among Begin, Kook, and Eri Jabotinsky had begun back in the days of the underground. Ze'ev Jabotinsky's son referred to Begin as a politician and not as his father's rightful heir. The tension between the two was never publicly aired, yet it was a well-known secret that harmed Begin's attempts to maintain a public image of unity in the party. As noted above, ideologically Kook and Jabotinsky saw Hebrewism as a substitute for Judaism and the common combination of religion and nation; they also demanded that Herut change its political orientation to a more straightforward Western policy, while Begin declared that Herut would rather maintain neutrality toward both the Soviet Union and the United States in order to differentiate itself from the Revisionist Party.[146]

In August Begin spearheaded a change in the election campaign—which was taking place in the shadow of war—and started touring the country and holding public meetings. Begin had a considerable advantage over Ben Gurion: the mysterious aura surrounding him at the time he commanded Etzel created a buzz, and many were eager to see him. Indeed, Begin and his followers had a shared interest: he wanted the cheering masses, and they wanted to cheer him.[147] During his public speeches he tended to descend from the stage and join the audience, a dramatic act foreign to the spirit of Mapai. When visiting Acre Prison, Begin stood in silence for several minutes in front of the gallows chamber, in an act he described as "communion with those hanged on the gallows."[148]

In front of thousands of cheering enthusiasts in Rishon Letzion, Begin said that the Jewish Agency leaders had been "ready to surrender" when they agreed to the Morrison-Grady Plan and argued that "only our battle prevented our country from becoming a ghetto." Begin sought to persuade the voters to support Herut not only because his party's policies were right and other policies were wrong, but also because Herut offered the possibility of an unarmed revolution against a hostile regime. During the speech in Rishon Letzion he accused Mapai of "kidnapping the country." He demanded that the Ministry of Police be abolished,[149] as well as the British emergency laws enacted in 1945: "Why do we need emergency laws in our country? Our people are disciplined but also free. We do not need Nazi emergency laws that have not been eradicated until today."[150]

When Herut organized a central assembly at the Gan Rina Cinema in Tel Aviv, Begin arrived with Aliza and his five-year-old son. Near him at the speakers' table sat Mrs. Stavsky, the widow of Avraham Stavsky, who was killed by the IDF fire on the *Altalena*. When Begin introduced her to the crowd, he presented her as living testimony of the affair. A blind Etzel soldier was also invited on stage, and the host introduced him as a soldier who "had lost both his eyes during the attack on Jaffa, and he has come to hear his commander and mentor." Begin's assemblies were undoubtedly the best show in town.[151]

Up to the date of the elections Begin continued to demand the extension of the democratic process and the cancellation of the emergency laws, on one hand, and that the government give backing to military actions on the other; he also demanded that a referendum be held—"the most democratic act"—on the issue of annexing Jerusalem. In an article he published in *Herut* he expressed his opposition regarding Count Folke Bernadotte's proposal to demilitarize Jerusalem and to position international inspectors in the city, calling the proposal "the final goal," thus evoking the Nazis' "final solution."[152] Begin's demand regarding the annexation of Jerusalem was rejected, and he ordered the Etzel soldiers stationed in the city to sign a petition supporting annexation. There is no certainty about the number of signatories, but the petition clearly influenced the atmosphere in the city.[153] According to *Hamashkif*, more than thirty thousand signatures were collected.[154] *Haaretz* referred to the petition as "grand and gaudy propaganda" and ridiculed Begin for his lack of political wisdom in his decision to ignore the United Nations while the government was attempting to annex Jerusalem in diplomatic ways.[155] Thus the struggle between Herut and Mapai became a battle between the realistic and the dramatic, between honor and purpose, between the white shirt and the khaki trousers.

Three days after the annexation petition was circulated, Begin toured Jerusalem. The combination of his speeches and his presence in the city intensified the effect of his rhetoric. While his speeches highlighted

Begin the leader, his physical presence exposed Begin the man.[156] On his second night in the city he spoke in Zion Square, where over fifteen thousand people gathered to hear him, according to *Hamashkif*. In his diary, Ben Gurion wrote of his anger at the momentum his opponent had gained during his visit.[157]

When Begin returned to Tel Aviv for a seminar regarding Herut's guidelines, he noted his goal: to conquer ever larger circles of Revisionists on the way to a position of power. By so doing, he presented his political platform: a coalition of the disadvantaged. During his tours of the country, Begin realized that the spirit of the Yishuv was alien to him—a fact reflected in his clothing, his manner, and his ideological preferences; he also realized that the monolithic guideline dictated by Ben Gurion displeased many and that a repudiation of Mapai was Herut's link to these people. "We must focus on the disadvantaged groups in our midst who are the real proletariat, unlike those who call themselves such yet in actuality are a bourgeois class of propagandists," he stressed, and even added, "Do not fear to stand against him [Ben Gurion] in a front with the Communists and even with Mapam."[158] On this matter he completely deviated from Jabotinsky's revisionist path[159]—a fact that bothered him not at all on his quest to gain constituents.

Hatzohar also noticed the disregard of the public for Mapai and in a party meeting with Ben Gurion claimed, "It is up to you if the Revisionists become a political party or an underground organization. . . . Their people are not being accepted into the system. . . . This strengthens Etzel." Ben Gurion was not convinced. He ignored the differences between the Revisionists and Etzel and was certain that "Etzel's identification with the *Altalena* affair has distanced even those who wished to support it."[160]

At the time, immigration from Islamic countries was still at its first stages, and masses of Mizrahi Jews (the Easterners), who had not yet heard about Etzel, had not yet arrived in Israel.[161] But Begin had already prepared the groundwork for when they arrived. He described Herut as "the popular movement," and in a brilliant maneuver labeled the socialist party, Mapai, as a bourgeois party, while his own party became known as the working man's party.

Begin's desire to expand his circle of supporters coincided with his approach to "benefit the people."[162] When speaking at a Tel Aviv hotel, he noticed that his audience was not dressed in fancy suits and quickly declared, "Means must be taken from the rich to benefit the poor." It was clear that he found pleasure in the position of patron to his people, although he never mentioned exactly how he planned to extract means from the rich; moreover, although he understood that the tradesmen to whom he was speaking were not the country's well-to-do, he failed to grasp that they were not necessarily fans of the Histadrut nor advocates of communism. The slogan "to take from the rich and give to the poor," usually associated with the Left, created great discomfort and wonder. As he stepped excitedly off stage, Begin searched Bader's face to see if he was impressed, but Bader's face was filled with indignation. Only after it was explained to him that his comments might distance the tradesmen and small manufacturers from Herut did Begin desist from mentioning extractions from the rich. After he returned from his first tour of the United States, Begin also gradually abandoned the notion of maintaining neutrality in the East-West conflict that was developing into the Cold War, and he returned to the stance of supporting the United States.[163]

In August, due to Begin's insistence on establishing a party separate from Hatzohar, as well as his rising popularity, most Revisionists slowly joined Herut. But this shift did not work out well, as many of the veteran Revisionist Zionists, including the senior members, found it difficult to accept Begin's unchallenged status, so eventually two Revisionist parties participated in the first elections.[164]

Meanwhile, the military situation in Jerusalem had become complicated. The Jews in the Old City had already surrendered in May, the roads to the city were blocked, and Etzel and Lehi continued to aggravate the IDF's task of organizing military operations. Begin continued to talk about the need to annex the city under any terms, ignoring Ben Gurion's declaration that state laws had already been applied to Jerusalem and that a military governor had already been appointed to the city.[165] The numerous Etzel commanders in Jerusalem wanted to dismantle their units and integrate into the IDF, but Begin objected to this.[166] Paglin traveled to Jerusalem to evaluate whether it was viable for Etzel to relieve the Old City and concluded that Etzel could not do it alone.[167] Even though Begin had formally announced that he no longer had any influence over Etzel in Jerusalem, he continued to berate Ben Gurion, whose policy, in his opinion, was too irresolute.[168]

The dispute over Jerusalem concerned more than just tactics. Begin saw it as one of many controversies between the advocates of practical Zionism, who preferred gradual progress and the deliberate and clandestine establishment of settlements, and the supporters of political

Zionism, disciples of Jabotinsky, who preferred a practical implementation of the righteous path. Therefore, when he visited Jerusalem, Begin mocked the appointment of a military governor and declared, "Just as you will not allow the demilitarization of Jerusalem, do not let it be occupied by the armies of Israel" (and once again found it difficult to utter the words "Israel Defense Forces"). "We need to liberate Jerusalem, not to conquer it. How can Jerusalem become an occupied city? There is no greater shame than allocating a military governor to Jerusalem."[169]

The IDF commanders continued to file complaints about Etzel activity in Jerusalem.[170] David Shaltiel, the Jerusalem regional commander, claimed that the organization was instigating provocations and that it might damage military operations. The government was split regarding the Etzel issue: ministers of the religious parties and the General Zionists preferred to seek a settlement with Etzel, while Mapai and Mapam ministers demanded the elimination of the organization by force if it did not disband on its own. "Warn them, and if they do not adhere, eliminate them by force," Ben Gurion wrote in his diary.[171] In early September, Foreign Minister Moshe Sharett, who was also tired of Begin's foot-dragging about the dismantling of Etzel in Jerusalem, burst out in the Knesset, "The question is not about Jerusalem.... The question is about Israel; is it a country or is it not? That is the question." The session adjourned without a decision, but the spirit of the words expressed in it indicated what was to come.[172]

On September 16, Count Bernadotte published a draft of his peace proposal, which recommended putting all of Galilee under the sovereignty of the State of Israel, establishing international rule in Jerusalem, and placing all of the Negev between Ashkelon and Beit Jubrin under Jordanian authority.[173] Ben Gurion and his government, with the consent of Etzel and Lehi, opposed Bernadotte's proposal. Lehi members in Jerusalem went so far as to publish in their party organ *Mivrak* (Telegram) a commentary about Bernadotte's hostility toward Israel, ending with the remark, "If he is not deported, who knows what will happen?"

On September 17, Bernadotte left Government House in Jerusalem, accompanied by a French officer. Between Katamon and Rechavia a jeep suddenly blocked their path. Four men wearing khaki shorts and armed with a submachine gun stepped out of the vehicle and asked them for identification. As Bernadotte reached in his pocket to retrieve his, one of the men shot him in the head.

Government ministers were horrified. A Jewish organization called Chazit Hamoledet (the Homeland Front) claimed responsibility for the killing, saying "Bernadotte was murdered because he worked for the British and carried out their orders." It was later discovered that the Lehi central committee—Shamir, Eldad, and Yellin Mor—had given the order to murder Bernadotte. Shamir and Yellin Mor denied any connection to the murder.[174] On September 19 the government ministers gathered for an emergency meeting, terrified of the imminent response from the United Nations. The hysteria that gripped them was successfully expressed by Minister of Transportation David Remez: "Since the crucifixion of Jesus we have not had such an accusation directed at us."[175]

Despite suspicion among the cabinet ministers that there was in fact no such organization as the Homeland Front and that Lehi was behind the assassination, Ben Gurion—fearing for Israel's position in the U.N. Assembly, which was scheduled to convene to discuss the assassination—decided to take the opportunity to achieve an ulterior goal. "We have finally decided to eliminate Etzel," the prime minister wrote in his diary.[176] On September 22 the cabinet activated the mandatory regulations for the prevention of terrorism, which included administrative detention without trial. (These regulations have not yet been abolished and are known as the Act for the Prevention of Terrorism.) On the day following publication of the new regulations Begin claimed that "these are laws that grant the new government dictatorial powers. . . . In fact, these regulations eliminate human and civil rights and the foundations of law in the state of Israel."[177]

In a meeting with Isser Harel, who was appointed head of the Israeli internal secret service (Shin Bet), Begin accused Lehi of "delivering a heavy blow" and did not wait for the ultimatum that Harel was about to issue. This time he refrained from declaring that he was opposed to civil war and flatly announced that Etzel's Jerusalem Brigade would be dismantled. "They have completely surrendered," Harel reported back to the government.[178] On September 23—four months after the establishment of the state, three months after the *Altalena* affair, and in the midst of the War of Independence—even the most extreme Etzel members understood that they had reached the end of the road.[179]

On October 19, the first meeting of Herut's national council convened in Ohel Shem Hall in Tel Aviv. For Begin, this was the most important meeting prior to the elections. On the stage were three portraits—of Herzl, Jabotinsky, and Raziel. Beside the photographs hung three maps: the partition map, with the caption "This is how the

Gentiles wanted it"; a map of the state, with the caption "This is what our soldiers accomplished"; and a map of the historical land of Israel, with the caption "We will fight until we achieve it." Some time before the meeting, Begin had wired a telegram to his comrades describing their missed opportunity in the War of Independence: "We could have reached the Jordan River and even crossed it, but the formal leadership has missed the opportunity."[180]

Begin entered the hall accompanied by the elderly Tamar Jabotinsky-Kop, Ze'ev's sister. He opened his speech with the Yizkor (memorial prayer) for all of Israel's fighters from the Left and the Right; specified Avraham Stern, "the commander, poet, and creator of Lehi"; and amazed his audience by saying the Yizkor for the fallen soldiers of the Haganah (though he quickly added that they "had fought for a brief period, during the resistance days, with the underground organizations"). He tried to portray himself as a national leader and not just the head of a political party, and he focused on two major issues. First, it should be announced "that the government of Israel is the government of the land of Israel"; by this Begin meant that war should be declared against King Abdullah's kingdom, "which covers four-fifths of our historic domain, and it is the task of the Hebrew government to rid the world of this thieving kingdom." The second issue was the nondemocratic character of Ben Gurion's government. "Herut will heal the country from the plague of despotism," he promised. "If the people give us their sanction, we will establish a government based on intellectual foundations that will not fall short of those on which the present government rests."[181] After the speech, the hundreds of participants, who had listened to his speech with bowed heads, sang the Beitar anthem.

Some of the attendees were not impressed with the festive atmosphere Begin had tried to create for the event. Abba Achimeir, a member of the maximalist Revisionist faction, warned against the frustrating differences between the underground and official political dealings.[182] He clarified that "we are moving from a period of heroism to small actions—a gray day," and that "it was easier to prevail over the British than it is to beat Mapai."[183] This was not the first time Begin found himself in opposition to the party's intellectuals, whose style was foreign to him. The hostility was mutual. Begin demanded a chance to respond to Achimeir's comments: "For God's sake, do not be afraid! Why are they trying to scare us with a shift from life underground to visible action and to frighten us with the demon of Mapai? We defeated the British. To defeat Mapai will be all the more simple." In response to Achimeir's argument that there was a gap between Begin's self-importance and the public's opinion of him, Begin replied that he was not interested in power at all: "We thought about the terrible war or of life and death" and concluded by saying, "The day is not far off when we will be in power."[184] Begin's conflict with Achimeir expressed the discomfort of many Revisionists and Etzel members who had not yet become familiar with the melodramatic aspects of Begin's personality. "He is an entirely different person," said Doris Lankin (she was then Katz's wife but they divorced, and in 1954 she became Eliyahu's wife); she expressed her disappointment with his political persona—a disappointment that resulted from her innocence.[185] She did not understand that Begin's audience had grown and changed and that Begin no longer needed to convince a handful of dedicated visionaries to act against the British but rather needed to speak to the hearts of hundreds of thousands of Israelis concerned with daily hardships. And in this niche Begin had no competitors.

When Paglin studied the list of Herut candidates for the Knesset, he could hardly believe his eyes. He was twelfth on the list. Begin himself had put the list together, guided by the belief that those who had been useful in the underground would not necessarily be suited to politics. Paglin had not believed for an instant that Begin, for whom he had left the Haganah, would disappoint him, and he did not understand how he had made the transition from commander to politician so swiftly. He could not bear to look at Begin, he was so disappointed. But he demanded no explanation, though there was actually no need for one; Begin's disregard spoke for itself. In conversations with friends Paglin would say, "I was his deputy, and this is how he treats me? This is how he destroys me?"

Unlike his days in the underground, Begin the politician was not interested in his comrades' advice. It was as though he unleashed everything he had suppressed during his days as a commander, and it all surfaced in his rapid political progress, the minor schemes he hatched and even personal quarrels.[186] When he became a Member of the Knesset (MK), he was sharply criticized by many of his opponents for the individual rule he introduced into the new party; they especially expressed astonishment that Herut members still called him "sir," a title they believed strengthened the party's dictatorial and militaristic public image. What they did not know was that Begin was a more authoritative politician than he was a commander, and the title "sir" was in fact more relevant to Begin the politician than it was to Begin the commander. At that time there were those who believed that there were "two Begins"—the commander and the politician—and many believed that when he emerged from the underground, he was mesmerized by the crowd's affection. The truth is that Begin had changed—he rarely listened to others, he became more focused, and he was more of a "man of the people" in mass gatherings—but only because his activities had changed.

Begin never aspired to be remembered in history as a warrior, but he envied and respected warriors. Compared to other leaders, he made a point to always be fair, just, and moral; these were values from which he drew his strength—in part because of his mental structure—but he exhibited them in every position he held—in Beitar, in the Anders Army, and in the underground. And he also made political calculations. Now that he was in politics, these factors just became more noticeable. Many Etzel members realized to their regret that the only thing remaining of his remarkable adaptive capacity to life in the underground and the ability to suppress his ego during his days as a commander—necessary qualities for a commander with no experience in military matters—was the impressive adaptive capacity—applied to politics.

Putting Paglin twelfth on the list of Knesset candidates after he had been second in command in Etzel aroused great indignation. Paglin's deputy in Etzel, Shraga Alis, decided not to stay silent and demanded an explanation from Begin: "Gidi was one of your favorites. How is this possible?" Begin was surprised but was adamant about his decision as he felt Paglin was too frenetic to fit into the tempo of parliamentary activities; he replied coldly, "There is a difference between fighting and politics; politics are something else." Landau, who witnessed the argument between Alis and Begin, remained silent, and Begin was very upset by his former subordinates' hostility. "Well, I can give Amichai seventh place," he said. "Either second place or nothing at all," replied Paglin when he heard the news.[187] Paglin's supporters recognized that his demand was excessive, so Begin had no difficulty in standing behind his decision. But the relationship between Begin and Paglin deteriorated until it ended completely. In 1977, when Begin became prime minister, he insisted on appointing Paglin as his adviser on terrorism, despite the opposition of the defense authorities, who claimed that "[Paglin's] military education has remained the same since the forties."[188] They did not know that when Begin appointed Paglin, he was motivated in part by guilt.

Begin was also adamant about his Knesset list because he already had a candidate for second place, a surprise that he had planned for a long time: he intended to nominate the poet Uri Tzvi Greenberg. His decision was not based on his taste in poetry but mostly on his talent for public relations. But Greenberg did not adapt to politics. He refused to attend Knesset committee meetings, and over the course of two years he made only four public speeches. During his tenure he became friends with Israel Eldad, the editor of *Sulam*, and he began to mock Herut for its loyalty to democracy and advocated the establishment of a monarchy.[189]

Putting Greenberg in second place exemplified Begin's political skills. Assigning the poet-prophet a place in the party softened Etzel's militaristic image and strengthened Begin's. And most important, Begin's number two had no political ambitions or aspirations to power.

Third on the Knesset list was Begin's deputy from Etzel days, Yaakov Meridor. Fourth was Arie Ben Eliezer, who had helped Begin with his discharge from the Anders Army. Fifth was Avraham Recanati, who was from Salonika (this choice was designed to attract the Sephardic Jews). Yochanan Bader was placed sixth, followed by Hillel Kook and Shmuel Merlin, Etzel staff members in the United States. Chaim Cohen-Maguri, an Etzel member who had emigrated from Yemen, was placed tenth, followed by Eliyahu Lankin and Shmuel Katz. Eri Jabotinsky was down in fourteenth place, and the only woman on the list—Esther Raziel-Naor, David Raziel's sister—was seventeenth. Meir Shamgar—an Etzel member who had just returned to Israel after being incarcerated in Kenya and who later became a Supreme Court judge—was assigned a symbolic eighty-fourth place (the Knesset has 120 seats, but no party believes that it will gain as many as 84).

A week after the publication of the list, Begin invited the first twenty members to a meeting at his house. To their surprise, he was anxious and nervous. He briefly spoke about the candidates' credentials and later incidentally asked them all to prepare letters of resignation from the party to be entrusted with him, as he might have to make changes in the list later on. Begin knew that this demand might be pushing the limit, but none of the candidates dared to complain. The term "political career" was looked down upon in those days, and Begin preferred to use the phrase prevalent in Mapai—"carrying out the party's will."[190] (After the elections he indeed used the letters in order to place Raziel-Naor in a higher position.)

Begin's individual rule of the party is also evident in the following story. Shmuel Tamir was sent to the United States to raise funds from the American Jewish community, but he failed to collect the required amount. His explanations did not satisfy Begin, so he invited Bader to a walk, during which he offered him an unusual job: "I want you to question Tamir as an investigating judge and find out what happened in the United States." Bader, astonished at the suggestion, argued that the head of a democratic party did not nominate one of its members to investigate another at his own discretion. "We are not in Etzel," he said. Begin realized that he could not carry out his plan, but he decided that he himself would go to the United States anyway.[191]

In December, a month before the elections for the legislative assembly, Begin took his first trip to the United States as a legitimate leader. On his return he described his impressions and spared no superlatives: "As our delegation stepped off the plane at the airport, we were met by such excitement that the Americans themselves say they have not seen such an enthusiastic crowd since the day Lindbergh crossed the Atlantic Ocean and landed at the very same airport. The crowd was delighted and blessed us both in their words and in their hearts."[192]

Begin often took advantage of the aura of an underground commander during his trip. For an entire day he did not speak to reporters, and his escorts whispered to them off the record that he was heading on an important mission—a secret meeting with President Harry Truman in Washington. The next day, when he showed up for a press conference in New York and was asked about his disappearance, he merely smiled, as if hiding a secret. In fact Begin did not meet with President Truman, although he was not exactly disappointed by the rumors of such a meeting because it strengthened his image as an important leader.[193]

In actuality, Begin was the object of a torrent of unpleasant criticism. On December 4, a commentary was published in the *New York Times*, signed (among others) by Albert Einstein and Hannah Arendt, claiming that Herut was "similar to the Nazi and Fascist Parties."[194] He also faced criticism about his dramatic gestures and his lack of intellectual depth, and when lecturing in English for the first time—a language he had learned by listening regularly to the BBC—he found himself in distress. So he summoned his sense of humor and declared, "Although Einstein is the kind of genius who appears once in a thousand years, I still understand more math than he understands politics." His ingenious tactic eased the tension between the two and shifted the conflict to an arena in which Begin felt increasingly confident—politics.

Before the elections Begin estimated that over 33 percent of Israelis would vote for Herut, giving it forty Knesset seats.[195] He was certain of this estimate based on his belief that his speeches excited his audiences and managed to crack the wall of public disdain against him. When *Haaretz* wrote that hundreds went to listen to him talk at the Esther Cinema in Tel Aviv, Begin kept the newspaper clipping and waved it about ceaselessly, proud of the media's recognition of his success.[196] Ben Gurion predicted that less than 32 percent of the voters would vote for Herut and the religious parties together.[197]

In the days remaining before January 25, the date of the elections, Begin stumped the length and breadth of the country. In addition to the party's main campaign slogan—"The Herut Movement—the only alternative to the old regime,"[198] which blasted across the country through loudspeakers mounted on vehicles—Herut members recited messages that were often more personal than ideological. Begin mounted a cunning political campaign, choosing to relate only to Mapai, as if the two parties were equal, although Herut was of course much smaller.[199] Mapai was depicted as a party shoving its greedy hands into its constituents' pockets to serve its own needs. "Mapai, listen," started a typical message from a loudspeaker, "Ben Gurion admitted in his Jerusalem speech that on May 15 only four hundred rifles were available for defending Jerusalem. Where have the millions donated by the Yishuv for our protection gone? Where have they disappeared? Where? Not for our protection! But into the Mapai accounts! To Solel Boneh, Tnuva, and Hamashbir [Histadrut-owned enterprises identified with Mapai]—that's where!"[200]

During a speech in Petach Tikva (considered an Etzel stronghold), Begin quoted a verse from Jeremiah 2: "I remember thee, the kindness of thy youth, the love of thine espousals, when thou wentest after me in the wilderness, in a land that was not sown."[201] He repeated this verse in May 1977, when he won his grand victory in the general elections. But in 1948 he spoke of the city of Petach Tikva, and in 1977 he referred to his wife Aliza.[202]

The first elections set the patterns of Herut's campaigns, and later those of the Likud, up until the present: a demand would be made to hold a referendum regarding the country's borders,[203] and a claim would follow that the Left would give up Jerusalem: "The enemy is still at the gate, and the danger still exists that the temporary authorities will give up Jerusalem," Begin repeatedly proclaimed.[204]

Begin was good at attacking his opponents, but he too was fervently targeted. His lashings out at his political rivals were mostly due to the intense hostility aimed at him during the election campaign. The Communist journal *Kol Haam* (Voice of the People) wrote that Herut was "Jewish fascism," and the socialist *Davar* wrote that "Herut is trying to revive a godforsaken and notorious spirit that brought grave disaster upon its homelands: England and Germany." On top of this, Begin was faced with unabashed disdain from many ministers. The day before the elections, Foreign Minister Moshe Sharett announced that Etzel's contribution to the establishment of the state was nil.[205]

When the balloting closed, Begin and his supporters gathered at the party's headquarters on Tchernichovsky Street in Tel Aviv. At first Begin was optimistic, as he had been during the entire election campaign, but as the hours passed, the words he threw into the air were replaced by cigarette smoke. Begin was dealt his first defeat in politics. Herut received only fourteen Knesset seats, and unlike in its forecasts, it became the fourth largest party in the country.[206]

The election results instilled deep disappointment in the entire Revisionist camp. Hatzohar did not pass the voter threshold and was shortly after assimilated into Herut.[207] The party of former Lehi members, Halochamim (the Fighters), received only one Knesset seat.

At first after the election results were published, the Herut members refrained from blaming Begin, who had handled the entire election campaign himself. However, as the days passed, the dam broke, and he was bombarded with criticism. During a party meeting, Landau hinted that Herut was perceived as an irresponsible party because of Etzel's actions in Jerusalem and that it was Begin's fault, as he had refused to disband the organization until after Bernadotte's assassination.[208] Jerusalem became a symbol of failure because despite the campaign's heavy focus on the city in its attempts to slam Mapai, the voting rate for Herut in the city stood at only 14.4 percent, half the figure of those who had voted for Ben Gurion.[209] *Haaretz* claimed that the election results indicated that the majority of the public was more moderate than Begin and even more reasonable than he, a claim that also became popular among Herut members.[210] Begin's attempts to arouse spirits before the elections did not succeed because the public was exhausted after the War of Independence, which claimed over six thousand Israeli fatalities—almost 1 percent of the whole Jewish population. Furthermore, the elections took place amid talks of a cease-fire with Egypt and before negotiations with Jordan, Syria, and Lebanon, which were soon to be held in Rhodes. The public yearned for peace and quiet and therefore preferred the diplomatic option of a possible cease-fire over Begin's insistence on military action to expand the country's borders.

It seemed that Begin did not yet grasp the general public's mood, although even if he had realized it, he would not have abandoned his belief in the righteousness of his chosen path, leading to "Both banks of the Jordan River." He was unable to compromise and maintained his objection to cease-fire talks even after the elections, as he believed them to be "disastrous."[211] Others accused Begin of a lack of political maturity. Bader argued that placing Greenberg second on the Knesset list had had no electoral value in the eyes of the general public and that dull Etzel activists who had also been placed on the list had not inspired the intellectual circles.[212]

Herut members were stooped in gloom. Begin assumed that Herut would be the major opposition party in the future and that if expectations had not been so high for success in the elections, they would not have been so disappointed with the results. His power within the tightly knit party prevented the members from publicly blaming Begin for the party's failure; he tried to calm matters by laconically stating, "We will serve the people in the opposition," and he turned his focus on repairing the internal damage.[213] In May the party held internal elections, and Begin was elected Herut chairman by an absolute majority.

While Herut's story is depicted in the newspapers as an utter failure, a pivotal fact regarding the results of the elections was overlooked—a fact that would have political implications twenty-eight years later and that was discussed in the meeting convened by Mapai to analyze the election results. "In ten neighborhoods in Tel Aviv, in which most of the residents are Sephardim, 2,500 of 3,300 voters voted for Herut," warned party activist Shraga Netzer, adding, "I hope we can change this." Another member added that "the majority of Yemenites who voted for Herut were not poor, but rather owners of factories and shops. Why is this so? Because of poverty and deprivation? No. They voted for [Herut] because they want to be in power. They want to go up on the public stage, and their way is blocked. Our party should pay attention to them, should give them a sense of equal rights, and should stop treating them as objects in need of care and charity." Zalman Aran, Mapai's secretary-general, concluded, "On this the state stands, and on this it will fall. That is to say: the next four years will be measured against our success in rehabilitating the life of the Sephardim in the country. If we can, we will have decisively defeated Herut for good. If we fail, a cancer will grow in the country that will endanger its very existence."[214]

SEVEN

REJECTED AND OUTCAST

Begin was rarely absent from the first Knesset, which resided in the Frumin Building on King George Street in Jerusalem. He used to sit casually, with his legs crossed and an expression of disdain on his face for politicians who had never led an underground resistance movement. After four years of solitude in Etzel he enjoyed public exposure. Those who met him were under the impression that he was in high spirits. Herut's defeat in the first elections had been forgotten. From his seat on the right-hand side of the government's table he would rise expressively only when he was called to the podium—usually dressed in a black (or sometimes brown) suit, with a pin in his lapel inscribed with the Etzel slogan, "Rak Kach," a stylish mustache adorning his face, his deep bass voice resonating through the chamber when he spoke. Less than a year earlier Begin had still been a wanted man and the public did not know him, and now his speeches were a public attraction.[1] Despite his being the leader of the fourth largest party in the Knesset, he forged a special position in the assembly based on his uncompromising standpoint on two main issues: Etzel's contribution to the establishment of Israel and the need to expand the state's borders.

Begin was an active MK. In July 1949, when the Rhodes Armistice Agreement was finalized, he was the first MK to submit a no-confidence motion against the government in response to the agreement dealing with the Hashemite Kingdom of Jordan, headed by King Abdullah.[2] He claimed that the agreement waived the Old City of Jerusalem and the West Bank. His no-confidence motion showed that Begin was a diligent parliamentarian, but the reasons he listed for his motion proved he was denying political reality. "This is an agreement with a country that has no right to exist," he explained, and he demanded that the government wage war to shift Israel's borders to the east bank of the Jordan River; moreover, as though the British Mandate had not truly ended, he expressed concern that the agreement would bring back the British.[3] For many years to come Begin persisted in his refusal to acknowledge Jordan, and until *Herut* closed down in 1964, it wrote the word "Jordan" in quotation marks.[4] Begin's approach indicated that although the election results had taught him that the public had had enough of war, he still did not see Herut as an alternative to the ruling party. "Who made you avoid sending the IDF to conquer the entire land of Israel?" he attacked the government members at a public rally on Mugrabi Square in Tel Aviv.[5]

Begin's position on expanding the country's boundaries was based on a rigid ideology quite detached from general public opinion. Therefore, it seemed that he had accepted his role as an oppositionist. As Etzel commander, Begin had been in contact with dozens of members, and after the establishment of the state his relations remained within the organization's framework, partly because many social and political circles considered him an outcast. Because of this separation from most of the public, he was tagged as an anachronistic leader, even though Ben Gurion was twenty-seven years older than he.

Following Ben Gurion's declaration on December 13, 1949, that West Jerusalem was Israel's capital, Begin insisted that this was not enough and demanded that a law be enacted that would unequivocally clarify the position to the "Gentiles"[6]—the term by which Begin still referred to the world's nations, as if he was living in a provincial village in Poland.

The focus of Begin's activity in the first Knesset was a struggle against Ben Gurion—another chapter in the historical rivalry between the Revisionist movement and the Labor Party that had started during the early 1920s. This chapter was the result of a struggle between two leaders who were completely different from one another—in their positions, their manner, and their actions—but were similar in the intensity of their charisma and the admiration or hatred they garnered from either their supporters or opponents. Begin was defeated in most of their confrontations, mainly because he was up against a cunning, older, and more experienced opponent, while Begin exhibited every possible weakness from which a young man could suffer in his battle against a sly fox. Ben Gurion belittled him, mocked him for his leadership skills, and referred to him as a "clown."

From the very beginning, when Ben Gurion started assembling the government, he stated that it would not include Herut or Maki (the Israeli Communist Party), arguing that "Herut and the Communist Party are extremist parties, and their attitude is foreign to Israel's spirit."[7] "Without Herut and Maki" was a policy to which Ben Gurion strictly adhered. When Begin took the podium, Ben Gurion usually left the plenum chamber; when he did listen to him and decided to respond, he referred to Begin as "the Knesset member who sits to the right of [MK] Yochanan Bader" and not by his name. "He even told one of his confidants that he "cannot stand Begin's voice, not just his words."[8]

Ben Gurion constantly attacked the frustrated Begin, who continued to file no-confidence motions about the Old City of Jerusalem. Once he even remarked, "We have heard from Mr. Begin a rhetorical question that did not lack in amusement or talent, but Mr. Begin should know that he is speaking in the Knesset and not in a Purim carnival. To speak in the Knesset one must be knowledgeable, speak the truth, and show some responsibility." "The division of Jerusalem will not pass," Begin shouted from his seat, "just as you voted against the establishment of the state of Israel, but it did come into being," thus hinting at the internal opposition within Ben Gurion's party in the decision to declare independence. Ben Gurion smiled, as if he had been waiting for this opportunity. "If we vote, it will pass. Just as"—he said in delight—"when we voted for the destruction of the *Altalena*, and it came into being."[9] Begin looked around him, as if to draw encouragement from his party members, stood up, approached the podium, and commenced yelling his response, which was barely heard because of the commotion he had created, all the while accompanying his shouts with threatening hand gestures. After the confrontation, once the atmosphere had calmed down and Begin had gone to the cafeteria, Ben Gurion went to sit in Begin's chair next to Bader and calmly began chatting with him, an act that made a clear point to everyone around: there were people in Herut with whom one could exchange opinions.[10] Several arguments between the two leaders became historic. As Ben Gurion interpreted Begin's actions, he was organically unable to distinguish between reality and fantasy, and his part in the battle for Jaffa was practically a military innovation: the strategy of advertising.

The debate on Etzel's part in another event—the expulsion of the British from Palestine—evoked in Begin the sense that he had been

Family portrait, Poland 1932. Begin (center),
his sister Rachel, brother Herzl, and parents Ze'ev-Dov and Chasia.
(Courtesy of Jabotinsky Institute Archives.)

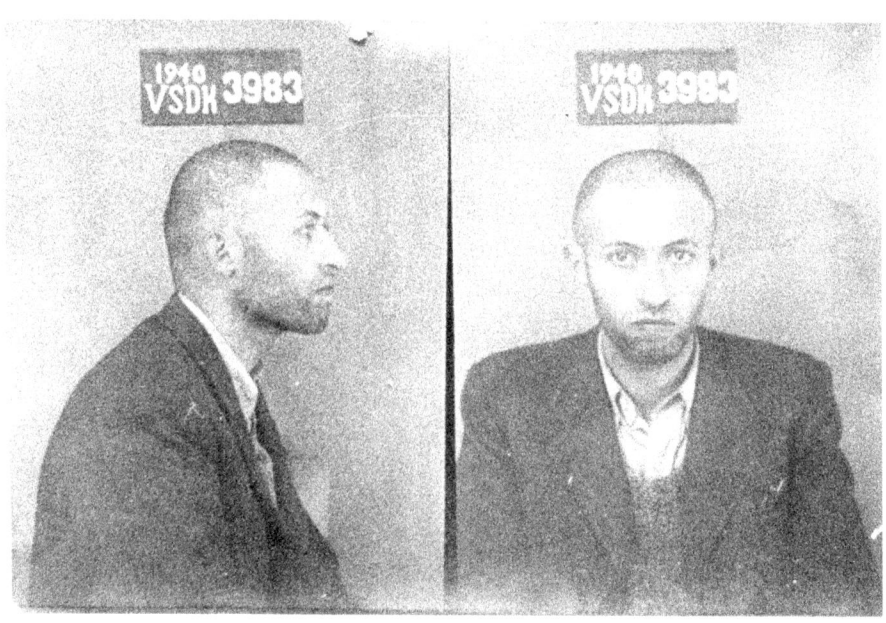

Begin in Soviet prison, 1940.
(Courtesy of Jabotinsky Institute Archives.)

Begin and Aliza on their wedding day, Poland, 1939. (Courtesy of Government Press Office [GPO].)

Begin in uniform while still in the Anders Army, with Aliza and friends, Tel Aviv 1942. (Courtesy of GPO.)

Begin "masquerading" as Rabbi Israel Sasover, with Aliza and son Benny, Tel Aviv, 1946. (Courtesy of Jabotinsky Institute Archives.)

Photos of wanted people from Etzel and Lehi in posters issued by the British police, February 1947. Begin is top row left. (Courtesy of Menachem Begin Heritage Center Archives.)

Begin's counterfeit ID bearing the name Jona Konigshoffer, 1947. (Courtesy of Menachem Begin Heritage Center Archives.)

Begin saluting Jabotinsky while reviewing an honor guard of Beitar commissioners in Poland. (Courtesy of GPO.)

The *Altalena* burning off Frishman Beach, Tel Aviv, June 1948.
(Courtesy of Jabotinsky Institute Archives.)

Begin kissing the Etzel flag at a ceremony marking the
dismantling of the organization, Jerusalem, September 1948.
(Courtesy of Jabotinsky Institute Archives.)

Members of the Herut Party at a meeting of the Constituent Assembly. Begin is third from right; Esther Raziel-Naor is to his right; behind her is Uri Tzvi Greenberg. (Courtesy of GPO.)

Begin while writing *The Revolt*, 1950.
(Courtesy of Menachem Begin Heritage Center Archives.)

Begin giving a speech at a Herut conference, 1948. (To his right, Chaim Landau.) (Courtesy of Menachem Begin Heritage Center Archives.)

Begin giving a speech at a political conference with his trademark clenched fist, 1949. (Courtesy of Jabotinsky Institute Archives.)

Begin at a mass demonstration against the Reparations Agreement, Tel Aviv, 1952. (Courtesy of GPO.)

Begin (far left) at the Knesset plenum in its first residence in Jerusalem. David Ben Gurion smirks at the government table. (Courtesy of GPO.)

wronged from a historical perspective, and it alienated him from the state of Israel in its early years. Begin claimed that establishing the state without conquering East Jerusalem was like "a third Tisha Beav (Ninth of Av, the day of mourning for the Holy Temple, destroyed once by Nebuchadnezzar and a second time by the Romans—both on the same day of the year)";[11] such claims, together with many others along this line of thought, distanced him from the mainstream, as the majority of people still considered the very existence of the country to be miraculous. Many Herut members also saw the damage his statements caused. "For God's sake, Menachem. You're falling into a trap," said Herut MK Shmuel Katz. "You're losing all these fights with Ben Gurion. He's exploiting your short temper to ignite impractical arguments. This is not the way to strengthen the party. Don't shout. Ridicule him. It's more useful than shouting."[12] Begin nodded but could not overcome his tendencies.

In November, unlike his custom, Ben Gurion did not leave the plenum chamber when Begin took the podium to talk once again about the importance of annexing East Jerusalem. Noting that the prime minister was still in the hall, Begin took a deep breath and after contemplating briefly, offered to recite the Shehecheyanu blessing (a common Jewish prayer used to celebrate special occasions—a sort of "Thank God") because "I got up on stage and the prime minister continued to sit in the hall." It seemed for a moment that he was expressing a longing for unity, for internal peace. He waited happily before glancing at Ben Gurion with an expression that testified that he was tired of their war, the war of David and Goliath.

Ben Gurion took the podium. "MK Begin recited the Shehecheyanu prayer," he said, "but unfortunately I cannot return his blessing after listening to his speech. Although this was the first time I have listened to his speech, it was not the first time I have heard this kind of speech, not in Hebrew, not in this country, [but] many years ago, before World War II."[13]

Begin was not offended by the comparison to Hitler and Mussolini—it was familiar to him—but he was hurt that the hand he outstretched in peace was rejected. He stood up, pointed to the visitors' gallery, raised his fist, and shouted that someone sitting there was a spy from the security service (know by its Hebrew initials—the Shin Bet) who was following him: "Don't patronize me and don't be conceited! Five years ago you promised to destroy us, with the help of the Gentile. And remember: without our help you would have been left with one title alone—that of an informant.... Those who haven't forgotten and will not forget are the Etzel."[14] No one knew whom he was talking about. He may have believed that he was being followed, but perhaps he just wanted to expose an illegal activity that was being conducted "without Herut and Maki." The sudden and strange change of subject—from the issue of Jerusalem to the charge that a Shin Bet agent was following him—strengthened the belief that Begin was a theatrical character. Such an image hid some of his moderate ideas. "I oppose any idea of a population exchange," he declared when MKs raised the idea of a transfer. "The Arabs must remain where they are; otherwise it will give legitimacy to the partition of the country."[15]

Ben Gurion, who saw Begin as a fascist, was not the only one who mocked him. The independent newspapers—*Haaretz*, *Maariv*, and *Yediot Ahronot*—ridiculed him and many times wrote "Beigin" instead of "Begin" to emphasize that he was of the Diaspora.[16] A *Haaretz* editorial, for example, advised Ben Gurion to continue ignoring Begin; otherwise he would "ascribe Herut with the power and sense of belonging that in fact it did not have."[17] *Maariv* wondered sarcastically, "How long will Begin stand on stage and talk about the times the Jewish Agency informants tipped off the British and about the King David Hotel bombing?"[18] *Davar* went further and described his speeches as "a mixture of incitement against the Israeli government, hypocrisy, and audacity."[19] The newspapers also ridiculed Begin for his looks. "His dwindling hair is long, wavy, and combed over. His eyes dart; his thick upper lip quivers like an animal's [when it is] about to charge madly," wrote Arie Gelblum, the senior *Haaretz* commentator at the time.[20]

In this hostile public environment Begin could either have softened his stance and changed his image or, in defiance, made his position more extreme. He chose to radicalize his position—a response typical of a Beitar member. His arguments with Ben Gurion deteriorated to personal insults. "The man who has never worked a day in the country" was how Ben Gurion referred to Begin during a discussion on October 16, 1950, in response to Begin's reference to Ben Gurion's pet name, "the Old Man": "It is not my fault that I was born thirty years after Ben Gurion, and were it not for the work I and my fellow members have done in this country, Mr. Ben Gurion would still be asking for interviews with the British Commissioner and would never have inherited his authority."[21] Herut party member Esther Raziel-Naor missed no opportunity to support Begin, but many other members were critical of his remarks.[22]

In the first years after the Declaration of Independence, Israel's foreign policy was influenced by the Cold War between the Soviet Union and the United States. During the first two years of the state's existence the Israeli government avoided taking an official stance in the struggle between these two world powers, but in reality Israel began to establish ties with the West and the United States. At the time, as noted, Begin preferred a neutral approach, despite the Revisionist movement's clear orientation toward the West.

In July 1950, after the Israeli government asserted its solidarity with the U.N. Security Council's decision to extend military aid to South Korea in its war against North Korea—an important assertion, as it was seen as a declaration of Israel's Western orientation[23]—Begin authorized his party's number two, Arie Ben Eliezer, to express his opposition to Israel's support of the West.[24] Surprisingly, his position revealed a distinct leaning toward the Left—although after only one year Begin resumed his condemnation of the Communist bloc—but more than anything, his viewpoint embodied one distinct and central idea: Greater Israel. And that was Begin's gravest missed opportunity. Despite the fact that Herut, as a party inspired by Jabotinsky's creed, had firm liberal views (unlike Mapai), Begin hardly expressed these in his speeches. His insistence on discussing only matters of defense harmed his image and prevented him from establishing an alternative to Ben Gurion's domestic policy. This failure is reflected mainly in the issue regarding the constitution. The Knesset was elected as a constituent assembly, after which it was expected to legislate a constitution and to dissolve itself in preparation for new elections. Herut supported the constitution and Mapai objected, but when Ben Gurion and his party drafted a law on February 16, 1950, that granted the Constituent Assembly permanent status as the Knesset, Begin settled for a weak opposition, devoid of protests and his usual dramatic outcries. Ben Gurion argued that the constitution would inhibit the new legislature and that the rule of law and the buttressing of democracy were enough to ensure stability, and he expressed satisfaction that he had defeated the opposition so easily. Ultimately, it was determined that the Knesset would legislate basic laws in a gradual process—a process that has lasted until this day.[25] The main reason for Begin's passivity was the fact that he was unable to formulate an agreement regarding the relations between state and religion, even within his own party. During the deliberations, *Haaretz* wrote, "It is strange to see how a political movement that by its very nature usually tends to strengthen the executive force is asking here to represent pure liberalism."[26]

The debate about the constitution within Herut created a rift with the original Revisionists and especially with the American group (Kook, Merlin, and Eri Jabotinsky), a rift that in retrospect was another step in Begin's disengagement from Beitar's ideology and the transformation of Herut from a bourgeois-ideological Right party to a populist, national-religious Right party. As noted, the American members, loyal to the ideas of Jabotinsky, saw Judaism as the remains of an obsolete ancient civilization, with an influence on the lives of individuals but certainly not on a country;[27] they attacked Begin for compromising on the constitution, which was as central to them as the idea of a Greater Israel and was intended to separate state and religion.

Begin strongly objected to their position. In his opinion it was impossible to separate religion from Jewish nationality. As he was unable to deny their claim that their position was an integral part of the Revisionists' tenets, Begin agreed that Herut would initiate a bill to allow civil marriages and to make things easier for children considered *mamzer* (bastard) according to the Halacha (strict Orthodox Judaic law). (Note: the Jewish definition of "bastard" is different from the Christian one; it does not refer to an "illegitimate" child but only to one born of parents whose marriage cannot be binding—such as that of two siblings or a Cohen and a divorcee; Cohens were the offspring of families who had served as saints in the Holy Temple and therefore should not marry women who were considered "impure.") But Begin agreed reluctantly and stated that the religious parties would in any event object—which they did.[28] Begin's differences with Kook and Eri Jabotinsky could no longer be brushed away.

Jabotinsky believed he had followed in his father's footsteps; he had gained a reputation for his contempt for religion, and he continuously argued with Begin over this issue. During a Herut party meeting Jabotinsky raised a vexing proposal: to allow non-kosher food into the Knesset cafeteria. Begin upheld kosher regulations even at home but did not want to publicly argue with "the son of." Because he valued symbols and saw Judaism mainly as a national symbol—a belief that did not require that one practice the religious decrees—he could not agree that his party would rally to put pork on the Knesset menu. He responded to Jabotinsky by saying that if Herut wished to strengthen its ranks, it would need to attract "religious people," and therefore there was no point in raising such a bill, which would only deter them.[29] The proposal was eventually rejected. The controversy reinforced his opponent's claim that Begin's ideology was shallow, but it became one of the cornerstones for the bridge Begin eventually built between himself and the hundreds of thousands of immigrants from Arab countries. Because he saw Zionism as a phase in the development of modern Jewish tradition, Begin—whose roots were in a family of Mitnagdim (religious Ashkenazi Jews who opposed the rise of early Hasidic Judaism)—identified with the traditional Jews.

The hostility between Begin and Eri Jabotinsky did not stem entirely from differences of opinion, but also from more personal reasons. Deep down, Begin believed that Eri was opposed to him out of spite, while Eri believed that Begin was not a worthy heir to his father.[30] But because the relationship was complex, the conflict was handled with great caution; it seems that a comparison with the former Beitar commander could harm them both. Among other reasons, Begin did not want to publicly display his profound differences with Jabotinsky junior because he feared that Jabotinsky senior's attitude toward his successor would then become known—namely, that his "teacher and mentor" had never expressed a desire for Begin to succeed him. Meanwhile, Eri saw Begin's policies as the reason for Herut's ailments and wanted to be rid of the heavy burden he carried as the son of the founder. The rivalry between the two—who resembled each other in their eccentric, theatrical gestures; their personal assurance in the justification of their ways; and their desire to be recognized for it—did not dissipate; it became more discreet.

Jabotinsky's son was not a lovable man. When his own son Ze'ev was born, Eri invited Begin and several other Herut members to the Brit Milah, and when they came to take part in the joyous occasion, Eri informed them that he had decided to forgo the Mohel (the circumciser). The Herut members were not happy with his decision and argued with him for two hours until he finally changed his mind.[31] In one Knesset debate he gave an entire speech in French, which most members could not understand, so as to prove that without a constitution the country did not have an official and understandable language. Had he not been the founder's son, Begin would have ridiculed him, as it was clear that his political views were somewhat bizarre: he aspired to make Israel the center of the Middle East while simultaneously freeing minority groups (especially the Kurds, the Maronites, and the

Alawites) from Islam's grasp. He believed that Begin had reduced the party's ideology to topics relating only to Jews and to the land of Israel: "Herut has become a branch of Hapoel Hamizrachi [one of the religious parties] and not a revolutionary movement. In fact, the religious should be no less of an enemy to us than Mapai." On one of the rare occasions when he dared to express his personal disapproval of Begin, he argued, "I do not care that he uses religious gestures in his speeches; it bothers me that Begin actually believes this nonsense."[32]

Was Begin God-fearing? This issue preoccupied many. Some interpreted his attitude to religion as charlatanism, and others believed his faith ran even deeper than he let on. In reality, Begin's adherence to religion sheltered him from the ravages of life, and it also had a streak of nationalism. His Zionist concept was not drawn entirely from Jabotinsky's writing; his father had educated him from childhood to integrate religion and nationality, and the Revisionist movement merely helped to develop his worldview.

Begin assisted ultra-Orthodox extremists who became entangled in criminal offenses; a perfect example of this is his struggle to help the Brit Hakanaim (the Covenant of Zealots), a group that in the course of the first year after the state's establishment torched cars whose owners were suspected of driving on the Shabbat. When the group members were caught, including Rabbi Mordechai Eliyahu (who later became the chief rabbi of Israel), they were held in prolonged custody without trial. They claimed that the guards abused them, and Begin, who often raised parliamentary questions in the Knesset, was instrumental in establishing an inquiry committee—the first such committee in parliament. Following the investigation, the committee confirmed the Brit Hakanaim's complaints: it was revealed that the members were emotionally abused while in police custody.

Begin was not very religiously observant. He went to the synagogue mainly on religious holidays, and although he refrained from smoking on the Shabbat, he talked on the phone and listened to the radio. His approach to religion was reflected in the meetings held on Saturdays: he would wear out his voice, refusing to use the loudspeaker so as not to desecrate the holy day of rest, but he did not go so far as to cancel the meetings.[33]

As mentioned above, Begin was the first person to file a motion of no-confidence against the government, and he was the first to bring about a parliamentary investigation committee, but his liberal views raised objections because of the way he expressed them. He referred to the place in which the members of the Brit Hakanaim had been held as a "concentration camp" and accused the government of using "Nazi emergency laws." "Perhaps," suggested Minister of Justice Pinchas Rosen, "you should be careful in the use of Holocaust terms in your arguments." "Every place where a man is jailed without legal proceedings is a concentration camp!" Begin declared.[34] He did not understand that as his words became more radical, his arguments were weakened, in part because he knew no other method of debate. In a similar way his father had called his opponents "poisonous bacteria."

Begin's world of imagery, based on a nationalistic-religious value system, finally defeated Eri Jabotinsky. In June 1949 Jabotinsky wrote to Begin that owing to his disappointment that Begin was not operating according to the movement's principles, he was going to resign from the party. (But he only really resigned in March 1951.) Jabotinsky and Kook announced that the party had gotten diverted from the righteous path and that they had decided to join a new group within Herut—Lamerchav—lead by Shmuel Merlin and Shmuel Tamir.[35] In his letter of resignation Jabotinsky wrote some of the most scathing words about Begin that any party member had ever said of him. He argued that Begin was leading a loud dictatorship lacking any content and that he treated the Herut newspaper as if it were his own; he even asked Begin to stop using his father's name.[36] Begin was offended but did not respond. He expressed his only demand of Jabotinsky by publishing an unsigned editorial in *Herut:* the dissident must retire from the Knesset as well as return his seat to his former party.[37]

Kook and Jabotinsky continued to attack Begin. At a press conference they claimed that "under [Begin's] leadership Herut is not a Revisionist movement" and that "youth and intelligence have both escaped the party."[38] Despite their declarations, Lamerchav did not become a new party and did not participate in the second elections, and Jabotinsky retired from politics in favor of an academic career (he became a professor of mathematics at Addis-Ababa Technical College). Upon Jabotinsky's retirement from the party, Begin's second political confrontation with Jabotinsky ended in his favor. This victory can be seen as the first step that paved the way for Herut to become a populist party and loosen its ties with the cradle of revisionism.

Some time earlier, in October 1950, a government crisis occurred over the compulsory state education law and education in the immigrant camps. Ben Gurion assembled a new government, but it collapsed in February 1951, when the Knesset voted against the proposition for registering children at schools. Ben Gurion resigned and the Knesset prepared for new elections, which were scheduled to take place after the first elections for local governments.

In those years Israel's economic situation was dire, and the hundreds of thousands of Jews who had immigrated to Israel, mainly from Islamic countries, did not find sufficient housing or jobs. Many of the immigrants were housed in hastily erected tents in transit camps under harsh conditions. In an attempt to overcome this difficult situation the government declared the Austerity Regime. Each family was allocated coupons to buy groceries, and the coupons were calculated in correlation to the number of persons in the family. "The Agriculture Ministry will allocate 700 grams of sugar a month for each family" was a typical headline in the newspapers in those days.[39] The Austerity Regime encouraged a black market and subsequently widened the gap between those with financial means—mainly Ashkenazim—and those who could not pay for their groceries. Long lines in front of the food stamp distribution stations made it clear to everyone that the situation would harm the ruling party. As expected, the economic crisis had implications in the social and cultural arenas. In many Sephardic families the traditional framework deteriorated, and fathers lost their status as heads of the family, which they had earned as sole breadwinners. Many immigrants from Arab countries found that the country they had longed and prayed for was not the land of milk and honey—at least not for them.

Therefore, it was not surprising that Herut saw the regional elections as something of a dress rehearsal for national elections to the Knesset, and Begin, who was facing his first political test as an MK, invested great efforts in the regional elections. He personally accompanied the Herut candidates for local governments and focused on the demand for "justice, freedom, and abundance." Despite the fact that during his first speech following the Declaration of Independence by Ben Gurion he had supported mass immigration, ignoring its financial implications ("even if they [the immigrants] have to sleep under the open sky"),[40] he blamed Mapai for the immigrants' situation. Mapai, Begin argued, was using the property seized in the War of Independence instead of transferring it to civilians. His main slogan—"Housing instead of transit camps"—was intended to win over the immigrants' support.[41]

Surprisingly, Herut suffered an appalling defeat in the elections for local governments—only 10 percent of the votes were for Begin's party. The defeat was doubly hard because, despite Mapai's similar failure (it received only 27.3 percent of the votes), Herut was not the benefactor, but rather it was the General Zionists, who won 24.5 percent of the votes and became the second-largest party in terms of the number of representatives it had in local municipal councils.[42] Begin was astonished but quickly played down the importance of the municipal elections. "The state's very existence is the fruit of our toil, and we will continue to reap what we sow," he declared, demanding a focus on the Knesset elections, as the failure in the regional elections was allegedly an unimportant mishap in the dress rehearsal.[43]

Herut viewed Kook's and Jabotinsky's retirement as a setback in the race for the second Knesset elections. The young and vibrant public image Begin had attempted to create was now tainted, and Herut mainly appeared as a torn and abandoned party. Begin also understood that the repercussions following the War of Independence and the financial crisis demanded that he focus his propaganda on internal matters. Unlike Ben Gurion, a "formative leader" who required the people to adapt to the new reality,[44] Begin was a "rewarding leader," meaning that he was able to identify the people's yearnings and to attempt to respond to them, as far as he could. When he described his concepts, he repeatedly referred to the need to "benefit the people," and in consultations with his colleagues, he determined that his plan was simply to "get rid of poverty."[45] But, just as he had done as Beitar commissioner in Poland, he would make a proposal and then say of its execution, "We will leave that to the experts," never specifying how to carry it through.

Begin had not yet broken out of his social circle; he did not go to the theater, and of course he did not go out for other forms of entertainment, even though he was only thirty-five years old. His lifestyle was monastic (he lived in a two-room rent-controlled apartment), the same as that of most Yishuv leaders at the time, but not because he was in touch with society. In fact, it was quite the contrary: he was out of touch with the common human experience, and as he had no ambitions to advance economically, he focused mostly on political activity. When he was required to join his party members to decide on various issues, he imposed the task of negotiation on Bader. "Begin knows how to give a speech, but you cannot reach a mutual agreement with him," Bader used to complain.[46] His confidants knew that he was open to all political advice, but for personal assistance they would have to turn to his assistant, Dov Halpert. Halpert was surprised when Bader approached him one day asking for "help on a personal matter." "What's the problem? Go to Menachem," he replied. "He is not attentive to such matters," said Bader.[47] Sometimes it seemed as though Begin loved the Jews as a people more than he loved the individual Jew. But Bader and the rest of his friends did not complain about this attitude since it was not personal, and in an age in which the ideological superseded the personal, they had no right to complain about the nature of their revered leader, who had led the battle against Ben Gurion.

Begin's detachment from personal and everyday matters was also his weakness in electoral terms. Even though he understood that he should focus on economic issues in his campaign because of the dire economic situation and the hundreds of thousands of new immigrants, he could not help talking mainly about his rigid political demands. His opinion that war was a valid possibility, provided that Israel could take over the West Bank, alienated the public.[48]

In the second legislative elections Begin continued to focus on the slogan "Both banks of the Jordan River" and on the liberalization of civil rights, especially the elimination of censorship and the emergency regulations. His campaign's most interesting demand was to eliminate the Shin Bet, which was filled with "informants, provocateurs, and sadists."[49] Of course, Begin's intention was to intermingle those serving in the Shin Bet with his own people and not to abolish the organization, but this demand highlighted the gap between the issues that plagued Begin and those that interested the general public, which was quite uninterested at the time with issues concerning the Shin Bet.

The results of the municipal elections had revealed that the General Zionists were more effective than Herut and that their socioeconomic plan was more cohesive. One of Begin's tactics to overtake them in the elections was to recruit two former Revisionist members, Arie Altman and Eliezer Shostak, into Herut.[50]

Begin's considerable contribution to the second legislative elections was in the realm of propaganda. He shifted the stage of the electoral campaign from movie theaters and town squares to the transit camps. Other leaders, including Ben Gurion, also understood the political importance of the camps, and Begin was not the only leader who made frequent visits to them. But the getting together of Begin and this great new audience, which was unfamiliar with the days of the underground, ignited a somewhat romantic relationship between them. A rumor that spread throughout Israel in the 1970s and 1980s that "Begin is Moroccan" took root in those days, despite the fact that his newfound relationship with the Sephardim was still not electorally fruitful.

In his memoirs Begin claimed that although "I have never calculated any statistics on this matter ... at least 25 percent [of Etzel members were] Sephardic Jews."[51] He was not yet referring to the political connection between himself and the Mizrahim, who had not yet immigrated to Israel, but mainly to that with the Yemeni and Sephardic communities. Mutual feelings of deprivation were not the only foundation for this affiliation. Even though Begin was raised in Poland, he shared a lifestyle and worldviews with the Jews who came from Arab countries. Like Begin, they were from a traditional background and worked mainly in small trade, respected their ancestors, and believed that Zionism had originated in the religious Orthodox faith. Even if most of the Yemenis in Etzel were not educated in Jabotinsky's liberalism, their former occupations in their land of origin increased their sympathy toward Beitar's bourgeois concepts.

Already at the first meeting of Herut's temporary center—that is, a core group that was comprised mainly of former Etzel and Revisionist members who were now the main political activists of Herut—the potential for connection between the party and the Mizrahim was emphasized. Yaakov Meridor argued that forcing the new immigrants to learn Hebrew was not a good idea and that pamphlets should be published in their native languages. There were those who suggested supporting the Mizrahim in a way that would nowadays be called "affirmative action," while others preferred the establishment of a sectarian faction that would work alongside Herut. In his unique way, Hillel Kook made an unusual proposal on how to solve the ethnic problem: "We should convene a meeting with the Sephardim and tell them that they do not constitute a special problem."[52] But in this case Begin actually preferred the approach of Ben Gurion, who advocated a melting pot solution, and he suggested that he would be satisfied with their full integration into the party as a natural process.

In the elections Begin planned to emphasize that Herut was capable of putting an end to the dire economic situation—he had added the Revisionist members to the Knesset list because they were experts on economic problems—while Mapai "is starving the masses" intentionally.[53] But the social and economic issues were not his priorities. "Luckily," in the midst of the campaign, on July 20, 1951, King Abdullah was assassinated at Al-Aqsa Mosque in Jerusalem, so Begin turned back to his favorite subject: the need to expand Israel's boundaries. "It will not be long before joyful parades of a liberating army will march through Amman and Jerusalem," he boomed during a speech in Haifa,[54] and in another speech he even promised "to evacuate the women and children during times of war," as if he had a ready plan for war.[55] But his words only frightened his audience.

Begin's insistence on clinging to the expansion issue had both short- and long-term effects. In the short term he struggled to create a dialogue that would captivate the Sephardim, who were mostly concerned with day-to-day problems and in whose eyes Ben Gurion was the legendary leader who had brought them to Israel on the wings of eagles. Paradoxically, in the long run, after his failure in the second elections, Begin became a symbol of discrimination by the establishment, especially for the Sephardim, who had not known him in his Etzel years and who still regarded him as one of the establishment leaders during the second elections. Gradually, once they had learned the story of Herut, they began to support his rigid principles on national affairs in the hopes that he would bring about changes that would grant them pride and dignity—on a national as well as a personal level.

On June 30, 1951, two weeks before the elections, Begin and an interpreter traveled to a transit camp in Rehovot that was populated mostly by Iraqi immigrants. (The trip was made in a Cadillac purchased by Etzel supporters from the United States.) When he stepped out of the car, wearing a hat, the people who gathered around him started to call out, "Yaish! Yaish! Yaish!" Because he feared that the crowd did not recognize him, he asked the interpreter, "Why do they call me Yaish?" The interpreter, assigned by Herut members who had neglected to verify whether he was fluent in Iraqi Arabic, told him they were iterating the word "Long live!" It was almost the last correct translation he conveyed. But it did not matter. The affection they showered on him, the candy thrown at him, the kisses and the shouts of joy, captured his heart. Before he mounted the temporary stage erected in his honor, he kissed every person who happened to be along the way.[56]

(The relationship between Begin and the Mizrahim had a sartorial side to it. Begin regularly wore suits, even in midsummer, and his dress code raised questions among the Yishuv leaders, who were not used to such formal attire. In contrast, his meetings with the camp inhabitants satisfied him immensely, as they saw his dressy suits as a sign of respect. Many of those who lived in the transit camps can recall their astonishment at the sight of the Yishuv leaders, including Ben Gurion, who came wearing shorts and short-sleeved shirts.)[57]

"We will guarantee you a better future," Begin roared during the June 30 speech, and the crowd responded with thunderous applause.

But even when he spoke about the harsh conditions in Israel, the crowd responded with thunderous applause. Now he exchanged glances with his interpreter. From the very first words he had uttered, Begin suspected that the translation had not been precise, judging by the crowd's responses, and now, when he saw the embarrassed look on the interpreter's face, he realized that he had been talking to the deaf. The interpreter was fluent in Egyptian Arabic, while the crowd spoke Iraqi Arabic, and he understood neither of them.

Begin decided to continue to speak despite the lack of communication and later spoke about the occasion facetiously. But as it turned out, what had happened was not accidental.[58] Choosing the wrong interpreter highlighted how little the hard-core "Polish" Herut members knew about the differences ranging among immigrants from the various Arab countries. This incident also illuminates the fact that although the Sephardim sympathized with Begin in Israel's early years, most of them cheered him because he was a Jewish leader and not because they agreed with his political ideology. They saw Begin as a member of the establishment who had come to help them and not as someone who was actually challenging the leading party, Mapai.

On July 30, 1951, when the election results were published, it became clear that Herut had failed miserably, and this time Begin could not ignore the results. Only 6 percent had voted for Herut, which now had only eight seats in the Knesset. (Mapai maintained its previous number of seats—forty-five.)[59] Unlike in the elections for the local governments, Begin did not know how to cheer up his supporters, so he remained silent. He expressed his opinion in a *Herut* editorial. He claimed that his party had suffered defeat because Mapai had bribed the residents of the transit camps, and he stressed that Herut's party mechanism was weaker than that of the General Zionists. He also blamed the public: citizens had gotten tired of the need to protect the homeland.[60]

Many Herut members opposed the assertion that the public was to blame. Begin's propaganda, wrote Kalman Katznelson in a commentary on Begin's editorial, was too extreme, terrifying, and detached from civic problems, and he added, "The vision he set with the intoxicating smell of the blood of those who were hanged on the gallows was too oppressive for the tired masses, weary of standing in line, counting their food stamps for their apportioned rations."[61] There were those who noted that Begin was ruling the party in an undemocratic way. Former party secretary Shmuel Merlin made the accusation that Begin was managing the party as an underground and that its political platform dealt only with Israel's redemption.

Begin had tremendous influence on the party center, and he could basically do whatever he pleased with the party. But his spirits were low. He had been slapped in the face by reality, and when he could no longer hide his failure, he argued, "The party is to blame; its members let me down." He even warned Bader, "Very soon you will be working without me."[62]

Begin's allusion to retirement was not only a threat but also a cry for help, and when no one came to his aid and the criticism increased, he neared a breaking point. Unlike in conflicts with opponents from other camps, which sparked his energies, Begin found it hard to accept his own colleagues' criticism, for he saw them as his family. He himself had coined the phrase "the fighting family."[63] It was no accident that he referred to Etzel and Herut members as "my brothers and sisters" rather than "my comrades," as was customary in Mapai; as far back as Beitar, Begin had considered membership in the party a moral obligation from which one could not escape.[64] Begin was not merely the party chairman; he was its father. Such was the radical Revisionist perception regarding the undisputed leader—a stance that stemmed from the radical right wing in Poland at the turn of the twentieth century.[65] Begin felt that the accusations against him were in fact a form of betrayal.

When Israel Eldad asked Begin to insert him into the party's parliamentary list, he noted, "You will never be in power, so you should at least show some uniqueness, a distinct voice." Begin suggested he should submit his candidacy to the party's institutions. "As you know, I'm not a party member," said Eldad. "And what's wrong with being a member?" Begin grumbled. Eldad could not understand why Begin was ready to accept the claim that he would never come to power but could not control his anger when Eldad pooh-poohed the idea of joining the party.[66]

Because he was convinced that his way was the right way, Begin was unable to adjust to the new reality taking shape before his eyes and could think only of escaping, hiding, or quitting. He consulted with Aliza, and the two decided to leave the country for a while; upon their return he would practice law in a private firm. Bader tried to dissuade him from his decision to retire, reminding him that this was the way of politics, and suggested that he try to calmly analyze the results and perhaps try to adjust. But Begin was unconvinced. "There are people who stood by me only when times were good, but when things took a turn for the worse, they saw me as a construction contractor. My decision is to resign, and that's final." Yet because he was still convinced that he was destined to serve a role in history, retirement was his way of punishing reality. Bader understood that Begin was tired and chose to let him go.[67] With the encouragement of Aliza, who did not hide her satisfaction at his leaving politics, Begin went with Bader to register as an intern for attorney Max Kritzan, the defense attorney for many Etzel and Lehi members.[68]

Begin was not happier after his decision to retire from politics, as it was not only an occupation for him but also a habit. Like his father before him, he was a politician in spirit, knowing no other way of life. On the contrary, Aliza was pleased. "Our entire life is still ahead of us," she said. Their planned vacation seemed alluring. Begin did not attend the inauguration ceremony of the new Knesset members on August 20, and he handed Arie Ben Eliezer a letter of resignation.

Bader was sure that Begin would retract his decision. Knowing him, he saw his retirement as an act of desperation more than a thought-out decision. At the party secretariat meeting after the inauguration ceremony Bader requested that the filing of Begin's resignation letter be postponed and that a temporary Knesset member not be assigned immediately in his place. His request was granted, and Herut functioned with an absent leader. Begin, who missed no details of occurrences in the party, ignored the suspension of his resignation. He told his friends that he was planning a vacation in Italy.[69]

Begin and Aliza sailed from the port of Haifa. They left their eight-year-old son Benny and their one-year-old daughter Chasia with a family friend. Aliza was on vacation, a holiday that she had dreamed about for years, while Begin, who still believed that he was meant to be a leader, saw this trip as a national event. The handshakes he exchanged with the longshoremen at the ship's departure from port left no doubt in his mind—here he was, the Etzel commander, abandoning his birthright, the citizens of his state, and the party activists who had done him wrong.

As Begin stood on the gangway admiring the lights of Haifa, a longshoreman shouted, "Mr. Begin, it's good that you're going; just don't come back." It seemed as though he was trying to make his friends laugh, but Begin did not find it funny at all. He turned toward the man; debated whether or not to respond; looked at his wife, who had a protective look on her face; and then stepped on board. During their journey he wrote the party's secretary a letter describing the incident as if it were a critical moment in his biography. (In one of the two suitcases they packed was a block of writing paper.) "Age is not without sadness, love is not without hate, and fulfillment is not without agony," he poeticized.[70] He then went on to criticize the Herut members who had accused him of focusing entirely on the political field and abandoning all other topics. He explained that his desire to liberate the land involved, among other things, the will to change the regime; therefore there was no need to "whine," for just like Etzel's policies had triumphed, so would Herut's.

The few weeks that Begin spent in Italy remain an unclear chapter in his history. There is no documentation of them, and none of his colleagues ever spoke of them, although a rumor later spread that he had spent time at a sanatorium in Switzerland.

The couple returned to Israel earlier than anticipated—on September 13, a little more than a month after they had left—and the short vacation strengthened the assumption that Begin had planned to return to politics all along. Bader and Ben Eliezer went to greet him and demanded that he return to lead the party, but he adamantly refused. Ben Eliezer did not give up, and the next time they met, at Begin's home, he repeated his conviction that there was no Herut without him and that the party he had created would be erased from the political map. The ease with which Begin refused—with a hint of arrogance—irritated Ben Eliezer, who started to shout. He reminded Begin that he had arranged his discharge from the Anders Army and had supported him when many were reluctant to believe that he could command Etzel.[71]

On September 21, Begin announced at a Herut secretariat meeting that he was determined not to return to the party. Most members urged him to retract his decision, and some even burst into tears. They reminded him that Herut was a family from whose ranks one could be released only by death. At the end of the meeting an official announcement was released to the media that Begin was taking an extended vacation. This did not please Begin. Ben Eliezer was appointed as his replacement.[72]

The truth was that Begin had not yet surmounted his crisis. After his return to Israel he decided to leave home. From September 1951 to January 1952 he lived in a rented room at the Arza Guest House near Jerusalem, where he studied for the bar exam and began writing about his days in a Soviet prison. (The house director recalled that Begin was mostly busy writing his memoirs, which were later published under the title *White Nights*.)[73] His decision to distance himself from his wife and children was surprising, as during his days in the underground he had found it very hard to do so. It looked as though Aliza supported his decision both because he had to study and because he had not yet fully recovered from the disappointments that had befallen him. She visited him regularly with Benny and Chasia. His self-imposed withdrawal from politics was difficult for him, and even in the guest house he often suffered from mood swings and canceled meetings with visitors.[74]

As acting party head, Ben Eliezer dealt with the rehabilitation of Herut, which had run out of money. His attempts to persuade Begin to return to politics decreased but did not cease entirely. Meanwhile, surprising diplomatic ties began forming between the governments of Israel and the Federal Republic of Germany over a compensation agreement for Holocaust survivors.

EIGHT

BE KILLED BUT DO NOT TRANSGRESS

> (The "three cardinal sins" of Judaism, which usually sanctify human life, require a person to be ready to give up his life and not to transgress the three sins.)

The beginning of negotiations between Israel and West Germany was initiated by a claim filed with the great powers by the Israeli government on March 12, 1951, and ended with the establishment of full diplomatic relations between the two countries in 1965.[1] Relations were achieved despite the fact that Ben Gurion had not sought an agreement with Germany at the beginning of the negotiations. Ben Gurion's purpose in filing the claim was to make Germany extend economic aid to Israel—which it desperately needed—without evoking a public dialogue about a possible agreement. The funds he sought were referred to as "reparations," testimony of Israel's desire for revenge and not for making amends. One of the interpretations of the word "reparations" is "revenge," as it is written in Deuteronomy.[2] "We will not permit that our murderers will also be our inheritors," Ben Gurion explained in his decision.[3] When filing the claim against Germany, Begin estimated that it would be possible to receive reparations without direct negotiations and thus joined the claim's supporters—including members of Mapam, Hapoel Hamizrachi, and Mapai—and even saw it as reclaiming "the nation's dignity."[4]

However, West Germany's first chancellor, Konrad Adenauer, set as his goal the establishment of diplomatic ties with Israel in order to regain international legitimacy for his country. Ben Gurion, encouraged by Nachum Goldmann, president of the World Jewish Congress, realized that if Israel did not enter into negotiations with the new German government, he would not receive any money. In December 1951, Goldmann and Adenauer secretly agreed on the beginning of negotiations for reparations. On December 30, the government approved the decision. Over time Ben Gurion coined the phrase "the other Germany," which established the moral grounds for negotiations but caused an uproar in Jewish communities across the world.

Ben Gurion and Begin differed in their views of the Holocaust, though it was a seminal event for both of them.[5] Begin thought about the victims, while Ben Gurion thought about the survivors; Begin sought to restore the national honor and the memory of those who had perished, while Ben Gurion looked to the future; throughout Begin's life the Holocaust was a present reality that served to strengthen his conviction and toughen the spirit, while Ben Gurion emphasized that after the State of Israel had gained its independence, the Holocaust became a distant memory, and he wanted Jews to look at the impressive aspects of their people's past.

The differences of opinion regarding the agreement, which in many ways bought forgiveness with money, spread across the various camps. The majority of the religious supported Mapai, whose own members were divided (for example, the renowned poet Natan Alterman opposed any contact with the Germans),[6] while members of Mapam, Herut, Maki, and the General Zionists stood in opposition.

On January 7, 1952, the day the Knesset was scheduled to convene for a vote on the approval of the negotiations, mass demonstrations were held across the country. Begin followed the developments from his guest house room and heard Ben Eliezer announce that Herut could not accept an agreement that made amends for the systematic murder of the Jewish people.[7]

As the Knesset vote drew near, Herut members understood that the issue of reparations was the silver platter on which Begin could run for leadership. The entire political spectrum needed a man to unite the opponents of the agreement. But it was not the only reason why they wanted to bring Begin back into the political ring. In December 1951 Herut had been caught up in a crisis yet again when Ben Eliezer suffered a heart attack and the leadership was entrusted to the party secretary, Yaakov Rubin, a dreary Revisionist politico. It was a critical moment in the party's history: the question was whether to continue or to desist. Moreover, the party's top officials realized that for the first time Begin could support a position crossing among the various camps.

Bader hastened to make a move. Just before the New Year he went to see Begin and immediately presented the most sentimental argument Begin had ever heard: "Menachem, this is not just a historical issue. This is your moral obligation to your family, your duty toward your murdered mother."[8] Bader had never before dared to raise personal matters with Begin, and Begin was stunned. The two parted with an embrace, but Bader did not yet know what the implications of their meeting would be.[9] Thus the most turbulent political battle Begin would ever wage, amid which he would consider reestablishing the underground, was evoked by a simple, sentimental statement about his mother. That very evening Begin wrote an article that was published on January 1. He claimed that approving a treaty with West Germany concerned not only his generation, but all Jewish generations to come and that if approved, it would bring "eternal shame on the Knesset."[10] Begin was once again at the peak of his form, as he had been when he had declared the rebellion: agitated, calling upon the sublime, and emphasizing the despicable.

Begin would have likely tried to return to politics in any event, as his decision to retire had not been a calculated, informed choice but rather had been based on the bitterness and deep disappointment that had overcome him and that had led to mental exhaustion. When he summoned up his strength, the Reparations Agreement established the ideological grounds for his return to the political arena. Begin saw the Israeli attitude toward the Germans as the most serious and important issue of the Jewish people of his generation and took on the role of a modern-day prophet of doom with the conviction of a man who belonged to a lineage of the prophets of Israel.[11]

On January 5, at Mugrabi Square in Tel Aviv, ten thousand demonstrators—some holding a Torah, some wearing a yellow star, some in tears—heard words that had never been heard before in the young country. Begin's first public appearance since his retirement was a direct threat to the government, since this was a man who had already proved his ability in the underground.[12] "I am warning you, Mr. Ben Gurion," Begin cried out; "I'm warning you with the people as my witnesses. If you dare do such a thing [accept the treaty], note the conclusion that every Jew will be permitted to draw: if such a thing is acceptable in Israel, anything will be allowed in the State of Israel.... There will be a turning point in the country's history if the agreement is approved. . . . It's time for Ben Gurion to be judged by the people for all his crimes. . . . Our people will not pay taxes anymore. . . . Even if the Mapai rule is by spears, Herut has the experience for breaking it down." Begin concluded his speech with a proposal for everyone to wear a yellow star, saying, "Remember what Amalek did to you" and urged the masses "to ascend the day after tomorrow to Jerusalem."[13] And they went in droves to Zion Square, to the demonstration that preceded the discussion in the Knesset.

Fifteen thousand people attended the demonstration in Jerusalem, despite the freezing cold. Some carried torches; many wore a yellow star; and some, mainly former Etzel members, confronted the hundreds of policemen surrounding them. From a balcony overlooking Zion Square, wearing a black suit, Begin argued that his opposition to a treaty had historical, philosophical, and moral significance, and he outlined the historical continuities from the days of the Bible to the twentieth century. "We have here with us Professor Klausner, one of the greatest historians in Israel, and he will tell us. Ever since the Battle of Gibeah [a biblical battle involving rape and murder, considered the first Israelite civil war according to the Book of Judges], has such an act of abomination ever been executed among the Jewish people? Has there been a deeper rift within our people over any other matter than this act? They say that Germany is a nation and not what it actually is: a herd of wolves who devoured our people as prey. . . . And thanks to our people's blood Ben Gurion became prime minister, that small tyrant and great maniac. . . . How will we look when our disgrace is exposed, as we turn to our fathers' murderers to receive money for their spilled blood?"[14]

The crowd began hurling stones at the hundreds of policemen who were keeping order, and for a moment it seemed that the demonstrators were going to lynch the MKs gathered near the square. (One of the stones hit Geula Cohen in the head, and the following day Begin hurried to visit her, calling her Jeanne d'Arc.)[15] Over one hundred police officers were injured, and in the midst of the commotion they were ordered to throw tear gas grenades at the crowd. "Gas! Gas! They're using gas against us!" many shouted, and Begin was quick to fan their anger. "From reports we have just received, Mr. Ben Gurion has deployed police officers carrying grenades and tear gas made in Germany, the same gases that asphyxiated our ancestors, and he has prisons and concentration camps."[16] In fact, Begin suggested in his speech an alternative to Mapai's "we"; this alternative "we" both united and separated the people. The memory of the Holocaust united the oppressed—among them Sephardim and a few Orthodox Jews and left-wingers—and separated them from Mapai.

Begin concluded his speech by saying, "Though Ben Gurion is older than I am, I am older than he in my experience in opposing the powers of evil. So I declare: evil is standing here before a just matter, and it will shatter like glass against a rock. For this, we are all ready to give our souls. We will be killed, but we will not transgress. There is no sacrifice we are not willing to make to thwart this plot. When you fired your gun at me"—he referred here to the *Altalena* affair—"I commanded: No! Today I will command. Yes! . . . You will not show us mercy, but this time we will have no mercy for you either; it will be a war to the death."[17] After his speech, Begin rushed to the Knesset, a walking distance away. Apprehensive of the possible consequences of the speech, Bader quickly replaced Begin on the balcony. He announced that the demonstration was over and asked the demonstrators to disperse.[18] But hundreds of excited protestors began to move on the Frumin Building, and clashes erupted between the Etzel veterans and police. When the protesters reached the Knesset gates, the police called for reinforcements. Stones were hurled toward the building, smashing the windows and penetrating the Knesset plenum. Knesset members, including Ben Gurion and Arie Ben Eliezer, who was brought in on a stretcher from the hospital, were frozen still.

When Begin took the podium—he had just recently renewed his parliamentary activities—he smoothed back his hair, as if he wanted to delay what was about to happen, and said, "Today, the Tenth of Tevet, is a memorial day for all of us, a memorial for my father and also a memorial day for the nation."[19] He thus took the discussion to a more personal and emotional level—unlike most of the participants in the debate on the Reparations Agreement. The Holocaust had shaped his Jewish identity, and he believed it should also shape the state's Jewish-national identity. Begin then stated his opposition to the agreement in a more reasoned way. He quoted a letter written by Foreign Minister Moshe Sharett to the leaders of the United States, Britain, France, and the USSR: "No progress can be made toward Germany's return into the family of nations until the matter of reparations paid to the Jewish people is straightened out." Begin claimed that the letter actually stated that Germany could buy absolution. He then turned to Ben Gurion and said, "As adversaries, there is an unbridgeable rift between us. There will be no bridge; it is a bloody abyss. I turn to you at the last minute, as one Jew to another, as the son of an orphaned nation, as the son of a bereft nation. Halt; do not go through with this act. This is the most abominable of abominations in Israel." And since he believed that the Holocaust was a Jewish-national matter, he asked Arab members of the Knesset to refrain from participating in the discussion: "You have a formal right to vote on this matter, but you should distinguish between your formal right and your moral right. This is our issue; the blood of our mothers, our brothers, and our sisters is involved. Let us decide on this matter." Finally, the secular Begin addressed the religious Knesset members. Only one of them voted against the agreement (some of the opponents preferred to abstain) and accused them of blasphemy: "How is the Torah connected to negotiations with Amalek? By supporting this agreement, you will erase an entire verse in the Torah, the Lord's war on Amalek from generation to generation."

The Knesset members listened to his speech, and unlike what usually happened, they let him clarify his views, despite the commotion taking place outside the building. Ben Gurion could not bear their silence, which he considered a sign of their cowardice, and he shouted, "Yes, and who brought these hooligans here?" "You. You are the hooligan," Begin shouted, and started a commotion in the Knesset plenum. Yosef Serlin, the Knesset vice speaker, asked Begin to apologize for the word "hooligan" and threatened that if he did not, he would not give him the floor. Begin refused. "If I don't speak, no one will speak here!" he yelled, shaking his fist. Begin continued to speak despite the turmoil: "I beg of you . . . as a Jewish believer and the son of a believer, do not go through with this," and he threatened, "I am telling you, there will be no agreement with Germany. There is one thing I learned from my father, which I too have taught others: some things in life are more precious than life itself. This is one of those things for which we will give our lives; for this we will die. We will leave our families and say goodbye to our children so that there will be no negotiations with Germany."

The Knesset members were concerned about what might happen, as in their eyes Begin was a leader of the underground more than he was a democratic leader. Minister of Health Yosef Burg, from the Hapoel Hamizrachi, advised Ben Gurion to escape from the Knesset plenum, fearing for his life. In answer Ben Gurion indicated he was afraid of something else: "If I leave, this will be the end of Israeli democracy."[20] Ben Gurion consulted with his assistant, Yitzhak Navon, and told him that he was not sure whether he should order the military to intervene, adding that what had occurred was "proof that Begin is capable of anything."[21] The meeting was suspended for three hours, and when it restarted, MK Pinchas Lavon (Mapai) said, "We have witnessed the preparation for a rebellion in Israel."[22]

Begin found it hard to carry the torch he had lit and chose to leave the Knesset in secret, accompanied by his assistant. "Let's go to the ultra-Orthodox neighborhoods," he said; "we'll draw some encouragement from them."[23] The next evening he went on a walk with Bader, and the two decided to cancel the demonstration that had been planned for the day of the Knesset vote on January 9. They knew that things were out of control. When they parted, Begin whispered, "We must not let the agreement pass." Bader nodded. Begin said, "We should think about going underground." Bader's response was decisive: "Menachem, on this, I will not be with you."[24] The topic was never raised again.

Bader's opposition was enough to make Begin abandon the idea of going underground, indicating that it was not a formulated plan. But the fact that he had thought about it and consulted with his confidant is enough to indicate that the thirty-nine-year-old Begin had not yet come to terms with leading a democratic party.[25] (In 2006 a book of memoirs was published by Eliezer Suditi, a former Etzel fighter who was involved in a failed attempt to assassinate Adenauer; in it Suditi claimed that Begin had confirmed the plan, although there are no official references to such a confirmation.)[26]

On January 9, the Knesset approved the start of negotiations with West Germany for a reparations agreement; sixty-one MKs favored the negotiations and fifty opposed them.[27]

Begin's associates were split regarding the turn of events at the demonstration against the Reparations Agreement. There were those who wondered why Begin had changed his position from the underground days—"There will be no fraternal war"—to a new promise—"We will leave our wives." Bader said that Begin was moody.[28] Menachem Porush, then a young activist in the ultra-Orthodox Agudat Israel party who attended the demonstration, said that Begin had lost his senses.[29] There is no doubt that Begin acted from his heart and really believed that such a reparations agreement went against Jewish values, but he also acted as he did partly because of the feelings he had held ever since he had immigrated to the country—that the establishment ostracized and humiliated him and saw him as an outsider—and partly because of his failure in the legislative elections, which had added to his disappointment. When he felt that the government was adopting policies antithetical to his even in regard to the Germans he hated, he snapped. All his pent-up frustrations, which had accumulated over the years, burst forth. However, it is reasonable to assume that he also understood that his opposition to the policy would have political benefits. "I will give speeches greater than this," he promised Eldad, who praised him for his speech at the demonstration the following day.[30]

After his speech in the Knesset Begin was suspended from Knesset sessions for three months. In protest, the rest of the Herut members halted their Knesset activities for the same stretch of time. His supporters saw Begin's suspension as another attempt to push him over the political fence. Paglin, now a businessman in the private sector, hastened to announce to Bader that he was willing to hang all members of the government "on a telephone line."[31] But Begin saw his suspension as an opportunity to reevaluate what had happened. Later, Herut members who believed that Begin had gone too far preferred to downplay what he said in his speech and on the following day.

The uproar Begin often caused during his term in the Knesset did not always help his political career. Among his opponents, both from the left of the political spectrum and from the extreme right, Begin was considered passionate and strident, but when he expressed his opposition to the Reparations Agreement, many of them found it difficult to ignore the force of his arguments. Furthermore, during the three months of his suspension, Begin returned to the all-too-familiar position of victim, from which he managed to deal with political issues and to elevate Herut to the status of an opposition party worthy of taking power.

Begin dedicated his free time to expanding the circle of Herut's supporters. His excommunication from the Knesset strengthened his desire to strengthen ties with all the country's deprived groups. Although he had asked the Israeli Arabs not to interfere in the vote on the Reparations Agreement, he summoned them to a meeting during which he spoke of the party's fight for "liberty for all in Israel."[32]

On January 20, in a speech during a demonstration at Mugrabi Square in Tel Aviv, Begin denied that he had gone underground and claimed, "If the agitated masses sought to break into the Knesset building to flog him who declares himself the Messiah with thirty-nine lashes—as written and deserved, according to Jewish law—they could have done it. . . . It is regrettable that a few stones fell on the Knesset, but don't make a tragedy out of it." However, just as he was refuting rumors that he had threatened to declare a revolt, he proved that he believed he had good reason to do so. "Look, my friends, a plane," he interrupted his flow of words, pointing to an aircraft that chanced to fly overhead,

"Let's bless it for its part in the demonstration." The hint was understood: the plane had been sent to spy on him, and the crowd, waving its hands, was thrilled. The demonstration ended with a march to the Great Synagogue on Allenby Street, where, surrounded by Jews clutching Torahs, Begin exclaimed, "If I forget the shame of destruction, may my right hand forget its skill."[33]

Over the months between the approval of the first draft of the Reparations Agreement and its actual signing, Begin continued to speak at various demonstrations, but he talked mainly about divine guidance rather than about politics. "The God of Israel will be the one to judge between Ben Gurion and me," Begin vowed in front of a crowd at a Mugrabi Square demonstration. He reiterated his appeal to Ben Gurion as "one Jew to another" and claimed that Israel did not require economic aid at all—even though the previous year he had been in favor of receiving reparations money without any negotiations. A *Haaretz* editorial expressed puzzlement about his style: "It is not a politician talking, but a rabbi gifted with the extraordinary talent to appeal to the masses."[34]

After the signing of the Reparations Agreement on September 10, 1952, by Foreign Minister Moshe Sharett and Chancellor Konrad Adenauer, the demonstrations subsided. A year and a half later, when equipment was shipped to Israel from Germany, Begin was in South Africa. Many wondered where he had gone, and there were those who assumed that he had planned his trip abroad with the intention of being away from the country when the shipment arrived in order to avoid the need to respond with new demonstrations. But Begin never admitted it.[35] It seemed as though he understood that he had stretched the rope too thin.

Yet Ben Gurion had not forgotten Begin's threats, even a decade later, as indicated in a letter he wrote to poet Chaim Guri: "Begin is a distinctively Hitleristic type. He is a racist who is willing to kill all the Arabs in order to gain control of the entire land of Israel. In his view, the sacred goal—absolute rule—justifies every means. I see him as a grave danger to Israel's internal and external security. . . . I cannot forget the little I know about his previous operations, which have a clear meaning. . . . I have no doubt Begin hates Hitler, but this does not prove that they are any different. . . . The first time I heard Begin give a speech over the radio, I heard the voice and the screaming of Hitler."[36]

There was a reason why Ben Gurion reiterated his warning about Begin ten years after the protests against the Reparations Agreement. With his thunderous speeches Begin gradually improved his image and gained influence as the greatest speaker in Israel at the time. He appealed to people's emotions and spirit of curiosity, even when speaking to educated listeners, and as his internal dialogue ran on both these levels of communication, he had no difficulty stimulating people's enthusiasm.[37] He even tended to insert Latin quotations in his speeches in order to impress the audience with the use of a language that not all of them understood.[38] The journalists who mocked him did not realize that Begin had figured out that his audience did not always need to understand everything that was being said. Rather, listeners preferred a leader who seemed to know more than they, and they viewed him as a father figure.

In his relations with party members, however, Begin continued to communicate in a monologue, demanding absolute obedience. When Shmuel Katz wanted to publish an article in *Herut* about the possibility of unification with the General Zionists, he discovered that Begin had demanded that the article be shelved. "He's not the same Begin he was in the underground. He cannot accept any criticism," Katz said angrily to other members. Begin had rejected the article not only because of its content. Katz belonged to a group of intellectuals who disliked Begin, and Begin believed they would never understand the wisdom of the common man. Katz claimed that because of "the isolation forced on him during the underground, he is intoxicated with the love of the masses."[39] Later on, psychologists would maintain that Begin needed the crowd's love also as compensation for the stern education he had received from his strict father.

One day in the summer of 1953 Israel Eldad told Begin that he was too preoccupied with "erecting monuments." Begin replied proudly, "This is history's mandate." "It's a mistake," Eldad responded. "It would be a better idea to establish a publishing house. We are losing the intellectual right-wing spirit." "We have no spirit?" Begin exploded. "What are you talking about? Did you see the rally we held at Mugrabi?" "Is the spirit of a political rally a spiritual thing?" grumbled Eldad.[40] Unlike Ben Gurion, Begin did not hold meetings with writers, nor did he rummage through ancient bookstores. He was never suspected as unintelligent; quite the contrary. However, as he continued down this populist path, he slowly and consistently alienated the intellectuals from Herut.

After Israel signed the armistice agreement with the neighboring Arab states, a phenomenon of Arab infiltration into Israel from Egypt,

Syria, and Jordan began. Between 1949 and 1954 over fifteen thousand people crossed into Israel every year. Most infiltrators did so in order to steal crops or visit relatives, but others entered with the purpose of harming Israeli civilians. Ben Gurion harshly criticized the phenomenon and blamed Jordan and Egypt for encouraging guerrilla warfare in order to wear out Israel. The infiltrators began to be called *fedayeen* (those who sacrifice themselves).[41]

From 1949 to 1956, over two hundred Israeli civilians were killed, and many residents abandoned the border communities in fear of the fedayeen attacks. When the situation deteriorated, Ben Gurion adopted a new policy of punishment: reprisals across the border. In 1953 a special unit was established, Unit 101, whose sole purpose was retribution. It was led by a young major named Ariel (Arik) Sharon.

On October 12, 1953, a grenade was thrown into a house in the village of Yahud, killing a mother and daughter. Unit 101 was sent on a mission of retribution to the village of Qibya in Samaria. By the end of the operation over sixty corpses were found in the village. When the number of casualties was published, the action was internationally condemned. Ben Gurion knowingly lied when he told the Knesset that Israeli civilians had probably carried out the operation on their own.[42]

Although Begin was a consistent supporter of military action, he adamantly objected to the doctrine of retaliatory actions. "Why is the killing of fifty Arabs, although no evidence points to their connection to the murder of Jews, considered an act of defense, while occupying land is considered an act of aggression?" he asked. Retribution, Begin clarified, is based on the incorrect theory that the killing of Arabs is a method for achieving stability along the borders. He suggested an alternative: the initiation of a war to seize land. Such a step would force the Arab governments, who allegedly had no respect for human life, to sign an agreement with Israel based on the recognition of its power.[43]

Even though Begin's assessment of the value of human life was more moral than that of the Mapai ministers, the press and the public continued to see him as bloodthirsty, mainly because ever since he had returned to the Knesset after his suspension, he missed no opportunity to propound a military strike on the Syrians, Jordanians, and Egyptians.[44] Unlike Ben Gurion, who established his decisions based on Israel's renewed strength, Begin based his demands for military action on the claim that "in every generation they rise against us to annihilate us" (a motif from the Passover Haggadah).

Yet Begin's attitude toward the Arabs had changed since the revolt against the British. Before the Mandate, Begin saw the British as the main obstacle in the way of establishing the State of Israel. However, after the British evacuated the area, the existential anxiety that shaped Begin's national perspective did not vanish, and the threat the British had once posed over the Jewish people's fate was now replaced in his eyes by a new threat—the Arabs. In fact, the successful struggle against the British, the establishment of the state, and the winning of the War of Independence were all interim periods in Jewish history in Begin's view. "There is one thing we must believe," he used to say, "and that is the Arab threat."[45] Every incident along the borders was part of the Jewish people's struggle against their indefatigable enemy. Begin's frequent use of the word "Amalek" made him appear as a figure of Diaspora mentality, a stranger to the new Israeli, impertinent and self-confident. This is one of the reasons Begin admired generals, as they embodied the Jewish-Israeli character he dreamed about.

During his term in the second Knesset Begin placed little value on determining the country's policies. In most of the important events at that time he was only an observer, and he could only voice his opinion, which was usually according to expectations. These were gray and dreary days for him, during which he continued to play the part of the constant complainer.

The attitude toward Begin did not change, even when Ben Gurion announced that he was retiring and went on vacation at the end of 1953. Foreign Minister Moshe Sharett was appointed as his replacement. Sharett, like Ben Gurion, disregarded Herut. But Begin's speeches, particularly the emphasis he placed on Jewish identity, seeped into Israeli society, itself involved in a search for identity. Unlike Ben Gurion, who aspired toward the development of a new Jew—a native, an Israeli not attached to life in the Diaspora—for Begin, the State of Israel had been established primarily as a Jewish state and was the center of the Jewish world, and all his ideas stemmed from this conception.

In late 1953 Begin traveled to the United States to promote the idea of a world Jewish federation. He believed that only a Jewish institution of world order could resolve controversial issues, such as the Reparations Agreement, through a referendum of all Jews in the world. Yet Begin did not turn his mind—at least not in public—to the practical aspects of organizing such a federation, nor the implications of such a move on the sovereignty of the State of Israel and the damage such an organization could do to the world image of Jews. His plan was not implemented, but the idea of a global Jewish association continued to fascinate him. On Israel's tenth anniversary Ben Gurion asked forty-six Jewish intellectuals in Israel and abroad to answer the question, "Who is a Jew?" Begin identified completely with the Orthodox position on the issue: "Although other nations can separate religion and nationality, this is not a possibility for the Jews. Why? There are many questions that do not need to be verbally explained. Only assimilated thinkers tried to bring up the option of a German Jew. The God of Israel has the right to determine who is Jewish—the Bible says so—and this is not a matter for political bargaining. Since the Jews do not separate nation and religion and the rabbis have the authority to determine who is Jewish, the government has no business dealing with this matter." But Begin fell silent when Ben Gurion reiterated the standpoint of Jabotinsky, who had argued, "Not religion, but national uniqueness is the sacred treasure our people has kept so stubbornly."[46]

The second Knesset ended its term with the exposure of the case first known as Esek Habish (the Unfortunate Affair); over the years, as it became more complicated, it became known as the Lavon Affair or simply the Affair.

The Affair, which became public knowledge while Ben Gurion was on vacation, is the story of the failure of a Jewish cell operating in Egypt in the early 1950s. The members of the cell, all of whom were local Jews, were assigned to plant explosives in cinemas and American and British information centers in Cairo and Alexandria so as to undermine the Egyptian government and disrupt its relations with Western countries. The cell members were caught before they could complete their mission, and the Egyptian authorities claimed that the Israeli government had sent them. Two members, Moshe Marzouk and Shmuel Azar, were sentenced to death, and the rest were sentenced to long prison terms.

Prime Minister Moshe Sharett apparently did not know about the operation. Defense Minister Pinchas Lavon claimed that he too did not know about it. Head of Military Intelligence Binyamin Gibli insisted that he had received an oral order from Lavon, and IDF Chief of Staff Moshe Dayan also saw Lavon as responsible. Sharett decided to establish a committee to investigate the affair and determine who had given the orders. The committee's conclusions were inconclusive, but the investigation led to Lavon's retirement and Gibli was removed from his position. On returning from his vacation, Ben Gurion was appointed defense minister in order to stabilize the system, but his sour relationship with Sharett sabotaged the government, eventually leading to Sharett's dismissal. A short while before the next general elections, Ben Gurion had been reelected as the leader of Mapai.[47]

The results of the third legislative elections, held in July 1955, after the surfacing of a new affair—the Kastner Affair—reflected the cumulative impact of Begin's protests against the Reparations Agreement. The results directed attention to the relationship between the Zionist establishment and the Jews in the Diaspora and Holocaust survivors.

In the 1950s, Malkiel Gruenwald lived near Zion Square in Jerusalem. Gruenwald used to send letters to members of the Hamizrachi religious party expressing his hatred of the Zionist establishment and Mapai because of their despicable incompetence during the massacre of European Jews. Nobody took his letters too seriously, not even Israel Kastner, a Mapai candidate for the Knesset and a spokesman for the Ministry of Trade and Industry, despite the fact that Gruenwald specifically discredited him: "Dr. Rudolf [Israel] Kastner must be eliminated. . . . The smell of rotting flesh scratches my nostrils. . . . It will be a funeral full of splendor due to his cooperation with the Nazis." Attorney General Chaim Cohen decided to file a libel suit against Gruenwald.[48]

The trial took place in Jerusalem in 1954; the presiding judge was Binyamin Halevi. Shmuel Tamir, a former Etzel member, was appointed Gruenewald's lawyer, and in a brilliant legal maneuver he managed to raise an issue that stirred the entire country: Had members of the Zionist establishment collaborated with the Nazis? Tamir claimed that Kastner had done so because he had hidden from the Jews in Cluj the fact that they were destined to be sent to Auschwitz, and in return for his secrecy the Nazis enabled him to smuggle Jewish dignitaries, including his associates, out of danger. Tamir further claimed that after the war Kastner negotiated with the Nazis, including SS officer Kurt Becher. When he presented Judge Halevi with his evidence (Kastner initially denied the allegations), the trial took a drastic turn.

Tamir argued that Kastner was only a symbol, a symptom of the policy of the Yishuv leaders—especially David Ben Gurion and Moshe Sharett. This position was supported by many right-wingers, the ultra-Orthodox Haredim, and members of Mapam, who took advantage of the opportunity to blame the Zionist establishment. In June 1955 Judge Halevi read his verdict and shocked the State of Israel. Quoting Goethe's Faust, he stated that Kastner "had sold his soul to the devil."[49] Prior to Kastner's trial, the issue of the Yishuv's efforts to save the

Jews of Europe had not been pursued in depth. The verdict strengthened Begin's criticism of Ben Gurion's government, and Herut made the most of the mood of the public, which was now inclined to support Begin. The party's main election poster showed a picture of Kastner and under it the slogan, "He votes for Mapai; you vote for Herut."

During the third election campaign, most major political parties were assisted by advertising consultants and artists—a sign of the embrace of American culture. Begin refused to make use of performance artists in his rallies, as it appeared that "the greatest actor in politics" (as Dan Meridor called Begin) feared that he would be eclipsed by them.[50] After all, the Polish Begin was the first Israeli politician to adopt the patterns of behavior of the American politician—he arrived at most rallies in an open Cadillac, he kissed children, and he inserted catchphrases in his speeches.

In late July 1955, just days before the election, Begin stood on a terrace in Dizengoff Square, looking at more than three thousand people who had gathered to hear him speak. He smiled and said, "I cannot but ask forgiveness from a particular segment of the public. All parties have given Israeli artists an opportunity to earn a great deal of money. I am not disregarding Israel's artists. They need a livelihood. Therefore I ask them to forgive Herut for not providing them with jobs. So I'm sorry, dear Shoshana Damari; the lovely Yaffa Yarkoni; the wonderful Meskin; the great cantor Koussevitzky. I am sorry, and ask for your forgiveness and atonement."[51]

The crowd was ecstatic, but Begin was sweating—the heat was a burden, and the only advantage of the suit he was wearing was the pocket, which always had a handkerchief in it. When he finished wiping the sweat off his face, Begin spoke to the policemen in charge of the rally's security. He asked them "to stop the traffic, because in a democratic country citizens are entitled to listen."[52] His request embarrassed the young democracy's policemen. No one had ordered them to stop the traffic during Begin's speech, but because he insisted, they catered to his whim. Begin addressed the police during every rally for two reasons: first, to impress the audience by pointing out that he had been assigned official security, and second, because he took pleasure in commanding security personnel—especially those who served under Ben Gurion's government.

The following day, during a rally in the Yemenite quarter in Tel Aviv, Begin again addressed the policemen before he began to speak. This time he asked them to leave: "I do not need any security, just as I did not need it in the underground. I trust the Almighty, and I would rather see you as friends than as bodyguards." The police did not leave, of course, and Begin turned to the crowd—over two thousand people, mostly Iraqi-born ("dressed in pajamas," as described condescendingly by *Haaretz* reporter Shimon Samet)—and asked a few rhetorical questions: "Do you remember how we walked together, armed rows of Yemenites, Sephardim, and Ashkenazim? Do you remember how we expelled the one hundred thousand British troops from the country?" Though most of them had only recently immigrated to Israel and knew nothing about the underground, they all responded in unison: "We remember, we remember." Begin often asked rhetorical questions in his speeches—and always when his speech had reached its climax. In his famous speech at Menorah Square in Jerusalem, he told the audience confidentially, "Until now the State of Israel has received $3 billion from various sources. According to this number, that would mean $2,000 a head—have you received $2,000?" He turned to one of the people in the crowd and asked, "Have you?" and then to another, "Have you?" and again "Have you?" When the answering shouts of "No! I did not receive it!" grew louder, Begin continued to ask more people, "Have you?" again and again—and there were those who swore that he asked the question at least sixty times during the speech.[53] "Here they come," Begin said at the end of his speech, referring to Mapai, "inventing a false theory, as if there is Yemenite blood, Ashkenazi blood, and Sephardic blood. I tell you: It's a lie. There is no separate blood. We all have one blood: Jewish blood."[54]

When Begin's critics said that one of his speeches bordered on demagoguery, he remarked, "They should try talking in front of ten thousand people in the square, the crowd standing on their feet, the sun beating down on their heads, and sometimes in the rain, and then they should try to give a scholarly lecture."[55]

The results of the third legislative elections, held on July 26, a month after Kastner was sentenced, were Begin's first political success. Herut now had fifteen Knesset seats, almost double what it had had in the second Knesset, while Mapai had forty seats, five seats fewer than in the previous elections. Herut's achievement was impressive mostly because it became the largest opposition party—despite the fact that the General Zionists had also made use of Kastner's trial to hurt Mapai and the fact that both Achdut Haavoda (Labor Unity) and some members of Mapam had supported the idea of a Greater Israel. Despite the fact that the alternative proposed by Mapam, Achdut Haavoda, and the General Zionists was more realistic—and perhaps because of it—Begin was the only one who actually threatened the government.[56]

The election results strengthened Begin's conviction that leadership of the country was attainable, and this conviction was reflected in the party center's decision, which Begin had proposed: disallow any violent means to achieve power.[57] Nevertheless, Begin hardly had any effect on Israel's policies.[58] He remained a laughing stock for the left wing because (among other reasons) he insisted on his semantics. For example, in June 1956 he released a statement to the Knesset journalists apologizing for his "regrettable error" in comments against the foreign minister's appeasement policy. The journalists expected something important, but Begin had not changed his position on the matter; rather he just noted that Sharett was "not my enemy, but my rival."[59] During a special Etzel conference marking the seventy-fifth anniversary of Jabotinsky's birth, Begin declared, "The former Etzel fighters are making themselves available to the Israel Defense Forces to resolve security problems requiring the special experience acquired during their years in the resistance."[60] The newspapers ridiculed his comments by wondering sarcastically when the fighters had acquired an understanding of military tactics, as they were experienced in terrorism, and why, if their help was useful, did they not serve in the reserve forces as all other citizens. In 1955, after Israeli soldiers kidnapped five Egyptian officers during a military operation, Begin called for a press conference and announced that there was sufficient evidence that Israel was "moving toward the ways of Etzel."[61] (Among Etzel veterans, Begin was not the only one who felt estranged from the establishment. During an Etzel fighters' conference Paglin argued that the government's decision to establish a mental institution within Acre Prison expressed the government's desire to erase the memory of the Acre Prison break; he thus demonstrated the lack of confidence felt by many of the former Etzel members toward state institutions.)

Earlier, in 1952, the Israeli government had begun implementing a selection policy toward the immigration of Moroccan Jews—preferring the young, healthy, and financially established—and the policy aroused indignation among Moroccan immigrants.[62] Begin was one of the leaders who opposed this policy. He stated that "*Pikuach nefesh* [the saving of souls] comes before development," compared the government's policy to "the handing out of certificates by the British administration," and claimed that no Jew in the state would object to a tax raise in order to finance Moroccan immigration. In mid-1955 Begin organized demonstrations across the country demanding the right of immigration for all North African Jews. He presented a clear plan: the "10 million program." The government would transfer 10 million Israeli lira from the state development budget to the immigration budget, and citizens would cover the deficit, each according to his ability.[63] Once again it was obvious that despite his hostility toward the "reds," Begin did not rule out a national-socialist economy. However, the plan he proposed reflected an ideal that he never bothered to examine in depth.

Even though Begin was aware of the possibility that the immigration of Moroccan Jews would strengthen Herut, his opposition to the selection policy and his proposal that citizens participate in funding unrestricted immigration stemmed from his strict worldview. In his eyes, Israel was primarily a shelter for the world's Jews, and from his first speech after the Declaration of Independence, he argued that immigration should be made possible for Jews the world over.

The Moroccan immigrants never forgot that Begin supported the immigration of all the Jews of Morocco and saw him as the one responsible for their immigration—despite the fact that he had focused on exacerbating the struggle against the British over accelerating the process of illegal immigration during his years in the underground and that he was in the opposition when the government was working to bring Jews to Israel.[64]

NINE

BUDS OF LEGITIMACY

During September 1955 Egypt tightened its siege on the Straits of Tiran and closed the air space over the Gulf of Aqaba. Furthermore, at the end of the month Egypt's president, Gamal Abdel Nasser, announced that Egypt was about to sign a large arms deal with Czechoslovakia that would transform the balance of power between Israel and Egypt.[1]

Ben Gurion, who had decided after the closure of the Straits of Tiran to respond with military action, sought the West's official legitimacy for the operation. In October 1956, after Nasser nationalized the Suez Canal, Ben Gurion convinced the British and the French, who had economic interests in the canal, that the nationalization was a result of Egypt's strengthened ties with the Communist bloc and that the circumstances for preventive war had ripened. In late October, during a meeting in Paris, Ben Gurion, French prime minister Guy Mollet, and British foreign minister Selwyn Lloyd decided to attack Egypt.

Ben Gurion told the members of his government of the plan—Operation Kadesh—only on the morning of the military operation, October 28, and for the first time he decided to update Begin of the developments as well. The ministers were upset by the late update, while Begin was extremely satisfied: Israel was going to war and he was part of the process.[2] After briefing Begin, the prime minister told him about a dream he had had in which "the Israeli Army crosses the Jordan River." The dream—a common prophetic tool of Israel's leaders throughout the Bible—increased Begin's enthusiasm. Several days later, in the midst of the military operation, Ben Gurion fell ill, and Begin, who thought that they were tending a newfound friendship, hurried to his bedside.³ Several Herut members felt that Begin was too quick to forget Ben Gurion's attitude toward him and that his dream was simply a manipulation—the use of Begin's own terminology in order to captivate him and to emphasize who was the boss.⁴

Operation Kadesh was hailed a success. By November 6 the entire Sinai Peninsula and the Gaza Strip were under Israeli control. The next day, Ben Gurion declared that the rise of the Third Kingdom of Israel was not far away, and that the Straits of Tiran were themselves the island of Tiran (also known as Yotvat), which harbored a Jewish kingdom in the sixth century.⁵ A few hours after Ben Gurion's speech, the U.N. General Assembly decided, by a vote of sixty-five to one—the one being Israel—that the IDF must withdraw immediately from the conquered territories. The United States threatened sanctions and the Russians said that they might respond with military action, and less than twenty-four hours later, the prime minister—this time in a recorded speech on the radio—announced that Israel would withdraw.

Begin felt belittled. He thought Ben Gurion's change of heart had been too sudden. During the Knesset debate he quoted the prime minister's victory speech, saying that this was a withdrawal from homeland territory. He was unsparing toward the army as well and demanded that the chief of staff "lay down his wand."⁶ "This is the first step in tearing the Negev from the state," Begin concluded and vowed to "support a budget increase for pensioning off the prime minister and the foreign minister."⁷

Ben Gurion was bitter because of the chain of events and resumed his fight with Begin. "Mr. Begin, the man who once said he would not allow anyone here to speak," Ben Gurion said as he recalled the events over the Reparations Agreement, "knows under all circumstances and at any time to give just one piece of advice—to start a war. . . . I do not believe the crocodile tears he has shed for the fallen soldiers. I am confident that the people of Israel will never give these irresponsible people the power to command our magnificent IDF." His comments, accompanied by Begin's heckling—"Phooey! Speculator in blood! Remember the holy canon! How many times have you initiated a war! You reckless person!"⁸—put an end to the brief idyll that had existed between them.

Begin went back to mass rallies, during one of which he was carried on the shoulders of his supporters, wearing black ribbons of mourning, all the way from Mugrabi Square to the Great Synagogue in Tel Aviv, with a Torah scroll in his arms. "The fate of Jerusalem will be decided in Gaza," he exclaimed, but this time he did not threaten a revolt.[9] Begin continued to believe that he was being spied on by the Shin Bet. When he complained about it in a Knesset speech, he was asked how he knew, and he replied, "We have received word from a member of the Mapai Secretariat whose name I will not betray."[10]

Meanwhile, the sense of alienation strengthened among the tens of thousands of new immigrants from Arab countries who were already somewhat familiar with Israeli politics and could not believe that the establishment wanted to help them. The gap between the Mizrahim, who did not assimilate into Israeli society, and the veterans of the Yishuv, mostly Ashkenazim—a gap that was widening (in part because of the reparations payments, which had begun to arrive)—became the focus of a new controversy that Begin started. He said of Finance Minister Levi Eshkol that "he is not even qualified to be a grocery store bookkeeper on Allenby as he is half illiterate."[11] He also started talking about the growing wealth of the Mapai members, saying that "Dov Yosef [a senior Mapai politician] has three villas, furnished with furniture that is not 'for everyone.' . . . The manager of Hamashbir [a chain of department stores owned by the Histadrut] owns a luxurious villa in Ramat Gan."[12] In this way Begin created a new division between the rich and the poor, although many advocates of the Revisionists were bourgeois, small traders who had a higher standard of living than the kibbutznikim.

Begin began to realize that the rivalry between Mapai and Herut went beyond the conflict between the Haganah and Etzel, so he focused the debate on the socioeconomic gap. He also started to seek unification between Herut and the General Zionists (headed by Peretz Bernstein), with whom Herut had no dispute regarding the principal social and economic issues. But the General Zionists, who were part of the government coalition, were apprehensive of accepting Begin's embrace as the prime minister still considered him a political outcast, and their fear of aligning with him sabotaged his efforts.[13] Begin waited for the right opportunity and for the time being focused on the following goal: achieving legitimacy as a national leader. Begin started objecting to Ben Gurion's slogan, "Without Herut and Maki," and declared that in fact there was a connection between Ben Gurion and the Communists because Sneh had joined Maki after retiring from Mapam. "Sneh was one of those who carried out Ben Gurion's orders to start the Saison," he clarified. Even his attitude toward Ben Gurion changed; during the 1950s, as his associates advised, he started to exercise restraint. "The MK seated to the right of Bader," as Ben Gurion usually referred to Begin, started calling the prime minister "the respondent."[14]

An example of Begin's change of style was exemplified in an argument that erupted during a Knesset debate in June 1958. "Begin belongs to the only political party that has a military wing even after the establishment of the state, a military that was disbanded only after an ultimatum was given," the prime minister reminded the ministers. However, when he raised his eyes toward the Knesset seatings, he saw that Begin was joking around with his associates, laughing and ignoring his provocation. "What is this laughter?" growled Ben Gurion. "It is because what you say is both funny and tragic," Begin peacefully explained.

Ben Gurion could not ignore Begin's apathy and continued talking in a grim tone. "The party's military wing remained active in Jerusalem until mid-September, while the state was established in May."

"But you only negotiated with me after the establishment of the state," Begin replied in a teasing tone.

"I did not negotiate with you, and I never will, and I will not speak to you."

"Which is why I am saying," Begin added, "that it's funny as well as tragic." Begin's laughter was hesitant at first but steadily grew louder and louder. The prime minister asked the Knesset chairman to admonish Begin for disorderly conduct, to which Begin reacted with triumphant smugness: "I did not disturb [the proceedings]. I smiled, and the prime minister got angry."[15]

In retrospect, it seems that this argument, which the MKs viewed as an amusing interlude, was important for the reshaping of Begin's new image. Begin made an effort to cultivate a more moderate party image as well. At the time, a student named Arie Naor (the son of MK Esther Raziel-Naor) wrote an article in *Herut* implying that the idea of expelling the Arabs from Israel was gaining support. When they met at Begin's open house, a tradition he maintained every Saturday afternoon at his home, Begin berated Naor in front of everyone and asked him, "Who taught you such things?" Begin was now careful to mute all extreme voices, though he was not the journal's official editor.[16]

Before the fourth legislative elections, held on November 3, 1959, Begin was optimistic. He was determined to market himself in new packaging, including a shaved-off mustache. The transit camps were gone, and by then most of their former residents were settled in the dozens of development towns erected in their place. Various party headquarters and all the newspapers speculated that the key to winning the elections lay in the development towns, and Sephardi candidates were placed on every political party's list of candidates.

Herut's leadership, however, was almost entirely Ashkenazi. Begin's rationale was that he did not want any discrimination and that a person's origins mattered not at all in his eyes. Begin had no problem because of this stance. Many journalists who visited the development towns were surprised that many of the residents were convinced that Begin was Moroccan and that he was responsible for "bringing us to Israel."[17] The Sephardim in the development towns were no longer new immigrants, and the situation in Israel was not strange to them. The youngsters among them had become familiar with the social gaps during their military service, and for them Begin was not only a beloved leader, but also a real alternative to the government.

During the fourth election campaign hostility in the developing towns toward Mapai became more obvious. For the first time, this was unconnected to the former Etzel members' hostility toward the establishment. The residents of Shtulim, for example, did not allow a Sephardic Mapai MK to come and talk in their moshav, while they welcomed Yaakov Meridor, an Ashkenazi, who was part of Begin's party.[18] The hostility toward Mapai did not begin, of course, in 1959, yet it was now much more evident—in part because it undermined the political status of the all-powerful Ben Gurion—and the riots that erupted in the Haifa quarter of Wadi Salib that year expressed its extreme aspect. Most young Sephardim did not know about Jabotinsky, and they certainly did not know about his teachings, but they knew they were not the only ones against whom the Mapai establishment discriminated. Therefore, despite the fact that Herut had an Ashkenazi majority and although there were "ethnic" parties with which these young Sephardim were naturally expected to affiliate, they preferred Begin, as they wanted to fit in, not to take over. Their radicalism was manifested in their aspirations for change and equal opportunity, not a revolution, as their views were built on national-traditional values rather than ethnic ideas. For this reason, for example, in the Tel Aviv Yemenite quarter only 9.3 percent voted for the Yemenite Association, while 43 percent voted for Herut. Furthermore, owing to their nationalistic perception, largely instilled in them by the institutional education system—that is, Mapai—the Mizrahi parties of the later years, such as the Black Panthers, failed to inflame the masses of Mizrahi Jews and to connect with the leftist parties, which also offered an alternative to Mapai. These parties were not considered "Jewish" enough, and their leaders' speeches about "social justice" were too broad-reaching to focus on the immediate problems of poverty and personal-national pride.

An Ashkenazi leader seeking equality while enjoying the Mizrahi culture was exactly what they desired.[19] Begin's main claim during the election rallies—"The government is implementing a tactic of dividing the nation between the Ashkenazim and the non-Ashkenazim"[20]—suited their desire to fit in rather than start a revolution. On the day before the fourth elections Begin appeared at four rallies in a matter of several hours. Because of the need to move quickly from place to place, Herut acquired two motorcycles to travel ahead of Begin's convoy and to make way for his Cadillac. Enthusiasts—teenagers from Tel Aviv's southern neighborhoods—joined the convoy. It seemed threatening. Begin enthusiastically waved in all directions, without knowing the damage his convoy would bring.[21] The election results—seventeen mandates for Herut, two seats more than in the previous Knesset—did not match the party's expectations. Against all expectations Mapai had grown stronger, and Ben Gurion, who achieved forty-seven mandates, was able to create a government. After the results were published, many believed that the motorcycle-led convoy deterred many who had considered giving Begin their vote. This was the last time Begin let motorcycles accompany his entourage.

The fourth Knesset too did not last out its term. The Lavon Affair made headlines once again, and the issue of Lavon's innocence was revived after the publication of the proceedings of a secret trial held for the "Third Man"—a double agent involved in the Affair in Egypt who was suspected of having exposed the mission operatives.[22] The government set up a committee to reinvestigate the Affair, and details from the committee meetings leaked to journalists revealed disorder and intrigue among IDF officers. In January 1961, after the committee ruled that Lavon had not given Binyamin Gibli the order (to plant explosives in Egypt) and thus was unaware of the mission, Ben Gurion resigned in protest and demanded that the Affair be investigated by "judges and not ministers."[23] Ben Gurion hoped that Begin, being a lawyer, would support his demand, but Begin did not do so, and he even ordered Arie Ben Eliezer to support Lavon's version of the Affair. He instead demanded a reinvestigation of the murder of Arlosoroff.[24] Begin's distancing from the Lavon Affair was based on political considerations, but his demand for a reinvestigation of the murder of

Arlosoroff expressed his tendency to engage in nostalgia. Begin loved to bring up old memories, and many Herut members said that during his open houses on Saturdays, they spent most of the time reveling in the past rather than discussing the present.[25]

After Ben Gurion's resignation, elections were set for August 15, 1961. Once again Begin tried to unite Herut and the General Zionists, only to suffer another failure. The General Zionists preferred to unite with the Progressives, creating the Liberal Party. Begin's failure disappointed many Herut members, who were fed up with being in the opposition. "He is a great leader in his speeches when it comes to clear and targeted tasks, like fighting against the British," said Kalman Katznelson in a provocative article published in *Haaretz*, but he fails when it comes to complex political situations, like during the Altalena affair or his attempts to unite Herut with the General Zionists. Therefore, "he who depends on Begin to perform the complicated and multi-sided task of overthrowing Mapai is simply mistaken."[26] Begin did not comment on the article, despite the controversy it aroused among Herut members.

The fifth elections did not really change the Israeli political map: Herut received the same number of seats (seventeen), and Ben Gurion once again created a coalition including Mapai, Mafdal (acronym for the National Religious Party), Achdut Haavoda, and several minority parties affiliated with Mapai. Yet the government had a majority of only sixty-eight seats, and Begin's optimism grew regarding the possibility of an overthrow.

During the negotiations for the establishment of a coalition under the direction of Levi Eshkol, Begin considered joining the government for the first time. Eshkol's offer to Bader, who represented Begin, was that Herut would join the government and receive marginal ministerial positions. A surprised Bader clarified that the proposal was not serious and that in any event he refused to join the government because of its fundamental guidelines. Eshkol commented, partly advising and partly predicting, that "if this is your stance, you will never come to power." When Bader reported the conversation to Begin, he made it clear that he had immediately informed Eshkol that Herut would not join the coalition. Yet to his surprise, Begin said that he was wrong and that he should have inquired which ministerial positions Eshkol was offering.[27]

Following the string of failures, Begin started joking about them. "They say that we hired an old Jew to call out every morning, 'Begin to power! Begin to power!' and when asked why he had chosen this job, he responded that it was a job for life. . . . He often told this joke, especially after the 'Reversal' in 1977, when he came to power."[28]

In the fifth Knesset Begin emphasized his party's liberal side, and he was the first leader of a Zionist party who proposed a diminution of the Military Administration (which was in effect from 1949 to 1966 over several geographical areas of Israel with a large Arab population), arguing that "one of the founding principles of a free country is that military commanders should monitor soldiers and civilians [should monitor] civilians." Begin did not go so far as to propose the dissolution of the Military Administration but he suggested civilian supervision over the Israeli Arabs, with a system of civil checks and balances.[29] But Ben Gurion objected, and the Knesset voted against it.

In 1963, because of growing tensions among the various generations of Mapai members, the exhausting differences of opinion, and the investigation of the Lavon Affair, Ben Gurion retired, and two years later he left Mapai and formed a new party—Rafi (acronym for the Israeli Workers' List). On June 26, Levi Eshkol, his deputy, was appointed prime minister.[30] Eshkol—a compromiser and a man of cheerful disposition—always tried to bridge the gaps among differing positions, and he was respectful toward Begin.[31] He saw Begin as a political rival, not a threat to the government, and was one of the few Mapai members who addressed him by his first name; the two would tell each other Yiddish jokes.[32]

At the end of 1963 Begin was introduced to the man who would become his confidant until his last day—Yechiel Kadishai. Kadishai, who had a sense of humor and a talent for telling stories, replaced Dov Halpert, an ultra-Orthodox convert who exchanged his typical ultra-Orthodox frock coat for a knitted yarmulke (he died of cardiac arrest in September 1963). Begin's chauffeur, Yoske Giladi, who knew Kadishai, recommended him for the job. Kadishai was first appointed as party secretary and shortly thereafter became Begin's confidant and personal assistant. Kadishai had a great impact on Begin, and it was thanks to him, in part, that Begin adopted a more subdued attitude toward his political rivals. When he first started working for Begin, Kadishai's major task was to decipher Begin's handwriting and to make his articles readable for the typist.[33] Their first joint mission was to transfer Jabotinsky's bones to Israel.

In his will Jabotinsky stated that he wished to be reinterred in Israel by order of the government. Ever since the establishment of the state of Israel, Begin had been requesting that the Beitar commander's remains be brought to the country, both to satisfy Jabotinsky's final wish and because he thought that Jabotinsky's reinterment in Israel would finally legitimize Herut. But Ben Gurion used to dismiss his request, saying that the country needed live Jews, not dead ones. When Eshkol became prime minister, during one of their first meetings Begin again requested that Jabotinsky's remains be brought to Israel. Eshkol most likely knew about Jabotinsky's will, but he said innocently, "Who is stopping you from doing so?" Begin explained that he would be violating the will if Jabotinsky's remains were reinterred without the government's permission. Eshkol saw this as an opportunity to mitigate the historic rivalry and asked to review the will.[34]

Without involving the other party members, Begin asked Kadishai to obtain a copy of the will. He formally handed it to Eshkol, who promised Begin that he would raise the topic at a government meeting and asked him to speak of it to no one. Begin returned from Eshkol's home to the Knesset cafeteria, and while trying to hide the smile on his face, he whispered to Kadishai, "They are about to bring the remains of Beitar's head to Israel." Kadishai promised not to tell anyone, although several days later he saw Begin huddled with one of the MKs. His facial expression indicated that he had told the MK and sworn him to secrecy as well. A few days later it was decided to approve Begin's request.

Before he instructed his men to start arranging for the reinterment, Begin asked Eri Jabotinsky if it was enough that the government had approved the request or if the will required that the government order it. Eri was satisfied with the government approval since he had received a private letter from Eshkol clarifying that the approval was actually an order. When Begin realized that the government would not make military vehicles available for carrying the coffin, he arranged to hire a private pickup truck and to paint it military olive green. After the funeral the truck was repainted its original color.[35]

"I inform the Jewish people in their country, and in the Diaspora from East to West, that forty-six years after he fought with a battalion of Hebrew soldiers for returning the land of Israel to its rightful owner—the people of Israel—and thirty-five years after he was exiled because of his battle for the establishment of a modern-day Jewish state, twenty-four years after his passing, and sixteen years after the removal of the foreign government from our land—Jabotinsky has returned to his homeland," Begin said at the state ceremony held in the presence of the president and a paratrooper unit. The burial ceremony for Johanna—whose remains were also brought to Israel—and Ze'ev

Jabotinsky on Mount Herzl was the dawning of a new era. As Begin had envisioned, bringing Jabotinsky's remains to Israel served as official recognition of the importance of the revisionist camp and legitimized his leadership.[36]

During the term of the fifth Knesset, Mapai and Achdut Haavoda were consolidated, and in 1965 they established the country's main Zionist party—Hamaarach (the Alignment). Beforehand, Begin had continued his efforts to unite Herut and the Liberal Party, the result of the unification of the General Zionists and the Progressives.[37] Begin was prepared for ideological compromise as well. As a disciple of Jabotinsky, who in the 1930s wrote his famous article "Ja, Brechen" (Yes, Break [in Yiddish]) in the publication *Chazit Haam* (People's Front) about the struggle against the Histadrut,[38] Begin decided that Herut would run in the elections for the Histadrut, despite the damage this could cause for the National Labor Federation in Eretz Israel (NLF), which was established by the Revisionists.

Most Herut members who convened for a conference in January 1963 to discuss this topic were against the decision, as they thought it would severely harm the party's anti-socialist tradition.[39] Begin was aware of the conference's historical significance and remained silent. He asked Ben Eliezer to address the crowd in his place. In his speech Ben Eliezer said that the Histadrut was "not what it used to be," so there was no point in remaining hostile toward the organization. But the shouts from the crowd—"That's what they say about Germany"—testified to the fact that Herut was not yet able to forget.[40] Only when things started spiraling out of control did Begin decide to address the crowd. "This is the best option for hitting Mapai in every place, even at its base. There are thousands, perhaps tens of thousands, of Herut supporters in the Histadrut; this decision will give them a home until the red flag becomes blue and white and Mapai gradually loses its power," he said. His speech calmed the few objectors to his proposal, which passed by a majority of a mere sixteen votes. Begin demanded a second vote to "demonstrate the movement's unity," and the proposal was accepted a second time, this time by a majority of eighty-eight votes.

This was not Begin's last ideological compromise. Because he found it hard to reach an agreement with Yosef Sapir, chairman of the Liberal Party, Begin agreed that in the platform common to the two parties, only Herut would be required to maintain the "indisputable right to the land of Israel."[41] This time he aroused the objections of his close associates, including Bader and Landau. "It would be disastrous for us if we compromised with the Liberals over the definition of the whole land of Israel," Landau said.[42] But Begin insisted, in a burst of surprising pragmatism that alarmed the former Etzel members, that this was the only path to power.[43]

Ahead of the sixth general elections, the "Gush [bloc (Hebrew)] Herut-Liberalim" (acronym Gahal) was established. To overcome the bureaucratic difficulties raised by the union, Begin decided to be satisfied with the establishment of a parliamentary bloc and did not establish a new party. The political statement in the establishment of Gahal was clear: one could manage without Herut, but would it be possible without Gahal?[44] When Gahal was established, the attitude to Begin changed. A *Haaretz* article titled "Has Begin Changed?" said that Begin was no longer a "violent dissident." It was an extraordinary article to be published in one of the nonpartisan publications that generally did not refer to Begin as a leader of stature. One of the first to identify the new trend was Ben Gurion, who led Rafi into the sixth elections alongside Shimon Peres and Moshe Dayan. Ben Gurion was quick to repeat that "Herut supporters are Nazi-Jews," but he sounded anachronistic, and Begin, who responded to his comments by pleading, "Jews, do not hate Jews," suddenly sounded more rational and conciliatory.[45] Before the elections Mapai distributed a photograph of Begin taken during his Zion Square balcony speech against the Reparations Agreement to remind the public that he was still a dangerous man. Begin himself added fuel to the fire by demanding a national day of mourning in May 1965, on the day Germany's first ambassador to Israel was to arrive; by so doing, he raised anew the debate over his conduct in 1952.[46]

But the main reason for the surprising defeat Gahal suffered in the elections (twenty-six seats; in the previous Knesset each party separately had received seventeen) is that the public was not yet ready for the alternative Begin offered, and the man with the problematic image was blamed for the damage caused to the new bloc. It was obvious that there was no substitute for Begin as a combative opposition leader; however, it seemed that in order to increase the number of Gahal voters it would be necessary to replace him with someone more conventional.

Gahal's defeat in the elections caused unrest mostly among the young party members. One of them was Ehud Olmert, a prominent activist in Herut's student wing and the son of Mordechai Olmert, a member of the third and fourth Knessets. During the June 1966 party conference, the young Olmert made an unprecedented proposal: remove the obstacle from the party—that is, dismiss Begin. This was the first time that a Herut member had demanded that Begin be dismissed from the party's leadership; in the past, his most prominent objectors, Hillel Kook and Eri Jabotinsky, had preferred to retire rather than challenge his leadership.

Members of Herut said that Olmert was personally avenging his father's fight with Begin, who had removed the senior Olmert from the list of candidates for the fifth Knesset because Olmert and Begin disagreed regarding the separation of religion from the state. However, the junior Olmert had dared to say what no one in Herut had had the nerve to say—that is, that Begin was unable to lead the entire nation and that he actually felt more comfortable in the opposition. Begin's announcement at the opening of the conference that "the movement does not need a leader who will guide it to power but to the path of truth and integrity" reinforced his opponents' claims, and they formed a group of dissidents led by Shmuel Tamir, Herut's rising star since the Kastner trial.[47] Paradoxically, Begin was also damaged by the failure of Ben Gurion, whose new party, Rafi, received only ten seats in the sixth Knesset. A new opinion was forming among the public that it was time to replace the old leaders, together with their ideological fixations, with some fresh political blood.[48] Ironically, *Herut*, the party's newspaper, shut down the same year (the official reason being economic difficulties).

Tamir walked on eggshells during his struggle against Begin. He asked to be elected executive chairman and expressed his support for another term of Begin's leadership, but as a member of the executive, he set himself the goal to increase his influence on Central Committee members who would be elected at the conference, thereby toning down Begin's power within the party. Tamir also disagreed with the ideological agenda of Begin, who in his speech at the conference tried once more to raise the issue of Greater Israel and Israel's relations with Germany. Tamir demanded the initiation of peace negotiations with Arab countries and a change in the income tax system. *Haaretz* reported that finally "a Herut MK is stirring the Knesset on current topics and isn't dwelling on the past."[49]

During the first two days of the conference, Amichai Paglin and Eitan Livni, two former Etzel officers, accompanied Begin, who wished to demonstrate who was the original and who was the imitation. But Tamir was equally cunning, and during his speech he pointed out incidentally that "Paglin too supports me." Although he sided with Tamir,

Paglin could not directly express his views against his commander and prepared to take the podium shortly before the vote in order to clarify his position. But to many delegates, Tamir's statement branded Paglin as a traitor to Begin, and they tried to beat him on his way to the podium. A riot broke out, and Begin himself stepped up to the podium saying, "I will defend Amichai; let him speak."[50] When the commotion died down, it turned out that Begin's dramatic gestures had not created the desired effect, and Tamir's proposal to be elected executive chairman was accepted.

Several minutes later Begin decided to retire, without consulting anyone. On June 28, the third day of the conference, Begin gave a speech full of rage and self-pity, saying that "a chapter in the movement's life had ended," among other things, and that if he were indeed standing in the way of the party's success, he would step down and give up his Knesset seat. It was a confused speech that reminded the party veterans of his speech after the *Altalena* affair. Begin asked the delegates, "Is this how Mapai would have treated Eshkol?" adding, "And what have I done to Ben Gurion that he hates me so?"[51] He spoke like a betrayed father and not like the head of a democratic movement,[52] and his opponents were reminded of Jabotinsky's nobility when the young Begin had defeated him in the Beitar conference in 1938.

Begin's speech created an uproar. Paglin and Livni tried to persuade him otherwise, and Ben Eliezer announced that Begin would always be a moral authority. But the turmoil did not die down, and the conference became a scene of fighting and cursing (the rebellious young Olmert ducked a second before being punched). Begin himself intervened between his opponents and his supporters, who were shouting "We do not accept your resignation, father," "A father doesn't leave," and "Don't go, father."[53]

Members loyal to Begin went up to the podium one by one, and the expressions of sorrow and grief demonstrated how much Herut was a family movement, patriarchal and undemocratic in its political culture. Esther Raziel-Naor said, with her voice breaking, that if not for Begin, they would not have managed to set up a party after the disbandment of the Resistance, and another party member bowed down to Begin, shouting, "You are God." The drama reached a peak when party delegate Shraga Yoram shouted, "Father, dear father, today we are going to the cemetery," and compared him to Moses, "who also did not quit when Korakh incited all the people against Moses." Begin listened to the appeals with a frozen expression, but upon hearing Yoram's exclamations, he said, without hiding his pleasure, "At least in terms of my age, I cannot be your father."[54]

The newspapers reported that the conference was "the best show in town," and Begin's supporters' melodramatic behavior was described with amazement and ridicule.[55]

As with his threat after the second elections, when he had announced that he was going to retire yet did not stick to his word, Begin again did not return his Knesset seat to the party but rather simply stopped functioning as party chairman. Meanwhile, he continued to attend the party's meetings, despite the fact that he was no longer the official leader, and to take part in purposeless activities—mainly in positioning members in the movement's internal courts. In his personal conversations he mostly employed an emotional blackmail bordering on mental violence. The party was paralyzed for almost eight months because of his presence-absence.

One of the party delegates left a meeting with Begin with tears in his eyes. He found it unbearably difficult to deny Begin, who told him, "This [topic of discussion] is a matter of life and death and I will never again turn to you on this issue."[56] One member of the Liberal Party could not understand what Begin meant when he approached him and said, "Who asked you to be loyal to me? Be faithful to the party." Begin repeated this statement in all his meetings with party delegates and activists, who did not understand the difference between faithfulness to the party and personal loyalty.[57]

During the months of his "retirement" Begin continued to harass his fellow party members. After seeing David Yotan, a friend from the Beitar days, applauding at the end of Tamir's speech, he wrote to him saying, "I cannot consider you as my friend any more. Do not approach me, neither directly nor by letter."[58] In one of the debates in which he participated he wondered aloud, "Who ignited such a fire in you, dear party? Wonderful party, who has sparked this foreign fire?"[59] Few knew that the reference to the "foreign fire" was taken from Leviticus 10:1, where a foreign fire possessed the tabernacle. By so saying, Begin insinuated that Herut was the tabernacle, and along these lines, it was not difficult to understand to whom he compared himself in the analogy. When a certain party activist would not carry out Begin's wishes, he told him not to look him in the eyes, as if he was unworthy of doing so. "Why are you looking at me all the time with those eyes? I've already seen that you have beautiful eyes," he said. He also blatantly insisted, more than once, "Do not call me by my first name."[60]

Aliza, who took the insults against her husband personally, was not inclined to forgive easily. She bore a grudge against Paglin and Shraga Alis, Paglin's deputy in the underground, and sent them a message that they were not welcome to attend her open house on Saturdays. Begin tried to appeal to her sympathy. He explained that these were the rules of the game in politics and that they did not object to him, as Tamir had claimed. But Aliza insisted: they had betrayed Menachem. Shortly before the Six-Day War broke out, when Begin was already a minister and the national atmosphere was one of unity, Paglin and Alis decided it was time for reconciliation. Since Paglin was by then a member of a new party, Hamerkaz Hachofshi (the Free Center), set up by Shmuel Tamir, he was too proud to call Begin. Therefore Alis phoned "Sir," which was how he referred to Begin directly, and told him that given the situation, "Amichai and I want to talk to you." Begin granted their request and invited them to his home, among other reasons because the Waiting Period before the war (a period of several weeks when the mobilized army waited expectantly under camouflage nettings and the public grew steadily more apprehensive, digging slit trenches and air-raid shelters in backyards and public parks) increased his sense of nostalgia for their joint days in the underground.[61]

Paglin and Alis knocked on Begin's door, but when Aliza opened it and saw who it was, she slammed the door in their faces even before they had a chance to say hello. They knocked again, embarrassed and hesitant. When Begin asked Aliza who was at the door, she would not respond. Begin understood, went to the door, and invited them into the living room. At the end of their conversation Begin opened a bottle of wine in light of their "reconciliation." Alis realized that the reconciliation would not be complete without Aliza's forgiveness and asked that she join them for a toast. Begin went to the kitchen, where Aliza was waiting, but after seeing her pensive expression, he returned to the living room and told his former subordinates, "Forget it; you know how it is with women."[62]

TEN

THE BREAKTHROUGH

In February 1967 Begin was reinstated as party chairman, almost by chance. An inquiry committee established at the request of Begin loyalists found that a slanderous letter against Begin, published in the letters to the editor section in *Haaretz* and purportedly written by a man named Chaim Amsterdam, was in fact written by one of Tamir's supporters, Shimshon Rosenbaum.[1] The commission was headed by Bader, who argued that this was an act of deception the likes of which had never been committed in the history of the movement. Begin himself remained silent, but when he was asked to rejoin the party to "clear the air," he agreed. (During the months after Begin's resignation Gahal did not have an official chairman as no one dared appoint a replacement.)

Herut was a democratic party and a legally elected institution, yet party members were loyal to Begin more than to any person or idea. Unlike the Mapai leaders, who utilized their political clout to appoint members to positions of power and to bestow favors, Begin drew his absolute power from personal relationships with party activists. He preferred personal interaction. "So how are the kids? The family?" he would flatteringly ask his political activists even during the most important political meetings. Like Ben Gurion, he utilized his superior memory during political gatherings, but unlike Ben Gurion, whose attitude was matter of fact, Begin would express his personal fondness for each member. But he also knew how to rapidly switch from personal interest to biting frost when someone displeased him. When he retracted someone's invitation to the open house he held at his home on Saturdays, everyone knew he was angry. That was the most severe punishment in a movement that valued militaristic ceremonies and leader worship. Through personal influence, Begin bypassed the party apparatus and his views became the party's direct ideology, even when they changed—like his decision to return the Sinai Peninsula to Egypt in 1978.[2] Begin's charisma was also based on the fact that he had become a symbol in his own lifetime. Party members believed that harming Begin was synonymous with doing damage to Israel and surrendering to the dictates of Mapai. Begin was a symbol in the eyes of his objectors as well, and everyone knew that without him Herut would never succeed.

When it became clear that Tamir was behind the letter published in *Haaretz*, the Herut management suspended him from the party for a year, and in response Tamir established Hamerkaz Hachofshi.[3] The majority of the members who joined the new party were former Herut intellectuals who had despaired of any possibility of making a change within Herut. The establishment of Hamerkaz Hachofshi hit Begin in his soft underbelly. Tamir emphasized that Begin had been opposed to the 1947 partition plan and to the group of liberals identified with Hillel Kook. He added that Begin had been opposed to the disbandment of the Etzel branch in Jerusalem even after the establishment of Israel and stressed that Begin was responsible for the eighteen-year delay in Herut's uniting with the Liberal Party owing to his adamant and bullheaded adherence to the slogan "Two sides of the Jordan River." Since the Hamerkaz Hachofshi leaders were Jabotinsky loyalists, their portrayal of Begin as a stumbling block and an anachronistic and stubborn leader damaged his image.

Tamir insulted Begin on a personal level too. He invited Amichai Paglin to join the party after he had previously announced that Begin was "no longer suitable to lead Herut" and that his leadership was undemocratic. Paglin also spoke publicly of Begin's reluctance to hang the two British sergeants during the underground days.[4] Furthermore, Eri Jabotinsky also joined Hamerkaz Hachofshi and pressured Begin to give up his seat, explicitly stating that Begin was not upholding his father's legacy.[5]

The hostility expressed toward Begin by the Revisionist intellectuals reflected the general public's attitude toward him. Because of his radical stance, Begin had few opponents or supporters and multitudes of admirers and haters. He was a contradictory leader. His speeches were venomous at times, but he also expressed humanitarian positions that were rare even among the leftist parties. He was careful to uphold his commitments but continued to engage in trivial political matters within the party. He interjected Latin quotations into his speeches, yet his cultural preferences were somewhat provincial; most of the books in his library were on history, and he read almost no philosophy, poetry, or art.[6] His austerity bordered on asceticism, but he also had an appetite for insulting and annoying his rivals. Outside party ranks, Begin's prolonged activity as the main opposition leader paradoxically testified mostly to his electoral weakness rather than to his seniority and experience. In fact, Herut had become Israel's conservative party, an almost historical nature preserve, and its politicos were not optimistic for its future. However, if the 1952 Reparations Agreement was the catalyst for Begin's rise to politics, in 1967 he was saved by the Six-Day War. Begin was inserted into the government—thus changing his image—not by the voters but by several hundred thousand Egyptian soldiers, thanks to whom he made his most important political move toward achieving legitimacy among the citizens of Israel.

On May 15, 1967, Israel's Independence Day, Egyptian troops advanced toward the Sinai Peninsula. Israel was surprised by the move. Yitzhak Rabin, chief of staff at the time, was updated on the developments while watching the Independence Day military parade, and he immediately reported them to Prime Minister Levi Eshkol, who was sitting by his side. Eight days later Egypt's president, Gamal Abdel Nasser, ordered his forces to block the Straits of Tiran.

Egypt's military actions heightened the tensions that had built over the recent months among Israel, Egypt, and Syria. The general staff deemed that a war would be the only way to relieve the tensions and that if Israel wanted to be victorious, it would have to conduct a surprise attack. The times in Israel were difficult: the economy had not yet recovered from a prolonged recession, and the prevailing atmosphere of fear grew with the feeling that Eshkol was too weak a leader for what was needed in those trying times. (*All the Eshkol Jokes*, a booklet ridiculing his abilities, was distributed across the country.) Senior IDF commanders took advantage of this situation and pushed for a military operation.[7] One of those who contributed immensely to the tensions during the Waiting Period preceding the Six-Day War was the first prime minister, David Ben Gurion. In 1967, the eighty-one-year-old Ben Gurion was the oldest and most bitter of the MKs. After Rafi's failure he often slandered Eshkol in interviews. His warnings against the prime minister's limited capabilities exacerbated the despair prevailing in the country.

Eventually it was understood that the Six-Day War broke out not only because of the Arab states' desire to destroy the Zionist state, as the Arab leaders arrogantly claimed. It was also the result of bad assessments and complex considerations, including Israel's interests unrelated to its security.[8] But during the Waiting Period, the Israeli public was affected by the threats of the Arab leaders, especially those of Egypt and Syria. "We will hang the last imperialist soldier by the intestines of the last Zionist," Radio Damascus announced in late May 1967, and the radio station Voice of the UAR from Cairo vowed that the day of the "destruction of Israel" was nearing.[9] The anxiety that gripped the public also affected the political system. Eshkol's precarious position led the government to search for a leader who would be strong and stable enough to rely on. In the last week of May, as Chief of Staff Yitzhak Rabin was swallowing anti-anxiety medication to overcome his stress and nicotine poisoning (the public knew nothing of this), Shimon Peres, then a Rafi Knesset member, presented an inspired idea: disband the government and create a coalition based on a union among Mapai, Rafi, and Gahal. According to the plan, Peres explained to Begin in the Knesset cafeteria, Ben Gurion would return as prime minister, and if Eshkol refused, Ben Gurion would at least return to the defense ministry and conduct the war.

Peres did not have to work too hard to convince Begin, who tended to see this event as a "historical hour" and who privately expressed anxiety for the fate of his people. "This is a profound threat," he described the situation,[10] and claimed that the Arabs should be believed, "at least when they say they intend to destroy us."[11] Begin also saw a golden political opportunity in Peres's idea, as this was the first time that Mapai leaders and Begin would possibly be seated in the same government. Peres estimated that Eshkol would object to Ben Gurion's return to center stage, yet in an effort to persuade him to abandon his personal considerations, Peres thought it would be fitting to send Begin—Ben Gurion's mythological rival, of all people—to talk to Eshkol. Begin agreed. He was even enthusiastic about it. They parted with a handshake, and Begin asked Kadishai to set up a meeting with Eshkol.

Unlike his image, Eshkol did not hesitate to respond. Because of his strained relationship with Ben Gurion he stated that "these two horses will never be able to pull the wagon together."[12] Nevertheless, Begin decided to check what Ben Gurion thought about the idea. He avoided convening the Gahal center and consulted no one. Begin knew that his effort to persuade Ben Gurion to return as prime minister or minister of defense would arouse speculation, despite the fact that it was an opportunity for him to join the government.

Begin's rare visit to Ben Gurion's house in the very middle of the Waiting Period did not raise too many questions among the general public, but his colleagues were not enthusiastic. Chaim Landau could not believe it when Begin told him where he was heading. "Why?" he wondered. He had not forgotten Begin's moving exclamation at the convention when he had announced his retirement: "What have I done to Ben Gurion that he hates me so?" Bader was also appalled. He believed that going to Ben Gurion was not that different from going to Canossa, and he tried to persuade him not to go. But Begin insisted that he needed to do it. Bader asked Ben Eliezer and Landau, "How did you allow him to do this?" They saw it as a humiliating surrender of the leader of the Revisionist camp.

Begin's decision to court Ben Gurion testified to his understanding of his position in the political hierarchy. Though he was aware of the great damage Ben Gurion could cause him, he recognized his authority and did not despise him as a person. "Though no one has hurt me more than Ben Gurion," he insisted during a conversation with his friends, who tried to convince him not to go, "these times call for a prime minister who has the people's trust, and that is Ben Gurion."[13] His insistence suggests that at times of need he knew how to ignore his personal resentments and act on the state's behalf. Begin's actions also testify to his impressive stamina for political maneuvering—after all, he was a skilled politician, as shrewd as his rivals. He knew all too well that Gahal was in distress, and just as he had supported the establishment of a faction of Herut in the Histadrut and during the merger with the Liberal Party, he was astute enough to abandon the old conventions in order to escape a political vacuum. He wanted, therefore, to take full advantage of the new situation and began to think aloud of the possibilities inherent in cooperating with his old rivals. But it was important to him to note that this was not only contemporary politics. He reminded his friends that Etzel knew that Ben Gurion had sent a messenger to ask him to announce the establishment of the state as the Etzel commander if Ben Gurion had political difficulty making the announcement,[14] proving that in fact their cooperation was not a new phenomenon.

Ben Gurion was bitter and angry in the meeting with Begin and accused the government of hastening to go to war without coordinating with the United States and the West, in contrast to his traditional policy. He claimed that a surprise attack should be executed only after U.S. approval and repeated that Eshkol must be dismissed immediately.

Only then did Begin realize that Ben Gurion, long considered the nation's powerful founding father, was even more doubtful about the preemptive military operation than Eshkol, who was considered indecisive.

Begin was disappointed by Ben Gurion's stance, and he also knew that the proposal to reinstate him as prime minister raised strong objections in Mapai, especially from Eshkol and Golda Meir;[15] nonetheless, he persisted in his efforts to persuade Eshkol to include Ben Gurion. Like he did in his speeches, he attempted to appeal to Eshkol's emotions. "The moral validity behind my request," he clarified, "is that things between me and Ben Gurion are more difficult."[16] (In other words, while Ben Gurion was also his opponent, in times of trouble for Israel, Jews should be united.) But Eshkol also refused to have Ben Gurion appointed as defense minister (even though Ben Gurion did not authorize Begin to discuss this personal matter with Eshkol). The possibility that the "Old Man" would return to the government was off the table for good.

Peres, therefore, presented a new proposal: the establishment of a national unity government that would include Rafi and Gahal, with Moshe Dayan, on behalf of Rafi, as defense minister. Eshkol was reluctant to give up his position; he agreed that Begin should join the government but expressed reservations regarding the inclusion of Rafi. But Begin, as well as the Mafdal, made it clear that he would not join without Rafi because it was important for him to be faithful to Peres, his partner in the political initiative; because he was in awe of Moshe Dayan; and because a unity government would be an opportunity to weaken Mapai's power. Unifying Gahal, Rafi, and the Mafdal might undermine Mapai—after the war, of course.

On June 1, five days before the war, after a meeting of the Mapai center, Golda Meir announced that the political situation had ripened for the creation of a unity government: Begin and Yosef Sapir of Gahal would be appointed ministers without portfolio, and Dayan would be appointed defense minister, over Eshkol's objections.[17] Nineteen years after he was first elected to the Knesset, Begin finally joined the government. The night before his first cabinet meeting Begin asked Ben Eliezer and Bader to join him for the journey to Jerusalem. In the midst of preparations for the war he stopped to see Rabbi Arie Levin, the underground prisoners' rabbi, to get his blessing.[18]

On his first day in the conference room Begin embraced Rabin—perhaps because he noticed the distress on Rabin's face or perhaps because he himself was excited—and said, partly on behalf of Herut and partly on behalf of the entire nation, "We are proud of you." Rabin, as usual, smiled embarrassedly.[19] Yet this time, for a change, Begin's dramatic gestures were taken positively; the anxious ministers needed encouragement.

No one expected that Begin, a minister without portfolio, would affect the course of the war. The operational plans had already been prepared, and his participation in the first meeting had been hastily arranged before the Knesset approved his appointment. His main contribution was to raise morale; the very fact that he was sitting in the cabinet was perceived as a consolidation of the people and as paving the way for Dayan's appointment as defense minister.

But sitting in the government considerably influenced his image and his political career. On June 4, a day before Israel attacked Egypt's airfields, the annual memorial service was held for the Olei Hagardom (underground warriors hanged on the gallows). For the first time in the history of the state an IDF unit presented arms in honor of Etzel fighters. This was also the first time Begin was absent from the ceremony because he was participating in a cabinet meeting, and his absence also had a symbolic aspect: the eternal opposition leader had chosen officialdom.[20] Despite the fact that in principle Begin supported a preventive attack, in the cabinet meeting the day before the war broke out he proposed that the chief of Mossad (the national intelligence agency) be sent to the Western capitals to explain Israel's predicament, even at the cost of delaying an attack by several days.[21] Despite the opinions he often expressed and despite his image, within the government Begin was cautious, and Eshkol and his fellow ministers valued his discretion.

The Six-Day War broke out on June 5, 1967. Within a few hours the Israeli Air Force (IAF) had destroyed the air forces of Egypt, Jordan, and Syria while they were still on the ground, paving the way for victory by the ground forces.[22] When the IAF's success became known, Begin encouraged Defense Minister Dayan to move ahead and seize Jerusalem. On the second day of fighting Begin could already imagine the entire cabinet and both the chief rabbis saying the Shehechyanu prayer at the Western Wall. "We must utilize this historic opportunity," he claimed. But Eshkol hesitated, and Dayan chose first to encircle the Old City, hoping it would surrender without a fight.[23] Begin's fantasy raised several eyebrows. But as usual, almost without fail, his intuition was on the mark: he immediately realized the war's historical significance and its consequences, though even in his euphoric moments he did not raise the possibility of conquering the eastern banks of the Jordan River, the long-held Revisionist wish.

Even as a minister Begin gleaned most of his information from the radio and compared what he heard with the chief of staff's reports. On June 7, the third day of the war, Begin had trouble falling asleep. He got up, turned on the radio, and listened, as usual, to the BBC. In the morning he heard that the Security Council was expected to declare a cease-fire. He was concerned that the military operation would end and decided to call Dayan. "Moshe, we must make haste and conquer Jerusalem," he warned.[24] Dayan, who was still a bit sleepy, referred him to the prime minister, not forgetting to mention bitingly that he "needed no advice on the matter." But Begin insisted, and Dayan promised that he would hold a meeting to discuss it.[25]

At a 7 a.m. meeting the next day, Eshkol, Dayan, Galili, and Allon decided that it was time to take the Old City. Paratrooper Brigade 55 conquered the city almost without resistance, and before noon brigade commander Mordechai (Motta) Gur made his now famous report: "The Temple Mount is ours!"[26] Jerusalem, the most important symbol in the history of the Jewish people, was reunited. Capturing the city evoked great excitement among Jews both in Israel and abroad—religious, secular, and members of Zionist parties of all shades of the rainbow.

During the war Begin was known for his influence as a peacemaker between rival ministers. In the government, unlike in the Knesset, he took it upon himself to be the national reconciler, a role he filled very successfully as most of the ministers still saw him as an outsider and therefore a neutral arbitrator. On the fourth day of the war, when the government learned that Dayan had ordered the IDF to conquer the Golan Heights without consulting with Eshkol, a debate arose over his bypassing the prime minister. "There is something of an aesthetic defect in this," Begin told Yaakov Shimshon Shapira, the minister of justice, in an attempt to quell his anger, "but we should learn from Austria's history." Begin told the ministers that during the reign of Empress Maria Theresa, a soldier who had committed a heroic deed while breaking discipline would be both reprimanded and issued a medal.[27] For the ministers, euphoric over the reports of the IDF successes, it was enough. But Begin did not have to relate stories from distant lands to appease the ministers; he could also tell them that during his days as Etzel commander, he had more than once accepted responsibility for actions executed without his prior approval. The outcome of the war strengthened Begin's legitimacy and status in the political system.[28] Israel's victories in the Gaza Strip, the Sinai, the Golan Heights, the Old City, and the territories west of the Jordan River in six days had great religious significance—and this was exactly what Begin had talked about in his days in the opposition.

After the battles subsided, Israeli citizens flocked to the Jewish holy places. Hundreds of thousands gathered at the Western Wall. The direct connection between biblical times and the days of the Palmach that Ben Gurion so much loved to talk about took physical shape before their eyes. In this prevailing atmosphere Begin's biblical imagery suited the vision of Ben Gurion and Mapai, who did not want to see the Holocaust as part of the continuity of Jewish existence and wished to establish a people proud of its heritage.[29] The change in mood in Israel after the war was extreme—a rapid shift from depression to mania, from fear to arrogance. The overwhelming victory, after an agonizing waiting period and tremendous anxiety, provoked a wave of happiness, admiration for the IDF and its commanders, and euphoria about Israel and its capabilities. And Begin was the right leader in the right time and place. His melodramatic character suited the general ambience.

When the war ended, Begin demanded, as minister without portfolio, to review all government documents dealing with the occupied territories.[30] "Even if we disagree about future proposals for resolving the conflict in the Middle East," Begin told Foreign Minister Abba Eban, "let's agree in the meantime that all drafts mentioning the option of giving back the territories should say to 'hand over' instead of 'return.'"[31] Begin's devotion to semantics and grandiose statements no longer raised ridicule (it was he who coined the phrase "the estate of our forefathers"). For example, he objected to the name chosen for the war—the Six-Day War—which was selected with Eshkol's consent, and preferred "the War of Redemption."[32] In his speeches he tended to refer wistfully to the Maccabean victory and saw the IDF triumph in the Six-Day War as equivalent to it. He also referred individually to many IDF officers as "Our Yehudah Hamaccabi."[33]

In the current situation Begin did not find it hard to explain his decision to remain in the government after the war had ended. In fact, the new national mood narrowed the political gap between Gahal and Mapai. Golda Meir expressed a willingness, in principle, to make territorial concessions and did not reject a future return of the occupied territories as part of a political agreement, but she estimated that the Arabs were not yet ready to enter a peace process, and this position also reduced the gap between Begin's viewpoints and those of the Mapai chiefs.[34]

But a large gap remained on one issue of principle: Mapai's leaders saw most of the occupied territories as a military security zone and a political bargaining chip, while Begin thought of them in metaphysical terms and saw himself as the protector of the walls of Israel. Thus, for example, he proposed to change the wording of the governmental decision for uniting Jerusalem as a municipal union and sought to emphasize the unification's historical aspect. "Jerusalem was not unified in order to solve the problem of garbage in the streets," he said.[35] But Begin's enthusiasm never distracted him from the issue of the population in the occupied territories. He was among the first to say in a cabinet meeting that the refugee issue was a "significant moral problem," yet he was satisfied with the tenuous solution of a mini-transfer. "Some of them should to be settled in El Arish," he said.[36]

The new political alignment in Israel after the war and the blurring of differences between Right and Left was particularly evident in the Movement for a Greater Israel. This new movement established a common ground among intellectuals from the Left and the Right who circulated a petition demanding that the occupied territories never be returned. Among those who signed the petition were S. Y. Agnon, Natan Alterman, Uri Tzvi Greenberg, Moshe Shamir, and Chaim Guri. In a letter Begin wrote to Chaim Herzog (a popular military commentator during the war, later president of Israel) he claimed that the new situation was a paradox connecting Achdut Haavoda and Herut.[37] The winds of nationalism blew across the board, not only among the leftists. As long as Chaim Moshe Shapira led the Mafdal, he prevented the approval of overt extremist positions. After the war it was no longer possible to avert the influence of Gush Emunim—the messianic political movement spearheaded by Chanan Porat and Rabbi Moshe Levinger—over the spirit of religious Zionism.

On some issues Begin became more moderate than the leftists in the Movement for a Greater Israel. When Moshe Dayan considered suggesting a vote on the annexation of "Judea and Samaria" (as the West Bank began to be called by the Movement for a Greater Israel and its supporters), Begin was one of the most vehement objectors. While he supported the annexation of Jerusalem, he claimed that the majority in the government would reject an annexation of "Judea and Samaria," and "We don't want to be placed in that position";[38] it was an argument that could not be more convincing, nor more in line with the Mapai spirit. He also objected for personal reasons: Begin could not remain in a government that formally rejected such a proposal, and he did not intend to leave just yet. Siding with Golda Meir, Begin became one of the major supporters of the decision that Israel "was in no hurry" to express its willingness for a political settlement.[39] After the war, Begin freely expressed his views in and outside cabinet meetings. At a Herut conference he showed that he had been influenced by the arrogance of most Israelis after the war. During the conference rumors spread that King Hussein of Jordan was planning to conquer the West Bank, and in response Begin declared, "Hussein's attempt to conquer the West Bank is suicidal, though there is no international law prohibiting suicide." His main argument was that the Israeli-Arab conflict was not territorial but rather that "our enemies aspire to commit a crime of genocide."[40]

In those days, Begin was supercilious, like many Israeli politicians, and was enthusiastic about state trips abroad to tell the story of the great victory. In September 1967 he set off for a private visit to Switzerland, and in November he went on a three-week trip to the United States, Canada, and Mexico.[41] In May 1968 he traveled to Latin America, and shortly after his return he took off for the United States.[42] Newspapers harshly criticized him for his many trips. Yet Begin traveled often not because he liked it, but rather because he finally had the legitimacy for which he had yearned. When in the opposition, he had hardly ever spoken to listeners other than the Revisionists, and he gained much satisfaction from the broadening of his audience.[43]

In 1968 the ninth Herut conference was held for the first time in Jerusalem, and it was also the first time Begin participated as a member of government. He arrived in his official car, evoking much interest and curiosity among the participants. At the conference, an announcement was made that for the first time, underground fighters would receive a national medal.[44] The previous conference and Begin's struggle for political survival were forgotten. This time, he announced that he would give a carefully weighed speech.

Begin entered the plaza like a king, smiling at everyone. After making his rounds, he mounted the stage and waited patiently, somewhat amused and somewhat polite, for the applause to end. As he had fallen in love with "the national responsibility now borne by the party," he began his speech only after reading Ben Gurion's blessing out loud. At the outset he asked the audience to stand at attention and pulled out a black yarmulke from his pocket. After reading some passages from the Book of Psalms, he announced in Latin, *O vos audite me, audite gentes—Jerusalem, et non perit resurrexit!* (Hear me O you peoples, listen O you nations—Jerusalem is not lost and has risen again!). But his words fell on the ears of delegates who did not understand Latin (except for maybe Yochanan Bader and several other veteran Revisionists). His use of Latin impressed the audience and testified to the fact that the crowd's admiration for him overshadowed all reason, as if there was no need to understand his words. Begin excited the audience, which took in his every movement and gesture. "Our goal in government is to ensure that we never withdraw to the June 4 borders," he declared,[45] and by so doing outlined the framework for discussion without touching on social or economic issues. His speech lasted two hours, and it seemed as though the prime minister was speaking, not a minister without portfolio. His bid to remain in the government—because if it had not been the National Unity Government, "we would not have been victorious in the Six-Day War"—was accepted almost unanimously, while the only one who dared to disagree with him was Bader, who demanded that he quit the government and declare a full merger with the Liberal Party. Begin's declaration that Israel would never withdraw from the territories was not merely a political slogan in his eyes, but also the basis of a realistic foreign policy.[46] Just like he had done in the fourth Herut conference, Begin focused on one issue: Israel's borders.[47]

On February 26, 1969, Prime Minister Levi Eshkol died at the age of seventy-four, and Mapai chose Golda Meir to replace him. Meir suggested to Begin that he remain in the new government without a common platform and without a portfolio, as he had been in Eshkol's government. Begin did not think he should resign from the government, though his relationship with Meir was influenced by past memories and the Saison and was in general less cordial than were his ties with Eshkol, but he decided to set one condition for remaining in government—that the prime minister include in her inauguration speech the words "the estate of our forefathers has been liberated." Meir had no problem responding to his request.[48]

Winning the war strengthened Israel's economy—through foreign investments, waves of both Jewish and non-Jewish tourists from around the world, and economic cooperation between Israeli businesses and Arab inhabitants in the territories. The establishment of settlements in Gush Etzion, in the Old City, in the Jordan Valley, in Sinai, and in the Golan Heights came on top of this. Economic prosperity overshadowed the question of political moderation, though demands from around the world—not just from the Arab countries—to solve the issue of the Palestinian refugees became more and more insistent. Already in November 1967 the U.N. Security Council had formulated Resolution 242, which demanded that Israel withdraw from territories occupied during the war in exchange for a peace settlement. The resolution referred to "withdrawal from territories occupied in the recent conflict"; the wording was considered an important accomplishment of the Israeli diplomatic team, led by Foreign Minister Abba Eban, because it did not specify withdrawal from "the territories" but from "territories"—meaning not all of them.[49]

Meanwhile, Deputy Prime Minister Yigal Allon formulated a document that later became known as "the Allon Plan"; it had several main points: the Jordan Rift Valley, some of the Judea and Samaria mountains, and the Golan Heights would be annexed to Israel, which in return would return two-thirds of the occupied West Bank. The plan was intended to solve the demographic problem and thus to be accepted by the Palestinian and Jordanian leaderships. Allon hoped that an agreement would lead to the establishment of a demilitarized autonomy linked to Jordan, with the Jordan River continuing to serve as the security border.[50] The Allon Plan, which up until the Oslo Accords of 1993 served as the political outline by which almost all Israeli governments worked,[51] was considered by Begin as the utmost transgression. Eventually it lay at the heart of the political rivalry between the Likud and Hamaarach.[52] The Allon Plan also shook up Gahal (Yosef Sapir supported the plan while Begin adamantly opposed it).

Begin did not only oppose the Allon Plan, but he was also an enthusiastic supporter of the establishment of settlements in the "administered territories." (Israelis referred to the West Bank and Gaza Strip as the "occupied" or "administered" territories according to their political leaning or simply used the more neutral term "the territories"; Greater Israel purists used the term "Judea and Samaria" instead of "West Bank.") In January 1969, in response to a parliamentary question by MK Uri Avnery, Begin argued that "settlements should be established all over Eretz Israel"—and he especially referred to Rafah, Jenin, Hebron, Nablus, and Qalqilya—regardless of security issues. He also rejected "the use of borrowed names like Palestine, as these are all Israeli cities."[53] Begin's stance reflected the gap between himself and Moshe Dayan and other Labor Party members who also supported the establishment of settlements in the "territories" but sought to solve problems of policy and security in so doing. Begin justified the establishment of settlements with God's promise to Abraham's seed, "therefore we can not pass on it."

Paradoxically, Begin's theological arguments later made him the more moderate member of government and the Movement for a Greater Israel after he was elected prime minister. For example, he believed that God had promised the Land of Israel to the people of Israel, and since the Sinai Peninsula was not a part of the Promised Land, he was willing to give it up. Despite his refusal to return the occupied territories, Begin did not overlook the problems involved in annexing more than a million Palestinians. And on this issue he also looked for assistance from the Almighty. "The Lord promised to gather the Jews from all over the world, and this will happen in our generation," he declared, referring to the anticipated opening of the Soviet Union to let Jews out.[54] He said that Jews needed to fight to bring the Soviet Jews to Israel (at the time there were an estimated 2–3 million), and for this battle he chose the slogan "Let my people go"—as Moses had asked of Pharaoh. But in cabinet meetings Begin presented other reasons to explain his attitude toward the demographic problem. He argued that according to the Allon Plan over six hundred thousand Arabs would remain in Israel and that the difference between that number and 1 million did not justify giving up the territories.

Begin thought of his position on the topic as a direct continuation of Jabotinsky's views as expressed in his essay "The Iron Wall," written in 1923.[55] "Our premise is a Jabotinskyesque assumption," he told Kadishai. "Peace between Jews and Arabs in Israel will come only after they understand that there is no chance of getting rid of us. For this to happen, we must always, but always, be stronger than the other side; but no less important, the other side should know it. Therefore, declarations are of paramount importance."[56]

Begin's office, located on the second floor of the Prime Minister's Office Building, was referred to by the press as "the office in the no-portfolio alley." Besides making proposals and giving statements, as a minister without portfolio, Begin could do nothing of significance except for three fund-raising trips on behalf of the government. Finance Minister Pinchas Sapir thought that sending the veteran member of the opposition would be an attraction abroad and would raise large sums for the state. Some people in Herut seriously thought that one of Begin's biggest achievements was heading the first ministry in which hung a picture of Jabotinsky.

Yet in Golda Meir's government, Begin's position changed. Eshkol liked him, and many times Begin was even asked to mediate between him and Dayan. Cunningly, Meir appointed him to committees of lesser importance, such as the Symbols and Ceremonies Committee. "He likes clarification of the matter, just as much as the matter itself," she was said to have said, half sarcastically, half with relief. And she was right: Begin even established a new committee, the Committee for Ministers' Statements, which he headed until it ceased to exist.[57] In most meetings Begin argued with Abba Eban. He used to surprise the ministers with a detailed review of Eban's speeches, listing all their faults. Once he read a document proposed by Eban and deleted every appearance of the word "withdrawal," replacing it with the expression "redeployment of the IDF." His office argued that this helped to prevent the return of land.[58] Meanwhile, the parliamentarian Begin disappeared from the political arena. Over the eighteen months he served in the government, he gave only one speech (about Polish Jewry) and displayed very little interest in Knesset affairs.[59] His attitude toward the Knesset sent a clear message: he was no longer the loud opposition MK.

Israeli television broadcasting began in 1968. Begin was among the first politicians to realize the new medium's power. Before the age of television, Begin had rarely given interviews to the print media, preferring that journalists quote from his speeches and press conferences. He knew that his speeches were more influential than his writings, and he was suspicious of most journalists owing to their views. Television broadcasts, however, substantially influenced his career.

Unlike many other leaders of his generation, Begin did not keep a diary, despite his fondness for historical documentation, perhaps because his statements were more effective when transmitted orally. It can be assumed that if he had kept a diary, his words would have lost their bite.

Toward the elections for the seventh Knesset, planned for November 28, 1969, the political map changed. In 1968, Mapai, Achdut Haavoda, Poalei Tzion (Workers of Zion), and most members of Rafi (which had split the previous year) established a new party—Haavoda (Israeli Labor Party). In 1969, when Mapam joined, it became Hamaarach. Ben Gurion also established a new party, Reshima Mamlachtit (the National List), with his loyalists from Rafi (those who had not returned to Mapai after Rafi split). Even before the election campaign started, the newspapers in Israel were curious about Begin's next steps, as this was the first time he was running as part of the government and not in the opposition. Until then his speeches had focused on the trampled personal and national honor of the Jewish people, and when he was not attacking the Gentiles, he was describing Mapai as the axis of evil; now he was collaborating with "the enemy."

Begin was prepared for the change and took advantage of the postwar spirit of nationalism and his seat in the cabinet to redefine Gahal and its leader. It was during this election that Begin entered the final stretch toward achieving public legitimacy. "The definitions of Left and Right are worn out and old-fashioned characteristics of reality after the Six-Day War," Begin claimed in interviews preceding the election. He also clarified that "there are more workers in Herut than in Mapam. Big businesses are controlled by the government and the Histadrut and not by the much-maligned small bourgeoisie."[60]

It was the culmination of a long process. Begin had started his political career out of a desire to be the main opposition leader, the government's stepbrother, albeit legitimate. Since the late 1950s he had aimed to cover up the harsher elements of his personality in order to advance from opposition leader to an alternative to the government, and now that he was a minister, he proceeded to the third step of the process: changing the old patterns of political debate and stepping into the center of the political arena. This process was also part of his personal status. More than twenty years had passed since the establishment of the state, and Begin, who just a decade earlier still believed the establishment was spying on him, became one of its integral parts. By 1969, the ideological rivalry had died down, Ben Gurion no longer ruled the country, and Begin was flesh and blood of the political establishment. The man who at first found it difficult to utter the words "Israel Defense Forces" and preferred to say "Israeli Army" now referred to its officers as saints, as Yehudah Hamaccabi's torchbearers. The results of the Six-Day War, which in his mind were a divine sign that his ideology was the correct one, facilitated the process in which he made his peace with the establishment.

Indeed, Begin avoided polemics during the elections, pointing his arrows mainly at the Arabs, saying, "We all want peace except the Arabs." His main argument was that the only party that would not return homeland territories was Gahal. His content became more moderate, but his style had not changed. Begin's sensitivity to everything written about him continued to shape his speeches. In a speech in Dimona, for example, he referred to an internal Hamaarach bulletin of which most of the six hundred attendees had no knowledge. "Do you know why the article's title is in red?" he asked about an article claiming that few participants attended his gatherings. "Because it's blushing with shame." In a tirade of witticisms he spoke of the U.N. efforts to achieve a cease-fire with Egypt and declared, "If the U.N. takes care of things, it gets You None of your needs." But it was obvious that without an opponent he could slam, his speeches were not the same. His becoming part of the government made his arguments lose their basis. While his use of language was still poetic, his speeches were less thrilling for his audience.[61]

Yet Begin was actually pleased with the new situation. From the start of the election campaign he wanted the public to see him as a national leader, a moderate and level-headed thinker. The seventh Knesset election results did not make dramatic changes to the political map, but the path taken by all the major parties paved the way to the Yom Kippur War. The arrogance of both Gahal and Haavoda led to an indifference regarding the need to resolve the issue of the administered territories. Begin opposed any deal involving the return of the territories and for the first time raised the argument that Hamaarach governments would argue all the way into the twenty-first century: peace agreements should include clauses about a full normalization of social and cultural ties, in addition to security arrangements. "In any other arrangement," explained Begin, "peace will remain a word on paper, just as the cease-fire agreement in Rhodes did not prevent an outbreak of war."[62]

From another one of Begin's promises during the election campaign it is apparent, in retrospect, how much he suffered from the hubris of Israel's leaders that led to the Yom Kippur War fiasco, a failure that eventually paved the way to the "revolution" that occurred in 1977. Begin trusted the IDF's strength and the strongpoints that were being erected on the banks of the Suez Canal (the Bar Lev Line), and more than once he ceremoniously declared, "I can announce that the Egyptian army will not be able to cross the canal. If they launch an offensive against us, they should expect a greater defeat than they suffered in the Six-Day War."[63]

As for Begin's personal life, in 1969 he was fifty-six years old, suffered from diabetes, and was a heavy smoker of French Gitane cigarettes. But his health, like that of all other leaders, was never discussed. In November, during a party meeting, he suddenly rolled his eyes, and seconds later his head dropped onto his chest. He had fainted. *Haaretz* reported in a played-down news item that Begin had been hospitalized for three days because of "fatigue." But Begin continued to lose strength, and after his discharge from the hospital his doctors recommended that he rest for two weeks at a hotel. After his hotel "vacation" he traveled to Switzerland, where he quit smoking.[64]

In December, after his return from Switzerland, his first grandson, Yonatan, was born, the first-born son of Benny and Ruth. (Yonatan was killed in 2000 in a plane crash.) Begin was the godfather. Benny insisted on a modest celebration at the Shaarey Tzedek Medical Center, yet the guest list included the prime minister and the chief of staff.[65]

Politically, Begin had no cause for either celebration or sorrow. The seventh Knesset election campaign was the mildest the country had ever known, and its results were consistent with expectations. Hamaarach won fifty-six seats, while Gahal retained its power with twenty-six seats. Despite the fact that the number of Gahal's MKs did not increase, it was clear that a unity government would be established once again. When Golda Meir invited Gahal to join the new government and receive four portfolios, it was considered an achievement for Begin.[66] This time Begin was not asked to join the government in a time of emergency; participating in the new-old coalition was a form of full rehabilitation and an abandonment of the traditional policy of "without Herut and Maki."

Many speculations surfaced regarding the position Begin would demand. In the previous government Begin had successfully fulfilled a ministerial role. Surprisingly, once again he was satisfied with the position of minister without portfolio. But only those who did not know Begin were surprised, as what interested him the most was foreign policy; moreover, he excelled as an analyzer and strategist more than an executive. There was another reason why Begin preferred a nonexecutive position: as a minister without a specific portfolio, he felt like a second prime minister dealing with the sublime—guarding over Israel—rather than with the trivial aspects of day-to-day leadership. His religious impulses also influenced him. Because he tended to act upon inspiration rather than information, it was more convenient for him to serve in an official post that was nonexecutive. In any event, his supporters saw his conduct as noble.[67]

Begin also made a surprising choice of ministers to serve in the government. The belief in Herut was that Begin would endorse Yochanan Bader, the veteran parliamentarian, but he opted for the loyal Chaim Landau for the position. Once again this reflected his familiar tactics—keeping the individualists and those with ideological influence away from the centers of power.

Herut members claimed that excluding Bader from the government was synonymous with Begin's move to exclude Paglin from the first Knesset list; at that time Begin's decision was reasonable—the hot-tempered operations officer was not suitable for political activism—but the decision about Bader was not. Even Golda Meir exclaimed, "Our party has been rife with foul deeds over the years, but such beastliness I have yet to come across."[68] Bader could not forgive Begin and decided to get revenge gracefully. They did not exchange a word for over a year. Bader was mainly offended because Begin referred him to the Herut administration to try to change the decision, even though everyone knew that almost all the party's decisions were made by Begin alone.[69] Yet as mentioned above, Bader was only a symptom. Landau's choice was in fact the result of Begin's long struggle against the intellectual camp in the party.[70] There is no doubt that Begin had intellectual advantages—he had an excellent memory, analytical skills, and wit—but between him and the Revisionist intellectuals lay a gaping abyss. Intellectuals, by their very nature, tend to be critical, and Begin detested their tendency to reject his proposals at face value and to examine his basic beliefs and the way he was doing his job. Furthermore, since his commitment to religion influenced his decisions, he found it hard to accept their tendency to rely on rationale alone. To all these must be added Begin's competitiveness. Like Begin, Bader was a lawyer by profession, was considered a master of phrasing, and was especially interested in foreign policy, and Begin preferred to keep this niche to himself.[71]

Nor did Begin's second selection for a ministerial position testify to his adherence to Revisionist grandeur. General Ezer Weizmann, head of the General Staff Operations Branch in the Six-Day War and previously commander of the air force, was disappointed that he was not promoted to chief of staff, so on December 15, 1969, he announced his retirement from the IDF. On the very same evening it was announced that he had been appointed minister on behalf of Gahal. Begin agreed to nominate him as minister of transportation without his being elected to the Knesset. Weizmann was the first general to join Gahal, and Begin could not refuse him. The newspapers noted that this move was a result of Begin's tendency toward self-deprecation in front of military officers. But this was not accurate. In fact, after their first meeting, Begin had many reservations regarding Weizmann's fiery temperament, and although he needed his battlefield glory, Begin did not admire him. Begin named him "that likeable rascal" to emphasize that he was liked by many but not a leader of stature.[72]

The difference between Begin's impression of Weizmann and other generals like Moshe Dayan, Ariel Sharon, and Rafael (Raful) Eitan indicated that the type of military man that appealed to him was not a pilot with technological skills but a field commander, a farmer, a man of the soil, rooted in the ground of the homeland—everything Begin himself was not.[73] It soon became apparent that in recruiting Weizmann into Gahal, Begin had acted on impulse. Introducing the "likeable rascal"—with a temperament quite opposite to Begin's—to politics heralded the beginning of a new era in Gahal, an age in which Begin slowly lost his tight grip of the party's reins.

The friction between Begin and Weizmann began the first moment Weizmann joined the government. Intellectual and ideological gaps separated the two men—if Weizmann was ever faithful to a clear ideology in the first place. The Sabra Israeli general found it difficult to accept the values and style in which the Polish Begin led his party. For example, during a vote to approve one of Foreign Minister Abba Eban's routine trips to Germany, Begin and Landau voted against the trip (as expected), even though they knew they could not prevent it. Weizmann passed a note to Begin saying that he had decided to support the trip, against the party's position, as it would contribute to Israel's interests. Begin replied in a note: "Long live Freedom."[74] Weizmann saw this as confirmation that he could vote as he pleased, but in fact Begin had used a play of words in which he meant that by voting as he wanted, Weizmann would be deviating from the traditional policies of Herut ("freedom")—that is, he meant "Long live Herut."

Weizmann was insensitive to Begin's attitude toward the Holocaust. He was surprised at the intense opposition his vote raised among Herut members and asked to speak privately with Begin. He intended to apologize and did everything he could to accept Begin's authority. "Sir, I made a mistake" he said. But Begin was in no rush to exonerate him. "Because of you I thought about resigning from the party," he said, wishing to teach him an agonizing lesson. Three years later, when they confronted each other at a party conference regarding the assignment of new members to the party center, Begin recalled the story in order to humiliate him. The audience was astonished by Weizmann's obsequiousness since until then he had been considered a strong and dominant personality, while Begin was happy that he had made the conversation public and managed to damage Weizmann's image.[75]

In the new government Begin did not hesitate to express his liberal views and was in fact one of the more enlightened ministers. However, when he said that Israel should give Israeli citizenship to every Arab who desired it if Israel were to annex the territories, he still surprised his audience.[76] Begin was also among the ministers who opposed Golda Meir's decision in the early 1970s to send Shin Bet investigators to the ministers' bureaus in order to find out who among them was leaking information to the media. "I will not answer you, my friends," Begin said several times before the Shin Bet officers left his bureau. "In a democratic country the secret services have no right to supervise the government," he said later, and when Minister of Justice Yaakov Shimshon Shapira supported Begin's stand, Meir backed down from hers.[77]

ELEVEN

ONCE MORE A REBEL

In January 1970 Begin's deputy and confidant in Herut, Arie Ben Eliezer, died of cancer. Ben Eliezer was Begin's close friend; he was the man who had had him discharged from the Anders Army, was responsible for Begin's appointment as Etzel commander, and was also the one who convinced Begin to return to the political arena after his retirement following the results of the second elections. After Ben Eliezer's death, Begin had no more old allies. Before the latest election, Begin's former Etzel deputy, Yaakov Meridor, chose to abandon politics and focus on his shipping company. Begin's relationship with Bader was at a low ebb after he did not appoint him as a Herut minister, and his relations with Weizmann were strained.

Begin engaged in many political fights in his life—these often filled him with energy—but always with the support of his party, his metaphoric family. When he realized that his own house, Herut, had stopped supporting him, he chose to retire, first when he was criticized in-house over the party's losses at the second legislative elections and then at Herut's eighth conference, when Tamir and Paglin voiced opposition. Now his loneliness at the top influenced his surprising decision to again retire. His essential justification was the Rogers Initiative, designed to bring about a cease-fire between Egypt and Israel in Sinai. Newly elected U.S. president Richard Nixon supported the initiative, together with Secretary of State William Rogers (after whom the initiative was named).

The Rogers Initiative was a new version of a proposal by U.N. mediator Gunnar Jarring, a Swedish diplomat who had been authorized by the United Nations to try to reach a Middle East peace agreement. The new initiative called for an immediate cease-fire in Sinai, an ongoing conflict that would soon be called the "War of Attrition." Jarring traveled to the capitals in the Middle East to prepare the groundwork for negotiations between Israel and the surrounding Arab nations, based on U.N. Resolution 242, which stated that Israel should withdraw from the occupied territories. Begin did not oppose the cease-fire but demanded all or nothing. He argued that if Israel signed a political agreement without a full peace treaty, the cease-fire would be one-sided and would benefit Egypt in preparations for a new war. As he usually did, he labeled the Rogers Initiative the "Munich Pact II."[1]

Begin's decision to retire after the government agreed to negotiate the Rogers Initiative aroused the anger of the Liberals within Gahal, and the prime minister expressed her surprise at his decision, as it was clear to all that the government's decision to negotiate the Rogers Initiative was mostly a political tactic, not a willingness on the part of Israel to return territories. However, Begin insisted on retiring, calling on his legal training to support his position. He stressed that while Israel relied on the English translation of Resolution 242 (which stated that Israel was not required to withdraw from "all the territories" but rather from "territories"), the preface to the draft of the Rogers Initiative created a legal obstacle. The preface stated that the principle of the "inadmissibility of acquisition of territory by force" should be taken into account—that is, there was no legal argument for annexing territory by force. Therefore, Begin said, by accepting the initiative, Israel recognized that it was required to withdraw from all the occupied territories, even if such a demand was not stated explicitly in the operative section of the initiative; it would be impossible to keep the territories except by force because the Arabs would oppose it.

Begin explained the initiative's problematic aspects with a victorious smile, as a man who had managed to reveal a plot by the Gentiles, and none of the ministers could ignore either his seriousness or his powers of legal analysis. But because more than five hundred IDF soldiers had already been killed in the War of Attrition being waged along the Egypt-Israel cease-fire line, most of the ministers felt that agreement to the initiative would afford them a cease-fire and in practice would not affect the future of the territories. Most of them—including the foreign minister and the prime minister—tried to persuade Begin not to resign, but Begin insisted.[2] When Golda Meir suggested that he remain in the government and vote against the initiative, Begin refused. "Such a proposal does not suit a man of truth," he explained. When the Liberal faction in Gahal, including Weizmann, agreed to the initiative, Begin argued that this was an opportunistic approach, unsuitable for ideologues.

On July 31, following the government's approval to negotiate the initiative, Begin convened the members of the Gahal center and proposed that the party immediately withdraw from the coalition.[3] "May my right hand forget its skill if I sign this proposal," he declared, expressing his disgust with this political manipulation.[4] Though Begin was not averse to stirring things up in matters pertaining to his political party, he distinguished between internal politics and statesmanship. Accordingly, when dealing with matters of principle he was more particular about the rules than when dealing with personal internal politics. The Liberal Party, which saw the Rogers Initiative as a step that would contribute to a cease-fire, demanded that more delegates be added to the party center in order to strengthen the party's position. Begin agreed since he believed that he had a magical effect on the party members who were still the majority in the center. On a hot summer day, his jacket hanging on the back of his chair and his white shirt soaked with sweat, before a sour-looking Weizmann, Begin announced that because accepting the initiative would result in tearing land away from the Land of Israel, he would resign from the government even if the party decided not to leave the government. Again he declared, "If I sign it, may my right hand forget its skill." Obviously his threat of resignation frightened Gahal. By a small majority of only five votes, it was decided that the entire party would withdraw from the coalition.[5]

Begin's decision to retire expressed a characteristic duality. On the one hand, he had showed gallantry and remained in the government even when it had approved Resolution 242, while on the other hand, he insisted on specific marginal clauses. He was always sure he was truly right, and his belief in his principles guided and strengthened his conviction throughout his life. There is no doubt that had he believed that his goal was purely political and not also moral, he would not have survived the political struggles. But he also wanted to advance politically; therefore he too had to fish in troubled waters and behave as a shrewd political activist.

In August 1970 Begin returned to the opposition in a good mood. Changes always instilled a sense of vitality in him. The prevailing view was that Begin simply did not want to take power, which simultaneously enthralled and disgusted him, and thus he was satisfied with being the alternative. In an article responding to the accusation that he was afraid of gaining power and therefore would never lead his party "to the Promised Land," he wrote that his party "wishes for power; [however], power does not mean gaining control of the people but rather serving the citizens."[6] It meant that even now Begin was torn between his desire to become prime minister and his tendency to entrench himself in the position of the Eretz Israel advocate, representing the people's will versus the left-wing government.

When Begin resigned, he returned to the imagery he often used for condemning the Labor Party. Thus, for example, because the differences between Herut and the left-wing Zionists were not differences of principle, he wondered aloud why Herut members were referred to as "annexists" while the leaders of Haavoda, who objected to returning the Golan Heights, were not. "Perhaps we should call them 'additionists'?" he mockingly asked upon taking the podium at the Knesset (which before the Six-Day War had moved to a new location). Simultaneously, Begin started attributing satanic qualities to Yasser Arafat, the leader of the Palestine Liberation Organization (PLO). He stated that returning the West Bank territories would bring "Arafat into our homes."[7] It was enough to see Begin's face distort upon mentioning Arafat's name and stressing the first syllable to understand the disgust he felt for him. Arafat, who was elected chairman of the PLO Executive Committee in 1969, had not been a popular figure in Israel, to say the least, since the founding of the PLO.[8] But Begin was the first to argue that Arafat was a demonic figure, and Likud officials continued to refer to him as the manifestation of pure evil until his death in 2005.

The former minister suddenly found himself with time on his hands. Like in his Etzel days, he resumed spending most of his time on his favorite hobby: writing. He devoted many hours to writing biweekly articles for *Maariv*. But when writing, unlike when lecturing, he found it hard to express his witticisms and show off his dramatic gestures. Begin insisted that nothing he had written be changed, and he often argued with *Maariv* editor Moshe Zak, who was not one of his opponents but sometimes wanted to delete a word, change a title, or shorten some text. "Menachem, I have a good idea for a different title," he would try to convince him, but Begin would fight for every comma.[9] Begin did not settle for just writing for the newspaper. On Mondays and Thursdays he and Kadishai wrote responses to almost all who had written to him. He felt he was more one of the people and more moral and decent when he treated every one of "the people of Israel" with respect, and he especially liked the vitality he felt as a result, though writing the letters was also a result of his inactivity.

Begin tended to stay in the Herut headquarters on the twelfth floor of Metzudat Ze'ev or in his room at the Knesset. His devoted assistant, Yechiel Kadishai, was always at his side. There certainly was no "glory" in his room in the Metzudat Ze'ev, which was in perpetual disorder, with letters scattered on the table and papers strewn on the floor—as in his days in the Anders Army.[10] Upon Begin's return to the opposition Kadishai advised him to hire a personal secretary. Yona Klimovitski, whose father was active in the Communist Party, was invited for an interview in which Begin focused mainly on her political beliefs. She fearfully admitted that she had received a left-wing education and was surprised when he said he had "respect for people with an ideology." The interview was brief, and the attractive young Klimovitski became his personal secretary and stayed with him until he retired as prime minister. Begin had a weakness for pretty women and for aesthetics in general and often treated people according to their appearance. In 1981, when he took part in the Mimuna (a Moroccan Passover celebration) in Migdal Haemek, he particularly admired "the beautiful women here."[11] His attraction to beauty was similar to his admiration of military people—they were endowed with features that nature had neglected to give him.

Klimovitski thought that the job was temporary and never imagined that she would eventually become the prime minister's secretary.[12] When she started working for Begin, she was again surprised by him. He often spoke to her about the Holocaust, in almost every context, and every time he heard a racial joke—the kind of joke that was popular in Israel in the seventies—he was quick to formally disapprove of it, as if surrounded by a gaggle of reporters. "No, it's not respectable to talk like that, not even as a joke," he would say.[13]

Begin's days in the opposition harmed his status in Gahal. The impatient Weizmann saw his return to the opposition as a mistake and believed that in order for Gahal to attain power, Begin's old loyalists had to be eliminated. "Sometimes I don't know what I'm doing here, among all these Poles," he blurted out more than once.[14] From his perspective Begin was rigid, intolerant, and anachronistic, and he believed that he had managed to survive in politics despite his weaknesses only because of his followers' absolute loyalty.

In order to bring about a real change in Gahal, Weizmann wanted to replace the entire management and cultivate new forces—more attractive to the general public—who would not be subordinate to Begin just because of the Etzel tradition. Begin was aware of the young major general's electoral power, but while he supported his appointment as executive chairman of the party, he was also careful to restrict his moves. Eitan Livni, who had served as Etzel operations officer before Paglin, was appointed as Weizmann's deputy for a clear purpose: to monitor him.[15] But Weizmann was not the only one who had reservations regarding Begin's actions. The bitter Bader attacked him regularly, claiming that serving in the government after the Six-Day War was "cheap opportunism."[16]

As often happens in politics, the weakening of his status encouraged many others to publicly oppose Begin. Mordechai Olmert stirred up a storm in Herut when *Haaretz* published a letter he wrote in which he accused Begin of not encouraging the establishment of settlements across the country since the days of the Yishuv.[17] As noted, when faced with in-house criticism, Begin always reacted by radicalizing his position even further, and the change would serve as a renewed source of energy for him. As also noted, his sentimentality affected his views, shaped his goals, and sharpened his words. And once again his extremism was soon to damage the moderate image he had been cultivating.

In February 1971, Begin attended the Jewish Councils conference in Brussels, a festive meeting intended mainly for public relations rather than real decision making, where he once again acted as an outlaw underground leader. It all began when Rabbi Meir Kahane, head of the Jewish Defense League in the United States, asked to attend the conference. Most council presidents were opposed to Kahane's violent tactics against the Arabs and decided to refuse his request. The decision was accepted with understanding and aroused little interest until Begin intervened. Although he had stated his opposition to Kahane's activities, Begin appreciated his motives, as if he were a brave Jewish ghetto warrior and not an extremist practicing violence in a democracy such as the United States. When word spread that the convention organizers had ordered the Brussels police to prevent Kahane from entering the convention hall, Begin remarked that there were Jews who were still willing to turn in a fellow Jew to the Brussels police—meaning that Jews were turning in Jews to Gentiles.[18] In an interview he said that Rabbi Kahane (he made sure to refer to him as "Rabbi") had a right to participate in the conference. Once again, the uproar he created made him appear as a rebel and dissenter, the image he had wished to change while he was part of the government. Only when he returned from Brussels did Begin realize that supporting Kahane was seen as an overly extreme position. He sought to play down the importance of his words by saying that he had never suggested that preventing Kahane from entering the convention was the betrayal of a Jew; he just thought Kahane had the right to participate. But the trap in which he was caught was inevitable. Though he understood that he should dissociate himself from Kahane, he could not break free from the past, from his days in the underground and the concept of "Jews against Gentiles."

In 1972 Begin flew to London for the first time, and there, like in Brussels, he caused mayhem. The official reason for his visit to the country in which he was still considered a terrorist whose hands were stained with the blood of British policemen was to visit Herut's British branch, a marginal group consisting of a mere 1,500 members. Many advised him to forgo the visit, mainly because of the turmoil he had caused in Brussels, as it was clear that his visit would generate demonstrations and protests throughout the United Kingdom. But Begin clung to his principles. "I intend to explain the situation in the Middle East to the British," he said in interviews and added that he intended to point out the "British errors from the days of the struggle." The British government decided to ignore his visit, but U.K. journalists did everything in their power to sabotage his trip. A *Daily Mail* headline read, "The Return of the Little Murderer," and a *Sun* headline advised, "Go home, Mr. Begin."[19]

But it appeared that Begin was pleased by all the fuss. He arrived in London accompanied by Israeli security personnel, and the larger the demonstrations against him, the more important he felt, as if he had returned to center stage. A dinner appointment scheduled in a London restaurant was canceled by the restaurant owners owing to public pressure, and when Begin referred to the bombing of the King David Hotel and accused the British government secretary of having given the warning of the bombing too late, he was threatened with arrest for war crimes. Begin attributed the claim that he was a war criminal and the threat to arrest him to pro-Palestinian organizations. Upon his return to Israel he solemnly pledged to return to London soon, yet in fact he returned only after he was elected prime minister.[20] What happened in London only strengthened his resolve: the more he was attacked, the more he felt that "the world is against us" and that Jews would always be persecuted.

Meanwhile, his status in his party had been weakened. Yosef Sapir died in 1972, and Elimelech Rimalt was appointed head of the Liberal Party. Rimalt aligned himself with Weizmann, as he thought that only a real change would enable Gahal to attain power. When Rimalt and Weizmann realized that under Begin's leadership they would not be able to propose a moderate political plan, they decided to focus on social and economic affairs.

In a speech Weizmann gave in June 1972 to Gahal members, he said that if Gahal wanted to be elected into power, it must focus on the most urgent problems: public housing, corruption among public officials, the economic situation, and social inequalities. And so, surreptitiously, instead of confronting Begin on his lack of willingness to compromise on political issues, Weizmann forced him to deal with issues in which he had little interest. Of course, Begin found it difficult to reject Weizmann's proposal to address internal issues. When he went to the podium to respond, he announced that he accepted the proposal. But when he talked about major social problems, it became clear how detached he was from the people. He stated, for example, that "rudeness and hypocrisy in the country" must be rooted out and spoke of a "new phenomenon" in Israel: people holding parties or walking the streets after midnight, making heaven-shaking noises and not letting the neighbors rest after a hard day's work. His poetic vocabulary—which his opponents mocked when he talked about foreign affairs and defense issues—sounded doubly disconnected when he spoke of social problems. When he added that he was "astonished that a Jew in his native country did not know how to behave," it was obvious to the journalists that the outdated leader needed to step down and let Weizmann take over.[21]

Weizmann did not want to miss the opportunity. When Begin said that sitting on the opposition benches was a sacrifice, that it was a national responsibility, that it educated people about democracy—"What have we not done for the people of Israel? What have we not sacrificed for them? How we have served as the parliamentary opposition! We represented democracy. . . . We do not want, and we do not need, to change"[22]—Weizmann argued that this was a Diaspora-like and defeatist attitude.[23] In Begin's absence he told the Etzel members in Herut that it was time for a change. The party veterans had not forgotten the ostracism to which they had been subjected before the establishment of the state and even after it and could not let go of the past, but Weizmann did not understand why they persisted in flaunting their teachings of democracy and their East European gentility. "We will never gain power this way," he said. Begin, who by that time knew exactly what was going on behind his back, never forgot that Weizmann tried to take away his leadership.

In 1972, on a surveillance of a group of Kahane's people in Israel who allegedly were planning to attack Arabs, the Ness-Tziona police discovered that some of the explosives found in the group's possession were manufactured in a private factory owned by Amichai Paglin. After their arrest, journalist Dan Margalit discovered that Paglin was among the detainees, and he intended to publish this scoop in *Haaretz*. Herut knew that such news would cause the party great damage, and before Margalit's article was printed, Shmuel Tamir, who had not spoken directly with Begin since being deposed and establishing Hamerkaz Hachofshi, summoned Alis, Paglin's Etzel deputy, and asked him to urge Begin to help get Paglin released. Alis hurried to phone his commander.

"Sir, your right-hand man from Etzel has been arrested," he told Begin on the phone, as if thirty years had not passed.[24] Begin listened to Alis, asked after his health, and surprised him with his chilly attitude toward Paglin. He was not moved. Paglin was no longer "the good Gidi" from the underground, but Tamir's partner, and therefore he had betrayed not only Begin and the party, but also the entire movement. Begin saw Paglin's distress as an opportunity. He took his revenge, as usual, in full Jabotinsky style. "You do not wake the justice minister at such a late hour," he told Alis. "We'll handle the matter tomorrow." Alis was obliged to agree with him.

The next morning Alis appeared at Begin's home, along with several former Etzel members. The justice minister's office said that he could not be reached, and Begin decided to appeal directly to Golda Meir. As he approached the phone, he fixed his eyes on Alis. "Weren't you among the stone throwers in the eighth conference?" he asked. Alis was surprised. Six years had passed since the conference, it was forgotten, and they had reconciled just before the Six-Day War. "What are you talking about?" he asked angrily. But Begin would not relent. "Yes," he said," I remember the riot." Once again, Begin's characteristic duality manifested itself. On the one hand, he showed gallantry, and despite the fact that Paglin supported Hamerkaz Hachofshi, he made his peace with him; on the other hand, during Paglin's hour of real distress Begin first bargained for a confession from Alis on a marginal and old issue before he would act. Alis raised his voice: "Sir, I have asked you for something on behalf of Amichai, one of your greatest fighters, and you are talking to me about [the stone throwing]?" The others present were also surprised by Begin's having chosen to bring up memories from the eighth conference at this time. Alis was offended and rose to leave; thus, after a delay of thirty years, the Etzel members were about to confront their commander. Meridor, who was also disappointed with the situation, pushed Alis back into the apartment and calmed everybody down.

When they had all settled down, Begin phoned the prime minister and asked her to release Paglin. "Mr. Begin, as an attorney, do you think it is right to grant special treatment to distinguished suspects?" Meir asked him. Begin, embarrassed, replied, "No," but he asked for his release nevertheless.[25] Paglin was released the next day and his trial was canceled.[26]

Meanwhile, encouraged by the power he had accumulated in the party, Weizmann continued to strive for leadership. He suggested a change in the electoral system—from proportional national elections to regional elections. He argued that as a political brand name Gahal would never beat Haavoda, "but," he told his followers, "we can put together a list that can defeat them in regional elections." Once again, members of the Liberal Party supported his position, which Begin strongly opposed. He believed that regional elections were just another one of Weizmann's many proposals to weaken Begin's control of the party and claimed that Gahal would be harmed by them. The members of the Liberal Party were disappointed, but Begin managed to prevent the proposal from being put into action. Weizmann saw it as further evidence that Begin was unable to adapt to the changing times. In fact, he said that Begin feared that changing the electoral system would force him to deal with young and attractive candidates who were not his loyalists.[27]

Weizmann would not give up. He set up a shadow government, as is customary in England, in which Begin was prime minister and he himself was minister of defense. Begin summoned his sharpest sense of humor to mock Weizmann's proposal. "Today, for the first time in my life, I was appointed prime minister by the celebrated former commander of the air force," he declared with a smile to Knesset reporters, "but what about the Liberals—don't they deserve anything?"[28] Weizmann realized that Begin, the skilled politician, had struck his Achilles heel—his reckless image. When he realized he could not jump over the hurdle Begin had set for him, he began to consider retirement. A year later he resigned from the party. "Sometimes it seems that Begin's influence on the party is the result of hypnosis," he declared and turned for a while to private business.[29]

Only the murder of eleven Israeli athletes from Israel's delegation to the Munich Olympics in September 1972 caused the Gahal ranks to unite internally.[30] "We will eliminate the murderers and liberate humanity from this disgrace," Begin swore in a speech in the Knesset. "Is it because of seven hundred nobodies, two-legged ravenous beasts, that Jews will once again bow their heads? Can it be that Israelis leaving for Europe are afraid of speaking Hebrew in the streets?"[31] In these words Begin revealed no state secrets, as he did not know that Golda Meir had ordered the Mossad to take revenge on the murderers. Begin was simply expressing his worldview: Bad people are murderers and good people are avengers. The realization of his belief shows exactly how deeply it was entrenched in the political establishment and that Begin and Meir were in fact more similar in their outlook than either one of them cared to believe. The difference was mainly in style.

Some of the younger members in Begin's party, whose generation had not experienced the Holocaust, were not excited by the words of a leader who had failed in the elections six times, and they were in fact fed up with him. The Israel of the seventies no longer remembered the Revisionist movement's struggles against the Labor movement, and Begin was considered a burden, an old-fashioned dogmatic leader out of touch with the times. As the election date approached—in late 1973—tensions increased between Begin's supporters and his opponents, not because of ideology but because of his personality and behavioral patterns. Even Geula Cohen, who had joined the movement and preferred the rigidity of Begin's national-religious ideology to Weizmann's calculated defense strategies, was among the opponents of "Beginism." Beginism, she explained, meant that Begin was the father of the movement, the supreme arbiter who could not be replaced or criticized.[32]

But Begin was incapable of change. He had been weaned on the perception that the leader was supreme during his days in Beitar, and it was no accident that every political change he made was based on Jabotinsky's writings. His old loyalists in Herut, of whom there were not many—about three hundred Herut center members, whose terminological world was identical to his—did not question his status.[33] For them there was no difference between the principles of loyalty toward the party and loyalty toward Begin, and with their support Begin ran the party with a firm hand.

In January 1973, ahead of the last Herut conference before the elections, Weizmann pushed his conflict with Begin even further. He openly declared in an interview in *Haaretz* that the "personality cult" was problematic and claimed that "even military appointments are decided in a more democratic manner."[34] Again, the conflict was about Begin's personality, but this time it took place during the internal elections for new delegates, when it might have detracted from Begin's power.

But Begin ruled that "what Weizmann regards as a revival is a matter of dismissal here." MK Matityahu Drobles was amazed when Begin summoned him for a private conversation and stated that it was "a matter of life and death." After two hours of speaking in detail about the history of the movement he made it clear that now it had boiled down to a simple question: "to betray the movement or not." In private conversations Begin tended to stir discomfort among his listeners, and Drobles had no choice but to give in to the pressure and vote against Weizmann.[35] Begin went on to summon many more party members and wore them down with his rhetoric. Once he invited Shmuel Tamir for a conversation (which began at 3 a.m. and ended at dawn), and whenever Tamir became angry, he addressed him as "Sir." Tamir said later that he never wanted to relive that experience.[36]

During the conference Begin threatened to resign and to establish "a party of our own." On top of his threat of retirement he added that he opposed a confidential vote, probably because he wanted to see who would dare to vote openly against him. Begin, like Ben Gurion in Mapai, achieved his goal by threatening to quit. But for him the threat of resigning was not only a maneuver that had become a habit because the idea of retiring, of disconnecting, tempted him. He believed that he was destined to play an important role in Israel's history, and due to this belief, as well as to his sense of moral superiority, he truly thought that his resignation would punish the people around him. Moreover, if his destiny to lead was not fulfilled, it would create a conflict with reality that could only be resolved by escaping it.

The party delegates gave in to Begin once again. Once the voting had ended, it was determined that Weizmann would run the campaign for the elections and that Begin would replace him as chairman of the party executive. This outcome undermined Weizmann's efforts to replace some of the delegates.[37] After the results became known, Weizmann decided to resign, but after talking to Begin, he reconsidered.[38] Once more, Begin won the battle within the party, but it was clear to everyone that his position had been weakened.

In this atmosphere Begin developed a tendency to adhere to his rigid etiquette, as if to spite those around him. For example, when asked to be interviewed on Israeli Television regarding the dispute with Weizmann, he agreed but on condition that he be allowed to say that "all eyes today are turned toward Bangkok" (where Black September militants had stormed the Israeli embassy and seized hostages). At the end of the interview he asked for assurance that his comments would be broadcast only after his official statement on what was happening there. "All political issues pale in comparison to the fate of the Israelis," he said. Herut spokesman Eliyahu Ben Elissar was asked to tell Micha Limor, the editor of the Mabat news edition (the official state television news edition) that if Begin's comments on Thailand were edited out, it would be better to shelve the entire interview. Begin was not naive. He knew that all interviews were edited and that because he was a member of the opposition, his stance on the events in Thailand was inconsequential. On the one hand, he was sensitive enough to realize that his battle with Weizmann cast him in the image of a party activist, certainly in light of what was happening in Thailand, while on the other, he actually believed that there was a difference between politics and statesmanship. This is why he acted as he did within his party and why in regard to existential issues he was careful to act as a statesman. This distinction also helped him overcome the dreariness of daily activities.

When Shmuel Almog, general manager of the Israeli Broadcasting Authority (IBA), heard about Begin's request, he said that not everyone could dictate the nature of an interview, certainly not while the government had yet to release an official statement about the events in Thailand. Former Etzel member Eli Tabin, one of the party activists, replied to Almog in all seriousness, "Don't you realize that Mr. Begin is not everyone?" In the end, the release of the hostages was announced before the broadcast, so this controversy dissipated.[39] But Begin's request to make a specific statement at the start of the interview eventually became a tradition; many politicians giving interviews on security incidents now say, "First, I want to wish a speedy recovery to the wounded" or "This evening we should not engage in politics." This was also the case with the symbolic act of praying at the Western Wall after Begin was elected prime minister; no prime minister has ever dared break this practice. These things of course became clear in retrospect. At the time, Begin's conflict with the Mabat editor testified to his gloomy political situation, and it seemed that his decision to resign from the government was a mistake. Once more, the outbreak of war rescued him.

TWELVE

AGAINST EXPECTATIONS

The Yom Kippur War caught the Israeli government by surprise.[1] After August 1, 1970, the designated day for the beginning of a cease-fire in the Suez Canal, the IDF focused on the northern border, and only after the IAF had struck Syrian military targets did the northern front calm down. Because Israel imposed a cease-fire without surrendering its political positions, the leadership thought that it was undefeatable and that the failure of political efforts was primarily an Arab problem. In September 1970, a month after the cease-fire came into effect, Egyptian president Gamal Abdel Nasser died, and his deputy, Anwar Sadat, was appointed president. The general perception that Sadat was a weaker leader than his predecessor increased the Israeli government's disregard for Egypt's military capabilities. Yet from the moment he came into power, Sadat did everything he could to express strength and determination, and among other things, he threatened not to renew the cease-fire agreement. He did not fulfill his threat but set 1971 as the deadline when he would decide whether to take his country toward a peace treaty or war. The India-Pakistan War, which broke out at the end of 1971, disrupted his plans.

Israel interpreted Sadat's threats as a sign of political and military weakness and estimated that Egypt would not go to war before it had prepared its air force to deal with the IDF. Regarding the northern border, Israel assumed Syria would not declare war on its own. In May 1973, Israeli intelligence learned that Egypt planned to declare war on Israel but estimated that chances were slim that war would actually break out. Being proved right strengthened the Israeli intelligence services' confidence in their assessments.

On September 13, 1973, the IAF engaged in battle with Syrian planes. The IAF shot down twelve Syrian planes and lost only one, strengthening the IDF's conclusion that Syria was too weak to harm Israel. In early October 1973 the IDF learned that Egypt was gathering vast military forces in the vicinity of the canal, but intelligence estimated it was a military drill. Only on the night of October 4, when Soviet advisers left Egypt and Syria, did Israel realize that it was about to be attacked. Yet still the IDF remained under only partial alert.

On October 6, 1973, the morning of Yom Kippur (the holiest day for Jews, when many Israelis fast and go to synagogues to pray), it became apparent that Syria and Egypt would launch a simultaneous attack that very day. The IDF began mobilizing its reserve forces, but the two Arab countries attacked at around two o'clock. Israelis were taken by utter surprise when air-raid sirens went off throughout the country.

Even Begin, who had announced in the prewar election campaign that Egypt would be defeated if it dared to attack, was surprised. Immediately after the alarm was heard, Begin arrived at the Knesset shelter in Jerusalem, where the Foreign Affairs and Defense Committee held frequent meetings. When the war broke out, Begin showed extensive knowledge about it and the various tactics employed, despite being in the opposition. "Why aren't we crossing the canal?" he asked repeatedly but never disclosed the source that had leaked him information about the events taking place at the front.[2] Many were surprised at the extent of his knowledge, and it eventually became clear that his source was none other than the commander of Division 143 in Sinai, Major General (Reserve) Ariel (Arik) Sharon.[3] It was the beginning of a beautiful "friendship," and they often helped each other to achieve their goals.

When Sharon was discharged from the army in July 1973, he was disgruntled for not having been appointed chief of staff. He wanted to join the political world and felt that he belonged in Gahal. He hastily set up a meeting with Begin, but following this he decided to join the Liberal Party. (Begin had a theory about Sharon's motives, but he kept it to himself until his old age.)[4] Sharon was reenlisted as a reservist when the war started, in spite of his shaky relationship with the IDF High Command.

It was not for the love of God that Sharon updated Begin about the events in Sinai. From the start of the war Sharon did not agree with the IDF senior commanders—especially Chief of Staff David Elazar and Shmuel Gonen ("Gorodish"), head of the Southern Command. He demanded that the IDF cross the canal and suggested that the enemy should be attacked while the army was still on the defensive.[5] Begin did indeed receive information from Sharon, but he also served as a pawn in the "generals' wars."

During the war Begin presented military proposals reminiscent of the showcase Etzel operations. On the tenth day of the war, when the IDF began to advance beyond the Israeli borders, the Foreign Affairs and Defense Committee debated the possibility of invading Damascus. The atmosphere in the committee was still grim, even though the IDF had moved from the defensive to the offensive. Yitzhak Navon and several Knesset members warned Israel Galili, the prime minister's security adviser, not to go there, but Begin had already started to fantasize about Israel closing a circle. "This is a golden opportunity," he argued, making a unique suggestion: to enter Damascus with tanks bearing the Israeli flag, to load all Jews onto them, and to bring them to Israel.[6] He was uninterested in the implications of his idea. But this time, because of the somber atmosphere, his romantic-messianic suggestion was not met with the usual anger but rather raised a smile on the faces of the meeting's participants. Galili did not respond.

Begin's main importance during the war, in addition to his activities in the Knesset's Foreign Affairs and Defense Committee, was in his official stance. Despite the public's recurrent requests for his comments about the war, as well as the frustrations over the leadership's failures, Begin refused to attack the government until the fighting was over because of his overall national approach. Shulamit Aloni, for example, one of the Mapai dissidents, already said on the third day of the war, "There has been a failure here."[7]

On October 17, eleven days after the war broke out, when it was clear that Israel was no longer defending itself but was on a full-blown offensive, Begin took to the Knesset podium and declared that he wanted the nation to be united. He mentioned that even if "there are questions and wondering, they will be addressed only after the eradication of the enemy." Earlier he had mainly blamed the Soviet Union for supplying weapons to Egypt and Syria and claimed there was a direct connection between the Ribbentrop-Molotov Agreement and the aid to Arab countries, for "In both cases, the Jews are the victims."[8]

On October 24, the Knesset approved a cease-fire agreement. Despite the fact that the approval was based on an acceptance of U.N. Resolution 242, Begin refrained from arguing over its significance regarding the future of the occupied territories. He explained that "as long as our troops are fighting, questions that many residents of Israel are asking will not be asked."[9] Once more, there was no disputing the fact that in order to prevent a national crisis, Begin was willing to forgo his personal interests.

At the end of the fighting, the Israeli public fell into a deep depression over the high death toll and the early battlefield successes of the Syrian and Egyptian armies. At least 2,693 soldiers had been killed in the Yom Kippur War, over 7,000 had been injured, 314 had been captured, and dozens had been declared missing in action. Furthermore, 102 Israeli planes had been shot down and 800 tanks destroyed. The sense of safety and trust in the country's leaders that had been predominant before the war was replaced by immense anxiety regarding Israel's future. The Israeli public—especially the reservists, who were shocked by the defects of the IDF and the horrors of combat—did not forget those who were to blame. The popularity of Golda Meir and Moshe Dayan plummeted drastically, and most citizens became fed up with the government. A survey conducted a month after the war revealed that the public thought that Yigal Allon was the most suitable man to be prime minister, and after him came Begin.[10]

Begin could not ignore these data and was completely energized. On November 13, during a special Knesset meeting for summing up the war, Begin made his first accusatory speech—the first step in his goal to take over the government. This speech, unlike his comments after the signing of the Reparations Agreement in 1952 or after the return of the Sinai Peninsula in 1957, was accepted with appreciation by the media, possibly because he was now part of the consensus. He asked again and again, "Gentlemen, why did you not advance the tanks? Why did you not advance the tanks?" And he did not desist, knowing too well what political treasure had fallen into his hands: "Our chief of staff, Lieutenant General David Elazar, said two days ago, 'Had the reserves been called up twenty-four or forty-eight hours earlier, there is no doubt that the war would have been different and that we would have had fewer casualties.' This is the IDF chief of staff's public statement. These things are simply terrible. . . . How did you become so irresponsible? Why is it that between Rosh Hashana and Yom Kippur you did not call up the reserves and you did not advance the tanks? Before this house you must answer the question: Why did you not call up the reserves; why did you not advance the tanks? Therefore, Madame Prime Minister, my advice to you, with all due respect, is this: Tomorrow, go to the President and tender your resignation." In fact, this was a campaign speech, though it was the first time Begin gave it knowing he had a chance to be elected. It was broadcast in full on the radio and was printed in *Haaretz* and *Yediot Ahronot*.[11]

Because of the war, the elections were delayed from October to December, and it suddenly seemed like Begin's biggest opportunity had come to be elected into power. Only after the war did it became clear just how lucky had been his decision to resign from the coalition and how much he had gained from not being part of the government's failure. In the December 1973 elections no one remembered that Begin himself had supported the "sit still, do nothing" policy that had paved the way to the war.

The election was also affected by what had happened in the political system before the war. While the personal conflict between Weizmann and Begin was being extensively covered by the newspapers, Weizmann and Sharon (who, as noted above, had joined the Liberal Party, which was part of Gahal), worked to establish a new party, the Likud (Unification), in response to the establishment of the second Hamaarach, created by parties from the Left and center.[12] (Originally, the Likud was named Hamaarach Hanegdi, the Opposing Alignment.) Weizmann and Sharon, whose affinity to the ideology of Begin and Herut was somewhat loose, made it their goal to merge Gahal, Hamerkaz Hachofshi, and Reshima Mamlachtit.

The truth is that Begin, who from that time on was considered the "number one Likudnik," was actually opposed to the establishment of Hamaarach Hanegdi. He knew the new party was a golden opportunity to seize power, yet he also understood that when the party's extended disposition was set up, his power would diminish and the Revisionist influence in Gahal would no longer be the same. In addition to his concern that the union would decrease his authority, Begin also disliked Tamir, who led Hamerkaz Hachofshi and with whom he had not really exchanged a word since the split in Herut after the eighth conference. Furthermore, Begin did not hold Weizmann in any particular esteem, and he found it hard to break his commitment to the Herut loyalists who opposed the union because they were afraid it would harm them and Herut's original ideology.

Kadishai did not dare criticize Begin too often. But like many Herut members, he found it hard to understand why Begin would agree to diminish the power of the party he had established with his bare hands by uniting with a party led by people who were not committed to

Herut's ideology. Begin knew that the establishment of the Likud was risky. But even so, because of the political opportunity, he came out in favor of this union. During one of his trips with Kadishai, Begin said that he too could make a good case for opposing the union, in addition to the disgust he felt for Sharon and Tamir, "but we have no choice if we want to be an alternative." That is, the greater the opportunity, the greater the concessions to be made. And it was clear that the pressure from both public opinion and the media, which were waiting for a change in power after the Yom Kippur War fiasco, influenced his decision to support the establishment of the Likud.[13] Begin indeed could not forgo the opportunity, although it was clear that his political power had diminished and this was practically his last chance. When he finally agreed to the unification, he made what would turn out to be a creative contribution: he changed the name of Hamaarach Hanegdi to Halikud Haleumi-Liberali (the National-Liberal Unification). Most of the rest was dealt with by Sharon and Weizmann.

Many Herut members, including David Levy (a Mizrahi Jew who later rose in the party ranks), Chaim Landau, and Yechiel Kadishai, told Begin they did not understand why he had forgiven Tamir.[14] Yet aside from his adherence to his own ideologies and views, Begin was also a skilled and cunning politician. He needed Tamir in order to establish the Likud. Moreover, Tamir's flattery of Begin was almost perfect. Every month or two, on a Saturday, Begin used to go to see a movie. Most people knew that he would walk to the cinema from his home in central Tel Aviv. When negotiations to establish the Likud began, Tamir offered to drive Begin to the cinema and back. On one of his trips abroad Tamir even carried Begin's suitcase. Chaim Landau considered his behavior subservient, while Begin saw it as a renewal of his loyalty to the movement.[15]

Begin's affinity for closing circles also played a part in his agreeing to establish the Likud. Just as he had invited Ezer Weizmann, the nephew of Chaim Weizmann, to join the party, so he agreed to include two former Rafi members in the Likud who supported the idea of a Greater Israel;[16] he declared, "Disciples of Ben Gurion are joining hands with disciples of Jabotinsky here."[17] He found it difficult to give up this pleasure.

When conditions ripened for the union, Begin supported it wholeheartedly. In September the Herut leadership approved the agreement, even though the number of candidates for the Knesset from Herut was relatively smaller than that of candidates from the other parties who joined the Likud.[18] Begin even announced that he was considering the inclusion of Rabbi Kahane in the Likud, though on this matter he would accept the decisions made by the centers of all the parties in the Likud.[19] Begin's nationalism was different from Kahane's fanatical nationalism, yet both focused on one important concept: the people of Israel are the sole value.[20] It was no surprise, therefore, that he did not regard Kahane as an outcast, although eventually the inclusion of Kahane in the Likud was shelved.

The formation of the Likud marked the end of a political era. While Herut remained the dominant faction in the party, Etzel veterans hardly had any influence. Bader reckoned that "ideologues have been replaced by merchants" and expressed his disapproval of Begin's surrender to the threats of Sharon, who did not hesitate to say that if the Likud did not come into being, he would strive for a unification of parties without Herut.[21]

When Weizmann repeatedly stated that the new party would focus on internal issues, Begin solemnly declared that the first thing he would do if he won the election would be to eliminate poverty[22]—and he actually intended to do so, so simplistic was his attitude toward economics. Previously, during all Herut gatherings Begin had pledged to "benefit the people," and unlike Ben Gurion and Meir, he did not demand anything from the people but preferred to give. It was a worldview, not just election propaganda. He argued that he was determined to eliminate poverty after listening to a radio broadcast in which a girl from Beit She'an said she was hungry. This was one of many times he used children as examples to justify his objectives. After the bombing of the Iraqi nuclear reactor in 1981 (discussed in chapter 16 below), he said that he dreamed of a small Israeli child thinking about his future. Begin's conceptual world was emotional, and he consistently reasoned irrationally. Already in 1955, during the fourth Herut conference, he blamed Mapai for the country's difficult economic situation; he made no concrete claims but spoke of the "malice" that had forced citizens to live in shacks. Good versus evil, right against wrong—that is how Begin perceived reality, especially in economics, a field that hardly concerned him.[23]

It seems that the contradictions in Begin's economic outlook came from his lack of interest in the topic and from the fact that he followed his instincts and emotions in the decision-making process. In a speech in May 1975 at a special conference of Tkhelet-Lavan (Blue-White), a Likud faction in the Histadrut, Begin chose to focus on foreign affairs and security issues. At the end of the speech he mentioned the economy and society, saying dryly, "I was assigned this evening to discuss social and economic problems," as if he saw them as marginal.[24] His position on economics was a combination of his desire to "benefit the people" and a capitalist-bourgeois perception. Back in 1965 he had stated that if there were no wage gaps, everyone would be lazy.[25] Yet he sometimes expressed a radical socialist viewpoint. For example, he declared that on entering the government, he would ban "luxury imports" and promised, "We will allow the use of foreign currency only in cases of real common and individual needs, so that each of us will serve as a personal model of frugality."[26] On another occasion, he accused the members of the kibbutzim of wanting to become millionaires and to laze about. He had no doubt about it; with his own ears he had heard "a heckler from Kibbutz Lehavot Habashan who called out in the middle of a meeting, 'I too want to be a millionaire.'"[27] Most citizens who voted for Begin were of a lower socioeconomic status, and in his speeches Begin would often swear to them that their lives under his rule would be better. But in practice, his party supported legislation that served the interests of the owners of property and wealth,[28] both because most of the members of the Revisionist movement were petit-bourgeois and because Begin aspired to promote his associates to a higher social status, and addressing the interests of the middle class served this end.[29]

Begin's first campaign as leader of the Likud was short because of the Yom Kippur War. Hamaarach's propaganda focused on the future, on the possibilities embodied in peace. Its spokespersons reiterated that Begin's support of the settlements was an obstacle for future peace agreements, and Minister of the Treasury Pinchas Sapir said explicitly, "Begin is incapable of achieving peace."[30] But such remarks were ridiculous given the outcome of the war, which had come about from (among other things) Meir's stubbornness. Begin, as usual, talked about the past, though this time he referred to the recent past. The Likud's propaganda focused on the military failure. "Had the reserves been mobilized in time, we would have had a great victory," Begin repeatedly argued, noting that he himself had warned against the war.[31] But this was 20/20 hindsight. The truth is that Begin always warned against war but in fact estimated that Israel would easily win.

Contrary to general expectations, the government was not replaced in the elections. The public, alarmed by the prospect that the IDF was not all-powerful—as it seemed to be after the Six-Day War—yearned for stability and reelected the known leaders. To remove Hamaarach from government would take a few more years. Meanwhile, the Likud gained significant ground—thirty-nine Knesset seats, more than in the previous Knesset, and the gap between the two major blocks had been reduced to twelve seats (compared with a gap of twenty-eight in the previous Knesset). Following coalition negotiations, Golda Meir established a government based on sixty-two MKs only. Begin told his associates that if they did not win the next election, he would retire. He was not accused of being a failure, but he was not credited with any success either. Some said the election results were a Likud achievement despite Begin, while others attributed it to him.

Meanwhile, a protest movement arose demanding that Meir and Dayan be deposed. The Agranat Commission, set up to investigate "The Failure" of the Yom Kippur War, found that on a political level no wrong had been committed, but this conclusion just aggravated the protest, which eventually led to Meir's resignation. In June 1974 the first Israeli-born politician became prime minister when Hamaarach candidate Yitzhak Rabin, IDF chief of staff during the Six-Day War and former Israeli ambassador to the United States, replaced Meir. Begin referred to the Rabin government as the "government of affront." He rebelled against what he called a "cosmetic change," "a deception," as in actual fact Mapai remained in power, and he demanded "in the name of the people" that new elections be held.[32]

Rabin's election deepened the political snare in which Begin was caught. Young Rabin was perceived as a breath of fresh air, a man who could clean up the stables of the old regime, while Begin was seen as a monument to obsolete leadership. Begin, unlike during the post–Ben Gurion era, chose to attack the prime minister directly, saying, "Rabin is a person who suffers from a serious functional defect—confusion. We see it up close in the Knesset, and it should not be kept secret." He was referring to the rumor that Rabin had collapsed at the beginning of the Six-Day War.[33]

Paradoxically, because Begin's views had hardly changed over the years, his image had softened (just like after the signing of the Reparations Agreement and the return of the Sinai Peninsula, he insisted that a referendum be held regarding the future of Judea and Samaria).[34] He was now perceived as a kind old man more than as the guardian of Israel. After the elections, even leftist publicists, such as Natan Donevich from *Haaretz*, suggested that he should be president. "His rhetorical skills, his fondness for rituals, his modest lifestyle will suit the job and will even strengthen the Likud without him," Donevich stated.[35] Even his colleague, Doron Rosenblum, who was known for his harsh criticism of Begin, noted that he could not seize power because he preferred the "guerrilla war of tongue lashing."[36] The articles written about Begin had already laid out his future path, as if his historical role had ended.[37]

In May 1975, twenty-one of the thirty-nine Likud MKs voted, in an open vote, against Begin's proposal to oppose the government's plan to devaluate the lira. A week earlier most of the Likud MKs had voted against his proposal to support the establishment of a settlement in Nablus.[38] Begin was embarrassed. This would not have happened in Gahal and certainly not in Herut. He was caught in a deadlock not only because he was at the head of a union of several parties, but also because he was worn out; he was the only party leader who had served in that role since the state was established.

Shortly after Weizmann retired, Sharon also decided to leave the Likud. Explaining that the country was facing a difficult war and that he wanted to serve in the IDF as a reservist, he decided he had to resign from the Knesset. Begin was embarrassed by the retirement of his most admired general. He presented Sharon as "a paragon of patriotism,"[39] but it soon became apparent that Sharon had retired from politics in order to establish a farm at Chavat Hashikmim (Sycamore Ranch), and in 1975 he was appointed Rabin's adviser on terrorism.

As noted, Begin had difficulty dealing with in-house criticism. In desperation, he chose to loosen the reins, and when MK Binyamin Halevi announced that he was willing to give back occupied territories—an issue that was of utmost importance to Begin—he refused to take punitive action against him.[40] It seemed that Begin had made his decision. In internal talks he vowed that if he lost the next elections, he would retire from politics permanently. He was a clever enough politician, and he understood that he was caught in a deadlock, but he was still ambitious enough to insist on trying one more time.

In regard to the West Bank, Begin remained entrenched in his position. When he visited the settlement of Sebastia in Samaria, journalists referred to the visit as a political statement, though it was a personal visit on his part. It was his favorite kind of party—national-religious poetry and dance. "The Lord Our Father is still alive, Our Father's still alive," he sang on the shoulders of the dancers during a three-hour visit at the settlement, in which he participated in the founding ceremony of two prefabricated buildings.[41] Begin now focused on developing the settlements, and he sought to hold the Herut conference in 1975 in Kiryat Arba (a Jewish settlement on the outskirts of Hebron), in spite of public criticism. During the conference, as expected, he announced his support for Israeli sovereignty "over all of Judea and Samaria." *Haaretz* reporters concluded, "As it was, so it will be."[42] But this conclusion was a large miscalculation since at the conference Begin revealed a big surprise: his position regarding withdrawal from Sinai.

Not many people noticed that in the conference's closing statement, Begin made an important distinction between the Sinai Peninsula and the lands of the homeland, the status of which, he declared, would "never be negotiated." Thus he expressed for the first time that he officially endorsed a compromise regarding Sinai.[43] Shmuel Katz, his colleague in the underground, was among the few who understood the implications of this decision. "Sinai is today's Iron Wall, and it is most dreadful that the conference did not include it in our national demands," he told Begin.[44] But Begin did not see the decision as a wavering in his position but rather a political solution for bringing peace and preserving the "land of our fathers." As noted, his worldview was derived from the belief that God had promised the Land of Israel to the people of Israel, and Sinai was not part of the Promised Land. He viewed Sinai and the Golan as a security solution that could be implemented through political arrangements. In fact, Begin was slightly more moderate than some of the Likud members, but his passion about Eretz Israel blurred his position.

Meanwhile, Begin strengthened relations with Moshe Dayan, and Yigal Allon even said, "It seems that Dayan is closer now to the Likud than he is to Hamaarach."[45] The relationship was not only an ideological connection. The admiration Begin felt for the lieutenant general did not diminish even after the Yom Kippur War. One day Begin was dining with a friend in the Knesset cafeteria and saw Dayan eating alone. Begin whispered, "Look, thus passes the glory of the world," and then a second later he added, as if he was speaking of himself, "It is merely a legend that some people are made of iron."[46] The low point in Dayan's status after the Yom Kippur War influenced what came to be called the Mahapach (Reversal; also called the Great Reversal) in the government because it dented the mythological image of the dauntless Sabra, long associated with the Labor Party, and paved the way for ostracized Herut members to enter the forefront of the public stage.

The damage to Dayan's image also enabled Begin to put forward his own national policy plans. In 1975, during a lecture at Tel Aviv University, he revealed for the first time his plan for a cultural autonomy that he had proposed during the negotiations with Egypt: direct negotiations with the "Eretz Israeli Arabs" (as Begin preferred to call the Palestinians because in his eyes they were not a nation). He tended to emphasize that he took this idea from the writings of Jabotinsky, who was indeed in favor of cultural autonomy for all religions in Israel, but he meant that the minorities would be able to integrate into the Jewish state that would be established in all the territory of the Land of Israel. When Begin was asked if his insistence on holding onto the occupied territories would not undermine Israel's Jewish character, he said that just as the Druze voted for Zionist parties, so would the Eretz Israeli Arabs.[47] Unlike Jabotinsky, who spelled out his views in his famous essay, "The Iron Wall" (in which he argued that the need for standing firm against the Arabs stemmed from a recognition of the power of their nationalistic aspirations), Begin continued to underestimate the power of Palestinian nationalism.

In May 1975, in a series of articles on Israeli television, reporter Dan Samama revealed that Herut had substantial debts, starting with the Tel Chai Fund, established back in Jabotinsky's time and designed to serve the party, in the same way that the Workers' Corporation served the Histadrut. The reports revealed that since the establishment of the fund, Herut had accumulated over 33 million lira in debt (mostly to banks, to the Jewish Agency, and to party members who were lured into lending money to the fund). It was more than Haavoda owed. The scandal triggered by Samama's reports was the hardest blow Begin had to deal with before being elected prime minister.

The difference between the debts of Herut and Haavoda was not only in the amounts. Herut, unlike Haavoda, had accumulated large debts in the private market as well. After the information was made public, debt collectors and suppliers flocked to Herut's offices, including Begin's office.[48] He shut himself in his room on the twelfth floor of Metzudat Ze'ev and tried to resolve the crisis. The first, instinctive, decision he came to was motivated by pride, as if he wanted to punish himself: he proposed to forgo his salary and demanded that the rest of the movement's Knesset members do so as well. And indeed, over the next six months he did not receive any salary, nor did Bader or Livni.[49] Begin, the master of rhetoric, whose signature was on many bounced checks, preferred to remain silent when the affair began. For the first time he had nothing to say to the media. He asked Yosef Kremerman, the party treasurer, to explain that the debt was primarily for funds distributed to the Etzel wounded and families of the fallen, who did not receive compensation from the newly established state.

When journalists demanded to be shown documents of expenditures, it turned out that none of the party's institutions had ever received or written a financial statement; Herut was not punctilious with its bookkeeping. There were those who accused Begin of mishandling the party budget, and there were those who said that he had been led astray because of his innocence.

When Begin decided he would personally respond to the crisis, he stated that over six hundred Etzel members had been killed. Yet some journalists were quick to note that Begin himself had written that only four hundred Etzel members had fallen.[50] Herut was in disarray. Not only did his own party members feel that he was not to be trusted, but the crisis also fed the doubts about the myth created during Begin's days in the underground. There were those who reminded the public that Etzel had obtained most of its funds through confiscations and raids of various kinds, and there were those who wondered what had become of the hundreds of thousands of dollars transferred by Hillel Kook to the party in Israel after the dismantling of the Etzel headquarters in the United States.

The conceited Begin never imagined that one day Mordechai Raanan, the Etzel commander in Jerusalem, and Amichai Paglin would claim he was lying. Although no one suspected him of lining his own pockets or of involvement in corruption, as the person responsible for the Tel Chai Fund, he was now perceived as a weak man who had little understanding of what was going on around him. Begin spent many days in 1975 abroad on fund-raising trips to cover the party's debts.[51] He left to Bader the unpleasant job of putting forward a bill in the Knesset for financing party debts, a bill that Hamaarach supported and that eased the crisis.[52]

With regard to political affairs, Begin's relations with young Rabin were not as friendly as his ties with Eshkol had been, but they were better than his ties with Golda Meir. The comfortable relationship between them was at its peak in June 1976, when Palestinians and Germans kidnapped an Air France airplane with ninety-eight Jews on board, including Israelis, and landed it in Entebbe, Uganda.

Rabin did as Ben Gurion had done before the outbreak of the Sinai campaign and updated Begin, as leader of the opposition, on the developments. Begin promised Rabin, as he had previously promised Ben Gurion, that he would support any decision the government made, whether it be to conduct negotiations with the terrorists or to embark on a military operation.[53] Once again Begin proved how statesmanlike he could be during times of crisis and how much he yearned for legitimacy—how his very inclusion in events, even in the most passive of ways, weakened his tendency to harm his opponents. In fact, despite his outspoken dislike of "Diaspora mentality" and his view that every position of compromise presented to the world by spokespersons from the Left was a surrender to the Gentiles, his willingness to support prime ministers who shared state secrets with him echoed that very same "Diaspora mentality"—as if he needed recognition and rehabilitation by those stronger than he.

Begin kept his promise and supported the government's decision to conduct a military operation. But he found it difficult not to talk about it. "Rabbi," he whispered to Shlomo Goren, Chief Ashkenazi Rabbi of Israel, as they prayed together at their synagogue a day before the operation to extract the hostages, "the people of Israel need a large blessing," and he disclosed the military secret to him.[54]

After the audacious and successful military operation, *Haaretz* published some of the details, including the exchange between Begin and Rabbi Goren. Though *Haaretz* tended to vilify Begin for his chattiness, this characteristic story also indicated his ability to understand his people better than journalists could. What appeared to the journalists as a clear breach of censorship was seen by many Israelis, most certainly in the midst of the post-operation enthusiasm, as including rabbis in the miracles that happened to the people of Israel.[55] Indeed, Begin was not harmed by revealing the secret, and in fact, there were those who claimed that the operation had been successful because of the rabbi's blessing.

The successful operation had a huge impact on the general mood in the country, which was low after the failures of the Yom Kippur War. Government ministers rushed to the airport when the plane with the former hostages arrived, as they thought the large crowd that had gathered at the site was there to express admiration for them. But the man the crowd chose to hoist up on its shoulders was actually Menachem Begin. The criticism against him for taking over the celebrations was overshadowed by the real story of the survivors. The enthusiasm at the airport was a prelude to the enormous change approaching in Israeli politics. It was clear that the people, through they recognized the government's achievement, preferred to rejoice with new leaders more popular than those of Hamaarach.

In fact, not only joy for the survivors and electoral considerations had motivated Begin to go to the airport. The importance he attached to Operation Entebbe—which took place more than four thousand kilometers from Israel—was also due to his attitude toward Germans, for here again were Germans attacking Jews (two of the hijackers actually belonged to the extreme leftist Baader-Meinhof Gang); the Jews had once again clashed with their enemy, and this time, they had taken the upper hand. The day after the operation Begin addressed the Knesset with a melodramatic speech, an almost theatrical monologue, in which he quoted some of the survivors' testimonies. "A German, a Nazi leftist, stands and indicates with his finger: these to the left, and those to the right," Begin began, eliciting shudders throughout the room. "Only thirty years have passed since the crematoriums and the boundless cemeteries were revealed before our eyes, while we remember Mengele standing between two rows of Jews, men and women, children and babies, indicating with his finger, right and left, right and left . . . and here it is again." Begin also made a practical proposal during his speech—the establishment of an international unit for ridding the world of terrorism—and even named it: Yud Kaf (Hebrew initials for "Honor Unit"), to which "thousands will volunteer, all of whom must remain anonymous."[56]

Begin's speeches were characterized by pomposity, exaggerations, and poetic phrases, but these were not simply a political tool; this was his style in personal matters and all other areas as well. He called his granddaughter "the nicest granddaughter in the world"; he opened the 1966 Herut conference with the words "Gentlemen, it is a time of trouble for Israel and it must be saved"; and in 1975, when Arabs tore pages from two Torahs, he said, "Never has such pain been felt."[57] The combination of self- and national pity with threats and demonstrations of force was integral to Begin's rhetoric, and this spirit was about to shape the state of Israel in the years to come.

THIRTEEN

GOD, YOU HAVE CHOSEN US TO RULE

The 1977 election results reflected the influence political disappointment had on the voters, mostly due to repeated conflicts among politicians, including Prime Minister Yitzhak Rabin and Defense Minister Shimon Peres; reports on corruption in Hamaarach; and the trauma after the war, which weakened the government. Before the elections, Simcha Ehrlich had replaced Elimelech Rimalt as head of the Liberal Party, Weizmann had returned to the political scene after ensuring his economic future, Bader had decided to resign from the Knesset, and Sharon had left the post of prime minister's adviser on matters of terrorism and returned to the Likud.[1]

The year 1976 saw an intensification of public demand to change the government and bring about reforms in the economy and society; the demands resulted in the establishment of a new party—Dash (acronym for Democratic Movement for Change). Dash, which symbolized disgust with the political framework, was headed by Yigael Yadin (head of the IDF Operations Branch during the War of Independence and later chief of staff). Begin attacked Dash over the "rudeness of its advertisements," as if he was personally offended as part of the system Yadin sought to refresh.[2] However, Begin rarely referred to a corruption scandal revealed in Hamaarach, despite the stir it had created, maybe because of the embarrassment caused by the Tel Chai Fund affair.[3]

It seemed that everybody wanted a change. Even Shabtai Tevet, Ben Gurion's biographer, wrote an article in which he claimed that it was time for a change of government.[4] The only question was whether Begin was the right man at the right time.

Among the skeptics who doubted Begin's ability to bring about a victory for the Likud was Ariel Sharon. Sharon was more ambitious than Weizmann (who wanted to change the party delegates in order to weaken Begin's dominance); when he returned to politics, he demanded secret internal elections in the Likud and rejected the offer to become number two. Sharon believed that only he could bring victory and even insisted that the Likud propose a bill to change the political system from a parliamentary form of government to a presidential regime, explaining that without a real change in the regime structure, "a change of power will not occur."[5] Begin saw in Sharon's proposal evidence of his nondemocratic nature and rejected it. In response, Sharon resigned and founded a new party—Shlomtzion.[6]

Begin did not reject Weizmann's demand to inject the party with new blood and agreed to let new young members join. He also agreed that the party center would select the list of candidates for the Knesset by a direct and secret vote. His willingness to compromise in matters of control over the party was a result not only of political considerations. He also knew this would be his last election campaign.

During a speech at Tel Aviv University, in which he was basically asking for one last chance, Begin promised, without being asked, to retire at seventy—that is, in 1983. He was so determined that he had already planned what he would do after retirement: he would write the history of the Holocaust and Israel's regeneration, "two thousand pages in three volumes." However, he would not discuss a successor. Yitzhak Shamir, who had joined the Likud after his retirement from the Mossad, tried more than once to appeal to Begin on this matter. He knew that Begin would not suspect him of trying to speed up his retirement and believed he could persuade him to reconsider the issue. "Although your position is undisputed, you might want to have people prepared for the future," he said, trying gently to persuade Begin, adding that "perhaps we should educate them."[7] Begin responded with disinterest because at that time (among other things) he despised Weizmann, who sought to supplant him.[8]

Begin refused to nurture a successor for political reasons as well. He did not want to miss his last chance. "Since the blood libel [Arlosoroff's murder], the Jabotinsky movement has not had such an opportunity," he said two months before the elections.[9] When he was in a good mood, he would explain that he was not leaving his old apartment in Tel Aviv because "I will eventually move to Jerusalem as prime minister."[10] When sitting in the Knesset cafeteria with Kadishai one day, Begin was approached by Eli Mizrachi, Rabin's bureau chief, who told him in passing that his father had been a member of Beitar in Tunis before he immigrated to Israel. Begin's eyes lit up and he said to Kadishai, "Don't you understand? Don't you grasp what he was insinuating?" Begin was experienced enough to realize that if people were demonstrating their connection to the Revisionist roots, it was due to their assessment that he was going to be the next prime minister. Undoubtedly, the political game and the race to connect with power had become familiar to him.[11]

Televised election propaganda had started with the 1969 elections, but at that time not many homes had televisions sets, and the influence of such propaganda was slight. Propaganda broadcasts focused mainly on speeches that did not excel in creativity. Even after the Yom Kippur War election campaigns were conducted mainly in newspapers and town squares. The 1977 election campaign was the first time that televised propaganda had some influence. The newspapers reported with amazement that 50 million lira—a fortune at the time—had been spent on televised campaigns.

Although Begin was at his best when giving public speeches in town squares, he believed that television might serve him, as he saw it as a means of bypassing the mediation of the print media. In November 1976, he proposed a televised debate (as was common in the United States). At the time he was unaware that Rabin would be forced to resign the premiership owing to the Dollar Account Affair involving his wife Leah and that eventually Defense Minister Peres, who would replace Rabin in April, would be the one to run against Begin in the elections.

Three months before the elections, which were due to be held on May 17, as Begin was preparing for a trip to the United States, he suddenly fell ill with stomach poisoning. After his recovery, he went through with the planned trip but fell ill again in Detroit. Upon his return to Israel his doctor requested that he report to the hospital immediately for testing. On the day he was scheduled to go to the hospital, he met with Dayan early in the morning. While going over some documents before leaving for the hospital, Begin suddenly collapsed. Kadishai, who was with him, realized at once that the situation was serious. Begin was rushed to Ichilov Hospital in Tel Aviv, where he was diagnosed as suffering from a heart attack and hospitalized in intensive care. For the first two days of his hospitalization, Begin's aides claimed that he had been hospitalized for routine checkups that had been scheduled in advance. However, when it became known that he was hospitalized in the intensive care unit, his personal physician made an official announcement that Begin had suffered "contractions in his blood vessels around the heart"—in other words, a heart attack.[12]

Begin stayed in Ichilov for two weeks after he was transferred from the intensive care unit. His hospitalization was explained as being due to fatigue. It was not common at the time for the media to pry into the personal matters of the country's leaders, so Hamaarach did not make an issue of his illness. When he was released from the hospital, Aliza said that "His curiosity about the election results is what brought him back to life," and by so doing, she hinted at the seriousness of the situation.[13]

Meanwhile, Dayan's position in his party, Haavoda, had become undermined because he insisted on adding a section to the party's political platform encouraging settlement in the West Bank as well as in the Jordan Rift Valley and Jerusalem. It was after his demand had been rejected that he met with Begin at the hospital. Begin wanted Dayan to join the Likud, but both Ehrlich and Shamir were against it.[14] They feared, as politicians often do, that Dayan would get a major portfolio that would harm their status; furthermore, they claimed that Dayan was an electoral drawback as he was held responsible for the perceived failures in the Yom Kippur War and thus his joining the Likud would weaken the party. In his physical condition it was difficult for Begin to convince his associates to accept Dayan into the party. Paradoxically, Begin's condition and his lack of involvement in the management of the campaign—during the 1977 elections for the first time the race was referred to as a "campaign"—contributed to his victory.

Weizmann, chairman of the campaign headquarters, took the reins. He was the right man in the right place. He was popular and energetic, he was in touch with the new Israeli spirit from which Begin was completely disconnected, and he combined a firm political stand with a willingness to compromise. With regard to the West Bank, he believed that "there is no difference between the areas we conquered in 1948 and 1967," but with regard to Sinai and the Golan Heights he explained that "there we can make an arrangement." During the months preceding the election he would say, "I have no time; I'm busy kicking Rabin out of office."[15]

The 1977 election was the first time in the history of the state that the political parties did not conceal their use of advertising agencies for their campaigns. The Likud, under Weizmann's aggressive management and with the assistance of the Dachaf Institute advertising agency, decided to focus the campaign on changing Begin's image—the party's major problem, according to Weizmann.

In the previous elections Begin had designed the party's propaganda posters himself,[16] and he would probably not have accepted Dachaf's dictates had he not been too weak to object. It was difficult for him to recover from the heart attack (and, as noted, he was also burdened by diabetes). "My pen almost fell out of my hand," he told his close friends who knew how serious his condition was.[17] Because of his physical weakness and because he assumed it was the last election campaign in which he would participate, he collaborated with the advertising agency. Before his heart attack Begin would wake up every morning at six, but after it he found it difficult to wake up and would arrive at Metzudat Ze'ev at eleven.[18] The optimism in his party lifted his spirits, yet he repeatedly promised that if he "did not supply the goods," he would resign.[19]

After regaining his strength, Begin found it difficult to hand over the propaganda baton to Weizmann and the advertising agency. "I know there will be problems with him, with Weizmann," he said.[20] But it became clear that Weizmann was "marketing" him wisely. For the first time Begin was presented as a grandfatherly figure rather than a former resistance leader, and he was photographed walking with his grandchildren on the banks of the Yarkon River, wearing a white golf shirt, without a jacket, and with new glasses.

Now that Weizmann and the advertising consultants were conducting the Likud's election strategy, many movement veterans realized that even if they achieved victory, it would not be theirs. Bader and Landau announced their retirement before the internal elections, and veteran member Eitan Livni was pushed to the back of the list in the internal vote. Begin was elected to the number one spot by the smallest number of votes since he had become chairman of the movement. Unlike in the past, when he was elected unanimously, this time only 511 out of 566 members voted for him. Weizmann was elected to second place, Shamir to third, followed by Moshe Arens, David Levy, Yoram Aridor, and Geula Cohen.

There was only one Mizrahi member among the top seven in the Likud list—David Levy—and he was placed only fifth. But the Sephardis' identification with Begin ran much deeper.[21] In fact, the number of Sephardi Knesset members in Herut was smaller than that in Mapai; when Begin served as prime minister, they were a minority in the leadership but not in the party center, thus creating the impression that they were not just window dressing. David Levy, a construction worker who began his career in politics in the Beit She'an branch of Hamaarach, was one of the only Mizrahi leaders in the Likud and was considered an authentic representative of the Sephardi Jews, while the Mizrahim who were part of Hamaarach's leadership—such as Shlomo Hillel, Shoshana Arbeli Almozlino, Yitzhak Navon, and Moshe Shahal—were considered Mizrahi elitists. Most Iraqi immigrants, who were generally more educated than other Mizrahim in Israel at the time, voted for Hamaarach, while most Moroccan immigrants, who came from villages in their country of origin, voted for the Likud. Israel Eldad often pointed out that in Poland Begin had inspired mostly the weaker and poorer levels of society. As his emotional rhetoric and lofty ideas had contributed to his popularity among the poor in Poland, so they did among the Mizrahim in Israel.[22]

The Mizrahim voted for the Likud despite the fact that there were hardly any Mizrahim on the party Knesset list because their positions were nationalistic, not social. Since the 1955 elections the Mizrahi voters had made up about 60 percent of Herut voters, but only 30 percent of the general Mizrahi population voted Herut. The turning point occurred in 1973, when the second generation translated the fear with which their parents regarded Mapai into hatred toward the establishment. That year, 50 percent of the Mizrahim voted for the Likud.[23] By voting for Begin the Mizrahim did not want a revolution but rather asked for recognition; therefore they did not fancy revolutionary ideas such as those offered by the Black Panthers but preferred the sense of a shared destiny, a fair distribution of resources, and fast improvement in their financial situation—as Begin offered. Begin could not offer them jobs and incomes while in the opposition; he could only offer them what he himself had sought during his days in the underground—respect and legitimacy, not a revolution. From the beginning, the Mizrahim and Begin were a perfect match.

As the election date approached, more viewers watched televised propaganda broadcasts. At the time, the term "rating" was not yet in use, and as there was only one channel, it was watched by millions. Yossi Sarid headed Hamaarach's public relations. As for the Likud, IDF Radio journalist Alex Ansky served as consultant for Weizmann and the Dachaf Institute. The newspapers criticized the Americanization of the propaganda broadcasts, although in retrospect—compared to today's marketing strategies—it could be said that it was a witty campaign. For example, Hamaarach introduced a video clip using the classic monologue "For Brutus is an honorable man" from the play *Julius Caesar*. The character playing Begin was asked, "Is it true that you will not change?" to which he replied, "Certainly not, as I am an honorable man!"[24]

Begin's first public appearance after his release from the hospital was eleven days before the election, during a Knesset discussion on the state auditor's report. The following day he gave interviews to all the newspapers in which he explained that rumors about his health had been spread by his political rivals who wished to create the impression that he was disabled, when in fact, his work filled him with "satisfaction and energy." Begin was careful to adhere to the professionals' advice and pledged "to contribute a lira from my pocket" to anyone who found the words "no piece [of land to be returned]" in his platform. However, during his last day of interviews as head of the opposition, Begin did not let slip the slightest hint regarding the change about to occur in the relations between Israel and Egypt. He claimed that Sadat was an "extreme leader who deters peace" and that a Palestinian state would become a military base for the Soviet Union and a bridge for the Iraqi army, adding that even "after the Six-Day War, Abba Eban called the 1967 borders the borders of Auschwitz."[25] Even Chaim Weizmann, he stressed in one of his interviews, promised the British High Commissioner that "one day we will liberate all the land of Israel," though in 1977 most voters had no idea what he was talking about.[26] Given such utterances, it was clear why Ezer Weizmann had kept Begin away from the public stage.

On May 15, 1977, two days before the elections, tension at the Likud was at its peak. The very notion that a change in power was about to occur increased the members' fears regarding the obstacle in their way—the televised debate.[27] The first one was about to take place between the two leading candidates, Shimon Peres from Hamaarach and Menachem Begin from the Likud. As noted, Begin was at his best when he could make dramatic use of his voice and hand gestures. Though Begin preferred television to the print media, it was foreign to him. Moreover, he had not yet completely recovered from his heart attack and appeared thinner than ever. Begin was apprehensive about the debate, and when he learned that he would not be facing Rabin but Peres, he no longer insisted on going through with it, but now Peres was enthralled with the idea.[28]

One of the Likud's fears regarding the debate was based on the debate between Nixon and Kennedy in 1960, the first televised debate in the United States. Nixon suffered from knee problems and swayed from side to side during the debate, making him appear as a feeble old man, while Kennedy was charming and full of charisma. To make matters worse, Kennedy wore a dark blue shirt because he knew the studio would be light, while Nixon wore a light shirt that blurred his image, was heavily made up, and sweated profusely. According to a survey conducted after the election, Nixon lost the debate among television viewers but won it among radio listeners (he lost the election by a very small margin). Likud strategists learned from the Nixon-Kennedy debate. Alex Ansky coached Begin for many hours in an effort to improve his physical appearance. In order to make him look more tanned, he wore, for the first time in his life, a pale blue shirt. "It was hard to get him one like that, as all his shirts were white," Aliza said.[29]

The debate, hosted by journalist Yishayahu (Shaike) Ben Porat, lasted over forty minutes. Each candidate was allotted three minutes to answer every question. Peres presented himself as a new figure in politics, "only four weeks at the head of the party" (as opposed to Begin's twenty-nine years), and promised to set up new ministries—science and technology, welfare and the environment—while Begin promised that the government would be made up of only twelve ministers and that he would reduce bureaucracy. Despite his opposition to land concessions, he said he would strengthen ties with the United States because Israel was a strategic asset in the area in light of the threat of a Soviet takeover of the Middle East. Peres said that he too wanted the River Jordan to be Israel's security border, but unlike Begin, he was in no hurry to make any extreme declarations. The two candidates were very excited, but Begin was clearly more so. When the debate first started, Begin's gaze constantly searched for the cameras. Furthermore, despite his blue shirt, he looked pale and weak and sweated just as profusely as Nixon had done in his debate. But the Israeli public is different from the American. What Americans perceived as a disadvantage was taken by the Israeli viewers as an advantage. The sweaty and excited Begin triggered sympathy. His appearance—which was ill-suited to the medium—actually made him seem to be a responsible and mature Jew who did not sleep at night because of his concerns for Israel. When the debate ended and the cameras were turned off, Begin could no longer resist some humor and remarked while Peres was removing his makeup, "Oh, look how beautiful he is." His associates burst into laughter.[30]

One of the greatest contributions to the Reversal, as Israeli TV announcer Chaim Yavin named the outcome of the exit poll results he announced on election day, was the 1967 war, which turned Begin's anachronistic aspirations to reality. Ten years after the war, Begin's claim—"The West Bank, the Golan Heights, the Gaza Strip, and Sinai are all ours"—was accepted by the majority of the public. But what contributed most to Begin's rise to power was the demographic change that had occurred in Israel, resulting both from the natural growth rate among the Mizrahim and the religious community—the potential Likud voters—and from a change that occurred among the working class: workers had become contractors, craftsmen had become factory owners, and vendors had become business owners. The socialist slogans were depleted of all meaning. Furthermore, Dash, which attracted many intellectuals, helped to create a shift in power as they preferred the new party over Hamaarach.

The significant demographic changes were apparent in the general election results ever since the state was established. In the first election in January 1949, Herut won a relatively impressive fourteen Knesset seats and was voted in mostly by Etzel activists and fans. In the second election Herut received only eight seats, as the immigrants from Arab countries gave their vote to Ben Gurion, who had brought them to Israel. But over the years, the public lost its dependency on legendary leaders. In 1955 Herut got fifteen Knesset seats, and in 1959 and in 1961, seventeen; in 1965 and 1969 the public voted Gahal in with twenty-six Knesset seats; in 1973, when the Likud was founded, the party received thirty-nine, and in 1977, forty-five (together with Sharon's party Shlomtzion, which joined the coalition the next day).

In fact, Begin was the first leader to say that the government must benefit the people, who have the right to demand and to receive, not only to give. For example, he promised after the election to strive for the establishment of neighborhood rehabilitation projects. (When Simcha Ehrlich, the prospective finance minister in Begin's government, asked where the money for such a project would come from, Begin responded that the rich Jews in the United States would not be able to refuse a request to help their oppressed brethren.)[31] Rabin's government—the first government whose members were not among the founding generation—was seen as a government of technocrats, heightening the public's desire for a paternal leading figure, an old-fashioned authority. Begin, therefore, was the right man at the right time.

All the changes described above were visible to all, yet their sudden expression in the polls on May 17, 1977, was astonishing. The hypothesis that a revolution takes place when a government is no longer able to solve society's fundamental problems while an alternative power rises at the same time applied in this case to Israel. The shock and disillusionment after the Yom Kippur War and people's disgust with the corruption in the stagnating establishment were the last straws.

As the election results became clear, it appeared that the former underground and opposition leader was about to form the next government and head it. Eliezer Jorabin from the Dachaf Institute informed Begin in the early evening that he should prepare a victory speech, but Begin insisted on waiting and even held off preparing an outline. "It's premature," he said. "You should know that it is 150 percent certain," Jorabin said. But Begin continued to object, and unlike in previous elections, he remained at home until the election results were published. A few minutes before ten, when Chaim Yavin declared the Reversal, Begin asked in a whisper, "If not now—when?"[32]

When the sample results came in, Begin had to adapt immediately to new security regulations. Although he lived only a couple of blocks from Metzudat Ze'ev, the police were uncertain how he would make his way there. He delayed the victory speech partly to have time to prepare it and partly to invite his wife and two daughters to the ceremonious event. He hurried to call his son Benny, his close adviser, who was completing a PhD in geology in the United States.[33] Only around midnight, surrounded by fans and admirers, did he arrive on foot at Metzudat Ze'ev, along with his wife, sister, and daughter Chasia.

Begin wore a gray suit, large glasses (not the ones he had worn during the television debates), and a black yarmulke. He was pale, but his eyes sparked. The crowd that gathered outside Metzudat Ze'ev shouted, "Begin to power!" They mocked Peres, singing, "Hoo-Ha! What is done, Peres lost and is gone!" as they had done after the Maccabi Tel Aviv basketball club's victory against the Russian basketball club CSKA, which had taken place earlier in the month. When the tumult began to get out of control, Weizmann asked the crowd "to demonstrate that we are worthy to rule." After all the hugs and kisses, Begin wondered, "Where's Ezer?" When he saw him, the two shared a long embrace. Then he turned to his party's Knesset members, who had all rushed to Metzudat Ze'ev, and asked each and every one of them the same question: "I haven't disappointed you this time, right?"[34]

When the citizens of Israel, huddled around their television sets, saw Begin speak for the first time, they saw a prime minister with an exceptionally different spiritual world from that of his predecessors, one who quoted verses from the Bible and praised Jabotinsky's theories. "Tonight, the history of the Jewish people and the Zionist movement took a turn, the likes of which we have not known for forty-six years, since the seventeenth Zionist Congress, in which Jabotinsky proposed that the goal of Zionism was to establish a Jewish state in our time," Begin said. "Jabotinsky devoted his whole life to this end. He did not live to see the establishment of the state, and he did not live to see today's change. His disciples, who in the name of his teachings and their implementation fought to liberate the nation, persisted with patience and faith in democracy and sought to change the country. With the ballot vote, with the ballot vote only, we have come to this moment."[35]

It is likely that most Israeli citizens did not understand what he was talking about. But at the beginning of his speech Begin was not addressing them but rather the Etzel members who had supported him for many years, his friends who were accused of trying to forcefully seize control of power, the Revisionist movement members who felt ostracized and were bitter because they felt they had sacrificed their lives for a country which had despised them. "From a loyal alliance with Chaim Weizmann's students, Menachem Ussishkin and Abba Hillel Silver," Begin added as he clung to the past, "with our friends from the Liberal Party, disciples of David Ben Gurion, devotees of the Greater Eretz Israel—we have come to power."[36]

At the end of his speech he called out, "Thank God, that he has heard my pleas." He then turned to his wife Aliza and said, "I remember the devotion of your youth, how as a bride you loved me and followed me through the desert, through a land sown with mines." He also thanked his sister Rachel, his two daughters and eight grandchildren, and said, "They wrote me that they were in favor of Begin because he is a good grandfather."[37] As he stepped down from the podium, still wearing a black yarmulke, he kissed Aliza's hand.

When the TV cameras turned to Jerusalem to document the celebrations in the Likud's main branch, the viewers saw a Hasidic band and an elderly white-bearded Jew blowing the Shofar. For an outside observer, it seemed as though the Messiah had arrived.

FOURTEEN

NO MORE WAR

Not since the days of Ben Gurion had a leader been so loved. The victory breathed new life into Begin. On learning the election results, he gave many interviews and found it hard to conceal his delight.

"What kind of leadership style will you bring to Israel?" he was asked before moving from his one-bedroom apartment on Rosenbaum St. to the posh Prime Minister's Residence in Jerusalem. "The usual style—a Jewish style," he replied, with a victor's composure.[1] Even concerning the future of Israel's relationship with Germany, Begin hastened to clarify that his actions as prime minister would not necessarily be the same as those that he had espoused in opposition. When asked what he would do when asked to shake the hand of a German politician, he replied, "I shall act like the prime minister."[2] The rage and impassioned delivery of his opposition days vanished as if they had never existed.

In the first days following the election Begin savored his victory. One of his first instructions at the Prime Minister's Office was that a portrait of Ze'ev Jabotinsky be put beside those of former prime ministers. He waited for the clicking of the cameras while he gazed upon the photograph, his face glowing with the sense of achievement of one who had completed a decades-long marathon. One of the photographs of him at this time shows a pile of newspapers on his desk, with the two left-wing dailies, *Davar* and *Al Hamishmar*, on top. He declared that nothing would change in his daily routine. "As always, I got up this morning at 5:30 a.m.," he would say.[3] It was important for him to express continuity, as if his rise to power was a natural culmination of an expected, preplanned chain of events. His satisfaction derived not just from his political achievement, but also from the belief that he now would be able to fulfill his historic mission, to carry out the divine directive in whose power he had believed since his teens.[4] As fate would have it, however, this historic mission was granted him at the age of sixty-four, while he was still recovering from a serious heart attack and with many of his friends—including Arie Ben Eliezer and Eliyahu Meridor—either dead or retired from politics. Bader had retired from the Knesset before the Great Reversal, Yaakov Meridor had turned to business, and Chaim Landau and Esther Raziel-Naor had turned their backs on political life. Begin had finally arrived—but alas, somewhat late.

Even before Begin assumed the official duties of his new position, it was clear from his comments—such as "Nothing, not even prime ministership, will equal my personal achievements in 1946–47"[5]—that he was not setting out to achieve great things as prime minister. After having waited so long in the opposition, one word that he repeatedly used was "patience." "We waited patiently for twenty-nine years in the opposition," he would say.

Although he had fervently wanted to win the election, when he had actually done so, it appears Begin was so taken aback that he sought to play down the event to allay fears of overly abrupt changes. This is one of the reasons why—much to their dismay—comparatively few Herut members made it into his first cabinet. Indeed, one of the first individuals he made a point of including was Ariel Sharon, whose new party, Shlomtzion, won only two seats in the election. Many within the Likud objected to the appointment of Sharon—including Simcha Ehrlich, the treasury minister and deputy prime minister designate on behalf of the Liberal Party, who muttered about political shenanigans. Sharon very much wanted a cabinet post, however, so on Begin's recommendation he quickly sent Ehrlich a letter of apology in a bid to make amends. Only later did he rejoin the Likud.[6]

Begin and Sharon had maintained a close affiliation since the Yom Kippur War, when Sharon (then a division commander in the Southern Command) had made sure to provide Begin with regular updates. Begin saw in him a model of the modern Jew—a man of the land and a fighter—but was also unsure of him. Sharon had been a favorite of Ben Gurion's, who said he was "an original thinker, who, if he only overcame his tendency not to speak the truth and distanced himself from gossip, would be a superb military leader."[7] Although Begin too admired Sharon's military skills and wanted him in his government, he hesitated to put him in charge of a national security portfolio, given Sharon's well-known difficulties in accepting authority.[8] He therefore declined Sharon's request to head up a new ministry in charge of the secret services, although in a private conversation with him before the government was formed he tried to alleviate Sharon's disappointment by heaping praise upon his capabilities as a military leader. But Sharon took this praise the wrong way and told his friends that Begin was about to appoint him minister of defense. Then, a while later, Sharon surprised Begin with another request: to head the Ministry of Agriculture. This greatly appealed to Begin, and he immediately agreed. Sharon's image suited the importance that he attached to that ministry as a means of establishing new settlements—particularly in the territories administered since the Six-Day War. Begin even asked Sharon to chair the Committee for Settlement Affairs.

After Sharon joined the government, his illegal actions in the course of establishing new settlements often upset Yigael Yadin, head of the new centrist party, Dash, and a leading prospective coalition partner.[9] Begin himself took pains to ensure that the law was respected but usually refrained from intervening in the confrontations between the two. To Yechiel Kadishai, his bureau chief, Begin said, "I'm willing to make concessions wherever possible when it comes to money, honor, and political status—all for the sake of the settlements."[10] Despite his reservations about Sharon's methods of operation, turning a blind eye was one of the "concessions" he was willing to make. In effect, in his own way, Sharon was fulfilling Begin's own goals.

Sharon was not a Herut man, but this did not bother Begin. In fact, he offered three of the five most senior government posts to individuals who were not from Herut: the Ministry of Defense to Ezer Weizmann, the Ministry of Agriculture to Sharon, and the Treasury to Ehrlich. Rumors that Begin intended to offer Moshe Dayan the position of foreign minister caused great bitterness within his camp. Likud officials realized that while Begin was happy to let them share in the struggle to reach power and in the victory celebrations, they were largely shut out when it came to sharing the spoils. Begin refused to flood not only the ministerial ranks with Herut officials, but the managerial ranks as well, and even within his own bureau he made few personal appointments. The party spokesman, Eliyahu Ben Elissar, was appointed general manager of the Prime Minister's Office and Kadishai, chief of staff of Begin's private offices; Klimovitski, as expected, was made his chief personal secretary, and Arie Naor, his aide, was made cabinet secretary.[11] However, in appointing the young Naor (as noted, the son of Esther Raziel-Naor, a Herut MK and the sister of David Raziel, the illustrious Etzel commander in the late 1930s), it was clear that Begin wanted to preserve the warm nest of the "Fighting Family"—as the collection of smaller anti-British underground groups was known—as a kind of Revisionist answer to Labor's Red Notebook.

Even Haavoda officials were amazed at how few political appointments were made in the new administration. They were sure that Mapai's old adversary would rush to "clear" the senior ranks of the old guard. Simcha Dinitz, the Israeli ambassador to Washington and a confidant of Golda Meir, was quick to phone the new prime minister and offer him his resignation. Much to his surprise, Begin asked him to stay on, thus allaying the anxieties of many other government officials.[12]

Likud grassroots activists, however—some of them party veterans—were not pleased, and they called a conference to vent their disapproval of Begin's appointments policy. Among them were many of his loyal companions, including Eitan Livni, who had stayed by his side through the long years in the political wilderness. They accused him of cowardice and sucking up to the establishment. A few even accused him of betrayal. They claimed that a regime could not truly be replaced without changing the people in the administration.[13] But Begin stood firm. "I did not attain power in order to hand out jobs to Etzel members," he replied angrily.[14] When one of his people expressed his desire for a "public career," Begin was aghast; the word "career" was not even in his personal lexicon.[15]

Begin himself was of course not entirely innocent and naturally had political goals of his own, but he did think that everyone had a duty of loyalty toward society, and therefore whoever sought to "make a career" out of public service must at the very least keep it to him- or herself. In conversations with grassroots activists he spoke about "majesty," "decency," and "civil servants" and declared, *"Banu lesharet—lo lareshet"* (We've come to serve, not to inherit). But his statesmanlike messages also came across as pompous. His audience was dumbfounded; it was hard to escape the feeling that his appointments showed a lack of appreciation of his own people or at the very least a lack of confidence in their ability to run the country.

Begin tended to pass over his fellow party members for three reasons. First, he indeed judged them ill-equipped to make the transition from critics to managers. Although he had already been a cabinet minister, he himself was not very good at managing his daily routine. When he began working as prime minister, his office staff discovered that he wrote down his daily agenda on little notes, that he did not even have a pen,[16] and that he also personally drafted every political missive, as if he were still the head of an underground organization and not the leader of a country in touch with dozens of foreign counterparts. It was only after some time in his new position that he understood that he would have to delegate.[17]

The second reason was Begin's notion of "civil servants." As an admirer of the British system, he believed that the civil service must be a professional body that does not change with every change in the party in power. This belief tied in with his particular notion of the state (inspired by the philosophy of Jabotinsky), which placed the state above the individual. His admirers saw this as a model of decency.

The third reason stemmed from the fact that by the time Herut had finally formed the government, it had lost many of its good people. For this reason, Begin decided to offer the position of foreign minister to Moshe Dayan, who had entered the current Knesset as a Labor MK. The two had known each other since their days in the underground, somewhat before the Saison, at a meeting in which Dayan represented the Haganah. Even then Begin had marveled at Dayan, who struck him as a modern Bar-Kokhba, the great historical military leader. In years to come, Begin would say how in those days he suspected that in his heart of hearts Dayan had identified with the Etzel fighters and that Dayan had told him that he admired Etzel for teaching Jews how to fight.[18] Since then, Dayan's and Begin's political views had also grown more similar. In this context, it should be noted that Begin had paved the way for Dayan to become minister of defense when the National Emergency Government was formed in 1967. Now, a decade later, Dayan realized that sitting in the opposition as a member of the Labor Party would hasten his political demise, given the knock that his reputation had received following the Yom Kippur War debacle.

While Dayan was looking to redeem himself after the war, Begin had his own reasons for extending him a hand. Although Dayan's prestige as a military leader was somewhat tarnished, Begin felt he needed a familiar and acceptable figure in his government because as soon as he took office, he received indirect signals from Washington that it was preparing for a change in its relationship with Israel.[19] The editorials in the world's major newspapers, which still regarded Begin as an opposition leader with a terrorist past, also played a part in his decision.

"A negative campaign is being conducted against me in the world's press," he told Arie Naor, "and appointing Dayan will give the government international legitimacy."[20]

Nevertheless, the partnership of Begin and Dayan was odd. Israeli politics had seen its share of party splits and defections before—even Ben Gurion, after all, had left Mapai to set up Rafi—but Dayan's jumping ship from Avoda to Likud in return for a senior cabinet post seemed like an extreme stunt, as did Begin's appointment of him. "Come back, Rachamim Kelanter—all is forgiven," wrote Hannah Zemer, editor of *Davar*, referring to the notorious Jerusalem council member who had defected for political gain twenty years earlier and whose name had become synonymous with political prostitution.[21]

Not only left-wing commentators were up in arms. When word first got out about Dayan's appointment, the families of those who had fallen in the Yom Kippur War organized a protest rally, and some of them even threw stones at the windows of Begin's apartment. Acting on Kadishai's advice, Begin went out to them, and with a hand over one eye—alluding to Dayan's famous eye-patch—explained in simple terms that the reason for his decision was Dayan's prestige in foreign circles. "The country needs a foreign minister who invokes respect," he said, adding that Dayan's aura was such that "foreign officials who know they're about to meet him make sure to put a crease in their trousers."[22] By implication, he was admitting that in his own party there were none who equaled Dayan in stature.

When forced to explain his appointment to those on the Right, however, Begin focused on Dayan's image as a fighter and said that he had chosen a foreign minister who "would make the Arabs shake in their boots."[23] Begin set great store in such matters of image, but there was one more motivating factor: appointing Dayan, who in his youth had already been tapped to be Ben Gurion's successor, was for him a kind of closing of the circle—and, as noted, Begin loved to close historical circles.[24] For this same reason he offered Yitzhak Shamir the position of Knesset chairman. He had little appreciation for the political skills of this introverted and suspicious man, but he told Kadishai that it was important to him that the former Lehi head finish his political career honorably. Shamir's appointment was not only a symbolic gesture, however. Begin relished the ceremonial moments of anointing his old comrades in new posts. "See?" he chuckled to Kadishai after Shamir had accepted his offer. "Our Michael [Shamir's underground code name] is now Knesset chairman thanks to us."[25]

Although civil service officials were not replaced with Revisionists, the Great Reversal was noticeable in other areas. Under Begin Israel became, as he had promised, more Jewish in character—starting with the makeup of the coalition. It was now clear that the Mafdal (under Zevulun Hammer) would join the government, as Hammer and Begin had agreed well before the election outcome was known. Ideologically, their respective brands of Zionism were similar, and the Mafdal still bore a grudge against Hamaarach for allowing the F-15 fighter planes that Israel had bought from the Americans in 1976 to land in Israel on the Shabbat—a move that had outraged Mafdal cabinet ministers and had led to their dismissal. Although the pairing of Mafdal and Likud was predictable, the cabinet post that Begin decided to give Mafdal was surprising; for the first time in Israel's history, the Ministry of Education would be given to a religious party, in addition to its traditionally held portfolios of the Interior Ministry and the Ministry of Religions. Under Begin, the national-religious camp would wield its greatest influence, despite the fact that he was encroaching upon its electoral base; with his own national-religious rhetoric, Begin vied with the Mafdal leaders, converting many traditionally Mafdal voters into future Likud supporters.[26]

Begin's main innovation with regard to the religious parties was his active courtship of the ultra-religious ones, which had shunned all overtures to join government coalitions in the past, following a 1951 resolution to conscript women into the army. Well before he even approached the centrist Dash party—the party that was supposed to be the senior coalition partner—Begin invited the ultra-religious Agudat Israel to join the cabinet. In this he deviated from a consistent position held by all previous administrations, but, as in so many other areas, his personal priorities dictated the political agenda. Moreover, because, as he saw it, all previous Israeli administrations had wandered too far from Jewish tradition, he gave in to many of the ultra-religious demands without demur. Thus, for example, he unhesitatingly acceded to Agudat Israel's demand that all El-Al flights on the Shabbat cease. Menachem Porush, the party leader, was astonished that Begin did not even ask for anything in return during their negotiations.[27]

El-Al immediately expressed concern about incurring losses as a result of this decision, so Begin appointed the designated coalition chairman, Chaim Corfu, to head a committee that would examine the extent of such losses. Corfu came to the conclusion that El-Al would indeed be adversely affected, but Begin had not intended to lose sleep over mere financial considerations. He dispatched a letter to Corfu: "When I was a boy at school, they tried to rub pork lard on my lips. I fought back with all my might and stood up to them." Indulging further in reminiscence, he added that throughout his school years—from elementary school through to university—he never once wrote on the Shabbat.[28] The message was clear: as long as Begin was prime minister, El-Al would not fly on the Shabbat. He had made up his mind and would not be budged on the matter. When it became apparent that Corfu took issue with his decision, Begin called him and with Porush by his side, asked him sweetly, "Chaimkeh, who told your wife about your new position?"

"You did," Corfu replied.

"So I'm telling you now: El-Al will not fly on Shabbat," Begin said and hung up.[29]

(Begin also objected to television broadcasting on Saturdays. "This is not Norway but a Jewish state," he explained. But he did approve of radio broadcasting on Shabbat because he strove to combine the secular way of life with a Jewish character and also because it had been his favorite means of communication since his underground days.)[30]

Thus, even before his cabinet was finalized, Begin changed the status quo that had existed in the prickly relationship between the religious and secular camps. His decisions were the outcome not only of coalition politics, but also of his own world outlook. He saw in the Jewish tradition a bridge linking the past, present, and future of the Jewish people, as well as all parts of the nation.[31] When he came to power, it became apparent that expressions such as *Be'ezrat hashem* (With God's help), which riddled his speech, were not merely an affectation, but a genuine part of his world outlook. The importance that he attributed to the Jewish character, as a value in its own right, merged with a sincere love of Jewish tradition. While personally not observant of Jewish religious law—ironically, only after becoming prime minister did he begin to use the telephone on Saturdays without apology[32]—his faith in God was evident in everything he did.

Not surprisingly, the spiritual leaders of Agudat Israel, the Council of Great Torah Scholars, gave it the nod to join the secular coalition—albeit not the cabinet itself. The large budgets that Begin promised for religious seminaries helped secure the support of Rabbi Eliezer Menachem Shach, the head of the Poniewiez Seminary and leader of the Lithuanian ultra-orthodox movement. When asked why he had given his support, Rabbi Shach cited a well-known parable by Rabbi Yisrael

Meir Hacohen (a.k.a. Hachafetz Chaim), who once said, "If you find yourself at a fair, grab anything that might be useful."[33] And with Begin, the ultra-orthodox could grab quite a lot. As part of the coalition agreement, the previous limit on the number of seminary students who could be granted exemption from military service (four hundred) was abolished, on the grounds of the same "His prayer is his craft" argument with which the ultra-orthodox had extracted the original concession from Ben Gurion. Begin probably had no idea quite how many would avail themselves of this exemption in the years to come, but the idea that young ultra-orthodox men formed Israel's "spiritual army" clearly appealed to him. The number exempted from military service swelled during Begin's time in office into the thousands, and no prime minister has since dared lay a glove on this arrangement with the ultra-orthodox.[34]

Begin's bouts of enthusiasm impacted his decisions in areas well outside matters of religion. When he met with Israel Eldad—who had criticized him more than once in the past but was quick to congratulate him on his win—he declared, "You'll see; by the time I'm done, I'll have five generals in my government!"[35]—by which he meant Dayan, Weizmann, Sharon, Yadin, and Meir Amit (of Dash). When Eldad reminded him that none of these were followers of the Jabotinsky doctrine, he replied simply, "Leave it to me."[36] Already during his Etzel days, Begin regarded senior officers as "experts" upon whom he could call to put his ideologies properly into practice. He hugely admired many of senior rank but, as noted, not all of them—especially not Ezer Weizmann, who still sought to succeed him. In fact, Weizmann, who had helped Begin win the election, was made minister of defense mainly because Begin was afraid that he would demand the Foreign Ministry, which Begin regarded as more important in deciding Israel's strategy.[37]

One of the first people to come to terms with the Reversal was Hamaarach leader Shimon Peres, who said in a radio interview the day after the Likud's historic win that his party should accept the results "like men" and called Begin to congratulate him. "On a personal level we shall remain friends, and in politics—opponents," said Peres, whose phone call was something of an innovation in Israeli politics. Priding himself in his gentlemanly gesture, Peres pointed out that Begin had never congratulated Hamaarach leaders when they were elected. But Begin responded with an innovation of his own by ending the exchange on a personal note: "And give my regards to your wife."[38] (Begin's chivalrous attitude toward women was also evident when he received the official mandate from President Efraim Katzir to form the new government. Katzir appeared embarrassed when Begin leaned toward Nina, his wife, and kissed her hand. Begin felt the need to conduct himself in this manner, despite the derision that his mannerisms prompted among Israeli journalists. But the president's wife appeared to be quite pleased with the gesture.)[39]

During Begin's time in office, Israel became a country whose style of government, including in matters of strategy, became more emotional, more ceremonial, and more given to the whims of its leader and his temperamental character. The Reversal belonged not to the Likud, but to Begin himself. He made little effort to confide in his designated ministers, and since his political standing within the party was rock solid, no one dared challenge his decisions. Although he would often consult Ehrlich on political matters and listened to Weizmann and Dayan, he made most of the important decisions on his own. As in his early days in politics, he believed that when it came to coalition negotiations, no one could get the better of him.

At first Begin conducted the coalition talks at his Knesset office. Just as in the days before his heart attack, he would rise early, before six, make himself a cup of Turkish coffee, and peruse most of the daily newspapers. He would then set off to his Knesset office, accompanied by Kadishai. His mood would then change: he would smile and reminisce about his days in the underground and once again tell the joke of the old Jew shouting for Begin to come to power.[40] And here they were, Begin having come to power earlier than the old man had predicted.

On emerging from his office, Begin would patiently answer questions put to him by the many reporters who waited to hear his latest pronouncements, and he would expound on his views, mostly in general terms, including declarations about peace, which "will come any day now."[41] He would often accompany these declarations with further promises, mainly about the settlements and "Judea and Samaria," as the West Bank now became known.

Well before the coalition talks were complete, Begin traveled to Kadum in Samaria, a civilian camp that served as the infrastructure for a new settlement. Hoisted upon the shoulders of dancing settlers, he declared, "The elections have brought about a turning point also with regard to settlements within the Land of Israel. Soon there will be no need for a temporary camp, and there will be many more like [the settlement] Alon Moreh!" When one of the dancing women declared in front of the cameras, "The days of the Messiah have come!"

Begin said nothing. Pictures showing him dancing with the bearded settlers were published in newspapers around the world. Ehrlich told Begin that his euphoria might harm Israel's image abroad and asked that he tone down his statements. Begin promised to try.

On June 20, 1977, about a month after the elections, Begin announced in the Knesset that he had formed a new government. At first, the coalition had the support of only 62 of the assembly's 120 members. Although Dash, which had won fifteen seats, had not yet joined the government, Begin predicted that it would eventually, despite unresolved disputes in negotiations. He therefore decided to put aside four portfolios for it and present his cabinet as it stood.

Begin presented his government and its founding principles for Knesset approval while members of his family and many of his former underground comrades sat in the visitors' gallery, clearly moved by the occasion. The founding principles included, for the first time in the history of Israeli governments, a statement that "the Jewish people have an eternal historic right to the Land of Israel, the land of our forefathers—an unassailable right."[42] In his speech, Begin emphasized the right of the Jewish people to settle throughout the Land of Israel—"our ancestors' beloved land," as he called it—but at the same time he dropped a hint at the compromise he was planning. Few among his listeners spotted the subtle gap in his speech between the people of Israel's ancestral right to settle in the Land of Israel and the duty to fulfill that right. True to form, Begin could not resist mentioning that Jimmy Carter, the recently elected U.S. president, had quoted from the Book of Micah in his inauguration address. He himself then chose a quote from the Book of Isaiah: "And they shall beat their swords into plowshares, and their spears into pruning hooks." No one foresaw the imminent changes in the relationship with Egypt and Begin's willingness to make compromises over the Sinai Peninsula.

Begin's first speech as prime minister was a mixture of euphoria, spite, and humor, all of which characterized him in moments of elation. It included a dig at Shulamit Aloni (leader of the left-wing Ratz party) over her reduced political base, as well as promises for a better future and national unity. He devoted a sizable part to the meaning of the Holocaust in the history of the people of Israel and once again recounted the story of how his father, along with five hundred other Jews of Brisk, was drowned while singing "Hatikva"[43]—a familiar story that his sister Rachel claimed was untrue. He also announced that he had decided that Israel would take in a group of Vietnamese boat refugees, in light of the lessons learned from the Holocaust. This decision proved to be the first in a series of resolutions that resulted from the impact the Holocaust had had on him.[44]

With the government sworn in, Begin continued a tradition that he had begun as a cabinet minister in the National Unity Government of 1967: he went to the rabbis for their blessing. This time he met with Rabbi Tzvi Yehudah Hacohen Kook, the spiritual leader of the nationalist Gush Emunim movement. Rabbi Kook indeed blessed the new prime minister in front of the television cameras and the next day sent him a letter in which he called the Likud's victory a "divine enlightenment."[45] Begin was thrilled; Mapai's election victories had never received such an endorsement.

Begin presented his new government as one of experts and professionals. He announced that cabinet meetings would be shorter, decided to make them smoke-free, and vowed to put an end to the phenomenon of leaks to the press. That, after all, was how meetings had been conducted in the underground. In his first meeting with Avraham Achituv, head of the Shabak (acronym for General Secret Service, formerly the Shin Bet), he listened as Achituv briefed him on ongoing operations; when Achituv had finished speaking, Begin told him bluntly, "I forbid you to use torture. I know that there is a price to pay in the results of investigations when torture is not used—I've been subjected to interrogations myself—but I want you to rely solely on the interrogator's guile."[46] No prime minister had ever made such a demand of the Shabak, but Begin, who during the election campaign had vowed to abolish the Ministry of Police on the grounds that it violated the freedom of the individual in a democratic society, was determined to achieve his aims concerning the rights of the individual.

No major disagreements emerged during Begin's meetings with the heads of the defense services, but there were certainly differences with regard to etiquette. Yitzhak Chofi, head of the Mossad, had planned to resign after Begin was elected, telling his wife, "I wouldn't be able to work with him."[47] But following their first meeting and the more they got to know each other, Chofi was impressed by Begin's seriousness and was persuaded to continue in his post. Every time he entered the prime minister's office, Begin would jump up out of his seat and greet him, "Commander Chofi!" The Mossad chief finally asked Begin to stop using the formal title and address him by his Palmach nickname, Chakah.[48]

A few months later, when Begin decided to appoint Amichai Paglin ("good Gidi") as his adviser on terrorism, his disagreements with the military establishment deepened. Paglin, an Etzel veteran who became an industrialist after independence, clashed with Chofi on many occasions over the methods of operation that Chofi was proposing, and Begin was forced to intervene. Although the conflicts were of a professional nature, the tone was reminiscent of the old underground hostility between the Haganah and Etzel. Paglin saw the chiefs of the Mossad and the Shabak as heirs to the leaders of the Palmach and Shai (the precursor to the Shabak during the British Mandate period) and found it hard to disguise his aversion toward them, thinking that part of his job was to teach them how to be decisive and resolute, in the Etzel spirit. For their part, senior defense officials wondered why Paglin had even been appointed, given that he had never done any regular military service.[49] A few months later, Paglin died in a car accident.

Even before his election as prime minister, Begin was unhappy with the Palmachnik mentality of military officers and the casual attire typical of Sabras. Since he believed in the power of new language to change reality, in the early days of his premiership he sought to call the IDF generals by a rare biblical term, Matzbi'im—that is, "captains of hosts" or "military leaders."[50] To his office staff he explained that in his view the heads of the army and the security services were on a par with the greatest military leaders of Jewish history, such as Bar-Kokhba and Yehudah Hamaccabi.[51] Many officers sniggered at this but admired him nonetheless for his decisive leadership style.[52] Begin's innovations extended beyond terminology to include dress style. The open-necked, short-sleeved white or light blue shirts of previous prime ministers were replaced with sober Western suits, and very rarely did Begin appear without a jacket. His suits were the stuff of legend long before his election as prime minister, even though they were old-fashioned and ill-fitting.[53]

In Begin's meetings with Chofi, the Mossad head raised the issue of Israel and its bond with Jewish communities around the world. Begin had no concerns regarding the future demographic ratio of Jews to Arabs within Israel since he predicted that the gates of the Soviet Union would soon open and millions of Jews would immigrate to Israel.[54] Therefore Chofi's suggestion—to urge the U.S. president to restrict the number of Jews allowed into the United States from both the Soviet Union and Iran (where the first signs of an imminent Islamic revolution had begun to appear) so that they would be obliged to immigrate to Israel—was strange. "Absolutely not," Begin said flatly. "Never shall I ask a Goy [Gentile] to refuse entry to a Jew into his country."[55] It was clear that Begin's approach was influenced by the Holocaust, when the Jews had no country and many world leaders denied them entry into their countries even though they were being persecuted. But now the Jews had a state, and Chofi was taken aback—not so much by Begin's position as by the fact that the prime minister was referring to the president of the United States as a "Gentile."

Begin's habit of viewing strategic issues in terms of Gentiles versus Jews was rooted, as we have seen, in a deep-seated worldview.[56] Thus, upon taking office he directed the Mossad to focus on fostering Jewish immigration to Israel since he believed that only Israel could provide Jews with a safe haven. He was also the first Israeli prime minister to order the transportation of Ethiopian Jews to Israel—and, as was his custom, he put out feelers to the rabbis to see what they thought of this. Only after they confirmed that Ethiopian Jews would be considered bona fide Jews under the Halacha did he give the order to redouble the efforts to bring them over.[57]

Begin was fascinated by the Jews of Ethiopia—due to their exotic appearance and their particular history—and on more than one occasion he pointed to their noble demeanor, as indicated by their willingness to accept authority.[58] He offered Mengistu Haile-Mariam, the Ethiopian military dictator at the time, considerable arms in return for allowing them to come to Israel (via Sudan). As far as he was concerned, bringing Jews to Israel was a mission of supreme importance. When he first watched a video showing Mossad operatives leading Ethiopian Jews to the seashore, he departed from protocol and invited Kadishai into the cabinet meeting room in the midst of a cabinet meeting: "Yechiel, you must come and see this film."[59]

Begin's style and frequent invocations of the Holocaust were not the only, or even the most significant, changes at the Prime Minister's Office. When he took over, few suspected that he would make any effort to establish peace with Israel's neighbors. When Naor, his cabinet secretary, was a guest at his home one day, they sat sipping tea and talking about upcoming events, and Begin surprised him with the revelation that his big dream—"since November 30, 1947, the day after the U.N. resolution to partition Palestine"—had been peace. "It's a fact," he said. "The decree in which Etzel announced that it would disband and establish a political party already stated that the Hebrew foreign policy would be a policy of peace—we underlined those three words."[60]

Begin's desire for peace should not have surprised anyone who knew him well. Unlike Ben Gurion, who before Israel was established dreamed of conquering southern Lebanon and after the 1956 Sinai campaign spoke of "the Third Kingdom of Israel,"[61] Begin was never an imperialist, in spite of his belligerent declarations. His combative positions were designed to protect the Land of Israel and to serve as counterweights for the Jews' helplessness during the Holocaust. Even as a cabinet minister during the Six-Day War, he did not suggest that the eastern bank of the Jordan be captured (although he regarded it as part of Greater Israel), and as Etzel commander he asked that certain operations—such as the conquest of Jaffa—be halted when he realized they entailed too many casualties. As a politician he was constantly initiating truces and new, moderate political frameworks, but because of his Etzel background, his fiery speeches, and the years in the political wilderness, he was nevertheless branded a militant.

The criticism leveled at him in the foreign media bothered him. "Well, what have they written about me in English today?" he would routinely ask Kadishai at the start of his first term—and the reply would often cause him to cry out in protest. He was used to critical editorials in Israeli newspapers, but the stream of invectives against him overseas, which focused on his past, pained him. "What, are they still calling me a terrorist? We're not terrorists—we were freedom fighters! Arafat—that Nazi—they call him a freedom fighter, and I'm a terrorist?"[62] Occasionally he reacted with humor. In his first days in office he would show reporters a letter written to him by James Callaghan, the British prime minister, which ended with the traditional closing, "Respectfully yours." Although Begin had a fair command of English, he quipped, "Look—even he respects me."[63]

Precisely because of the concerns expressed in the Israeli and foreign media over his extremism, it appears that Begin regarded a breakthrough in foreign policy to be his most important mission. "Precisely because" are the operative words here.[64] Eldad, who concluded from Begin's words that he was headed for a compromise on the foreign policy front, believed that one of his main motivations was the desire to prove that he could do something of which no one thought him capable or willing.[65] Moreover, since his role model and mentor, Ze'ev Jabotinsky, was first and foremost a political figure—a diplomat in the Zionist statesman tradition of Theodor Herzl—he wanted to leave his mark on history as a statesman and not just as the Etzel commander.[66]

Such was the importance that Begin attached to his image that when he appointed Dayan foreign minister, he hastened to offer Shmuel Katz (the former Etzel official in charge of liaison with the foreign media) the post of minister of information and asked him to go to the United States on a public relations tour to soften Begin's image.[67] When Katz asked him what he should focus on, Begin said that he should say that his government would honor U.N. Resolution 242. Katz was surprised because honoring the resolution meant making territorial concessions in return for peace. At the time, Begin had not yet informed his cabinet that he was planning to do just that—seek peace—with the exception of Dayan, who was his sole confidant in planning his foreign policy moves.[68] He treated his party colleagues as mere messengers. When Katz asked Begin how he understood the resolution, Begin would say no more than "You know the rest as well as I do."[69]

Generally, from the moment he was elected prime minister, Begin began his speeches with a declaration that, at the time, sounded noncommittal: "I shall devote all my energies to the peace agreements." In addition, he abandoned the traditional Herut claims over Transjordan. In conversations with Minister of Agriculture Sharon, he rejected Sharon's suggestion to resolve the refugee problem by viewing the Kingdom of Jordan as the Palestinian state. "Our ancestral right over Transjordan as part of the Land of Israel still holds true," he explained. "But it must not get in the way of our aspirations for peace with King Hussein." When asked if he was therefore abandoning the Jabotinsky doctrine, he replied, "A peace agreement is not necessarily a recognition of Jordan's right over Transjordan—merely a recognition of the objective political situation of our time."[70]

A month after presenting his government, Begin publicly announced that it would accept Resolution 242, the acceptance of which had been the pretext for his resignation from Golda Meir's cabinet a decade earlier. The reason for acceptance, he explained, was a matter of democracy: a government cannot renege on the resolutions of its predecessors. None of his ministers dared contradict him—partly because none of them had imagined that he would implement the decision so soon. The same leader who had forged his view on peacemaking on Jabotinsky's essay "The Iron Wall"—namely, maintaining unyielding military might vis-à-vis the Arabs—had now reached the conclusion that Jabotinsky had intended for the wall to turn into a bridge once the Arabs recognized the existence of the Jewish state and agreed to negotiate with those whom they regarded as having taken their lands.

Begin saw the negotiations between Israel and Egypt as "Phase Two" in the Iron Wall philosophy—that is, the phase in which the Egyptians would be willing to come to the table because they understood that Israel was too powerful to overcome militarily.[71]

There was another reason for Begin's decision to accept Resolution 242. He was alarmed by hints from the American administration about an impending crisis in U.S.-Israeli relations that might result in international pressure to return all occupied territories. "Shmuel, what do you want—a fallout with America?" he retorted when Shmuel Katz expressed concern about his planned compromise.[72] Katz, realizing that Begin was headed for concessions over Sinai, argued that as far as the rest of the world was concerned, there was no difference between Sinai and the Land of Israel, and therefore accepting Resolution 242 would be interpreted as Israel's willingness to withdraw from all the territories it had conquered during the Six-Day War. But Begin disagreed; he saw compromise over Sinai as a suitable means of relieving much of the international pressure over Judea, Samaria, and Gaza.[73]

In a bid to underline the distinction between Sinai and the West Bank and Gaza Begin commissioned a position paper from Professor Yehuda Blum, an expert on international law at the Hebrew University in Jerusalem. Blum came to the conclusion that since the international community (with the exception of Great Britain and Pakistan) did not regard the boundaries of Judea, Samaria, and Gaza as borders in the proper sense, they were technically not occupied territories—in contrast with Sinai and the Golan Heights, whose boundaries were considered international borders. The statement was strictly correct in the narrow legal sense, and Begin thought it an achievement and cited it at every opportunity, but when he brought it to President Carter's attention and saw Carter wince involuntarily in response, he understood that this legalistic sleight of hand would not go down well in the international community.[74]

This anecdote typified Begin's foreign policy initiatives. Although he had decided to establish peace even at the price of territorial compromise, he found it hard to break free of the bonds to his past and his commitment to the Land of Israel. At a meeting of the Zionist Executive Committee in Jerusalem—the first since Begin had come to power—he emphasized that there was no contradiction between his agreement to Resolution 242 and the right of the Jewish people to settle throughout the Land of Israel because that right was not a precondition to negotiations.[75] He also declared that when he retired, he would move his domicile to Neot-Sinai, one of the Beitar settlements in the Sinai Peninsula—much like Ben Gurion before him, who had retired to Kibbutz Sdeh Boker in the Negev.

Begin was, in fact, in a quandary. Throughout his life he had dreamed of becoming prime minister, of leaving his mark upon the country—and when his dream finally came true, the main goal he set himself—to compromise, to make concessions—ran counter to the positions that he had held since his youth. His contradictory declarations were interpreted by journalists as a political gimmick, but in fact they were the start of a process in which he gradually distanced himself from positions that he had held through most of his years in the opposition.

About a month after his government was sworn in, Begin prepared for an important political meeting—with U.S. President Jimmy Carter. Begin's rise to power had surprised the American administration as much as anyone else, and Begin's image as a former terrorist raised both concerns and curiosity. Carter's primary goal was to establish peace in the Middle East. He believed that Israel should retreat from all the territories it had conquered during the Six-Day War and that it must recognize the Palestinians' right to self-determination. Unlike his predecessors at the White House, Carter viewed the Israeli-Palestinian dispute as the heart of the broader conflict between Zionism and the Arabs, and as a Baptist Christian, he attached great importance to the fate of the Land of Israel and the Jewish people.[76]

In his meeting with the U.S. president, Begin—whose diplomatic skills were acquired by listening to BBC broadcasts during his days in the underground—had his first opportunity to draw upon his skills as a statesman. Hitherto, no one outside Israel had considered him very important, and the meeting with Carter appeared to legitimize the Reversal that had taken place in Israeli politics. Knowing that the road to peace ran through Washington, Begin prepared for this visit very thoroughly.

A week before the meeting Begin revealed his political game plan to his cabinet. Aware of the impact his announcement would have on his ministers, he told them that he was proposing to carry out a significant withdrawal in Sinai and that he might even agree to a token withdrawal in the Golan Heights—in return for peace, of course. This was the first time his ministers heard him say explicitly that he was willing to make territorial concessions. But such was his authority among the new ministers, most of whom had adjusted by now to their new status, that something happened that was very unusual in the history of Israeli politics: none of them challenged his intentions, nor was his announcement leaked to the media. None of the journalists who were to cover the meeting at the White House had any inkling of its significance. On the contrary, they continued to dwell upon Begin's mannerisms and quirks of etiquette. As he made his way along the tarmac to the plane heading for Washington, Begin bowed slightly toward the national flag—an unprecedented gesture that underlined how foreign his mannerisms were to the Israeli spirit. But in doing so, Begin was signaling his respect not only for the flag, but also for the historic significance of his forthcoming meeting.

Prior to Begin's departure, Dayan arranged to meet with Samuel Lewis, the U.S. ambassador to Israel at the time, to prepare the groundwork for the visit and minimize the risk of a confrontation between the two leaders. Dayan recommended that the president use the meeting to move matters forward on the Egyptian rather than the Palestinian front. Lewis passed on this recommendation to the administration in Washington, which accepted it.[77] Although Begin feared a confrontation with the United States, it is clear that Washington, too, wanted to avoid a showdown with what it regarded as its primary strategic outpost in the Middle East.

July 19, 1977, was a special day for Begin. On that day, he arrived at the White House as prime minister of Israel. Begin longed for international legitimacy and was determined not to fumble this opportunity. The meeting took place at first in private. Begin put forward no plan but agreed to accept Resolution 242 and to take part in an international conference in Geneva. The two leaders agreed to strive toward establishing a comprehensive peace and not be content with intermediate agreements. Begin saw this as an achievement; he was against intermediate agreements, lest these entailed making territorial concessions with no real return.

But the agreements reached between Begin and Carter did not entirely eclipse their differences. Begin not only ruled out any possibility of withdrawing from Judea, Samaria, and Gaza, but he also tried to apply his persuasion techniques upon Carter. He pulled out a map and explained why a withdrawal would expose Tel Aviv to the danger of Katyusha rockets from "PLO terrorists." Nor was the map the only ploy. When Carter raised the issue of the settlements in the territories, Begin replied by listing American towns and cities with biblical names and asking if the president would consent to the authorities of those towns banning Jews from living there. Carter did not reply but suggested that Begin agree at least to freeze any further construction in the existing settlements. On this subject, too, they reached no agreement. Although Begin agreed to participate in the planned peace conference in Geneva, he insisted that the Jordanian-Palestinian delegation comprise only Palestinians from the administered territories—whom he referred to as the "Eretz Israeli Arabs"—who were not PLO supporters. At the end of the meeting he raised two further issues that struck Carter as somewhat odd—at least in the way in which they were presented: "We must be concerned about the fate of the Christian minority in Lebanon and about the Ethiopian government, which has to contend with Muslim rebels. These goals are most important to me because in light of what it experienced in the Holocaust, the Jewish people cannot stand by in silence when minorities are being mistreated."

At a dinner held later in the presence of many guests, Begin told the president, by the by, that if the peace conference idea did not come to fruition, he would be happy to meet personally with President Sadat of Egypt. At this stage Begin had no definite plan in mind beyond a summit at which he would persuade Sadat to agree to his peace terms. Carter thought the idea was a nonstarter and contented himself with wishing Begin good luck with that. At the end of the dinner, as they bid each other farewell, Begin renewed his efforts to convene the Geneva conference after October 10. Carter asked him why only then, and Begin replied happily that in the weeks until then the entire Jewish people would be busy celebrating the Jewish holidays of Tishrei (first month of the Jewish year, with Rosh Hashanah, Yom Kippur, and Sukkot).[78]

In the days following their meeting, Begin reported that he had had a successful discussion with Carter, despite the differences of opinion. He favorably surprised the American media, not least for refusing to grant an interview to a network whose technicians were on strike, lest he undermine their labor action.[79] American officials also let it be known that unlike Rabin, who had declined to give a good-night kiss to Amy, Jimmy Carter's young daughter, Begin was demonstrably warm toward her. The Israeli press, too, had the impression that the visit was a success, and an article by Dan Margalit in *Haaretz* was indicative of a sea change in the attitude of most journalists toward Begin. "What we are seeing," he said, "is the most authoritative prime minister since Ben Gurion."[80]

During his U.S. visit, Begin also met with leaders of the Jewish community in New York, and these meetings reflected the winds of change that were beginning to sweep through Israeli politics. He was not the first Israeli prime minister to visit rabbis in the United States, but he was the first to kiss the hands of the Lubavicher Rabbi; of Rabbi Moshe Feinstein, one of the leading authorities of Agudat Israel; and of Rabbi Soloveitchik, an accepted authority for the religious-nationalist movement in Israel. These were not merely working meetings but also ceremonial tours of their courts. It was as if he was asking to share his prime ministerial position with the spiritual council of the Jewish people—an idea that he had proposed as far back as the 1950s. Although not religious himself, Begin had grown up in a traditional home, and his yearning for religion made him revere anyone who could at once inspire people to faith and cite chapter and verse in its support.[81] Begin objected in principle to the notion of separating church and state, and in all the debates on this subject he sided with the Orthodox proponents.

"Conversion to Judaism must be in accordance with the Halacha, because the very concept is taken from the Halacha," Begin used to say. But being nonobservant himself, he also met with rabbis from the Reform and Conservative movements, including the Reform rabbi Alexander Schindler, chairman of the Conference of Presidents of Major American Jewish Organizations (CoP). Schindler demanded that the administered territories be returned and was concerned that Prime Minister Begin would be hostile toward the most popular religious movement among American Jews but was favorably surprised by Begin's warm attitude toward him. After the meeting he noted that this was the first time he had met an Israeli prime minister for whom being Jewish meant more than being Israeli.[82]

Begin was, indeed, the most "Jewish" of Israel's prime ministers. At a meeting with members of the CoP during one of his visits to New York, at the height of the crisis in talks with the Egyptians, he noted the criticism leveled at him in foreign circles, then sighed and suddenly said in Yiddish, "Wass willen zei fon uns?" (What do they want from us?) in the manner of the persecuted Jews in the Diaspora. His audience was duly impressed.[83]

On returning to Israel, Begin was so enthusiastic about his visit that he likened his meeting with President Carter to his introduction to Jabotinsky.[84] Such hyperbole was characteristic of him. It stemmed from his buoyant mood and his giddiness at the compliments he had received in the foreign media. He then immediately sought to downplay what he had said but too late; his veteran comrades muttered angrily at the comparison.[85]

When Begin learned that the Arab countries who were set to attend the Geneva peace conference were demanding that PLO members be allowed to be part of the Palestinian-Jordanian delegation, his optimism evaporated. To resolve the issue, he dispatched Dayan to meet with King Hussein of Jordan. At the meeting, which took place in London, Dayan offered to support Jordan on the issue of sharing the civil administration of Judea and Samaria. Hussein was firmly opposed; Jordan, he said, would never agree to sharing authority with Israel over the West Bank without the participation of the Palestinians, for if it did, it would be accused of selling Arab land to the Israelis and sacrificing the rights of the Palestinians. After the meeting, Begin and Dayan realized that talks with Jordan would lead nowhere, and they decided therefore to focus their attention on direct talks with Egypt.[86]

In July 1977, when it seemed that peace talks had reached a dead end, Begin asked Ion Cabac, the Romanian ambassador to Israel, to arrange a meeting between him and Nicolae Ceausescu, the Romanian president, who was on close terms with the Egyptian president. Begin hoped to secure the Romanian dictator's help in preparing the ground for a meeting with Sadat. Ceausescu invited Begin to a meeting in Romania on August 25.

To all outward appearances, the meeting between the two was insignificant, and on setting off to Romania, Begin even avoided the usual ceremonial fanfare of which he was so fond. He had briefed his ministers on his readiness to make territorial concessions even before his meeting with Carter, but none of the ministers—except Dayan—nor any of the senior national security officials was privy to the specific moves that were being contemplated (Minister of Defense Weizmann heard about the substance of the meeting in Romania only after the event).

Begin tended to operate and make decisions on his own—partly because he felt that he had the power and the mandate to do so, but also because (as noted) his old Herut colleagues had either retired from politics or were no longer alive. The sight of his cabinet colleagues and the military officers surrounding him made him feel nothing but nostalgia for the common language that he had shared with the "rebellion gang," his former comrades-in-arms of the underground and the early days of Herut; they spoke his language of the pogroms, the Holocaust, the uprising against the British and the Tkumah (Resurrection), as they referred to Israel's independence—a language that was foreign to his ministers and advisers.[87]

The critical meeting in Romania was held according to Ceausescu's whims, which included discussions while sailing on a lake. Through an interpreter, Begin asked Ceausescu to arrange a meeting between him and Sadat, telling him he was fully aware of all the implications of a peace agreement with Egypt,[88] thereby hinting that he was amenable to a full withdrawal from Sinai.

This secret channel of talks yielded results very quickly. Within two months of Begin's visit to Romania, Sadat visited there too. Ceausescu tried to persuade him that Begin—of all people—was willing and able to conclude a treaty between Israel and Egypt. Sadat listened but gave no clear answer; later in his memoirs he wrote that by the time he had left Romania to fly on to Iran, he had made up his mind: negotiations with Israel would kick off with a meeting with Begin.[89] Years later, he justified his astonishing decision to come to Jerusalem on the grounds that "70 percent of the conflict was a psychological barrier that needed to be surmounted."[90]

The peace talks directly between Israel and Egypt were the outcome of the shared political interest of both parties to hold them. Egypt had incurred heavy debts and needed American aid, and Sadat had reached the conclusion—even before Begin came to power—that an alliance with the West was preferable to close ties with the Soviet Union and that the road to the superpower of the West went through Israel. Already during Rabin's premiership, Egypt's deputy prime minister, Hassan Tohami, had asked for a meeting with Minister of Defense Shimon Peres, but this meeting never came about—partly because Rabin had doubts about Egypt's true intentions.[91] Sadat also understood that he would not achieve his goal of recovering Sinai within the framework of an international peace conference since this would entail Israel's withdrawal from the Golan Heights as well—something that Israel would undoubtedly reject. (For this reason he also turned down Syria's demand that all the Arab countries take part in an international conference as a unified Arab delegation.) To make progress on the Egyptian front, he understood that he must go it alone, independently of other Arab countries. For his part, Begin chose to negotiate with Egypt first and foremost because he saw a compromise over Sinai as a realistic alternative to making concessions over Judea and Samaria, to which he objected on ideological grounds.

The two leaders' desire for direct talks was also the result of a similarity in their personalities. Both were fond of political drama and grand gestures. Both saw their individual charisma as a means for achieving strategic goals. Begin in particular preferred direct negotiations because he was confident in his powers of persuasion. He thought that he could sway the Egyptian president just as he did the audiences of his speeches at home.

Begin was so eager to achieve a breakthrough that he was no longer content to rely upon Ceausescu's mediation. In September he dispatched Dayan, in disguise, to several meetings with King Hassan of Morocco. Among other things, Israel's foreign minister offered to arrange a lower-level meeting between himself and Egypt's foreign minister to prepare the ground for a meeting between Begin and Sadat. With King Hassan's help, such a meeting was indeed arranged between Dayan and Tohami, at which the latter asked whether, should such talks take place, Israel would agree to withdraw from the whole of the Sinai Peninsula; that would be the condition for a public meeting between Sadat and Begin. Dayan refused to make an explicit commitment on this point and replied in vague terms.[92] Dayan and Tohami agreed that they would report to their respective leaders.

While the Dayan-Tohami meeting was going on, the media both in Israel and abroad focused on the attempts to convene the Geneva peace conference, while the ministers in Begin's cabinet debated Sharon's plan to increase the number of settlements in the administered territories and the new economic plan put forward by Finance Minister Simcha Ehrlich. Vigorous activity by each of the cabinet ministers in his own domain was typical of the Reversal spirit, with Begin leaving his mark by approving grandiose plans. In anticipation of Israel's thirtieth anniversary the following year, he announced that he was going to revive the custom of a military parade on that day (it had been suspended in 1973 for reasons of cost and the need to recruit reservists for the purpose).[93] In addition, he announced that he would go ahead with the Sea-to-Sea Canal Project (a scheme to conduct water from the Mediterranean or the Red Sea to the Dead Sea by using the thirteen-hundred-foot drop in elevation to produce electricity) and raise funds to search for the tombs of the Maccabees, the remains of which had been found near the new town of Modi'in. These initiatives created the impression that Begin was busy with showcase projects and that the changes he would bring about while in office would be mainly in internal matters. The peace process initiative with Egypt was kept hidden both from the media and from government ministers. Begin and Dayan kept the secret between them and on occasion brought Weizmann in on it.

On October 30, Begin went to a meeting with Ambassador Lewis to discuss developments concerning the peace conference. He smiled to reporters on his way to his car, but once inside, his head fell on his chest, and he mumbled to his cabinet secretary, "The machine is tired."[94] But Naor had no idea quite how much.

Begin's meeting with Lewis was difficult. The ambassador asked that Begin agree to limit the conference to reaching certain security arrangements rather than full peace and normalization, as he had demanded. This angered Begin, who, as always, was concerned that intermediate agreements would force Israel into making territorial concessions without adequate gains in return. Utterly exhausted by pains in his chest, he suddenly exclaimed, "Do you expect me to stick a knife in my heart for the sake of friendship with the United States?" Lewis was taken aback, but in a bid to relieve the tension, he replied jokingly, "No, no, no—not for the sake of the friendship, of course—but for the sake of peace."[95] Begin did not smile. At the end of the meeting, still in an emotional turmoil brought on partly by pain, he hurriedly summoned the members of the Ministerial Committee for National Security. Briefing them solemnly, he explained that Israel had found itself in a complicated situation. But before he finished speaking, his face screwed up in pain, and he grabbed his chest, leaned on Naor, who sat on his right, and sighed, "Mama'leh, mama'leh." The ministers froze. None of them knew how to react. Nearly a minute passed until Brigadier General Efraim Poran, his military secretary, came to his senses, and Begin was moved to his office to wait for a doctor. Only an hour later was he able to stand on his own two feet and was taken to the hospital. The doctors diagnosed pericarditis (inflammation of the heart membrane).[96] The ministers told no one about what had transpired in the meeting, and the media did not report that Begin had collapsed—merely that he had checked himself into the hospital. The prime minister spent two days in intensive care, and his office reported only that he was suffering from weakness brought on by fatigue.

Pericarditis generally afflicts people after heart surgery, and to overcome it Begin had to take a great deal of medication, including steroids, which are well known to cause mood swings.[97] Begin was released from the hospital two weeks later, looking gaunt from weight loss. Although the country was told that nothing would change in his daily routine, after his collapse he made fewer public appearances and he gave up spending time at the Knesset cafeteria in favor of napping at home. In addition, he had to submit to a weekly medical exam by a doctor.

Surprisingly, Begin's physical weakness was to his political advantage. Coalition talks with Dash had run into problems, but since the government clearly lacked a stable, significant, and secular partner, he still held off from appointing ministers for the justice, transportation, communications, and labor portfolios in the hope that Dash would still join. By this time the head of Dash, Yigael Yadin, was offended by Begin's attitude toward his party, but Shmuel Tamir, who had joined Dash as the head of Hamerkaz Hachofshi before the elections and had been trying to persuade Yadin to accede to Begin's terms, now had a further argument that Begin's associates would never forget: "Begin is ill. If you become deputy prime minister, you might need to replace him fairly soon."[98] Yadin said nothing, but on returning from a visit to the United States not long after Begin was discharged from hospital, he agreed that Dash would join the government. In return, Begin promised Dash free voting rights in matters of foreign policy and national security. On concluding the coalition agreement, Yadin argued that if Dash had not joined, he would have feared for Israel's future.[99]

On November 9, 1977, President Anwar Sadat astonished the members of his parliament with the following announcement: "I am willing to go to the ends of the earth—even to their house, to the Knesset—and to argue with them there. We have no time to waste."[100] His announcement was so surprising that even Yasser Arafat, the head of the PLO who was visiting the Egyptian parliament at the time, joined in the enthusiastic applause. Only when the full significance of Sadat's words sank in did the first murmurs of objection begin to emerge.

While Sadat was astounding the entire world (two days earlier he had alerted Carter to the possibility of such an announcement, but the American administration had not taken him seriously),[101] Begin and his wife were watching television, as they usually did in the evenings. Begin was in the habit of watching American series and was particularly fond of *Dallas*. When Kadishai showed him a piece by Michael Handelsaltz in *Haaretz* in which the critic poked fun at Begin's taste, Begin was unabashed. "Let them laugh. So what? Should I be embarrassed? What, am I supposed to be looking for Schopenhauer on the tube?"[102]

The news of Sadat's announcement was relayed to Begin by his communications adviser, Dan Patir, but it was only the next morning, while shaving, that Begin understood quite what a stir it had caused. Journalist Shlomo Nakdimon—who would later become his adviser—

called and asked him for a response. Begin replied that he would respond only after seeing a full transcript of the speech. Nakdimon insisted, however, and pointed out that all the news agencies in the world were commenting on it. Begin relented and said, "I shall be happy to meet with Sadat anywhere, including in Cairo, and if he wants to come to Jerusalem, he's welcome."[103]

This off-the-cuff response became Israel's official response and was broadcast on Kol Israel, the state radio.[104] Sadat's announcement effectively ruled out any hope that Begin had had for a discreet private meeting. He understood that he had to respond with an equally dramatic gesture. On arriving at his office, he first asked that a press conference be called as soon as possible.[105] Before it took place, however, he made a request that attested to his difficulty in understanding the psychology of the other side: he asked experts in Middle Eastern affairs at the Hebrew University to provide a written opinion on the Koran's attitude toward Jews. When he was told that in the Koran the Prophet Mohammed speaks of the right of the Children of Israel to live in their own country,[106] he was quick to tell everyone about it, as if he had stumbled upon the most decisive piece of evidence that would impact upon the peace accords. He repeated the quote frequently,[107] stopping only when he realized that the Egyptians were rankled by such incessant invocations of the holy book of Islam. Three days later, Sadat was handed an official invitation to visit Jerusalem, through the American Embassy in Cairo. The American administration, which had been caught off guard, quickly adapted to the new situation and announced, with a hint of disappointment, that if this was what Israel and Egypt wanted, it would help them.[108]

Begin believed that Sadat's declaration vindicated his hard-line position in foreign affairs, inspired by the Iron Wall philosophy. The facts seem to bear him out: the president of Egypt, who for many years had been considered a stubborn enemy, wanted to come to Israel and make peace. While Begin was chatting in his Knesset office with Shmuel Katz, Ambassador Lewis called to verify that Israel was indeed prepared for such a visit. After that, Begin went back to talking with Katz but found it hard to keep his mind on the conversation. He kept pacing around the room and then said, proudly, "Shmuel, you see? He's coming all the way to me."[109] He was bursting with ill-concealed exhilaration.

After a meeting with a delegation from the U.S. Congress, Begin stood in front of the cameras and, swelling with pride and pleasure, announced that he would of course be happy to visit Egypt—especially the pyramids, "which our forefathers built, you know." This statement immediately provoked an entirely avoidable incident with the Egyptians, who were upset not so much by the blatant historical error—the pyramids had been built long before the Israelites even arrived in Egypt—as by the patronizing attitude inherent in Begin's facetious remark. Israel therefore found itself having to apologize to Egypt even before Sadat arrived in the country. Of course, it was not Begin's intention to jeopardize the chances for peace; he was merely expressing his worldview and the meaning that he attached to Sadat's visit in the wider context of the history of the Jewish people, which to his mind was a mirror of his own life.[110]

Several days after Sadat declared that he would come to Jerusalem, the Israeli cabinet held its weekly meeting and officially announced that the Egyptian president would be welcome, as Begin had already said. Immediately after that, Begin and Sadat were interviewed on CBS Television. When the interviewer pressed Sadat to reveal the date of the meeting—"Are we talking about a week or so?"—the president said yes, while Begin hastened to promise, "I shall escort the president to the speakers' platform at the Knesset," and added, "No more war, no more bloodshed."[111] No Israeli leader before him had made such deliberate use of television to achieve his goals. (The interviews were broadcast again and again throughout the world, to great acclaim.)

These were Begin's days of glory. His popularity among the Israeli public reached new highs. "Look, Yechiel. Have I changed in any way? Do I look different? Talk differently?" he asked Kadishai, reveling in the changed attitude toward him.[112] The sense that they were witnessing a historic moment suited his personality. The territorial significance of peace—namely, the return of the Sinai Peninsula to Egypt—was pushed to the margins of public debate, which focused on Sadat's visit itself. Begin's good spirits overcame the physical frailty that had brought on his heart inflammation, and, as always, he expressed his vigor by being magnanimous toward his political opponents. Officially he did not need the Knesset's approval, but nonetheless he asked the assembly to ratify the invitation to Sadat. Since the day of the event happened to coincide with the anniversary of the death of Ben Gurion, he declared, "It is only fitting that we hold this debate on this day, of all days, as we honor the immortal memory of David Ben Gurion."[113]

The term "immortal memory" is one that Begin had hitherto used exclusively with regard to Jabotinsky—certainly not for his political arch-opponent—but at that moment he could not resist the temptation. Such was the man. Just as he could debate endlessly over trivia, so also was he capable of showing enormous empathy in his greater moments. In fact, these were two sides of the same coin. When he finished his speech, he even said that Ben Gurion was the first Israeli leader to express willingness to meet with Arab leaders to talk about peace[114]—implying that he, Begin, was following in Ben Gurion's footsteps, much to the dismay of Herut veterans.

In Begin's office and among the military there was still great uncertainty surrounding Sadat's arrival because the strategic decision to work toward a peace treaty with Egypt had been made by Begin alone, and he had confided only in his foreign minister.[115] The degree to which the rest of the Israeli leadership was surprised and somewhat disconcerted by events was evident in part in an incident on November 17. Yadin—who was acting defense minister while Weizmann was recovering from injuries from a car accident—asked to meet with Begin urgently. At the meeting he explained that the chief of staff and the head of army intelligence were afraid that Sadat's visit was nothing more than a bluff—a ploy designed to catch Israel off guard, as had occurred at the start of the Yom Kippur War. In support of his theory, he pointed out that the Egyptian armed forces had been placed on high alert, and he recommended calling up Israeli reservists immediately in response. Begin listened to him attentively, laid a hand on his shoulder, and dismissed his concerns. He had no qualms about disputing the assessments of the Israeli intelligence services because he was not part of the government that had ignored the warnings in the run-up to the Yom Kippur War and because he knew full well that Sadat's visit was the culmination of months of political initiatives about which the ministers and the heads of the armed forces knew nothing.[116] It later transpired that the Egyptian army had indeed been put on high alert but specifically for the purpose of maintaining public order within the country while the president was away.[117]

On November 19, two hours after the Shabbat, the door of the Egyptian president's plane opened at Ben Gurion Airport, and millions of Israelis, who were watching the proceedings live on television—which were being broadcast without sound—waited for him to emerge. Lined up along the red carpet laid out at the foot of the stairs of the plane stood the prime minister and all other cabinet ministers, the heads of the army, and former Israeli leaders. The Egyptian president, partly hesitant, partly excited, in a gray suit and dotted tie, accompanied by his entourage, walked down the steps and waved to his welcoming committee, headed by Menachem Begin. At the same time, citizens lining the route intended for the president and prime minister's convoy opened bottles of wine and broke into the song "Hevenu Shalom Aleikhem" (We've Brought Peace upon You). The peace process had begun.

Begin and Sadat embraced each other somewhat diffidently, as if unsure how to treat an enemy-turned-friend.[118] Begin accompanied Sadat as he proceeded down the red carpet, on his left, but the orderly proceedings quickly began to unravel. Yadin banged angrily on the roof of a car when he found himself pushed behind the row of VIPs who were waiting to shake Sadat's hand.[119] Since the broadcast was without sound, viewers felt as if they were watching something quite unreal.

The president of Egypt—the largest of the Arab countries—made a point of exchanging a few words with each of the waiting dignitaries. Golda Meir said to him, "We've been expecting you," and Sadat replied, "And now I'm here." To Sharon he said that if he ever again tried to cross the Suez Canal, he'd have him arrested, to which Sharon replied, "Oh, no, sir. Now I'm just the minister of agriculture." To Chief of Staff Mordechai (Motta) Gur, who had voiced fears that Sadat's visit was nothing but a ploy, Sadat could not help but quip, "You see? I wasn't bluffing."[120]

The images broadcast from the airport hypnotized viewers at home. Sadat's estimate that 70 percent of the Israeli-Arab conflict was psychological proved true. Peace was no longer a utopian vision. The peace treaty might still be some way away, but the way to it had been paved.

The agreement's broad principles were set out as early as the first, unofficial, meeting between Begin and Sadat, about an hour after Sadat's arrival, at the presidential suite of the King David Hotel in Jerusalem. Right at the outset, Begin proposed that they announce that there would be no more war and that any disagreements in the future would be settled only through negotiation. Sadat agreed but asked that Begin first commit to a full withdrawal from Sinai. Begin—in his first-ever direct response—replied that he would agree to a withdrawal from Sinai but not from all of it and only on condition that it be demilitarized. Sadat insisted that in that case he would expect Israel to demilitarize on its side of the border too. When Begin asked, in jest, if he meant right up to the River Jordan, Sadat smiled, hinting that he had not expected Israel to concede on this point. Such was the excitement of the two at the historic significance of the occasion that in the smiling verbal ping-pong that ensued, agreement was reached on three principles: Israel's withdrawal, the demilitarization of Sinai, and an undertaking to settle differences in the future by peaceful means only.

Begin had not needed to meet with Sadat in order to trust him. He guessed that the Egyptian president had set himself the goal of signing a peace treaty mainly because Egypt's economy was so shaky and in desperate need of American aid.[121] But what Begin regarded as the main achievement of his first conversation with Sadat—the fact that Sadat had not made the peace conditional upon an agreement with the Palestinians—was an illusion, a result of the brevity of their conversation and their being caught up in the moment. By the following day, before the negotiating teams had even been put together, this optimism evaporated.

In spite of Sadat's promise never again to use the threat of war and despite the huge excitement and thunderous applause that greeted him as he made his way to the speaker's platform at the Knesset, his speech was not music to Israelis' ears—and certainly not to Begin's. Sadat stressed the Palestinians' right to self-determination and made it clear that unless the Palestinian issue was resolved, the Israeli-Arab conflict would also never be resolved.

Begin, somewhat irked, went up to the platform after Sadat and delivered an equally dogmatic speech in which he focused on the Jews' historic right to the whole of the Land of Israel and gave the impression that he was not about give up Israel's assets in Sinai just because of Egypt's goodwill gestures. His words did not bode well, and it was apparent that peace was perhaps not as close as it had seemed. Nonetheless, Sadat's very presence in the Knesset overshadowed anything that was being said. Much to Begin's satisfaction, Sadat visited Yad Vashem, Israel's chief memorial for the victims of the Holocaust. Sadat was moved by what he saw and heard, but he dismayed Begin when he wrote in the visitors' book that what he had learned at the site was that suffering of all kinds must be prevented—and he did not single out the tragedy that had befallen the Jews.

At the end of Sadat's visit in Israel, which lasted two days, Sadat invited Begin to Ismailiya to launch the actual negotiation talks. He avoided extending an invitation for a reciprocal visit by Begin to the Egyptian parliament, probably because he knew that the peace initiative met with considerable opposition both within Egypt and in other Arab countries.[122]

Well before the negotiation talks began, Begin asked Dayan to prepare a detailed list of Israel's interests in the context of a peace process.

The result, had it indeed been used to guide the peace process, would have slowed it down. Dayan and Begin agreed to withdraw from Sinai but only in stages and over several years. As for the future of Judea and Samaria, Dayan proposed that Jordan and the Palestinians assume the civil administration of their inhabitants while official sovereignty and military authority would remain in Israel's hands. Begin accepted Dayan's plan for Palestinian autonomy and made it clear that it was based on the one envisioned by Jabotinsky. He believed that in this way he could resolve the issue of land ownership. Unlike Jabotinsky, Begin did not insist on extending Israel's sovereignty over the West Bank and the Gaza Strip, but he hoped that in return the Palestinians would be content with having rights on the land rather than rights to the land—or as he put it, "the Eretz Israeli Arabs would have administrative autonomy, and Israeli Jews would have true security."[123]

Meanwhile, Begin flew to the United States for a second time, this time to persuade Carter to support the autonomy plan. Such a plan would abolish Israel's military administration of the occupied territories, he told Carter, and lead to the establishment of an administrative council whose members would be elected by the inhabitants and that would manage their civilian lives. In addition, he proposed that the Palestinians be allowed to set up a police force whose job it would be to keep public order, and he also proposed that they choose between being citizens of Israel or of Jordan. In return, Israeli citizens would be entitled to purchase land in the territories, and Palestinians who chose Israeli citizenship would be allowed to settle within Israel's borders. Since Begin did not recognize the notion of a Palestinian nation, he saw his plan as a means by which Israel could maintain its sovereignty and Palestinians could join the Israeli Arab community.

The autonomy plan was controversial, both within the cabinet and within the Israeli defense establishment. Sharon and Motta Gur were concerned that it would lead to the formation of a Palestinian state. Defense Minister Weizmann was peeved mainly because he had not been privy to the plan during its conception (since he had been in the hospital), but he supported it in principle. Begin, Dayan, and Yadin supported it wholeheartedly because they thought it was the best solution.

Begin's political vision, which he had still not made public, was of confederation with Jordan. With confederation, he hoped, the western bank of the Jordan River would remain under Israel's control, the Arabs would manage their own civilian affairs within an autonomous framework, and the eastern bank—Transjordan—would in effect also be linked to Israel as part of the common confederation.[124] He shared this vision only with those closest to him personally and ideologically because publicly proposing such an arrangement at the time might have come across as a challenge to the Hashemite kingdom of Jordan, leading to a change in its character, given that two-thirds of its population were Palestinian.

Begin returned from Washington satisfied with the support that he had received. He declared his proposal "a plan that is praised by anyone who sees it" and predicted that in light of Washington's support Sadat would find it difficult to reject it. Not content with the Americans' support, however, Begin flew on to the United Kingdom to share the proposal with British prime minister Jim Callaghan.

Britain's influence upon the plan was negligible, and in any event it would not have acted contrarily to the Americans on this matter. But Begin marveled out loud at the contrast between the positive reception he now received and the demonstrations that had greeted him during his previous visit in 1972.[125] It was clear that he enjoyed being able to prove to those who had called him a "terrorist" that he was now a respected statesman. "Just as in his youth he proposed to return to bombed-out Warsaw only because he had been denounced for running away, he now chose to share his plans with the prime minister of Britain to show how the man whom they had perceived as a terrorist was now the one bringing the peace," muttered one of his associates who now opposed his initiatives.[126]

On December 25 that year, Begin, Dayan, and Weizmann left for Ismailiya to continue the peace talks. This was the first time an Israeli delegation had ever arrived in Egypt on an official visit. But unlike Sadat's visit to Jerusalem, the atmosphere at these talks was decidedly cooler. Sadat listened to Begin's description of his autonomy plan and responded drily, "I've heard what you have to say. Now I'll propose my plan, and then we'll start negotiating." He had been influenced by Boutros Boutros-Ghali, his hard-line foreign minister,[127] as well as by the hostile public opinion in the Arab world, which opposed any solution that did not include a declaration of the Palestinian right to self-determination.

The first talks in earnest ended in disappointment but failed to dent the upbeat mood of Begin, who continued to relish the very fact that the peace process had begun. On his return to Israel he told reporters that he had left for Egypt as a concerned prime minister and returned a happy citizen. He took exception to reports that the talks had reached a dead end and insisted that he had heard no refusal in principle.[128] However, the television cameras caught Dayan shrugging his shoulders upon hearing Begin, and the feeling grew among the Israeli public that Begin was being too optimistic and that the peace process would be long and arduous.[129] Someone in the Israeli delegation leaked to the media that ever since Sadat's visit, Begin had been in a state of euphoria that made him detached from reality, and his old underground comrade, Chaim Landau, was obliged to come to his defense and explain that Begin was happy simply because "he's always been optimistic."[130] At this point, one of Israel's vulnerabilities in the negotiations with Egypt became apparent. The start of the process—Sadat's visit to Jerusalem—had been so dramatic that everything in its aftermath was doomed to be an anticlimax, and long and grueling negotiations could only give rise to disappointment.

At a dinner held during the visit of the Israeli delegation to Egypt, Begin referred to Ibrahim Kamal, Egypt's new foreign minister who had replaced Boutros-Ghali, as a young man who, because of his youth, did not remember the Holocaust and so did not understand the Jews' need for security. Kamal was offended and left the room in protest, and Begin expressed surprise since he did not think he had insulted him. This was how he was accustomed to dealing with political crises—by alternately teasing and giving fatherly "compliments," as required.[131] After Kamal had left, he joked, "I wish I had been called a young man."[132] During Sadat's visit to Jerusalem Begin's manner had appeared to suit the dramatic occasion, but now it looked as though his personality might undermine the process. At the same time, there were those in Israel who said that Kamal had used the occasion as a pretext to withdraw from talks on the political issues, when Egypt might be called upon to make concessions too.[133]

As disagreements mounted between Israel and Egypt during the talks, cracks began to appear in the national consensus within Israel as well. Those on the Right were concerned about the autonomy plan and a full withdrawal, while those on the Left were concerned that overly hard-line positions would delay the signing of a treaty. Begin's main problem, however, was the criticism leveled against him within his own party. Moshe Arens, head of the Knesset's Foreign Affairs and Security Committee, opposed the talks on the grounds that without Sinai, Israel's strategic value to the United States would be greatly diminished. The young Geula Cohen, true to form, declared that giving up Sinai would be tantamount to treason. At a conference in

Begin, an Etzel pin on his lapel, during preparations for elections for the second Knesset, 1951. (Courtesy of Menachem Begin Heritage Center Archives.)

Begin mocking Mapai at an election rally, 1959. (Courtesy of GPO.)

Begin (second from right) and Prime Minister Levi Eshkol (center) toasting at a ceremony at Mevo Beitar, 1965. (Courtesy of Matityahu Drobles.)

Begin (center) signing the coalition agreement with the Golda Meir government, 1969. On his left, Shimon Peres and Moshe Nissim. On his right, Yigal Allon and Yosef Burg. (Courtesy of GPO.)

A government meeting before the Six-Day War. From left to right: Moshe Dayan, Tzvi Sherf, Yosef Sapir, Begin (at that time a minister without portfolio), and Moshe Kol. (Courtesy of GPO.)

Ezer Weizmann speaking at a Herut conference after joining the party, December 14, 1969. Eitan Livni is on his left, Begin on his right. Weizmann is framed by portraits of Jabotinsky (to his right) and Herzl (to his left). (Courtesy of GPO.)

Begin kissing Aliza's hand after his historic victory speech following the Reversal, May 17, 1977. (Daughter Leah to her mother's right.) (Courtesy of GPO.)

Shimon Peres shaking hands with Begin at his inauguration, June 21, 1977. (Courtesy of GPO.)

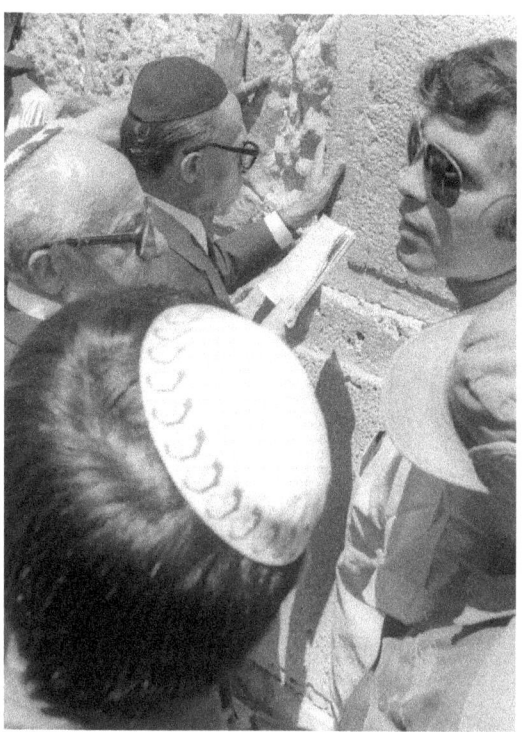

Begin (top left) praying at the Western Wall after his victory, May 1977. (Courtesy of GPO.)

Begin in his study glancing at the left-wing *Davar* on his first day as prime minister, June 21, 1977. (On his left, Bureau Chief Yechiel Kadishai.) (Courtesy of GPO.)

Begin conversing with Yigael Yadin, his deputy, during a discussion concerning the Jerusalem Law, July 1980. (Courtesy of GPO.)

Begin leafing through newspapers at the Waldorf Astoria in New York City just before his first visit to the White House, July 16, 1977. (Behind him, wife Aliza.). (Courtesy of GPO.)

Begin and President Anwar Sadat of Egypt departing a negotiations meeting in Ismailiya, December 1977. (Courtesy of GPO.)

Begin (center front with his daughter Leah) visiting the city of Yamit, September 1977. (Courtesy of GPO.)

Begin, Sadat, U.S. President Jimmy Carter and their wives after the signing of the Egypt-Israel Peace Treaty in a ceremony at the White House, March 1979. (Courtesy of White House.)

Begin, Aliza, and daughters Chasia (on the right) and Leah during the Jewish holiday Sukkot, October 1979. (Courtesy of GPO.)

the settlement of Ofrah in Samaria, the settlers' leaders claimed that Begin had lost his way in his pursuit of a Nobel Peace Prize.

Begin found it hard to ignore those upon whom he had depended during his long years in the political wilderness under the rule of the Labor Party in its various guises (first Mapai, then Hamaarach). In his entire political career he had encountered serious criticism within his party only twice, and on both occasions he had responded by stepping down. He thought of himself and "the movement" as one and the same, so that he regarded any criticism of him as a betrayal of the cause. But this time the criticism was leveled against a position that he himself had always drummed into his followers: "No to withdrawal." He was torn. Although he wanted his followers to support him, he secretly admired them for expressing their objections because he had always urged them to stick to their principles. He therefore stuck to his own position that those who were against his initiative were misinterpreting the Revisionist ideology. "Look," he said to Moshe Arens, in an attempt to win him over, "Sinai is after all not part of the Land of Israel, and the advantages of peace are enormous, including the chance of a defense alliance with the United States." But Arens replied that if they made concessions in Sinai, they might as well give up the Gaza Strip so as to rid themselves of the demographic burden of such a large Arab population. Begin was aghast. "But Gaza is also part of the Land of Israel!" he exclaimed. At that moment, Arens realized that they were not talking the same language.[134]

Begin needed the support of someone from the old guard. In this hour of need, he decided to add Chaim Landau, his old friend and comrade since Etzel and the early days of Herut, to the cabinet. But this contemplated step only highlighted the extent to which his authority had weakened within his own party.

Shmuel Katz vehemently opposed the peace negotiations and decided to put himself forward for the position that Begin had designated for Landau. At a stormy meeting of the Herut caucus, when it looked as though matters were moving in Katz's favor, Begin made an appeal to him straight out of the "fighting family" playbook: "How could you do this to Chaim?" With Katz, as with many in the Likud party, such "family"-based arguments from the opposition days no longer cut any ice. Seeing this, Begin then repeated what he had said to Arens: "But Sinai is not part of the Land of Israel, even according to the Bible!" Katz was dumbfounded. "What does this have to do with the Bible?" he shot back. "I mean, you can use it to prove almost any borders you want!"[135]

As long as Herut was in the opposition—a minority party whose members felt they were doomed forever to struggle against the mighty powers of the (Labor) establishment—Begin's authority in it was secure. Now its members had acquired power—they were now the rulers—and there was no longer any need to stick together in the face of the powers-that-be. Thus, paradoxically, now that he had become prime minister, Begin's authority within the party was undermined. In response, Begin fell back on his familiar reflexive ploy and threatened to resign if Katz were elected. However, this time it did not work, and despite his threat he was unable to have his way easily.[136] Although in the final analysis most caucus members did vote for Landau, the difficulties that Begin had encountered at the meeting indicated the erosion in his status.

Begin saw Katz's position on the issue as treasonous and refused to speak to him again until virtually his dying day. Katz, noting that he had given up in the face of the "anti-democratic approach of that vindictive and begrudging man," retired from politics.[137] Ironically, Begin soon realized that Landau, supposedly his faithful representative in the cabinet, was also opposed to the emerging treaty, and the conviviality with which he used to greet him—"My good friend"—was replaced with the more formal "Mr. Landau" or occasionally "Engineer Landau" (owing to his profession).[138] Begin now understood that his authority alone would not suffice to bring around his caucus members but decided that he would nevertheless not give in to the opponents within his own camp. He was no longer the head of a minority party but the prime minister, a popular statesman both within Israel and abroad, and the greater the resistance he met with, the more he stood his ground. He fought back.

"I told the people of Gush Emunim, 'I love you today and will continue to like you tomorrow too, but you've developed a Messiah complex,'" Begin said during a Knesset debate on his autonomy plan.[139] Accusing Gush Emunim of messianism was no easy thing for Begin, and it came about only because of the emotional turmoil that was raging within him. He knew that the settlers' position stemmed from the positions he himself had held over the years since it was he who had always preached assertiveness with regard to territories that Israel had conquered. But he also felt betrayed because they were hampering him at the greatest moment of his life and because he believed that with Israel's withdrawal from Sinai he was saving other parts of the historical Land of Israel.

Begin's plan was ultimately approved in the Knesset by a large majority, thanks to the support of Hamaarach.

The main stumbling block in the talks with Egypt was Begin's objection to any compromise whatsoever in Judea, Samaria, or the Gaza Strip that deviated from his autonomy plan. It quickly became apparent to him that the American administration was leaning toward Sadat's position, and although President Carter supported the autonomy plan, he planned to use it as a breakthrough toward establishing a Palestinian state. After Carter's speech in support of the Palestinians' right to self-determination during his visit to Egypt—which became known as the Aswan Declaration—Begin felt trapped between a rock and a hard place; as always in such situations, he lost his composure and did things just in spite.

No new settlements had been established in Sinai since Begin had entered office, but in January 1978, in the face of pressure from both sides, he reversed his position on this matter. Sharon and Dayan believed that over time, as the peace talks progressed, Sadat would soften his stance and allow the Israeli settlements in Sinai to remain under Israeli sovereignty. To put their theory to the test, Sharon suggested that they give the go-ahead for infrastructure projects that would expand the existing settlements without actually setting up new ones. "This way, we can see how the Egyptians react without the risk of being accused of undermining a possible peace accord," he said. At that time, Begin was abroad, and Sharon sent him a letter asking for his approval. Begin's response was brief and to the point: "Approve wholeheartedly." Although Weizmann had warned that any expansion of the settlements would be seen by Egypt as an Israeli provocation, most cabinet ministers supported the proposal; moreover, Sharon pointed out that if the Egyptians objected, work would be halted, and "If not—well, we would have had to strengthen our hold there anyway." But neither Cairo nor Washington made any distinction between expanding settlements and establishing new ones. The Egyptians were outraged, and negotiations were suspended.[140]

The peace process was plagued with such crises—both because of the Egyptians' insistence on Israel's full withdrawal and recognition of the Palestinians' right to self-determination and because of Begin's contortionist antics, as he woke up to the price he would ultimately have to pay while trying to walk between the raindrops—attempting to calm his conscience and reassure his own camp while working toward a withdrawal. In March 1978, 350 army officers, fearing Begin was not working toward a peace deal, sent him a petition demanding that he agree to withdraw from the whole of Sinai in return for peace. After delivering it, they launched a series of demonstrations that gave birth to the Peace Now movement.

In the fall of 1978 it looked as if the peace process was going nowhere. The dramatic impact of Sadat's visit had dissipated, and Begin sank into a daily routine. He was always at his peak in extreme situations—at times of crisis or upon scoring a victory—and now he seemed to be wilting. His frustration at the conflict in which he found himself—between wanting to sign a peace accord and fearing that Dayan, the Americans, and the Egyptians would pressure him into making concessions to which he objected—became apparent in a very undiplomatic outburst during his visit to the White House in March 1978. During one of his meetings with Carter and his national security adviser, Zbigniew Brzezinski, one of those present began to say, "The Egyptian Mustafa says that—," but he never got to finish his sentence. Begin, who was listening to the Americans' demands with pent-up anger, interrupted him: "Well? What did the Gentile Arab say now?"[141] and proceeded to let everyone know that with the Americans, too, he no longer felt among friends and wished now to return to his natural constituency—the one that saw the world in terms of "us" and "the Gentiles," the good guys and the bad guys.

Although it was ignored, Begin's outburst deepened the tension in the room. When the meeting was over, there was a sense that it would be impossible to mend the rift that had opened up between the Americans and the Egyptians, on the one hand—who demanded that Israel withdraw from the whole of Sinai, remove the settlements that it had established there, and provide the Palestinians with an autonomy that would serve as the basis for a future Palestinian state—and, on the other hand, Begin, who was now being called "The Compromiser" by his own camp and "stubborn" by the media.

After Begin's visit to the White House, a source there leaked to Israeli journalist Shalom Kital that the Americans were disappointed with the prime minister. Kital broadcast the item on *Yoman Haerev*, Kol Israel's early evening news program. Begin's advisers were livid. Kadishai called Kital and told him that Begin liked him and saw him as a trustworthy journalist. "Why are you broadcasting unsubstantiated news items?" he asked through gritted teeth. Kital insisted that his reports were substantiated and expressed confidence in his sources. Kadishai ended the conversation with, "Begin is angry with you," and hung up.[142]

The next day, Kital's item was published in the newspapers as well, and on Begin's return to Israel he was asked by journalists about the confrontation with the U.S. president. Begin, however, was neither angry about the leak nor concerned to deny it, and he even sought out Kital in the crowd and told him, "Thanks for that item you published. It shows the kind of forces we're up against. You did a great service for the Jewish people." Kital was embarrassed and now found himself suspected by his colleagues of being Begin's stooge and publishing the item with his knowledge. The prime minister, meanwhile, proved once again that he knew a thing or two about how to manipulate the media in order to strengthen his position within the right-wing camp.[143]

As political and media pressures grew upon Begin, so too did a decline in his health. In May 1978, he once again collapsed at home, following attacks of dizziness and weakness. The cabinet was told only that he had come down with a cold, and it was only two days later that his doctor, Marvin Gottesman, announced that Begin was resting at home due to complications of the pericarditis.[144] This time the flood of rumors and theories surrounding his health and ability to function was hard to ignore. In an article in *Time-Life* a senior doctor at Hadassah Hospital, on condition of anonymity, was quoted as saying that Begin's health problems were affecting his mental condition: "The problem is that he has to take conflicting medications—some dealing with his diabetes, others with heart problems—and as a result he's suffering from frequent and extreme ups and downs in mood swings." Hospital staff denied the rumors, which at the time still sounded fanciful.[145]

Rumors about Begin's health have never been verified, but it is known that the steroids that he had to take to treat the pericarditis do affect mood—usually for the better but with a sharp slump when the patient stops taking them. An article presenting these medical facts was published—inconspicuously—in *Haaretz*, and within both political circles and the media there seemed to be a tacit agreement not to inquire too deeply into the subject. The rumors nevertheless went on making the rounds.[146]

Begin returned to work after a recuperative leave of absence, but his poor health continued to dog him, and meanwhile talks with Egypt were making little discernible progress. In light of Begin's frail condition, Dayan took charge of the peace process and made various compromise proposals in a bid to revive the talks. In June 1978, he flew to Leeds in England to meet with Ibrahim Kamal and U.S. Secretary of State Cyrus Vance.[147] Dayan knew that Begin would not accept any changes to his autonomy plan, so he suggested that Egypt accept it as it was. On this issue, he explained, Begin would not budge an inch. To overcome the objections, he undertook to add to the autonomy plan a clause to the effect that five years after autonomy was established, Israel would agree to discuss the permanent status of the administered territories. He had not secured Begin's agreement to this suggestion before making it, hoping that the Egyptians would accept it in the belief that Israel's position would soften over time. When he presented it to Begin, he told him there was nothing in it obliging Israel to loosen its control on the ground. "When it comes down to it, when we discuss the permanent status of the territories, Israel will be entitled to stand her ground. On the contrary: it would now be clear that Israel could determine the fate of the territories on her own."[148]

Begin, who was mentally as well as physically worn out, listened and surprisingly—given his previous insistence on precluding any detail that might open the door to relinquishing Israel's sovereignty—accepted Dayan's proposal. His consent was owing to a clear political need: at this stage, it would serve his main goal of warding off international pressure. Begin understood that he could not go back on his agreement to the peace process without inflicting enormous political damage to Israel, and Dayan's proposal was a convenient escape route. But another reason for his acceptance was his poor health and mood, as evident from his reservations about this clause after signing the accord with Egypt and his request that the government declare in advance what its position would be in relation to sovereignty over the territories five years down the road.

In effect, Begin was the first Israeli prime minister to give de jure recognition of the rights of the Palestinian people.[149] The right-wing government that he headed was the first in Israel's history to cast doubt on Israel's right to control Judea, Samaria, and Gaza, and it sparked off a debate on the issue of sovereignty over these regions. It is clear that had it not been Begin himself who paved the way to negotiations with Egypt, the hard core of Herut would not have been able to digest this change of direction, which Begin himself admitted was "the biggest ideological break with the past."[150] Begin's advantage was that over many years he had based his leadership on the perception that he had been entrusted with Jabotinsky's ideological legacy—a perception that he managed to instill thanks to his rhetorical skills. Therefore, when he did deviate from the path—albeit for tactical reasons—his followers saw it as part of the ideology. For this reason the grassroots activists of the Likud and most of its younger MKs supported Begin, while those who opposed him were the movement's ideologues, including Moshe Arens and Shmuel Katz, who had firsthand knowledge of Jabotinsky's writings without Begin's mediation. However, they lacked the political clout to organize any real opposition.

Begin and Dayan continued, therefore, to conduct the negotiations as they saw fit, and the government ministers played but a minor role. Begin took care to observe the nominal conventions of democratic rule by reporting his decisions to the cabinet and explaining his positions to the ministers, but he did not involve them in foreign policy meetings. Dayan was his sole partner in the process from the start of the government's term, although he did also listen to Yadin, Weizmann, and Sharon. In his private offices he went on conducting small talk with Kadishai and Naor, who spoke his language—the language of the underground and the early days of Herut—and on Saturdays he continued to entertain underground veterans at his home. But he involved almost no one in his foreign policy plans—partly because he was powerful enough to do so and partly also, as we have said, because he had no common language with the politicians surrounding him.[151]

The clause put forward by Dayan, which had the effect of giving Egypt a temporary reprieve of its need to protect the rights of the Palestinians in the eyes of the Arab world, gave new impetus to the negotiations. In August Vance visited Israel and Egypt and invited Begin and Sadat to a conference at Camp David in September. At this presidential retreat in the Catoctin Mountains in Maryland, north of the capital, the three leaders were to finalize the details of the agreement. Begin accepted the invitation immediately and began preparing for the conference, declaring, "I shall go to the peace conference at Machaneh David [literal Hebrew translation of Camp David]."[152]

The Camp David Conference was supposed to be the climax of the talks. All parties concerned knew that it would herald the decisive moment. Begin became reenergized, and his mood improved at the prospect of signing a peace accord between Israel and Egypt. Great missions of this sort had always had such an effect on him. Before leaving for the conference, he convened his cabinet and chaired the meeting with firmness. The ministers authorized those attending the conference to pass the necessary resolutions, and red lines were drawn up that could not be crossed and that were supposed to prevent a confrontation with Egypt: there would be no compromise over Jerusalem, Israel would not agree to foreign sovereignty over any part of the Land of Israel, and there would be no withdrawal without full peace.[153]

Aliza was among those going to Camp David. Since Begin's election as prime minister she had devoted her time to the Yad Sarah organization and other charities dedicated to helping the disabled. Like her husband, she was modest and frugal in her personal needs and spent much time visiting poor neighborhoods. But her main concern was to provide total and absolute support for her husband. Menachem and Aliza were an exceptional couple, both within the political arena and outside it. The love and consideration that they showed each other were unique. Their relationship was like bastion walls protecting them from the upheavals of Begin's political career.

Aliza's influence on Begin was enormous—in part because she was cold and calculating, in total contrast to her tempestuous and emotional husband. Unlike him, she never managed to overcome her addiction to cigarettes and smoked on average two packs a day, despite the severe asthma from which she had suffered since childhood. She kept an inhaler permanently in her handbag and a breathing machine at home. Despite her physical frailty, it was she who spurred him on in difficult times and brought him back to earth in his moments of euphoria.[154] Unlike him, she usually kept her feelings to herself, and to her friends it seemed as if her introversion stemmed from a desire to offset her husband, who was given to outbursts.[155]

Begin needed such a counterbalance. Aliza raised the children and managed the household, but she was also involved in the personal aspects of her husband's political life. On the political front her position was equally uncompromising: she opposed any concessions regarding the Land of Israel. It should be noted in this context that Begin always took care to keep politics and domestic matters separate; although he listened to Aliza and let her in on his decisions, he made it clear that the political domain was exclusively his. Before the election, as he lay in the hospital, she agreed to represent him at an election conference in the town of Bat Yam. When asked to make a speech, however, she declined. "In our house," she explained, "only one person does the speaking."[156]

Begin had no doubt whatsoever that Aliza should join him in Camp David.[157] Nor was this his only deviation from ceremonial convention. The Americans had chosen Camp David in order to offer a relaxed atmosphere, but Begin's idea of casual attire was a tailored shirt with no tie. On arriving at Camp David, he was taken aback to see some of the Egyptian delegation wearing tracksuits.

In his final consultation with the Israeli delegation members in New York before leaving for Camp David, Begin promised them that no settlements would be removed, and he made it clear that if the other side insisted on such a concession, they would pack their bags and go home.[158] But in fact he did not intend to return from the conference empty-handed. He estimated that it would go on for a week and told them, "I have no intention of storming out of the proceedings."[159]

The makeup of Begin's delegation reflected his resolve. With the exception of Kadishai, none of his old Herut comrades was among the advisers. Dayan and Weizmann were more moderate than he, and the addition of Simcha Dinitz, the Israeli ambassador to Washington, and Major General Avraham Tamir was a further indication of his willingness to compromise. He was determined to bring about a profound change and to achieve the goal set by the Israeli establishment since the days of Ben Gurion: peace with the largest Arab country.[160]

The Camp David Conference began on September 5. Begin treated his first meeting there with Sadat and Carter as if it were the final and decisive stage. This was, after all, a battle over his country—which is to say over his own life. Sadat was tense and started the proceedings by reading a document that included a demand for Israel's full withdrawal from the territories that it had conquered during the Six-Day War. Although he was clearly merely stating his opening position, after listening to him, Begin defiantly announced that he rejected all of Sadat's demands. Seeking to lighten the mood, Carter then quipped, "Well, all's that needed now is for Begin to pull out a pen and sign"—whereupon Begin and his colleagues burst out laughing. But the laughter did not relieve the leaders' tension in the run-up to the second meeting. Begin asked that Israel be allowed to keep the airports that it had built in Sinai, explaining to Sadat that his request stemmed from a national security need, in case Sadat's successor, whoever he might be, "persuade the Egyptian people to throw us into the sea, as happened in 1967." Sadat replied that he too feared the future: what would happen if Begin was replaced by Sharon? "Sharon is a good man," Begin replied.[161] Thus, in a mixture of hardball and affability, Begin conducted the negotiations. "A mixture of biblical prophet and European courtier," observed Cyrus Vance. "One moment he could be blunt and sarcastic, the next convivial and generous."[162]

Despite the pastoral surroundings, the early days of the conference were fraught with tension. Sadat wondered why Israel was not making a gesture of its own after his visit to Jerusalem, and Begin replied that it had in fact done so with the warm welcome that it extended him in

Israel. In a moment of anger, Begin asked that the Egyptian president not speak to him as if he were the leader of a "defeated nation." The remark was a further indication, if such was needed, of his utter lack of understanding of the psychology of the other side. The words "defeated nation" made Sadat jump because he wrongly misinterpreted them to mean that Begin was implying that Egypt was the defeated nation. "We are not a defeated nation—not a defeated nation!" he said, raising his voice. Carter, embarrassed and concerned at the shouting, realized that no good would come out of such one-on-one meetings, and thereafter Begin met directly with Sadat only once more—on the final day of the conference. From this point on, the talks were conducted exclusively by the teams of both sides.[163]

As noted, there was no disagreement per se on the issue of withdrawal from Sinai in return for peace. The dispute was over the extent of the withdrawal and over Begin's demand—still with the support of Weizmann and Dayan—to leave the Israeli settlements in Sinai intact even after the withdrawal. Begin pointed out that even if he did consent to dismantling the settlements, he would not be able to get such a resolution ratified by the Knesset. At one of the dinners held during the conference, Carter tried to flatter Begin by saying that if a leader of Begin's stature recommended such a motion to the Knesset, it would accede to his demand. But Begin insisted that in fact such a proposal would result in his being ousted from power.

The delegation members failed to reach agreement after a week of talks. Begin became disillusioned and retreated into his cherished world of associations. He began to refer to Camp David as "Camp Detention"[164] and began conducting his verbal exchanges accordingly, as if he were back in the Siberian prison camp where he had been held and interrogated in the first half of World War II. When Carter raised the issue of Jerusalem, noting that both Dayan and Weizmann agreed to have "an Arab flag" fly over the mosques on Temple Mount, Begin objected vehemently: "Never!" "Why not?" Carter wondered. "And what will happen when the Messiah comes? After all, that's where we are supposed to build the Temple, and agreeing to an Arab flag would mean giving up on our faith." When the Jerusalem issue came up again, Begin told the well-known story from the Jewish prayers during the Days of Awe between Rosh Hashanah and Yom Kippur, about Rabbi Amnon of Magentza (Mainz), whose legs were cut off for refusing to convert. Carter was shocked at the comparison.[165] The religious zeal in Begin's words, however, caused the Americans to avoid any further debate on the subject.

Begin did not always intend his words to have the effect that they sometimes had. For him, figurative speech was a matter of style. When his son Benny heard about the pressure being put upon his father to agree to a full withdrawal from Sinai, he goaded him in a similar manner: "In the gulag they couldn't make you sign—so at Camp David you will?" Despite his bluntness, it was not Benny's intention to challenge his father; this was simply the way they were accustomed to speaking at home.

The members of the Israeli delegation were also unhappy with Begin's pronouncements. Ambassador Dinitz, who by now had become used to the new ways at the Prime Minister's Office, was less surprised by Begin's style of delivery as by his belief that what he was saying would yield results. After one of his conversations with Carter, Begin noted to Dinitz, "I had a very good talk with the president," and Dinitz remarked that it looked to him as if the disagreements between the two sides had only widened. Begin agreed but explained that the talk was good nonetheless "because the president finally heard things the way they really are."[166] When Yosef Burg, head of the Mafdal and the interior minister in Begin's cabinet, heard that Begin was substantiating the Jewish people's right to rule in Jerusalem on the grounds that it is mentioned hundreds of times in the Bible but only in a handful of instances in the Koran, he asked him to stop making that argument because "the dispute is a political, not a theological, one."[167] But Begin continued to do so nonetheless.

Begin spoke the way he did even after becoming prime minister because he still acted as if he were in the opposition, and he believed that the Achilles heel of all previous Israeli statesmen had been their desire to please and their avoidance of presenting "the historical truth" in their pursuit of diplomatic compromises. He, by contrast, set out to defend Jewish honor—with expressions such as "May my right hand wither if I sign such a document" and a host of stories from Jewish tradition.[168] In practice, however, he agreed to make concessions.

Begin did indeed believe in his powers of persuasion. As with Jabotinsky, his political career was founded from the outset upon protest speeches, and those protests now created a problem: he was a hard-liner heading a team of compromisers, while in the Egyptian delegation the reverse was true. This led to many complaints on the Egyptian side. In his memoirs, Boutros-Ghali made no attempt to hide his disappointment with Begin's attitude or his surprise at the contrast between the personalities of the leaders of the Israeli and Egyptian delegations: "Begin's difficult personality was evident in every word he uttered and in every movement he made. Begin, who was a statesman and diplomat, was also belligerent and struck me as a danger to peace. Weizmann, who was a distinguished military man, charmed us with his cheerful style, and his presence had a calming effect. Dayan was unpredictable. One moment he could be arrogant and bitter, and the next moment he would come up with creative solutions."[169] Carter complained that Begin was deliberately telling him stories in the hope perhaps of tiring him out, and as time went on he distanced himself from Begin and grew closer to Sadat.[170] For his part, Ambassador Lewis judged Begin's tactics to be an intellectual stratagem. "Begin simply drives anyone who disagrees with him up the wall," he concluded.[171]

During the conference, at the height of the tension and the pressure, Begin often sought comfort in conversations with members of his family and with his friend Kadishai. Aliza made sure to strengthen his resolve and persuade him not to give in and strove, with Kadishai's help, to counter Dayan's influence.[172] His son Benny continued to urge him to resist the removal of Israeli settlements in Sinai.[173] The frequent consultations between father and son were also the outcome of a deterioration of Begin's relationship with his own cabinet ministers—particularly Weizmann, who had a tendency to urge the negotiators to compromise and disregard or concede points of legalistic phraseology. Begin had become fond of Weizmann and would affectionately call him "Mon général," but Weizmann's conciliatory tendencies appalled him.[174]

Tension between Begin and Weizmann ultimately disrupted the functioning of the Israeli delegation. Weizmann complained that "Begin treats me like an unloved son" and that "Begin's legalistic niceties are driving me nuts."[175] Begin, for his part, thought that both Weizmann and Dayan were too inclined to make concessions,[176] and he particularly resented Weizmann for turning his back so easily on the political platform of the party that had gotten him elected.[177] This mounting hostility is one reason why one evening Begin made a surprise request of his delegates to sing "underground songs." This caused deep embarrassment; Kadishai and Begin ended up singing alone because only they knew all the lyrics.[178] For Begin, the singing was like mental therapy; once again, as in the underground days, he was standing alone against the rest of the world and the Labor establishment.

In the second week of the conference, Begin insisted on preventing the removal of the Israeli settlements and airports in Sinai, as the Egyptians had demanded, even if it meant leaving them under Egyptian sovereignty. In an attempt to break the deadlock, Dayan asked the

Egyptians to let the fate of the Israeli settlements be decided after the first stage of withdrawal, not before the accord was signed, but the Egyptians were adamant: the settlements had to go and without delay.

The Egyptian delegates did little to make things easier. Hassan Tohami, an amateur astrologist and mystic, kept saying that his positions were revealed to him in his dreams by the Prophet Mohammed. He even handed slivers of gray ambergris—found in whale intestines and used in the preparation of perfumes—to his team members, claiming the slivers would strengthen their resolve if they dissolved them in their tea. He also promised Begin that the day would come when he would enter Jerusalem riding a white horse.[179] Seeing Begin's partiality to formal attire, he tried to bring him around to his way of thinking by using an allegory about a suit: "To return Sinai with the settlements kept as they are would be like handing in a suit for dry cleaning and having it returned with all sorts of stains," he said. Begin was not impressed. Two days before the conference ended, in a fit of anger, he even accusingly said to Ambassador Lewis that he had believed the conference would consist of three parties but he now saw that Carter and Sadat were in cahoots.[180]

Of course, Begin was in a difficult spot. He was entrenched in a position that only he held, and he was facing pressure from Dayan, Weizmann, the Egyptians, and the Americans all at once. Moreover, Benny Begin, whose military service had been in intelligence, told his father that he guessed that the Americans were eavesdropping on the delegates' telephone conversations, so Begin took to conducting quite a few of his consultations outdoors on the walking paths around Camp David.

On September 14, when it looked as though the talks were about to break down, there was a surprising turnaround in Begin's position. Arik Sharon, who had stayed in Israel and had opposed the removal of the settlements, called him to say that removal would have no adverse effect on Israel's national security and that for the sake of a peace agreement they were dispensable. Begin thanked him for calling.[181] He did not need Sharon to reach a decision since he had already made up his mind he would not return home without an agreement. In all likelihood he understood that Sharon's support for removal stemmed also from Sharon's wish to score points over Weizmann, who saw him as a competitor. He also surmised that the phone call was a ploy, made at the request of one of the Israeli delegates, but getting the green light from the person seen as the father of the Israeli settlements in the territories was hugely valuable to him nonetheless.[182] Although Dayan and Weizmann were military icons in their own right, only with Sharon's support could Begin confront the might of the settlers' opposition since he was of the same camp as they. Sharon's approval also fulfilled a personal need. Begin needed someone to share the responsibility of removal since in his heart of hearts he was deeply unhappy about it. After all, during the delegation's final consultation before leaving for Camp David he had promised that they would pack up and leave if it came to this point. His son, who once again voiced opposition to the proposal, made his predicament worse. The idea that Begin himself would give the order to remove Jews from their land was intolerable to him, so even after the conversation with Sharon, he proposed to Carter and Sadat that he present the issue for a vote in the Knesset, "and whatever the Knesset decides—so be it." Carter was not satisfied with this proposal and asked if the prime minister would recommend the settlements' removal to the assembly, and Begin replied, "I shall make no recommendations whatsoever. It will be a free vote, up to each MK to decide."[183]

Begin was being truthful when he stressed the democratic importance of making his proposal to the Knesset, but fundamentally, as we have noted, his position reflected an inner conflict. Even a year after the signing of the accord, after having commissioned the Foreign Ministry's legal adviser to prepare a propaganda booklet about the peace, Begin hastened to ask that corrections be made to a paragraph that stated that at Camp David Israel had agreed to give up the Sinai settlements. "After all, it was the Knesset that decided that," he said, and the paragraph was rewritten.[184]

As a result, the Camp David Conference ended not with a final peace accord but rather a declaration of principles called *A Framework for the Conclusion of a Peace Treaty between Egypt and Israel*—whose final form was supposed to be signed within three months—and a framework for an autonomy agreement to be concluded within five years. The signing ceremony for the framework agreements was set for Saturday evening, September 17, 1978, but in the eleventh hour, a new crisis arose: the Egyptians, with the Americans' support, asked that all settlement activity in the administered territories be halted during negotiations over the autonomy. Begin agreed only to refrain from any new settlements and only for three months, the time allocated to signing the peace accord. Carter saw this as yet another one of Begin's subterfuges, but Begin refused to budge on this point, even at the risk of returning home without an agreement. He had agreed to full withdrawal from Sinai and to the dismantling of the settlements, but this was about defending the Land of Israel.

Thus on the morning of the scheduled signing it looked as if the ceremony would be called off. Knowing his phone was tapped, Begin called his aides in Israel and told them he was packing to go home. Sadat, who unlike Begin had no patience for timetable details, gave in and agreed to be content with a three-month freeze.[185] The accord was signed, but the dispute over the settlements sowed the seeds of a crisis that was yet to flare between Carter and Begin.

On returning to Israel, Begin was greeted with many demonstrations for and against the agreement, but this time, it was the opposite of previous occasions: the Peace Now movement staged rallies in his favor, while those on the right unfurled black umbrellas in protest at his surrender—in allusion to Neville Chamberlain after the 1938 Munich Pact with Hitler. Opinion polls revealed that 82 percent of the public supported the agreement, a statistic that no politician could afford to ignore.[186] Nevertheless, many wondered how it had come to pass that Begin—who seven years earlier had resigned from the government over the mere hint in the Rogers Initiative that Israel should make territorial concessions—had agreed to give up the whole of the Sinai Peninsula.

There is no doubt that Begin was convinced he was doing the right thing. In a bid to leave his mark on the history of Israel, he had achieved the seemingly impossible: a peace accord with the largest of the country's enemies. He had been stubborn during the negotiations and had agreed only very reluctantly to the removal of the settlements, but he never once had any qualms about withdrawal from the peninsula. On the contrary, in a personal conversation with the cabinet secretary he confided that never since his proclamation of rebellion against British rule in 1944 had he been more at peace with any decision he had made.[187] Even after his retirement from politics he claimed that the agreement that he achieved was "very good."[188]

Begin had made a distinction between Sinai and the rest of the Land of Israel while still in the opposition. As far as he was concerned, the distinction was at once ideological, historical, and religious. He also justified his support for the agreement on national-democratic grounds: since previous Israeli governments had accepted Resolution 242, he could not repeal it. Furthermore, by signing the agreement, he was now in a position to sign a strategic memorandum with the United States.[189] He regarded the withdrawal from Sinai as a diplomatic maneuver to head off international pressure over the return of the territories conquered in 1967 because he felt that if he withdrew from Sinai, the pressure to do so from Judea, Samaria, and Gaza would diminish.[190] In other words, the pullback from Sinai was not a precedent but a final chapter. Like Sharon's "disengagement" plan from Gaza in 2005, Begin's unspoken aim was to hold on to most of the territories by emphasizing the part that he would give away.

At the same time, Begin could not ignore the argument that returning Sinai was indeed a precedent, and this left him conflicted.[191] The Left's rejoicing embarrassed him; author Amos Oz wrote to him saying that he admired his decision even more knowing that in Begin's heart he "plucked a different string," but Begin wrote back thanking him but stressing that the appreciation was unwarranted since his decision was in keeping with his previous views.[192] Nonetheless, Begin was alarmed—very alarmed—by the idea that he had changed his principled objection to territorial concessions per se. It is no coincidence that immediately after signing the Camp David Accords he sent an unofficial document to the Israeli team at the autonomy talks to the effect that all settlers in Judea, Samaria, and Gaza would in future be subject to Israeli authority and that they (the negotiators) should conduct the talks accordingly. The document, to which Dayan and Weizmann both objected, in particular underlined Begin's fear of the implications of the withdrawal, and it was the start of a process that culminated in the departure of both figures from the government. The mental difficulty Begin experienced was also evident in his wish to hold two separate votes in the Knesset—one over the peace issue and another over the dismantling of the settlements. When asked what would happen to the agreement if the Knesset approved the peace but rejected the withdrawal, he replied, "I shall explain the democratic decision to Carter and Sadat," although he knew full well that this would spell the end of the agreement. It is reasonable to assume that the double vote, which may well have scuttled the accord, was not what he really wanted, but his conscience troubled him so much that even after the signing at Camp David he hoped that in the matter of the withdrawal he would be led rather than lead. Ultimately, at the insistence of Hamaarach, whose votes he needed to pass the resolution, he abandoned the two-vote idea and agreed to put the entire issue to a single vote.[193]

On returning to Israel, buoyed by a peak in public support, Begin attacked his own party with the same rhetoric that he had previously used against his opponents on the Left. When Yosef Rom, one of the Likud MKs, argued that withdrawing from Sinai would diminish

Israel's strategic value in American eyes, Begin shouted at him, "Maybe you should take your hands out of your pockets when addressing the prime minister?" His words revealed his need to demand satisfaction for the harm done to his mythical status within the party. At the same time, he rejected the option of invoking party discipline and allowed a free vote on the issue. This decision, which was a model of democratic rule, stemmed from his wish to underline that in this matter he was the prime minister, speaking not on behalf of Etzel or Herut but the nation or, as he put it, "My duty is to all the mothers."

The issue of dismantling the settlements, however, continued to trouble Begin, and in his speech before the Knesset vote on September 28—whose outcome was foretold—he stressed that there was no choice in the matter. He noted that the peace accord would entail a measure of distress and pain, like "the greatest thing in the universe—the birth of a child—which is brought forth in sorrow." He added, "My heart grieves for the settlements." At the same time, he underlined the benefits of the accord: peace with the most powerful Arab country, assured passage for Israeli ships through the Suez Canal, demilitarization of the Sinai Peninsula, and the continued control of Judea and Samaria by the IDF. He ended his speech with a commitment: "After the Jewish New Year, we shall be able to say, the year of peace has arrived—peace upon Israel."

Eighty-four of the 120 MKs supported the agreement; nineteen were opposed and seventeen abstained (the latter mostly from Begin's own camp). MK Ehud Olmert was among those against, as were Moshe Arens, Geula Cohen, and Moshe Shamir. Yitzhak Shamir, Eitan Livni, Dov Shilansky, and Yoram Aridor abstained. Rabbi Kook, who until recently had been Begin's closest rabbinical authority, denounced the accords as "a desecration of the sacred name of peace." But Begin stood his ground. When he made a decision, he stuck by it. This was Begin's finest hour. He confronted his associates, cited the decision in every speech he made, and demonstrated a leadership that astonished many who only a year before had thought that his militant stance would destroy the country.

Although the framework agreed upon at Camp David called for a signing of the completed accords within three months, in reality the process concluded after six months or so. The delay was due in part to a row over a defense alliance that Egypt had entered into as a member of the Arab League and that committed it to come to the aid of any other Arab country that found itself at war with Israel. That Egypt should make such a commitment after signing the peace accords with

Israel made no sense whatsoever, and it came about because Sadat had found himself in political distress. Contrary to his expectations, his bold move to make peace did not inspire other Arab leaders to follow his lead but rather caused him to be marginalized. However, Sadat decided to demonstrate leadership and acceded to Israel's condition that he withdraw from the alliance, even at the expense of Egypt's expulsion from the Arab League.

Sadat—who unlike Begin was not a micro-manager—preferred to run the proceedings from behind the scenes and put his advisers and ministers front and center, especially in view of the resistance his initiative had met within the Arab world. For this reason, on receiving an invitation to Oslo to receive the Nobel Peace Prize along with Begin, he declined on the grounds that a crisis in the talks would make his going to Oslo inappropriate and asked his son-in-law, Hassan Sa'id Mar'i, to receive the prize on his behalf.

Sadat's decision posed a problem for Begin. In view of Sadat's planned absence, most Israeli newspaper columnists suggested Begin too forgo the ceremony—particularly since the difficulties in the talks largely robbed the prize of its meaning. The debate in foreign publications over the misgivings that the Nobel Committee had in honoring him given his part in the Deir Yassin massacre of 1948 also weighed on him. Editorials in the London *Times* and the *Guardian* went so far as to propose that the prize be given only to Sadat and Carter on the grounds that Begin had merely done what Israel was obliged to do anyway.[194] Begin was deeply hurt. He felt that the honor inherent in the prize came only at a price of having subjected himself to humiliation as well.

"What do you think—should I really not go?" he asked Kadishai only days before the ceremony. His impulse was to react as he had always done when facing criticism within his own camp: throw in the towel and quit. But Kadishai had a short and potent argument why he should go: "To spite them! Make them have a fit!" he said to him in Yiddish.[195] This notion hit home. The sentiment suited how he felt. "Like a child starved for his mother's love," is how Begin's secretary summed up his mood before the ceremony.[196] Years of political ostracism had heightened his yearning for legitimacy, his ardent wish no longer to be seen as a warmonger, and the Oslo ceremony was his chance to change that distorted image forever.[197]

Decked out in a dark suit and white tie and accompanied by his wife and sister, he who had been considered an outcast within his own country showed up to receive a prize that gave him respect and honor throughout the world. Begin understood the significance of the occasion both on a national level (no Israeli had received the Nobel Peace Prize before) and personally, and he accordingly delivered a poetic and emotional speech. "Peace is the beauty of life," he said, and compared his life history to the resurrection of the Jewish people. He linked the idea at the root of the Nobel Peace Prize to the essence of Judaism; noted that its first laureate, Jean Henry Dunant (in 1901), was an admirer of Theodor Herzl; and ended by saying that the prize did not belong to him but "to the entire Jewish people, which has suffered so much throughout history."[198] Since material comforts were of no interest to him, he dedicated the monetary proceeds of the prize ($85,000) to create a fund—the Menachem and Aliza Begin Nobel Peace Prize Foundation—to support disadvantaged students.

After receiving the prize, Begin returned to the dreary routine of policy dilemmas created by the peace talks. Sadat, as noted, had instructed his ministers and advisers to wrap up the talks without him, but the teams were finding it hard going, and Begin's legalistic nitpicking continued to pose stumbling blocks. The Egyptians, doing everything they could to prove to the rest of the Arab world that they were looking out for the interests of the Palestinians, insisted on strengthening the link between the autonomy plan and the withdrawal from Sinai by setting up a liaison office in Gaza. Begin was opposed to this idea. He made sure that every English version of the agreement had the words "people of Palestine" (with a lower case "p" in "people") rather than "Palestinian People," to underline the distinction between the inhabitants of Palestine—that is, the Arabs of the Land of Israel—and the Palestinian nation, which he did not recognize.[199] Another cause for delay was Begin's demand for full normalization between Israel and Egypt as early as the first stage of withdrawal. The Egyptians insisted that the process be gradual.

In March 1979, Carter came to the Middle East for a visit dubbed as "crucial" because both sides were worn out from the peace process and negotiations had reached an impasse. During his visit to Israel he was invited to take part in the weekly cabinet meeting, at which he thought he noted a hint of rebuke from several ministers who voiced their opposition to positions he had expressed during the talks. In a fit of pique, he let slip something along the lines of, "You will do whatever the United States tells you to." The embarrassed ministers fell silent and looked at Begin, who was incensed by Carter's outburst. Once again, he was the proud Jew facing up to the oppressive Polish feudal lord. "We are a sovereign country," he said defiantly. "No one will tell us what to do, and I shall not sign any document that this government does not approve."[200] Stung by the apparent scolding, Carter stood up to leave, but Burg and Tamir prevailed upon him to stay.[201] The incident proved to be important, however, because Carter understood at this point that Begin was in political trouble domestically and could not make any further concessions. On arriving in Egypt, he persuaded Sadat to drop his demand for a liaison office in Gaza because Begin saw it as an infringement on Israel's sovereignty. Agreement was also reached over the supply of Egyptian oil to Israel.

The final point of dispute was over the control of Taba—an area of less than a quarter acre on the shores of the Red Sea on the Egyptian side of the border near the Israeli city of Eilat, at which an Israeli resort had been established. It was decided that this would be resolved through international mediation some time later. In addition, it was agreed that negotiations on the autonomy would commence a month after the signing of the accords. The date of the signing was set for March 26, 1979, at the White House.

A photograph of the three-way handshake among Carter, Sadat, and Begin—one of the most famous images of the twentieth century—immortalized the high point of one of the most emotionally moving days in Middle Eastern history. In its thirty-first year, after five wars, the State of Israel was signing a peace treaty with the largest Arab country. Menachem Begin had left his mark on history. Contrary to all expectations, none other than the former Etzel commander—whom the first Israeli prime minister had compared to Hitler, no less—became the first Israeli leader to sign a peace accord with an Arab country.

In his speech at the signing ceremony, Begin noted that this was the third greatest day of his life. The first was May 14, 1948, when Israel declared independence. The second was the conquest of East Jerusalem during the Six-Day War. Before finishing his speech, he donned a black skull cap and read a verse from Psalms 126: "When the Lord restored the fortunes of Zion, we were like those who dream."[202] Once again he chose to wear the black yarmulke of the ultra-Orthodox—not a crocheted one of the religious nationalists, with whom he bore a closer political affinity—because in his eyes the ultra-Orthodox represented the unbroken historical Jewish tradition, of which he and his party and the modern state were merely an extension. This was part of the determinist philosophy to which he subscribed, and to his followers he explained that peace was the emanation of the divine power steering Jewish history.

Now, approximately two years into his first term in office, Begin was at his height. For the first time in his life he enjoyed the support of virtually all sectors of the Israeli public, and even foreign newspapers were complimentary of him. On returning to Israel, he was invited to dinner with newly elected president Yitzhak Navon, who asked him, "How did you succeed where previous prime ministers failed?" "It's all in the timing," Begin replied. "Making the most of the right moment."[203] He was not being modest. At the height of his career, Begin found himself in an odd situation: he had achieved the glory that he so wanted but only at the price of a decision that caused him great pain and that went against everything he believed concerning the right of Jews to settle and live in security wherever they pleased.

His determination to prove that his legacy would not be limited to the returning of territories and to the dismantling of settlements would be a decisive factor in the new initiatives that he now had in store.

FIFTEEN

DETERIORATION

In the summer of 1979, after he had signed the peace treaty, it seemed as though Begin had reached his summit too early. It soon became clear that the "peace shock" was undermining the government's stability. Several Likud members, including Geula Cohen and Moshe Shamir, resigned in protest over the treaty and established Hatechiya (the Revival), a secular right-wing party. Dash began to disintegrate because of internal disagreements, and Dash member Meir Amit, the minister of transport, resigned. Even Minister of Trade and Tourism Yigal Horowitz, a Likud member, resigned over his opposition to the agreement. In response, Begin made several changes in the government. Landau, who was a minister without portfolio, was appointed minister of transport, and David Levy, the immigration absorption minister, was also appointed minister of housing and construction. Yitzhak Modai, the minister of communications, was persuaded not to resign in exchange for receiving the energy portfolio. The Mafdal also went through changes; Gush Emunim, the core supporters of the party, found it difficult to cope with the withdrawal from Sinai, and Mafdal leaders Burg and Hammer, who supported the agreement, had to deal with serious complaints. Clashes among the ministers during cabinet meetings occurred more frequently, a fact that leaked to the press. Begin called these conflicts "breakdowns" and pledged to stabilize the ranks, but he soon realized that his great achievement was a difficult burden to bear.

Senior newspaper commentators predicted that Begin would be the Israeli De Gaulle and that he would sign a peace treaty with the Palestinians, but they were mistaken, as it turned out that Begin was actually planning on strengthening Israel's presence in the administered territories. After signing the agreement, he did say that he expected to see an Arab judge sitting on the Supreme Court bench (gaining him some admiration from the Left),[1] but he was not about to compromise on the issue of the Palestinian autonomy, although the right-wing camp (which had not yet recovered from the disappointment of the peace treaty) did not cease pressuring him to resign.

When politicians attacked him, Begin usually expressed his contempt for them, but his meetings with the leaders of Gush Emunim deepened his internal conflict because he believed their intentions were pure.[2] He met with them often, as if out of an impulse for self-flagellation or an attempt to make amends, though he knew they considered him a traitor. His bureau chief objected to these meetings and would often ask him to stop them while they were already in progress, although he knew that Begin wanted to suffer to the sound of their claims.[3]

The peace agreement also deepened the divisions among the senior ministers. Dayan and Weizmann hoped to complete the process and establish a Palestinian autonomy, while Sharon pushed in the opposite direction and planned to build new settlements in order to prevent a separation between Israel and the administered territories. Begin could not control his ministers. He tended to side with Sharon but did not want to sabotage his government's international status by establishing settlements via questionable means. His many dilemmas threatened his mood. He started once again to alienate those around him and tended to shut himself in his office for hours on end. He continued to adhere to his principles and to manage the peace process, but no longer as a modern prophet leading his people. The change did not affect his ability to function, and it was not visible to the public, but his former elation had turned into frustration that at times made him indifferent.

Yosef Burg, the interior minister, was one of the first to speculate that Begin's mood swings were a result of changes in blood pressure caused by diabetes.[4] Klimovitski, his secretary, said he was not the same man she had known and noticed that at times he was uninterested in whatever was happening around him. She asked Bader, who had already retired from politics, what his spells of depression could mean. "Don't worry. This is Begin, a man of moods," he calmed her.[5]

On the eve of July 20, 1979, yet another event took place that exacerbated Begin's fluctuating moods. While he was at home with Aliza, he suddenly felt dizzy and was unable to stand up straight. A doctor was called and he suggested that Begin be transferred to the emergency ward, where it was discovered that he had suffered a stroke.[6] Today such an event would stir a storm of public reaction, raise concerns regarding the prime minister's ability to function, and be smeared across the newspapers' front pages. But the spirit of those times and the blackout regarding Begin's health that his associates had imposed since his previous heart attack dictated a different approach. His stroke was described as a minor matter. Two days after his hospitalization, Professor Silvio Lavi, head of the Laboratory for the Study of Blood Vessels at Hadassah Hospital, announced that a small vessel in Begin's brain was damaged and that it would affect only the vision in his right eye. "It's quite normal," he explained to reporters, and noted that Begin's driver's license would most likely be revoked. The term "stroke" was not mentioned. The Israeli newspapers wrote that there had been "an improvement in Begin's condition," and his "dizzy spell" was concealed. The *New York Times* reported that Begin's condition was worrisome, but Israelis believed his spokesmen, who denied it.[7] *Haaretz* published an article in which the risks of blocked blood vessels in the brain were discussed, but the prime minister's condition was not specifically mentioned.[8] TV and radio broadcasts and the other major newspapers, *Yediot Ahronot* and *Maariv,* only hinted at the stroke.

In the first week of his hospitalization only Begin's family visited him, and Professor Asa Harel, the director general of Hadassah Hospital, said that "Begin is still suffering from a blockage in one artery in the brain." Again the word "stroke" was not mentioned. Harel added that Begin was being treated with blood-thinning medications that would prevent the formation of blood clots and that it was a "small blockage of a minor artery."[9] During this first week Begin found it hard to read the documents brought to him and was updated by oral reports alone. A week later, while still in bed, he began to meet with his senior government ministers. In retrospect, it is difficult to evaluate whether the stroke caused Begin any mental impairment, and if so, to what extent. Weizmann was the first and most vocal politician to opine that Begin was dysfunctional after suffering a stroke, and he called him "the deceased" behind his back.[10] However, the knowledge that Begin tended to suffer from mood swings, as well as his undisputed status in his political camp, caused those around him to ignore the deterioration in his condition.[11]

In mid-August 1979, two weeks after his release from the hospital, Begin returned to his office. He was intent on maintaining the existing political situation. He conducted the autonomy negotiations like a man who has already sold off all his stock. Furthermore, after signing the peace treaty, he retracted his consent to Dayan's proposal that the final status of the territories would be discussed five years after the establishment of a Palestinian autonomy. The peace treaty with Egypt had been signed, and Begin allowed himself to announce in the name of his government that after five years Israel would demand to exercise its sovereignty throughout the territories.[12] Begin stressed to Yitzhak Zamir, the recently appointed attorney general, that he was referring to a "personal" autonomy and not a "territorial" one. Absurdly, the talks over autonomy for the Palestinians—"the Eretz Israeli Arabs," as Begin referred to them—took place between Israel and Egypt alone, as the Jordanian-Palestinian delegation refused to participate in talks based on the agreed contour lines.[13]

Zamir's reports about "empty talks that are not progressing" did not particularly upset Begin. Despite the rising tension between Israel and Egypt over the failure of the peace talks with the Palestinians, Begin was pleased, as he had not undermined the peace treaty with Egypt, to which he was committed.[14]

Begin was appalled by assessments that he had actually agreed with the Palestinians about their right to self-determination. He reiterated to Kadishai that the results of the autonomy agreement would depend on "how and who conducts the talks in the future."[15] In this respect, Dayan changed from an asset to a burden. Now, unlike during the negotiations with Egypt, Begin no longer needed Dayan's creativity, and he did not trust his knowledge of the details that would prevent the autonomy from forming a state in the future. Therefore, in the summer of 1979 Begin offered to appoint Burg as head of the team leading the autonomy talks. Some members in Burg's party—the Mafdal—viewed giving up Sinai as intolerable and pressured him to turn down Begin's offer. Begin saw Burg as a man whose stand regarding Judea and Samaria was more rigid than Dayan's. Moreover, the mere placement of the autonomy issue in the hands of the interior minister symbolized that the subject was an internal Israeli concern.

The surprised Burg asked for time to consider the offer. Begin said he did not wish to sabotage the autonomy plan but clarified that he had offered him the job because for him "the Land of Israel is not a term from a geography book but a worldview, part of the commandments, the prayers." Finally, he added a convincing argument. Begin told Burg that he had received advice to appoint him from a "wise man." "Who?" wondered Burg, and Begin replied, "My son, Binyamin."[16]

Dayan was furious at Burg's appointment. He did not believe Begin's statement that he had appointed Burg in order to strengthen his position within his party, and he understood that the prime minister wanted to keep him away from the hub of decision making. Dayan knew that the idyll between him and Begin was over; when he confronted him by saying that those who opposed any concessions in Judea, Samaria, and Gaza did not really want the autonomy talks to succeed, Begin proposed that he join Burg's team—an insulting suggestion that pulled the plug on Dayan's participation in the talks for good.[17] Shortly afterward it was discovered that Dayan had cancer, and his motivation to participate in the talks naturally declined. "I had an interesting life until the age of sixty-four," he concluded in his usual cool and collected manner.[18]

The conflict between Begin and Dayan over the autonomy talks was preceded by a bitter argument about the Elon Moreh settlement, in which Begin's worldview about the settlements was clearly expressed. Already in September 1977, Sharon had presented the ministers with a settlement project plan he had prepared (which he called "Sharon's settlement plan"), and he executed it with his typical determination. It was largely based on a plan proposed by architect Avraham Bachmann in 1976; Rabin had rejected it because he opposed the establishment of settlements in areas of dense Arab population. When Sharon presented his plan to Begin's government, he explained that the three main objectives of establishment were urban settlements on the mountain ridge in order to control the coastal plain, settlements along the Jordan Valley in order to protect Israel's eastern border, and settlements around the Arab neighborhoods in Jerusalem in order to strengthen Israel's capital city. Sharon stressed that the establishment of settlements had no political meaning but rather that it would be a direct continuation of the settlement project that had begun with the start of Zionism in the nineteenth century. Beyond the stated purposes of the plan, Sharon, like Begin, hoped it would prevent attempts to divide the country,[19] but unlike Begin, Sharon would not be afraid to break the law in order to execute it. On October 2, supported by Begin, the government approved the plan.[20] It was approved despite the differences of opinion among the four senior ministers—Begin, Sharon, Weizmann, and Dayan—regarding the settlements. Weizmann and Dayan opposed the erection of settlements in areas of dense Arab population and often commented that Sharon was cooperating with Gush Emunim and helping to build settlements in areas not mentioned in the plan. Weizmann preferred a concentration of 5–6 settlement blocs so as not to expropriate private land.[21] In principle, Dayan supported the Jews' right to settle anywhere, even in areas of dense Arab population, but in practice, he demanded that settlements be erected only for necessities of defense. Sharon, as noted, sought to use them to upend any compromise that might be suggested, while Begin sought legal validity so as to attain public legitimacy for the establishment of the settlements.

Disagreements escalated over the question of Elon Moreh, which became a symbol for all the settlements. Sharon and representatives of Gush Emunim urged Begin to stand by his obligation to establish the settlement. Begin agreed and decided to allocate land for its construction near the Kadum army base. Part of the land needed was expropriated from its Arab owner. Israeli law allows such expropriations for security reasons, but Defense Minister Weizmann refused to sign the permits. He argued that the establishment of Elon Moreh was not a security necessity and that it would only complicate Israel's political position. Begin then decided to directly contact the new IDF chief of staff, Rafael Eitan, who had replaced Motta Gur on Weizmann's recommendation. Eitan wrote an affidavit stating that it was indeed a security necessity, contrary to his superior's position.

Leftist organizations petitioned the Supreme Court on behalf of the landowners and claimed that the expropriation was not a security necessity and submitted an affidavit signed by former IDF chief of staff Chaim Bar Lev, then a Knesset member for Hamaarach. In July 1979, the court ruled that the expropriation was illegal.[22] Begin, who held the judicial branch as highly important, declared, "There are judges in Jerusalem" and stated that he intended to uphold the law. Unlike Sharon, who had planned from the start to erect the settlements in deceitful ways, Begin believed that legal approval was necessary and ordered the IDF to find state-owned land. An alternative plot was eventually found on a mountain near Nablus and was approved by the Supreme Court. Nonetheless, the Elon Moreh affair still presented the Israeli government as breaking the law and evoked international rebuke.

Dayan also objected to the establishment of the settlement, to Rafael Eitan's affidavit, and to the alternative plot of land. Because of criticism from the United States and Egypt, Dayan saw the establishment of Elon Moreh as damaging to the peace process and the developing relations with Egypt. He argued that the search for alternative ground indicated that no security consideration was involved and that Elon Moreh was only a provocation.[23] On October 2, after the Elon

Moreh incident and his exclusion from the autonomy talks, Dayan tendered his resignation to Begin.[24] Begin never fired ministers,[25] but he certainly knew how to get rid of them through political trickery. He parted cordially with Dayan, but they agreed that they were no longer suited to working together.

Begin found it hard to find a replacement for Dayan. He wanted to appoint Yigael Yadin, who headed a disintegrating party, but Yadin refused to take responsibility for the settlement policy. Begin then sought to appoint Burg, but the Mafdal would not give up the interior ministry. He was forced to leave the foreign portfolio in his hands and eventually offered it to Knesset speaker Yitzhak Shamir.[26] Shamir was not afraid to say that his appointment bode ill for those in favor of a peace agreement in return for land concessions.[27] Weizmann was now the only senior minister who believed in a territorial compromise, and a change in Begin's government began to emerge.

In 1979, Begin set his mind on a grandiose idea conceived by Weizmann—to produce an Israeli fighter plane. The plane, called the Lavi (Lion), would have huge technological advantages, and it ignited the imagination of the air force officers. Although the Treasury warned that the production costs would be too high, Begin was keen on the local development of an innovative plane that would be the most advanced fighter in the world. He could not resist such ideas. As usual, he overlooked the problematic details and held onto the overall concept. In the meeting that determined the issue, the IAF chief presented the plane's advantages to the cabinet and the finance minister claimed that the government would not be able to pay for production. Begin decided the issue in his typical way: he asked the IAF commander if he really needed the plane, and when he said he did, Begin turned to the finance minister and told him that it was his job to find the funding. The 1986 State Auditor's Report noted that the management and planning of the ambitious project were inadequate: "The decision in February 1980 on the construction of the Lavi did not consider the economic aspects, including employment considerations, financing, and export prospects compared to other alternatives."[28] In 1987, the unity government cut the project despite the fortune that had been spent on it, and hundreds of engineers found themselves unemployed.

Begin often accepted the whims of his ministers and members of his coalition and supported far-reaching proposals even when he did not completely support them. Such was the case with the Jerusalem Law, initiated by MK Geula Cohen.[29] On July 30, 1980, the Basic Law:

Jerusalem the Capital of Israel was approved; it stated that the united Jerusalem was Israel's capital and the official location of the Knesset, the government, and the Supreme Court and that no transfer of authority to a foreign entity would be made unless through legislation involving the law's cancellation. This brought on the world's outrage. The U.N. Security Council condemned the law, noting that it was "meaningless and must be abolished";[30] the United States avoided vetoing the U.N. resolution, and subsequently some foreign embassies in Jerusalem were relocated. Nevertheless, Begin supported the bill and publicly praised it as if it was an achievement because he believed in its impact even though Jerusalem had been united before the law and the law only deepened the international criticism of Israel.

The government's weak point was not Israel's political situation but its economy. During the period in which Begin had been focusing on the peace process, significant changes had occurred in the economy. On October 29, 1977, Begin argued in support of a new program proposed by Finance Minister Simcha Ehrlich. Called the New Economic Reversal, it was intended to bring about a tremendous change in the Israeli economy, and it was based on the spirit of free enterprise in the teachings of Jewish American economist Milton Friedman, who was appointed as government adviser on the subject. Like all plans proposed during Begin's term as prime minister, it stimulated a great amount of public interest. Ehrlich stated that Israel would become the "Switzerland of the Middle East," and Friedman described the changes as "daring as the raid on Entebbe."[31]

Indeed, the first stage was far-reaching. Most of the subsidies provided by the government—especially for basic goods, for which subsidies had been an integral part of the Israeli economy since its inception—were eliminated. The guiding principle for abolishing the subsidies was to allow market forces to determine prices. When Ehrlich was asked about potential harm to the weaker layers of society, many of whom had voted for Begin, he explained that in his opinion it was better to help them by specific and limited aid since the subsidies, which also served those with means, created distortions that affected the market forces. The plan also canceled foreign currency controls. For the first time in Israel's history every citizen was entitled to hold foreign currency and to trade freely. The Finance Ministry hoped the cancellation of the controls would convince rich Jews in the Diaspora to invest in Israel and thus stimulate the country's trade. In addition, the plan offered exchange rate flexibility. Foreign exchange rates would now be determined on a daily basis by market forces, according to supply and demand.

It was a bold plan, one that contradicted the socialist spirit that Mapai had sought to create in the state. The planners were well aware of the risks; from the start, concerns were raised that loosening the reins of the economy would increase the government's deficit and deepen the gaps between rich and poor. By Friedman's optimistic predictions the market forces would stabilize the Israeli lira and thus prevent a deficit in the balance of payments, but as a precautionary measure, the government raised the Value Added Tax (VAT) from 8 to 12 percent in order to absorb excess funds from the public and reduce the government deficit.

As in the Etzel days, Begin was carried away by the general idea and glossed over its details. He explained that the plan would "benefit the people and open up new economic opportunities." Because of the importance he attached to political issues, he did not bother to delve into matters of economics, preferring to rely on one of "our experts"—Ehrlich—whose economic point of view, as head of the Likud's liberal faction, was already a lot less socialist than that of Herut.[32]

Begin's lack of interest in economics was exemplified in a press conference held before the withdrawal from Sinai, when he was asked how the government would finance the withdrawal and the demolition of the abandoned settlements. "Ah," he said, smiling broadly, "we will take a loan from the Americans and return every penny."[33] Begin did not remember that during the preparations for the withdrawal, Israel's Finance Ministry and U.S. government officials had agreed that $800 million of the estimated $3 billion cost of the withdrawal would be a grant, not a loan. These $800 million were forgotten for the same reason the memory tends to neglect other facts: lack of interest. In any event, the Finance Ministry was horrified to hear that Begin had offhandedly dismissed the agreement it had reached, and at the end of the press conference it immediately released a statement announcing that the prime minister's response had been only an answer in principle.[34]

Israeli citizens were now allowed to open foreign currency bank accounts, and the amount of funds they were allowed to take out of the country was raised significantly. But few people benefited from the possibility of trading in foreign currency. Immediately after the plan was implemented, a sense of relief became obvious among the upper and middle classes. The cancellation of the travel tax made traveling abroad a "legitimate" pastime; it was no longer considered contrary to the economy's interests. And new products imported from abroad and offered at reasonable prices filled the shelves. Liberalization also significantly assisted the business sector, and the stock market recorded rising share prices. But the change did not benefit the people as Begin had declared it would.

The cancellation of subsidies raised the prices of basic products and aroused resentment against the Likud for hurting its constituents, the people of the poor neighborhoods and development towns. It soon became clear that the plan's primary objective—the removal of economic restrictions in order to speed up economic activity and generate more revenue for the government—would not be achieved. The combination of the increased VAT, the cancellation of subsidies, and the sudden rise in the U.S. dollar exchange rate triggered an unprecedented wave of price increases and created an inflationary spin. The demand for cheap imported products raised prices by 12 percent within two months. In early 1977 the inflation rate was 42.8 percent; in 1978 it increased to 48.8 percent, in 1979 to 111.4 percent, and in 1980 it rose again to 132.9 percent.[35] The increase in the deficit weakened the economic infrastructure, and less than a year after the plan's implementation the country was caught in a crisis that the government was helpless to alleviate. On the evening of July 17, 1978, the ministers convened an emergency meeting to discuss the deterioration in the balance of payments. TV crews waited outside the conference hall to confirm rumors of an emergency plan and the imposition of new taxes. But Begin himself halted the proposed economic decrees. He argued that "you cannot manage the economy over the housewife's back." Near dawn, when the cabinet secretary announced that the ministers had actually decided not to decide, Begin's government appeared to be incompetent and an economic failure.[36]

The economic program, initially supported by liberal economists outside of Israel, failed primarily because it harmed the economic mechanisms that had kept the gaps in the Israeli society relatively small—for example, through subsidies—and also because the government did not muster the courage to fully implement Friedman's recommendations. The desire to create a free market in an economy that had not known many changes since the establishment of the state was expressed, among other things, in the fact that the linkage mechanism that compensated wage earners for price increases and that had been in existence since the days of Mapai was not eliminated, thus negating the effect of the built-in mechanism of inflation, by which rising prices were supposed to reduce demand and inflationary pressures.

Begin was torn between a liberal economic approach and a desire for social justice.[37] It was no accident that before the first elections he had declared that a government he headed would "take from the rich and give to the poor," in the spirit of Robin Hood. In many ways he was more of a socialist than Hamaarach. For example, since the 1970s he had requested several times that a minimum wage law be enacted, but Hamaarach was against such a law on the grounds that only the Histadrut was permitted to determine minimum wages. In 1971 Moshe Bar'am, the minister of labor in Golda Meir's government, slammed MK Yoram Aridor, claiming that Begin had ordered Aridor to suggest a minimum-wage bill and that "the Knesset will not interfere in matters of wages. We need to entrust the determination of minimum wages to the Histadrut."[38] Begin's vision for minimum wages was eventually implemented in Haavoda's political platform in 2006.

Yet, in fact, Begin opposed socialism as an idea because he adhered to the principles of civil liberty and free enterprise. "I want social justice without socialism," he told the finance minister. "The socialism I oppose is the type that turns every person into an employee. Our Left causes situations in which employees work for socialist conglomerates instead of for private enterprises. What's the difference? In terms of the employee, he is still an employee. And the combination of ruler and provider of livelihood is a means for perpetuating this rule."[39]

The fear of harming the weaker sectors of society also prevented the privatization of many public companies. Although the government made infrastructure plans for the privatization of public sector enterprises, during Begin's six-year tenure only eighteen companies were privatized.[40] Furthermore, Ehrlich's efforts to curb government spending failed. To curb it Ehrlich would have required the prime minister's support, but Begin did not understand the economic program's full significance and often supported ministers who refused to cut their own ministry's budget. The result was that in November 1979, two years after the plan's implementation, the balance of payments deficit had increased by $900 million to $3.4 billion, and Friedman eventually disassociated himself from the plan. He explained that since all parts had not been completed—that is, the state budget had not been cut and the public sector had not been reduced, as required—the plan as implemented was not the original plan he had recommended. In November

1979 too, because of the economy's grave situation, Ehrlich resigned as finance minister.[41]

Yigal Horowitz, who had previously resigned as minister of trade and tourism in protest against the peace agreement, was persuaded to return to the government as finance minister.[42] Horowitz did not find it hard to turn his back on Ehrlich's economic ideas, as if he had found a magic solution for the ills of the previous plan. There was a considerable difference between the refined Ehrlich and the hot-tempered Horowitz. Unlike Ehrlich, Horowitz believed that the deficit was Israel's most serious problem, and he refused to increase government spending. He became known for his blunt statements, such as "Madmen, come down from the rooftops," in which he expressed his disapproval of the ministers who demanded budget increases while the economy was collapsing.[43] Because of his insistence on cutting government costs, even at the expense of the weaker sectors, he was called "Yigal Ein Li" (Yigal I've got nothing). Begin was aware of the burden of inflation and the deficit created in the balance of payments, and he sided with Horowitz when he decided to convert the Israeli pound into the shekel, yet because he aimed for a perfect, victimless solution, he did not agree to new taxes or cuts in government spending that would harm the weaker sectors.

When Horowitz insisted that without a tax increase and the cancellation of further subsidies the deficit would grow, Begin replied, "You do not impose too harsh decrees on the public," adding, "Even the Polish government would not behave like that."[44] Various economic advisers also asked Begin to cut government spending, but he continued to refuse, giving mostly symbolic reasons. Although the advisers explained that it was necessary to reduce subsidies because of the increase in inflation, which automatically brought on an increase in subsidies,[45] Begin adamantly refused to cancel the subsidies on bread and public transport because he felt he had to repay his debt to the disadvantaged population that had brought him to power.[46] His refusal placed him in frequent conflict with Horowitz. "David Levy has many children," he argued. "Think how much he needs to pay just for bread."[47]

Differences of opinion among the ministers on economic issues deepened after conclusions were published from the Etzioni Commission, which had been established at the beginning of Begin's term to discuss improving the education system. The commission recommended, in part, that teacher salaries be raised. Horowitz objected, arguing that the economy did not allow such a recommendation to be implemented, while Education Minister Zevulun Hammer (from the Mafdal) insisted that it did.

Begin was in despair. In late 1980, after two heart attacks and a stroke and after the resignations of several ministers, he now had to deal with economic difficulties. He chose to share his sentiments with Egypt's President Sadat, of all people, and wrote him a letter expressing his feelings at the sight of an X-ray image of his heart. "I will allow myself to tell you something that's on my mind in light of the sudden illness that has struck me. . . . Well then, what is the human heart? Simply put, it is a pump. I thought, Lord in Heaven, as long as this pump is working, a human being feels, thinks, talks, loves his family, smiles, cries, enjoys his life . . . but when the pump stops, this is no more. What a wonder of the cosmos is the fragility of the human body, without which even the mind becomes dormant, helpless."[48]

Begin delayed responding to the Etzioni Commission's recommendation to raise teacher salaries because he was unable to decide. He eventually accepted the recommendation and explained the decision in legal terms; according to the law, he said, the recommendation could not be ignored. Now it was Horowitz's turn to resign, just a year and two months after his appointment. In January 1981, he claimed that he was unable to function under Begin, and he never again returned to serve as finance minister.[49] The most accurate description of the economic situation at the time was given by Dayan, who said, "The world already sees Israel as an economic corpse."[50]

Begin's claim that the government was legally obligated to accept the recommendations of the Etzioni Commission was not an excuse. Legal-ethical principles had guided him throughout his public life, and his faith in them gave him the courage to do everything he had done. To support a recommendation that would raise teachers' salaries despite the economic crisis was typical of him. He loved grandiose projects and attractive slogans—Money for teachers! Money for the neighborhoods!—but he often overlooked the consequences. This approach instigated a number of worthy projects. For example, in April 1978 the Knesset approved the Law for Free Education for youth up to the age of seventeen, backed by Begin, despite opposition by the Finance Ministry.[51] With his usual determination, Begin led one of the government's most successful and broad projects, the Neighborhood Rehabilitation Project, initially entrusted to ministers Yigael Yadin and Gideon Patt and then to minister David Levy and aimed at the restoration of 127 Israeli slums. Begin's approach was innovative and successful. He determined that donations for the project would be transferred neither to the government budget nor to the Jewish Agency but rather directly to the budget managers of the various rehabilitation subprojects. Thus it was decided that the Jews of London would contribute to the neighborhoods in Ashkelon, South African Jews to Jerusalem's Bukharian Quarter, and so on. Through his vision and enthusiasm Begin raised hundreds of millions of dollars from Jewish communities the world over, strengthened the ties between Israel and the Diaspora, and improved the implementation of the rehabilitation project, as donors could directly supervise their donations.[52]

Within several years many of Israel's poorest neighborhoods, in which oftentimes five people lived in one room, were renovated. No one doubted the need to invest in the neighborhoods; the main question was whether it was better to invest in social rehabilitation and community involvement, as suggested by Yadin, or in the improvement of living conditions, as suggested by Levy.[53] Begin sided with Levy, who advocated that proper housing elevated human dignity and would ultimately benefit education and employment, "for it is impossible to encourage one to do homework when five or six people have to share the same room."[54] It was clear that Begin was pleased with the newfound relationship he had forged between the rich Jews of the Diaspora, many of whom were Ashkenazi, and the Sephardi immigrants living in the neighborhoods that were included in the project; in fact he saw this relationship as an achievement as great as the actual rehabilitation.[55]

The Neighborhood Rehabilitation Project made the residents of the neighborhoods feel that the government was concerned about them and that they could extricate themselves from a distressing situation. In 1977, the proportion of Jewish families who lived in homes in which more than three people shared a room stood at 2.9 percent, while in 1983 it had dropped by more than half to 1.2 percent.[56] Over sixty-nine neighborhoods were renovated during Begin's tenure as prime minister, and despite the criticism against the project on the grounds that it did not educate the population of the neighborhoods or increase employment possibilities, many of the inhabitants maintained that rehabilitating their homes first, without trying to educate them or put them through Ben Gurion's melting pot, was an expression of the respect Begin had for their culture, not needing to mold them into something else.[57] The project reflected Begin's attitude—under his leadership the Jewish identity defined what it meant to be Israeli, and thus he included the Mizrahi Jews in the definition—and contributed to the residents' sense of belonging and self-esteem.

But the poverty issue was not resolved during Begin's time as prime minister. Moreover, three years after he came into office, it became clear that the number of poor in Israel had increased. According to the National Insurance Institute, in 1977 the proportion of Israeli citizens living below the poverty line was 2.2 percent, while in 1980 it had tripled to 6.6 percent.[58]

The economic issues accelerated the rate of the government's disintegration. In May 1980, Defense Minister Weizmann resigned due to his disappointment over Begin's support of Sharon's position regarding the settlements and the delay in the autonomy talks. As noted, Weizmann believed he deserved to be prime minister, and because Begin supported Sharon, his main rival, Weizmann chose to bring forward the battle of succession. Since the start of 1980, Weizmann had held many conversations with Likud MKs in order to form a force that could overthrow Begin. He joined Begin's critics both in the press and in the Likud, saying that Begin was harming the peace process and was unable to spur a recovery in the economy, and he suggested that internal elections be held for the Likud chairperson. Rumors began spreading in the Knesset that Weizmann would be the next prime minister, but Begin's status within the party prevented many from openly opposing him. The short-tempered Weizmann despaired of mustering enough support within the party to back his plans and gave up the fight.

Many Likud members urged Begin not to exacerbate the conflict with Weizmann in order to not harm the government's image in the global community, mainly because they feared that Sharon would become number two instead of Weizmann. But the exhausted and despondent Begin lost his patience.[59] The crisis with Weizmann, the man who had helped him into power, added to his mental strain, and he decided to fight back. During Begin's 1980 visit to the White House he heard that Weizmann had said in a television interview in Israel that Begin was denying Israel the enjoyment of the fruits of peace. Upon his return he quickly declared that he supported the finance minister's proposal regarding required cuts in the defense budget. Weizmann took the hint. He announced he would resign because of the potential damage to national security.[60] Begin was not sorry to part with him, and Weizmann was not sorry to go. But this time, unlike with Dayan's retirement, the separation involved emotional turmoil. After announcing his resignation, Weizmann made a scene while leaving the Prime Minister's Office and tore a peace poster off the wall shouting, "No one here wants peace."[61] He claimed to reporters that Begin was not fit to serve as prime minister because of his failing health, a fact that was hidden from the public. Though the public perceived Weizmann's comment as typical hyperbole, Begin saw it as a personal betrayal. He could not forgive the criticism against him from within his own camp, let alone the personal criticism.[62] Up until 1991, a year before his death, Begin did not exchange a word with Weizmann. In 1991, Begin called him to offer condolences on the death of his son Shauli in a car accident.[63]

The defense minister's resignation was a golden opportunity for Ariel Sharon. He wanted the job; the new situation, without Weizmann and Dayan, should have given him an advantage in the succession battle. Sharon told Begin that unless he was appointed defense minister, he too would resign;[64] despite his exhaustion, Begin refused to appoint him and was willing to risk his resignation—another one of many. He admired Sharon as a military leader and a minister, and Sharon had helped to establish the settlements, but Begin was still concerned about his character. When one of Sharon's associates leaked news about Sharon's expected appointment to *Maariv*, Begin, holding the paper, told his secretary, "If that were true, my office would have already been surrounded by tanks."[65]

Begin did everything he could to avoid appointing Sharon as defense minister. He hoped to persuade Shamir to take that portfolio instead of the Foreign Ministry, but Shamir refused, and he also warned Begin that Sharon did not adhere to the rules of democracy.[66] Moshe Arens also refused the job, but Begin still preferred to hold onto the portfolio rather than offering it to Sharon. On May 28, 1980, Begin started to also serve as defense minister, just like Ben Gurion in his time. But his was a completely different situation, both emotionally and politically. Begin stood at the head of a bruised government during a huge economic deficit, and his stints of depression affected his energy levels and his ability to function effectively.

In Begin's first speech as defense minister, Ben Gurion was the star; in times of difficulties, as usual, he abandoned the future and focused on the past. The day after he appointed himself, Begin participated in a memorial service for those who had fallen in the *Altalena* affair. He arrived without a tie, the collar of his white shirt sticking up outside of his jacket. He was agitated and tired but took advantage of his position "as Israel's defense minister, in the name of Israel's defense forces," to apologize retroactively to the surviving *Altalena* immigrants; he accused Ben Gurion, this time officially, "for the IDF's actions against the *Altalena*." Naor, who accompanied him, felt that Begin was experiencing, as it were, an act of atonement by reincarnation, as if he were Ben Gurion: "I have come here, my glorious brothers, as prime minister and defense minister of Israel, to ask in the name of the Israeli Defense Forces for forgiveness, pardon, and atonement."[67]

Even when he was Etzel commander, Begin had stayed uninvolved in operational planning and focused instead on general policy. But such a lack of involvement was not the only problem with his decision, made out of necessity, to appoint himself defense minister. He could not find anyone suitable for the job while tensions were high along Israel's border with Lebanon, and the country needed a full-time defense minister. When asked how he could function in both offices, he said with vexation, "I will dedicate Thursdays to the Ministry of Defense, and the rest of the week it will be run by Deputy Minister Mordechai Tsipori. Besides," he added, "the chief of staff can call me anytime."[68] Journalist Nachum Barnea expressed the public's dissatisfaction on the matter. He claimed that in light of Begin's statement he did not know when he should be more concerned—on Thursdays, when Begin was defense minister at the Kirya (the government center in Tel Aviv where the Defense Ministry and IDF headquarters are located) or during the rest of the week, when he was in the Prime Minister's Office.[69]

A year before the 1981 elections it seemed as though Begin had lost the ability to rule correctly. He went into a decline in his office and often closed himself off at home. Journalists were given many different stories and excuses: he has a cold, he has a fever, and the like. From the stern and dominant prime minister who had signed the peace agreement, only kindness and cordiality in private conversations were left. His interlocutors felt he was contemplative and distant. When he did go to his office, he rarely intervened in matters on the agenda, and his behavior tainted the atmosphere among the cabinet members. Clashes in government meetings grew more and more frequent, and words the likes of which had never been spoken before were exchanged. For example, one time Sharon said to Yadin, "I will strip you bare at the table" when Yadin once again accused Sharon of violating the law in the territories.[70] Such exchanges were leaked to the media and created a general atmosphere of stagnation. The media raised fears about an extremist Likud government, and the fears grew when individual MKs started introducing strange bills in the Knesset. Yechezkel Flumin, the deputy finance minister, proposed to forbid newspapers from freely choosing their reporters and to grant press cards only to journalists who passed a state examination. When Yosef (Tommy) Lapid was appointed director general of the IBA, journalists were surprised to learn that he intended to focus on reducing the freedom of speech rather than expanding it.

Begin did not reprimand the ministers who tarnished the government's image.[71] In fact, he had come to terms with his likely defeat in the upcoming elections, and in cabinet meetings it often seemed as though the issues on the table did not concern him.[72] Ministers were used to his indifference. His office attributed his mood to the Likud's dire situation in the polls, though the office saw his decline as a temporary condition, for mood swings had been typical of him.[73]

The silence that Begin's close associates imposed on themselves testifies to the atmosphere at that time. Claiming that someone—let alone the prime minister—had mental health problems was considered a serious accusation, almost a betrayal. Some psychologists from the Left, knowing that Begin's condition was bad, mulled over the option of publishing professional opinions and arguing that the prime minister was not mentally fit for his job, but ultimately they decided that publicizing opinions about a man they had not personally examined was an ethical breach.[74] Begin continued to go to his office, despite his condition, but in practice he would spend only several hours a day there and then leave. In his desperation, he sought refuge in the past, as he usually did. And he thought about the Arlosoroff case.

On Friday, June 16, 1933, at 9:30 p.m., Chaim Arlosoroff, head of the Jewish Agency's Political Department (forerunner of the Foreign Ministry), and his wife Sima went for a walk on the beachfront in Tel Aviv. As they approached the mouth of the Yarkon River, Sima noticed two men walking behind them and drew her husband's attention to them. The couple decided to turn the other way, and when they thought they had lost their tail, they returned to the beach and headed back south, toward the center of Tel Aviv. But they were wrong. The two men were still following them, and the shorter one drew a gun and shot Arlosoroff. The assassins ran away from the scene. Arlosoroff was taken by a private vehicle to Hadassah Hospital, where he died shortly afterward, having lost much blood. The murder of Arlosoroff, a prominent young leader of Mapai, was considered the culmination of a struggle within the Yishuv between the Labor camp and the Revisionist camp.

In 1933, after the Nazi party had risen to power in Germany, Arlosoroff understood that the Jews were in grave danger, and he did everything in his power to make an agreement with Nazi Germany that would enable the Jews to retain their assets and immigrate to Israel in exchange for large financial donations—contributed by Jews from around the world. The Revisionist newspaper *Chazit Haam* (the People's Front), which was among the main opponents of the agreement, published headlines such as "The Stalin-Ben Gurion-Hitler Union" and "A Knife in the Back of the Nation" and "[Arlosoroff] The Red Diplomat." The claim that Arlosoroff was trading the honor of the Jewish people for money split the Jewish community and stirred up many demonstrations. After he was murdered, the entire Revisionist camp was blamed for allegedly inciting the assassination.

Shortly after the murder, two suspects were arrested who were among Jabotinsky's followers: Tzvi Rosenblatt and Avraham Stavsky. In a police lineup Arlosoroff's wife said she had seen the two during the assassination, and they were charged with murder. Abba Achimeir, founder of the rightist faction Brit Habiryonim (the Toughs' Alliance), was accused of incitement to murder in his articles criticizing Arlosoroff's plan, but he was acquitted.

Two Arabs, Abd-al-Majid and Isa Darwish, confessed to the murder, but before their verdict was read, they claimed that Rosenblatt and Stavsky had offered them 1,000 lira to claim responsibility. In June 1934 the court convicted Stavsky and acquitted Rosenblatt. Stavsky was sentenced to death, but he appealed and won the appeal because under British Mandate law, a person could not be convicted of murder based on one person's testimony alone. Stavsky left the country and in 1948 was killed in the firefight on the *Altalena*.

In 1981, Arlosoroff's murder was considered one of the many chapters in the history of Zionism. In the winter of that year, when Attorney General Yitzhak Zamir was vacationing with his family in northern Israel and was notified that he should contact the Prime Minister's Office, he did not imagine that Begin would instruct him to establish an investigative committee into Arlosoroff's murder. Zamir told Begin that by law he could set up a committee only about current affairs, but Begin insisted. He told Zamir about a recently published book by Shabtai Tevet that insinuated that the Revisionist camp had incited Stavsky and Rosenblatt. "You see," he explained to the surprised Zamir,

"Arlosoroff's murder is still a relevant issue for Israeli society." Zamir promised to examine the subject.[75]

Begin indeed thought that it was necessary to find out the truth about the murder and saw the accusations against the Revisionists in 1933 as leftist propaganda that had continued to his days as prime minister. Yet his desire to probe into the incident was also based on a promise that he had made many years before that upon his election as prime minister he would establish an investigative committee to look into the murder. Once he had come to terms with his likely defeat in the upcoming election, he wanted a chance to deliver on his prior commitment. Zamir prepared the groundwork for the committee, but it began its work only a year later because an angry citizen petitioned the Supreme Court over whether the committee was necessary; after many deliberations the court allowed its establishment. The committee's conclusions were ambiguous, mainly because most of those involved in the affair had died and the few existing testimonies were vague and contradictory.[76] The widespread belief today is that Arlosoroff's killers were Arabs, members of the Palestinian Communist Party.

In the winter of 1981, Begin was sure his days in politics were numbered. He saw the polls' predictions of his downfall as ingratitude. "Why do they oppose me?" he desperately asked his advisers.[77] Three months before the election, after reviewing the assessments of the expected downfall of Likud, Begin met with U.S. Ambassador Lewis, who had become his friend during the peace talks, and opened his heart to him. "I," he said decisively, "am not afraid to lose my job. Just as I took command of Etzel from Yaakov Meridor, so I can hand over the premiership to him."[78] This was the first time, even in private, that Begin had named who he thought would be his appropriate replacement. Lewis hastened to act as an ambassador should upon hearing these intimate details and summoned Meridor for an introductory meeting.

Begin's statement—"I'll return the command to Meridor"—once again expressed his fondness for closure as well as his mental state. Meridor was a figure from the past, and that was how most of the public saw him, but Begin fixed on him. His momentary vision about his successor might have materialized had Meridor not sounded the death knell on his political future. Several days before the election, on a Saturday night, he was interviewed in a special television broadcast and announced, full of the significance of the moment, that he had acquired the rights to a rare invention to generate electricity and energy. He added that a one-watt light bulb could illuminate "all of Ramat

Gan" and that Israel could gain enormous economic profits from the invention. In an interview on Kol Israel he also warned that spies were after information about the invention. Within several months Meridor's fantasy became a joke. It turned out that he had been misled by a con man who had fraudulently collected money from him for the "discovery." So ended his promising political future.

SIXTEEN

THE BEGIN DOCTRINE

On January 21, 1981, before his designated successor was known, Begin appointed his third finance minister. His decision to give the portfolio to Yoram Aridor, who had been appointed as minister of communications only two weeks before, resulted mainly from the political situation. Although Aridor was the first finance minister with a bachelor's degree in economics—"an expert" according to Begin—he was appointed mainly because "now we need a political finance minister," as Eliezer Shostak, the minister of health, told Begin.[1] Aridor had had a great success two weeks before with his first decision as minister of communications. He had canceled a ban on color television broadcasting, an anachronistic regulation that mainly derived from an attempt to prevent the import of new televisions. It was a brilliant decision as broadcasting in color helped the public forget the sorry economic situation at least for a little while at a time.

Aridor's appointment led to a turning point in the economy. Unlike Horowitz, who considered saving in foreign currency and eliminating the deficit as the main goals, Aridor actually thought that inflation could be eliminated by loosening the reins. In this way he promised Begin "to benefit the people."[2] And indeed, as finance minister, Aridor increased the range of services offered to the public. He believed that taxes need to be lowered—especially on consumer goods—in order to reduce the deficit and stimulate the economy; lowering prices—mainly on cars and imported electrical appliances—would increase the trade turnover and eventually increase the state's revenues.

The changes initiated by Aridor, including increasing the subsidies on basic products—which had been decreased by his predecessor—

immediately bore fruit. The prices of many imported products were reduced within a few weeks—especially those of VCRs, televisions, pianos, and cars—and the public swarmed to buy them. Begin viewed these steps as supporting the low-income population. The public, especially the middle class, cheered.[3] Aridor's economic policy also changed the mood among those who thought a magic solution to the economic woes had been found.[4] Begin reacted to his critics by saying that it was not election economics but a plan aimed at economic recovery. While the public's purchases increased the state's revenues somewhat, inflation surged, and the value of the Israeli currency decreased.[5]

The improvement in the public's mood was demonstrated in the elections for the Histadrut on April 7. The leaders of the Likud saw the election results as a sample poll for the Knesset elections. Unlike in previous forecasts, the number of voters for the Labor Party increased by only 7 percent, and the Likud was harmed less than expected—25 percent voted for it.

The results were much better than Begin had anticipated. He said, "If every fourth worker votes for Likud, there is a chance for victory." The change in his mood was quick. Suddenly, his goal to continue to rule was within reach, and he was invigorated.[6] He perceived the change in the public mood—as displayed in the elections results—as satisfaction with his actions as prime minister. As in his struggle against the Reparations Agreement, he seemed to awaken from a long, deep sleep and became energized.

Begin launched an aggressive election campaign that caused the second dramatic change in Israeli public opinion within the less than three months remaining until election day. He started this campaign with an appearance on *Moked*, the main political TV program at that time. He was assisted by David Garth, an American adviser.[7] Surprisingly, he promised on the show that even if elected, he would retire after two years, at the age of seventy—as he actually did, although under circumstances unforeseen by him. He refused to mention the name of a successor. He explained that a successor would be democratically elected.[8] The announcement of a retirement date even prior to the elections was awkward, and many within the political arena were surprised. His statement was the result both of a realization that he was tired and that he accepted Garth's assessment that the public would find it difficult to give him up if he announced the retirement only after two years.

In 1981, Israel was light years away from the 1950s, when participation in political gatherings was considered an entertainment. Nevertheless, Begin instructed his people to organize meetings for him as during his days in the opposition, when he had inflamed the masses. Kadishai objected.[9] He tried to convince him that the time of speeches in public was over. He was also aware of how weak Begin was. Begin insisted. He wanted to see an audience that was excited by his words, and not only for electoral purposes. He was driven by the audience.

So Begin returned to stirring up the public's emotions, contrary to Kadishai's advice. He declared during a gathering in Kiryat Malachi that "we will change Israel's defense perspective and strike the terrorists in their bases"[10] in the midst of clashes with PLO terrorists in Lebanon and while Syria was placing missiles in the Lebanon valley. His ambition grew, and he repeated this promise time and again, although he acceded to Sadat's request to allow mediators to try and resolve the missile crisis by diplomatic means.

The threats that Begin made against the terrorists were not new. What surprised the reporters who were present at a gathering in Netanya and the members of the Knesset who read his comments in the newspapers the following day were Begin's remarks against Helmut Schmidt, the chancellor of Germany. The chancellor had roused Begin's anger when he declared during a visit to Saudi Arabia that Germany had a moral obligation toward the Palestinians because of the injustice they had suffered upon the establishment of the State of Israel, which he claimed was the outcome of the Holocaust. Begin's response was definitely undiplomatic. "He is greedy," he said, and the crowd cheered. "He seeks two things. To buy oil cheaply and to sell weapons dearly. He talks about moral obligation to the Arabs? The obligation to the Jews will never end."[11] Begin's words and his aggressive stance were a throwback to the days of demonstrations against the Reparations Agreement.

Begin was denounced worldwide for his tongue-lashing of Schmidt, but opinion polls made it apparent that the public in Israel identified with him. His words were intended not only to incite his audience. They were a mixture of his objection to Schmidt's comments and his revulsion of Germans. When MK Amnon Rubinstein of the Shinuy (Change) party proposed a discussion about Begin's agenda, the prime minister replied, "Happily for you, Professor Rubinstein, your mother and father raised you in the land of Israel. My mother and father never were in the land of Israel. They dreamt about the land of Israel, and I will not tell you their fate. Mr. Schmidt, who swore allegiance to the Fuehrer, was then in the eastern front, where a city called Brisk of Lithuania stood. Can I know for certain that he was not there?"[12] Rubinstein fell silent in the face of Begin's outpouring. What could he tell a prime minister who mourned his parents before everyone?

Begin continued to attack his opponents. A month before the elections he invited Tommy Lapid, general manager of the IBA, to a meeting and reprimanded him for the programs on Channel 1: "Who placed you as the opposition to the government? Why do you invite all the 'has-beens'—Eban, Dinitz, and Hertzog? What is the meaning of the title that you gave Bar Lev—'a candidate for the defense minister's post if and when Hamaarach returns to rule?' What is this 'if and when'?"[13] The polls suggested that support for the Likud increased the more Begin intensified his stand, strengthening his self-confidence. He did not heed the rumors regarding his mental weakness. But it became clear that he was aware of the changes in him on an interview at Kol Israel on May 7: "I have never felt better.... Mentally, morally I feel much better today than I have felt in the past four years since now I'm fighting. It has been so all my life."[14]

Begin participated in the celebrations in the city of Ariel in Samaria on the thirty-third anniversary of the State of Israel and delivered a speech before thousands of people. In his speech he praised "the architect of the settlements, Sharon." He explained that any piece of land that was handed over to King Hussein would eventually end up in Arafat's hands. Suddenly, in a moment of overexcitement, he raised his right hand in the air, became silent, and then swore, "I, Menachem, son of Chasia and Ze'ev Begin, give my word that as long as I am the prime minister, we will not hand over any land to foreign rule." The audience began to rhythmically chant "Be-gin! Be-gin! Be-gin!"[15]

During Hamaarach's election campaign, Peres stated that Begin was running wild and that he was dangerous. MK Chaika Grossman (Mapam) said that the prime minister talked like the leader of a gang.[16] However, Begin did not intend to moderate his style. Peres called Begin "a leader of motorcyclists" during one of the last pre-election discussions, which was dedicated to the goings-on in Lebanon. Peres referred to Begin's election parade in 1955. Begin's response, while standing on the podium, was reminiscent of Ben Gurion as prime minister. However, this time Begin played the role of Ben Gurion, while Peres was Begin.

> *Begin:* "Well, Mr. Peres, you view me as a leader of motorcyclists. The one who quotes will be quoted. Let's see what kind of leader you are. I'm reading from a book—"

MK Shmuel Toledano: "Is it a discussion about Lebanon?"

Begin: "Oh-ho, you don't even know what book I'm talking about."

Left-wing MK Yossi Sarid makes an unclear interjection.

Begin: "MK Sarid, you will not disturb my reading from a book. Well, 'Peres is renowned for his lust for publicity. He constantly and intentionally builds himself up, being undeterred by any difficulty—'"

Gad Yaakobi: "He [Begin] is able to read only from one book."

Begin goes on: "'—by nurturing relationships with reporters, [seeking] publicity, and giving interviews—'"

Interjections.

Begin: "It will not help you. I will read from the book.... '—and taking care to publish them.'"

Toledano: "Is this a discussion about Lebanon?"

Peres: "You're lying!"

Begin: "My God, how ugly. This was published in Moshe Sharett's book [*A Personal Diary*, the former prime minister and foreign minister's monumental no-holds-barred diary, encompassing his years in the government], volume 8, page 3215, and you tell me that I'm lying?! Here's the book."

Peres was surprised. He, like the members of his party, expected Begin to read from Yitzhak Rabin's famous book, *Pinkas Sherut* (*The Rabin Memoirs*), in which he defamed his opponent in the party. The prime minister exploited Peres's embarrassment and said, "People have said that I'm sick. I have already been buried. And here I am resurrected from the dead. Thank God; do you see the miracle that has come to me? Mr. Peres will certainly say that I suffer mood swings, ups and downs. Thus, I should not be given the reins. Oh-ho, he has suddenly become a seer. What is his profession? I do not know. How much time did he study medicine? But he said he did.... Let the people judge between us." And he descended the podium with a winner's smile on his face.

One month before the elections the polls still predicted that Hamaarach was going to win, although the gap between it and the Likud was narrowing.

The problem posed by the Osirak nuclear reactor near Baghdad had already been raised during handover discussions between Yitzhak Rabin, the outgoing prime minister, and Begin. Rabin briefed Begin on Iraq's efforts to develop a nuclear bomb and on Israeli intelligence's surveillance of the developments. Since the Holocaust and anxiety for the fate of the country were his prime motivators, Begin regarded the Iraqi nuclear reactor as a danger to the entire Zionist enterprise.[17]

On August 23, 1978, shortly before leaving for Camp David, Begin convened the Ministerial Committee for National Security Affairs to decide how to act. Sharon, the most decisive of all, proposed that any Arab country that attempted to develop nuclear arms would be regarded as initiating war and demanded that Israel prepare to bomb the Iraqi reactor. Yadin had the most misgivings. He argued that Iraq's plans to develop a bomb could not be thwarted by military means and suggested that the diplomatic channels be exhausted first. Supporting Yadin's position were Shlomo Gazit, head of IDF intelligence, and Yitzhak Chofi, head of the Mossad. Both argued that a long time would pass before the reactor became operational, and they expressed concern that a military operation would harm Israel's international standing and the peace accord with Egypt. Begin too dismissed Sharon's proposal, and in the end it was decided that Dayan would leave for secret talks with France in an attempt to prevent by diplomatic means the development of an Iraqi bomb and that the matter would be reviewed in a future meeting of the committee.[18] In the meantime, Begin and his senior ministers focused on the peace process.

On April 6, 1979, three days before a French ship was scheduled to set sail with components for the Iraqi reactor, a mysterious explosion went off at the facility where they were hidden, near the town of Toulon. French newspapers blamed the Mossad for the incident, but Israel made no comment. The attempt to sabotage the components failed.[19]

In October 1979, Begin instructed Chief of Staff Rafael Eitan to prepare an operation to attack the reactor. Eitan charged David Ivry, the air force commander, with planning the operation, and in April 1980 Ivry announced that bombing the reactor was operationally feasible. In September of that year, after the Islamic revolution in Iran and the rise to power of the fundamentalist religious leader, the Ayatollah Khomeini, war broke out between Iran and Iraq, which was headed by Saddam Hussein. On September 27, at the height of the war, the Iranians bombed the Iraqi reactor, but Israeli intelligence informed Begin that the reactor had suffered only minor damage and would soon return to operational status.

On October 14, 1980, Begin once again convened the Ministerial Committee for National Security Affairs, and once again the intelligence chiefs voiced opposition to a military operation. The chief of staff was in favor, however. Begin proposed two options, both difficult, he warned. One was to bomb the reactor, a move that might invoke a confrontation with Egypt and other countries in the world. The other was to limit Israel's response to diplomatic negotiations, which might or might not ensure that the Iraqis did not achieve nuclear weapons capability. Begin pointed out that the Iranian bombing had delayed the development of the reactor and reduced the risk of radioactive fallout that might have resulted from its destruction, so if the first option was chosen, it would be better to carry it out sooner rather than later. "This is an operation of long-term strategic importance," he explained, "because it will deter other Arab countries from attempting to acquire nuclear weaponry." Due to his concern that bombing the reactor might lead to radioactive fallout, Begin stressed that it was better to attack before the nuclear fuel rods were loaded because "the children of Baghdad are not our enemies."[20]

Yadin (himself a former chief of staff) continued to express strong opposition to a bombing of the reactor. After listing the military risks involved in such an operation, he estimated that the Soviet Union might respond with a military action against Israel, that Egypt would be accused by other Arab countries of collusion, and that the United States might respond by delaying the supply of arms to Israel. Finally, he asked that the debate be opened up to include the entire cabinet. Begin agreed and two weeks later presented his proposal at a general cabinet meeting. The military chiefs raised arguments for and against, but as in the peace process with Egypt, Begin did not need their unswerving support. He maintained that it was his duty to confront the greatest threat to have ever loomed over the State of Israel. Since Israel's territory was small, he explained, the principle of the balance of terror (mutually assured destruction) that prevented war between the Soviet Union and the United States did not apply in the case of Israel versus the Arab world. He therefore insisted that the reactor be bombed. In the ensuing vote ten ministers voted in favor and six against, and the resolution was passed.[21] The chief of staff therefore gave the IAF the go-ahead to prepare for the operation, which was to take place in January 1981.

After the meeting, Begin was excited. On his way to work that day he had justified his proposal before the cabinet secretary and the military chiefs with an argument that he had not raised during the cabinet meeting: "This morning, when I saw Jewish children playing outside, I decided: 'No, never again.'"[22]

In view of the weightiness of the decision, Begin invited Shimon Peres, the head of the opposition, for a discussion on December 30 and briefed him on its details. He told Peres about the planned operation, albeit without mentioning any date. Peres was surprised and mainly listened, but he believed that Begin was embarking upon a political stunt that would jeopardize Israel's standing in the world.[23] He too was aware of the threat inherent in Iraq's nuclear ambitions, but he believed that it was better to focus on diplomatic tactics because a military operation in itself would not be enough to foil Iraq's plans to acquire nuclear arms. He pinned much hope on political estimates that the presidential elections in France—which had helped Iraq build and operate the reactor—would be won by François Mitterand, who he believed would prevent its further development.[24]

Begin did not ask for Peres's opinion. In the meantime, he had decided to postpone the operation date for fear that launching it so close to the inauguration ceremony of the new American president, Ronald Reagan, would be seen as a provocation. But preparations for the operation continued. On April 6 Begin met with the new U.S. defense secretary, Alexander Haig—alone, without a stenographer at hand, and with some details written only on notes. He asked Haig what the United States could do to prevent Iraq's development of a bomb. "Our efforts to date have been in vain," Haig replied, and Begin understood from this that the new U.S. administration was indirectly giving him the green light.[25]

On April 8, 1981, with preparations for the operation complete, Begin convened the Ministerial Committee for National Security Affairs for a decisive meeting. The previous day the results of the elections for the Histadrut had become known. While one minister was expressing his position, MK Moshe Nissim, who had been active in the Likud's campaign for those elections, entered the room. Before he sat down, he heard Begin calling him and saw him make a victory gesture with his hand. Begin was in a fighting mood—sharp, assertive, and energetic—and it seemed as if his decision about the bombing suited his improved mood.[26]

However, on April 28 the Israeli Air Force shot down two Syrian transport helicopters over the skies of Lebanon during an IDF operation, and the northern border suddenly went into high alert.[27] A military operation in Iraq, it seemed, would push things over the edge. Minister Nissim remarked, "The fact that we have the capability to carry out this operation doesn't mean that we should act like a superpower," and the rest of the cabinet, with the exception of Sharon, agreed. Begin agreed to postpone the operation in light of the developments. However, since he did not want to risk having it canceled altogether, he asked for and received the cabinet's authorization for the prime minister, foreign minister, and defense minister—namely, Begin and Yitzhak Shamir—to decide when to give the OK.[28] The two then decided to carry out the operation on May 10, close to the elections.

On that day, while the pilots were in their planes waiting to take off, they heard a surprising order: the operation had been called off. The reason was apparent in an urgent handwritten letter that Begin had received from Peres: "Dear Prime Minister," it began. "At the end of December 1980, you summoned me to your office in Jerusalem and informed me of a most serious matter. You did not ask for my reaction, and I myself chose not to respond under the circumstances at the time. However, I feel this morning that it is my supreme civil duty to advise you, after profound and serious consideration and with the national interest at heart, to refrain from doing [what you proposed]. I speak from experience. The proposed dates that have been reported by us are not practical. One material may be substituted with another. What is intended to be a preventive [measure] may prove to be an incentive. Israel, on the other hand, will find itself as a 'heath in the desert' (Jeremiah 17:6). And it too has reasons to be concerned. I add my voice—and it is not just mine—to those who say to you not to do this and certainly not at the present time or in the present circumstances."[29]

Although the brief missive was highly cryptic due to the secrecy involved, it was clear that Peres knew that in the government and among the military there were disagreements over the operation and that he knew exactly when the planes were set to take off. Since there was a risk that the secret was no longer a secret abroad as well, the operation was canceled.

The general election date, June 30, was approaching, but Begin pushed for the reactor to be bombed before the polling stations opened. He knew he would be accused of launching the operation as an election gambit. When MK Zevulun Hammer asked him if it would not be possible to carry it out after the elections, he answered truthfully, "I don't know what the election outcome will be. No one can know. For all I know, a month from now, Shimon Peres will be sitting in this room. From his letter it's clear to you that he certainly wouldn't carry out this operation, and I'm not willing to leave the stage knowing that I left this problem hovering over our children."[30]

Begin supported the operation even taking into account the possibility of its going wrong. During one of the final discussions before the operation, the air force chief was asked if, in his estimation, all the pilots would return home safely. He said no. Begin listened with an inscrutable expression on his face. He knew that failure in the operation might inflict huge electoral damage to his party, but he was not willing to concede in what was for him a matter of principle: never let an enemy country possess a nuclear weapon.[31] Unlike the head of the Mossad, who had agreed to the operation but objected to its latest date (June 7) because three days before it Begin was to meet with Sadat, Begin insisted that the Egyptians would not be accused of collusion and approved that date for the attack.[32] The date—a Sunday—was chosen on the assumption that French and Russian technicians at the reactor site would not be working there on the Christian Sabbath.

On June 4, Begin visited Sharm-al-Sheikh for a summit with Sadat. Aliza, unusually, did not accompany him on this occasion. She was in the hospital for treatment of pneumonia; when Begin phoned her at the hospital from the summit, he was told that she was hooked up to an oxygen respirator. In this state of mind—concerned about his wife's condition and the impending attack on the reactor—Begin posed for photographs with the Egyptian president, but he smiled and was pleased at the thought that Sadat preferred to meet with him rather than with Peres, perhaps because he thought only Begin could find a solution to the autonomy issue. Begin said that the meeting was a success, and clips of it were used in the Likud's election campaign, but of course nothing was said about the impending operation in Iraq.

On the day of the operation Begin was at home in Jerusalem, waiting for updates. He told his secretary to summon the ministers to a meeting only when the planes were already in the air. When they arrived, the prime minister was excited but focused and decisive. "What we have done is unprecedented, but we did it for our children's sake," he told the ministers, who were surprised by the timing. Eight F-16 fighters had taken off in the afternoon from Etzion Air Base in eastern Sinai in the direction of Iraq. They flew low, in close formation, avoiding detection by the radars of Jordan, Saudi Arabia, and Iraq. At 5:30 p.m. they reached their target. The attack lasted only two minutes. Sixteen one-ton bombs were dropped on the facility. Not a single rocket was fired at the planes, and the Osirak reactor was utterly destroyed.

As soon as the chief of staff was told that the reactor had been bombed and the planes were on their way home, he called Begin and updated him. The ministers raised a toast. At his home in Caesarea, former defense minister Ezer Weizmann, who had opposed the operation, could barely contain his anger at not being told when the operation would take place, even though his own son-in-law was one of the pilots involved.[33] On this occasion, Peres too was taken by surprise by the timing.

At 6:47 p.m. Begin was informed that all planes had returned to base. The question that preoccupied the ministers now that the operation had been a success was whether Israel should accept responsibility for it. It was no longer possible to ignore Begin's desire to reap the maximum political benefit from the military achievement. The prime minister, unlike most of his cabinet colleagues, who feared the consequences of officially accepting responsibility, insisted that an official announcement must be made. He explained that the operation's success would strengthen Israel's deterrence capability and added that the IDF did not operate "like a thief in the night."[34] In the meantime, he withdrew to draft the announcement. At the end of the announcement he noted, "We shall not allow our enemies to develop weapons of mass destruction against our people." This declaration became known as the Begin Doctrine, according to which Israel would not allow any Arab nation to acquire nuclear arms. Its principles have been adopted by all Israeli governments since.[35]

Only the next day, after Israel's operation was reported on Jordanian radio, did Begin instruct his office staff to announce it on Israeli state radio, and he waited for it to be broadcast. Much to his surprise, programming went on as usual. Was the state radio not aware of the historic importance of the operation? In fact, the news editors at the IBA did not believe what they had heard. Uri Porat, the new communications adviser to the prime minister, phoned to find out what was holding up the announcement, but since his voice was unfamiliar to the news editors, they were convinced that it was a hoax. Finally, journalist Immanuel Halperin, Begin's nephew, decided to call his uncle, and thus in an intimate conversation between Begin family members, the announcement that would cause a furor throughout the world came to light. But it was broadcast, of all places, in a news flash on Radio 3—the IBA's pop music station—at 3:30 p.m., and Begin had to wait yet another half hour to hear it in an official IBA newscast.[36]

In the evening, Begin turned his attention to the international arena. Virtually all members of the United Nations were condemning Israel—including the United States, whose new president, Reagan, immediately ordered, as Yadin had predicted, a delay in all supplies of fighter aircraft to Israel. Begin wrote a strong and emotional letter to Reagan: "A million and a half children were killed by Zyklon B gas during the Holocaust. This time, it was Israeli children who were about to be poisoned by radioactivity. For two years now we have been living under the nightmare of this danger.... I was not sleeping at night.... It could have been a new Holocaust."[37]

One of the main problems at this point was how Sadat would react. As noted, he had met with Begin only three days earlier and knew that the photos of them posing together would help Begin in his bid for reelection. He now felt betrayed and possibly feared being labeled a collaborator to boot in the eyes of his opponents. Begin therefore sent him a message through Moshe Sasson, Israel's second ambassador to Egypt. Two days after the operation, Sasson appeared before Sadat, who was at his retreat on the outskirts of Alexandria. Later, in his memoirs, Sasson noted that this was the tensest political meeting of his career.[38] The president lit his pipe and immersed himself in reading Begin's message, while Sasson sat and waited for his response.

"The purpose of peace was to break the psychological barrier, but the IDF's operation once again presents the arrogant Israel with its invincible might," Sadat eventually said, adding that Begin had turned back the wheel of history. But before Sasson had time to respond, Sadat added in Arabic, "God forgive you, Begin" and vowed that Egypt would not violate the peace agreement even though the operation would strengthen the extremists in the Arab world. When Sasson reported Sadat's response to Begin, he told him he had the impression that the Egyptian president was not sorry that the reactor had been destroyed.[39]

Begin himself paid no attention to the psychological impact the operation would have upon the Arab world. His determination to go ahead with the attack was not an election ploy, as his opponents from Hamaarach claimed, but its success did fill him with enthusiasm, and he did everything to boost the Likud's electoral appeal. Nor did he shy away from humiliating Peres by instructing Naor to publish the secret letter that Peres had sent him months earlier. For its part, Hamaarach in its campaign stressed that the operation had been unnecessary and that it would have been possible to achieve results by diplomatic means, but the publication of the letter was a low blow and presented Peres as a defeatist.

Peres's opposition to the reactor bombing even after the fact was a political blunder because in this matter many Israelis sided with

Begin, who claimed that Hamaarach was opposed to it purely for electoral reasons. The pilots who took part in the operation, whom Begin thanked personally on their return to base, resented that it was being used for political gain, and they said so. When Begin arrived at the air force base, he saw Hamaarach stickers on several of the pilots' cars.[40] He did not mind this too much; he knew that other air force staff supported him. A reservist pilot, Major Dan Chalutz, and one of his fellow pilots made a point of sending Begin a telegram to congratulate him and to suggest that he "make it clear to Shimon Peres that his words lead to irresolution and doubts about whether we are in the right—even among the military." They also stressed that they and their friends in the Phantom fighter squadron "are expecting vigorous responses against Hamaarach's attempt to sow dissension within the nation."[41] In 2005 Chalutz—then commander of the air force—was appointed IDF chief of staff.

SEVENTEEN

KING OF ISRAEL

Three months before the 1981 elections, public opinion polls indicated that Hamaarach would defeat the Likud by over 25 percent, yet three weeks before, the polls revealed that the two would most likely end up almost even. Begin did not intend to end his efforts to achieve victory. This time, unlike in the previous elections, in which he was marketed (under the instructions of his advisers and Weizmann) as a moderate, responsible, and mature leader, Begin returned to his methods in Zion Square and lashed out at Hamaarach, the Arabs, and the Gentiles, especially the Germans. He was the prime minister, but he behaved as though he was still in the opposition. In his speeches he appeared as the representative of the outcast and the underdogs, not as a leader, thus heightening his listeners' identification with him.

A week after the bombing of the Iraqi reactor Begin spoke at a meeting in Netanya. More than ten thousand enthusiastic fans greeted him, chanting "Begin, King of Israel." At the start of his speech he asked that they thank "our God in heaven for giving us such wonderful pilots." The crowd excitedly joined in. As was characteristic of him, he responded to Hamaarach's claim that the bombing was an election tactic by doing what he did best—appealing to the personal aspects of the operation. He spoke as though he was an old and concerned Jew who had sent "the boys" to battle, not as a prime minister who had made a weighty strategic decision. "Fellow Jews, you have known me for over forty years," he said; "could you imagine that I would send the best of our sons to face the danger of death—or worse, the danger of captivity—with these barbarians, who commit terrible tortures, to win the election?" When talking about the missiles deployed by Syria in the Lebanese Beqaa Valley—perceived by Israel as a threat, especially as it believed they would endanger the IAF's photo flights—Begin shared the secrets of his political contacts with the crowd, as if seeking their approval. He spoke of the efforts of American mediator Philip Habib to settle the dispute between Israel and Syria in order to prevent a flare-up in the region and suggested a solution less cumbersome than diplomacy. "When Habib comes to me," Begin told his audience, "I'll ask him whether the missiles will be moved or not. Are you going to move them? Or should we move them?" The enthusiastic audience shouted back, "Move them!" Begin listened to the crowd with a tight face and declared, "The Syrians are afraid of the Israeli Army"—he had returned to the days when he had struggled to refer to it as the IDF—and warned, "Assad beware! Yanush [Ben Gal, head of the Northern Command] and Raful [Rafael Eitan, chief of staff] are waiting for you!"[1]

The next day journalists and the opposition complained about Begin's use of IDF officers for political purposes. (General Ben Gal's wife sent Begin a letter asking him not to involve her husband in his political campaign.) [2] But the personal angle in his speeches served its purpose. The tensions along the northern border became a simple matter—good versus evil, black against white—and his audience had no choice but to support the struggle.

But the Syrian president was Begin's secondary rival in this election. During a cabinet meeting Begin called Shimon Peres (who had announced that Begin's actions endangered Israel's international status) an "inciting, sycophantic briber of voters."[3] Because of the public enthusiasm over the Iraqi operation and Begin's claims that the children of Israel had been saved from "demise," the letter Peres had sent to Begin urging him against attack on the reactor made Hamaarach's candidate appear as a danger to national security, almost a traitor. Thus, just as Begin had slandered Arafat as the very symbol of the dangers inherent in Palestinian nationalism, so he now claimed that Peres was responsible for Mapai's failures over the generations—its condescension toward the Sephardim, its defeatism in its relations with the Arab countries, its calls for delay in the destruction of the Iraqi reactor—and he let the listeners draw their own conclusion that these failures were the very reason that the Syrians had dared to threaten Israel with missiles. "Even Sadat says the Syrians are to blame," Begin told five thousand people who had gathered to listen to him in Hadera. "Sadat says that, but what does Hamaarach say? That the Syrians are not to blame, that the Israeli government is to blame. I am ashamed and embarrassed by the opposition. As a Jew, I am ashamed to see them in this moral decline of theirs."[4]

In early June 1981, the televised election propaganda began, and it suited the most passionate election campaign in the history of the state. The Likud broadcasts focused on distressed neighborhoods that had not yet been renovated in the Neighborhood Rehabilitation Project, and the announcer explained that such misery was the result of "thirty years of Mapai's neglect." It was not by chance, then, that the Likud chose the slogan "You must choose fast—continue forward or return to the past." This slogan, steeped in the myth of the hated Mapai, stirred emotions from times long past, and once again Israeli society split into two camps, right and left, Mizrahim and Ashkenazim. Words of hate spread like wildfire, and the country was swept in a pre-election wave of violence. In Beit Shemesh, tomatoes were thrown at Peres, and in Petach Tikva, Begin supporters did not allow Peres to deliver a speech by cursing him off the stage. They saw Peres as the bad guy, a member of the old establishment that had made them socially and economically inferior. Peres lost his temper on more than one occasion. "Great, great," he said furiously to an angry crowd in Petach Tikva who raised their hands in offensive gestures; "this is what the people look like, Begin's nation, a nation of Oriental gestures." (A hand gesture similar in meaning to "flipping the bird" is termed in Israel "an offensive Oriental gesture.")[5]

In his anger, Peres fell into the trap set for him. Unlike the Likud leader, who presented himself as one of the people, Peres created a buffer between himself and "Begin's nation, a nation of Oriental gestures." This reaction, quoted in all the newspapers, was proof that Hamaarach was patronizing. Furthermore, its propaganda broadcasts repeatedly aired violent incidents and pictures accompanied with the slogan, "You've got to choose the right team—Beginism or an enlightened regime," on the assumption that such propaganda would tarnish Begin's image and clarify that his rule endangered the future of Israeli society. But Begin took advantage of the situation. For example, during a meeting in Haifa ten days before the elections, Begin responded as follows to a broadcast in which Herzl Chanukkah, a resident of Petach Tikva, was seen making the improper gesture toward Peres: "One young man behaved badly," Begin told the audience, "and along comes Hamaarach and films it, and it is sent out to the world. Yes, even to America. Is that the way to treat a man who made a mistake? After all, he who embarrasses a man in public is equal to him who spills his blood.... And we know about [Hamaarach's] violence from the days of the Saison and the *Altalena*." But when the agitated crowd started cursing Peres, Begin put on the mediator's cloak and appealed to them to stop: "I do not like this behavior. When Peres comes to you, accept him with dignity.... You are free men, no longer under Mapai rule, so listen quietly. Then, after he has spoken, go and vote Likud, until Hamaarach learns how to behave in the opposition for another four, eight, or sixteen years." The crowd, realizing once again the extent of their leader's greatness—teaching tolerance even for his opponents—parted singing "Begin, King of Israel." A satisfied Begin explained in the car to his assistant, semi-seriously and semi-ironically, that he did not like the song. "After all, I have been a republican all my life; why are they singing a monarchist anthem for me?"[6]

The assemblies invigorated Begin. He appeared happy and full of vitality for the first time since Sadat's visit. During a tour of Migdal Haemek, wearing a striped tie and in high spirits, he told reporters, "What are you filming me for? Film the beautiful women here."[7] When only one week remained before the election date, Begin utilized his rhetorical abilities to their maximum and slammed the media and his political opponents. His admirers claimed that "Begin is at his prime." He responded smugly to claims that he was inciting violence: "How beautiful democracy is. How beautiful these wonderful people are. People go to the polls, cast their votes, come home, and wait for the outcome. But in recent weeks they have tried to smear the Israeli democracy. A people often argue aggressively. There are one or two such incidents; is this a reason for violence? Is this why there is no democracy?"[8]

In a conference at Metzudat Ze'ev Begin confessed to his party members that he was frustrated by the prevalent rumors about his condition. "Hamaarach said I am not functioning. If this were true, then I would be a case of the resurrection of the dead," he said as a roar of laughter came from the man who had been chosen as number two in the list of Likud candidates, Ariel Sharon. "I have not been this strong for years. Healthy as a horse," he added.[9]

During a more relaxed meeting at Tel Aviv University, Begin was asked why his comments were so blatant; he replied, "I do not regret my remarks. As for those bleeding hearts who wrinkle their noses, they will remain with wrinkled noses." His companions laughed. He repeatedly used the term "bleeding hearts." When answering a question by Yaakov Achimeir, the Israeli TV reporter, he wondered, "Do I speak in a loud voice? I say everything I have thought of saying, even if it's not liked by the 'bleeding hearts,'" and he pulled a face.[10] The message was received: there are the bleeding hearts, who deal with tiring criticism, and there are those who work for Israel, like Begin and his party. Thus he changed the image prevalent in the Yishuv in which the Labor camp was productive and the Revisionists excelled only in criticism.

Five days before the voting began, Begin and Peres participated in a televised debate. Ze'ev Schiff was the host. This time, unlike in the previous debate, Begin was vigorous, aggressive, and a little smug. Peres answered one of the host's questions by saying, "This has been one of the most violent, insulting, and difficult election campaigns in the history of Israel. This government has turned into an election headquarters." Begin responded immediately by saying, "Mr. Peres began talking in such an aggressive tone, I almost fell off my chair. But whoever opens with aggression will get an answer. Honorable Mr. Peres, tell me, do you or do you not recognize me as the prime minister of a democratic country? I, for one, have read that you don't recognize me as prime minister. What kind of education are you giving your friends? I recognize you as the head of the opposition. Even after four years I will recognize you as holding that position. . . . And Mr. Peres does not see me as prime minister. Suppose that all his comrades take his path; what will become of democracy in Israel? This is a highly perturbing anti-democratic expression. And then later on he spoke of violence. Are you talking about violence, Mr. Shimon Peres, huh?"[11] The next day the polls revealed that the public considered the debate as ending in a draw, but the conflict was just a continuation of the Likud's momentum, which grew stronger and stronger until the elections.

Three days before the election, demonstrations marking the end of the election campaign took place consecutively in the Kings of Israel Square in Tel Aviv, now Rabin Square. During Hamaarach's election rally, held on a Saturday night, comedian Dudu Topaz gave Begin the greatest gift he could have received. Topaz sought to sever the tie the Likud had tried to forge between the bombing of the reactor in Iraq and the achievements of the Likud; he said that Begin was ignoring that most of the IDF officers and fighters were Hamaarach supporters, whereas Likud voters were only rear-echelon privates and evaders of military service whom he called Chach'chachim (riffraff), a derogatory name for Mizrahim in widespread use in Israel at the time.[12] Begin was unfamiliar with the Israeli parlance, and up until that evening he had been unaware of that term, which had apparently originated from a mockery of Moroccan accents (the first and third "ch" in the term are pronounced as in English; the second and fourth are the Hebrew letter *chet*).

Begin did not hear Topaz's speech live, but he read about it in *Haaretz* the next morning. Thanks to his sharp political sense, he immediately understood the incident's potential. He asked Kadishai the meaning of the word.[13] Upon entering his car on the way home for a rest before his speech in the square, he again asked his driver the meaning of the word. In the afternoon he wrote down the outline of his speech. He wrote down the word "Chach'chachim" on a note pad so as not to pronounce it incorrectly.[14]

"Last night, at this square, stood a young actor; what's his name? Dudu? Yes, his name is Dudu, David Topaz," Begin's voice thundered over the tens of thousands gathered in the square. "And here he said the following—." The crowd responded with cries of scorn, but Begin asked for silence. "Now silence! Let us not hear a fly; total silence. Listen! Dudu Topaz, in front of one hundred thousand Hamaarach members, said the following: 'The Chach'chachim are at Metzudat Ze'ev. They are barely Shin Gimelim. The soldiers and commanders of the combat units are here.' I confess to you that until this morning I had never heard the word 'Chach'chachim,' and I did not know what it meant. . . . In the underground, in the days of the Resistance, as we were planning actions against the British rule, Galili from the Haganah, after consultation with Natan Yellin Mor from Lehi, asked me, 'How did you solve the problem of the Mizrahim in Etzel?' And I looked at him confused and said to him, 'Israel, what are you asking? What problem?' And he said: 'What, don't you know? Haven't you heard? The problem of the Sephardic Jews.'

"So I said to him, 'What problem? We do not have a problem! We are all brothers; we are all Jews; we are all equal, all of us! . . . One of our great area commanders—a Yemenite!—Uzi was Sephardic. Gidi, who executed the historic operation at the King David Hotel, was Sephardic. The man in charge of all the prisoners at Latrun Prison was a Yemenite, and all the boys stood at attention before him! What problem? We do not have one!'

"But listen, when . . . what's his name? Du-du To-paz made his foolish, empty, and spiritually devoid comment, the entire crowd that was here last night cheered. Now I'll tell Dudu Topaz who he was referring to. Our Sephardim were warriors, heroes. Even in the underground.

Some of them were among the Olei Hagardom, who up until their last minute alive sang 'Hatikva' and amazed an entire world with their bravery. They went to prison, to concentration camps; they fought and did not break; they cried out to the British judges, 'We do not recognize your rule. The [British] must leave this place, the land of Israel!' Feinstein was of European origin—what's it called? Ashkenazi. Moshe Barazani was a Sephardi from Iraq.

"Ashkenazim? Iraqis? Jews! Brothers! Warriors!

"Can every actor hired by Hamaarach stand here and utter blasphemy in vain? Sephardim are the best fighters in the IDF; they, along with Ariel Sharon, crossed the Suez Canal and moved over to the other side on the Yom Kippur War. He commanded them, the best fighters in Israel! . . . Yes! Blasphemy! And the audience cheered. And where was Mrs. Shoshana Arbeli [Almozlino], placed second on Hamaarach's list? And where were the others? Why did they not leave the assembly in protest? . . . No one has hurt the dignity of an entire tribe of Israel as Hamaarach did last night at this place. . . .

"I ask you, tomorrow, from morning till evening, take a phone and call your friends. . . . Just tell them what Dudu Topaz said here. All the people of Israel must know of this, just one sentence: 'The Chach'chachim are at Metzudat Ze'ev.' And I say: I'm happy and proud that they are at Metzudat Ze'ev."

This speech is one of the most fascinating that Begin ever delivered. The inclusion of Israeli tradition; imagery from the underground; a family-oriented tone; grimaces; Begin's ability to appear as a leader who, on the one hand, had never heard the common parlance, while, on the other hand, was in touch with the pulse of the public; his tying in of Arbeli Almozlino (originally from Iraq) to Hamaarach's denigration of the Mizrahim; and his ability to vilify the opponent's camp while simultaneously uniting the people—all these and above all his closing statement—"I'm happy and proud that they are at Metzudat Ze'ev"—attest to Begin's rhetorical virtuosity.

Unlike Ben Gurion, who urged the Mizrahim to enlist in commanding positions in the IDF and expressed hope that one day a Yemenite would be appointed IDF chief of staff, Begin offered a different approach. He provided a sense of belonging and opened his political camp to all Mizrahim while demanding nothing in return. In their eyes, this was the secret of his charm.

It is difficult to assess the impact the speech had on the election results. But when the balloting was over, two days later, on June 30, 1981, it became clear that the leader who only four months earlier had sought to appoint a successor had won again, albeit by a narrow victory: the Likud received forty-eight Knesset seats while Hamaarach received forty-seven. Nevertheless, it enabled Begin to form a coalition.

Because of the tiny voter margin between the Likud and Hamaarach—some ten thousand votes—Begin arrived late at Metzudat Ze'ev on June 30, as he wanted to make sure there had been no mistake. While at home, he watched the images broadcast from Hamaarach headquarters, where it was incorrectly declared that Peres was the new prime minister of Israel. When Begin finally arrived at Likud headquarters, he did not forget to insult Peres for the premature celebrations. "Where's the kiss that Mr. Peres gave Mr. Rabin? Will Mr. Peres take back his kiss?" he wondered amid his admirers' laughter.[15]

This victory tasted less sweet than his first one, but it had a greater effect on Begin's self-confidence. He knew that this time it was his victory more than the Likud's, and his experience as prime minister reinforced his assurance that in this term he would not have to rely on the mercy of strangers as he had had to do in the era of Weizmann and Dayan. But politically the situation was more complicated than in the previous Knesset. The disappearance of Dash—some of its members had joined Shinui, which received only two Knesset seats—shifted the balance that had characterized the previous government. With the Mafdal (six seats), Agudat Israel (four seats), Tami (a Sephardic party that gained a surprising three seats), and Telem (the party founded by Moshe Dayan—two seats),[16] Begin could only form a hard-pressed majority.

Sixty-three Knesset members supported Begin's new government, established on August 5. The government's weakness in terms of the number of parties supporting it was well compensated by political cohesion and the fervor of a common ideology. The confidence Begin drew from his victory and his achievements as prime minister of the previous narrow right-wing coalition government made the new government even more extremist than the previous one. This time, unlike in his first term, Begin ensured that members from his ideological camp would be appointed to important positions. Matityahu Shmuelevitz, from Lehi, replaced Ben Elissar as general manager of the Prime Minister's Office, and Ben Elissar was appointed ambassador to Egypt. In the middle of the term, Yehuda Lapidot, a former Etzel member, was appointed head of Nativ, the liaison office with the Soviet Union. Moshe Arens was appointed ambassador to the United States, and Begin's military secretary, Efraim Poran, who had completed his term, was replaced by Brigadier General Azriel Nevo, the son of a Revisionist family. These appointments indicated that Begin's second government would be the government the Left had feared when he was elected prime minister for the first time.

The appointment of cabinet ministers turned out to be a simpler task. It was clear that Shamir would continue to serve as foreign minister, Yoram Aridor as finance minister, Yosef Burg as interior minister, and Ehrlich as deputy prime minister. David Levy, the housing and construction minister, was angry because the immigrant absorption portfolio was taken from him. Only when he locked himself up at his home in Beit She'an did Begin agree to his request to appoint him deputy prime minister alongside Ehrlich.

Begin's most difficult decision was the appointment of the defense minister. Only two former generals were serving in the new government: Brigadier General (Reserve) Mordechai Tsipori, deputy defense minister in the previous government, and Ariel Sharon. Begin did not see Tzipori as an important public figure and preferred to appoint him communications minister. With regard to Sharon, Begin was still hesitant.

Sharon, who was ahead of Levy and Shamir on the Likud candidate list for the Knesset, did not intend to give up his position. Even before the elections he had recruited his supporters in the Likud and held many press briefings regarding his suitability as defense minister. During the coalition negotiations Sharon hinted that Begin's continued tenure as defense minister would be irresponsible and that regarding matters of security other people's opinions were more important. In a conversation between Begin and Sharon following this statement, Begin quoted from George Orwell's *Animal Farm*, saying, "Nobody is more equal here." The cabinet secretary believed that Sharon did not understand that Begin had used the pig analogy from the book to suggest something about Sharon's character.[17] Sharon, in any event, was unfazed.

Begin believed that the best man for the job of defense minister was Moshe Arens, but Arens reiterated that he did not want to be the one who would have to evacuate the Sinai settlements. Begin's dilemma was exacerbated when on top of pressure from Sharon, many ministers appealed to him not to appoint Sharon. The fear that Sharon would be appointed motivated Dayan, who was dying of cancer, to hurry and meet with Begin in order to caution him: just not Sharon. "I know him. He will entangle the IDF in Lebanon," Dayan warned. Full of confidence, Begin dismissed his concern. He told Dayan that he would maintain direct contact with Eitan, the outgoing IDF chief of staff whose tenure he had extended by a year. Dayan concluded, "He's no better." Ehrlich too tried to sabotage the nomination and warned that Sharon tended to work without authorization. Begin promised his deputy, "If Sharon acts without my authority, I will fire him."[18] Motta Gur also tried to persuade Begin to do otherwise.[19] Nevertheless, Begin decided to appoint Sharon.

Why did Begin choose Sharon? Primarily because the peace agreement Israel had just signed with Egypt required it to evacuate all the Sinai settlements by April 1982. Because of the threats by the Gush Emunim and the settlers in Sinai—namely, that they would oppose an evacuation by force—Begin held onto the promise by Sharon (whom he saw as an authority regarding settlers' matters) that he would evacuate the settlements without bloodshed.[20] Furthermore, he needed the militant Sharon, who, like Begin himself, believed that the PLO, which was based in Lebanon and continuously fired Katyusha rockets at northern Israel, needed to be destroyed. Moreover, since Begin's government relied on sixty-three MKs alone, he feared that an angry Sharon would undermine it. Above all, Begin was convinced that if it became necessary, he could handle Sharon. After all, he had already signed a peace treaty, bombed the Iraqi reactor, overcome illness, and won another election. He was so confident that on the day that Sharon took office, Begin told the employees at the defense ministry, "You are getting someone better than me," adding that Sharon "is a craftsman" when it come to security matters.[21]

Sharon also was familiar with the art of persuasion. The Prime Minister's Office, where he was quite disliked by the military secretary, the cabinet secretary, and Begin's personal secretary, was surprised that as the coalition was being formed, a different, mild-mannered, and gentle Sharon appeared before them. He called Begin several times a day to consult on everything and did everything he could to express loyalty and obedience.[22] Begin was convinced that he could control his defense minister and had no fear of his disobeying him.

A month after the establishment of his new government, Begin traveled to Washington for his first meeting with Ronald Reagan, the newly elected president of the United States. The new administration saw the

PLO and Syria as part of the "Axis of Evil" led by the Soviet Union, a worldview that accorded with Begin's perception of the political situation—good against evil.

Conceptually, the new administration altered Carter's approach to the Middle East. Carter saw the Israeli-Arab conflict as a struggle apart from the conflict between the Western and Communist blocs, but Reagan formulated a global strategy that aimed to reduce the Soviet influence everywhere in the world. While serving in the first Knesset, Begin had preferred to remain neutral in the international struggle between East and West, but now he enthusiastically supported the establishment of a Western front against the Soviets. Furthermore, Begin had a better personal relationship with Reagan than with Carter. The Republican president, a former movie star, saw Begin as a brave leader and a moral ally. Unlike Carter, who had refrained from saying that Israel was an ally, Reagan used the term frequently.[23] Begin was aware of his ideological ties with Reagan. It is likely that he would not have dared to say to Carter, "If you had had a general like Sharon in the Vietnam War, you would have won"[24]—as he said to Reagan, like a friend giving good advice.

Encouraged after his meeting with Reagan, Begin flew from Washington to New York and met with Yanush Ben Gal, the general who he thought was a worthy candidate to be the next IDF chief of staff. Begin surprised Ben Gal when sketching what he considered to be a possible solution to the problem of rockets that were being fired on northern Israel by the PLO: "We go into Lebanon, catch the bearded man, get him out of his bunker, and put him on trial in Jerusalem. Just like Adolf Eichmann."[25] The "bearded man" was obviously Yasser Arafat. Ben Gal nodded, under the impression that Begin was not referring to a specific plan and that his frailty was affecting his concentration. Begin's daughter Chasia, who had accompanied him, arranged with Ben Gal in advance that she would signal when she noticed that her father had grown too weak to continue, and Ben Gal would ask to end the meeting. Indeed, they did so. When Ben Gal left the hotel, he thought to himself that the prime minister was not in his prime.[26]

On October 6, 1981, Egypt held a military parade commemorating the "October Victory." Since the signing of the peace treaty, Sadat's regime had struggled with threats from radical Islamic organizations that were opposed to the agreement and had even tried to assassinate Vice-President Hosni Mubarak during his visit to Ethiopia a year earlier. Thus the security services had taken special measures for the event. While they surveyed the parade, the president and vice-president sat behind a concrete wall designed to protect them from any assassination attempts. A short while after noon, in the middle of the parade, several men in military uniforms approached the reviewing stand. One of them, Khaled al-Islambouli, raced toward the president. Sadat assumed that the officer wanted to salute him and stood up, exposing his head. He was wrong. The assassin managed to shoot him before the guards could respond. Mubarak, who had learned from his experience in Ethiopia, dropped to the floor and survived.

Begin heard about Sadat's assassination on his office radio. At first it was unclear whether Sadat had survived or not, and Begin, in shock, waited for official confirmation. There was no need to be an expert in international relations to understand that Sadat's death could endanger the peace treaty. Israel had not yet finished evacuating several settlements, as required by the agreement, and two of the signatories, Sadat and Carter, had disappeared from the political arena. Egypt was aware of the concern in Israel. Even before the funeral, Mubarak conveyed a message to Israeli ambassador Moshe Sasson that his country would still adhere to the peace agreement. Meanwhile, Begin reiterated that Israel would meet all its withdrawal commitments.[27]

A question was raised about whether or not Begin should attend the funeral. After Sadat's assassination, Egypt seemed dangerous, and it would be difficult to guarantee the protection of Israeli guests. But Begin insisted. "I'm the only one of the signatories left in office, and it is my responsibility," he said. He declared that the peace agreement had been signed between nations, not between leaders, but he knew that traveling to Egypt at that time would be a sign of stability. Ezer Weizmann also requested permission from the Prime Minister's Office to attend the funeral, out of respect for Sadat and to emphasize that the peace treaty had not collapsed. Begin refused. He had not forgiven Weizmann for the insults and preferred that Burg and Sharon accompany him as the government representatives.[28]

Begin consulted with his wife about participating in the funeral, and she told him that he should go. Explaining that "Aliza said so," he then convinced Burg, who did not want to appear a coward.[29] Despite the concerns, Begin refused to wear the flak jacket the Shabak ordered for his trip. His decision went along with his character. The very sense that he was risking his life for peace, for his life's goal, gave him the necessary transcendental strength for his actions. During the funeral procession Begin chose to walk, so as not to desecrate the Shabbat.[30]

During his condolence visit with Sadat's family, Begin met Egypt's new president, Mubarak. Already at their first meeting it was clear that a beautiful friendship would not develop. Upon his return to Israel, Begin recalled that Jehan, Sadat's widow, had told him that shortly before his death Sadat had become interested in Judaism and even recited the Ten Commandments to himself.[31]

On November 26, 1981, Begin slipped in the bath and broke his pelvis. It was a strange injury. Burg raised the suspicion that he had stumbled because the oxygen supply to his brain was briefly interrupted because of the stroke he had suffered.[32] Begin's advisers stressed that because of his modesty he had never demanded a renovation of his official residence and suggested that he had slipped because the bath was old. Whatever the reason, Begin was hospitalized and managed government meetings from his room at Hadassah Hospital. Sometimes, due to the painkillers he was taking, he would doze off during the meetings, and the perplexed ministers would wait for him to wake up.[33] This embarrassing fact was not leaked to the media, and the ministers did not dare challenge the prime minister's ability to function.

While Begin was hospitalized, the Israeli media dealt with every aspect of the final steps of the evacuation from Sinai, set for April 1982, and the thought of the evacuation soured his mood. For one thing, the settlers' threats to resist the evacuation by force had grown more frequent; for another, the discussion had spread to the implications of the withdrawal on the future of Judea, Samaria, and Gaza. Begin was concerned that he, who had prevented a civil war during the Saison, would as prime minister be the cause of bloodshed and conflict among Jews, and he especially protested the claim that he had created a precedent by which Israel would be forced to withdraw from the rest of the territories.

Before he had left for Camp David, Begin had announced to the ministers that he would be willing to withdraw from some areas in the Golan Heights, but now he changed his mind. While he was in the hospital he decided that Israel should apply its sovereignty to the Golan Heights. He did not consult with any of his ministers, and as always his decision stemmed from political, emotional, tactical, and historical considerations. In fact, he mainly wanted to punish Syria over its deepening involvement in Lebanon and its deployment of missiles in Lebanon's

Beqaa Valley. Since a political crisis broke out in Poland just then and the entire world turned its gaze there as it feared that the Soviet Union would invade Poland, Begin believed it was a perfect time to apply Israel's sovereignty.

With this decision Begin also laid a political trap for Hamaarach because its leaders claimed at the time that he preferred to invest in Judea and Samaria over the Negev and the Golan Heights. He thought the decision would force Hamaarach leaders to vote for sovereignty over the Golan Heights, and if they objected, he would reap domestic gains because he could blame the Israeli Left for abandoning northern Israel. Yet he knew that the implementation of the decision would not be simple. It conflicted with the U.S. position, and it seemingly shut down any chance of a peace agreement with Syria. But Begin was so confident and enthusiastic that he did not wait until his release from the hospital and informed the interior minister about his decision while still in the recovery room. "What's the rush?" Burg asked and suggested that he wait until his release before going ahead with it.[34] But Begin was too eager. As if trying to recover from both his health problems and political issues, he summoned Minister of Justice Moshe Nissim to Hadassah on the day of his release. He made an exceptional request: that Nissim prepare to approve the decision within one day. The following day the other ministers gathered at Begin's house, and, with his plastered leg resting on the table, he explained the urgency of approving it to avoid international pressure.

On December 14, the prime minister, who chose to file the bill himself, was transported to the Knesset in a wheelchair. He seemed euphoric to those who had not seen Begin in the Knesset for over a month.[35] In his speech he said that this was a festive day, that the Golan Heights had been a part of the Land of Israel for generations, and that it was only an arbitrary decision that had separated them from the territory under the British Mandate at the end of World War I. He could not ignore the argument that he was harming the chances of a peace with Syria, and he said that if the Syrians wanted—at the "end of days"—to negotiate, "putting the territory under Israeli civil administration would not prevent negotiations."[36] He persuaded most MKs, while Hamaarach agonized about how to vote. Ultimately, it chose to abstain. The bill was approved by a majority of sixty-three against twenty-one. Begin was satisfied.

The Golan Heights Law aroused serious riots among the Druze in the Golan Heights, who burned their ID cards, and it drew harsh criticism abroad. The United Nations approved a resolution stating that Israel was not a peace-seeking country, and after urgent consultations with his government, U.S. ambassador Lewis announced to Begin that the president had decided to suspend the signing of a strategic memorandum of understanding between Israel and the United States by which the two countries pledged to coordinate intelligence and military information.[37] Lewis expected that Begin, for whom one of the motives for signing the peace treaty with Egypt had been the strategic agreement, would try to persuade the president to change his decision. But he was in for a surprise. Deep in his heart Begin felt that all the nations of the world were Gentiles not to be relied on, and he also feared that the strategic agreement would bind Israel's hands and turn it into an aid-seeking country. "I will not be the Jew who relies on the Polish landowner," he said. Thus, agitated and aggressive, he amazed Lewis with his response: "If the United States suspends the agreement, we prefer to cancel it entirely. My knee is broken," he added proudly, "but Israel will never bend over."[38] Furthermore, he surprised the cabinet secretary with his demand that the confrontation with Lewis be published; in contrast, most of Israel's leaders tried to play down differences with the United States. It seems that Begin took out on Lewis the anger that had been brewing within him over the evacuation of the settlements

The Golan Heights were now under Israeli sovereignty, but Begin did not yet internalize the biblical prophecy that "Out of the north an evil shall break forth" (Jeremiah 1:14).

EIGHTEEN

"THERE WILL BE NOT A SINGLE KATYUSHA"

The Lebanese population in the 1980s was made up of Shiites, Sunnis, Christian Maronites and Catholics, Druze, and more than three hundred thousand Palestinian refugees who had no civil rights. Although most Lebanese are Arabs and the predominant language is Arabic, many Lebanese citizens do not tie their personal fate with that of the Arab nation. Maronite Christians, for instance, argue that they are descendants of the Canaanites, Phoenicians, and other peoples who lived in Lebanon before the arrival of the Arabs in the seventh century. Ben Gurion believed that because of the composition of the Lebanese population an alliance could be formed with the country's Christians. Before the War of Independence he wrote the following in his diary: "The Lebanese Christians are in a similar state to ours, and it is important for both of us to be neighbors. . . . There is a need for a common political border with Lebanon. A land that has a large Christian community will barely be able to exist in a Muslim ocean."[1]

Indeed, there are similarities between the histories of the Christians in Lebanon and the Jews. Fleeing Muslim persecution, Maronite Christians came to Mount Lebanon in the seventh century and aspired to form a country that would be a refuge for the Christians in the Middle East, just as Zionists saw Israel as a refuge for all Jews. But the historical analogy did not affect relations between Lebanon and Israel. Even though many Christians had contact with Zionists, they preferred to maintain normal relations with the Muslims and refrained from forming alliances with the Jews. Already during the War of Independence, Ben Gurion's hopes had been dashed that the Maronites would rebel against the Muslim leaders and eventually form an alliance with Israel, although he had believed that the Muslim rule was "artificial" and would be easy to destabilize.[2] In 1955, when he was defense minister, Ben Gurion once more raised the idea of a military alliance with the Christians, but Prime Minister Moshe Sharett said that this was a "chimerical and adventurous plan that was amazingly crude and unrealistic," and he rejected it.[3]

In the late 1960s, the balance of power in Lebanon started shifting. Palestinian terror organizations headed by the PLO moved into Lebanon and began to train in camps set up in the south and in Beirut. These camps served as bases from which terrorist attacks were perpetrated against Israel. In 1969 Pierre Gemayel, leader of the Christian Maronites in Lebanon, agreed that the Palestinians in the country could implement the Cairo Agreement, which allowed them to hold weapons in the refugee camps. But when he realized that the PLO was not going to recognize Lebanon's sovereignty and in fact was busy establishing a state within a state, violent clashes erupted between the Lebanese Army and Palestinian militias.

In Jordan, Palestinians also clashed with the authorities. After the bloody events of September 1970—known as Black September—King Hussein put an end to the activity of Palestinian organizations in his country, and thousands of Palestinians fled to Lebanon.[4] The Maronites and the Catholics feared that their country would fall into a demographic imbalance, and when the PLO began to establish itself in areas having a Christian majority, clashes erupted between the two groups. That same year the PLO kidnapped Bachir Gemayel, Pierre's son, but he was eventually released. Gemayel's hatred toward the PLO did not go unnoticed by the Israelis, who kept a close eye on the events in Lebanon.

By 1975 the Lebanese people had split into ethnic/national groups, each fighting for the country's identity, and in the midst of this civil war, Maronite Christian phalanges fought against the PLO militias. At this point Hafez al-Assad's regime supported the Christians, but the policy gradually changed. In 1977 violent clashes broke out between Syria and the Lebanese Christians, and Syria began helping the PLO.[5] In 1978 the IDF's intelligence chief reported to the Foreign Affairs and Defense Committee that in one day a Syrian tank brigade had fired thousands of shells at Ashrafiya, a Christian neighborhood in East Beirut.[6] Reports of the Christians' suffering were horrific, though the Christians were not threatened with extinction, as Syria's goal was to warn them and strengthen its influence in Lebanon based on the "divide and conquer" principle.[7] During the 1970s many PLO terrorists set out from Lebanon on attacks against Israel, so Israel had a clear interest in helping the Christians.

Relations between Israel and the Christians in Lebanon began to take shape on two tracks. One line of contact was established with a Maronite Christian phalange active in Beirut and led by the Gemayel family; the second was established with the Free Lebanon Army, led by Saad Haddad and operating in southern Lebanon. Israel began to assist in the training of Haddad's forces during the days of Rabin's first government, and simultaneously it opened the border crossing into Lebanon as part of what was known as the "Good Fence," aimed at sending humanitarian aid to residents of southern Lebanon during the civil war.[8]

Between 1977 and 1981, as the Lebanese civil war subsided, PLO terrorist penetrations of Israel's northern border increased, and the IDF responded by shellings, raids, and aerial bombings throughout Lebanon. On March 15, 1978, after the hijacking of an Egged bus on the Tel Aviv–Haifa highway, an attack in which thirty-five passengers were murdered, the government ordered the army to launch Operation Litani to push the terrorists away from the border. Within a week, three IDF brigades took over the entire area between the Israel-Lebanon border and the Litani River, killing and wounding hundreds of PLO militants and capturing dozens.[9]

Israel achieved its goal in Operation Litani, and the results created a new reality in southern Lebanon. The PLO was pushed back beyond the Litani River, and two forces were put into place to prevent their return to the border. A ten-kilometer strip north of the border was created as an enclave clear of any PLO men and was now dominated by the Christian militia headed by Saad Haddad. The militia was assisted with equipment and training and became a semi-regular force called the South Lebanon Army (SLA). The territory beyond the ten-kilometer enclave up to the Litani River was manned by the United Nations Interim Force in Lebanon (UNIFIL) in accordance with U.N. Resolution 425, which also called for Israel's full withdrawal from Lebanon in exchange for the removal of the threat of Katyusha rockets.[10] In response to Operation Litani, however, Syria had increased its military actions against the Christians in Beirut and its aid to the PLO, as it feared that Israel would control Lebanon through the Christians.

Begin came to power after relations between Israel and the Christians had begun to develop, and he expanded them. In September 1977, despite the opposition of IDF chief of staff Motta Gur, Begin set a precedent when he ordered the IDF to participate in an attack initiated by Haddad's forces on a PLO post in southern Lebanon.[11] Haddad's men, who up to that time had received only indirect assistance, seized the post with the support of a paratrooper battalion reinforced with armor and artillery. The success satisfied Begin, who called the new approach "a transition from retaliation to initiative" or sometimes "preventive initiative." During the Chach'chachim speech in Kings of Israel Square—which because of its proximity to the elections was remembered particularly for the social-ethnic debate it provoked—Begin also introduced his security strategy, which hinted at a plan regarding the northern border. "We have changed the method of defense," he asserted. "During the days of Hamaarach governments it was retaliation. We do not belittle that. We have changed the system. There is no more retaliation. There is preventive initiative. We go toward them, penetrate their bases, and punish them. We no longer wait for them to come to us."[12]

But the main change Begin made in Israel's policy was expressed not in military tactics alone, but also in the country's political-moral vision regarding the situation of the Christians in Lebanon. During his first term in power Begin reiterated his position that "we must show the world that Jews save Christians."[13] On this issue, just like on the issue of an international peace conference in the 1970s, Begin compared the situation to what had ensued with the Munich Pact in September 1938, when British prime minister Neville Chamberlain and French prime minister Édouard Daladier agreed to Hitler's demand to transfer the Sudetenland to German authority, thus abandoning Czechoslovakia. Begin reiterated that he and his government would not be like Chamberlain and Daladier. Although it was not the first time he had made this comparison, it was interesting that this time, unlike in the 1970s, he did not equate the Maronite Christians with the Jews before the Holocaust. Because his confidence in Israel's military strength had grown after the attack on the Iraqi nuclear reactor and because a resolute defense minister and chief of staff served beside him, this time the Christians were equated to the Czechs, Syria and the PLO to the Germans, and Israel to the Allies—no less.

Begin believed that protecting the Christians would showcase the Jewish people's transformation from persecuted to saviors and that the country's military might would emphasize the Western countries' indifference to the suffering of Christians. He ignored the fact that the Lebanese Christians were not united, that the Lebanese civil war was not about the good guys versus the evil guys, and that all those involved had committed atrocities. His vision, based on a moral concept, was consistent with the security concepts and *realpolitik* of some defense officials, particularly the deputy chief of the Mossad.[14] These officials believed that Israel should join forces with the Christians in Lebanon to thwart Palestinian plans to attack Israel from within Lebanon or that it was better to help the Christians to take over Lebanon and later establish a peace agreement with them.[15] Yet the defense establishment was not in consensus on the matter. Toward the end of Begin's first term, Yadin objected to the Mossad's assessment and warned that the Lebanese Christians and Israel did not share a common interest. Yadin said that the Christians wanted to inflame the region so that the IDF would be forced to fight in their place against the Palestinians and the Syrians, while Israel needed the region to remain peaceful. Even Yehoshua Sagi, the head of military intelligence, and Mordechai Tsipori, the deputy defense minister, agreed with Yadin. But Yadin was not part of the new government, and the defense minister was Sharon, who advocated an alliance with the Christians. The relationship between Begin's historical-moral concept and the country's political-security interests developed and matured into a policy regarding the northern border.[16]

During Begin's second term, unlike in the days when Ben Gurion was serving as defense minister, there was no significant political figure such as Moshe Sharett to restrain Sharon, who urged the government to launch an operation to assist a transfer of power in Lebanon into the hands of the Christian Maronites and later to replace the weak president, Elias Sarkis, who was susceptible to Syria's influence and was incapable of handling the PLO.[17] Begin and Sharon projected their hopes onto Bachir Gemayel, the Maronite Christian militia commander. They were not the only ones. During the Rabin government in 1976, intelligence officers, including Colonel Binyamin Ben Eliezer, saw him as a strong and reliable leader with whom a treaty could be made.[18]

Since being appointed defense minister, Ariel Sharon had tried to bring about an invasion of Lebanon in order to accelerate the desired political changes in the country. He started to raise moral arguments that sounded as if they had come directly from Begin's mouth and that sometimes brought smiles in the prime minister's office. "The Syrians are massacring innocent Christians, and the murder of innocents is a red line," he said in an interview with *Yediot Ahronot*.[19] But he did not act on his own. In early 1980 Begin passed a secret message to Gemayel saying that if the Syrian Air Force were to attack his troops, the IAF would give them direct support. On June 3, 1981, Begin made his promise public during a speech in the Knesset. "Christian security is essential to Israel's security," he ruled and stressed the moral aspect of his policies.[20] Begin knew that with his promise he imposed a role on the IDF of helping foreign forces, contrary to its lawful duties. Therefore, he based his position on Herzl and explained that "Herzl had already written that the Jewish state would help to liberate the peoples of Africa because Zionism is a human ideal."[21] Gemayel was less concerned with the Zionist ideal than was Begin. He realized that his militia would not be able to oust the Syrians and the PLO from Lebanon, and thus he strived to entice the Syrians into a battle that would force Israel to intervene, as Begin had promised it would. But the Syrians wanted to avoid a direct military confrontation with Israel. The deployment of batteries of anti-air missiles along the Beqaa Valley and Scud missiles near Damascus was meant mainly to warn Israel that it should avoid exacerbating the situation. But Begin saw the deployment as a real threat, in part a threat to the IAF photo flights over Lebanon. By April 30, 1981, the government had already approved a decision to bomb the missiles, but due to weather conditions the decision was not implemented. Meanwhile, U.S. mediator Philip Habib tried to reach an agreement for a withdrawal of the missiles, but Assad refused to compromise.[22] This was the background during the election campaign, in which Begin promised to remove the missile threat by force.

On July 10, shortly after the elections, the IAF resumed bombing PLO targets in southern Lebanon. The PLO responded by firing Katyusha rockets at northern Israel. When the PLO bombarded the northern city of Nahariya, Begin approved the bombing of Beirut neighborhoods where, according to Israeli intelligence findings, many members of the PLO were situated. The results were harsh. The world media reported more than one hundred dead and hundreds wounded among Lebanese civilians. Reagan threatened Israel with sanctions, and the PLO responded by firing at additional northern Israeli communities. After two weeks six Israelis were killed and fifty-nine injured. Many Kiryat Shmona residents, fervent supporters of Begin and the Likud, claimed they had been abandoned and left the city, while the residents who remained struggled to adapt to the situation in neglected shelters. The IDF was unable to eliminate the air fire, and Begin had to settle for a cease-fire, achieved via Habib and mediated by Saudi Arabia. Begin called the cease-fire a "cessation of hostilities" to avoid the impression that he had negotiated with the PLO. But his terminology did not obscure the fact that his government had been unable to eliminate the PLO in southern Lebanon and destroy the Syrian missiles; moreover, the negotiations with the PLO, although indirect, contributed to the organization's political prestige. Begin considered the agreement a humiliation. He consulted with the chief of staff, who told him that the only way to put an end to the rockets was to send ground forces into Lebanon to push the terrorists beyond the range of the Katyushas—approximately forty kilometers.[23]

On July 23, before having completed forming a coalition government, Begin visited Kiryat Shmona, where he was taken to one of the shelters. Ever since his heart attack Begin had tried to avoid sweating, on his physicians' orders, and he lasted only five minutes in the shelter. "What about some air?" he asked his escorts, and they rushed him out. He was appalled by the conditions in the shelter. After his visit he was adamant: "A little more, a little more time, and there will be not a single Katyusha in Kiryat Shmona."[24]

Sharon estimated that the cease-fire would not last long, and he criticized the agreement at every opportunity. He called it "a temporary solution" and aspired to establish a new order in Lebanon that would affect the entire region. Naor assessed that Sharon believed that if the PLO was expelled from Lebanon, Palestinian refugees would flee to Jordan, which would eventually become a Palestinian state.[25] Publicly Sharon spoke only about pushing back the terrorists beyond the range of the Katyushas, but in upper-echelon military discussions he was more explicit about his comprehensive plan, in the spirit of Ben Gurion's vision from the 1950s: remove the Syrians from Lebanon, expel terrorists from the country, and pave Gemayel's path to power so that he could establish a pro-Western government that would make peace with Israel.[26] During a political convention at the Likud headquarters in September 1981 Sharon explicitly said, believing that his words would not be made public, that "Israel's goal is to make Lebanon an independent state that will live with us in peace and to solve the problem of the Syrian presence there."[27]

Sharon told the General Staff to focus on two plans already in the works for solving the Katyusha problem.[28] The first, Little Oranim (Pines), proposed an invasion of southern Lebanon up to the Zahrani River in order to put an end to the PLO's activities in the area while avoiding contact with the Syrians. The second, Big Oranim, proposed a large-scale operation in which the IDF would enter Beirut, join forces with the Christians, and cut off access to the Beirut-Damascus road in order to weaken the Syrians' hold over the area. Because the PLO headquarters, many of its units, and its arms caches were concentrated in Beirut, it was clear that anyone interested in destroying the organization could not be satisfied with a forty-kilometer range; however, a deeper penetration was not possible without conflict with Syria, whose forces stood between the Israeli border and Beirut. The Syrians suspected that Israel was planning to launch an attack close to the elections in Lebanon (which were to take place in August) so as to push Gemayel, their enemy, into power. It was difficult to assess whether or not they would respond to Israel's operations in Lebanon. Sharon claimed that the IDF would be able to avoid direct confrontation with Syria by outflanking its forces.[29]

The issue of who was responsible for the war in Lebanon and whether Sharon deceived Begin, causing him to enter into a war he did not want, can be traced back to this exact point. There is no doubt that Begin's vision, as he put it to Ben Gal in 1981, suited the Big Oranim plan.[30] He even asked Sharon to present the plan to the government ministers. When Sharon did so, on December 20, 1981, many expressed their opposition, including Ehrlich, Burg, and Tsipori, who were shocked that Sharon would not be satisfied with simply removing the Katyusha threat and had instead suggested a plan by which Israel could end up reaching Beirut and confronting Syria. Begin wanted unanimous support for the operation, so when he heard the reactions, he ruled that "the plan is not ripe." After that the plan was not put to a vote.[31] Later, when it became clear that the IDF had reached Beirut after all, Sharon rightly argued that the ministers knew about the plan, but he ignored the fact that it had not been voted on.[32]

Meanwhile, military preparations for the operation continued. Sharon and Chief of Staff Rafael Eitan, who tended to be self-deprecating beside the powerful defense minister,[33] pressured Begin to approve the limited Little Oranim operation. During a cabinet meeting on January 28, 1982, after the discovery of a Palestinian terrorist band that had infiltrated from Jordan into Israel, Sharon proposed a strike against PLO leaders in Lebanon. This time, Begin voted against the proposal, along with most of the ministers, because he feared an escalation with Syria and U.S. opposition.[34] Two months later, during a cabinet meeting on March 25, Begin said, in response to the hurling of a grenade onto an IDF jeep in Gaza, that it was time to embark on a mission in

Lebanon. But most ministers opposed such a move, noting that the grenade attack had taken place in Gaza and not in Lebanon.[35] Ehrlich realized that Sharon was looking for an excuse to invade Lebanon and was outraged, accusing him of wanting a grand operation at all costs. When Begin realized that the proposal was still controversial, he left the meeting before it ended, claiming that he needed to deal with urgent matters. A vote was avoided.[36]

At this point, Begin simply attempted to maneuver between Sharon and the opposing ministers. On the one hand, he supported the operation and also did not want a confrontation with Sharon before a completion of the withdrawal from Sinai and the evacuation of the Yamit settlements planned for April 21; on the other hand, he disapproved of embarking on an operation without the consent of a majority of the ministers and without American support. As time went by, Begin understood that Operation Big Oranim would not be approved, and he adhered to the limited version. He decided to focus on preparing for Operation Little Oranim, which aimed at forcing the PLO back forty kilometers from the border.[37]

Meanwhile, another hurdle stood before Begin: the evacuation of the settlements in the Yamit bloc, with the town of Yamit as the largest settlement. The need to uproot Jews from their dwelling places was difficult for him, though he did not even know the distance between Jerusalem and Yamit. During one of the discussions regarding compensation for the evacuees, Begin suggested to one of the settlers' representatives that he stay overnight in Jerusalem so as not to travel late at night. When asked what he thought the travel time from Jerusalem to Yamit was, Begin replied six to seven hours. It was in fact only two hours.[38] It seems that the leader who had forced his men to show restraint during the Saison and now led a country that exerted force so that its decisions would be implemented did not like the job that history had thrust upon him. The pressure was enormous. "How dare you return Israeli territory," Arie Ben Eliezer's wife Judith shouted at him when he met with the evacuees. Begin, embarrassed, did not reply.[39] In order to appease the evacuees and to carry out the evacuation without violent confrontations, Begin approved increased compensations for them and repeatedly complimented them. The threats from settlers and from Gush Emunim members who joined them during their protests—that they would use firearms as a means of resisting the evacuation—frightened him, and he was even willing to accept the assistance of Rabbi Meir Kahane, who was summoned from the United

States to convince the settlers to evacuate (and a helicopter was put at his disposal for the task).[40]

Despite Begin's efforts to ease the settlers' plight, he agreed with the attorney general that those who threatened to break the law should be indicted in military court, as all his life he had attributed major importance to the judiciary system. "Fulfill your role as you see fit," Begin said when Zamir went to him with the issue.[41] The more threats there were to break the law, the angrier Begin became, and when one of the leaders of Gush Emunim phoned him on the evening before the evacuation, Begin told him that it was late and that he was violating his privacy and slammed down the phone.[42]

The evacuation took four days. Despite the threats of the Gush Emunim and the evacuees and despite the clashes between soldiers and settlers—some of whom barricaded themselves on rooftops, threw torches at the soldiers, and had to be lowered from the rooftops in huge iron cages—the evacuation ended without blood being spilled. Regarding his success in evacuating the settlers without bloodshed, Begin said it was the most important decision of his life.

In an unconnected move, that same month Begin appointed Dan Meridor, the son of Herut Knesset member Eliyahu Meridor, as the cabinet secretary, replacing Naor, who resigned for personal reasons.

After the withdrawal from Sinai was completed, Begin believed that he had the legitimacy to increase the attacks in Lebanon. On May 9, when Sharon proposed that the IAF bomb terrorist camps in Lebanon, Begin approved the plan. In response, the PLO fired rockets toward northern Israeli communities, but this time there were no casualties. Intelligence reports raised the possibility that the PLO had missed intentionally so as to avoid escalating the situation, but Begin was enraged and convened the government to decide on an appropriate response.[43] Levy and Ehrlich, his deputies, still opposed a ground invasion, and Begin, who still wanted a unanimous decision, assured Sharon that the Little Oranim proposal would be put to a vote later on. The more the operation was delayed, the clearer it was that it eventually would be executed. Begin did not know that during a general staff meeting on May 13, the head of military intelligence had expressed doubts about the effectiveness of the operation. In this meeting Sagi predicted, almost exactly, the results of Little Oranim. He argued that it would be impossible to avoid confrontation with the Syrians in the Beqaa Valley, that the Christian phalanges would not fight the PLO, that the IDF invasion of Lebanon would split the Israeli public, and that it would be harder to leave Lebanon than to enter it.[44]

The defense minister did not give an update of Sagi's forecast to Begin, who at the time was engaged in efforts to convince U.S. officials of the operation's importance. A week after the general staff debate, Begin sent Sharon to the United States to persuade Secretary of State Alexander Haig to support the operation after approval by the Israeli government. At that time Haig was Israel's most ardent supporter in the Reagan administration. When he began to serve as secretary of state, he said that Israel was the largest and most effective American aircraft carrier: there were no Americans on board, it was unsinkable, and it cruised in a region essential to the security of the United States.[45]

Sharon did not intend to return empty-handed from Washington. He claimed there was a connection among the Soviet Union, Syria, and the PLO, and he emphasized the correlation between Israel's interests—to harm the PLO in Lebanon and end Syria's influence in the country—and the strategy of the Reagan administration, which sought to halt the Soviet influence in the Middle East through its allies. Already in April Haig himself had said, following a meeting with Begin, "Do not tell me there is no connection between the Soviet Union and the PLO."[46] He was inclined to support Israel's planned operation, but he also feared that an extensive invasion would hurt the Lebanese government, which was influenced by the United States. During a conversation with Sharon on May 20, Haig clarified that only "a terrible provocation" would be grounds for the operation and asked that the exact objective be determined. Sharon answered vaguely, "Wherever the need takes us." After the meeting, Haig agreed to support Israel's operation, provided it was quick and short.[47] Sharon was pleased and hurried to update Begin that Haig had given the green light. Ambassador Arens also worked to ensure the U.S. government's support, and in late May he too informed Begin that the U.S. approved the operation intended to push the PLO beyond a forty-kilometer range from the border.[48] Begin realized he had been given the legitimacy he wished for. After a string of meetings he understood that he could obtain U.S. support provided the operation was limited in scope.[49]

But there were still those in the U.S. administration who continued to fear Israel's plan, the most prominent of them being Secretary of Defense Caspar Weinberger, who opposed the secretary of state's pro-Israel position. Therefore, Begin was invited to Washington for further discussions with Reagan in mid-June. Haig sent him a message before the visit saying that the United States demanded that Israel restrain itself in order to prevent a conflagration, but it did not explicitly object to operations forty kilometers into Lebanese territory. Begin believed that it would be better to start the operation before the meeting so that the United States would not pressure Israel to postpone it again, and thus Israel would avoid embarrassing the Americans by holding a meeting in the midst of a military operation. He assumed he could finish the operation before the meeting and fulfill his promise: "Just a little more, a little more time, and there will be not a single Katyusha in Kiryat Shmona." There was nothing more stopping him and Sharon except to decide on what kind of provocation would be reason enough for the operation.

On the evening of June 3, 1982, after a banquet at the Dorchester Hotel in London, Shlomo Argov, the Israeli ambassador to England—who was considered a brilliant diplomat—left for his car, parked on Park Lane. He did not notice that three men were following him. Before he could open the car door, one of the three approached him and fired a bullet into the back of his neck from a few steps away. Argov was fatally injured, both physically and mentally. He was in a coma for three months and lived the rest of his days in hospital. The attempted assassination seriously disturbed Begin and the entire Israeli public. But it was impossible to blame the PLO this time. Argov's attempted assassination was the handiwork of another Palestinian organization, this one headed by Abu Nidal, who was considered Arafat's rival. In fact, at the time Abu Nidal's goals were quite similar to Israel's: to weaken the PLO's power in Lebanon. Abu Nidal believed that if he could escalate the situation in Lebanon, it would speed up the Israeli operation in which the PLO would be severely harmed, after which he would be able to take Arafat's place as the Palestinian leader.[50] Israeli intelligence quickly fingered Abu Nidal's organization: the assassin had fired a Polish-made submachine gun that was used only by the members of his organization.

The government convened an emergency meeting on June 4. Avraham Shalom, chief of the Shabak, suggested to the ministers that one of his staff deliver an overview of the history of the Abu Nidal organization. Although Begin usually respected members of the security services, he interrupted Shalom immediately and determined that there was no need for a review. He saw the assassination as the "provocation" that he had discussed with Haig, and he spoke about the larger picture. "Harming the ambassador is harming Israel, and we will respond. They are all PLO," he said. The chief of staff came to Begin's defense and ruled, with his usual brevity, "Abu Nidal, Abu Shmidal—we need to screw the PLO."[51] Begin and Eitan had agreed before the meeting to launch Operation Little Oranim, an agreement that was reached both because they saw eye to eye on this issue and because of the relationship between the two. Everyone knew Begin respected the chief of staff, the figure of the peasant warrior that had always attracted him.[52] In Begin's eyes, Raful, the man with the strong military appearance who spoke slowly and laconically with self-confidence, the ideal Jewish soldier, was the successor to Gidi from the underground. Begin appreciated Eitan's humility, considered him a decent man without political motivations, and trusted his judgment. Eitan was the first chief of staff appointed during Begin's tenure as prime minister, and Begin saw him as his faithful representative in the military.

They had not yet discussed how to embark on the planned operation. The chief of staff proposed bombing several targets in Beirut and southern Lebanon and believed that when the PLO reacted, it would be considered cause for an invasion. He also asked the government to postpone the operation by a day, as he believed the PLO officials had gone into hiding after the attempted assassination out of fear of Israel's response. Begin was interested in the overall operation more than in the particular bombings. He wanted to respond that same day and believed that it was a political opportunity before the pressure to avoid action restarted. Deputy Foreign Minister Yehuda Ben Meir added that Rabbi Goren permitted heading out on such an important operation even before the end of the Shabbat. This was the first time Begin smiled in the meeting.[53]

In this meeting the government approved most of the bombing targets. The expectation that the PLO would respond, thus preparing the ground for Israel's response, was right on the money: two hours after the bombing started in southern Lebanon, the PLO launched Katyusha rockets into northern Israel. It was clear that it was the right time for the invasion of ground forces.

But the man responsible for the sequence of events was not present at the meeting. At the time, Sharon was on a secret visit to Romania; when the ministers were to gather, he hastily made his way to Israel.[54] On Saturday night, June 5, after Sharon landed in Israel, the ministers were invited to the Prime Minister's Residence for an urgent meeting. When they started arriving, Begin embraced Yaakov Meridor, who had visited that day in Kiryat Shmona and had a rocket explode near him. Begin was full of dramatic gestures during the meeting.

"The alternative to the operation is Treblinka, and we agreed that it would never happen again," he told the ministers. Before the meeting officially started, heads of the defense establishment raised various ideas, including the eradication of the PLO in Beirut. The head of military intelligence and Chofi, the head of the Mossad, warned against a deterioration leading to the invasion of Beirut. Chofi stressed the political aspects of occupying an Arab capital and warned that there would be heavy casualties if the troops were forced to fight inside the city. Begin, despite his reference to Treblinka, agreed with Chofi. He concluded that the defense minister would present the limited operation plan to the government. When the meeting ended, Dan Meridor, the new cabinet secretary, asked Chofi if he was pleased with the decision. Chofi replied that he was but added that because of his knowledge of the people involved, he was afraid that the operation might deviate from the plans, and that would be, as he put it, "the Likud's Yom Kippur."[55]

There is no doubt that in the decisive meeting on June 5 Sharon asked the ministers to approve Little Oranim. He specifically said there was no intention to confront Syria, stressed that the IDF would not penetrate into Lebanon beyond the forty-kilometer limit, and projected that the operation would continue for only a day or two. But he certainly did not tell the ministers what Brigadier General Ehud Barak had said in a discussion about the planned operation during a general staff meeting on March 12: "I do not see any possibility or circumstances that would enable us to avoid combat with Syria; therefore I suggest planning the engagement with them."[56] Moreover, on May 4, 1982, a month before the operation was to begin, in a conversation with officers from the Northern Command, Sharon said, "The operation against terrorists must not be limited to artillery arcs but should be viewed in terms of the elimination of the military power, including military and political headquarters, [so that it] will take us to Beirut."[57]

Minister Tsipori understood immediately: to complete the occupation of a forty-kilometer strip, the IDF would have to fight the Syrians. After the presentation of the plan, Tsipori said, "Such an operation means attacking Syria." The prime minister expressed his impatience: "It has been clarified that we will not initiate a conflict." "Yes," Tsipori said, "but that's what will happen in light of the planned route. The Syrians will not ignore the activity taking place near them." Begin dismissed Tsipori's comment. He thought Tsipori opposed Sharon's plan only because Sharon had been appointed defense minister and he, Tsipori, had to make do with the position of minister of communications.[58]

Did Sharon know that the operation would lead to a battle with the Syrians but chose to mislead the government? This question remains a mystery to this day. Ben Gal, who was summoned from the United States to command the corps operating in the eastern sector of southern Lebanon, where the Syrians were concentrated, was convinced of the following:

> The defense minister and chief of staff wanted to avoid confrontation with the Syrians. Thus, when they presented the plan to the prime minister, the idea was raised to outflank the Syrians through the Chouf Mountains and force them, by flanking, to withdraw without a fight. As the man responsible for the operation, I argued that it was not applicable. And indeed, the Syrians retreated only after heavy battles. But in my opinion, even though they wanted to avoid it, both Sharon and Raful did not believe that an outflanking alone would allow for the occupation without combat. But I would not describe it as "fraud" or "deception." When military commanders try to convince the political leadership they always "have to sell the plan in a convincing manner." In any event, Begin, who said that the goals of war would be determined as time goes by, approved all plans.[59]

Tsipori not only cast doubt on the success of the operation, but also raised the fear that Sharon was planning to initiate an escalation and would force the IDF into Beirut to strike the PLO beyond the forty-kilometer range. Sharon responded smugly to Tsipori's doubts regarding the scope of the operation, saying that the exact number of kilometers was not forty but forty-two, a distance that could be "measured by a pair of compasses up to Sidon." Sharon was eager to go into battle and wished to mock Tsipori, who was also his deputy in the Defense Ministry. Two days later, when they met again, Sharon told Tsipori that his questions reminded him of his days at school, when students were required to bring rulers to class.[60]

Some of the ministers were not impressed by Sharon's determination. Ehrlich specifically asked, "Is there any chance we will reach Beirut?" Sharon replied, "Beirut is out of the picture." Yet Begin, who tried to reassure the ministers, came to Sharon's aid: "The government will be on the alert. If the need arises to conquer Beirut, the government will make that decision. Nothing will just happen out of inertia, as happened in the previous Israeli governments."[61]

The ministers now had to vote. Ehrlich found it hard to believe Sharon and abstained. Yitzhak Berman, who was not convinced of the connection Begin had made between Argov's attempted assassination and the operation in Lebanon, also preferred to abstain. Tsipori eventually decided to support the plan, and Burg, who also had reservations about the plan, made the suggestion to attack only from the air. This time Begin did not wait for a unanimous decision. He instructed the cabinet secretary to compose the government's official announcement that the operation would be instigated. The statement did not mention the word "war." "The Israeli government has decided to order the military to take on the task of removing all settlements in the Galilee out of firing range of the terrorists, who are concentrated, they and their headquarters, in Lebanon," stated the first clause,[62] the very clause that was later used by the chief of staff to justify the need for the army to enter any area in Lebanon if necessary since there was no mention of a specific range.[63] The second clause stated that the operation was named "Peace for Galilee" (Begin himself chose the name); the third clause stated that "at the time of this decision the Syrian Army must not be attacked unless they attack our forces"; the fourth clause indicated a grandiose plan to change the regime in Lebanon: "Israel continues to pursue the signing of a peace treaty with an independent Lebanon, while preserving its territorial integrity."[64]

On the morning of June 6, 1982, there were no signs of any crack in the consensus uniting the Israeli society. Newspaper headlines, which reported on Ambassador Argov's condition and on the Katyushas fired in response to the air strikes in southern Lebanon, fanned the flames of war, and the general feeling was that Israel was fighting a justified war to destroy the terrorists. Begin was filled with the spirit of combat. Here he was once again, leading his people under a broad national consensus in an operation that would save the good from the clutches of evil. He decided to stay in the north for two days and called his wife to inform her that he would return home "in two days, after we banish the terrorists from the border."[65] Aliza wished him luck, and unlike anything she had done before and without the knowledge of her husband, she called the military secretary and asked him to ensure that only Arie Giladi, his personal driver, would drive him because he was the only driver in the Prime Minister's Office who knew how to handle Begin and which pills he should take to ease the pain in his leg.[66]

Begin then proceeded to call the heads of Haavoda—Rabin, Peres, and Bar Lev—to his office to update them on the details of the operation. He stressed that the final destination was a forty-kilometer range.

The three had no objection in principle, although Bar Lev warned against a confrontation with Syria and an invasion of Beirut. Begin explained that Beirut was not an objective,[67] and he alluded sarcastically to the development of the wars during Hamaarach's reign in power, adding that his government was responsible for this operation "not developing on its own."[68] At the end of the meeting they agreed to join forces so the operation would succeed. Rabin, who went on a reconnaissance along the border with the corps commander, was the most ardent supporter of the government's decision among the opposition leaders.[69]

At the beginning of the operation it was clear that Begin did not want it to continue for long. "The IDF will damage the PLO's power, and its fighters will be pushed away from the border to a distance of forty kilometers," he wrote in a letter to President Reagan when the operation began.[70] This was what Sharon had assured him, and he certainly did not intend to mislead his wife over the phone. The IDF operation order, which took into account the possible complications, specified that "The IDF will strike the terrorists, will destroy their foundations in southern Lebanon . . . will be ready to join forces with the Christians, will be ready to destroy the Syrian Army in Lebanon. . . . There will be no shooting at the Syrians or entering combat with them for at least twenty-four hours."[71] However, this order was not brought to Begin's attention. No doubt the prime minister did not know that Sharon had told the officers of Northern Command at noon of the operation's first day, "I do not believe that we will reach the Sidon line, that forty-kilometer line, and that the firing will then cease. Everyone here should consider themselves on alert for further action."[72]

At 11:00 a.m. the IDF forces began to cross the border between Israel and Lebanon. Seven divisional task forces were deployed. The PLO forces and other Palestinian organizations in Lebanon, an estimated fifteen thousand warriors, knew they could not defeat the IDF. However, Arafat hoped to inflict heavy casualties on it, to harm the residents of northern Israel by rocket fire, and to force the Arab states to intervene so that the Security Council would impose a cease-fire and thus strengthen the PLO's status in Lebanon as an organization that did not surrender to Israel.

Two days later, the IDF forces reached the outskirts of Tyre. The city itself was occupied on June 9, despite difficulties. The PLO warriors used civilians as human shields and hid in the city alleys; the IDF soldiers had trouble orienting themselves in the alleyways and had to issue warnings via loudspeakers before each assault so that the Lebanese civilians could flee.[73]

On the morning of June 7, Sayeret Golani (the recon company of Infantry Brigade 1, Golani Brigade) completed the conquest of Beaufort Castle, an important outpost overlooking the Upper Galilee and the security zone. During the decade preceding the operation, IAF planes had bombed the crusader-built fort dozens of times but had failed to put an end to the rockets launched from it into Metulla and Kiryat Shmona. The Beaufort conquest was not easy. PLO soldiers, with the advantage of the higher ground, fought bravely in a face-to-face battle and refused to surrender. Six Golani soldiers were killed in the Battle for the Beaufort.

The truth is that the fortress was conquered by mistake because of poor communications among the IDF forces. An order from Amir Drori, the head of Northern Command, to cancel the plan to conquer the fort did not reach its destination in time, causing a chain of mistakes. Sharon did not receive an update on the price of conquering the Beaufort and was swift to report to Begin that "none of our troops were hurt."[74] Begin was full of admiration and decided to visit Lebanese soil for the first time and transfer the command of the fort to Haddad's militia in a festive ceremony. His helicopter landed at the fort, and he walked about, grasping a walking stick. "This is a high place; you can breathe mountain air here," he commented to Sharon and his aides.[75] After a brief tour he was introduced to one of the Golani officers, who was downcast because of the death of his friends. Begin did not notice this and showered him with questions. He was interested, for example, in whether the Palestinians had employed "gun-machines" (an approximate translation of the obsolete World War II Hebrew term he used), arousing some ridicule by the media people documenting the visit. When he asked, "Did all the terrorists surrender here?" Begin was disappointed by the response: "They did not surrender; they fought to the death." The disappointment was replaced by embarrassment when the Golani officer told Begin and Sharon (who had noted to the reporters that the fort was taken without casualties), "What's wrong with you? Six comrades were killed."[76] This was Begin's last visit on Lebanese soil. When he realized he had been misled, though accidentally, he ordered that he be personally notified of every soldier killed.

That night Begin called for Sharon, the chief of staff, and the head of intelligence for a consultation regarding the IDF's activity in the Jezzine sector, the southern Lebanese region in which Syrian Division 1 troops were stationed. Their presence prevented the IDF from accomplishing the forty-kilometer objective in the eastern sector. Sharon explained that outflanking them from the north and surrounding them would force the Syrians to withdraw without a fight.[77] "This is Hannibal's tactic," he said appreciatively.[78] The head of military intelligence, in turn, made it clear once again that progress in the area of Jezzine would be like "a drive under fire," but Begin did not comment.[79]

After a consultation between the defense minister and the head of military intelligence on June 7, Sagi ruled, "The movement of Division 162 will invite Syrian fire and will thus create an image of Syrian involvement," while Sharon said that "the division's movement up to the forty-kilometer range from the Israeli border, even if it provokes clashes with the Syrians, is grounded in the government's decision."[80] Sharon was right. The third clause in the government's statement on the eve of the operation noted that Israel wanted to avoid confrontation with Syria, but if Syria opened fire, it would respond. Sharon acted like a skilled solicitor: he saw in this clause a legitimate reason to attack the Syrians should they open fire.

Meanwhile, Begin himself continued to be impressed by the "Hannibal tactic." On June 8, two days after the operation began, Begin went to the Knesset determined, energetic, and feeling as if he owned the place. Twenty-five soldiers had already been killed, seven were missing, and ninety-six were wounded, but the achievements were impressive. The IDF was about to complete the forty-kilometer mission, apart from the eastern sector, and Begin notified the MKs that when the goal was reached, the operation would come to an end. "We want only one thing: that nobody ever harm our communities in the Galilee again . . . that they not fear sudden death from a rocket called Katyusha."[81] In response to heckling by MK Tufik Tubi[82] regarding the large number of casualties on both sides, Begin clarified that "It was not easy to send soldiers into battle. Yes, this is not a war, but it is a campaign, and we knew it would not be a walk in the park."[83] Thus, it is clear that even at the height of the operation Begin believed that it was not a war but a mission of limited duration. At this point he probably did not think that the IDF was going to reach Beirut, and he even asked Habib to send a message to Assad saying that Israel wanted to avoid a confrontation.[84] But the "Hannibal tactic" he had counted on did not prove reliable. When he declared from the Knesset podium that the forty-kilometer line was the objective and called for Assad to order his army not to harm Israeli soldiers so that no harm would come to his troops, the

Syrian forces had already noticed that the IDF forces were attempting to outflank them, and they opened fire. A heavy battle ensued. Some of the Syrians retreated while the IDF surrounded the rest.[85] Israel's entanglement in the operation began with this battle, and ironically it was the very moment at which Begin announced that the operation was almost completed.

Sharon argued that because the Syrians had opened fire, the IDF had to respond, relying on the third clause in the government's statement.[86] However, Brigadier General Amram Mitzna, chief of staff of the Northern Command corps fighting in the eastern sector, claimed that he heard Sharon demand that his officers blur the marked maps he was supposed to present to the government because he knew in advance that the idea of outflanking the Syrians would bring about a confrontation. Mitzna said, "The order to avoid contact with the Syrians was not compatible with the route of advance specified for the forces. This order seems strange to me since it is clear that you cannot pass by the Syrians without coming into contact with them."[87]

While the battles were raging, there was no time for inquiries. Damascus was furious; Assad placed a further five missile batteries in the Beqaa Valley and ordered his troops to attack Israeli tanks that approached the Syrian posts.[88] After Begin had given his speech, Sharon informed him of the situation, explained that Syria's missiles were endangering the IAF aircraft; in his opinion they must prepare to attack the missile batteries. Begin believed that the IDF was trying to avoid a battle with the Syrians and viewed the missile deployment as an extreme response. He therefore agreed with Sharon that they should return fire, despite the blatant deviation from the operation plan.[89]

On the morning of June 9, Sharon explained in a cabinet meeting that Assad was taking advantage of Israel's restraint to increase the threat of a missile attack. The operational plan for the destruction of the missile batteries was ready, and Sharon pressured for approval to activate it. Back in November Begin had boasted that "without conceit, by knowing the facts, Israel can destroy the missiles in two hours without risking any losses to our air force,"[90] and in the cabinet meeting he supported the defense minister's proposal. Sharon added that in response to the incident in Jezzine, Ben Gal's divisions had begun to outflank Syria's armored divisions in order to reach the Beirut-Damascus road and weaken Syrian control over the territory. It now became clear that the forty-kilometer objective had been replaced by another one: cutting off the Syrians from the Beirut-Damascus road. But the ministers' main concern was the destruction of the missiles.⁹¹ They found it hard to reach a decision mainly because of the chief of staff's reservations about attacking the missile batteries, an act he thought could lead to war with Syria. Only when the IAF deputy commander guaranteed that the operation would be completed successfully was it decided to approve the attack. While reviewing the operation that day, none of the ministers heard what the Northern Command commander told the general staff: "Just a bit further, another ten kilometers, we could have reached the forty-kilometer mark without [attacking] the surface-to-air missiles, without a general war, nailed the terrorists, and finished the war quietly."⁹²

The operation to destroy the missiles in the Beqaa Valley, which the air force commanders had had ready for a long time, started at noon on Wednesday, June 9, shortly after the cabinet meeting. Within two hours, fourteen out of nineteen missile batteries were destroyed, and three were heavily damaged. The Syrians sent planes to protect their batteries, and twenty-four of them were shot down. None of the IAF planes suffered any damage. To this day, the method by which the missiles were destroyed remains a secret. It is thought that Israel employed electronic warfare, cluster bombs, and long-range missiles.⁹³ It was a great achievement in military terms. Marshal Pavel Kotakhov, commander of the Soviet Union's Air Force, was rushed to Syria to inspect the damage, fearing that NATO forces would be able to destroy missiles in Eastern Europe.⁹⁴

But Israel's blow was one victory too many. Begin had no time to savor the achievement. Under Soviet pressure, Reagan sent Begin an urgent telegram in which he claimed that IDF forces had penetrated deeper than had been agreed into Lebanon, adding that Leonid Brezhnev, president of the Soviet Union, had threatened to intervene. Reagan did not intend to quarrel with Begin and demanded an immediate cease-fire.⁹⁵ Begin received the telegram at 2 a.m. and was horrified by the severe tone. He ordered the cabinet secretary to arrange an emergency cabinet meeting within two hours.

The half-asleep ministers arrived bleary-eyed at the prime minister's official residence. The prime minister and ministers wanted to respond to Reagan's demand, while Sharon said coolly that they should never surrender to an ultimatum. He explained that the IDF had not yet completed its mission—that is, to position its forces on the forty-kilometer line in the eastern sector—that in order to complete it they had to suppress the terrorists, and that the IDF would need only one more night to reach that goal. Begin tried to find a middle ground between Reagan's demand and Sharon's request. He suggested telling the U.S. president that in principle Israel accepted his demand but that the Syrians would have to push back the PLO forces forty kilometers from Metulla. In a telephone conversation with Haig, Begin reminded him that the forty-kilometer pushback had been the campaign's initial goal and stressed that Israel would not compromise over this matter.[96] The proposal was brought to Assad's attention, but he insisted that Israel withdraw its forces from Lebanon immediately.[97]

The IDF used the hours in which the cease-fire discussions were taking place to move deeper into Lebanon. It launched an offensive in order to reach the Beirut-Damascus road. In response, the Syrians sent the First Armored Division into battle. Until a cease-fire agreement went into effect—at noon on June 11—the IDF managed to destroy the Syrian armored division and its air defense system but did not complete its goal, in part because of a setback in a battle at Sultan Yakoub. By the end of this battle twenty IDF soldiers had been killed, dozens had been wounded, and three were missing.[98]

The government unanimously approved a proposal for an immediate cease-fire. The most prominent issue now on the agenda would be to reach a good enough agreement that would prevent PLO forces from returning to their previous posts while convincing Israel to withdraw its forces. When the cease-fire went into effect, Begin announced that the operation had achieved its objectives. In the western sector, the IDF forces came to three kilometers south of Beirut Airport, after occupying Tyre and Sidon, while in the eastern sector they came within a few kilometers of the Beirut-Damascus road. The IDF had already transgressed beyond the forty-kilometer range.

The exchange of fire ceased in the eastern sector on Friday at noon. In the western sector, however, two hours after the cease-fire went into effect, Begin received reports that the terrorists had not held their fire. Begin approved returning fire.[99] PLO fighters who had fled from IDF forces were concentrated in the area between Sidon and Beirut, refused to surrender, and occasionally attacked the Israeli forces. When the IDF cut off traffic routes between Lebanon's coastal plain in the west and the Beqaa Valley in the east, the terrorists could retreat only to Beirut. On Friday night Sharon flew to Jounieh to convince Gemayel that his men should eliminate the PLO people in Beirut and take over the capital. But Gemayel turned him down.[100] Sharon was disappointed.

On Saturday, June 12, a day after the cease-fire went into effect, fighting broke out between PLO and IDF forces, and in response Israeli forces advanced toward Baabda, the presidential palace overlooking Beirut. Begin received reports about exchanges of fire between the IDF and the PLO but was surprised when he also received a phone call from U.S. ambassador Lewis, who asked why the IDF forces had reached Beirut. Lewis warned Begin that this could lead to the fall of Sarkis's government and demanded that firing cease immediately and that all IDF forces withdraw. Begin protested. "No IDF soldiers are in Beirut at all," he stated. But Lewis insisted. "Impossible," Begin said.

Begin did not need to talk to Lewis to understand that the operation had exceeded its prescribed framework, but until this point he had at least been updated on all the developments. At the end of the conversation he immediately called Sharon. Sharon, to his surprise, confirmed Lewis's claim but tried to appease Begin by pointing out that the presidential palace was outside the official municipal jurisdiction of Beirut and that IDF troops had reached it only because of the necessity to protect the beleaguered forces.[101]

As a general rule, Begin's sweeping trust in senior military officers and defense establishment officials compromised his ability to see the whole of a picture or to contradict the military's stance. A useful example is his one-time intervention in a debate between senior IDF officers before the Lebanon war. When the chief of staff reported to him that the head of military intelligence had quarreled with the commander of the Northern Command because the latter had approved, on his own accord, an action in southern Lebanon, Begin summoned the three to meet with him and made inquiries in his characteristic manner. "My general, did you act without the approval of the Israeli government?" Begin asked the Northern Command commander as if he were a judge. The major general replied, "Prime Minister, it is all with the approval of the chief of staff." Begin looked straight at Eitan, who was gazing at his watch and remained silent. "Chief of Staff, say something," Begin pleaded, but Eitan continued to play with his watch. Begin looked at the two generals, then glanced at the bewildered chief of military intelligence, and immediately resolved the issue: "I assert that the celebrated major general Ben Gal is telling the truth. He has given an officer's word of honor."[102]

During the war Begin was not familiar with the operational maps, and therefore he could not argue with Sharon, but he was convinced of the need to protect the soldiers. Begin grumbled to Minister Nissim that he had received the information about IDF forces in Beirut only after the fact, but he did not reprimand Sharon.[103] On the contrary, when he phoned Lewis, he justified the IDF's progress with arguments

Sharon had raised, as if the advance had been his own decision. In an interview on the *Moked* TV program on June 15, Begin expressed his absolute support for Sharon and denied rumors that Sharon had embroiled him in a war he did not want. "Yaakov, it's a lie," he told interviewer Yaakov Achimeir. "Vanity and chasing the wind. Just empty talk. This is a functioning government. All the facts were presented before it. No one dragged us into it. Why should the defense minister, a man experienced in battle, a true patriot dedicated to the nation heart and soul, drag the government into something behind its back, and so on?"[104]

Why did Begin back Sharon completely? First, it was clear at the time that questioning Sharon's actions was like questioning the entire government, and no one thought that there was a conflict of interests between the defense minister's aims and the objectives set by the government.[105] In addition, Begin believed that even if Sharon was not precise at times in his reports, his actions were crucial for Israel and for the safety of the troops.

This was not the first time that Begin accepted retroactive responsibility for the actions of his subordinates. This had been his way of controlling the people he led ever since he began his political career: strict liability in exchange for absolute loyalty. Though he was surprised by the developments in the field, he did not intend to cut off Sharon's credit because of a one-time exception. But many people close to Begin started raising doubts about Sharon's actions.

On the morning of the war's seventh day, while the exchange of fire continued, Azriel Nevo, Begin's military secretary, realized that Sharon was not going to make do with keeping terrorists away and had his mind set on destroying the PLO in Lebanon. Nevo believed he had to warn the prime minister, but he did not dare criticize the defense minister. He consulted with Kadishai, who suggested that he should send the prime minister a personal letter. In his letter Nevo warned Begin that developments in Lebanon could lead to war with Syria, adding that he thought the operation should be terminated at its current stage. He personally handed the letter to Begin. Begin's response surprised him. The tremendous pressure Begin had been under had started to show: Begin tore up the letter before Nevo's eyes and ruled, without referring to its content, "Soldiers cannot criticize the political echelon." Nevo later regretted not collecting the pieces of the letter from the floor in order to preserve them as evidence.[106] Of course, the letter's destruction did not solve the problem. The battles with the Syrians stopped, but Sharon said in a press conference that "we have not signed a cease-fire with terrorists" and instructed the troops to move further in order to join forces with the Christians in Beirut.[107]

At this stage it was clear that Begin's promise to Reagan, to the Knesset, and to his wife had been broken, as the operation would not be as short as he had declared. The main question now was whether to continue with it. The gaps in communication between Begin and Sharon showed even in the communiqués issued by the IDF spokesman. One of them stated that according to Begin, "Israel fulfilled its goals when it pushed the PLO forces more than forty kilometers from the border. The only remaining task left for the IDF forces is to ensure that the status quo ante, which was unbearable, will not return. An Israeli withdrawal could happen within two weeks if we receive the proper assurances." However, Sharon said, "As long as there are terrorist headquarters in Beirut, it is unlikely that the IDF's task is completed."[108]

But since Begin had not managed to bring about a political agreement that would not detract from the IDF's achievements—that is, a transfer of control of the area occupied by the IDF to a foreign body that would prevent the PLO's return to southern Lebanon—and since continuing the fighting was presented to him as a necessity for protecting the troops under attack, he authorized the continuation of the offensive. On top of that, Begin could not resist Sharon's proposal to link up with the Christian Maronites in Beirut so that they themselves would destroy the PLO because the proposal matched his own vision. "I felt that there was an understanding in principle between them about what was happening beyond the forty-kilometer line," said Ben Gal, who participated in many military discussions.[109]

On June 14 the head of the IDF Human Resources Branch announced that more than 214 IDF soldiers had already been killed and over 1,114 wounded. The public suddenly understood that Israel was paying a heavy price for Operation Peace for Galilee and was shocked. The IDF had encountered serious difficulties while maneuvering around Beirut, mainly because of its unfamiliarity regarding terrain compared to the Syrians and the PLO, and on June 19, Sharon ordered the chief of staff to send two divisions to Aley and Bhamdoun, where Syrian and Palestinian forces were stationed, to sustain the deployment along the Beirut-Damascus road.[110]

On June 21, Begin left for Washington to meet with Reagan. The U.S. president was grumpy and angry. He accused Israel of harming American interests—that is, ensuring Sarkis's rule and avoiding war with Syria. Moreover, Reagan slammed Begin for harming innocent Lebanese civilians. Begin protested that Israeli troops refrained from harming civilians, unlike the terrorists, who were hiding behind them. But his objections sounded empty in light of the casualties in Lebanon.[111]

While Begin was being reprimanded in Washington, the IDF continued to consolidate its position on the Beirut-Damascus road. Meanwhile, it also engaged in firefights with the Syrians and Palestinians. Haig demanded that Begin instruct the IDF to agree to a forty-eight-hour cease-fire so that an agreement could be reached with Sarkis to deport the terrorists from Beirut in exchange for the withdrawal of both the IDF and the Syrians. Begin accepted the American proposal to send U.S. Marines into Beirut to supervise the evacuation of the terrorists.

Begin's weakness was not reflected in his consent to the American proposition—the best offer under the circumstances—but in his inability to keep the promises he had made to the U.S. administration. He told Ehrlich to order a cease-fire; two hours later Ehrlich phoned and said he had not succeeded in getting hold of the defense minister, as he was in the field. Begin told him to notify the chief of staff, but he too was not available. It turned out that Israel, which only a month earlier had destroyed the Syrian missile batteries and amazed the world with its technological capabilities, was totally inept in its internal organization. The cease-fire began two hours after the agreed-upon time, and by then the IDF had already reached the Beirut-Damascus road.[112] There were those in the U.S. administration who blamed the pro-Israeli Haig for the severe deterioration of the situation. On June 25, he was forced to resign, and his successor, George Shultz, applied heavy pressure on Begin and Sharon.

Begin returned to Israel on June 24 and immediately convened the ministers. They were bitter. Levy, Ehrlich, and Tsipori expressed the bluntest criticism regarding the moves Sharon had made without government approval.[113] They believed that had Begin been in the country, Sharon would not have acted as he had, and they now expected the prime minister to impose his authority on him.

The defense minister claimed that the advance had been necessary to protect the soldiers due to their inferior knowledge of the terrain. He was truthful when he said that as a result of the advance the forces were able to deploy under more suitable conditions, but Minister Berman was more impressed by his political tactics: "Why don't you just tell us now what you are going to request from us the day after tomorrow so that we can defend the things you wish to have approved tomorrow?" "You have a sense of humor," Sharon replied.[114] The prime minister was silent. Burg felt that Begin's silence stemmed from his distress.[115] Ultimately Begin had no choice but to retroactively approve the "defense minister's and chief of staff's suggestion to gain control of the Beirut-Damascus road from Aley to el-Bader."[116] On June 25, thanks to the control the IDF now had over the Beirut-Damascus road, its forces surrounded West Beirut, where the terrorists had gathered.

Meanwhile, the Israeli public's and the troops' doubts about the war increased. When Deputy Chief of Staff Moshe Levy went to offer encouragement to the reserve paratroopers who had already reached the Beirut-Damascus road, the soldiers were bitter and severely criticized the sequence of events. Many interrupted him and wondered what the road had to do with "Peace for Galilee."[117] The atmosphere among the general public was equally charged. Every evening more reports came in of casualties among the troops, who were challenged by improvised explosive devices and ambushes on unfamiliar terrain. In an interview with Raya Harnik, mother of Guni Harnik, the commander of Sayeret Golani who was killed in the Battle for the Beaufort, she said, "I would shoot Arik Sharon," and her words inflamed others. The war had now become a part of the political struggle between Left and Right, and the Likud's *Weekly Journal* published the reaction of a bereaved mother to Harnik's comment: "I would shoot Yossi Sarid."[118] No military campaign had been as controversial as this operation, and in no other campaign had such criticism raged during the fighting. But the more the operation was attacked, the more Begin barricaded himself into his position—full support for Sharon.

The tension evoked by the operation was also apparent among the senior military officers. The doubts expressed by General Mitzna since the beginning of the operation matured into a recognition that Sharon was misleading the government. Mitzna believed that the advance on Beirut had been planned beforehand and that Sharon's goals were fundamentally different from the goals set at the beginning of the operation. Mitzna remained in his position but was embittered and claimed that an IDF led by Sharon was corrupting its own long-held values. He was especially embarrassed when an IDF spokesman announced that the cease-fire was being violated by enemy fire, as he believed that many incidents were the result of orders for the IDF to proceed toward Beirut under the guise of defensive actions and an improvement of positions.[119] Struggles among the generals were not new to Israel at times of war, but the outcome of the Likud's first war was severe: a crisis of faith between several senior officers and the defense minister.

Mitzna's frustration was not enough to cause Sharon to hesitate or stop. After its forces were positioned along the Beirut-Damascus road, Israel declared another cease-fire with Syria, and a new strategy was applied: laying siege to Beirut. The objective was to remove fifteen thousand combatants from Beirut, including five thousand Syrian soldiers who were barricaded near the ammunition caches. The question was how. Begin and Sharon wanted the Christian phalanges to conquer terrorist-infested neighborhoods in Beirut, especially in the western part of the city, and that the IDF only support them. But they were divided regarding the scope of the support. Begin preferred support with artillery fire, psychological pressure, and damage to the electricity and water infrastructure in Beirut. Sharon preferred to utilize the air force. At this point no one spoke of a penetration of Beirut by ground forces, as it was feared that engaging in the necessary house-to-house fighting would cause many casualties. Because of the lack of trust between several ministers and Sharon, the former feared that Sharon would find a pretext for involving the IAF despite Begin's decision to the contrary. Minister of Education Zevulun Hammer sought to ensure that a directive to avoid IAF intervention would be explicitly noted in the government protocols, and Sharon blurted out, "There's no need; we understand." Begin intervened and ruled, "I said things clearly, and so it will be noted. Without the air force."[120] This was the first time Begin explicitly and openly expressed his dissatisfaction with Sharon's course of action, but it was not the first harbinger of a change to come. Begin continued to support Sharon in the decision to tighten the siege on Beirut.

There is no doubt that as the situation worsened, Begin wanted to solve the military problem by applying more and more force. He agreed with Sharon that under the circumstances, it was better to conclude the operation with the removal of all terrorists from Beirut.[121] Colonel Eli Geva, commander of Armored Brigade 211, believed that the plan to invade Beirut if the besieged terrorists did not flee on their own accord would involve many unnecessary victims. He clarified to the chief of staff that if his brigade received the order to enter Beirut, he would give up the command and fight as a private. "I will not be responsible for unnecessary casualties," he said. Some estimated that an invasion of Beirut would result in hundreds of casualties, if not even a thousand.[122] The chief of staff was not in favor of occupying West Beirut, but as usual he avoided confronting Sharon.[123] Geva went to the defense minister. Sharon referred him to Begin. Begin received Geva in a different manner than he usually received military officers. "How many casualties are expected in your opinion?" he asked stiffly, and Geva said, "Dozens."

"So, you disagree with the chief of staff's assessment," Begin concluded.

Geva nodded, adding that he believed an invasion of Beirut would lead to the murder of entire families. Begin asked angrily, "What, did you get an order to kill children?" Geva said no.[124] It seemed as though Begin was fed up with the criticism he had heard from the public, and he hurried to finish the meeting. Later, the chief of staff decided not to accept Geva's request to fight with his unit as a private and had him discharged from the army.

Why did Begin react so strongly to those who dared criticize Sharon? Why did he still prefer to rely on him despite knowing that the plans had been disrupted, as he admitted in a private conversation with Minister of Justice Nissim, saying that he too was not satisfied with Sharon's reports? At this point, the relationship between Begin and Sharon resembled that between King Saul, the gloomy warrior, and the young David. It seemed as though in his plight Begin had developed an emotional dependence on the man who was similar to him in his certainty of the righteousness of his path and whom he envied for his capacity to act and focus on his target.

The comparison between the prime minister and the defense minister highlights the question of Begin's responsibility for an operation that developed into a war. No doubt Begin did not mean for things to turn out the way they had. Throughout his political career he had been careful to tell the truth and was therefore an exception among politicians. He most certainly did not dare deceive Reagan in the letter that stated the goal was to remove the terrorists forty kilometers away from the border, and he certainly did not intentionally mislead his wife.[125] But neither were Sharon's arguments doubtable. The government had approved, albeit in retrospect, the advance toward Beirut, as well as all the steps expanding the scope of the operation in light of developments on the ground. No wonder that the two people closest to Begin, his son Benny and his assistant Kadishai, are divided to this day on the matter of Begin's actions. Benny is of the opinion that his father was misled, while Kadishai believes that he knew and approved all the moves. The difference in their positions lies in their attitude toward the term "the leaders' truth." Benny rightly says that his father meant for the operation to be short, and it is more than likely that Sharon knew that it could develop as it did. Kadishai is correct in saying that Begin, though he was not always updated in detail or in time, supported all the resolutions put forward because of the developments on the ground. "There were times when he said that there were things he knew about before and things he heard about after, but in general during the operation, he hoped and expected that Arafat and his forces would be removed even further north than Beirut," Kadishai said.[126]

In a Knesset speech about a month after the beginning of Operation Peace for Galilee, Begin admitted, although not explicitly, that the operation's goals were no different from the goals of Big Oranim: Israeli military assistance to bring Gemayel to power, removal of the PLO from Lebanon, and peace with Lebanon. He argued that meeting these goals should be very simple, and he dismissed the argument that the internal situation in Lebanon was too complex to be solved by "crowning" the Christians. "There are those who say the Lebanese fight among themselves. So what? Don't Jews fight? We all fight among ourselves a bit," he said. "So what? They will reach an agreement among themselves, a Lebanese government will be formed, they will establish an army, the United States will help equip the army with modern weapons, we'll help if need be, [and] then we will sit down with the Lebanese government and sign a peace treaty. Gentlemen, that is what we want."[127] Sharon could have understood, therefore, that Begin was asking him to fulfill the more important goal—exactly as when the settlements were established, when he was appointed chairman of the Committee for Settlement Affairs—and that the means were less important. Sharon even admitted this explicitly in a Foreign Affairs and Security Committee hearing on June 28: "You are not allowing us to finish the job for which we went to war, and that is the destruction of the PLO. We are very close to that end."[128]

The two major questions raised by the operation are the following: Was Begin actually forced to fulfill his vision by Sharon's stratagems, or did he in fact want it fulfilled? And did Sharon already know when the government approved the limited operation that it would eventually require executing Big Oranim? Over the years, as Sharon himself changed his publicly aired version, it has become impossible to answer these questions. It is likely that Sharon saw what was coming and often took advantage of Begin's lack of familiarity with the details in order to approve the troop advances. But the responsibility rests with Begin, who already in 1959 had said, "The captain becomes known in the storm, the maestro in the playing, and the statesman in his observations, his foresight."[129]

On June 29, when the IDF tightened its siege on Beirut, Begin reported to the Knesset in a completely different mood from the one he had been in when giving his first speech after the war began, on June 8. He now headed a confounded government that was not supported by the public, and the opposition did not cease attacking him. Everyone expected him to explain the developments that he had pledged to avoid. At this stage of the operation, which had become a war that resulted in many casualties, the consensus was completely undermined, and Begin stood before a stormy and agitated Knesset. He started his speech by admitting that the IDF was continuing to operate, and then he outlined actions that contradicted the promise he had made on the second day of the operation ("If we reach forty kilometers, then our mission is complete"). He justified the deviation from the plan by the technical constraints in the field: "I want to ask the wondering Knesset members who have asked the question of what happened to the forty-kilometer line. The army has reached it, so why is the war continuing? . . . We have ceased our fire. . . . [They] have continued to fight, continued to try to kill our soldiers. [So I ask] what should we do, we, the government? What should the troops have done? The answer is clear. And so the war has continued."[130]

Begin's distress was apparent, and uncharacteristically, he avoided arguing with the MKs. He addressed Rabin and Peres by their first names, suggested that his job weighed heavily on him, that matters were spinning out of control, and that he was considering retiring:

> Yitzhak, my dear opponent and friend, did you not yourself say that the government is the army's commander in chief? How can you separate them? There was the praised Operation Entebbe; I came to the Knesset. Did I try to separate them? Shimon, you were minister of defense. Did I not praise you for your decision to send troops to Entebbe at the risk of their lives? . . . I do not demand that you say such words to me. Who am I, what am I? An old Jew. I will soon step down from the stage, but before then I will stop limping, so that I can move smoothly. I do not ask for such words, but to separate the government from the army? The enemy

did not allow us to cease fire, and the political echelon gave the army an order to continue fighting; this is how we've reached this situation. So what?

Begin added that "the IDF found itself surrounding Beirut out of necessity," and it seemed that he wanted to end his part in the history of Israel after the expulsion of the terrorists and the troops' return home. "Yes, I announced that I do not want to enter Beirut.... We certainly do not want to enter Beirut. I said that. The government has not yet made a decision to enter Beirut. But, for heaven's sake, you are all experienced. As I have described, as a result of developments that were inevitable, we are now near Beirut, and the terrorists are being captured.... After all the effort we've made, after all the victims among us, will seven thousand murderers remain in Lebanon, equipped with tanks, artillery, heavy gun-machines, and other weapons of destruction? One day we will leave Lebanon; there is no doubt about it. So what will they do? They will move southward." He announced that Israel would agree that the terrorists could leave Beirut with their personal weapons, like medieval knights, who conditioned their surrender on keeping their swords strapped to their hips, and he even expressed compassion for Arafat, his nemesis: "We do not want to humiliate the terrorists.... They are vile murderers, there is no doubt about it, especially the one with the hair on his face, the lowly one, the killer of children. But they are people too, and every man should be valued, every human being." Begin then referred to the many victims and clarified that he could not apologize on this matter. "Israel can survive, with God's help, only by devotion," he said, "on the willingness to sacrifice the best of our sons. Without it we would not have gained independence.... We cannot comfort the bereaved families. Only God can comfort them—and me." He ended unambiguously: "Blessed are the people who have such an army. Blessed is the state that has Ariel Sharon as its defense minister. I say this with all my heart."[131]

More than expressing something about the defense minister, Begin's remarks indicated something about himself. Despite his reservations about Sharon's methods, Begin admired his adherence to a goal, his toughness, his ability not to give in under pressure—everything that characterized Sharon and no longer characterized him. His words of praise for the defense minister also expressed his desire to refute the claim that he had been dragged by him into the war. There is no doubt that it was easier for Begin to deal with the Left's argument that he was complicating Israel in a bloody war than with the claim that he was Sharon's puppet. He was already used to being vilified as a warmonger—this accusation had been hurled at him since his early political career, and the current accusations were, in his view, part of the Left's hostility toward the Right. But the worst damage to his dignity was the claim that he was detached from what was happening on the ground, precisely because it had a grain of truth.

The siege of Beirut was imposed in late June and lasted nine weeks. Thousands of terrorists, led by Arafat, were besieged in Lebanon's capital. In July, at the height of the siege, Begin had a political success. As a result of the deepening rift between Left and Right, Mordechai Ben Porat decided to retire from the Telem movement and join the government, and shortly after that, Techiya acquiesced to Begin's overtures and joined the coalition.[132] In exchange, Begin appointed Yuval Ne'eman, one of the three Techiya MKs who joined the coalition, as minister of science and development—a new post. The coalition now had sixty-seven MKs. When they gathered to vote on Ne'eman's appointment, Begin wished to refute the argument that the government had no control of what was happening and insisted that all the moves had been legally approved. "What is this? Why is it said that [the IDF's action] has not been planned, that it just happened? Far from it.... Nothing just happened. We progressed in face of the enemy's fire.... We announced that the goal was to ensure peace for the inhabitants of the Galilee. There is peace for the Galilee. But if the fighting continues, peace must be guaranteed for Israel."[133]

There was a reason for Begin's bitterness at the public criticism. From his experience as a minister in the National Unity Government in 1967 and from his knowledge of the ways that Israel's wars had been managed in the past, he knew that this was not the first time things like this had happened. After all, he himself had assuaged the ministers who were enraged with Dayan when he, on his own accord, had ordered David Elazar, the Northern Command commander, to conquer the Golan Heights on June 9, a day after the government had decided not to do so.

On July 12, two weeks after imposing the blockade of Beirut, Begin accepted the proposal of Sharon and the chief of staff that the IDF troops enter Beirut in order to speed up the PLO's removal. Begin and Sharon had no choice. The Israeli public was tired of Operation Peace for Galilee, and because of Arab propaganda, which disseminated harsh images from Beirut, public opinion in Israel and the world was divided regarding the necessity of the blockade, its morality, and its effects. Begin's and Sharon's assessment was that a quick mission would cause less damage to Israel's image than the sights of the siege.[134] But the government opposed the proposal and prevented the operation.

The change in the public mindset was signified by Yitzhak Rabin, who had initially supported the campaign and now published an article in *Yediot Ahronot* titled "Against the Occupation of West Beirut."[135] Begin and Sharon realized that the government would be unable to continue the siege without severely harming its status at home and abroad and wanted to end it immediately, but they had a stubborn adversary—Yasser Arafat, who refused to leave and threatened to blow up three hundred ammunitions caches and destroy Beirut. Even Arafat had no choice because the Arab states refused to accept his fighters.

Meanwhile, the Americans attempted to resolve the siege by political means. They prepared an evacuation plan in which the PLO members would leave for Tunisia and Israel would guarantee their safety while they were leaving. On July 29, the member-states of the Arab League approved the plan. Begin was pleased with the agreement, but Arafat held his ground. Beginning on August 1, the IAF carried out 127 air strikes on Beirut; these were accompanied by ground forces attacks to make it clear to the terrorists that the IDF would not back off despite external pressures. The Americans continued to pressure all those involved in the war to agree to their plan, and on August 10 the Israeli government approved the evacuation plan and waited for Arafat's response.

Begin saw the agreement as a considerable achievement: the removal from Lebanon of the PLO and his longtime enemy Arafat with the consent of the Americans and the Western world. But he had little time to enjoy it. On August 11, when the IAF returned to bombing Beirut, the image of a young girl who had survived the bombing and was found among the rubble had a dramatic impact on world public opinion. At noon that day, while resting in his room in the Knesset, Begin was called urgently to the phone. Reagan was on the line. The president told Begin, "You are causing a holocaust." "No one can preach to us about the Holocaust," Begin replied. The president slammed the phone down in his ear, and Begin went back to his room, his face contorted.[136] He did not dare admit to Reagan that he had not approved using the IAF.

In an inquiry between the ministers and the defense minister, Sharon said that the use of the IAF had not exceeded the approval to increase military pressure.¹³⁷ Following this comment, Burg, whose reservist son had been called up by emergency order, slammed Sharon, saying, "What is happening in Lebanon goes against the government's decisions." Sharon replied, "You cannot wage a war based on reports from relatives." Burg also accused Sharon of leaking information. "In fact, you are the one who leaks [information]," Sharon responded, and Burg suggested asking the members of the government who did the leaking. Ehrlich could not stand the commotion and asked Begin, "What's going on here, sir?" Begin was tired and only remarked to Sharon, "It is not you who is managing things here." When Sharon asked for permission to take over a few more buildings in Beirut and explained that the request was based on the need to protect the soldiers, Begin said ironically, "Sometimes precisely when advancing there might be casualties." At the end of this contentious meeting, in which the ministers accused each other of failures, Begin decided that he himself would have the authority to activate the IAF and armored forces in East Beirut, and this, in fact, was the first time he forced his will on Sharon. Yet he never considered dismissing him.

Shortly after Arafat announced his agreement to the evacuation. Sharon claimed that the bombings had led to the decision, and because of it, Begin had no choice but to agree with him. At the end of the day, Sharon had cunningly fulfilled Begin's wish "to remove Arafat from the bunker," but Begin gave up the idea of putting him on trial. "From my observation, in contrast to the way many others viewed things, including my good friends who assisted in promoting this theory in public opinion [that Sharon was running things] by accusing Ariel Sharon or Rafael Eitan," stated Kadishai, "Begin wanted to remove the PLO from Lebanon with no remnant left behind. It is true that he said in the Knesset that he wanted this [operation] to end at the forty-kilometer line. But immediately afterward it became clear that it was not only about the forty kilometers and that if the PLO remained in Lebanon at the fifty- or sixty-kilometer line, they would return."¹³⁸

On August 12 Begin delivered a long speech at the National Security College—one of the most important speeches of his life—in which he responded to criticism that he had entered into an unnecessary war; the speech sounded like a document intended for the judgment of future historians. He spoke like a victor, following the agreement on the terrorists' evacuation from Lebanon, noting that his security strategy had not changed since Etzel had captured Jaffa. He reminded his listeners that even before the establishment of the state, he had called for a liberation "from the Maginot Line of defensive psychology" and now claimed that as head of the government he preferred to go to war over a threat to the country rather than wait for an attack. "There is no moral imperative that a nation is required or allowed to fight only with its back to the sea or even to an abyss. Such a war could be a disaster, if not a Holocaust, for the entire people and [could] cause terrible losses. On the contrary, a free, sovereign nation that hates wars and loves peace must create conditions in which war, if necessary, shall not be out of no-choice," he said, adding that the advantage of a war of choice lay in avoiding the casualties of having been forced to fight because of no other choice. He characterized Israel's wars in the past according to this criterion. The War of Independence, the War of Attrition, and the Yom Kippur War were no-choice wars, he argued, while the Sinai War and the Six-Day War were wars of choice, as was Operation Peace for Galilee. "If all of Israel's wars were wars of no-choice," he said, "today we would be a nation deprived of its best youth, and we would have been left without strength to stand up against the Arab world."[139] Begin rightly stated that his argument stemmed from a fundamental approach he had already expressed in the past, and he was not apologetic regarding Israel's entanglement in Operation Peace for Galilee. Back in 1954, when Arab gunmen had attacked a bus on Maale Akrabim (Scorpions' Pass) in the Negev, Begin had suggested the government respond by military action: "Had we initiated, by a counterattack, an open frontal war, we would have done nothing wrong, but rather [would have had] a righteous war."[140]

In accordance with the agreement, evacuation of the terrorists began on August 21. Within eleven days more than nine thousand Palestinians had left Beirut, headed by Arafat, on their way to Arab countries (many of them went to Tunisia). The five thousand Syrian soldiers in the city also left Beirut and were redeployed in northern Lebanon and the Beqaa Valley. The PLO was not eliminated, but it was expelled from Beirut, a feat not to be underestimated. The achievement had taken a heavy price: by the time the PLO departed from Lebanon, three hundred Israeli soldiers had been killed and more than fifteen thousand had been wounded. Among the Syrian soldiers there were four hundred dead and fourteen hundred wounded or captured. Hundreds of Syrian tanks had been severely damaged, and the IDF had destroyed about a hundred of their planes. Among the Palestinians and the Lebanese residents over twenty thousand had been killed and more than thirty thousand had been wounded.[141]

But the war did not end even after the PLO was removed from Beirut. Although Begin declared that he would be willing to withdraw the IDF troops, intelligence estimated that over two thousand terrorists had outsmarted the international forces supervising the evacuation and remained in Beirut with large weapons caches, so Begin agreed to Sharon's demand to get rid of them too.[142] Meanwhile, groups of Shiites who objected to the IDF's and the Christian militias' control over southern Lebanon replaced the PLO terrorists. The Shiites planted numerous explosive devices along the roads, and there were casualties among the Israeli soldiers almost on a daily basis. No solution for the mess in Lebanon was in sight. Israel sought to withdraw its troops but conditioned its withdrawal on the evacuation of all other forces from Lebanon—namely, the Syrian army. Assad refused.[143]

On August 23, just days after the evacuation, Begin was informed that the next step in Sharon's vision had started taking shape. Lebanon's parliament chose Bachir Gemayel as the new president in a vote of sixty-two to fifty-seven. His election did not indicate that Lebanon had become a proper democracy. Syrian newspapers stressed that IDF soldiers had had to escort several delegates to the polls to protect them against Gemayel's opponents.[144] Begin thought that Lebanon's new ruler, a friend of Israel, would remove the PLO and the Syrians from the country and sign a peace treaty with Israel; it would be Begin's second agreement with an Arab country, a successful conclusion of his term as prime minister, an achievement that would surely put an end to the acute criticisms over the death toll. Begin wanted a political achievement. A week after Gemayel was elected as the Lebanese president, Begin was on vacation with Aliza in Nahariya, which was no longer under the threat of missiles, to demonstrate the start of a new era of peace, and he was about to meet the new president. Gemayel came to Israel on an IDF helicopter. He was less enthusiastic than Begin and agreed to meet on condition that the meeting would be secret.

When preparing for the meeting, Begin was told that Ambassador Lewis wanted urgently to meet with him. The prime minister asked that the meeting be postponed. Lewis insisted. "It is about an important message from the president," he stated. In their meeting the ambassador handed Begin a letter from Reagan in which the president wished to update Begin about a new regional peace plan he was going to suggest. The plan proposed an arrangement under which Israel would withdraw from Judea and Samaria and a state with affinity to Jordan would be established in the territories. The Americans saw the plan as compensation to the Arab League for its support of the PLO's evacuation from Beirut.

Reagan's plan was a political defeat for Begin. It drained the underlying purpose for fighting in Lebanon of all content—crushing the PLO in order to moderate the Palestinian demands for a state on the territory of Eretz Israel. Begin was appalled. Not only had the war become muddled, but "a battle over the Land of Israel" had just started, he told his aides.[145]

When Gemayel landed in Israel, he was tense and preoccupied by the efforts to stabilize the government in his country and because he knew what Begin was going to ask of him. "Allow me to address you as a father to his son," Begin began after a toast to Gemayel's presidency.[146] It was his way of expressing warmth and respect, as he had done in calling Egyptian foreign minister Ibrahim Kamal "young man" at the beginning of talks on the peace treaty with Egypt. Like Kamal, Gemayel was embarrassed by what sounded to him as a patronizing gesture. He restrained himself but objected to the date Begin proposed for signing an agreement for the establishment of peace—December 31. He explained that it would endanger his position if he signed an agreement with Israel at the beginning of his term because he could be boycotted by the Arab countries. He added that he first intended to restore order to Lebanon and remove the Syrian noose around his neck. He also rejected Begin's request that he visit Jerusalem, or at least Tel Aviv, and opposed open formal negotiations. "There is no justification for a quick signing of a peace treaty," he said. "I first have to work on an agreement with the Sunnis in West Beirut and formulate an arrangement by which the Syrians and the Israelis will withdraw from Lebanon." Begin was furious. He did not grant Gemayel's request that a large number of Christian fighters be allowed to enter the Chouf region to suppress the Druze militia—a move that could have harmed Israel's relations with the Druze. He suggested that Gemayel appoint Haddad, the commander of the Christian militia in southern Lebanon, as chief of staff. But Gemayel saw his suggestion as an intervention in Lebanon's internal affairs; moreover, he said that Haddad was harming the Christians' interests and that he intended to try him on charges of desertion from the Lebanese Army.

Now it was clear to Begin that his dream was not about to be realized. He did not understand why the Christians were not uniting into one camp, and the pressure he was under left its mark: he reddened and shouted at Gemayel; his outburst was heard outside the room.[147] Sharon, who also attended the meeting, inflamed the confrontation by reminding Gemayel of his position. Gemayel was also upset. He pressed his hands together and said wryly, "Handcuff me. I'm your vassal."[148] Eventually, the three agreed to form a committee to discuss future relations between Israel and Lebanon, but at the end of the meeting they all seemed uncomfortable. Gemayel was offended by Begin's demands. He told his aides that the Israeli prime minister had treated him condescendingly,[149] and he told U.S. secretary of state George Shultz that Begin was interested in a "puppet government."[150] The next day the media reported on the secret meeting, and Begin's response was, "You don't ask a married gentleman where he spends his nights."[151] It was one of his last witticisms in the history of Israeli politics.

Begin returned depressed to Jerusalem. He had set many goals in this war, and an alliance with Lebanon was the most important of them. It would have been a utopian achievement that would have immortalized the entire operation as a success. He also believed that Gemayel was ungrateful because he was certain that Israel had freed the Christians from Syria and the Palestinians and had helped him get elected. Gemayel's ingratitude was further testimony of the bitter fate of the Jews. "Begin was never the same man after that," said Shamir.[152]

Meanwhile, the IDF remained in Lebanon. Israel was late to sober up from the illusion of a treaty. The IDF had to deal with the Palestinians who remained in Lebanon; with leftist Lebanese groups; and especially with organizations of radical Shiites, which had initially welcomed the entrance of the IDF because they thought it would release them from the control of the PLO but which ultimately, with Syrian support, rebelled against the Israeli soldiers, whom they saw as their new occupiers. The main organization in Lebanon was the Shiite Amal, but a new and more extremist organization of Shiites had started forming: Hezbollah (God's Party), which had gained strength since its members had been forced to flee to southern Lebanon.

The large number of casualties in the war, the disappointment with Gemayel, and the Reagan plan were too much for Begin. He refused to discuss Reagan's proposal, and he decisively stated when putting it to a vote in the government on September 2, "The plan has died before it was born. For me it does not exist."[153] The government rejected the plan as well, and at the meeting's end Begin drafted a response to the U.S. president stating that his proposal had sparked a sense of betrayal and persecution in the prime minister. He accused the United States of ingratitude—a word Begin tended to use often at the time—following the sacrifice of 340 Israeli soldiers in return for the destruction of

Soviet tanks and aircraft. Reagan replied that he was hurt by Begin's criticism of a realistic peace proposal, while in his diary he indicated that Peres seemed "more rational than Begin."[154]

Even after the meeting with Gemayel, Sharon did not intend to abandon his goal of cleansing West Beirut—in other words, eliminating the munitions caches and removing the remaining Palestinian extremists, especially in the refugee camps. Because of the heavy price Israel had paid and since Gemayel had already been elected, Sharon preferred that the Christian phalanges finish the job, so he sent the IDF commanders and senior Mossad officials to coordinating meetings with the militia commanders. Begin sided with him. In a conversation between Nachum Admoni, deputy director of the Mossad, and Eli Hobeika, who led the phalanges' security mechanism, Admoni stressed that "the Palestinians should not be treated with the generosity of winners."[155] Hobeika, who was not known for his gentleness but rather for his cruelty toward his enemies, did not need motivational speeches. At the time Begin refrained from intervening in the talks with the Lebanese and did not dwell on their details. However, when he read intelligence reports noting that thousands of terrorists remained in the city after the PLO's evacuation from Beirut, he told the Foreign Affairs and Defense Committee that Israel would still seek to expel the "hostile elements" remaining in West Beirut.[156]

Sharon strove once again to realize the goal Begin had set. On September 13 he met with Gemayel, and the two decided that the terrorists remaining in West Beirut needed to be expelled from Lebanon. Gemayel saw the Palestinians who remained in refugee camps as a contentious element that would come between the Lebanese Christians and Muslims and believed that their removal would make it easier to control the country. But he was outsmarted. On September 14, while he was in his party headquarters in East Beirut, a huge explosion shook the building, which partly collapsed. In the evening it became clear that the recently elected president had been killed in the explosion, caused by a device that had apparently been planted by a Syrian intelligence agent.[157]

Gemayel's murder was yet another link in the chain of failures as Begin and Sharon saw it, as he was the Lebanese leader closest to Israel and the most reliable of them, despite their differences. That night Begin called Sharon and the heads of the defense establishment for an urgent consultation. He feared that the murder would lead to a coup in Lebanon and that the Shiites or groups affiliated with Syria would rise to power. He was also concerned that international forces that might be sent to Beirut to keep order in the Lebanese capital would make it difficult for IDF troops to capture the terrorists still hiding there. The only option for preventing this possibility, Sharon told Begin, was to regain control of West Beirut. Begin agreed. The new argument for the return of IDF forces into Beirut was the need to prevent bloodshed and revenge the campaigns of Christians and Muslims alike.[158]

On September 16, the IDF completed its takeover of West Beirut, and as Israel prepared to celebrate Rosh Hashanah, Sharon and the phalange commanders agreed that they would complete the task and would "mop up"[159]—that is the term Sharon used—the terrorists in the refugee camps. It was a precedent in the relations between the Christian phalanges and the IDF. Until that time the phalanges had preferred to let the IDF fight the war; besides, the IDF had not been eager to cooperate with them, in part because it lacked trust in their military capabilities and feared they would draw the IDF into unnecessary battles. The activation of the phalanges was partly a consequence of the criticism from Israel that the phalangists were sitting on their hands while Israeli soldiers were dying and partly the phalangists' wish for revenge. That same day in the afternoon, before sending his men out, Hobeika met for one last briefing with division commander Amos Yaron. Yaron warned him not to harm civilians[160] and ordered a mortar battery to fire illumination rounds to light up the phalanges' way to the refugee camps.

In the evening the Israeli government convened for a last meeting before the holiday. The ministers complained that the IDF had taken control of West Beirut without their approval; Begin explained, as Sharon used to explain, that the constraints on the ground did not allow them to be convened before the operation. Sharon himself reviewed the sequence of events but did not say a word about the phalanges' operation. The chief of staff informed the ministers about the action, noting dryly that it was also "an outburst of revenge."[161] Minister David Levy was the only one who thought the chief of staff's report was important. "When I hear that the phalanges are entering a certain neighborhood and I know what the meaning of 'revenge' is for them—a slaughter—no one will believe that we went in there to enforce order, and the burden of guilt will be on us," he said.[162] But even after Levy's conclusion not one of the ministers said a word. Begin remained silent as well. The ministers rushed off to celebrate the holiday.

The next afternoon, Chief of Staff Eitan spoke with Hobeika and inquired as to what was happening in the refugee camps. Hobeika informed him that a battle was raging, but Eitan was not interested in details. IDF soldiers at observation posts were the first to understand that something odd was going on, but they still assumed it was a regular battle.[163] Only the next day, when IDF officers entered the camps with foreign reporters, was the horror revealed. Some of the women had been raped, babies had been trampled with hobnailed boots, and hundreds had literally been slaughtered. It is estimated that Hobeika's men killed over eight hundred Palestinians in the refugee camps of Sabra and Shatila.[164]

On Rosh Hashanah, which fell on September 18, Begin spent most of the day at the Great Synagogue in Jerusalem. He knew nothing about what was happening in the refugee camps. Senior Israeli politicians and defense officials who had learned about the massacre did not bother to inform him. When journalist Ze'ev Schiff from *Haaretz* heard what had happened, he called Minister Tsipori, who then updated the foreign minister. Shamir did not believe the issue was important enough to update Begin. Begin learned of the massacre only at 5 p.m. while listening to the BBC news after he had returned home from the synagogue. He phoned Sharon immediately. Sharon said the details were correct but explained that the action was over and that the phalanges had been removed from the refugee camps. Begin did not yet realize the massacre's political implications. He believed that the media storm would pass and that the massacre would eventually be considered an internal Lebanese affair since the killers were not Israeli soldiers. But he was wrong again. The images broadcast around the world were horrific.

The next day Begin went again to the synagogue. When he finished praying, he saw hundreds of protesters, including Knesset members from the Left and bereaved families. They shouted at him, "Beirut—Deir Yassin" and "Begin—a child killer." He looked at them in silence and walked home with an alienated smile on his face and with dozens of police and soldiers escorting him.[165] Only then did he realize the significance of the massacre.

At 9 p.m. the government convened for an emergency meeting. Sharon claimed that he could not have predicted the developments and said he had approved the phalanges' operation because he did not want to risk the lives of Israeli soldiers. Begin agreed. Allegations against him and his government only increased his feeling that he and his people were suffering an injustice. He saw the criticism as evidence of the "deterministic hatred" of Gentiles toward Jews and the hostility between the Left and the Right. In the meeting he formulated the government's announcement, expressing its "deep regret" over what had been done "by a Lebanese unit" and emphasizing that the charges of IDF responsibility were a "blood libel against the Jewish state and its government."[166] The next day, in a meeting with Yehuda Lapidot, his friend from the underground, he complained that the Jews were always given the blame.[167]

But Jews too accused the Jews. Mitzna was sure that Sharon should have understood the meaning of the phalanges entering the refugee camps, and he sent the chief of staff a letter saying he no longer had confidence in the defense minister. The chief of staff referred Mitzna to the prime minister. A surly Begin received Mitzna in his office. Mitzna was emotional. He told Begin that he believed that he had not been told everything about what was going on on the ground and that Sharon had told the officers to blur the marks on the operational maps to confuse the ministers. His allegations were stunning in their blatancy and should have shaken the prime minister enough to discredit the defense minister. But Begin looked at Mitzna blankly and made do with a short response: an officer cannot make a no-confidence statement against the defense minister. He also asked Mitzna to retract his words and to write a letter of apology. Mitzna agreed to apologize for the harshness of his statement but not for its content. When Begin read his letter of apology, he told him that it was not satisfactory. But this time Mitzna was determined, and Begin agreed to listen to him. He was particularly interested in understanding why Mitzna did not believe Sharon. Mitzna concluded from the prime minister's refusal to adhere to Sharon's request—to dismiss Mitzna from the army—that Begin believed him but was struggling to impose his authority on the defense minister.[168]

There is no doubt that Begin was shocked by the massacre. Even his political opponents such as Shulamit Aloni could not suspect him of discounting human lives. But the notion that Jews were the eternal victims was so deeply rooted in his beliefs that he could not accept, even within himself, that the Jewish people too were responsible for evildoing.[169] Before the Knesset he repeated his complaint against the modern-day "blood libel" and refused a demand to establish a commission of inquiry. "There is no one to blame in Israel. There is no fault in the IDF. Only a disaster," he said. "Disasters happen [even] in Israel, not only in Lebanon. There is currently a blood libel against Israel and the Israel Defense Forces. A disaster. . . . But does this mean that the Jews are to blame?"[170]

Many Israelis saw the horrific pictures from the refugee camps as the final straw. On September 25, hundreds of thousands of Israelis gathered in Kings of Israel Square in Tel Aviv—*Haaretz* estimated that there were 400,000 people,[171] but it was probably closer to 150,000—to protest Israel's involvement in the massacre and to demand the establishment of a commission of inquiry. Although the demonstration had concrete demands, it was clear that the public was expressing general abhorrence against the war, and Begin and his government could not ignore their wrath.

The day after the demonstration, under pressure from the Americans and Israeli public opinion, IDF soldiers withdrew from West Beirut and returned to their positions from before Gemayel's assassination. International forces then entered Beirut to help Amin Gemayel, the new president, who was elected on September 21. Unlike his brother, he objected to the relations Bachir had forged with Israel. Begin was embittered and felt that the failures were threatening to overcome him. In a conference of the IDF's senior command, Amos Yaron accused the entire system of apathy.[172] On September 27, Minister Berman announced his resignation in protest against Begin's refusal to establish a commission of inquiry. The intervention of President Yitzhak Navon also weighed on Begin. Navon demanded the immediate establishment of a commission of inquiry on the grounds that only through an investigation could the moral stain clinging to Israel's reputation be removed. Begin argued that the very establishment of a commission would be an admission of guilt and agreed only to appoint an investigating judge on behalf of the army. The members of government were divided in their opinions.

Begin succumbed to pressure only when President Navon made his position clear on a national television broadcast.[173] On September 28 he announced, as if coerced by the devil, that the government had approved the establishment of a commission of inquiry headed by Justice Yitzhak Kahan. The other commission members were Reserve Colonel Yona Efrat and Aharon Barak, Begin's favorite from the days of Camp David. Thirty-four years after having been accused of responsibility for the massacre at Deir Yassin, Begin—who believed with all his heart in his morality, a belief that was a psychological crutch—was accused once again of responsibility for murder.

These were Begin's most difficult days as prime minister. He who had raised legal arguments to justify all his actions, who only a year and a half earlier had ordered the establishment of a commission of inquiry into the murder of Arlosoroff, now had to testify as a suspect before the commission. He who had spoken so intensely of saving the Christians was now seen as the man who had corrupted them, as someone who had collaborated with them in the massacre. He disliked the idea of having to rely on the assistance of a lawyer, and unlike most of the witnesses, he appeared before the panel alone, although the cabinet secretary, who was a lawyer by profession, helped him in preparing his testimony. He rarely smiled, tended to withdraw into seclusion, and avoided interviews and political meetings.[174]

In his testimony before the committee, which sometimes caused discomfort, it became clear that Begin was detached from his role. In his defense he argued that he had no idea that the phalanges would do what they had done, but when asked what he meant by saying that the IDF would take over West Beirut in order to prevent bloodshed, he replied that he feared that the phalanges might take revenge, thus contradicting his previous claim. He even argued that the defense minister had not informed him that the phalanges had entered the camps, but when asked if he thought Sharon should have updated him, he said no.[175] It is not clear whether he was acting gallantly or whether he wanted to justify his lack of knowledge of the details on the grounds that he was not supposed to know them.

While the commission was completing its investigation, the differences of opinion among the government ministers grew deeper. Yaakov Meridor was convinced that the Likud had no reason to fear the conclusions. He believed that if the committee concluded that the IDF was guilty of the massacre, it would be better to declare new elections because such a conclusion would only strengthen the sympathy for the Likud and help it gain victory.[176] Tsipori believed that if the committee did its job properly, it would be clear that Sharon had wanted a slaughter in order to intimidate the Palestinians and make them flee to Jordan.[177] Begin rejected both assessments.

NINETEEN

THE DOWNFALL

Even when he had returned home during the days of the commission meetings, Begin could not be comforted. Aliza had developed severe pneumonia, and her condition deteriorated rapidly. She was hospitalized again and again, and Begin spent long hours at her bedside.[1] At home she often had to use a respirator and a wheelchair. Begin found it hard to see the champion of his youth so weak, and her condition affected his ability to conduct meetings. He needed no medical knowledge to understand that the woman he loved, who had given him the strength he had needed to cope with the difficulties he encountered, was fading away. In a conversation with the U.S. ambassador to Israel before a meeting with Reagan in November 1982, Begin said that he preferred to resign and "devote my time to her in the time she has left," but Aliza encouraged him to continue in office.[2]

Reagan wanted to meet in Washington to discuss the peace plan, about which he and Begin were in disagreement. Before the meeting Begin was scheduled to deliver speeches across the United States and to raise funds. Amid preparations for the visit Begin split his time between the Prime Minister's Office and Aliza's bedside. At the beginning of November her condition took another turn for the worse, and a breathing tube was inserted into her throat. Because she could not speak, she communicated by writing notes. Begin wanted to postpone his scheduled visit and stay by her side until she recovered. At that time Begin's relationship with Burg got closer, and Burg too believed he had to postpone the trip. But Aliza wanted to bolster him, as usual, and after hearing allegations that he was unable to perform his duties, she encouraged him to go.³ Before leaving for the United States, Begin went to say goodbye. Aliza was connected to an oxygen pump. When she noticed that he was leaning toward canceling the trip in order to stay with her, she wrote, "Don't worry; everything will be fine; you have to go." Begin kissed her and said goodbye. She fell asleep immediately afterward.⁴

Begin did not go alone to the United States; his daughter Leah replaced Aliza. On Saturday, December 13, Begin was expected to speak at a large event in Los Angeles. He prepared his outline, as usual, and in the afternoon he went to the synagogue to pray with the Jewish community.

Benny learned about his mother's death while Begin was in his hotel room. He hurried to call the Israeli consulate in Los Angeles and spoke with Kadishai, who suggested first notifying Begin's doctor, who was at the synagogue and had a beeper, but he did not notice a message that arrived while he was reading the Torah. Only upon the doctor's return to the hotel did Kadishai tell Begin succinctly, "I got a call from Benny. Aliza has passed away." Begin locked himself in the bathroom, and when he finally came out, he wanted to change his tie. Leah entered the room and began to cry, and he muttered, "I shouldn't have left her."⁵

Kadishai organized their return to Israel. Begin asked him to make sure Aliza would be buried on the Mount of Olives, near the graves of underground fighters Meir Feinstein and Moshe Barazani, who had been sentenced to death and committed suicide before the verdict was executed. (He purchased the burial plot for himself and Aliza following her death.)⁶ The flight from Los Angeles to Israel took sixteen hours, and Begin spent the entire flight in the bedroom on the plane. His world had fallen apart. He knew that nothing would ever be the same.⁷ The funeral took place when he returned to Israel. He walked silently behind Aliza's coffin, wearing a gray hat and supported by the weeping Leah. Begin sat shivah at the Prime Minister's Residence in Jerusalem. He kept the mourning customs, did not shave during the thirty days of mourning, and did not hesitate to cry on the shoulders of guests who came to comfort him. President Navon described how Begin "attacked" him with hugs, as if to hold onto every shoulder offering him support.⁸ It was clear to his friends that Begin would find it difficult to survive without Aliza, and his guilt at leaving her in her final moments added to his sorrow.⁹

Despite his deep grief Begin decided to return to work full time, and when the days of mourning ended, he also returned to conducting meetings with a firm hand, as if to prove he had not lost his power.[10] But his guilt never left him, and neither did the grief over Aliza's death. The frustration evoked by the outcome of the war, the loneliness, and the mental fatigue that gripped him were evident in all his actions. "You suddenly see what a person is worth," he told Foreign Minister Shamir while feeling some weakness when climbing the stairs to the cabinet conference room.[11] When he participated in a meeting of Northern Command officers, he fell asleep just a few minutes after it began, and the perplexed officers tried to wake him. Ben Gal pushed the table, while another officer made a loud noise on purpose. Begin woke up and fell asleep again. "As soldiers say, he caught some z's," said Ben Gal. When he awoke, before the meeting's conclusion, Begin asked, among other odd questions, "How do you communicate with the soldiers?" and "What's the difference between wireless and a two-way radio?"[12]

Begin tended to express distress and to share his health issues with those around him. He told Burg that he had had some bleeding and that "a genius Sephardi doctor" had told him that it was caused by the aspirin he was taking for headaches. Burg was surprised by both his candor and his childlike naivety and told his wife, "Aspirin causes bleeding only if one suffers from some other major problem. Does he really think that without aspirin he will get better?" Burg believed that Begin would not be able to function as before and discussed his thoughts with Ehrlich. After one of the meetings in which Begin seemed distracted, the two decided to turn either to the attorney general or to the president if his condition did not improve within a week. However, Begin conducted the next meeting like his usual self, resolutely and firmly. Because of his constant mood swings it was difficult to tell whether his distress was a temporary state that would pass with time or whether it was a sign of irreversible mental and physical deterioration.[13]

On February 8, 1983, the Kahan Commission's report was published. The commission ruled that members of the Christian phalanges were responsible for the massacre but added that the Israeli government was indirectly responsible. Regarding Begin, the report stated, "We cannot accept his claim that the threat of a massacre was completely absent from his mind.... The prime minister's lack of involvement in the matter casts a degree of responsibility upon him," but it did not suggest that he should resign.[14]

The report got prominent media coverage throughout the world. The February issue of *Koteret Rashit* sported the headline "Remove the

Government of Evil from the Land." Nachum Barnea, the magazine's editor, wrote that the prime minister was described in the report as an "uninvolved zombie."[15] Feeling that the burden of Jewish history was on his shoulders, Begin was hurt most of all by the comparison that the commission had made between Israel's responsibility for the events in Sabra and Shatila and the responsibility of the authorities in Russia and Poland toward the Jews who were massacred in those countries in the nineteenth century.[16]

Begin shut himself up in his room after receiving the report, and after reading it, he told Government Secretary Dan Meridor that he should resign. This was the first time he explicitly expressed a wish to retire, but the justice minister and the government secretary persuaded him to go on.[17] Meridor did not ignore Begin's distress signals, but he was convinced that under the circumstances, there was no greater leader in the country at the time and that in any event, he could not retire at a time when his reputation was being tarnished.

Begin was not the only one criticized in the report. The commission noted that it did not suggest that IDF chief of staff Eitan should be dismissed only because he was about to end his term. It also said that Sharon—who claimed that he did not consider that the phalanges, "who had among them lawyers and engineers," would take the military term he had used, "mopping up," as permission to commit a massacre[18]—had been negligent and recommended that he should not continue to serve as defense minister.

On Thursday, February 10, the government convened to decide on its response to the commission's recommendations. Sharon suggested that the recommendations be rejected and that preparations for elections begin, but other ministers opposed his proposal. Since the commission was satisfied with a recommendation alone, Begin had the burden of deciding on his own whether to dismiss Sharon from the defense ministry or not. Now that he had the opportunity to be rid of Sharon, it was too late; he could no longer make major decisions, and he asked the attorney general to decide. The AG ruled that Sharon must resign but added that he could serve in a different ministry.[19] Sharon anticipated Begin and resigned as minister of defense.

Two days after the publication of the Kahan Commission's conclusions, the Shalom Achshav (Peace Now) movement organized another demonstration in Jerusalem against the war in Lebanon and demanded that the commission's findings be implemented. The protesters planned to march to the government building, but shortly after word of the march spread, the rightists organized a demonstration in support of the war. In the midst of the demonstration, a right-wing activist, Yona Abrushmy, threw a hand grenade at the marchers heading for the government building. Emil Grinzweig, a thirty-three-year-old reserve officer who had fought in Lebanon, was killed. Avraham Burg, son of the interior minister, was wounded. The grenade throwing was the culmination of a wave of violence and hatred that swept Israel—the result of the deep disagreement between supporters of the war and its opponents. Begin learned about the fatal incident during a cabinet meeting. He condemned the murder but refused to give a televised speech, claiming he had not shaved that morning. Only after his aides pressured him to do so did he agree. He said that the murder was "a terrible tragedy." "God save us from taking the path of violence," he concluded and returned home.[20]

Despite the intense public opinion and the commission's conclusions, Begin did not dismiss Sharon from the government; he appointed him a minister without portfolio and a member of the security cabinet. And despite all this, Sharon still believed that Begin had abandoned him. He believed he was paying the price for a war for which they were both responsible.

As a minister without portfolio, Sharon no longer had any decisive influence in the government, and he expressed his frustration in a meeting he initiated with Begin in the summer of 1983. He went to Begin's office when he learned that another Israeli soldier had been killed in Lebanon. "A tragedy, a tragedy," Begin muttered and looked at Sharon. But Sharon did not blink. "The role of the leader is not to cry but to lead," he told Begin, and before the prime minister could respond he added, "But that's not why I came to see you." Sharon told him that when he left the defense ministry, he recalled his father, who had begged him on the day he was recruited to the Haganah never to hand over Jews to foreigners. Therefore, Sharon said, he had avoided joining the Palmach, which had fought against Etzel. "But you, Menachem—you turned me in," he said. Journalist Uri Dan, who was Sharon's media adviser at the time, claimed that Sharon told him about this meeting with great satisfaction and later saw it as the last straw regarding Begin's retirement.[21]

The year 1983 was a bad one for Israel. In late February Moshe Arens, Israel's ambassador to the United States, replaced Sharon as defense minister. Begin preferred him over the other candidate, Reserve

General Israel Tal. When Arens was appointed, many IDF troops were still stationed throughout wide areas of Lebanon. Arens changed the deployment of forces, ordered the IDF to prepare for a withdrawal and redeployment on the Awali River line, and decided that the SLA would be deployed throughout the security zone. The plan was delayed twice at the request of the Americans, who wanted to allow the Lebanese Christians to strengthen their status in the country. The IDF began withdrawing its forces in August, after which Syria resumed control over the Beirut-Damascus road, and the Druze started fighting the Christians for control of the Chouf Mountains.

Israel's economy was also in poor shape. Mass strikes erupted sporadically, including a doctors' strike that lasted three months and a strike of El Al employees. The country's external debt soared to $21 billion,[22] and the inflation rate rose to 191 percent. According to a National Insurance Institute report, about half a million people were living below the poverty line.[23]

Another danger posed to the Israeli economy was the unrealistic rise in share prices in the stock market, resulting from the method of their adjustment. During the 1970s Bank Hapoalim began regulating the price of its shares and recommended their purchase to its clients. These purchases enabled the bank to increase its capital for providing loans, for investments, and so on. In order to convince customers to continue to invest in its shares—that is, to make them an attractive investment opportunity—the bank itself bought its shares, creating the impression that they were in great demand. The bank also offered its customers generous credit for buying shares, making further profits from the interest. Share price adjustment through the creation of artificial demand appeared to the banks as an easy method for raising huge sums. Gradually, Bank Leumi, Discount Bank, Hamizrachi Bank, Bank Igud, and the General Bank joined Bank Hapoalim in the regulation of share prices. The only major bank that did not regulate its shares was Bank Habeinleumi (International Bank). Under pressure from the Israel Securities Authority, the banks reported the adjustments in their annual reports, but because of the need to hide the adjustments from the public, the reports were often partial, misleading, and sometimes false. The purpose of the adjustments was to create a steady increase in share prices regardless of the state of the economy. The artificial rates created an economic bubble, as the public continued to invest huge amounts in the shares but got diminishing returns. From January to March, Finance Minister Yoram Aridor and Ezra Sadan, the ministry's general manager, appealed several times to the heads of the banks to gradually reduce the adjustments. But treasury officials feared that if the public knew about the adjustments, it would lead to a real collapse, so they therefore refrained from publicizing the fact that they were pressuring the banks on this issue. Begin himself was uninterested in the financial situation and allowed Aridor to manage the economy as he saw fit. By that time he was completely indifferent to what was happening around him, and in the meetings he chaired it was clear that "only his body was present."[24]

The pressure on the banks was not fruitful, so to put an end to the adjustments, the treasury officials sought to significantly devaluate the shekel. In August 1983 the currency was devaluated by 8 percent, but this was not enough to stop the share price adjustments. By this time public selloffs of shares had increased, reaching their peak in September. The public converted bank shares into dollars, and the banks failed to convince them to stop. On October 9, the stock market collapsed, and the stock exchange was closed until October 24. Meanwhile, the shekel had depreciated by 23 percent. From the public the Bank of Israel bought shares whose value had depreciated by dozens of percentage points.

The direct result of the share price adjustment crisis was disastrous. One-third of the public's investments went down the drain, and the government bought the banks with public funds. Although the stock market actually collapsed only after Begin's resignation, the process leading up to the collapse was the result of his detachment from the situation. If he had been functioning properly, he may have been able to pressure the Ministry of Finance to eliminate the adjustments since it had already noticed signs of the impending crisis earlier in the year. In 1984, after the bank shares were put in order and before a stabilization plan was formulated by the new government, the inflation rate was 445 percent, and the shekel's depreciation against the dollar amounted to 493 percent. The economy was in danger of bankruptcy.[25]

The ministers blamed one another for the frequent scandals, and the cabinet meetings seemed like a dueling arena. Begin struggled to steer the ship of state effectively. His despondency grew, and he sometimes seemed tired of his job and lost his main psychological resource—hope. His condition became so serious that in one incident in which soldiers were killed, his military secretary, Azriel Nevo, and his secretary argued whether or not to update him from fear that he would collapse.²⁶ His eyesight, damaged during the stroke he had suffered, weakened and faded; his chronic leg pain exhausted him, and the pain relievers he took slowed down his reactions.²⁷ One day, while Begin was reading an article by Yoel Marcus in *Haaretz* that said the situation of the state was terrible, Dan Meridor entered his office. To Meridor's surprise, as he finished reading the article, Begin said to him, "What can we do? Marcus is right."²⁸

Begin gradually let go the reins of control and enclosed himself in silence. His passivity was rarely reflected in public, and his condition was also kept hidden. For example, at a dinner party during a private visit by former U.S. president Jimmy Carter, Begin did not eat or speak. He ignored Carter and those around him mainly because of his anger at Carter's statements condemning the war in Lebanon, but this attitude was not so much a thunderous silence as an expression of his despair and lack of will to enter into confrontations. Burg, who was also invited to the dinner, had to initiate topics for conversation.²⁹

In May, Begin was invited once again to a meeting with Reagan, but he asked to postpone it. Now he could not hide his mood,³⁰ and when he realized that there was no easy solution to the issues of Lebanon, he fell deeper into despair and sometimes did not even bother to go to the office in the mornings. He grew very thin and ceased to dye his hair as frequently as before. Batya Eldad, Aliza's friend, said to Ruth, Benny's wife (who worked with her at a welfare organization), "Begin is acting like someone who wants to die," adding that in her opinion his suffering was more intense because he was unable to express his distress. Eldad asked Ruth to convince his family to get him psychological help.³¹ Not only did Begin reject help from everyone, but it even seemed as though he was purging himself through self-punishment.³² When the interior minister suggested that he order the police to remove protesters from Shalom Achshav who had placed a board outside his house on which they continuously updated the increasing number of IDF soldiers killed in the war, Begin insisted that it was their democratic right, although it was clearly making him suffer.³³

On May 17, after lengthy talks with Amin Gemayel, U.S. secretary of state George Shultz was able to conclude a draft agreement between Israel and Lebanon in which Syria and Israel would withdraw their forces from Lebanon in exchange for a peace agreement between Israel and Lebanon. Although it was clear that Gemayel would not be able to implement the agreement and remove the Syrians from his country,

Shamir and Arens saw it as a political success. Begin, despite his aspirations to sign such an agreement with Bachir, was no longer interested. When Arens and Shamir presented him with the agreement, they argued that it was the most important achievement of the war, if only for its mission statement.[34] But Begin, who throughout his life had preceded actions with words, was not convinced. He only listened, and as he handed the signed agreement to the president, he said, "Here is the agreement that is not worth the paper it was written on." He was right. In the spring of 1984 the Lebanese government canceled the agreement, and it was never implemented.[35]

After the publication of the Kahan Commission report Begin rarely gave interviews or made public appearances, but on July 7, after having refused several times, he agreed to the request of some old friends from Herut to participate in a political debate on the war in Lebanon. Begin surprised the audience not only because of his presence but mainly because of what he said. For some reason he chose to focus on the claims of a citizen who had published a newspaper article expressing his opposition to Jabotinsky's theories. There was no doubt now that Begin was having trouble dealing with reality. "As for Lebanon—it is a tragedy," he concluded and stepped down from the podium. By purposely selecting the word "tragedy," he meant that this was a drama that would have an inevitably sad end because of wrong decisions that had led to the entanglement. It was his way of saying he could not change the results and therefore was taking responsibility for them.[36] Begin's last speech in the headquarters of the party he had founded lasted about five minutes. The participants were startled. He looked thin and pale, the jacket he wore did not match his shrinking frame, and after his speech, he sat and stared without uttering a single word.[37]

The following day *Haaretz* published an interview with Shlomo Argov, the ambassador whose attempted assassination had been the pretext for the war. Argov criticized the conduct of the war and said it had been a "military experiment."[38] Begin refused to respond to his remarks. When Begin met with Miriam Gross, the mother of a soldier from the Nahal infantry brigade who had fallen captive to Lebanese terrorists, she asked him to begin negotiations with terrorist organizations, including the PLO and Ahmed Jibril's organization. Begin remained silent and she threw herself down on the floor and burst into tears. Begin was in a hurry to get to another meeting, but he refused to leave the room until Mrs. Gross got up.[39] These moments were sad and embarrassing, and they had a crucial effect on Begin's mood. The next day the diaspora affairs adviser went to visit Begin in his office. Begin ate crackers, drank water with lemon, and said nothing. Upon leaving the room in shock, the adviser told Kadishai, "He is ill."[40]

Even Kadishai was worried. Unlike before the elections, he suggested to Begin that several public rallies be held. He clung to the hope that once again Begin would find a cure in the love of the masses. But Begin objected. He did not justify his opposition with the idea that the era of public rallies was over—as Kadishai himself had claimed before the election—but he simply believed that they would serve no purpose. Kadishai tried to persuade him, to elicit some enthusiasm, but Begin told him, "Yechiel, you cannot force someone to laugh."[41] Meridor too noted Begin's sorry state, but he was convinced that Israel had no other leader of his stature who could replace him. Kadishai still hoped he would recover. He saw Begin's loneliness after the death of his wife as the main predicament. After a consultation between Kadishai and Avraham Shapira from Agudat Israel, Shapira turned to the rabbi from Gur for advice. He returned to Kadishai and promised, "Do not worry; the rabbi said that only after Shalosh Regalim [the three pilgrimage festivals in Judaism] do you get over grief, and Begin will recover."[42]

But Begin was unable to overcome the difficulties in which he was entangled, and he no longer bothered to hide his condition. When he acceded to a request by David Danon, a former Etzel member, to host a delegation of Jews from the United States in his office, Danon was alarmed by his condition. The prime minister leaned on him, was deep in thought, and preferred to listen to those present rather than to give a speech.[43] The prime minister's condition was an open secret among his friends. Everyone knew but kept silent. The myth he had become was greater than the man. "We were simply afraid; we feared that it would make a big noise," Foreign Minister Shamir in retrospect explained the silence of the ministers, who continued to serve a malfunctioning prime minister.[44]

They were not the only ones who kept silent. During a meeting with Begin, President Chaim Herzog noticed that Begin did not respond in his usual manner. He told Klimovitski, Begin's secretary, that he thought Begin was suffering from depression and suggested either that treatment be organized for him or that the pressure he was under be minimized. Klimovitski responded the same way all of Begin's close associates responded to such comments, as if it was chutzpah to interfere in personal matters.[45]

THE DOWNFALL

But the U.S. president's request to meet with Begin could not be called chutzpah. When Begin rejected the meeting scheduled in May, the administration set a new date. But Begin did not have enough strength to meet with the president in June either, and he had no proper excuse. To avoid damaging the special relationship with the United States, Begin called the president directly and made it clear that the reason for the cancellation was personal, and he promised that a new date would be determined soon. "I just cannot go to the United States, and even Reagan understands me," he told his office.[46]

In June Begin avoided public appearances and asked that cabinet meetings take place mostly without him.[47] He was now carrying out minimum functions as the prime minister. His physical condition deteriorated further, and he now struggled even to take off his shoes.[48] His military secretary, Kadishai, and Meridor took care of most of his business. After Aliza's death, his daughter Leah moved back home. But he accepted emotional support from no one. He kept the reasons for his decline completely to himself. His secretary blamed Sharon because he had deceived him.[49] The foreign minister was convinced that the Lebanese Christians' betrayal had undermined him and attributed his tendency to withdraw to his home to his physical weakness.[50]

Although Begin's condition was well hidden from the Israeli people, the U.S. administration grew angry about the repeated delays of the meeting with Reagan. Ambassador Lewis met with Meridor to emphasize the importance of Begin's trip to the United States and urged him to encourage him to go. When Meridor spoke to Begin about it, Begin said, "You're right; the prime minister has to visit Washington." Only in retrospect did Meridor understand that Begin was trying to tell him that he was no longer suitable for office.[51] Kadishai also tried to find out, with awe and compassion, if Begin was ready to meet with Reagan, in part because he believed that the meeting would bring him back to life. "Look at my collar," Begin interrupted him; "I can fit two fingers between my throat and my collar. Can I go to Reagan in my condition?"[52]

In August Begin was due to celebrate his seventieth birthday, the date on which he once, when strong and self-confident, had promised to retire. The government secretary believed that this date was critical. He thought that Begin, who appreciated closure, would take advantage of the symbolic date and would retire in a dignified manner. But Begin was not interested in a celebratory retirement. At his office everyone made an effort to cheer him up and made him a cake. He struggled to cut the cake and his secretary helped him. The image of them slicing the cake together was published only in the weekly tabloid *Haolam Haze;* it was a symbolic picture. Begin's associates pressured him to continue, to believe, to be optimistic, but he could no longer continue. "Enough, enough," he told Kadishai in August. Kadishai, his trusted aide, held on to the hope that Begin would regain his spirits, as had happened in the past. "What's the rush? You'll overcome this," he said.[53] Begin's other associates also held to the hope in his mental strength, reflected in his ability to bounce back after all the defeats he had suffered in his life. The myth of the great and powerful Begin had not dissipated even in his old age; his departure from the scene was seen as the closing of a curtain on an era in Israel's history, on an entire camp, a sentence they all had difficulty passing on themselves.

Meanwhile, the rift in Israeli society deepened. Since June 1980, an organized group of Jews, who later became known as the Jewish Underground, had been executing terrorist attacks against Palestinians in Judea and Samaria.[54] When the group carried out an attack at the Islamic College in Hebron in August 1983, Begin had to agree with the attorney general that they must act against the group under the terms of the emergency regulations, and the events only reinforced his feeling that he had no way out.[55]

On August 27, 1983, German flags were hoisted over the Prime Minister's Office building in honor of a visit by Helmut Kohl, the new German chancellor. The night before the visit Begin decided that the following day, in the government meeting, he would announce that he wanted to resign. When his adviser on diaspora affairs entered his office, Begin said, as he looked out the window at the German flags blowing in the wind, that he had solved the dilemma of a visit from a German. Begin was clearly no longer thinking as a prime minister who had promised upon taking office that when it came to relations with Germany, he would act as a head of state; rather he now spoke to Horowitz as Begin the Jew, a civilian who did not want to shake hands with the German chancellor.[56]

The next day, the most decisive he had been for a long time, Begin got up early and stood in his office awaiting Kadishai's arrival. When Kadishai stepped into the office, he seemed satisfied with Begin's appearance, as he looked much better than before; at that moment Begin announced, "It's good you've come. I want to tell you that today I will quit my job."[57] Kadishai was the first to hear of his decision, but he was not surprised. He assumed that Begin would have the final word on the matter, and perhaps he too was relieved. He did not say a thing about it to anyone. On his way to the meeting in which Begin was going to tell the ministers that he was resigning, he ran into Matityahu Shmuelevitz, the director of the Prime Minister's Office, who told Kadishai that it would be a long meeting as it would deal with the economic crisis. Kadishai said, "No, it will be a short meeting." Only then could he no longer hold in the news and informed Begin's military secretary of the expected announcement. He too remained silent. Meanwhile Kadishai updated the government secretary. Meridor was concerned and would not give up hope. As he entered the conference room, Kadishai sent Yaakov Meridor a note saying he would try to convince Begin to postpone his decision.

The other ministers knew nothing about the projected retirement. For them this was supposed to be just another regular meeting. In the middle of the meeting an argument erupted between Sharon and Arens, and Sharon stormed out of the room and slammed the door behind him. Begin did not respond. He allowed the ministers to say what they had to say, and when they had finished, he asked for permission to speak.[58]

"The reason for my announcement is personal," he began. "But I feel I can no longer wait to deliver it, so I will make it according to the law. First of all, I ask for forgiveness, absolution, and atonement. Whether it will be granted to me, I do not know. . . . Gentlemen and friends, I am informing the government of my intention to resign. I did not think I would come here today. I came specifically to deliver this message because only then can the legal process begin. I repeat: I can no longer fulfill this role." He used the words "this role" almost in disgust, quietly, and in full confidence of his decision. Minister Meridor interrupted, "Mr. Prime Minister, I suggest the government does not accept your announcement." Begin was quick to interrupt his old friend: "Yaakov, there is no legal possibility that the government will not accept my announcement."[59]

Later many ministers, whether fearing for their political careers or for Begin himself, tried to convince him to retract his resignation. "We have followed you through thick and thin; take it back," Shamir said. "Sir, all members of the government request that you reject this announcement, that you reconsider," Justice Minister Moshe Nissim said. Yitzhak Modai could not resist mentioning that Begin's resigning would harm "our" shared objectives, meaning the Likud's rule. Tsipori was more direct: "The government may be put in Peres's hands." David Levy said, "The people love you." And Eliezer Shostak, a veteran Revi-

Begin raising the Euroleague Basketball Cup with Lou Silver, Maccabi Tel Aviv basketball player (right), March 1981. (Courtesy of GPO.)

IDF chief of staff Rafael Eitan (right) welcoming Begin upon his return from the United States March 1981. (Behind Begin, Yitzhak Shamir.) (Courtesy of GPO.)

Begin and IDF chief of staff Rafael Eitan at a press conference following the bombing of the nuclear reactor in Iraq, June 1981. (Courtesy of GPO.)

Begin (left) visiting the city of Ariel during the 1981 campaign. (On Begin's left, David Levy; on Levy's left, Yaakov Meridor.) (Courtesy of GPO.)

Begin bowing before President Yitzhak Navon and his wife Ofira just before his second inauguration, July 1981. (Courtesy of GPO.)

Begin (left) toasting Ariel Sharon (second from right) on his first day as minister of defense, August 1981. (At Sharon's left, his wife Lily.) (Courtesy of GPO.)

Begin with U.S. president Ronald Reagan at the White House, September 1981. (Courtesy of White House.)

Begin alone in his wheelchair during a Knesset discussion on annexing the Golan Heights, December 1981. (Courtesy of GPO.)

Begin (right) and Sharon (center) visiting Beaufort Castle after its occupation, Lebanon, 1982. (Courtesy of IDF.)

Begin (at table to right) testifying about the Sabra and Shatila massacre, November 1982. (On his left, Dan Meridor, secretary of state; on his right, Kadishai, bureau chief.) (Courtesy of GPO.)

Begin celebrating the Mimuna (a Moroccan Jewish festival), April 1983. (Courtesy of GPO.)

Begin (standing) in his last coalition meeting after resigning from the government, August 30, 1983. (Courtesy of GPO.)

Dan Meridor (center left) and Benny Begin (center right) in the Knesset, December, 1995. (Courtesy of GPO.)

Begin (now seventy-five and aided by daughter Leah) during a memorial service for his wife Aliza, August 1988. (Courtesy of GPO.)

Tens of thousands pay their last respects at Begin's funeral, March 9, 1992. (Courtesy of GPO.)

Begin on his birthday, August 1983. (His secretary, Yona Klimovitski, helps him cut the cake.) (Courtesy of GPO.)

sionist, to everyone's surprise, responded: "I'm afraid your position is correct; it's hard for me to ask you to retract it." Begin listened to everyone with a blank face, thanked them, and said, "Do you think I didn't consider it before? The session is closed."[60] He hurried to closet himself in his room and drafted his letter of resignation.

The government secretary provoked consternation among reporters when he told them that "The prime minister has announced his resignation." There was a great commotion, but Begin just wanted to leave the Prime Minister's Office. Many ministers chased him, as though they wanted to see him off one last time. He said a weak goodbye to the photographers who were already waiting near his car and sat down in the back.[61] Begin was operating out of a sense of urgency, like someone trying to get rid of a heavy burden.[62] As he went on his way, ministers gathered in Kadishai's room to obtain information about the resignation.

Kadishai did not know more than the ministers. "Begin said he can't take it anymore," he explained. But there were ministers who insisted on phoning him at home, including Burg. On the phone Begin only said again, "I can't take it anymore."[63] Kadishai concluded as follows: "Apart from the claim that he regretted the Lebanon war and the peace treaty with Egypt, all things said about his motives for resigning are true. Everything caused him to physically weaken. He said, 'I can't [take it] anymore.' . . . So naturally the next question is: But why couldn't he take it anymore? My answer is that he could not continue. Why? Because he was a perfectionist. He wanted to do things perfectly, and he felt that he no longer had the energy—neither to meet Reagan nor to appear before an audience nor to have a serious discussion with the gusto he was used to. So he retired from political life and went home."[64]

Begin truly could not take it anymore, but the main reason for his retirement was repentance—knowing that he was unable to end the war the way he wanted, the way he had dreamed. However, he believed that imposing responsibility on Sharon would increase his negligence. And his conscience tormented him. He knew that as prime minister he should bear "another gram of responsibility," and he therefore refused to disclose the details behind his decision to resign. But many ministers and associates hoped that this time, as in 1951 and in 1966, he would yield to their pleas and return to center stage.

After the announcement of Begin's retirement his adherents suggested that owing to the shock thousands of fans would flock to the Prime Minister's Residence and demand that he retract his resignation.[65] By noon over two hundred people had gathered there, and some carried signs reading, "Begin—you are our king." But as evening descended, the masses had not turned up, and the few who gathered near the house went their separate ways. It seemed that those who loved Begin were exhausted and understood his motives. By that night, the only people who remained were the protesters from Shalom Achshav, who continued to note the number of casualties of the war.

The next day, the coalition members met in the Knesset, and many of Begin's friends from the underground joined them.[66] Begin decided to attend the meeting. The rumor of his arrival made everyone a little optimistic about the possibility that he might retract his resignation. He arrived wearing a dark jacket over an open-collared white shirt, and it was apparent that he felt relieved. He did not come in order to talk about his motives or to be talked out of resigning, but to take his leave of politics and the Knesset he loved so dearly, maybe even to savor his final moments in the Knesset, in which he felt so much at home. "There is only one reason I cannot continue," he said. "Please let me go to the president." Minister Meridor was quick to respond again, "You said 'Please let me.' Well, we will not." Begin smiled at him. "Yaakov, it will not help," he said. Little attention was paid to the dialogue between Meridor and Begin and more to the minister who had stormed out of the cabinet meeting on the day Begin announced his resignation and was now again present.

Ariel Sharon was well aware that Begin's associates held him responsible for the retirement, and he also had something to say. "With all due sorrow, the prime minister's resignation does not mean the dissolution of the party," he concluded. He asked Begin, in his characteristic level-headed manner, to technically delay his resignation so that it would be possible to form a new government.[67] It was clear that Begin was disappointed by Sharon's comments, but he did not express it. He shook hands with everyone and never returned to the Knesset.

Sharon's remarks were politically important. Because of changes that had taken place in the factions during Begin's term, Sharon feared that the president would ask Peres to form a new government. For this reason Begin agreed to delay the delivery of his letter of resignation to the president until the Likud could choose a new candidate.

Begin continued to serve officially from August 28 until Yitzhak Shamir replaced him on October 10, but he remained at home. He dissociated himself from the ministers and even refused to meet with Defense Minister Arens. He ran the country through his secretaries. It was clear that he was fed up with his job and did not want to make even practical decisions. "Use your own discretion. If it seems okay, then it's okay," he told Nevo. The intelligence reports brought to him for review were returned without comments. He suffered from a skin rash, which was perhaps psychosomatic, and because he could not shave, he would not even go out beyond the yard of his residence.[68]

Two Likud members were candidates to replace Begin: David Levy, who declared himself Begin's heir, and Shamir, who avoided personal statements but said he could lead the government properly. Begin refused to voice support for either of them. Although he respected Levy in many ways, he used to say in private conversations, "He only knows French," as if to politely express his dissatisfaction that the deputy prime minister did not know English well. He believed that the country would benefit more from Shamir's skills. Most of his associates in the party chose Shamir.

On September 15 Begin was due to report to the president to submit his letter of resignation, but still he refused to leave his house. The government secretary was surprised. It was not typical of Begin, who all his life had attributed much importance to ceremonies. His relatives tried to convince him that he was worthy of stepping down from the stage in a more elegant, formal manner. But Begin insisted that the beard he had grown to cover the rash on his face did not allow him to leave the house. It was the first time a resigning prime minister refused to personally submit his letter of resignation to the president. When a loophole in the law was found, it was decided that Meridor would submit the letter for him. His close friends believed that he would not be satisfied with just the resignation and feared that he literally wanted to disappear.

The government secretary submitted the letter three times to the president, at the request of photographers who documented the scene. Now Begin was officially no longer prime minister. Now began the last chapter in his life's journey. The next day, the eve of Yom Kippur, Begin did not pray at the synagogue.

TWENTY

SELF-FLAGELLATION

Yaakov Meridor did not hesitate for a second before he picked up the phone to call the Prime Minister's Residence in late 1983. It was after midnight, but he could not resist. It had been almost four decades since he and Begin had served together in Etzel, and he wanted to report to his "commander" about the historical turning point—that their adversary from the days of the Resistance, Yitzhak Shamir, one of the three leaders of Lehi, had been elected to lead the Likud.

To some extent, Begin and Shamir respected each other. They began their public careers in the Beitar movement, and their loyalty to the Land of Israel was never questioned. But Begin was motivated by justice as he perceived it, while Shamir was motivated by effectiveness. They also differed in their nature, as Begin saw Shamir as a gray man who was not destined for great things, while Shamir was unimpressed by Begin's tendency to be emotional and thought he attached more importance to manners than he did to actions.

Meridor believed that Begin would not fall asleep before he knew who had been elected to replace him. Like many Begin supporters in the Likud, he preferred the uncharismatic Shamir, in part because he believed that his tenure would serve as a sort of surety until Begin decided to return to the political arena. But he was wrong. Begin had dissociated himself from politics, his life's joy, in one blow. He did not intend to return to public activity, and on the day of the election he was in fact preoccupied with the importation of religious artifacts from Poland to Israel, and he went to bed early. He listened impatiently to Meridor's report on Shamir's victory.[1] The following day, when Shamir phoned him to get his blessing, Begin merely wished him success. He was reluctant to be overly effusive not because he was opposed to Shamir's election, nor because he wanted to hurt him, but because he thought it would be improper to express his opinion on the matter. In the first weeks after his resignation Begin was constantly asked to publicly express support for Shamir in order to strengthen his position, but he rejected all requests. "I'm not a king, and I have no heirs," he insisted, while Shamir himself declared that the leadership's reins were a "surety" in his hands.[2]

Begin's comments were brief at the time, just as when he had said, "I can't take it anymore," a brief response that expressed all the reasons that had forced him to retire. He could no longer lead the people and could not bear the personal failure. He shared his thoughts only with his family, with Dan Meridor, and with Kadishai, and even with them he shared only some of his thoughts.[3] His withdrawal, his guilt over the fact that under his leadership Israel was caught in an impasse in Lebanon, his etiquette, Aliza's death—all these contributed to the emotional whirlwind in which he was trapped. The respect his associates held for him and the aura that had formed around him made it difficult for them to ask the difficult questions, the intimate questions.[4] However, it was clear that he was bitter and despairing. His performance in his last months in office embarrassed him. He knew that until he had mustered the courage to resign, he had functioned only partially. He knew that he had not led his government properly and that he had become embroiled in a war he did not desire, and he knew it was his responsibility. Furthermore, he knew that those around him had witnessed his deterioration, yet none of them had dared say a word and actually had helped him to retire with dignity.

There were those, including Kadishai and Meridor, who continued to believe that there was no substitute for Begin in his generation, despite his obvious weakness, but many ministers also benefited from his condition. Begin felt exploited, especially after his decision to retire. He realized that his poor functioning was a relief for many of the politicians surrounding him. But he was mostly overwhelmed with pain because of his entanglement in Lebanon. He never regretted the underlying strategic idea of Operation Peace for Galilee, which became a war, but his retirement was an act of contrition, of taking full responsibility for the results—an act that contained both the sentencing and the self-flagellation. Just as in his youth he had considered divorcing his wife so that she could lead a normal life after he was sentenced to prison in the Soviet Union, in his old age he did not deviate from his habit of taking responsibility. But in the Soviet Union Begin had still had optimism about the future, and now he had no hope left. Now he asked for nothing but to soothe his aching soul. But because he struggled to cut the deep roots he had planted in politics, he understood that he needed to withdraw completely. Only then, he knew, would his disengagement be complete.

The mythological Begin turned overnight from an admirable and vital figure to an old and dysfunctional man. The man for whom speeches had been his daily bread and who had even violated safety precautions during the underground days in order to be with people was now exhausted and asked to be excused from publicly expressing his opinions, to utter not one unnecessary word. Begin had been a public figure almost all his life, and when he decided to break away from the public, it was as though he had simultaneously decided to break away from life itself. His acquaintances did not know him anymore, and those who tried to get him to talk were all disappointed.[5] When Burg called for a second time, Begin invited him to his home, mainly to get rid of the nuisance. Burg decided to let go.[6] Similarly Begin agreed to meet with Geula Cohen, and she told him that an important historical role was still ahead of him. Begin smiled wearily.[7] He did not want to express his feelings and reiterated the same "I can't take it anymore" to all who came to call. After a while the number of people who wished to talk to him diminished, as he refused to talk to most of them.

The first anniversary of Aliza's death came in November, two months after Begin's formal resignation, and he had to decide whether to expose himself to the public or to persist in his withdrawal. He chose not to participate in the memorial service. His family said he did not want to be seen with the beard he had grown due to his rash and that made it difficult for him to shave. He told Kadishai that the beard might appear as a sign of mourning. His son explained his surprising absence for "personal reasons," and rumors about his condition grew.

Despite the mystery of his resignation, one thing was clear: Begin desperately wanted to be left alone. He also knew he would find no peace as long as he lived in the official Prime Minister's Residence. But because he had never dealt with the management of a home—nor had he accumulated assets—he could not immediately leave the official residence. The apartment at 1 Rosenbaum Street, which he had held under rent control, had been sold, and his friends and family started searching for a suitable apartment for him in which his privacy would not be invaded. In December, Chaim Corfu, the transportation minister and a former Etzel member, found a suitable place. An apartment had been vacated in the building in which he lived on Shlomo Tzemach Street in Jerusalem. The rent was $500 a month. Members of Begin's family signed the lease.

Begin's younger daughter, Leah, a stewardess with El Al who had lived with him since Aliza's death, also moved to the apartment on Shlomo Tzemach Street. The withdrawn and shy Leah had never married, a fact that had troubled Aliza prior to her death.[8] Begin too was unhappy over this, but he respected her privacy and never bothered her on the matter. They got along well, and in the evenings they watched videos Leah would take out from a nearby library.

But even in the new apartment Begin found no solace. The newspapers Kadishai brought him daily presented a bleak picture. In 1984 there were so many scandals having to do with the economy, defense, and public integrity that it seemed that the country would collapse. The stock market crash, corruption in the coalition, and political difficulties had a terrible effect on Begin's mood, but what bothered him most was the situation in Lebanon. The daily reports of more casualties among Israeli soldiers, as well as bereaved families' continuous accusations against him, which did not stop even after his resignation and impinged on his honor, turned his dissociation into seclusion. Lacking Aliza's support and still growing physically weaker and isolated emotionally, Begin no longer had any motivation to recover, and he could respond only as he had been educated, in the spirit of the Polish nobility, with an acceptance of responsibility and self-flagellation.[9] This was how he sought redemption.

Since his fall from greatness, it was natural that Begin's spirits would be marred, but no one expected him to be taken over by darkness and gloom. The contrast between the man who several months earlier had been the strongest in the country and the pale and weak man who spent most of his days in pajamas, rarely leaving his room, was terrible. He was weak and his achievements were a thing of the past, while his present was full of failures. This was not the way he had imagined his departure from the political stage during his twenty-seven years in the opposition. He wanted to be remembered as a hero, a leader revered by his people because of his achievements. But he had left behind him a divided nation, immersed in a war with no end in sight, an embattled government, and a shaky economy. The admiration he needed like he needed air to breathe had vanished as if it had never been. All his life he had believed in grandiose deeds, majestic and glorious, and in his imagination his retirement should have been a successful conclusion to his years of action—otherwise he would not have announced in the early 1970s that he planned to retire from public life and devote himself to writing his memoirs. There were those who continued to shower him with love. "It's not you who is responsible; it is your role," his former secretary told him, but Begin was inconsolable.[10] Kadishai and Meridor suggested that he realize his plan to write his memoirs. "Soon—shortly. It's not time," he would say to evade them.

Begin was comfortable in his solitude. When he needed something, he would ask his family or Kadishai to get it. He felt that the politicians who still sought to see him wanted to exploit him. Kadishai explained that he did not meet with them because he feared they would use him for their personal interest. "I know what will happen when they leave the apartment," he said. "This politician will say I agreed with him, and that politician will say that Begin, on the contrary, agreed with him. And I wish neither to deny nor to confirm nor to argue. I will not be Ben Gurion, who continued to stir up trouble even after his retirement."[11]

Routine gradually took over Begin's daily agenda. He walked around the apartment in pajamas or trousers and a robe when he had visitors, and he often lay in bed and read.[12] He entertained his acquaintances in the living room. For lunch he ate chicken and potatoes prepared by his maid. As mentioned, the only people who met with him regularly, apart from his family—his children Benny and Chasia visited him almost every day—were Kadishai, who brought him newspapers and letters, and Dan Meridor. Meridor became his loyal friend and updated him on the happenings in the government. There were those who wondered about their relationship, as Meridor had been appointed government secretary only eighteen months before Begin's retirement. Few knew about the close connection that had lasted for years between the two families (when Aliza had immigrated, she had lived with Meridor's grandmother for several months). Their work together in the government bridged the age gap between Begin and Meridor. Begin treated him like a father. After Begin's retirement Meridor hardly ever missed a weekly meeting with him on Shabbat evening. Begin talked to him about his feelings, his attitude toward Sharon, politicians, his public policies, and his state of mind, and shared with him his experiences from the distant past. The reverence in which Meridor held Begin made him privy to Begin's confidences without any fear he would disclose them. Meridor listened, valued their conversations, and updated Begin discreetly about Shamir's government.

Begin asked Kadishai to turn away most people who wanted to meet with him. He himself never said "Never" but would respond to callers with "Now is not the time."[13] His phone number was known only to a few, and most conversations were coordinated with Kadishai. But sometimes Begin had to respond to callers, and he did so with great reluctance. "Hello, how are you? Thank you so much for calling, thank you" was how he started and ended many calls.[14] He agreed to meet only with his old friends. Corfu and his wife, his neighbors, used to visit him every Saturday night after he moved to Tzemach Street. Corfu's wife would bring a honey cake she had baked especially for him. They were occasionally joined by Yaakov Meridor and his wife Tzippora; Meir Kahn, who had taken care of all his needs in the underground; Rachel Kremerman, whose husband Yosef was among the founders of Herut; and Esther Raziel-Naor. These were intimate encounters of old friends whom Begin counted on. The members of this group were all made of the same stuff, and they did not dare ask him why he had opted for complete withdrawal or what his behavior meant. "He chose not to bring up the subject; it was his secret," concluded Kahn.[15] In the world in which he lived, an expression of weakness was shameful and mental health was a private matter. The national aspect was more important than the personal, and in their eyes, Begin was first and foremost a national symbol. They understood that although Aliza's death weighed on him, it was not the primary reason for his retirement and seclusion.[16] Although he had lost his emotional support and joy for life along with his wife, he avoided talking about her. He occasionally mentioned her name, yet as the memories floated to the surface, he was quick to mention, in Yiddish, that in Brisk they used to say that one did not "toy with the dead."[17]

Over time the "Saturday night club" was formed, a prestigious group of Begin's confidants and loved ones. The difference between those close to him and those who remained distant caused many hurt feelings, like the differences formed during the opposition when he hosted his friends on Saturdays. Harry Horowitz, Begin's adviser on diaspora affairs, became angry with Kadishai because he (Harry) could not understand why for over forty years he had been able to speak to Begin about anything and suddenly he could not. Kadishai suggested he call Begin himself. Begin invited Horowitz to join the "club." But even as the group expanded, the most intriguing question was still not raised: Why had Begin chosen to retire? The Saturday gatherings focused mainly on what was happening in the world. Begin was extremely interested in the changes occurring in the Soviet Union and often spoke about Nelson Mandela. Nobody dared speak to him about current events in Israel.[18] Because Begin did not hide his moods, they refrained from asking him questions that might be considered an invasion of privacy.[19] Thus the issue of his self-imposed confinement was not resolved.[20]

In retrospect Begin's seclusion was not surprising. He tended to shy away from society after a failure. This had happened after the *Altalena* affair and after the second election debacle. It had also happened after he was criticized in the 1966 Herut convention. His mood swings were a well-known response to his public struggles.[21] Therefore many people compared him to Shabtai Tzvi.[22] What surprised his friends, however, was the intensity of his withdrawal, as several months had passed and Begin had still not recovered.

The truth is that Begin had not meant to withdraw for so long. He had initially hoped that there would be a change in his condition and thought he could sequester himself until he recovered. But the longer he remained silent and sheltered, the deeper his isolation grew. At first, he believed he would devote himself to writing his memoirs once he recovered. He had already chosen a name for the book—*From Holocaust to Rebirth*—in which he wanted to incorporate his life story with the history of Israel, starting from the 1930s. He told Kadishai that the first part—the days of the underground—had already been documented in his book *The Revolt*. He intended to complete the rest of the narrative and said, "I've got it all in my head."[23] But what was in his head, although he had a phenomenal memory, was no longer enough. He lacked the passion to live and the ability to carry out his plans. His secretary guessed he did not write it because the end of the story was not worthwhile. Unlike *The Revolt*, which ended with the establishment of the state, the book he planned to write would not have the happy end he had dreamed of: the elimination of the PLO and a peace agreement with Lebanon.[24]

Meanwhile, the IDF was finding it difficult to extricate itself from the mud of Lebanon, the peace agreement signed in 1984 had been canceled, the stock market had collapsed, and Begin's public image had become that of a captain who had abandoned his sinking ship. The man who had always drawn his strength from the feeling that he was just and moral, who believed that divine providence had ordained him a role in history, was ready, owing to his failure, to sacrifice himself and his reputation and accept his punishment.[25] His conscience guided him to accept total responsibility. Thus he did not explain his detachment and refrained from imposing blame on others as he could have.

The coalition Shamir had formed was disbanded a few months later, and an election date was set for July 1984. In meetings Shamir held across the country he was greeted with calls of "Begin! Begin!" but these calls no longer concerned the former prime minister. Begin refused Shamir's request to make him the last candidate on the Likud's Knesset list (traditionally a "place of honor").[26] His detachment from the party remained unexplained, even when senior Likud members called to tell him that without his public support Israel was in danger. He was familiar with this argument; he himself had used it to convince people to join the party. But he stuck to his decision—complete disengagement—and was preoccupied mainly with the physical therapy that enabled him to walk more often and more steadily.[27]

Only when a reporter called Begin on election day did his political drive kick in, and he said that he supported Shamir and the Likud. But from the Likud's perspective, it was too late. Before the elections Yaakov Meridor had also resigned from the Knesset, and now the curtain had fallen almost entirely on the senior politicians who had been among Begin's friends and contemporaries. Begin did not even consider voting, and his son Benny yet again said it was for "personal reasons." The Likud members were angry. But he could not act as an outside observer. His identification with the movement, with the party, was so absolute that he felt that if he was no longer a part of it, the party itself was as good as gone for him. Unlike the times before he had retired from the premiership, this time Begin was not only fed up with current events, but had also lost his drive to make a mark on the past, thus going against his well-known fondness for closure. He was often confronted with historians who wanted to ask questions—among others, historians who were researching the history of Ben Gurion and Etzel—but he asked Kadishai to politely turn them away.[28]

In August 1984 Begin turned seventy-one, and his associates sought to cheer him up. But when they phoned to wish him a happy birthday, he hardly responded. His silence expressed his agony. These were the most difficult days of his life; he was sliding down a steep slope, and his growing disconnection was taking its toll. He was examined every month by Doctor Efraim Meltzer from Sha'are Tzedek Hospital. He rarely ate, a fact that contributed to his poor health. As mentioned above, he had had a stroke and suffered from heart disease and diabetes, and his vision was damaged. His pelvic fracture also continued to bother him, and he often needed painkillers to ease his discomfort. He was physically weak and felt more comfortable at home.[29] In addition, he was preparing for prostate surgery.[30] His health problems were interlinked with his low spirits, and he sometimes struggled to conduct a short conversation on the phone. When Batya Eldad phoned and asked why he had resigned, he replied, "How long can I continue to debase myself?"[31] This response revealed how much he was aware of his failure, and he saw no point in debating the issue.

In late 1984 Begin underwent successful prostate surgery. After leaving the hospital, he agreed to talk to the many journalists who had gathered at the entrance, said he was well, and thanked them for their interest. Physiotherapy treatments also improved his mood, as he could now walk much further. On November 24 the annual memorial service marking Aliza's death took place, and Begin believed that owing to the successful surgery, he could attend a public event for the first time since he had retired. He went to the cemetery accompanied by his son and daughters, wearing a black hat, a dark suit, and matching tie. He also made sure to shave. While his son said Kaddish, Begin simply stared, and after the prayer he agree to shake hands with the participants and thank them for coming. It was difficult not to notice the huge gap between the resolute prime minister and the old Jew who wanted to avoid contact with the participants at the ceremony. Soon after, he returned to his apartment and to his daily routine.

Yet in 1985 Begin was overcome with passion. Operation Moses, in which thousands of Ethiopian Jews were brought to Israel, excited him, and he wanted to hear about it from a primary source. After the elections, when Hamaarach and the Likud received the same amount of votes, the parties agreed to form a unity government, with each party's leader serving as prime minister in rotation. Shimon Peres acted as prime minister until 1986 and appointed a new government secretary to replace Meridor, who was elected as an MK for the Likud. Therefore, to get updates Begin invited Azriel Nevo, his former military secretary, to his apartment. Nevo had opposed the war in Lebanon and believed that Sharon had misled Begin; therefore he was determined to find out the reasons for Begin's seclusion and his opinions about what had happened during the war. Begin lay in bed but was alert. After some polite small talk they went right to the point. Nevo answered Begin's questions about Operation Moses, but when Nevo tried to divert the conversation to the subject that interested him, Begin interrupted: "I thank you very much for coming. Say hello to the family from me." Nevo took the hint and quickly said goodbye.[32] Thus with cold politeness, Begin blocked any possibility of a personal conversation.[33]

Two years after his retirement Begin was in better shape, both physically and emotionally, and he began to adapt to his lifestyle. He agreed to widen his circle of visitors and even agreed to meet with politicians he trusted. But the conversations still did not deviate from the subjects he agreed to discuss. "Do not introduce current events" was the condition Kadishai set for anyone who wanted to meet with him.[34] This condition was a mark of Begin's persistence; he was determined to dissociate even when he felt better. In fact he created a new world with strict rules, and only those who did not violate them were allowed to see him. He did not want to deal with loud and vocal admirers or bereaved mothers blaming him for the failures of the war. He had had enough struggles before his retirement.

In October 1986 Shamir returned to serve as prime minister, in accordance with the rotation agreement with Hamaarach. Shamir still attached public importance to his link with Begin, and this time he received his blessing. From that moment on, Shamir would visit Begin once or twice a year, mostly upon his return from a state visit abroad. Shamir, who was not one of Begin's admirers, raised only general issues during their conversations, in part because he knew that Begin did not want to talk about what was happening in politics and in part because the introspective Shamir did not ask personal questions.[35]

Begin's life ran on a fixed schedule, and what seemed to others like withdrawal was for him refuge. As the days passed, his mood improved, and he gradually expanded the range of topics he was willing to talk about. His mind was clear, his memory was sharp, and he talked a lot about the past. During meetings with his associates on Saturday nights he began to retell the stories of his talks with Carter and of the autonomy agreement, though his nostalgia was confined to his first term in office. His sense of relief was manifested in his willingness to express opinions regarding political matters. In 1986, he told Corfu that he opposed a change in the electoral system from proportional to regional for fear of an erosion in the power of the big parties and the creation of many small parties that would represent marginal sectors.[36] When a reporter called him about the right wing's demand to pardon the Jewish underground militants in exchange for freeing terrorists, he said that he "opposed this linkage."[37] In 1987, when Foreign Minister Shimon Peres and King Hussein of Jordan signed the London Agreement—which proposed a Jordanian-Palestinian confederation in the territories and a peace treaty with Israel—Begin expressed his opposition to the agreement, as he believed it would pave the way for a Palestinian state. When the Intifada broke out in December of that year, he opposed the Palestinians' right to self-determination and saw their struggle as part of the Arab-Israeli conflict. He was particularly angry at the comparison between Etzel's activities and those of the Intifada, arguing that the goal of the Palestinians—"Eretz Israeli Arabs" in his words—was the indiscriminate killing of Jews, while Etzel had tried to avoid harming innocent civilians. "They are not liberators of the homeland as we were," he stated.[38]

As Begin's condition improved, Horowitz tried again to convince him to write his memoirs. He even offered to record his words on tape to avoid the agonizing process of writing. But Begin still refused. One day he told Horowitz about a book he had been reading that documented the correspondence between Franklin D. Roosevelt and Winston Churchill, and the enthusiastic Horowitz suggested that Begin should publish his correspondence with Sadat. Begin didn't reject the proposal but wondered if there were enough letters for a book. Horowitz hurried to get the letters from the Prime Minister's Office and returned with the assurance that there was enough material and that the letters were interesting. Begin asked to review them. Contrary to the belief of many on the Right—including Geula Cohen—that one of the reasons Begin retired was his regret for returning Sinai, he was proud of the peace agreement with Egypt to his last day and regarded it as an achievement of historic importance. Three weeks later, Begin told Horowitz that the letters were indeed interesting but were not enough for a book. He even rejected the proposal to add both the leaders' speeches, starting from the beginning of the negotiations until the signing of the agreement. "Maybe in the future," he said.[39]

Since Begin's withdrawal his relationship with his younger daughter, Leah, had grown closer. As mentioned, the two would watch videos together when she returned home from work. Leah chose the films herself—Begin did not have any preferences.[40] His relationship with the rest of his family was close as well. They continued to insist that his seclusion was "not strange," as his public role was over and he did not want to be exposed to the public any longer. Benny added that just as

Begin had known how to restrain himself during his days in the underground and the many years he had waited in the opposition, he had managed to overcome his political impulses and end his life as one of the people. His family refused offers to be interviewed about him.[41]

Although he had recovered physically, Begin left his home only to participate in the memorial service for his wife Aliza, and immediately after the service ended he hurried to return home. Sometimes it seemed as though the public had forgotten him, although from time to time the media would discuss "the riddle of Begin." They attributed his silence to (among other things) his regret about the war in Lebanon, his feelings that he had been deceived, Aliza's death,[42] and his recurring depression. He did not respond to rumors about his condition, nor to speculation about the reasons for his silence, but he knew his seclusion provoked curiosity.

It would be difficult to disregard the sense that Begin's behavior was connected to the manic-depressive streak that had run in his personality since youth. He often shifted between depression and elation; the decisions he made and the actions he executed reflected his mood. As in the case of many creators, Begin's political creations mirrored the turns in his soul and were a direct expression of his strengths and weaknesses. Manic depression itself is a genetic disease and may worsen or improve with professional treatment. When a patient is in the manic stage, he may feel he has unrealistic powers, characterized by aggressive behavior, self-confidence, and euphoria. Alternatively, when the patient is suffering from depression, he may experience mood swings and irregular sleeping habits that bring on fatigue and a decline in energy. The patient then feels a sense of worthlessness and guilt, as well as a decreased ability to concentrate or think. Doctors believe that during these times the level of anxiety increases, alongside thoughts on the worthlessness of life and thoughts about death. It could be said that Begin's depressive tendencies were aggravated in his old age, and the opportunity old age offers to evaluate one's life did not help him. From Begin's life during this period—isolation, withdrawal, and a loss of interest in current events—a strong link can be seen between his behavior and the patterns of manic depression. But it is important to note that he was neither diagnosed nor treated by a psychiatrist, making it difficult to establish such an assessment; therefore, it should be treated with relative caution.

TWENTY-ONE

"SHARON WAS AFRAID OF ME"

Begin had never liked Sharon. After his resignation as prime minister he still appreciated Sharon's military contribution to the State of Israel but had reservations about the measures he took to achieve his goals, as well as his lack of commitment to the people around him and to moral values. Begin saw Sharon as an uninhibited manipulator, and when his name came up in conversations, he would point out that when Sharon left the army and entered politics, he joined the Liberal Party because "Sharon was afraid of me. He knew I was strong and preferred to avoid me."[1] The more Begin emphasized how much Sharon was afraid of him in the 1970s, the more he crystallized his opinion on their performance together in the second government: Sharon had taken advantage of his weakness, but Begin still emphasized the fear he imposed on him when he was at his peak, rather than Sharon's ability to do as he pleased when Begin weakened. Begin coped with his failure through the things that remained unsaid, not by what he uttered.

In 1984, Sharon filed a libel suit in a New York court against *Time* magazine, which had claimed that a secret appendix to the Kahan Commission report stated that he had spoken with members of the Gemayel family about the need to avenge Bachir Gemayel's death. In January 1985, the court ruled that the information published by *Time* was incorrect and that the publication reflected negligence but not malice. (Because U.S. law requires proof of malice, the court denied Sharon's claim for compensation of $50 million.) Sharon saw this as a victory in principle, and Begin, who had followed the case, was also pleased with the result, as he saw Sharon's victory as his own and the entire state of Israel's; he believed the moral stain with which Israel had been tainted after the Sabra and Shatila massacre had slightly faded. He sent a telegram congratulating Sharon, who was in New York. The following day he once again strayed from the patterns he had established and gave an interview to Israel Radio. He told the interviewer that Sharon's victory was very important and that it was an "absolute moral victory."[2]

The support Begin expressed for Sharon, a cunning politician who had contributed significantly to Begin's resignation as prime minister, was surprising, as Begin knew that the former defense minister had issued commands during the war without his approval. But because the Left in Israel, in the Arab world, and in the West saw Sharon as the symbol of Israel's responsibility for the war, Begin had no choice but to side publicly with him.[3] His support for Sharon was also a result of his mental complexity and his belief that he needed to distinguish between the need to protect a national symbol and his disregard for Sharon as a human being. His response was in line with Jabotinsky's formalities: the acceptance of responsibility and support for one's subordinates. There was yet another consideration: had Begin blamed Sharon or washed his hands of him, he would have perpetuated his own image as a weak prime minister who had been forced into unwanted military moves.

In early August 1987 Sharon phoned Begin and told him that he intended to give a comprehensive lecture at Tel Aviv University, marking five years since the outbreak of the war in Lebanon, and that he intended to give his full version of the events leading up to the war. He added that he would be happy to show Begin the text and hear his comments. Begin told him politely that he did not want to see him but that he would look into the text. Sharon sent the text to Begin by courier. Begin was disgusted that the country had to continue to deal with the war, and despite the curiosity Sharon's lecture stirred in the public and in the media, Begin did not even bother to review the text when it arrived. Because he did not hear from Begin, Sharon assumed that he had approved it, acting just as he had during his tenure as defense minister.

Sharon spent many months preparing the lecture and saw it as a golden opportunity to present the truth.[4] It had been understood from Sharon's earlier comments that the operation in Lebanon had turned into a war because of developments on the ground. However, in the lecture Sharon declared publicly for the first time that the government had actually planned to move beyond the forty-kilometer strip that was purportedly the limit of the operation. He claimed that the target of the operation had been planned according to the "Rolling Oranim Order"—that is, the invasion of Beirut had been preplanned and implemented in stages, and he said explicitly that "removal of the artillery threat on the Galilee" was considered merely a "minimum achievement."[5]

Sharon's lecture made the headlines and generated a great deal of controversy. When Channel 1 broadcast the lecture on the news, Begin was already deeply asleep. His son Benny, who was in Be'er Sheva, immediately understood that Sharon's version of events was completely different from his father's and from the operation order drafted in the cabinet meeting on June 5, 1982. Benny was suspicious of Sharon's version not only because he was the prime minister's son, but also because he had been called up during the war as a reserve intelligence officer and realized that the events on the ground did not match his father's goals and declarations. But before Sharon had made plans to deliver a lecture, Benny had not intended to publicly disclose his conclusion that Sharon had misled his father and gotten him into a war he did not want. Sharon's lecture, though, was the last straw for Benny, and he saw it as an opportune moment to speak out. Two days after Sharon's lecture he visited his father and asked what he thought of Sharon's remarks. Begin insisted that the published version of the lecture was the result of a misunderstanding and that it was impossible that Sharon had initially planned to enter Beirut. Although he believed that Sharon had embroiled him and the army in actions that could have been prevented, he did not believe that he had planned to do so. Benny explained that that was exactly what was implied in the lecture, and only then did Begin tell his son that Sharon had sent him the text of the lecture and that he still had not looked at it.

Begin's disregard of the text Sharon had sent to him was just another aspect of his withdrawal—though on a minor scale. The reason behind his decision to ignore the lecture was also the reason for his withdrawal, his silence, and his disregard of current affairs: he had accepted responsibility but could not contain the outcome. He refused to publish his version of the events, although Sharon's associates pressured him to do so. As father and son read Sharon's text together, Menachem rose agitated from his chair and said what his son had tried to hint to him: "If it is so, Sharon says I'm lying. Did I lie to the heads of the opposition, to the Knesset, and to the president of the United States?" he asked, referring to the government's decision at the beginning that the target of the operation would be a forty-kilometer range. "These statements are baseless," he added and reiterated again and again in anger, "There is no basis for this."[6]

Upset by his father's reaction, Benny decided to act. Without consulting his father, he turned to *Yediot Ahronot* and asked to publish a comment on Sharon's remarks. Five days after Sharon's lecture, in his polite style, Benny compared the operation order as formulated by the government on June 5, 1982, to Sharon's statements in his lecture and pointed to the contradictions that arose.

Begin was pleased with the article written by his son. When they met later, Begin handed Benny a record of the questions and answers that took place after Sharon's lecture (Sharon had also sent the record to Begin) and suggested he read it. Begin himself refused to comment on Sharon's remarks, but he allowed his son to participate in the great debate that ensued and set the record straight. Only then did he finally realize that Sharon had presented him with unclear facts about the situation on the ground at the time of the operation in Lebanon. Before that he had often said that there were many times when he was presented with facts that forced him to make decisions in order to protect the lives of soldiers and that these moves had actually exacerbated the entanglement. But now, after Sharon's lecture, he could finally prove that the defense minister had planned an operation Begin had not wanted at all. However, he thought that as prime minister he should have tightened the reins on his appointed defense minister, and therefore he had no moral right to blame Sharon alone.

Benny, who was exempt from all responsibility, set out on a public campaign. He published another article, this one in *Maariv*, in which he claimed, this time with more severity, "Either Mr. Sharon is lying now, or the Israeli government lied then."[7] He based his argument on the wording of the government's decision, the Knesset announcement, and Reagan's letter. He also mentioned that since Sharon did not deny in his lecture that he had ordered the bombing of Beirut on August 12 without the government's knowledge, it was sufficient to question his credibility.[8] After Sharon's lecture Menachem Begin continued to reject Sharon's requests to meet with him, and the rejections only hinted at his displeasure.

Benny was convinced that Sharon had deceived his father and that his father knew it, certainly in retrospect. Many saw his decision to run for the Knesset with the Likud in the elections of 1988, just months after Sharon's lecture, as part of his desire to constrict Sharon's movements. But Benny realized it would be a mistake to focus on a personal vendetta and refused to continue the quarrel with Sharon. Before entering politics, he consulted with his father, as he always did before making important decisions. Begin welcomed Benny's decision to run but refrained from talking about it publicly, and in 1991, in one of his last interviews in the media, he hinted that Dan Meridor would be a worthy leader for the Likud after Shamir. "Meridor has leadership potential," he said.[9] Although Meridor was touched by Begin's comment, he never talked to him about it. Benny and Dan were close friends. Menachem Begin's position in relation to the Likud leadership did not distance them from one another; rather they saw it as noble: he would not exploit his position to promote his son.

When he turned seventy-six, Begin started to reconcile himself with the past. Among other things, he agreed to recommend Shlomo Lev Ami to the president for a special honor. Lev Ami had commanded Etzel between the tenures of Begin and Eliyahu Meridor; he had rejected outright the "myth of Begin the Etzel commander" and had bitterly criticized Begin many times. Lev Ami saw Begin's recommendation as an attempt to thank those who had been pushed aside in Etzel's history.[10] Begin even acquiesced to MK Motta Gur's request to answer questions about the occupation of Jerusalem during the Six-Day War. He responded to the questions in letters that he wrote by hand, and Kadishai passed them on to Gur. Begin thought that the questions were meant to assist Gur in research he was doing and was disappointed when he found out that Gur was helping a friend who was researching the Battle of Ammunition Hill. Begin reprimanded Gur in a phone call. He reminded him that when Gur was chief of staff, he had expressed concern over Sadat's visit, arguing that Sadat was planning to go to war and that the visit was merely a façade, but he—Begin—did not accede to the defense minister's request that Gur be dismissed from office as a result. Gur was embarrassed and claimed he had never heard this before.[11]

Begin also agreed to talk to Shmuel Katz, who had stopped talking to him when Begin began negotiations with Egypt. Katz believed that his mere appeal to Begin after so many years of estrangement would thrill Begin and also open his closed heart. He was wrong. Begin was satisfied with laconic answers—"It will be fine," etc.—and the conversation between the two was short.[12] But Begin refused to meet with Carter, who came to visit Israel. The attorney general suggested to Carter that he should call Begin. Begin wished him luck and thanked him for the call, but the conversation was over in less than a minute. Despite the brief conversation, Carter, like many others who got a chance to talk to Begin even for a moment, said that he enjoyed talking to him.[13]

In 1990, Begin fell in his apartment and broke his hip for a second time. He was hospitalized in Shaarey Tzedek Medical Center and underwent surgery. After the surgery, doctors recommended moving him to the Rehabilitation Department of Ichilov Hospital in Tel Aviv. The news about his transfer to Ichilov was leaked to the press, despite efforts to conceal it, and when he arrived, dozens of photographers and journalists were waiting for him. When Begin heard about the media's arrival, he wanted to wear his black suit. He sat in the back of his car and did not speak with reporters. He looked thin and weak, his hair was disheveled, and the cameras caught the puzzled look on his face when he realized that he had aroused such interest, as if he had just rediscovered what was happening beyond his own world.

Begin's physical condition was poor. He could not stand up, and the first directive upon his arrival at Ichilov Hospital was that he be fed enough so that he could gain at least ten kilograms. He was also assigned a young physical therapist, Reuven Bett, at whom he snapped angrily at their first meeting. Over time it became clear that Begin's stay at the hospital was good for him, not only because of the medical treatment he received, but also because he could not abstain from human contact, which softened him. Little by little Begin started to cooperate with Bett and began correcting the doctors' Hebrew. ("You should not say 'Sure' but 'Of course,'" he told them; "Do not say 'Lift your leg' but 'Raise your leg,'" and so forth.) He even asked them to stop addressing him as Adoni (Sir) as that was the name of God (Adonai).[14] After his treatment sessions Begin would retire to his room for an afternoon nap and read books and newspapers. Every day he was visited by Merav, Benny's daughter, and by Rachel Kremerman, who would bring him his favorite apple compote.

In August 1990, when Saddam Hussein ordered his army to invade Kuwait, Begin was still hospitalized. For his seventy-seventh birthday Kadishai brought a cake to the hospital, but the hordes of photographers that gathered outside were disappointed when they discovered they could not document the event.

On January 16, 1991, when the Iraqi Army fired missiles at Israel, Begin went to a shelter with the rest of those hospitalized and wore a gas mask along with everyone else. He was not alarmed and did not express his opinion about the missile firing, even though it reminded many people about his decision to bomb the Iraqi reactor. Kadishai continued to bring him the daily newspapers, and when he showed him an article by Tommy Lapid in *Maariv* in which he had written that Begin was now the real hero because owing to his decision Iraq did not have nuclear weapons, he replied dryly, "Well, yes."[15] Nor was he excited by a letter of appreciation signed by one hundred MKs, including Yitzhak Rabin, acknowledging his important decision. (Peres did not sign the letter.)

Begin was released from the hospital in March 1991. He had gained ten kilos and he could walk, but he preferred to use a walker. Furthermore, his mood had improved. His family decided to allow reporters and photographers to cover the joyous event of his release from Ichilov, and for the first time since he had withdrawn to his apartment the citizens of Israel saw the former prime minister in a televised interview. The sight was a sad one. Begin looked weak and he walked slowly, his hair had dwindled and was completely white, and his wide eyes expressed partly joy and partly panic at the bustle around him. But his vitality surprised his audience. The prominent voice of Yaakov Achimeir, the television reporter, stood out from the barrage of questions as he asked Begin, "Why have you not left your house in recent years?" Begin chose to answer wittily, "I left the house but not often." "Sir, you owe the people of Israel an answer," Achimeir was adamant. "Why did you not leave your home?" "Oh, there were personal reasons of course," Begin replied, as he smiled while he descended the stairs, forgetting to hold onto the rail to his left. When he heard the doctor's reminder to hold onto the rail, he replied, "I never lean to the left."[16] The audience laughed at his answer, and for a moment it seemed that his spark had reignited. He even managed to express his opposition on a possible return of the Golan Heights—there was a rumor at the time that Israel would negotiate a peace agreement with Syria—before his daughter Chasia urged him to end the interview.

Begin never returned to his apartment in Jerusalem. During his stay in the hospital his family rented a new apartment for him in the Tel Aviv suburb of Neot Afeka at 4 Glicksberg Street. They thought that he was receiving excellent treatment in Ichilov Hospital and wanted him to live nearby. Leah also moved in with her father, and they continued to watch movies together. In one of the films they saw a lesbian couple. He wondered if there were indeed women who were like that.

The move to Tel Aviv agreed with him, and Begin recovered. He began walking from time to time in the adjacent streets or in the house's yard, and he always greeted his neighbors and inquired as to their well-being. His daily routine had not changed. He was still an early riser and he still read newspapers (although Kadishai avoided bringing him the local newspapers so as not to upset him with their aggressive style). He answered letters, had a daily nap, and read history books. He usually went to bed around 10 p.m.[17] Every Saturday evening he continued to meet with Meridor, who was already justice minister and was busy putting in place a new bill, Basic Law: Human Liberty and Dignity.[18] Begin saw this law as the "intelligent application of the tension between individual freedom and national importance," as he pointed out in a lecture that was included in the booklet *On National Perspectives and Personal Perspectives*.[19] Begin reminded Meridor that when Ben Gurion was about to instruct the Shabak to arrest Uri Avnery for his radical leftist opinions, he told Isser Harel, head of the secret service at the time, that he would raise a public outcry if a journalist were arrested for his views. Once in a while Begin also expressed his appreciation of rival political figures. He was particularly impressed by Yossi Sarid's Hebrew and explained that despite their differences of opinion, he preferred Yitzhak Rabin to Shimon Peres.

On Passover Eve 1991, Begin convened his entire family and close friends for the Seder. He sat at the head of the table and conducted the Seder, reading the Haggadah all the way to the end. None of his relatives doubted the evident improvement in his mood. In May, Kadishai and Meni Peer from Channel 1 agreed that Begin would participate in a festive television show marking the fiftieth anniversary of Jabotinsky's death. Begin refused to come to the studio, preferring a telephone interview, but said that he would answer every question he was asked. This was the first time he had agreed to a proper interview since his retirement, and excited Beitar members gathered in the hundreds in the studio to listen to him speak.

"Jabotinsky taught splendor," he said, "and we are so far from that splendor, especially in recent times, in the Knesset. We have faults and weaknesses. But we shall overcome these too." When Peer asked what was left to achieve from Jabotinsky's teachings, Begin said, "The war for the Land of Israel," adding that "it's a pity Jabotinsky did not live to see the immigration of the Ethiopian Jews and the Jews of the Soviet Union, of which he dreamed."[20]

The more Begin dared open up, the stronger he grew. He began expressing his opinion on current events. In July he agreed to be interviewed again, in light of the inauguration of the Etzel Museum. It was his last interview, and it was conducted over the phone. "I am well, thank you very much," he told David Dayan, the interviewer, who asked about his health.[21] When the interviewer implied that there might be no difference between Etzel members and Intifada activists, Begin interrupted: "That's blasphemy. What, did we kill civilians? Did we target British civilians? After all, what they are doing is killing any Jew because he is a Jew."

"Making the decision to start a rebellion against the empire is not a simple act," said the interviewer.

"It was not difficult at all. You have to remember Britain's situation at the time," Begin replied. "It was extremely weakened and eventually left mighty India. But this was not how we figured it. After all, we were a persecuted and destroyed people. What had to be done in those days to bring about the liberation of the nation? We could only achieve our holy goal through war. Only by resistance, by rebellion."

"When may a minority that believes in its way act on it, despite the decision of the national institutions?" the interviewer asked.

"It's a question of faith, and we had an unchallengeable faith that only through war could our people gain freedom and security."

"Does every armed rebellion achieve something?"

"I'm not talking about any rebellion. I've always said that not all ends justify the means. But our situation was so unique that there was no other way."

"Do you remember your most difficult decision as Etzel commander?"

"Yes. It involved an act of cruelty—I admit it was cruel. [Begin meant the hanging of the British sergeants.] It was in response to the hanging of our friends. And indeed, after the brutal act there were no more hangings of Jews in Palestine."

"The happiest moment you remember?"

"I was certainly happy when we formed the government in 1977."

"And as Etzel commander, were there any actions or acts that caused you satisfaction?"

"In terms of actions, the Acre Prison break."

When asked about his relationship with Ben Gurion, Begin said, "We were rivals, not only politically, but there were times that we even became friends. It was so during the Six-Day War. We walked together in the Knesset, and I told him the details—he did not know them exactly—about what had happened and about the victory." Begin sounded like a new person in the interview: refreshed, coherent, hungry for a recognition that he had been right. He insisted, "Those who wrote that we did something wrong, a provocation, they were wrong, and we were right."

In August 1991 Begin turned seventy-eight. For the first time since his retirement he celebrated his birthday with over 120 old acquaintances who gathered at his home. Most of the time he sat in an armchair in the corner of the living room, but he made many jokes, reminisced, and spoke of the future. At the time the Likud, headed by Shamir, was being sharply criticized, and both in the media and among the public the slogan "Crooks, enough of you!" was the focus of many demonstrations. Begin's admirers knew his condition had improved and began to fantasize that he would return to politics.

About this time Begin was informed that his granddaughter Orit had fallen in love with his security guard, Alon Chadad, who was of Moroccan descent and that they had decided to marry. Begin was very attached to his granddaughter and was happy for her newfound happiness, as well as for the merging of the ethnic groups. He decided to surprise her by participating in her wedding. He arrived at the wedding accompanied by a doctor from the Ichilov orthopedic department. "Doctor, see how I can walk," Begin said proudly and even approached the dance floor and clapped his hands to the Mizrahi music. A few days later the images were broadcast on TV—the wedding photographer had decided to make some extra money.

In his final months Begin had a reawakening. During the eight years of his withdrawal, he had rejected all proposals to perpetuate his name while he was alive, but now he was intrigued by an idea proposed by Shraga Alis to buy the house in which he had hidden during the underground and establish a museum similar to Ben Gurion's House. Begin was excited. He began to reminisce and eventually said he would allow his name to be commemorated while he was alive on one condition—that the project would be financed by donations and not by state funds. Roni Milo, Chaim Corfu, and Yechiel Kadishai accepted the challenge but found it difficult to raise donations.[22]

During this time Begin also met with his old friend Yochanan Bader. The two had first met in Poland, and their friendship had known many ups and downs, yet now they seemed like a loving couple who had not seen each other for a long time. Bader was almost completely deaf, and

Begin could not raise his voice. Mediated by Kadishai, they exchanged notes, but they mainly sat and looked at each other, laughed and smiled, and found it hard to part even when they had nothing more to say.[23]

In March 1992, with the primary elections approaching, the Likud held a stormy meeting at its headquarters in Tel Aviv to prepare a list of candidates for the Knesset. Foreign Minister David Levy went against the agreement of cooperation between the camps of Sharon and Shamir, and his supporters were pushed to the end of the list. Without the paternal figure, it seemed as though the party was falling apart; personal conflicts had become harsher and more visible than ever before. Begin followed the developments closely on the radio. He managed to hear only that his son Benny, who was trying to bolster Levy's camp, was booed off the stage and left the meeting. Levy's supporters accused him of partnering up with Ariel Sharon, the man who was being blamed for destroying Menachem Begin. "Shame on you," they shouted, "You have betrayed your father." The following morning Kadishai phoned Benny and told him that his father had suffered a heart attack and was hospitalized in Ichilov's intensive care unit.

On March 9, Menachem Begin died. He was seventy-nine years old. Kadishai rushed to his own apartment, where he kept a will that Begin had given him a few years earlier. He invited Benny, Chasia, and Leah to read the will. It was short—only three lines. He asked to be buried beside his wife on the Mount of Olives, near the graves of the executed freedom fighters Meir Feinstein and Moshe Barazani. He did not want a state funeral and did not want to be buried in the Burial Ground for Leaders of the Nation. For his family, this decision represented the man he was more than any other decision he had made in his life—he was a simple Jew who had done what he had to do for his people.

The news of Begin's death was broadcast on the radio at seven in the morning, and the funeral took place only a few hours later. No eulogies were delivered at his funeral. The man for whom ceremony and splendor were part of his very nature requested that his funeral be humble and low-key. Nevertheless, tens of thousands of people went to the Mount of Olives to pay their last respects to him. Hundreds of people gathered around the grave, and in the growing commotion and emotional turbulence they nearly trampled the grave of the man who had become a legend in his own lifetime.

EPILOGUE

In terms of his impact on the character of Israel, Begin is second in importance only to Ben Gurion. A quarter of a century has passed since he retired from political life, and by all indications he was the last ideological leader of his kind. His style of leadership would be ill-suited for the Israel of today. His ability to captivate crowds, his devotion to duty, the importance that he attached to his principles and to the ideological traditions in which he grew up—all these belong to another time that is unlikely to return. Begin abruptly ended his political career nine years before his death when he suddenly withdrew into his apartment, but only his death marked the true end of the era. It is probably no coincidence that three months after his death, in June 1992, Israel witnessed what became known as the Second Reversal—when, after fifteen consecutive years of Likud rule, Haavoda, under Yitzhak Rabin, returned to power, having spent most of that time in the opposition.

Not long after that, in September 1993, Israel signed a treaty with the PLO. Begin had regarded the conquest of the West Bank and the Gaza Strip during the Six-Day War as a return to "the land of our forefathers," and he clung to the notion of Af Sha'al (Not an Inch). It is safe to assume that he would have been against the Oslo Accords. But in point of fact, the Oslo Accords were no more than a sophisticated variation of the agreement that he himself had conceived and signed along with the peace treaty with Egypt regarding autonomy for the Palestinians. Indeed, ironically and unwittingly, Begin—who spoke of the sanctity of the Land of Israel and for whom the autonomy agreement that he signed was the most ideologically wrenching occasion that he had ever experienced (as one of his aides put it)—was part of the political process that was set in motion in Oslo.

Begin's links with that historic agreement—even if today it is regarded as debatable—are also the result of a dualism within his own personality and his political path since his youth. In fact, what appeared to be the big surprise of his first term in office—the signing of a peace treaty with Egypt by someone who had been regarded as a dogmatic nationalist and a one-dimensional personality and whose rise to power raised fears that Israel would be led into war—is less surprising when one examines Begin more closely. The dualism in his personality was also evident in other aspects of his worldview. He sought to bring together nationalism and the notion of individual liberty; he had an aversion to socialism but a desire for social justice; and he upheld the judicial branch of government while defying the establishment, which prior to his rule had always been Labor-dominated. In his personal lifestyle too there was considerable contradiction: he lived simply, almost ascetically, while his speeches were grandiose and occasionally almost ostentatious.

Even in his forthright views on the Holocaust—in which nearly his entire family perished—and in his aversion to Germans, Begin concealed a significant detail that came to light only years later courtesy of his sister Rachel: his father, Ze'ev-Dov, was an ardent admirer of German culture and had even hoped that the German Army would invade Poland. It is hard to imagine the shock that the young Begin must have felt when he realized that his father, whom he sought to emulate, was murdered by the very people he had admired. Contrary to his popular image, therefore, Begin's personality was complex and tangled.

Just as in a Greek tragedy, Begin's personality governed his actions and his destiny as a leader. He began his political career at the age of sixteen and was a public figure in every fiber of his being, but had he not chosen this path, he most likely would have become a stage actor. And like every great actor, small roles never would have suited him. On the most humdrum of days he would dream up his grandest initiatives. He chose to lead Etzel in a revolt against British rule in Palestine at a time when the organization was nearly completely paralyzed. Many people made fun of his "Palaver"—as his proclamation was known—but at the time he was helped by people who knew how to make it happen. He was not a great military leader and was often in favor of mounting symbolic showcase operations. At times he was even completely cut off from events—as, for example, during the *Altalena* affair and during the massacre at Deir Yassin.

Indeed, there was a huge disparity between Begin's beliefs and intentions (as expressed in his pronouncements and speeches) and his ability to lead accordingly. His capacity to galvanize his followers and crowds in fire-breathing speeches was matched by an equal inability to manage affairs in practice or to ensure that his instructions were followed accurately. In fact, in every position that he held he was more a spiritual leader with a distinctive style than an executive leader in the true sense of the word. But his followers never questioned his authority—which over the years grew to nearly mystical proportions—thanks to the particular nature of his leadership: rather than closely monitor his subordinates' actions, he offered them the protection of blanket responsibility for their actions in return for their absolute loyalty. Throughout his career until his resignation as prime minister, he refused to recognize his distinct shortcomings as a leader.

Begin collapsed under the strain many times in his life, but he always knew how to recover. During the infamous Saison period, when the two main Jewish underground organizations captured and turned each other's members in to the British, he even suggested to the Etzel operations officer that they put an end to the senseless struggle by mounting a heroic mass suicide, as was done at Masada, in the manner of the Zealots besieged there by the Romans two thousand years ago. Long before he retired as prime minister, he abdicated twice from the leadership of his party, Herut. Of the first occasion, in 1951, the unknown still outweighs what we know. The second time—in 1966—he did so because he could no longer take the criticism leveled at him within his own party. Begin's political path was, in any event, never exactly strewn with roses. Ben Gurion, Israel's founding father, despised him and made every effort to undermine the legitimacy of his party. In 1952, after Israel signed the controversial Reparations Agreement with Germany, Begin marched on the Knesset building at the head of thousands in a stormy demonstration and in private conversations with his aides even spoke of going underground again.

Nevertheless, from a historical perspective one can say that Begin was good at keeping his urges in check. In spite of all the difficulties, he made sure to instill in his people the principle of the primacy of the law and the judicial system and to put his trust in the emerging democracy of the young state. "The sacred slip of paper" is how he referred to the election process, and he believed the day would come when he too would rise to power.

Begin was an ideologue with a clear vision and unyielding principles, but he was also a pragmatic politician. He knew how to forge new political frameworks and to steer a course in line with the winds of public opinion, and over time he understood that he would have to moderate his views if he wished to rise to power. In his bid to acquire political legitimacy—to be no longer the extremist opposition leader but a realistic alternative in government—in 1965 he signed an agreement to establish Gahal, from a merger of Herut with the Liberal Party, for which he was willing to abandon the traditional Herut position of "Both banks of the Jordan River."

The Six-Day War was a turning point in Begin's career. The deep-seated fear in Israeli society during the Waiting Period before the war led to the establishment of a National Unity Government, in which Begin was an active partner. The war's spectacular outcome meant that his messianic way of speaking became the new norm in the country; the dream of returning to "the land of our forefathers" had become reality. Nevertheless, the prize of the prime ministership was still far off, and Begin continued to forge his way toward it by attuning himself to the masses—with whom he conducted a tempestuous relationship—and through the use of religious symbols and comportment. In this way he helped to forge a bridge between the Ashkenazim and the Mizrahim; many of the latter felt they needed such a bridge in the face of the ongoing discrimination they encountered under Mapai rule.

In 1973, under pressure from Ezer Weizmann and Ariel Sharon, Begin set up the Likud party—the final stage in a long process in which Herut finally parted with the Revisionist platform that had been its bedrock in favor of one with a broad populist base. Before the election campaign of 1977, Begin promised that it would be his last. He was tired, and to top it all he had suffered a severe heart attack in the run-up to polling day. But just at that moment, fate chose to smile upon him. Thirty years after first suffering the indignities of a spurned parliamentarian—"the Clown," as Ben Gurion had referred to him—Begin won the elections and became prime minister. His victory came about thanks to profound changes within Israeli society, but it was also the product of his own toil, patience, and persistence.

After taking office, Begin became the first Zionist leader to return territories and to establish peace with the largest of Israel's enemies, disproving the apocalyptic forecasts of some at the start of his term. He took the first tentative steps toward peace almost by himself, bypassing the military establishment and in the face of vehement objections within his own party. At that time, his authority was strong and unshakable. His ability to lead while swimming against the current was the outcome of years in the wilderness of the opposition, as well as of his tendency to cling to an idea. In his underground days, his integrity and naivety were the secret to his mental resilience, his dreams an effective antidote to the harsh and seemingly impossible reality. They now helped him implement his ideas during his first term as prime minister. They also led to his downfall in his second term. Begin's insistence on destroying the PLO in Lebanon and on signing a peace treaty with the heads of a new regime that he dreamed would emerge in that country ensnared Israel in a long and bloody war. In striving for social justice while liberalizing the economy—without due attention to the details of the inherent contradictions between the two goals—he nearly brought about the collapse of the Israeli economy.

Ultimately, however, Begin will not be remembered for the autonomy agreement or for his greatest political achievement—the peace agreement with Egypt—or for the bombing of the nuclear reactor in Iraq or for his failure in Lebanon. More than anything else, he will be remembered for putting his stamp on the Jewish character of the Israeli state. He injected a new speech aesthetic into the public debate. He saw himself as part of the Jewish nation across the ages, a kind of new and modern prophet, a link in a chain stretching across the generations whose hard-line views were inspired by the Jewish Holocaust and who restored to the public debate images and views from the Diaspora—in stark contrast to the direct link between the Bible and the Palmach, which the Laborite Zionist establishment had previously cultivated. With his foreign mannerisms and etiquette and the religious-nationalist vocabulary that he left behind, Begin forged a bond among the various working-class sectors of the Israeli society and restored in the Mizrahim a sense of belonging based on a shared Jewish history and religion. In effect, in this way he also foiled Ben Gurion's ambition to forge a new Israeli pioneer society and contributed much to the nation's transformation from a frugal society of pioneers to an urban bourgeoisie and a move away from agriculture and industry to the business professions. Although he had not intended for this to happen, from the time of his term in office onward, Israelis have felt increasingly disinclined to subject their personal desires to the good of society as a whole.

In spite of his modest lifestyle and although he championed equality and personal liberty even for Arab citizens, Begin's impassioned speeches, his fiery language, and his belief in the sanctity of the Jewish people darkened the atmosphere in the public domain. What for him was an issue of style—he spoke in a dramatic fashion within his own family—was interpreted by many Israelis as content. It is perhaps no coincidence that while he was in power, the first political murder in Israeli history took place, the ultra-nationalist Jewish Underground was born, and the first whiffs of racism began to stalk the land.

Since his youth, Begin spoke much about an ideal nation and strove to reward the people rather than reconcile it with reality. Such was his belief in the uniqueness and power of the Jewish nation that in his second term as prime minister he found it hard to differentiate between his aspirations and reality. By this time, his physical and mental frailties had also begun to play a part in his failures.

Begin was a unique leader. He was willing to take risks for what he regarded as the greater glory of Israel, but he was poor at assessing those risks, and for this failing he ultimately paid the price in his twilight years. To his credit it must be said that by resigning his post as prime minister, he assumed total responsibility for what had happened during his time in office, and his withdrawal appears to have been a form of self-flagellation. When the time came, he let down the curtains on his political life with the same drama with which he had conducted it all along.

NOTES

CHAPTER I. POLITICAL TALENT

1. Rachel Halperin, Menachem's sister, Menachem Begin Heritage Center, June 2000.
2. Rabbi Chaim Soloveitchik (1853–1918) preferred to focus on religious studies and rejected the idea of Zionism; see Immanuel Etkes, *The Gaon of Vilna: The Man and His Image* (Zalman Shazar, 1998), 164–222. His son, "Brisker Reb," Reb Velvele (1886–1959), went his father's way and said, "Even if our prime minister were the 'Chafetz Chaim,' we should not accept the idea of a Jewish state before the return of the righteous messiah." See *The Wall*, a collection of essays to strengthen religion, vol. 45; Neturei Karta pamphlet, 2000, 4.
3. *Hebrew Encyclopedia*, vol. 9, 901.
4. During the uprising, brought about by the Ukrainian authorities in 1648–1649 and led by Bogdan Chmelnitski (1595–1657), tens of thousands of Jews were murdered and many women were raped. The surviving Jews migrated west and suffered drastic changes to their way of life. After many Torah centers were destroyed, interest grew around the secret doctrine of the Kabbalah, and many Hasidim joined the mystical movement established at the time; for more details see Mordechai Vurembrand and Betzalel S. Ruth, *The People of Israel: 4,000 Years* (Massada, 1966), 292–293.
5. Rachel Halperin, Menachem Begin Heritage Center, June 2000.
6. A document from 1904 signed by Ze'ev-Dov has been preserved in the manuscript section of the National Library in Jerusalem. In the document, written in Yiddish, Ze'ev-Dov bluntly condemns the prohibition to eulogize Herzl in synagogues and accuses the religious leaders of Brisk of corruption in their election process.
7. Rachel Halperin, Menachem Begin Heritage Center, June 2000.
8. Aviezer Golan and Shlomo Nakdimon, *Begin* (Yediot Ahronot, 1978), 13.
9. Dov Levin, "The Crossroad in the Relations between the Lithuanians and the Jews in World War II," *Kivunim Chadashim, Journal of Judaism and Zionism*, 1976, 30.
10. Headlines such as the following appeared in newspapers at the time (translated from the Yiddish): "Failed Attempt at Blood Libel in Chabli" (*Di Yiddishe Shtime*, March 17, 1938); "Hooligans Attack Jews" (ibid., November 13, 1938); "Not a Day Passes without the Beating of a Jew" (*Falk Blatt*, March 31, 1939).
11. Rachel Halperin, Menachem Begin Heritage Center, June 2000.
12. Rachel Halperin, Menachem Begin Heritage Center, June 2000. During World War I, Henry Morgenthau Sr., father of U.S. treasury secretary Henry Morgenthau Jr., was known for his sympathy for the Jews. He wrote to his

son in the midst of the Armenian genocide: "When I read the report on the inhumane treatment of the Armenians I feel a deep sadness. It seems a very similar fate to the fate of the Russian Jews, and belonging myself to the persecuted race, I hold great sympathy for them." Henry Morgenthau, *United States Diplomacy on the Bosphorus: The Diaries of Ambassador Morgenthau 1913–1916* (Princeton and London: Gomidas Institute, 2004), 320.
13. "Brisk of Lithuania," in *Encyclopedia of Exile*, vol. 2, ed. Eliezer Steinman (Encyclopedia of Exile Company, 1954), 249.
14. Quoted in Golan and Nakdimon, *Begin*, 12.
15. Ibid., 16.
16. *Hebrew Encyclopedia*, vol. 9, 904.
17. Quoted in "Brisk of Lithuania," *Encyclopedia of Exile*, 308.
18. Rachel Halperin, Menachem Begin Heritage Center, June 2000.
19. Quoted in "Brisk of Lithuania," *Encyclopedia of Exile*, 249.
20. *Maariv*, June 17, 1977.
21. Rachel Halperin, Menachem Begin Heritage Center, June 2000.
22. Ibid.
23. "Brisk of Lithuania," *Encyclopedia of Exile*, 249.
24. From an interview with Menachem Begin, *Maariv Lanoar*, May 31, 1977.
25. From an interview with Menachem Begin, *Bamachane*, April 13, 1972.
26. Rachel Halperin, Menachem Begin Heritage Center, June 2000.
27. Ze'ev-Dov sent a postcard to his friend Yona Ettinger on the occasion of the latter's wedding, January 15, 1907. Menachem Begin Heritage Center Archives, Personal Archives and Collections, Document No. 188.
28. "Brisk of Lithuania," *Encyclopedia of Exile*, 251.
29. Rachel Halperin, Menachem Begin Heritage Center, June 2000.
30. Ibid.
31. Ibid.
32. *Haaretz*, September 2, 1982.
33. See note 6, above.
34. From an interview with Menachem Begin, *Yediot Ahronot*, June 10, 1977.
35. Aharon Tzvi Propes, Beitar Commissioner in Poland during 1933–1939, said Begin was particularly ambitious; see Golan and Nakdimon, *Begin*.
36. Israel Eldad, Israel State Archives, December 8, 1993.
37. Yaakov Markoviski, *The Irgun Lexicon* (Ministry of Defense, 2005), 25.
38. The WZO was founded at the First Zionist Congress (1897) by Theodor Herzl as an umbrella organization for all the Zionist movements. Its main goal was the creation of a national home for the Jewish people in Palestine. For the period we are discussing, the WZO was headed by Chaim Weizmann (1921–1931). Jabotinsky founded the Revisionist party called the Alliance of Revisionists-Zionists (Hatzohar) in 1925. (Beitar, its youth movement, was established in 1923.) Jabotinsky had differences of opinion with Weizmann and the labor parties on several issues: he demanded the foundation of an overtly military Jewish force in Palestine; he criticized Weizmann's political cooperation with the British; he asked that more aggressive demands be made to the British Mandate (he claimed that the British had

not helped the Jews build their national home as they had promised in the Balfour Declaration in 1917); and he strived to change the official goal of the WZO from the building of "a national homeland" (which he considered an ambiguous term) to the clear objective of building "a Jewish state." Eventually, in 1935, Jabotinsky and his party left the WZO because of the differences.

39. Menachem Begin, *White Nights* (Dvir, 1995), 58.
40. High school diploma displayed in the Menachem Begin Heritage Center Archives, Personal Archives and Collections, Document No. 16.
41. A document from the Menachem Begin Heritage Center Archives, Personal Archives and Collections, dated February 13, 1933, indicates that Ze'ev-Dov was unemployed, had lost his assets, and was struggling to pay his two sons' university tuition.
42. Worth today approximately NIS (New Israeli Shekels) 50.
43. Meir Kahn, Israel State Archives, September 6, 1993.
44. Begin, *White Nights*, 251, where he quotes from Mitskevich's "Pan Tadeusz."
45. Yonatan Shapira, *Chosen to Command* (Am Oved, 1989), 15–50.
46. "The character of Garibaldi is in my eyes a significant figure of a freedom fighter, a hater of wars who fought for freedom. A republican in consciousness, but for the unification of Italy he agreed to royalist rule. I do not deny that I read Herzl's diaries with excitement. And although I never saw him, his work and his suffering affected me very much." Quoted in *Yediot Ahronot*, June 10, 1977.
47. Yaakov Shavit, "Between Piłsudski and Mickiewicz: Policy and Messianism in the Zionist Revisionism," Zionism 10 (1984): 33–37.
48. Israel Eldad, Israel State Archives, December 8, 1993.
49. *Beitar Book*, vol. 2, ed. H. Ben Yeruham (Committee for Publishing Beitar Books, 1973), 618.
50. After the failure of the coup in Italy in 1834, Garibaldi, one of its perpetrators, was forced to escape to South America, and during the ten years he was there he fought in several wars of liberation. During the revolutions of 1848 he returned to Italy and with Giuseppe Mazzini took over Rome with the goal of declaring an Italian republic. Intervention by Austria and France thwarted these intentions, and Garibaldi fled to America. In 1860 he returned to Italy and fought for unification. His soldiers—about a thousand volunteers—excelled mainly at guerrilla warfare. They all wore red shirts and thus were called "the Thousand Red Shirts."
51. *Beitar Book*, 404.
52. Golan and Nakdimon, *Begin*, 35.
53. Ada Amichal-Yavin, *Sambatyon* (Beit El, 1995), 54.
54. *Beitar Book*, 442.
55. Israel Eldad, Israel State Archives, December 8, 1993.
56. "Beitar and Their Petition to Jewish Parents," *Beitar Book*, 345.
57. *Maariv*, June 16, 1977.
58. Daniel Carpi, ed., *Ze'ev Jabotinsky's Letters* (Jabotinsky Institute, 2000), vol. 5, *January 1926–December 1927*, 143–144.

59. *Beitar Book*, 412.
60. Jabotinsky Institute Archives b/3–6–35.
61. Yochanan Bader, a member of the Revisionist Party in Poland, Israel State Archives, December 9, 1992.
62. *Beitar Book*, 579.
63. Jabotinsky Institute Archives b/33–1–1.
64. In Polish they shouted, "*Bolda!*"—false.
65. In a letter dated November 6, 1936, Beitar member Shalom Rosenfeld's mother wrote her impressions from one of Begin's lectures: "Officer Begin really bewitched us in his speech. . . . Some tried to interrupt him by heckling, but they failed because he stopped them firmly. . . . I was fascinated" (translated from the Yiddish). See Menachem Begin Heritage Center Archives, Personal Archives and Collections, Document No. 79, 20.
66. Avraham Caspi, a member of Beitar who was present in the lecture hall; Menachem Begin Heritage Center Archives, October 17, 2004.
67. *Hametzuda*, no. 4, July 1937.
68. Shlomo Yunitzman, a leader of the Revisionist movement, claimed that in a conversation with Ze'ev Jabotinsky the leader had already talked about the possibility of retiring and marked Begin as the potential successor, but there is no reference for this claim; see Golan and Nakdimon, *Begin*, 40.
69. Israel Eldad, Israel State Archives, December 8, 1993.
70. Yehuda Lapidot, *In Flame of Revolt* (Ministry of Defense, 1998).
71. *Haaretz*, July 17, 1938.
72. *Beitar Book*, 856.
73. Shmuel Katz, *Jabo* (Dvir, 1993), 1045.
74. *Beitar Book*, 862–864.
75. Avraham Caspi, Menachem Begin Heritage Center Archives, October 17, 2004.
76. Quoted in *Beitar Book*, vol. 2 (Committee for Publishing Beitar Books), 862–864.
77. Yochanan Bader, Israel State Archives, December 9, 1992.
78. Israel Eldad, ibid., December 8, 1993.
79. Shmuel Katz, ibid., August 6, 1993.
80. Yitzhak Shamir, ibid., January 3, 1995.
81. Israel Eldad, ibid., December 8, 1993.
82. Amichal-Yavin, *Sambatyon*, 64.
83. Israel Eldad, Israel State Archives, December 8, 1993.
84. Shmuel Katz, ibid., August 6, 1993.
85. Avraham Stern, then a member of Etzel, sought to give Polish Jews basic military training with the help of the Polish government in order to help forty thousand Jews emigrate to Palestine by surprise, after military exercises in Poland. According to the plan, the Jews were supposed to attack the British along with Etzel and then declare the establishment of a Hebrew state. See Yochanan Bader, *My Journey to Zion: 1901–1948* (Jabotinsky Institute, 1999).
86. Shmuel Katz, Israel State Archives, August 6, 1993.
87. Israel Eldad, ibid., December 8, 1993.

88. Yitzhak Shamir, ibid., February 6, 1995.
89. Israel Eldad, ibid., December 8, 1993.
90. Begin's views were gathered in 1952 in the booklet *National Perspective and View of Life*, based on a comprehensive lecture in which he expressed his worldview. The booklet is in the Menachem Begin Heritage Center Archives Personal Archives and Collections, Document No. F. 20, and it includes the following statement: "If we were asked, 'Individual freedom or social reform, which is better?' we would respond without hesitation: the two are not mutually exclusive. Indeed, woe to the nation sacrificing individual freedom for slogans of social reform; on the other hand, woe to the nation that ignores social problems by placing individual liberty on the sacrificial altar."
91. *Haolam Hazeh*, September 29, 1983.
92. *Maariv*, June 17, 1977.
93. Quoted by Benny Begin, introduction to Menachem Begin, *White Nights*, 16–17.
94. Jabotinsky Institute Archives, Personal Archives and Collections, 20.
95. Benny Begin, introduction to Menachem Begin, *White Nights*, 16–17.
96. Batya Eldad, Israel State Archives, January 1, 1994.
97. Benny Begin, introduction to Menachem Begin, *White Nights*.
98. Batya Eldad, Israel State Archives, January 9, 1994.
99. Ibid.

CHAPTER 2. A COMMANDER'S GETAWAY

1. Ada Amichal-Yavin, *Sambatyon* (Beit El, 1995), 64.
2. *Haolam Haze*, September 21, 1984.
3. Author's conversation with Yaakov Banai, November 1, 2005.
4. Quoted in Amos Perlmutter, *Life and Times of Menachem Begin* (American University, 1987).
5. Amichal-Yavin, *Sambatyon*, 69.
6. Ibid.
7. Information in this and the preceding paragraph from Israel Eldad, Israel State Archives, December 8, 1993, and Batya Eldad, ibid., January 9, 1994.
8. Israel Eldad, ibid., December 8, 1993.
9. Yechiel Kadishai, ibid., January 5, 1993.
10. Batya Eldad, ibid., January 9, 1994.
11. Ibid.
12. Israel Eldad, ibid., December 8, 1993.
13. Ibid.
14. Ibid.
15. Batya Eldad, ibid., January 9, 1994.
16. Menachem Begin Heritage Center Archives, Personal Archives and Collections.
17. *Ha'ir*, April 17, 1992.
18. Menachem Begin, *White Nights* (Dvir, 1995), 30.
19. Ibid., 133.

20. Ibid., 12.
21. Investigation file, Jabotinsky Institute Archives, Personal Archives and Collections, 14–20.
22. Menachem Begin, *The Revolt (Achiasaf, 1956)*, 16.
23. Begin, *White Nights*, 30.
24. Begin, *The Revolt*, 10.
25. Begin, *White Nights*, 67–71.
26. Begin, *The Revolt*, 10.
27. Begin, *White Nights*, 123.
28. Benny Begin, introduction to Menachem Begin, *White Nights*, 19.
29. Begin, *White Nights*, 122–126.
30. Begin, *The Revolt*, 19.
31. Begin, *White Nights*, 113.
32. Begin, *The Revolt*, 17.
33. Investigation file, Jabotinsky Institute Archives, December 16, 1940.
34. Begin, *White Nights*, 55.
35. Investigation file, Jabotinsky Institute Archives, December 16, 1940.
36. Ibid., December 11, 1940.
37. Ibid., September 18, 1940.
38. Begin, *The Revolt*, 18.
39. "In prison he developed a habit that became his nature: organizing his thoughts by walking to and fro." Benny Begin, introduction to Menachem Begin, *White Nights*, 21.
40. Begin, *The Revolt*, 23.
41. Begin, *White Nights*, 239. The term "enchanted baby" (*tinok shenisba*) is from the Talmud and describes someone who sins inadvertently because he does not know what he is doing.
42. Ibid., 11–23.
43. Investigation file, Jabotinsky Institute Archives, December 13, 1940.
44. Begin, *White Nights*, 147.
45. Ibid., 134.
46. Protocol of the argument between Yaakov Schechter and Menachem Begin, Jabotinsky Institute Archives, December 17, 1940.
47. Begin, *White Nights*, 14.
48. Begin's file 782783 was photographed in 1992 by Isabella Ginor and brought to Israel. The protocols from the investigation were concise and spare, some handwritten and some in print, and they do not contain all the conversations. In *White Nights* Begin described many interrogations, but the file indicates only eleven, in the period September 8–27, November 22, and December 11–18. Not all documents are dated, and there are photographs and fingerprints.
49. Begin, *White Nights*, 170.
50. Ibid., 200.
51. Ibid., 204.
52. Ibid., 210.
53. Ibid., 215.

54. Ibid., 226.
55. Ibid., 260.
56. Ibid.
57. Ibid., 270.
58. *Maariv Lanoar*, April 15, 1975.
59. Batya Eldad, Israel State Archives, January 9, 1994.

CHAPTER 3. GOING UNDERGROUND

1. David Engel, "The Failed Alliance: The Revisionist Movement and the Polish Government-in-Exile, 1939–1945," *Zionism* 11 (1986): 333–360.
2. Moshe Aridor, Menachem Begin Heritage Center, January 8, 2003.
3. Yochanan Bader, Israel State Archives, December 23, 1993.
4. Ibid.
5. Hochman served with Begin in the Anders Army; Menachem Begin Heritage Center, June 17, 2002.
6. Ibid.
7. *Ha'ir*, April 17, 1992.
8. Yitzhak Hochman, Menachem Begin Heritage Center, June 17, 2002.
9. Ibid.
10. Ibid.
11. Israel Eldad, Israel State Archives, December 23, 1993.
12. "Where is your place, young Hebrew? In one of the corners, or in the center, in the place where the war over the damned piece of paper is being conducted?" Quoted in "Commanders' Platform," 20.
13. *Ha'ir*, April 17, 1992.
14. Israel Eldad, Israel State Archives, December 21, 1993. The original family names, Yazernitski and Shayeb, were changed into Hebrew names in a process known as the Hebarization of surnames, part of the Zionist approach of erasing the exile patterns of Jewish life.
15. Sarah Yotan, David Yotan's wife, *Ha'ir*, April 17, 1992.
16. Menachem Bocwitz, ibid.
17. Jabotinsky Institute Archives, Personal Archives and Collections, 20.
18. Raziel, upholding his decision that Etzel should help the British forces in their struggle against the Nazis, chose to head a team—including Yaakov Meridor, Yaakov Sika-Aharoni, and Yaakov Theresi—whose goal was to blow up fuel depots on the outskirts of Baghdad in use by the Luftwaffe. The operation was decided upon after pro-German Iraqi nationalists, headed by Rashid Ali Al-Keilani, rebelled against British forces in Iraq and the Germans quickly offered them help. Raziel also wanted to kidnap the Mufti of Jerusalem, Haj Amin al-Husseini, who had found refuge in Iraq, and to set up Etzel cells among Iraqi Jews. But this ambitious plan was not properly prepared, and as the team was moving into Iraq, a German plane bombed their car and Raziel was killed. His death raised questions as to whether the attempted abduction had really been needed and whether the demolition of the fuel depots had been important.
19. Shlomo Lev Ami, *The Guilty Ones* (Friedman, 2000), 179.

20. Eliyahu Lankin, *The Story of Altalena* (Hadar, 1974), 65–68.
21. Yitzhak Shamir, Israel State Archives, January 3, 1995.
22. *Ha'ir*, April 17, 1992.
23. Meir Kahn, Israel State Archives, September 6, 1993.
24. "In my opinion, Begin saw it as a need to maintain the framework." Israel Eldad, ibid., December 8, 1993.
25. Yad Vashem Archives, 025/72. See the letter from the head of the Polish Political Department to General Tukhachevsky in the Defense Ministry, January 10, 1944.
26. Engel, "The Failed Alliance."
27. David Niv, *Battle for Freedom: The Irgun Tzvai Leumi* (Klausner Institute, 1973), vol. 3, 242–276; Eric Silver, *Begin: The Haunted Prophet* (Random House, 1984).
28. To this day, Begin's status vis-à-vis the Polish authorities is unclear. Kahn said he was never called up again, with the consent of the Poles. A letter from the head of the Polish Political Department stated that "Begin is wanted by the Poles and the British for acts of terrorism," and an attachment referring to two other soldiers, Terller and Kushyk, who were supposed to have gone with Begin to the United States, noted that they could not be summoned to military duty as "they are in hiding and cannot be served with a warrant." However, the document does not refer explicitly to Begin. See Engel, "The Failed Alliance."
29. Quoted in "The Hebrew War of Independence" (Etzel manual, n.d.), 16.
30. Meir Kahn, Israel State Archives, September 6, 1993; Lankin, *The Story of Altalena*, 64–68.
31. Meir Kahn, Israel State Archives, September 6, 1993.
32. Ibid.
33. Lankin, *The Story of Altalena*, 65–68.
34. Eitan Livni, *Hamaamad* (Yediot Ahronot, 1987), 56.
35. Yerachmiel Halevi, February 21, 1969, in Shlomo Lev Ami, "The Etzel Headquarters during the Revolt" (master's thesis, Bar Ilan University, 1993).
36. Livni, *Hamaamad*, 110.
37. Author's conversation with Shlomo Lev Ami, April 25, 2007.
38. Ibid.
39. Meir Kahn, Israel State Archives, September 6, 1993.
40. Yochanan Bader, ibid., January 21, 1993.
41. Yosef Evron, *Gidi: The Jewish Insurgency against the British in Palestine* (Ministry of Defense, 2001), 51.
42. Aviezer Golan and Shlomo Nakdimon, *Begin* (Yediot Ahronot, 1978), 77.
43. Yosef Schechtman, *The Life and Times of Vladimir Jabotinsky* (Jabotinsky Institute, 1959), 17.
44. Benny Morris, *Righteous Victims* (Am Oved, 2003), 165–170.
45. Eli Shaltiel, *Moshe Sneh: Life* (Am Oved, 2000), 139.
46. The Biltmore Program was conceived in the Biltmore Hotel in New York in May 1942, during a special conference of American Zionists, and it specified the first explicit demand for a Jewish state in Israel. The plan was approved at a meeting of the General Council in Jerusalem in November 1942.

47. Quoted in Jacob Coleman Hurewitz, *The Struggle for Palestine* (Schocken Books, 1969), 213.

CHAPTER 4. DECLARATION OF REBELLION

1. Tzippora Kessel, Menachem Begin Heritage Center, September 18, 2000.
2. Shlomo Lev Ami, "Minutes of the Irgun Tzvai Leumi, July–November 1944," *Zionism* 4 (1976): 392. The protocols, saved in a cellar in Tel Aviv belonging to Etzel, were revealed by Lev Ami and transferred to the Jabotinsky Institute after the founding of Israel. Protocols from January–July 1944 were destroyed by the British during an operation in July 1944 in Petach Tikva. Transcription ceased because of the Saison.
3. Shlomo Lev Ami, "Etzel Headquarters during the Revolt" (master's thesis, Bar-Ilan University, 1993).
4. Israel Eldad, Israel State Archives, December 21, 1993.
5. Yochanan Bader, ibid., December 23, 1993.
6. Eliyahu Lankin, *The Story of Altalena* (Hadar, 1974), 64–65.
7. Menachem Begin, *The Revolt* (Achiasaf, 1956), 58–60.
8. Efraim Even, "The Underlying Ideology of the Etzel Revolt and Its Conflict with Reality," *Haumma* 2 (1974): 209–220.
9. From Moshe Sneh's report on his meeting with Menachem Begin, October 9, 1944; Appendix 17 of *History Book of the Haganah* (Maarachot, 1973), vol. 3, 1887–1893.
10. Quoted in Lankin, *The Story of Altalena*, 64–68.
11. Ibid.
12. *Ha'ir*, April 17, 1992.
13. Begin, *The Revolt*, 58–60.
14. Lankin, *The Story of Altalena*, 64–68.
15. The manifesto is displayed at the Gidi Museum in Jaffa.
16. Begin, *The Revolt*, 60–62.
17. Tzippora Kessel, Israel State Archives, June 3, 1993.
18. Lankin, *The Story of Altalena*, 69.
19. Eitan Livni, *Hamaamad* (Yediot Ahronot, 1987), 57.
20. Ibid., 67.
21. Lev Ami, "Minutes of the Irgun Tzvai Leumi."
22. Ibid. Weapons were taken from the police building near Hadera, a gun battle took place near Haifa, buildings were damaged in Qalqiliya, and in Beit Dagan the attackers failed in their mission and withdrew.
23. Yaakov Shavit, *The Season of the Hunt* (Hadar, 1976), 23.
24. Quoted in *Davar*, November 10, 1944. Golomb suggested combining a warning about an operation against Etzel and a call for the entire Yishuv to ostracize the members of the organization: "The Yishuv must be encouraged not to support them, to cast out those who act on their own accord, without public authority, and possibly this will help prevent [civil war]. The way must be guarded from loose action."
25. Quoted in *History Book of the Haganah*, 533.
26. Shraga Alis, Menachem Begin Heritage Center, January 29, 2001.
27. Yechiel Kadishai, Israel State Archives, February 23, 1993.

28. Aviezer Golan and Shlomo Nakdimon, *Begin* (Yediot Ahronot, 1978), 108.
29. Testimony of Miryam Ravid. Begin's comments are quoted in Moshe Sneh's report on his meeting with Begin on October 9, 1944, in *History Book of the Haganah*, vol. 3, appendix 17, 1887–1893. See also Yehuda Lapidot, *The Saison: The Hunting Down of Brothers* (Jabotinsky Institute, 1994), 123.
30. Begin, *The Revolt*, 114.
31. Lankin, *The Story of Altalena*, 64–69.
32. Ibid.; see also Begin, *The Revolt*, 114.
33. Testimony of Miryam Ravid; see Lapidot, *The Saison*, 120.
34. *Yediot Ahronot*, October 18, 1984. For his entire life Begin did not abandon the habit of listening to the BBC, and he even learned about the Sabra and Shatila massacre from listening to broadcasts from the British station.
35. Quoted in Lev Ami, "Minutes of the Irgun Tzvai Leumi."
36. Quoted in Chaggai Segal, *Dear Brothers: History of the Jewish Underground* (Keter, 1987), 38.
37. Begin, *The Revolt*, 384.
38. Ibid., 177.
39. Ibid., 390.
40. Ibid., 391.
41. Haganah Archives, 112/1117.
42. Begin, *The Revolt*, 155.
43. Anita Shapira, *Yigal Allon: The Spring of His Life* (Hakibbutz Hameuchad, 2004), 249.
44. Quoted in Haganah Archives, 112/1117.
45. Begin, *The Revolt*, 194.
46. Ibid., 193.
47. Quoted in ibid.
48. Eli Shaltiel, *Moshe Sneh: Life* (Am Oved, 2000), 16.
49. From Moshe Sneh's report on his meeting with Begin, October 9, 1944; Appendix 17 of *History Book of the Haganah*.
50. Ibid.
51. Livni, *Hamaamad*, 57; Begin, *The Revolt*, 117.
52. From Moshe Sneh's report on his meeting with Begin, October 9, 1944; Appendix 17 of *History Book of the Haganah*, 1887–1893.
53. "The first thing that Begin would do was something that all headquarters members waited for with anticipation. He would give an overview, a political overview, a review of our activities, a review of our actions, and an overview of the current events in the U.S. and in England itself. He would give ... a survey that also included the results of these actions, what the results were, what we could vote on. These things would appear later as well, in a simpler manner more acceptable for the general public, in the newspaper we published for the general public, called *Herut*, or on the posters we would hang up on the walls of houses in the streets." Betzalel Amitzur, Menachem Begin Heritage Center, June 7, 2000.
54. From Moshe Sneh's report on his meeting with Begin, October 9, 1944; Appendix 17 of *History Book of the Haganah*, 1887–1893.

55. *Haaretz*, November 12, 1944.
56. Shaltiel, *Moshe Sneh*, 143.
57. From a lecture by Professor Shlomo Aharonson, Department of Political Science at Hebrew University, as part of a seminar on Begin; Menachem Begin Heritage Center, July 23–24, 1999.
58. *Maariv*, July 11, 1991. In his last interview, on July 10, 1991, on Army Radio (host: David Dayan), marking sixty years since the establishment of Etzel, Begin said, "The Etzel fighting unit was the factor, as Dr. Silver once said, without which the State of Israel could not have been established."
59. Morris, *Righteous Victims*, 418–444. Gazit estimated that Sadat was planning a war and that the desire he expressed to come to Jerusalem was intended to mislead Israel.
60. From Moshe Sneh's report on his meeting with Begin, October 9, 1944; Appendix 17 of *History Book of the Haganah*, 1887–1893.
61. Ibid.
62. Lev Ami, "Minutes of the Irgun Tzvai Leumi."
63. From Moshe Sneh's report on his meeting with Begin, October 9, 1944; Appendix 17 of *History Book of the Haganah*, 1887–1893.
64. Ibid.
65. Begin, *The Revolt*, 197.
66. Lankin, *The Story of Altalena*, 64–68.
67. Quoted in Lev Ami, "Minutes of the Irgun Tzvai Leumi."
68. Protocol from a meeting of the Jewish Agency leaders, Central Zionist Archives, April 2, 1944.
69. Quoted in Lev Ami, "Minutes of the Irgun Tzvai Leumi," 428.
70. Altman headed the Revisionist movement in Palestine.
71. Lapidot, *The Saison*, 43.
72. *Haaretz*, October 17, 1944.
73. Quoted in Lankin, *The Story of Altalena*, 85.
74. Quoted in Lapidot, *The Saison*, 58.
75. From Moshe Sneh's report on his meeting with Begin, October 9, 1944; Appendix 17 of *History Book of the Haganah*.
76. Cyrus Vance, secretary of state under U.S. President Jimmy Carter, who often spoke with Begin during the peace negotiations with Egypt, wrote about Begin in his diary that Begin was deeply affected by the anti-Semitism in his youth in Poland. Morris, *Righteous Victims*, 419.
77. Material from this and the following two paragraphs is taken from Lankin, *The Story of Altalena*, 83–86, and Lev Ami, "Minutes of the Irgun Tzvai Leumi," 432–440.
78. Ibid., 85.
79. Lev Ami, "Minutes of the Irgun Tzvai Leumi."
80. David Niv, *Battle for Freedom: The Irgun Tzvai Leumi* (Klausner Institute, 1973), vol. 4, 93.
81. Quoted in Lev Ami, "Minutes of the Irgun Tzvai Leumi."
82. Israel Oron, *Death, Immortality and Ideology* (Ministry of Defense, 2002), 75–79.

83. Quoted in Niv, *Battle for Freedom*, 84.
84. Ibid., 88.
85. Yitzhak Shamir, Israel State Archives, January 3, 1995.
86. Quoted in Lev Ami, Minutes of the Irgun Tzvai Leumi, 423. Begin also noted: "Our success depended a lot on the Yishuv's support, at least its tacit support, and now it will largely be destroyed.... Of course, in this case they will not distinguish between us and the 'deviators' [the nickname for the Lehi underground]; we all have to bear the consequences and this fate is inevitable.... We cannot forgive them; this is cheating in every sense of the word; we must draw our conclusions from it.... [But] in our communiqué we will inform the public that the authorities are also responsible for the action in Cairo."
87. In *Book of the Palmach*, vol. 16, ed. Zrobavel Gilad and Mati Meged (Hakibutz Hameuchad, 1956), 803–805.
88. Material in this and the following two paragraphs is from David Ben Gurion, *In the Battle* (Mapai, 1950), vol. 2, 289–298.
89. The Partition Proposal was a plan suggested by the United Nations Special Committee on Palestine (UNSCOP), set up by the United Nations to partition the area administered by the British Mandate into two states and an international zone. The plan was accepted by the U.N. General Assembly on November 29, 1947. The plan called for a Jewish state consisting of almost 55 percent of Palestine and an Arab state encompassing almost 45 percent. Less than 1 percent, the area of Jerusalem and Bethlehem, was to be under U.N. control. Some of the leaders of the leftist Hashomer Hatzair movement preferred a two-nation state, and several leaders of the Hakibbutz Hameuchad, also a socialist movement, were opposed to the partition plan, together with parts of Etzel and Lehi. In any case, the Arabs in Palestine and the Arab states rejected the proposal and began a war against the Yishuv, which they lost. The state of Israel was established over a larger area. The Partition Plan was preceded by a plan proposed by the Peel Commission, set up by the British government, which had also recommended partition but allocated only 17 percent to the Jewish state. This plan caused controversy among the Jews. It was supported by Ben Gurion. However, it was rejected by the Arabs and was never carried out.
90. *Hamashkif*, January 4, 1945.
91. Quoted in Begin, *The Revolt*, 202.
92. Shavit, *The Season of the Hunt*, 80–100.
93. Ibid., 101–120.
94. The night of the massacre of the Huguenots in Paris by the Catholics on August 23, 1572.
95. Niv, *Battle for Freedom*, 99.
96. *History Book of the Haganah*, 540.
97. Regarding the motives of the Palmach fighters in the Saison, see also *Against Terrorist Groups* (pamphlet, Hashomer Hatzair Party Headquarters, June 1946).
98. Quoted in Shavit, *The Season of the Hunt*, 89.

99. *Lehi Writings* (Yair, 1959), 904–905.
100. Moshe Shamir, *Yair* (Zmora Bitan, 2001), 269.
101. Niv, *Battle for Freedom*, 100.
102. Yaakov Meridor, *A Long Road to Freedom* (Achiasaf, 1978), 14.
103. Lapidot, *The Saison*, 80–120.
104. The Etzel finance department was located on the roof of a building on 16 Herzl Street in Tel Aviv.
105. Yitzhak Avinoam, Etzel member, Menachem Begin Heritage Center, March 29, 2001.
106. Batya Eldad, Israel State Archives, January 9, 1994.
107. U.S. President Jimmy Carter, who was present at the Camp David summit in 1978, described Begin as a person who considered himself a man of destiny, a biblical character carrying the future of his people on his shoulders; see Morris, *Righteous Victims*, 435.
108. Quoted in Lev Ami, "Minutes of the Irgun Tzvai Leumi," 423.
109. From a proclamation written in 1944 that also read: "With a gloomy face the faithful Jew asks himself and his neighbor: Will we be beaten for this too? Will a fraternal war break out in Palestine? Will our home be destroyed before it is built? 'Us or them,' said Ben Gurion, 'and all means are acceptable to destroy them.' Yes, the faithful Jew's anxiety is understandable. What will the persecuted do who have been sentenced to such terrible decrees? These are serious questions, and we find it our duty to give an answer, in our names and in the name of Etzel: Be quiet, loyal Jews; there will be no fraternal war in this country." (A poster of the proclamation is at the Gidi Museum in Jaffa.)
110. Quoted in Lev Ami, "Minutes of the Irgun Tzvai Leumi."
111. Yaakov Amrami, *Things Are Greater Than We Are* (Hadar, 1994), 60.
112. Meir Kahn, Israel State Archives, September 6, 1993.
113. Yaakov Sika-Aharoni in *Hayarden* 203 (November 2002): 1–8.
114. Livni, *Hamaamad*, 56.
115. Lankin, *The Story of Altalena*, 67.
116. Quoted in Yaakov Sika-Aharoni in *Hayarden* 203 (November 2002): 1–8.
117. Livni, *Hamaamad*, 122–124.
118. "You are raving, Cain. In the streets of Jerusalem, the streets of Tel Aviv, in town, in the village, and in the Moshav roam thousands of your messengers.... We, the soldiers of Zion, our eyes are turned today—especially today—to brotherly love, to the nation's redemption, to internal peace and external war." Begin wrote the proclamation; see file of pamphlets in Menachem Begin, *In the Underground*, vol. 1 (Hadar, 1959), 221–223.
119. Livni, *Hamaamad*, 110–124.
120. Ibid.
121. Ibid.
122. Ibid.
123. Quoted in ibid., 124.
124. Quoted in Geula Cohen, *Historic Meeting: Haganah, Etzel and Lehi Chiefs around the Table* (Yair, 1986), 72.

125. Quoted in Livni, *Hamaamad*, 122–124.
126. Ibid., 123–124.
127. Ibid., 123–124.
128. *History Book of the Haganah*, 906–931.
129. Quoted in Livni, *Hamaamad*, 123–124.
130. Begin, *The Revolt*, 205.
131. Shaltiel, *Moshe Sneh*, 158, and Shavit, *The Season of the Hunt*, 117–120. Sadeh was also the Haganah's chief of the general staff from 1945 until the end of 1946 and one of the founders of the Israel Defense Forces at the War of Independence.
132. Shaltiel, *Moshe Sneh*, 158–159.
133. Quoted in Shavit, *The Season of the Hunt*, 117.
134. *Haaretz*, February 9, 1982.

CHAPTER 5. A BOMB IN THE HEART OF THE EMPIRE

1. In a letter regarding the union between Lehi and Etzel that Begin sent to Nathan Yellin Mor on September 4, 1944, he wrote, "The differences—methods of war—were emphasized between us on March 19, this year." He was referring to the death of Lehi militant Yerachmiel Aharonson, who was killed in a crossfire with British police officers after they found a gun in his pocket; see Shlomo Lev Ami, "Minutes of the Irgun Tzvai Leumi, July–November 1944," *Zionism* 4 (1976): 416. See also Yaakov Banai, *Anonymous Soldiers* (Yair, 1958), 182.
2. "The children grew up in an uneasy atmosphere. Aliza went with him [Begin] into hiding. I did not. I remained alone with the child I supported. To go by a different name and raise children. . . . I'm surprised they came out fine." Batya Eldad, Israel State Archives, January 9, 1994.
3. "When I would arrive, the little boy Benny would call to me, 'Uncle Shimon, Uncle Shimon, what did you bring me?' Every time I went I would bring with me a little toy so the boy would have something to do. He was miserable; he had no friends; he had nothing." Betzalel Amitzur, Menachem Begin Heritage Center, June 7, 2000.
4. Meir Kahn, Israel State Archives, September 14, 1993.
5. "I helped Ella; I went to the grocery store for her and things like that. Every now and then I had to type things Begin wrote." Tzippora Kessel, ibid., June 3, 1993. See also Kessel, Menachem Begin Heritage Center, September 18, 2000.
6. Shmuel Katz, Israel State Archives, August 6, 1993.
7. "For years, he did not enter a store. When he received a check, he gave it to Aliza." Harry Horowitz, ibid., November 15, 1993.
8. "He had a monthly account, and when he needed a larger amount, I would demand it from Chaim Landau. He is from Krakow, and the Krakowians are known as stingy people. But I insisted. I would bring groceries from the grocery store on Ben Yehuda. I would bring baskets to Aliza so she would not have to leave the house." Meir Kahn, ibid., September 14, 1993.
9. Betzalel Amitzur, Menachem Begin Heritage Center, June 7, 2000.

10. "He was brought newspapers, cigarettes; even when riding the bus he would travel with someone who paid for him. He wanted only small change in his pocket for tips." Harry Horowitz, Israel State Archives, November 15, 1993.
11. Tzippora Kessel, ibid., June 3, 1993.
12. Meir Kahn, ibid., September 14, 1993.
13. Lev Ami, "Minutes of the Irgun Tzvai Leumi," 424.
14. "He used to sit many hours listening to the radio; not a day would go by without the BBC mentioning Etzel or Lehi. Sometimes they would sit and analyze what was said. If he had ready material, there was material for posters. I did not like the style. He used bombastic words. But it was important. He wrote 95 percent of the posters. Eulogies and bereavement prayers. He also had a part in writing the report to UNSCOP. He did not sign all of them; sometimes he would make do with 'Ben David' [Begin's pen name]." Shmuel Katz, Israel State Archives, August 13, 1993.
15. Aviezer Golan and Shlomo Nakdimon, *Begin* (Yediot Ahronot, 1978), 108.
16. Ibid.
17. "There was reason to believe that during a certain period after Stalin's death, the clash between his supporters and opponents would ripen.... The centrifugal tendencies of the national minorities would become stronger.... All these factors could lead—not immediately—to extreme changes in the governing regime of the Soviet Union." Menachem Begin, *White Nights* (Dvir, 1995), 322.
18. Benny Morris, *Righteous Victims* (Am Oved, 2003), 171.
19. Ibid., 170–174.
20. Menachem Begin, ed., *In the Underground* (Hadar, 1959), 28, 30, 52, and elsewhere. Similar labels given to the British appeared in all issues of *Herut*.
21. Israel Eldad, Israel State Archives, December 21, 1993.
22. Eli Shaltiel, *Moshe Sneh: Life* (Am Oved, 2000), 201–207.
23. Menachem Begin, *The Revolt* (Achiasaf, 1956), 260.
24. Ibid., 265.
25. Ibid., 262.
26. The committee members were Rabbi Y. L. Fishman (Maimon), who was elected chairman; Moshe Sneh, deputy chairman; Peretz Bernstein, Levi Shkolnik (Eshkol); Israel Edelson, and Yaakov Riftin. David Remez, head of the National Committee, was appointed committee adviser.
27. David Niv, *Battle for Freedom:* The Irgun Tzvai Leumi (Klausner Institute, 1973), vol. 4, 174.
28. Meir Kahn, Israel State Archives, September 14, 1993.
29. Yaakov Markoviski, *The Irgun Lexicon* (Ministry of Defense, 2005), 244.
30. For example: "May I suggest that the 'Resistance' movement also respects one of its anonymous members who fell while fulfilling his duty. Goodbye, and I hereby shake your right hands. M." Quoted in Shaltiel, *Moshe Sneh*, 218, from Moshe Sneh's private archives, January 11, 1945.
31. Ibid.
32. Begin, *In the Underground*, vol. 1, 90–92. A pamphlet written by Begin and published by Hadar on November 29, 1947 (in ibid., vol. 1, 116–118), stated

the following: "To our Arab neighbors! We do not see you as enemies. We would like to see you as good neighbors.... There is room in the land of Israel for you and for millions of Jews who have no life but in this country. The Hebrew government will give you equal rights.... The Muslim religion and holy places will be subject to your inspectors' supervision.... [But] beware of listening to agitators' advice. Do not try to raise a hand on Jewish life or property.... We'll have to hack it off.... Together we'll advance with the free nations in the world toward justice and freedom.... Our Arab neighbors! We extend our hand to you in peace and brotherhood. Do not reject it!"

33. Avi Shlaim, *The Iron Wall* (Yediot Ahronot, 2005).
34. "The Hebrew War of Independence" (Etzel manual, n.d.).
35. Anita Shapira, *The Army Controversy, 1948: Ben Gurion's Struggle for Control* (Hakibbutz Hameuchad, 1985), 10–13.
36. Morris, *Righteous Victims*, 173.
37. Jacob Coleman Hurewitz, *The Struggle for Palestine* (Schocken Books, 1987), 249.
38. Shaltiel, *Moshe Sneh*, 230.
39. Ibid., 242.
40. "Though Sneh said to halt preparations for an action to stop the planned response to 'Black Sabbath,' he did not forward a similar provision to Etzel and Lehi.... He was satisfied with a plea to pause the action for a few days." Yigal Elam, *Hahaganah, the Zionist Way to Power* (Zmora Bitan–Modan, 1979), 242.
41. Yosef Evron, *Gidi: The Jewish Insurgency against the British in Palestine* (Ministry of Defense, 2001), 221–289.
42. "The idea to sabotage the building housing the British military headquarters was raised in a meeting between Etzel and Lehi before 'Black Sabbath.' Sneh showed signs of agreement. When the Etzel and Lehi members left, I said to Sneh: 'You were hasty to disclose signs of agreement, and you have now stepped into their trap. You must ensure the support of Jerusalem and the Agency for such a thing. King David is not a usual part of the struggle.'" Israel Galili, Yad Tabenkin Archives, May 25, 1983.
43. See the photocopy of the document in Evron, *Gidi*, 103.
44. Shaltiel, *Moshe Sneh*, 280; *History Book of the Haganah* (Maarachot, 1973), vol. 3, 860–864.
45. Evron, *Gidi*, 154.
46. David Robovich, who was inside the hotel on the day of the blast, told me the following on March 20, 2005: "I continued with my work.... A few minutes later Colonel Colley entered the room and told us, 'Everybody is to be confined to his seat.' About ten minutes later an explosion shook the entire ward in the building."
47. One of the archive documents of the Haganah's intelligence service from July 30, 1946, states the following: "We learned ... that immediately after the first explosion, Hamburger, the hotel manager, approached Shaw (the British cabinet secretary) and told him that the building was in danger and

that they should get people out, to which Shaw answered, 'I do not take orders from Jews.'"
48. Quoted in Golan and Nakdimon, *Begin*, 117.
49. Shmuel Katz, Israel State Archives, August 6, 1993.
50. Quoted in Evron, *Gidi*, 157.
51. Yehoshua Freundlich, *From Destruction to Rebirth: The Zionist Policy after World War II and the Establishment of Israel* (Mifalim Universitaim, 1994), 42–49.
52. Morris, *Righteous Victims*, 172.
53. *History Book of the Haganah*, 935–959.
54. Israel Eldad, Israel State Archives, December 21, 1993. Eldad continued: "The significance of national pride was deeply rooted in [Begin], as it was in Jabotinsky. The flogging was an insult to our honor; what could be more offensive than that? It was worse than harming the body. Lehi had no such considerations."
55. He added, "For seventy generations the Gentiles have been whipping us in seventy Diasporas." Begin, *The Revolt*, 318.
56. Chaim Gilad, *In the Shadow of the Gallows* (Hadar, 1978), 7–20.
57. Begin, *The Revolt*, 317, 320.
58. Ibid., 317–325.
59. Shraga Alis, Menachem Begin Heritage Center, January 29, 2001.
60. Ibid.
61. "[Begin] believed that we should accept Jabotinsky as the supreme arbiter, though he no longer existed. It did not seem appropriate. In Lehi we accepted people who were far from the Revisionist movement, willing and committed to fight with weapons against the British—that was the condition; the rest was less important. He did not like the war against imperialism. He was a disciple of Jabotinsky, who nevertheless saw, almost to the end, friendship with Britain as one of the principles of his policy. From the beginning, this did not exist in Lehi." Yitzhak Shamir, Israel State Archives, January 3, 1995.
62. Ibid.
63. "I was surprised, as I did not know, regarding human life, anyone less objective than Begin," Yellin Mor said. Quoted in Uri Avnery, "Begin," *Haolam Haze*, September 20, 1977.
64. Yitzhak Shamir, Israel State Archives, January 3, 1995.
65. "More than once I saw Begin sitting slouched, but once people gathered in front of him, he would light up. People were his fuel. Put before him a crowd of thirty people, and he will always start speaking." From author's conversation with Yanush Ben Gal, April 15, 2005.
66. Quoted in Golan and Nakdimon, *Begin*, 150.
67. Ibid.
68. Ibid., 148.
69. Ibid., 149.
70. "Begin wrote almost everything. I, Shalom Rosenfeld, and Shlomo Skolsky contributed." Yochanan Bader, Israel State Archives, January 21, 1993.

71. Meir Kahn, ibid., September 6, 1993.
72. Luca Wax, Menachem Begin Heritage Center, August 14, 2000.
73. Ze'ev Jabotinsky, *Hadar* (Ari Jabotinsky, 1961).
74. Tzippora Kessel, Israel State Archives, June 3, 1993.
75. Shmuel Katz, ibid., August 6, 1993.
76. "Menachem was closed in himself. He had a light in his eyes when someone talked about a subject that fascinated him, but when his interest subsided, his ears would not hear and he would start to mutter. I would bet that he could not repeat the last word he heard." Meir Kahn, ibid., September 14, 1993.
77. Batya Eldad, ibid., January 9, 1994.
78. Yona Klimovitski, Begin's secretary when he was prime minister, ibid., July 24, 1994.
79. Yitzhak Avinoam, Menachem Begin Heritage Center, March 29, 2001.
80. Morris, *Righteous Victims*, 174–175.
81. Quoted in Michael J. Cohen, *Palestine: Retreat from the Mandate: The Making of British Policy 1936–45* (Holmes and Meier, 1978), 223.
82. Morris, *Righteous Victims*, 175.
83. Markoviski, *The Irgun Lexicon*, 136.
84. Ibid., 170–171. (The break-in was executed on April 4, 1947.)
85. Begin, *The Revolt*, 406.
86. *New York Times*, May 10, 1945.
87. Quoted in Golan and Nakdimon, *Begin*, 148.
88. Morris, *Righteous Victims*, 177.
89. Avshalom Chaviv, Meir Nakar, and Yaakov Weiss.
90. *Haolam Haze*, September 20, 1977.
91. Quoted in Golan and Nakdimon, *Begin*, 172.
92. Quoted in Morris, *Righteous Victims*, 176.
93. Transcript of interview on Army Radio on the day marking sixty years since the establishment of Etzel, *Maariv*, July 11, 1991.
94. *Davar*, October 16, 1947.
95. Niv, *Battle for Freedom*, 176.
96. Yitzhak Avinoam, Menachem Begin Heritage Center, March 29, 2001.
97. Jabotinsky, *Hadar*.
98. "Protocols from the Irgun General Headquarters from July to November 1944," *Zionism* 4 (1976): 400–405.
99. Israel Eldad, Israel State Archives, December 21, 1993.
100. Ibid.
101. *History Book of the Haganah*, 906–931.
102. Yitzhak Avinoam, Menachem Begin Heritage Center, March 29, 2001.
103. *Davar*, July 4, 1947.
104. Yitzhak Avinoam, Menachem Begin Heritage Center, March 29, 2001.
105. Yitzhak Greenbaum, Institute of Contemporary Jewry, December 11, 1965; Yaakov Shavit, *The Season of the Hunt* (Hadar, 1976), 138–140.
106. Shaltiel, *Moshe Sneh*, 388–390.
107. Begin, *The Revolt*, 366.
108. Ibid., 362–370.

109. Ilan Assia, *The Core of the Conflict: The Struggle for the Negev, 1947–1956* (Yad Ben Tzvi, 1994), 37–38.
110. Amichai Paglin, Institute of Contemporary Jewry, November 27, 1970.
111. Lev Ami, "Minutes of the Irgun Tzvai Leumi."
112. Amichai Paglin, Institute of Contemporary Jewry, November 27, 1970.

CHAPTER 6. JUBILATION AND DISAPPOINTMENT

1. Yehuda Lapidot, one of the commanders of the operation, Menachem Begin Heritage Center Archives, August 3, 2000.
2. Ibid.
3. Ibid.
4. Benny Morris, *Righteous Victims* (Am Oved, 2003), 199–202.
5. Uri Milstein, *History of the War of Independence* (Zmora Bitan, 1989), 258–268.
6. Yaakov Markoviski, *The Etzel Lexicon* (Ministry of Defense, 2005), 117.
7. Shraga Alis, Menachem Begin Heritage Center, January 29, 2001.
8. Menachem Begin, *The Revolt* (Achiasaf, 1956), 435–436.
9. Ibid.
10. Meir Kahn, Israel State Archives, September 6, 1993.
11. Begin, *The Revolt*, 428.
12. Shraga Alis, Menachem Begin Heritage Center, January 29, 2001.
13. Quoted in Chaim Lazar, *Conquering Jaffa* (Shelach, 1971), 122.
14. Begin, *The Revolt*, 452.
15. Meir Kahn, Israel State Archives, September 14, 1993.
16. Shmuel Katz, ibid., August 20, 1993.
17. Amichai Paglin, Institute of Contemporary Jewry, November 27, 1970.
18. Morris, *Righteous Victims*, 204.
19. Shraga Alis, Menachem Begin Heritage Center, January 29, 2001.
20. Morris, *Righteous Victims*, 204.
21. Begin, *The Revolt*, 425–426. The Provisional State Council (Moetzet Haam) was the temporary legislature of Israel from shortly before independence until the election of the first Knesset in January 1949. There were thirty-seven members, representing all sides of the Jewish political spectrum. A separate body, the Provisional Government of Israel (Minhelet Haam), was set up as the proto-cabinet, all of whose members were also members of the Provisional State Council; it was headed by Ben Gurion.
22. Menachem Begin, ed., *In the Underground*, vol. 4, 245–247, 325–326.
23. Quoted in *Davar*, May 16, 1948.
24. Jabotinsky Institute Archives.
25. "Words Spoken by the Etzel Commander," *Herut*, no. 97 (May 15, 1948).
26. Markoviski, *The Etzel Lexicon*, 151–154.
27. Yochanan Bader, Israel State Archives, January 21, 1993.
28. The principles of the party included a desire that the state extend from both sides of the Jordan River, a national economy based on a free economy, a separation of the Histadrut's economic enterprises from the professional unions, and the workers' right to join unions. In addition, the party favored a state medical service, the denial of strikes as a means to resolve labor disputes, and

the introduction of compulsory national arbitration. The party's international orientation was toward the West, but it stated that Israel must remain neutral with regard to the conflict between East and West. It should be noted that the principles often stressed equal rights for minorities, and they also included a clause requiring compulsory education for both Jews and Arabs in both Hebrew and Arabic.

29. *Hamashkif,* May 17, 1948. Katznelson was born in 1907 in Babruysk, Russia, and immigrated to Israel in 1923. From 1928 he was an activist in the Revisionist movement and served as its columnist, and he was also active in Herut when it was established.
30. Yechiam Weitz, *From a Militant Underground to a Political Party* (Ben Gurion University, 2003), 22.
31. Dubi Bergman, "The Herut Movement: From the Underground to Politics," (master's thesis, Tel Aviv University, 1978), 33.
32. Yochanan Bader, Israel State Archives, March 4, 1993.
33. Yitzhak Alfasi, *The Etzel: A Collection of Sources and Documents* (Jabotinsky Publishing, 1990), 528–543.
34. *Maariv,* May 27, 1948.
35. Yosef Agassi, *Between Faith and Nationality* (Tel Aviv University, 1993), 117–177.
36. In *Protocols of the Knesset,* vol. 4, July 8, 1956.
37. Weitz, *From a Militant Underground to a Political Party,* 22. Mapam was originally a party with a Marxist-Zionist outlook and represented the left wing. Its pro-Soviet views did not endear it to Ben Gurion; it was not included in the governing coalition, and it became the main opposition to Ben Gurion with nineteen seats in the first Knesset.
38. "Words Spoken by the Etzel Commander," *Herut,* no. 97 (May 15, 1948).
39. In 1925 Ze'ev Jabotinsky established the Revisionist Zionist Party. Three principles stood out in the party platform: reestablishment of the Hebrew legions and a nurturing of the military spirit among the youth; the opening of the borders of the land for mass immigration; and a renewal of the Jewish Colonial Trust Fund and opposition to the Zionist Federation. In 1935, the party resigned from the World Zionist Organization and founded the New Zionist Organization. In 1946, after Jabotinsky's death, it returned to the World Zionist Organization on the grounds that the requirement of establishing a Hebrew state had been fulfilled.
40. Yochanan Bader, *My Journey to Zion: 1901–1948* (Jabotinsky Institute, 1999), 17–18.
41. With the appointment of a political leader to head Etzel, the organization no longer needed Revisionist policy guidelines.
42. "Words Spoken by the Etzel Commander," *Herut,* no. 97 (May 15, 1948).
43. Menachem Begin, "On the Living Teacher," *Haumma* 18 (September 1980): 338–343.
44. Quoted in a Shai report, June 15, 1948, Haganah Archives, 112/1230. (The very fact that the Shai—headed by Isser Harel—continued to keep track of political opponents such as Begin is evidence that it had not yet internalized the essence of democracy.)

45. Weitz, *From a Militant Underground to a Political Party*, 80.
46. Ibid., June 16, 1948.
47. Alfasi, *The Etzel*, 571–572.
48. Weitz, *From a Militant Underground to a Political Party*, 61.
49. Chaim Landau and Shmuel Katz also participated in negotiations on behalf of Etzel, while Yitzhak Greenbaum, Rabbi Yehuda Leib Fishman, David Tzvi Pinkas, David Remez, and Moshe Shapira represented the Jewish Agency and the National Committee. The other participants, besides Remez, a Mapai member, represented the Right and the religious parties.
50. David Ben Gurion, *War Diary* (Israel Ministry of Defense, 1982), 43.
51. Begin, *The Revolt*, 423–424. The agreement also stipulated that it would be necessary to approve and coordinate Etzel actions, including procurement activities, although Begin would be authorized to raise funds, but "the institutions in Israel and abroad would confirm that Etzel was not receiving any funds from the collections made for general security needs."
52. *History Book of the Haganah* (Maarachot, 1973), 1556. The essence of the agreement was as follows: "Etzel will declare disbandment as a military organization when a government is established. It will not attack the British or the Arabs without prior consent. In fronts where Etzel has been positioned it will take orders from our [Haganah] commanders. It will not employ violence or theft. The purchase (of arms and munitions) [will be] only by consent. [It] will carry out the actions assigned to it."
53. Even after the agreement was ratified, many coordination meetings were required to carry it out.
54. Quoted in Weitz, *From a Militant Underground to a Political Party*, 68.
55. Ben Gurion had already issued the order to establish the IDF on May 26.
56. There were six clauses to the agreement: Etzel members would enlist in the IDF in accordance with orders and pledge allegiance to the army; weapons, equipment, and weapons production facilities would be transferred to the army; a temporary headquarters would be established whose members would be Etzel officers, to work on behalf of the army until completion of the enlistment of Etzel members; Etzel operations and headquarters as a military unit in Israel and under Israeli governmental jurisdiction would cease, as a free decision made by the organization; independent procurement operations would be suspended; Etzel weapons plants would be transferred to the IDF. See Weitz, *From a Militant Underground to a Political Party*, 71.
57. Shai report on the Etzel commanders' meeting with Begin, June 8, 1948, Haganah Archives, 112/1230.
58. Quoted in Weitz, *From a Militant Underground to a Political Party*, 72–73.
59. As noted above, the agreement stated that Etzel would transfer all production facilities and weapons to the IDF and would dismantle all such facilities in "the entire state of Israel and in the jurisdiction of the Israeli government." But the parties had different interpretations of the clause about the Etzel presence in Jerusalem: Etzel believed that the city was not legally annexed to the country, while the government saw in the appointment of Dov Yosef as military governor of the city confirmation that the city was included in the "governmental jurisdiction." It should be noted that it was agreed that

Etzel headquarters would continue to operate for one month, until the final incorporation into the IDF; see details in David Niv, *Battle for Freedom: The Irgun Tzvai Leumi* (Klausner Institute, 1973), 213–214.
60. Shlomo Nakdimon, *Altalena* (Yediot Ahronot, 1978), 13.
61. Eli Tabin, *The Second Front* (Hadar, 1973), 193.
62. Meir Pa'il and Pinchas Yorman, *The Test of the Zionist Movement 1931–1948: The Political Leadership's Anger at the Dissidents* (Cherikover, 2002), 311.
63. Nakdimon, *Altalena*, 60.
64. Ibid., 56.
65. Pinchas Vassa, *The Mission: Procurement* (Maarchot, 1967), 206.
66. Uri Brener, *Altalena* (Hakibbutz Hameuchad, 1978), 86–70.
67. The French government recognized the Israeli government only toward the end of the War of Independence, in January 1949. Until then it refused to allow the Israeli government to establish diplomatic representation in France. On the letter of recognition of Etzel, see Tabin, *The Second Front*, 137.
68. The headquarters were on 9 Yehuda Halevi Street, Tel Aviv.
69. Ben Gurion, *War Diary*, 429.
70. Shmuel Katz, *Day of Fire* (Karni, 1982), 359.
71. Brener, *Altalena*, 70–85. Ariel was a member of Beitar in Romania and was among the organizers of the illegal immigration operation on the SS *Struma*. From 1946 on he was the overseas official responsible for organizing illegal immigration on behalf of Etzel headquarters abroad and acted as the headquarters' "foreign minister."
72. Morris, *Righteous Victims*, 225–226.
73. Quoted in Pa'il and Yorman, *The Test*, 365.
74. Nakdimon, *Altalena*, 109–133.
75. "In retrospect it became clear that Etzel would not have disclosed the purchasing connections even if there were no communications failures, due to the confidentiality promised to the French authorities." Niv, *Battle for Freedom*, 253.
76. Shmuel Katz, Israel State Archives, August 6, 1993.
77. Begin, *The Revolt*, 212.
78. Tzippora Kessel, Menachem Begin Heritage Center, September 18, 2000.
79. Eliyahu Lankin, *The Story of Altalena* (Hadar, 1974), 312–314.
80. Based on Etzel records, the ship was carrying 5,000 British guns, 3 million rounds of ammunition, 250 Bren guns, 250 Sten submachine guns, 150 Spandau machine guns, 50 81-mm. mortars, 5,000 mortar shells, and tons of explosives; see Nakdimon, *Altalena*, 130.
81. Begin, *The Revolt*, 212–213.
82. Betzalel Amitzur, an Etzel member who was involved in the negotiations, Menachem Begin Heritage Center, June 7, 2000.
83. Ben Gurion, *War Diary*, 522.
84. Vassa, *The Mission*, 210.
85. Aviezer Golan and Shlomo Nakdimon, *Begin* (Yediot Ahronot, 1978), 187.
86. Shraga Alis, Menachem Begin Heritage Center, January 29, 2001.

87. Meir Kahn, Israel State Archives, September 14, 1993.
88. Nakdimon, *Altalena*, 160–161.
89. The full text of the telegram is as follows: "I do not know what happened this morning, but this time we cannot make any compromises. Either they take orders and obey them or we shoot. I am opposed to any negotiations or agreement. The moment for agreement has passed forever. If you have power, you must enforce it without hesitation." The telegram is displayed at the Yad Tabenkin Archives.
90. Quoted in Nakdimon, *Altalena*, 185.
91. Quoted in Brener, *Altalena*, 129–131.
92. Golan and Nakdimon, *Begin*, p 189.
93. Brener, *Altalena*, 142–144.
94. "Our slanderers talk about the defection or escape of Etzel soldiers. Shame on them. They have named as deserters fighters who have for years without a break risked their lives for the nation. They received horrific news that their brothers were surrounded, attacked, shot, and they ran to their aid. Who was humanly entitled to require them to act differently? I also undertake full responsibility," said Begin; quoted in Nakdimon, *Altalena*, 323.
95. The text of the letter is as follows: "Greenbaum dear, Unfortunately I cannot enter into negotiations with Etzel now for two reasons. 1. There is a government decision. 2. It's late. We informed the United Nations that it was not we who brought weapons into Israel but a group of dissidents. Now is not the time to enter into conspiracies with Etzel about hidden weapons. Etzel stole some cars today and moved part of the army that came from Etzel against the government and its army. And according to *Yediot Ahronot* they have already attacked our army in several places, and I would not be surprised if they attacked government buildings. I appreciate your good intentions, but I doubt whether it is advisable for any government member to meet with an Etzel official under such circumstances. Yours, D. Ben Gurion. The letter is on display in the Ben Gurion Archives and was published in *Davar*, June 9, 1965.
96. Harry Horowitz, Israel State Archives, November 15, 1993.
97. "Begin: Because of the demand that we give an answer regarding surrender within ten minutes, we decided not to accept such a stupid ultimatum." *Hatzofe*, June 23, 1948.
98. Quoted in Nakdimon, *Altalena*, 199.
99. Shraga Allis, Menachem Begin Heritage Center, January 29, 2001.
100. Begin, *The Revolt*, 248.
101. "Lankin: The fire was not intentional; it was very well felt." *Yediot Ahronot*, June 19, 1964.
102. Nakdimon, *Altalena*, 231.
103. Shraga Allis, Menachem Begin Heritage Center, January 29, 2001.
104. Vassa, *The Mission*, 222.
105. Ben Gurion Archives, June 22, 1948.
106. Roman Frister, *Without Compromise* (Zmora Bitan, 1987), 185.
107. Nakdimon, *Altalena*, 240.

108. Pa'il and Yorman, *The Test*, 387.
109. In response to a question asked at a press conference Begin said that he hoped Tel Aviv residents would come to his aid and that "the Etzel members did consider that if they anchored opposite the U.N. offices, the army would not attack the ship in order to avoid injuring U.N. personnel." *Al Hamishmar*, June 24, 1948.
110. *Davar*, June 23, 1948.
111. *Hamashkif*, June 23, 1948.
112. David Ben Gurion, *The Renewed State of Israel* (Am Oved, 1969), 182.
113. Nakdimon, *Altalena*, 253.
114. Quoted in Lankin, *The Story of Altalena*, 320.
115. *Davar*, June 23, 1948.
116. *Hatzofe*, June 23, 1948.
117. Brener, *Altalena*, 224.
118. *Herut*, June 23, 1948.
119. Brener, *Altalena*, 230–231.
120. David Recanati, *Deceitful Bridge* (Hadar, 1977), 143.
121. Golan and Nakdimon, *Begin*, 190.
122. Brener, *Altalena*, 240–241.
123. From comments David Tahori made to journalist Roni Hadar, *Tel Aviv* (newspaper), June 16, 1986.
124. Israel Eldad, Israel State Archives, December 21, 1993.
125. "The speech was long. It was misunderstood; Begin's voice broke. He cried. Many felt that his words were not connecting. Who can blame him for crying, but why could he not send another man to the microphone?" Katz, *Day of Fire*, 415.
126. *Hamashkif*, June 23, 1948.
127. Israel Eldad, *First Tenth* (Hadar, 1976), 351.
128. Shmuel Katz, Israel State Archives, August 13, 1993.
129. Meir Kahn, ibid., September 14, 1993.
130. Begin, *The Revolt*, 251.
131. Ben Gurion, *War Diary*, 540.
132. The five arrested were Yaakov Meridor, Eliyahu Lankin, Betzalel Amitzur, Moshe Chasson, and Hillel Kook.
133. *Herut*, June 24, 1948.
134. David Danon, Israel State Archives, February 17, 1994.
135. *Davar*, June 24, 1948.
136. Doris Lankin, Menachem Begin Heritage Center, February 25, 2001.
137. The disagreement among Etzel members is evident from differing reports. *Al Hamishmar* had the following: "Hundreds of Etzel members announced that they were leaving the organization and would remain in the defense force; many have expressed their opposition to their leaders' actions and their disillusionment after the ship affair" (June 25, 2948). In contrast, Etzel historian David Niv wrote: "Once again voices from the Etzel barracks expressed demands to fight back. Among those demanding [were] even those among the top brass.... The Etzel commander threw in all his weight to prevent civil war" (*Battle for Freedom*, 278).

138. Shmuel Katz, Israel State Archives, August 6, 1993.
139. Doris Lankin, Menachem Begin Heritage Center, February 25, 2001.
140. Katz, *Day of Fire*, 418–419.
141. "Those who will pledge allegiance [to the army] must be treated as all soldiers and trusted until it is discovered that one must not be trusted. Of those who do not pledge, some will be sent to work in the Negev and the Galilee, and some will be handed over to police custody. Particular focus must be placed on the VIPs so they do not escape." Ben Gurion, *War Diary*, 547.
142. Yochanan Bader, Israel State Archives, January 21, 1993.
143. Kol Haherut Radio Broadcast, July 21, 1948; Jabotinsky Institute Archives, H1/10/32.
144. *Hamashkif*, August 27, 1948.
145. Israel Eldad, Israel State Archives, December 26, 1993.
146. Weitz, *From a Militant Underground to a Political Party*, 83–85.
147. Chaim Corfu, Menachem Begin Heritage Center, June 21, 2000.
148. "Menachem Begin in Acre Prison," *Hamashkif*, August 23, 1948.
149. *Herut*, January 13, 1949.
150. Document No. 21, September 8, 1948; Jabotinsky Institute Archives.
151. Weitz, *From a Militant Underground to a Political Party*, 88.
152. *Herut*, July 29, 1948.
153. Minutes from the provisional government meeting, Israel State Archives, August 1, 1948.
154. *Hamashkif*, August 2, 1948.
155. *Haaretz*, August 2, 1948.
156. Chaim Corfu, Menachem Begin Heritage Center, June 21, 2000.
157. "The Revisionists in Jerusalem received 3,300 votes for [the Zionist] Congress. From then on, sympathy for Etzel grew, especially after Begin visited the city." Ben Gurion, *War Diary*, 644–645; *Hamashkif*, August 10, 1948.
158. Jabotinsky Institute Archives, P/1-12-20.
159. Yechiam Weitz, "The Revisionist Criticism of the Yishuv Leadership during the Holocaust," *Yad Vashem Studies* 23 (1984): 271–291.
160. Ben Gurion, *War Diary*, 648–649.
161. Avi Picard, "The Beginning of the Selective Immigration in the 1950s," *Iyunim Bitkumat Israel* 9 (1999): 338–394.
162. Arie Naor, *Begin in Power: A Personal Testimony* (Yediot Ahronot, 1993), 22.
163. Yochanan Bader, Israel State Archives, March 4, 1993.
164. Among the prominent Revisionists who remained in Hatzohar were Arie Altman, Meir Grossman, Eliezer Shostak, and Shimshon Yunichman.
165. Pa'il and Yorman, *The Test*, 424–425.
166. Weitz, *From a Militant Underground to a Political Party*, 91; Nakdimon, *Altalena*, 402.
167. Katz, *Day of Fire*, 438.
168. Dov Yosef, *Loyal City* (Schocken, 1960), 319–320.
169. *Herut*, August 4, 1948.
170. Central Zionist Archives, s127-55 511.
171. Ben Gurion, *War Diary*, 644–645.

172. Minutes from the provisional government meeting, September 5, 1948.
173. Folke Bernadotte, *To Jerusalem* (Achiasaf, 1952), 107–108, 186–193.
174. Only in 1993 did Joshua Zatler, the Lehi commander in Jerusalem, admit in an interview published in *Yediot Ahronot* (September 11, 1993) that he had ordered the murder of Bernadotte, but he refused to admit that Lehi leaders took command of the action. In his autobiography Yitzhak Shamir wrote: "The idea to remove Bernadotte from the scene was born among our friends in Jerusalem, and we did not express any objection" (*Summing Up: An Autobiography* [Yediot Ahronot, 1994], 98). Eldad is the only one who, in 1979, claimed responsibility for the murder. He also said that in February 1949 he met with Yellin Mor at a café; when the latter said, "I do not recall that we decided on Bernadotte," Eldad decided to stop talking to him (*Monitin*, September 13, 1979).
175. Minutes from the provisional government meeting, September 19, 1948.
176. Ben Gurion, *War Diary*, 704.
177. Quoted in Weitz, *From a Militant Underground to a Political Party*, 161–163.
178. In Ben Gurion, *War Diary*, 705.
179. Yitzhak Avinoam, Menachem Begin Heritage Center, March 29, 2001.
180. Menachem Begin, "Shnat Geula Shlema," Jabotinsky Institute Archives, H1-10-3.
181. *Herut*, October 20, 1948.
182. In 1930, Achimeir had established the Brit Habiryonim (the Toughs' Alliance), the first anti-British underground. He was arrested after Arlosoroff's murder and after his release devoted himself to writing.
183. Quoted in Weitz, *From a Militant Underground to a Political Party*, 146–148.
184. *Herut*, October 20, 1948.
185. Doris Lankin, Menachem Begin Heritage Center, February 25, 2001.
186. Shmuel Katz, ibid., August 6, 1993.
187. Shraga Alis, ibid., January 29, 2001.
188. Testimony of Moshe Arens; see Yosef Evron, *Gidi: The Jewish Insurgency against the British in Palestine* (Ministry of Defense, 2001), 350.
189. Kalman Katznelson, *Occupiers in Distress* (Anach, 1983), 53.
190. Israel Eldad, Israel State Archives, December 21, 1993.
191. Yochanan Bader, ibid., January 21, 1993.
192. "Begin at the Gathering in Jerusalem," January 6, 1949; Jabotinsky Institute Archives, P1/-11-20.
193. *Haaretz*, December 17, 1948.
194. Quoted in Weitz, *From a Militant Underground to a Political Party*, 182–184.
195. Bergman, "The Herut Movement."
196. *Haaretz*, January 16, 1948.
197. Ben Gurion, *War Diary*, 967.
198. *Herut*, January 20, 1949.
199. Weitz, *From a Militant Underground to a Political Party*, 199.
200. Jabotinsky Institute Archives, H/2-1-14-1.
201. *Book of Jeremiah* 2:2.

202. *Herut*, January 20, 1949.
203. The demand to hold a referendum resurfaced in 1952, during negotiations for an agreement for reparations from Germany; in 1956, after the withdrawal from Sinai; and in 2004, when members of the Likud demanded, this time in opposition to Prime Minister Ariel Sharon, that a referendum be held on the withdrawal from Gaza and northern Samaria.
204. *Herut*, January 24, 1949.
205. *Kol Haam*, January 25, 1949; *Davar*, January 25, 1949; "Shertok's [Sharett's] Talk," *Davar*, January 24, 1949.
206. The voting rate for Herut was 11.5 percent (49,782 voters out of 434, 694). Mapai received forty-six seats, Mapam nineteen, the United Religious Front sixteen. The election results showed that the major power centers of Herut were in Netanya, Safed, Jerusalem, and Petach Tikvah, where it was the third largest party. In the southern neighborhoods of Tel Aviv too it achieved considerable success—in the Yemenite Quarter more than 50 percent voted for Herut, and in the Hatikva neighborhood over 30 percent voted for it. But compared to the previous elections in October 1946—for the Twenty-Second Zionist Congress—the rate of Herut voters was even lower than that of Hatzohar.
207. Only 2,844 people, 0.7 percent of all voters, voted for Hatzohar. Weitz, *From a Militant Underground to a Political Party*, 230–231.
208. Jabotinsky Institute Archives, H1/1–1.
209. *Yediot Ahronot*, January 27, 1949.
210. *Haaretz*, January 27, 1949.
211. *Herut*, January 16, 1949. See also *Hamashkif*, January 27, 1949.
212. Yochanan Bader, Israel State Archive, January 21, 1993.
213. Jabotinsky Institute Archives, P1/12–20.
214. Minutes from the Mapai Center meetings, Labor Party Archives, Beit Berl College, January 27–30; see Weitz, *From a Militant Underground to a Political Party*, 226–227.

CHAPTER 7. REJECTED AND OUTCAST

1. *Haaretz*, June 26, 1949.
2. Talks began in January 1949 and ended in July 1949. Israel signed an armistice agreement with Jordan, Lebanon, Egypt, and Syria. This led to the official end of the War of Independence.
3. Protocols of the Knesset, vol. 1, April 4, 1949, 289.
4. Arie Naor, *Begin in Power: A Personal Testimony* (Yediot Ahronot, 1993), 102.
5. "We have the Greater Land of Israel," *Herut*, April 30, 1949, 4.
6. Protocols of the Knesset, vol. 3, December 13, 1949, 283–284.
7. Ben Gurion decided on this position with the establishment of the Provisional People's Assembly, and he wrote about it to Israel's second president, Yitzhak Ben Tzvi, on February 27, 1951; see also David Ben Gurion, Path and Vision (Mapai, 1953), 70–71.
8. Arie Gelblum in *Haaretz*, June 26, 1949.
9. Protocols of the Knesset, vol. 3, March 1, 1950, 411.

10. *Haaretz*, April 1, 1950.
11. Ibid., January 6, 1950.
12. Shmuel Katz, Israel State Archives, August 13, 1993.
13. Protocols of the Knesset, vol. 3, November 15, 1949, 125–126.
14. *Herut*, November 26, 1949.
15. *Haaretz*, August 12, 1948.
16. Ibid., February 2, 1950.
17. Ibid., January 6, 1950.
18. *Maariv*, January 5, 1950.
19. *Davar*, July 1, 1950.
20. Arie Gelblum in *Haaretz*, August 26, 1949.
21. Protocols of the Knesset, vol. 7, October 16, 1950, 13–37.
22. Shmuel Katz, *No Courage No Glory* (Dvir, 1981), 10.
23. The government's decision was made on July 4, 1950.
24. Protocols of the Knesset, vol. 6, July 4, 1950, 260–261.
25. Ron Harris, "The Israeli Law, the First Decade," in *The First Decade*, ed. Tzvi Tzameret and Hannah Yablonka (Yad Ben Tzvi, 1991), 244–245.
26. *Haaretz*, February 8, 1950.
27. Shalom Ratzabi, "Jabotinsky and Religion," *Israel* 5 (2004): 31–32.
28. Shmuel Katz, Israel State Archives, August 13, 1993.
29. *Herut*, July 5, 1949.
30. Shmuel Katz, Israel State Archives, August 13, 1993.
31. Meir Kahn, ibid., September 6, 1993.
32. *Herut*, July 5, 1949; *Haolam Haze*, September 20, 1977.
33. Moshe Nissim, Menachem Begin Heritage Center, September 27, 2000.
34. Protocols of the Knesset, vol. 9, May 28, 1951, 1806–1808.
35. Yochanan Bader, *The Knesset and I* (Yediot Ahronot, 1979), 49.
36. Letter from Eri Jabotinsky to Begin, June 8, 1949; Jabotinsky Institute Archives, A/5/4/3.
37. *Herut*, September 2, 1951.
38. "Kook and Jabotinsky at the Press Conference," *Herut*, December 3, 1951.
39. *Maariv*, September 21, 1950.
40. "Words Spoken by the Etzel Commander," *Herut*, no. 97 (May 15, 1948).
41. "Municipal Platform," *Herut*, November 2, 1950; "Begin at a Mass Rally," ibid., October 15, 1950.
42. Yechiam Weitz, "The Turnover That Never Was," *Panim* 9 (1998): 98.
43. *Haaretz*, November 16, 1950.
44. Nadir Tzur, *The Rhetoric of Israeli Leaders in Stress Situations* (Hameuchad, 2004), 24–29.
45. Naor, *Begin in Power*, 22.
46. Yochanan Bader, Israel State Archives, February 17, 1993.
47. Yehoshafat Halpert (Dov's brother), Menachem Begin Heritage Center, August 17, 2004.
48. *Haaretz*, July 6, 1951.
49. For the full text of the party platform, see Jabotinsky Institute Archives, H1–E2/1/14.

50. For the Knesset list, Yaakov Meridor was assigned second place, followed by Yochanan Bader, Binyamin Avniel, Arie Altman, Arie Ben Eliezer, Chaim Landau, Esther Raziel-Naor, Eliezer Shostak, and Chaim Cohen Maguri.
51. Menachem Begin, *The Revolt* (Achiasaf, 1956), 119.
52. Temporary center meeting, October 7, 1948; Jabotinsky Institute Archives, H1-1-1.
53. *Haaretz*, August 5, 1951.
54. *Herut*, July 22, 1951.
55. Ibid., February 27, 1951.
56. Ibid., July 17, 1951. In this election, unlike in the first one, most of the reports of Begin's speeches in *Herut* focused on the excitement they stirred and not on their content.
57. From an interview with my mother, Sima Shilon, and my family, immigrants from Iraq, April 1, 2005.
58. Begin's lecture on November 28, 1974, Institute for the Study of Zionism, Tel Aviv University.
59. Other results were as follows: General Zionists—twenty seats; Mapam—fifteen seats; Hapoel Hamizrachi—eight seats. See Amos Carmel, *Everything Is Political* (Dvir, 1996), 548–549.
60. *Herut*, January 8, 1951.
61. Kalman Katznelson, "Reshit Sikum," *Herut*., November 17, 1950.
62. Quoted in Naor, *Begin in Power*, 91.
63. Ibid., 21.
64. Yonatan Shapira, *Chosen to Command* (Am Oved, 1989), 44.
65. Ibid., 28.
66. Israel Eldad, Israel State Archives, December 8, 1993.
67. Bader, *The Knesset and I*, 58–59.
68. Yochanan Bader, Israel State Archives, January 21, 1993.
69. Bader, *The Knesset and I*, 58–59.
70. Jabotinsky Institute Archives, Personal Archives and Collections, P20/22/1.
71. Arnold Sherman, *Ke'esh Beatzmotav* (Yediot Ahronot), 175.
72. *Herut*, September 23, 1951.
73. Begin finished writing his first book, *The Revolt*, while serving in the first Knesset; see Oren Rosenberg, "Begin and the Herut Movement, 1949–1952," master's thesis, University of Haifa, 2002.
74. Bader, *The Knesset and I*, 49–50.

CHAPTER 8. BE KILLED BUT DO NOT TRANSGRESS

1. In September 1952 Israeli foreign minister Moshe Sharett and West German chancellor Konrad Adenauer signed the Reparations Agreement by which Israel would be paid 3,450 million marks between 1953 and 1965 as compensation for the suffering and material damage caused to the Jews in the Holocaust. Furthermore, West Germany also undertook fixed monthly payments for Holocaust survivors to finance their medical expenses and as compensation for their having been in concentration camps; see Neima Barzel, "Israeli-Germany Relations, from Boycott Policy to Complex Relationships," in *The*

First Decade, ed. Tzvi Tzameret and Hanna Yablonka (Yad Ben Tzvi, 1991), 202–204.

2. Deuteronomy 32:35. Professor Dina Porat, in a conversation on May 5, 2005, told me that her father, a Mapai politician, after consulting with Nachum Goldmann (president of the World Zionist Congress) in a private conversation during the negotiations, chose the word *shilumim*. The word's biblical meaning is "revenge," but in modern Hebrew it is more like "money for compensation."
3. Protocols of the Knesset, vol. 3, January 7, 1952. See also Yaakov Sharett, ed., *Moshe Sharett and the German Reparations Controversy* (Society to Commemorate Moshe Sharett, 2008), 51.
4. Yechiam Weitz, "The Alternative Flag: Israel's Ties with Germany in the Herut Movement," *Zion* 16 (2001): 435–436.
5. The Holocaust was Ben Gurion's main motivation behind his decision to build a nuclear reactor.
6. Natan Alterman in *Davar*, March 16, 1951.
7. *Herut*, October 28, 1951.
8. Yochanan Bader, *The Knesset and I* (Yediot Ahronot, 1979), 58.
9. Yochanan Bader, Israel State Archives, February 17, 1993.
10. *Herut*, January 1 and 6, 1952.
11. Ibid.
12. From a lecture by Dr. Neima Barzel about Begin and his attitude toward the Holocaust; Menachem Begin Heritage Center, March 20, 2002.
13. *Haaretz*, November 11, 1952. Begin's speech was published in full only in *Herut*, and there was a complaint filed against the newspaper for incitement, but in November, at the peak of the storm, the attorney general dismissed the complaint.
14. *Haaretz*, November 11, 1952. For the full text of the speech, see Tamar Brosh, *A Speech for Every Occasion/Against the Reparations Agreement* (Yediot Ahronot/Open University, 1993), 130–135.
15. Geula Cohen, Israel State Archives, March 9, 1992.
16. *Haaretz*, November 11, 1952.
17. Ibid.
18. Israel Eldad, Israel State Archives, December 26, 1993.
19. Quotations in the next several paragraphs are from Protocols of the Knesset, vol. 3, January 7, 1952.
20. Yosef Burg, Israel State Archives, May 8, 1994.
21. Yitzhak Navon, Menachem Begin Heritage Center, December 18, 2000.
22. Protocols of the Knesset, vol. 3, January 7, 1952.
23. Yehoshafat Halpert, ibid., August 17, 2004.
24. Yochanan Bader, Israel State Archives, January 21, 1993.
25. Ibid.
26. *Haaretz*, June 13, 2006.
27. Ibid., January 8 and 9, 1952.
28. Yona Klimovitski, Begin's secretary when he was prime minister, Israel State Archives, July 24, 1994.

29. Menachem Porush, Menachem Begin Heritage Center, May 29, 2002.
30. Israel Eldad, Israel State Archives, December 26, 1993.
31. Yochanan Bader, Israel State Archives, February 2, 1993.
32. *Haaretz*, January 20, 1952.
33. Ibid., March 26, 1952.
34. Ibid., May 26, 1952.
35. Kalman Katznelson, *Israel after the Sinai Campaign* (Hadar, 1957), 150.
36. Chaim Guri published the letter in *Al Hasin'ah* 2 (1997): 6–7.
37. Israel Eldad, Israel State Archives, December 8, 1993.
38. Ibid.
39. Shmuel Katz, ibid., August 20, 1993.
40. Israel Eldad, ibid., April 1, 1994.
41. Benny Morris, *Righteous Victims* (Am Oved, 2003), 255–259.
42. Ibid., 262–265.
43. *Haaretz*, October 16, 1956.
44. Ibid., March 3 and April 20, 1954.
45. Yechiel Kadishai, Menachem Begin Heritage Center, February 6, 2002.
46. *Haaretz*, November 9, 1958.
47. See more in Eyal Kafkafi, *Lavon: Anti Messiah* (Am Oved, 1998).
48. See more in Yechiam Weitz, *The Man Who Was Murdered Twice: The Life, Trial, and Death of Dr. Israel Kastner* (Keter, 1995).
49. Roni Stauber, "The Controversy in the Political Press over the Kastner Trial," *Zionism* 13 (1988): 219–247. Kastner appealed to the Supreme Court, but in March 1957 he was murdered in the doorway of his home on Emmanuel Boulevard in Tel Aviv. The assassin was Ze'ev Eckstein; Dan Shemer waited for him in the car. The Shin Bet suspected that Yosef Menkes, a former Lehi militant, had planned the murder, but he denied involvement. As Kastner hung between life and death, Gruenewald sent him a telegram in which he wrote, "A speedy recovery despite the fundamental contradictions." Most of the judges sitting on the panel discussing the appeal changed the ruling and held that although Kastner had testified after the war on behalf of the SS officer, the things Judge Halevi wrote about him "deserve to be struck out." In 1969, after retiring from court, Halevi was elected to the Knesset on behalf of Herut.
50. Dan Meridor, quoted in *Begin*, ed. Meron Isaacson (Yediot Ahronot, 2003), 72.
51. *Haaretz*, July 25, 1955.
52. Ibid.
53. Ibid., February 11, 1963.
54. Ibid., July 25 and 26, 1955.
55. Yechiel Kadishai, Begin Heritage Center, February 6, 2002.
56. Analysis of election results. See series of articles "From Day to Day," *Haaretz*, July 1955.
57. Minutes from the Herut center meeting, Jabotinsky Institute Archives, H-1, February 27, 1955.
58. *Haaretz*, August 16, 1955.
59. Ibid., June 20, 1955.

60. *Herut*, October 9, 1955.
61. *Haaretz*, November 8, 1955.
62. Yaron Tzur, *A Torn Community: The Jews of Morocco and Nationalism, 1943–1954* (Am Oved, 2001), 406.
63. *Haaretz*, September 2, 1955.
64. Ibid., September 9, 1955.

CHAPTER 9. BUDS OF LEGITIMACY

1. See further details in Motti Golani, *There Will Be a War This Summer: Israel on the Road to the Sinai War 1955–1956* (Ministry of Defense, 1997).
2. Yehoshafat Halpert, Menachem Begin Heritage Center, August 17, 2004.
3. Aviezer Golan and Shlomo Nakdimon, *Begin* (Yediot Ahronot, 1978), 217.
4. Shmuel Katz, Israel State Archives, August 13, 1993.
5. Benny Morris, *Righteous Victims* (Am Oved, 2003), 280–282.
6. *Haaretz*, January 10, 1957.
7. Ibid., April 3, 1957.
8. Ibid., March 14, 1957.
9. Ibid., March 5, 8, and 17, 1957.
10. Ibid., June 20, 1957.
11. Ibid., November 2, 1957.
12. Ibid., April 20, 1957.
13. Ibid., July 22 and August 11, 1958.
14. Ibid., January 8, 1959.
15. Ibid., June 13, 1958.
16. Arie Naor, Menachem Begin Heritage Center, January 26, 2000.
17. Naftali Lavie, "The Great Mystery: Development Areas," *Haaretz*, November 26, 1958.
18. Naftali Lavie, "In All Colors of the Rainbow," *Haaretz*, March 20, 1959.
19. *Haaretz*, November 26, 1958, and March 20, 1959.
20. Ibid., August 11, 1959.
21. Ibid., July 1, 1959.
22. Chaim Israeli, *A Life Story* (Yediot Ahronot, 2005), 333.
23. During the trial of intelligence agent Avri Elad (Avraham Zaidenberg, "the Third Man"), which was held behind closed doors because he was suspected of having collaborated with the enemy, the defendant claimed that he commanded a squad that operated in Egypt in 1954 and that upon his return to Israel he gave a false report—ordered by Defense Minister Pinchas Lavon—at the request of his superiors. Judge Binyamin Halevi believed that he was lying and sentenced him to prison, and a copy of the testimony was sent to the attorney general. Lavon, who had already been ousted from the government and was appointed secretary-general of the Histadrut, demanded that his name be cleared. A ministerial committee headed by Minister of Justice Pinchas Rosen stated that he was innocent and that the order had been given by Chief of Military Intelligence Binyamin Gibli. Ben Gurion refused to accept the commission's findings, claiming that they did not uncover the truth, and he therefore resigned.

24. Chaim Arlosoroff, head of the political department of the Jewish Agency, was murdered in 1933 on the beach in Tel Aviv. At the time he was trying to negotiate with senior Nazis to rescue the Jews of Germany, and the Revisionists often attacked him over this matter. Two Beitar members, Tzvi Rosenblatt and Avraham Stavsky, were accused of the murder. Stavsky was convicted and Rosenblatt was acquitted. Stavsky appealed the verdict and was then acquitted for lack of evidence. Over the years, the belief grew that Arabs, not the Revisionists, had murdered Arlosoroff. For further discussion, see chapter 15, below.
25. *Haaretz*, July 7 and August 23, 1960.
26. Ibid., August 22, 1963.
27. Yochanan Bader, Israel State Archives, February 17, 1993.
28. Arie Naor, *Begin in Power: A Personal Testimony* (Yediot Ahronot, 1993), 27.
29. *Haaretz*, August 22, 1963.
30. Even before the 1961 elections, Ben Gurion accepted the roles of prime minister and defense minister only on the condition that Lavon be dismissed as Histadrut secretary; the party agreed to his demand and dismissed Lavon from office.
31. Dan Giladi, *Eshkol as a Leader* (Cathedra, Yad Ben Tzvi, 1985), 16–168.
32. Harry Horowitz, Israel State Archives, August 15, 1993.
33. Yechiel Kadishai, Menachem Begin Heritage Center, February 6, 2002.
34. Ibid.
35. Ibid.
36. *Haaretz*, August 11, 1964.
37. Yochanan Bader, Israel State Archives, February 17, 1993.
38. *Haaretz*, September 25, 1964.
39. Yonatan Shapira, *Chosen to Command* (Am Oved, 1989), 136–142.
40. *Haaretz*, January 24, 1963.
41. "Gahal Platform," Jabotinsky Institute, Herut Archives, H1/16/2, August 1965.
42. Quoted in Y. Shapira, *Chosen to Command*, 137.
43. Yechiel Kadishai, Menachem Begin Heritage Center, February 6, 2002.
44. Moshe Nissim, ibid., September 27, 2000.
45. *Haaretz*, November 13, 1963.
46. Ibid., May 21, 1965.
47. *Mabat Chadash*, June 7, 1966.
48. *Haaretz*, March 11, 1966.
49. Ibid.
50. Shraga Alis, Menachem Begin Heritage Center, January 29, 2001.
51. Quoted in Tedi Frois, *Begin in Power* (Keter, 1984), 28.
52. Israel Eldad, Israel State Archives, December 21, 1993.
53. *Haaretz*, June 30, 1966.
54. *Maariv*, June 30, 1966.
55. *Yediot Ahronot*, June 29, 1966.
56. Matityahu Drobles, Institute of Contemporary Jewry, April 19, 1973.
57. *Yediot Ahronot*, January 19, 1973.

58. *Davar*, September 13, 1966.
59. *Haaretz*, September 11, 1966.
60. Ofer Yehoshua in *Sefer Haoved Haleumi* 2 (1983): 111.
61. Shraga Alis, Menachem Begin Heritage Center, January 29, 2001.
62. Ibid.

CHAPTER 10. THE BREAKTHROUGH

1. *Haaretz*, August 27, 1967.
2. Minutes from the third Herut conference, Jabotinsky Institute Archives.
3. Tamir's partners in establishing the party were Arie Altman and Eliezer Shostak.
4. *Haaretz*, February 21, 1967.
5. Ibid., January 26, 1967.
6. Begin's library is exhibited at the Menachem Begin Heritage Center Archives.
7. Tom Segev, *Israel in 1967* (Keter, 2005), 111–112.
8. Benny Morris, *Righteous Victims* (Am Oved, 2003), 286–327.
9. Ibid., 293.
10. *Maariv*, June 20, 1969.
11. Yechiel Kadishai, Menachem Begin Heritage Center, February 2, 2002.
12. Quoted in Aviezer Golan and Shlomo Nakdimon, *Begin* (Yediot Ahronot, 1978), 223.
13. Yochanan Bader, Israel State Archives, February 17, 1993.
14. "Begin told me that during May 1948 Eliezer Livne approached him, on behalf of Ben Gurion, and suggested that if Minhelet Haam would not declare a state, Etzel should do so. Ben Gurion never confirmed this, of course." Shmuel Katz, ibid., August 13, 1993.
15. Segev, *Israel in 1967*, 291.
16. Author's conversation with Yechiel Kadishai, November 2006.
17. *Haaretz*, January 2, 1967.
18. Golan and Nakdimon, *Begin*, 224.
19. Segev, *Israel in 1967*, 340.
20. *Haaretz*, June 5, 1967.
21. Segev, *Israel in 1967*, 357.
22. See further details in Michael B. Oren, *Six Days of War: June 1967 and the Making of the Modern Middle East* (Dvir, 2007).
23. Eitan Haber, *Today War Will Break Out* (Yediot Ahronot, 1987), 229–230.
24. Yosef Burg, Israel State Archives, May 18, 1994.
25. Yechiel Kadishai, Menachem Begin Heritage Center, February 6, 2002.
26. Quoted in Segev, *Israel in 1967*, 381.
27. Ibid., 413.
28. Ibid., 439–470.
29. *Haaretz*, June 16, 18, and 28, 1967.
30. "He saw his role as the final formulator and authority of every letter or document of political significance." Yosef Burg, Israel State Archives, May 8, 1994.

31. Quoted in Segev, *Israel in 1967*, 515.
32. Ibid., 473.
33. Yechiel Kadishai, Menachem Begin Heritage Center, February 2, 2002.
34. *Haaretz*, January 26, 1970.
35. "Begin told me, 'After two thousand years, they are creating a united Jerusalem because of the garbage on the roads?' He reformulated the wording. He felt like Israel's guardian." Harry Horowitz, Israel State Archives, August 15, 1993.
36. Quoted in Segev, *Israel in 1967*, 551. Under the mini-transfer Palestinians would not be moved by force; rather, a part of the Palestinians in the Gaza Strip, who had lived under Egyptian rule before the war, would be convinced to settle in El Arish on the Sinai Peninsula, which had also been under Egyptian rule before the war.
37. Ibid., 574.
38. Quoted in Arie Naor, *Begin in Power: A Personal Testimony* (Yediot Ahronot, 1993), 44.
39. Segev, *Israel in 1967*, 528.
40. *Haaretz*, September 7 and 11, 1967.
41. Ibid., September 19 and November 1, 1967.
42. Ibid., May 5 and 24, 1968.
43. Yechiel Kadishai, Menachem Begin Heritage Center, February 2, 2002.
44. *Haaretz*, May 11, 1968.
45. Ibid., May 27, 1968.
46. *Hayom*, June 24, 1966.
47. Minutes from the Herut center meeting, Jabotinsky Institute Archives, E-1, February 27, 1955.
48. Golan and Nakdimon, *Begin*, 226.
49. According to the French version of the resolution, it could have been seen as a demand to withdraw from all the "territories."
50. Yigal Allon, "Israel: The Case for Defensible Borders," *Foreign Affairs* (1976): 41–47.
51. Daniel Dacre, "Defensible Borders: The Return of Repressed Strategy," *Azure* 21 (Fall 2005): 64–87.
52. Hamaarach, an alliance of the major left-wing parties, was first established in 1965 as an alliance of Mapai and Achdut Haavoda; it was dissolved three years later when the two parties and Rafi formally merged into the Israeli Labor Party and then reestablished in 1969 through an alliance of the Israeli Labor Party and Mapam.
53. *Haaretz*, January 2 and 9, 1969.
54. Ibid., November 21, 1968.
55. Ibid., January 1, September 29, October 4, and November 21, 1968.
56. "[Begin] said that everything was based on Jabotinsky's well-known essay 'The Iron Wall' and on 'The Morality of the Iron Wall'—two articles published in 1923 that are the basis for our need to be strong, always stronger than the others. This is the fundamental and principal concept of his school of thought, a school of thought in which you must be strong to survive. In

order to move forward, you must believe that that one [the Arabs] really wants to drive you away. So you have to be strong and avoid a situation of being attacked. Do not panic. The other side should know that." Yechiel Kadishai, Menachem Begin Heritage Center, February 2, 2002.

57. Simcha Dinitz, director general of the Prime Minister's Office during the tenure of Golda Meir, ibid., November 13, 2002.
58. *Haaretz*, November 22, 1968.
59. Ibid.
60. *Maariv*, June 20, 1969.
61. *Haaretz*, September 1, 1969.
62. Ibid., June 12, 1969.
63. Ibid., October 21, 1969.
64. Ibid., November 9 and 28, 1969.
65. Ibid., December 29, 1969.
66. Yochanan Bader, Israel State Archives, February 17, 1993.
67. *Yediot Ahronot*, June 7, 1974.
68. Yochanan Bader, Israel State Archives, February 2, 1993.
69. Ibid., March 4, 1993.
70. "Bader was among the intelligent ones and was very hurt. It was tremendously painful. But Begin expelled all the intelligent members, everyone who had some weight." Israel Eldad, ibid., December 21, 1993.
71. "In matters of foreign policy he saw me as a rival, and in his field of expertise, Bader the jurist overshadowed Begin's leadership." Shmuel Katz, ibid., August 13, 1993.
72. Arie Naor, Menachem Begin Heritage Center, January 5, 2001.
73. Ibid.
74. Ibid.
75. *Yediot Ahronot*, January 19, 1973.
76. *Haaretz*, January 23, 1970.
77. Ibid., May 23, 1973.

CHAPTER 11. ONCE MORE A REBEL

1. In Begin's view, in the original Munich Agreement the Western powers basically agreed to let Nazi Germany occupy Czechoslovakia.
2. Arie Naor, Menachem Begin Heritage Center, January 5, 2001.
3. *Haolam Haze*, August 5, 1970.
4. Arie Naor, at the time assistant to the minister of development, Menachem Begin Heritage Center, January 5, 2001.
5. Aviezer Golan and Shlomo Nakdimon, *Begin* (Yediot Ahronot, 1978), 226–227.
6. *Maariv*, January 5, 1973.
7. Yechiel Kadishai, Menachem Begin Heritage Center, February 2, 2002.
8. The PLO, established in 1964 as an initiative of Arab countries, was headed by Ahmed Shukeiri. Arafat headed Fatah, a faction in the organization, and in 1969 he was elected as head of the PLO Executive Committee and as leader of the organization.
9. Yechiel Kadishai, Menachem Begin Heritage Center, February 2, 2002.

10. Yona Klimovitski, Israel State Archives, July 24, 1994.
11. Israeli Television Archives.
12. Yona Klimovitski, Israel State Archives, July 24, 1994.
13. Ibid.
14. *Haaretz*, March 17, 1971.
15. Ibid., October 10, 1970.
16. Ibid., November 11, 1970.
17. Ibid., August 2, 1970.
18. *Yediot Ahronot*, March 5, 1971.
19. Quoted in Tedi Frois, *Begin in Power* (Keter, 1984), 94.
20. *Haaretz*, January 13 and 14, 1972; *Yediot Ahronot*, January 12, 1972.
21. *Haaretz*, June 30, 1972.
22. *Yediot Ahronot*, January 19, 1973.
23. "Weizmann did not respect him. Begin did not know until the last minute how many loyalists had moved over to Weizmann's camp." Yochanan Bader, Israel State Archives, March 4, 1993.
24. The episode as related here is from Shraga Alis, Menachem Begin Heritage Center, January 29, 2001.
25. *Haaretz*, September 18, 1972.
26. Ibid., October 2, 1972.
27. Ibid., August 15, 1972.
28. Ibid., December 21, 1973.
29. *Maariv*, December 22, 1972.
30. On September 5, 1972, Black September, an organization led by George Habash, murdered eleven members of the Israeli Olympic delegation, and in response the Israeli government decided to assassinate the killers.
31. *Haaretz*, September 15 and 29, 1972.
32. Geula Cohen, Israel State Archives, September 1992.
33. In 2006 there were two hundred founding members in the Likud, gathered in the Tagar (Challenge, Defiance) group. (The name was taken from a Beitar song: "Tagar—al kol Maatzor Vemeitzar.") Members of this group continue even today to examine the candidate list for the Likud according to one criterion—loyalty to Begin's way (from author's conversation with Eli Shitrit, Yossi Nachmias, and Avraham Appel, members of the Tagar group, January 2006).
34. *Haaretz*, January 2, 1973.
35. See Yoram Lichtenstein, "The Herut Movement, Internal Processes and Structure," master's thesis, Hebrew University, 1974.
36. Ibid.
37. *Haaretz*, January 2, 1973.
38. Ibid., January 15, 1973.
39. Ibid., January 19 and 31, 1973.

CHAPTER 12. AGAINST EXPECTATIONS

1. Numerous books and studies have been devoted to the Yom Kippur War and the mistaken perception that led to its outbreak. In writing this chapter, I relied mainly on Uri Bar-Yosef, *The Watchman Fell Asleep: The Surprise of the*

Yom Kippur War and Its Origins (Zmora Bitan, 2001); I was also aided by data from Henry Kissinger, *Crisis: The Anatomy of Two Major Foreign Policy Crises* (Shalem, 2004), 18–259, and Eitan Haber and Ze'ev Schiff, *Yom Kippur War Lexicon* (Dvir, 2003).

2. "What was strange, what seemed strange at the time, was that during the meetings you would suddenly hear the positions of MK Begin and Landau, Chaim Landau, who had information from the front: 'It's not like that. As we crossed the canal, the situation was such-and-such.' They received all kinds of information. Then it turned out it was Arik. Arik Sharon was calling and giving [them] information." Yitzhak Navon, Menachem Begin Heritage Center, December 18, 2002.
3. Yechiel Kadishai, ibid., February 6, 2002.
4. From an interview with Dan Meridor, May 9, 2007.
5. Haber and Schiff, *Yom Kippur War Lexicon*, 406.
6. "When we moved to an offensive in the Golan Heights and were not too far, a few dozen miles from Damascus, I expressed my opinion in the presence of Minister Galili, who was Golda's adviser for security affairs: Be careful not to go to Damascus; Damascus is the lady of all kingdoms in the Arab world, and if we enter Damascus, we will have a war against all Arab countries. Begin said, 'I would like us to go to Damascus with the tanks, take the Jews, put them on the tanks, and bring them here. I would like that.' He was a romantic. It was so unrealistic, so impractical, but it was romantic." Yitzhak Navon, Menachem Begin Heritage Center, December 18, 2002.
7. Yona Klimovitski, Israel State Archives, July 24, 1994.
8. *Haaretz*, October 17, 1973.
9. Ibid., October 24, 1973.
10. Ibid., November 23, 1973.
11. Ibid., November 13 and 16, 1973; *Yediot Ahronot*, November 14, 1973.
12. Moshe Nissim, Menachem Begin Heritage Center, September 27, 2000.
13. "He was not naive. He was smarter. One day during the 1973 campaign, I accompanied Begin and Yechiel in the car during one of their trips. It was a gathering in Ashdod. On the way Yechiel and I talked as if between ourselves about how this move cannot be made and how we cannot rely on Tamir and how we cannot accept what Arik is doing, etc. Begin would sit next to the driver during these trips and we, in the back. At one point he turned to us and said, 'You think I can't raise all these arguments? Believe me, I can raise them better than the way you are putting them now, but there are other reasons.' He thought at the time that Gahal had no choice, and if Gahal did not make the move, then he would lose his chance to really create an alternative and [Gahal] could even reach a stage of internal disintegration. The pressure of the media was significant in this decision-making process." Arie Naor, ibid., January 8, 2001.
14. *Haaretz*, August 3, 1973.
15. Yoram Lichtenstein, "The Herut Movement, Internal Processes and Structure," master's thesis, Hebrew University, 1974.
16. The former Rafi members were Yigal Horovich and Tzvi Shiloach.

17. Quoted in Arie Naor, *Begin in Power: A Personal Testimony* (Yediot Ahronot, 1993), 23.
18. *Haaretz*, September 4 and 5, 1973.
19. *Yediot Ahronot*, August 10, 1973.
20. "Love of Zion is above and beyond everything. The pride in being Jewish." Rachel Halperin, Menachem Begin Heritage Center, June 2000.
21. Yochanan Bader, Israel State Archives, March 4, 1993.
22. *Haaretz*, August 9 and 10, 1973.
23. Naor, *Begin in Power*, 22.
24. Quoted in Yonatan Shapira, *Chosen to Command* (Am Oved, 1989), 158.
25. *Herut*, March 13, 1965.
26. *Yediot Ahronot*, January 13, 1975.
27. Y. Shapira, *Chosen to Command*, 158.
28. Ibid., 98–106.
29. Arie Ziv, "About the Image of the Herut Movement," *Haaretz*, July 6, 1951.
30. *Haaretz*, April 19, 1973.
31. Ibid., December 10 and 17, 1973.
32. Ibid., June 4, 1974.
33. Ibid., January 16, 1975.
34. Ibid., April 12, 1974.
35. Ibid., September 8, 1974.
36. Ibid., December 20, 1974.
37. "We were raised on a tradition of revolutions—the Russian, and that which preceded it, and it was easy to slide into it in political life. There was a fear, not only among opponents of the underground, about the attitude of those who had experienced the underground to the basic elements of civil life. Begin was the first leader who taught and preached democracy, and he did it from the opposition." Yitzhak Shamir, Israel State Archives, January 3, 1995.
38. *Haaretz*, July 5, 1974.
39. Ibid., April 9, 1974.
40. Ibid., January 8, 1975. Halevi stayed in the Likud with the status of a faction with a single member and was not required to return his seat to the party.
41. Ibid., December 4, 1975.
42. Ibid., January 7 and 14, 1977.
43. "At one point I went up to Begin's room and asked him his opinion. He told me some things he would like to have written in the resolutions, including the wording that 'Israel's borders will be determined in negotiations for the signing of peace treaties, and the border will pass in Sinai and the Golan Heights.' Meaning, for the eyes and ears of those who did not yet notice the nuances of these wordings, that Begin no longer talked about complete control of the territories that we liberated from our enemies during the Six-Day War—the War of Redemption, as he called it; rather he talked about the border within Sinai, the possibility of territorial compromise. There was also a possibility of territorial compromise over the Golan Heights. No cease-fire lines." Arie Naor, Begin Heritage Center, January 8, 2001.
44. *Haaretz*, January 13 and 26, 1975.

45. Ibid., June 3, 1976.
46. Quoted in Naor, *Begin in Power*, 46.
47. *Haaretz*, June 6, 1975.
48. Israeli Broadcasting Authority (IBA), May 17, 1975.
49. Yehoshafat Halpert, Menachem Begin Heritage Center, August 17, 2004.
50. *Haaretz*, March 17, 1975. The figure of four hundred is discussed in Menachem Begin, *The Revolt* (Achiasaf, 1956), 514–520.
51. Ibid., May 25, 1976.
52. Ibid., March 18, 19, and 20, 1975.
53. Ibid., July 14, 1976.
54. Quoted in Tedi Frois, *Begin in Power* (Keter, 1984), 37.
55. Ibid.
56. *Haaretz*, July 5, 1976.
57. Quoted in Frois, *Begin in Power*, 139.

CHAPTER 13. GOD, YOU HAVE CHOSEN US TO RULE

1. *Haaretz*, April 5, 1976.
2. Ibid., January 6, 1977.
3. Ibid., October 22, 1976.
4. Ibid., April 9, 1976.
5. Ibid., October 17, 1976.
6. Nir Chefetz and Gadi Bloom, *The Shepherd* (Yediot Ahronot, 2005), 303–311.
7. Yitzhak Shamir, Israel State Archives, February 6, 1995.
8. "What did Begin call [Weizmann]? A likeable rascal. He did not understand much in matters of state. Anyway, maybe he understood, but he did not take them seriously. He did not help politically. He had a halo; as commander of the air force, he had the aura of a so-called friend among friends who people loved being around . . . but his remarks regarding political matters were not always appreciated by Begin. Begin refused to hear Ezer's comments about peace, as if it could be made quickly. Water runs slowly in such matters, . . . and you need to think and to think again. . . . Therefore he was not the most popular person. Begin wanted him in the frame, not to jump ahead too far." Yechiel Kadishai, Menachem Begin Heritage Center, February 6, 2002.
9. Quoted in Arie Naor, *Begin in Power: A Personal Testimony* (Yediot Ahronot, 1993), 18.
10. Yehoshafat Halpert, Menachem Begin Heritage Center, August 17, 2004.
11. Arie Naor, ibid., August 17, 2001.
12. *Haaretz*, March 27, 1977.
13. Ibid., April 6, 1977.
14. Yechiel Kadishai, Menachem Begin Heritage Center, February 6, 2002.
15. *Haaretz*, March 10, 1977.
16. Ibid., March 27, 1977.
17. Quoted in Naor, *Begin in Power*, 20.
18. "He was sick and thin. Arrived every morning at ten, eleven, and asked, 'What's up?'" Yona Klimovitski, Israel State Archives, July 24, 1994.
19. "He always said it. If it does not work this time, I'm retiring." Yona Klimovitski, ibid.

20. Shmuel Katz, ibid., August 20, 1993.
21. For more details see a thorough discussion in Efraim Ya'ar and Ze'ev Shavit, eds., *Trends in Israeli Society* (Open University, 2001), 533–579; Yochanan Peres, *Ethnic Relations in Israel* (Sifriat Hapoalim, 1976); and Chanan Haber, Yehuda Shenhav, and Pnina Mutzpi Haller, eds., *Mizrahim in Israel: A Critical Observation of Israel's Ethnicity* (Hakibbutz Hameuchad, 2002).
22. Israel Eldad, Israel State Archives, January 4, 1994.
23. Asher Arian, *The Elections in Israel 1977* (Academic Press, 1980), 277–280.
24. The play *Julius Caesar*, written by William Shakespeare, was put on by the Cameri Theater in 1977.
25. *Haaretz*, May 6, 1977.
26. *Yediot Ahronot*, May 6, 1977.
27. For more details, see Alex Ansky, *The Selling of the Likud* (Modan, 1978).
28. *Haaretz*, April 25, 1977.
29. Ibid., May 16, 1977; *Maariv*, May 16, 1977.
30. *Haaretz*, May 16, 1977.
31. Naor, *Begin in Power*, 22.
32. Ibid., 17.
33. Yona Klimovitski, Israel State Archives, July 24, 1994.
34. Quoted in Naor, *Begin in Power*, 26.
35. Israeli Broadcasting Authority (IBA), May 17, 1977.
36. Ibid.
37. Ibid.

CHAPTER 14. NO MORE WAR

1. Israeli Broadcasting Authority (IBA), May 30, 1977.
2. *Ha'ooma*, 58, 4 (1987).
3. Yaakov Achimeir's words at a seminar in the Menachem Begin Heritage Center, March 19, 2002.
4. "He believed that there was some sort of Providence, that we didn't stay alive for nothing [after the Holocaust]. He had a purpose. That's how he saw himself." Batya Eldad, Israel State Archives, January 9, 1994.
5. *Yediot Ahronot*, May 19, 1977.
6. Arie Naor, *Begin in Power: A Personal Testimony* (Yediot Ahronot, 1993), 31–32.
7. Quoted in Nir Chefetz and Gadi Bloom, *The Shepherd* (Yediot Ahronot, 2005), 146.
8. "[Begin] feared Sharon; it was love mixed with hesitation. In the movement he wanted him in any form, and he pressured me, as head of the organization department, to let him in. But he wasn't the first choice for minister of defense. I wasn't excited either. I've seen in him 'inconsideration toward the other and disrespect toward citizenship.' But he [Begin] insisted it aroused fear in the Arabs." Yitzhak Shamir, Israel State Archives, February 6, 1995.
9. Naor, *Begin in Power*, 58.
10. Yechiel Kadishai, Menachem Begin Heritage Center, February 6, 2002.
11. Naor, *Begin in Power*, 67.
12. Ibid., 28–29.

13. Harry Horowitz, Israel State Archives, November 15, 1993.
14. Yitzhak Avinoam, Menachem Begin Heritage Center, March 29, 2001.
15. From an interview with Dan Meridor, *Eretz Acheret* 36 (October–November 2006): 33.
16. Yehuda Avner, Menachem Begin Heritage Center, April 13, 2005.
17. Ibid.
18. Israel Eldad, Israel State Archives, January 4, 1994.
19. Avi Shlaim, *The Iron Wall* (Yediot Ahronot, 2005), 344.
20. Arie Naor, Menachem Begin Heritage Center, January 8, 2001.
21. Quoted in Tedi Frois, *Begin in Power* (Keter, 1984), 40.
22. Yechiel Kadishai, Menachem Begin Heritage Center, February 6, 2002.
23. Harry Horowitz, Israel State Archives, November 15, 1993.
24. Arie Naor, Menachem Begin Heritage Center, January 8, 2001.
25. *Chadashot*, August 2, 1991.
26. Yosef Burg, Israel State Archives, May 8, 1994.
27. Menachem Porush, Menachem Begin Heritage Center, May 29, 2002.
28. Chaim Corfu, Menachem Begin Heritage Center, June 21, 2000.
29. Menachem Porush, Menachem Begin Heritage Center, May 29, 2002.
30. Yosef Burg, Israel State Archives, May 8, 1994.
31. Yitzhak Shamir, Israel State Archives, January 3, 1995.
32. Moshe Nissim, Menachem Begin Heritage Center, September 27, 2000.
33. Quoted in Naor, *Begin in Power*, 51.
34. Tal Committee report for the formulation of an appropriate arrangement regarding the recruitment of yeshiva students, vol. 1, April 2000, 23–24.
35. Israel Eldad, Israel State Archives, January 4, 1994.
36. Ibid.
37. Arie Naor, Menachem Begin Heritage Center, December 26, 2000.
38. Quoted in Naor, *Begin in Power*, 33.
39. Government Photography Archive (NPC), June 7, 1977.
40. The old Jew used to stand at the door of the Herut headquarters when the party was in opposition and shout, "Begin to power! Begin to power!" When asked if he found the job worthwhile, he replied, "The pay isn't great, but at least it's a job for life!"
41. The discussion here and in the next paragraph is from Naor, *Begin in Power*, 34–35.
42. Quoted in ibid, 47.
43. Ibid., 66.
44. Ibid, 76.
45. Ibid., 53.
46. Related by Dan Meridor at a seminar in the Menachem Begin Heritage Center, February 19, 2002.
47. Yitzhak Chofi, Menachem Begin Heritage Center, January 11, 2002.
48. Ibid.
49. Yona Klimovitski, Israel State Archives, July 24, 1994.
50. Israel Eldad, Israel State Archives, January 4, 1994.
51. Yona Klimovitski, Israel State Archives, July 24, 1994.

52. Told to me by Yanush Ben Gal, April 14, 2005.
53. Ibid.
54. Yitzhak Shamir, Israel State Archives, January 3, 1995.
55. Yitzhak Chofi, Menachem Begin Heritage Center, January 11, 2002.
56. Yehuda Lapidot, Menachem Begin Heritage Center, August 3, 2000.
57. Harry Horowitz, Israel State Archives, November 15, 1993.
58. Yona Klimovitski, Israel State Archives, July 27, 1994.
59. Yechiel Kadishai, Israel State Archives, February 4, 1993.
60. Quoted in Naor, *Begin in Power*, 97.
61. David Ben Gurion, *War Diary* (Am Oved, 1969), 102.
62. Yehuda Avner, Menachem Begin Heritage Center, April 13, 2003.
63. Related by Yechiel Limor at a seminar in the Menachem Begin Heritage Center, March 20, 2002.
64. Harry Horowitz, Israel State Archives, August 15, 1993.
65. Israel Eldad, Israel State Archives, January 4, 1994.
66. Ibid.
67. Shmuel Katz, Israel State Archives, August 20, 1993.
68. Yitzhak Shamir, Israel State Archives, January 23, 1995.
69. Shmuel Katz, Israel State Archives, August 8, 1993.
70. Quoted in Naor, *Begin in Power*, 104.
71. "From Begin's point of view, over time, what Jabotinsky had written in 'The Iron Wall' in 1923 had come true, and it was possible to promote the process that ended with the signing of the peace agreement in March 1979." Yechiel Kadishai, Israel State Archives, February 10, 1993.
72. Shmuel Katz, Israel State Archives, August 8, 1993.
73. Shlaim, *The Iron Wall*, 344.
74. Naor, *Begin in Power*, 115.
75. Ibid., 117.
76. There was an assumption in the Carter government that peace agreements between Israel and the Arab countries would reduce the known effect of the Soviet Union on these countries. See Jimmy Carter, *Keeping Faith: Memoirs of a President* (University of Arkansas Press, 1995), 173–174.
77. Naor, *Begin in Power*, 120.
78. Ibid., 122.
79. Frois, *Begin in Power*, 42.
80. Quoted in ibid., 42–43.
81. Shmuel Katz, Israel State Archives, August 6, 1993.
82. Naor, *Begin in Power*, 113.
83. Ibid., 127.
84. Yitzhak Shamir, Israel State Archives, January 23, 1995.
85. Yechiel Kadishai, Israel State Archives, January 5, 1993.
86. Shlaim, *The Iron Wall*, 345.
87. From an interview with Chaim Corfu, *Yediot Ahronot*, February 22, 2002.
88. Shlaim, *The Iron Wall*, 346.
89. Naor, *Begin in Power*, 129.
90. Benny Morris, *Righteous Victims* (Am Oved, 2003), 421.

91. Shlaim, *The Iron Wall*, 337.
92. Yechiel Kadishai, Menachem Begin Heritage Center, February 6, 2002.
93. After many of arguments at the top of the ministry of defense, it was agreed to cancel the parade. Begin settled for a military parade and a march of underground veterans at the Hebrew University in Jerusalem.
94. Quoted in Naor, *Begin in Power*, 134.
95. Ibid.
96. Ibid., 135.
97. Noted by Professor Avinoam Reches in Michael Karpin's film *I Can't Take It Anymore*.
98. Quoted in Naor, *Begin in Power*, 57.
99. Frois, *Begin in Power*, 43.
100. Quoted in Morris, *Righteous Victims*, 423.
101. Ibid., 421.
102. Yechiel Kadishai, Israel State Archives, January 5, 1993.
103. Ibid.
104. Naor, *Begin in Power*, 140.
105. Yechiel Kadishai, Israel State Archives, January 5, 1993.
106. Ofer Grosbard, *Menachem Begin: A Portrait of a Leader—A Biography* (Resling, 2006), 187.
107. Yechiel Kadishai, Israel State Archives, January 1993.
108. Naor, *Begin in Power*, 142.
109. Shmuel Katz, Israel State Archives, August 6, 1993.
110. Carter, *Keeping Faith*, 330.
111. Quoted in Naor, *Begin in Power*, 140.
112. Yechiel Kadishai, Israel State Archives, February 10, 1993.
113. Ibid.
114. Naor, *Begin in Power*, 143.
115. Ibid., 144.
116. Morris, *Righteous Victims*, 423.
117. Naor, *Begin in Power*, 145.
118. Israeli Broadcasting Authority (IBA), November 19, 1977.
119. Frois, *Begin in Power*, 50.
120. Quoted in Morris, *Righteous Victims*, 425.
121. "Begin believed that Sadat wanted peace, knowing that Sadat's situation was very bad internally, in regard to the Egyptian population. A special chemistry had grown between them." Yechiel Kadishai, Israel State Archives, March 2, 1993.
122. Naor, *Begin in Power*, 146–149.
123. Ibid., 150–156.
124. Yechiel Kadishai, Israel State Archives, February 10, 1993.
125. Frois, *Begin in Power*, 95.
126. Shmuel Katz, Israel State Archives, August 20, 1993.
127. Moshe Dayan, *Shall the Sword Devour Forever? Breakthrough: A Personal Account of the Egypt-Israel Peace Negotiations* (Yediot Ahronot, 1981), 80.
128. Naor, *Begin in Power*, 162.
129. Ibid., 163.

130. From an interview with Chaim Landau, *Yediot Ahronot*, December 20, 1977.
131. "I didn't like that when there were arguments inside the movement, his tone of voice was as if kids were fighting in front of their father." Shmuel Katz, Israel State Archives, August 20, 1993.
132. Quoted in Frois, *Begin in Power*, 53.
133. Comments of Dan Patir at a seminar in the Menachem Begin Heritage Center, March 19, 2002.
134. Comments of Moshe Arens at a seminar in the Menachem Begin Heritage Center, March 21, 2002.
135. Shmuel Katz, Israel State Archives, August 20, 1993.
136. Ibid.
137. Ibid.
138. Yitzhak Avinoam, Menachem Begin Heritage Center, March 29, 2001.
139. Quoted in Naor, *Begin in Power*, 163.
140. Ibid., 166.
141. Elyakim Rubinstein, Israel State Archives, May 5, 1994.
142. Shalom Kital at a seminar in the Menachem Begin Heritage Center, March 19, 2002.
143. Ibid.
144. *Haaretz*, June 27, 1978.
145. Ibid., June 25 and 26, 1978.
146. Ibid., August 18, 1978.
147. Dayan, *Shall the Sword Devour Forever?* 119–127.
148. Ibid.
149. Yona Klimovitski, Israel State Archives, July 27, 1994.
150. Comments of Dan Meridor at a seminar in the Menachem Begin Heritage Center, March 21, 2002.
151. From an interview with Chaim Corfu, *Yediot Ahronot*, February 22, 2002.
152. Quoted in Naor, *Begin in Power*, 174.
153. Ibid., 173–174.
154. Batya Eldad, Israel State Archives, January 9, 1994.
155. "There was some modesty and closedness in her. Even as the prime minister's wife she came to my office and didn't meet at her place. It suited her. She liked going to people from the Katamon neighborhood, helping the challenged and the poor. She pushed Menachem but didn't like to stand out in her way of life." Batya Eldad, ibid.
156. Sarah Doron, Menachem Begin Heritage Center, May 7, 2001.
157. Yona Klimovitski, State Archives, July 27, 1994.
158. Elyakim Rubinstein, Israel State Archives, May 5, 1994.
159. From the diary of Dan Patir, September 3, 1978; cited in Menachem Rahat, *13 Days in September* (Menachem Begin Heritage Center, 2004).
160. Shlaim, *The Iron Wall*, 92–94.
161. From the diary of Dan Patir, September 7, 1978; cited in Rahat, *13 Days in September*.
162. Quoted in Morris, *Righteous Victims*, 419.
163. Ibid., 439.
164. Yechiel Kadishai, Menachem Begin Heritage Center, February 6, 2002.

165. Ibid.
166. Simcha Dinitz, Menachem Begin Heritage Center, November 13, 2002.
167. Yosef Burg, Israel State Archives, May 8, 1994.
168. From the diary of Dan Patir, September 13, 1978; cited in Rahat, *13 Days in September*.
169. Quoted in Shlaim, *The Iron Wall*, 353.
170. Yona Klimovitski, Israel State Archives, July 24, 1994.
171. Sam Lewis at a seminar in the Menachem Begin Heritage Center, March 21, 2002.
172. Yechiel Kadishai, Israel State Archives, February 10, 1993.
173. Simcha Dinitz, Menachem Begin Heritage Center, November 13, 2002.
174. Yechiel Kadishai, Israel State Archives, February 10, 1993.
175. Yona Klimovitski, Israel State Archives, July 24, 1994.
176. Yitzhak Shamir, Israel State Archives, January 23, 1995.
177. Yechiel Kadishai, Israel State Archives, February 23, 1993.
178. Elyakim Rubinstein, Israel State Archives, May 5, 1994.
179. Shlaim, *The Iron Wall*, 358–359.
180. Shmuel Katz, Israel State Archives, August 20, 1993.
181. Naor, *Begin in Power*, 176–177.
182. "Begin: I really did wonder about the phone call. He [Sharon] said that we could agree about the settlements in Sinai. I've been told Ezer asked him to call me." From the diary of Dan Patir; cited in Rahat, *13 Days in September*.
183. Meir Rosen, legal adviser to the Foreign Ministry, Menachem Begin Heritage Center, August 28, 2001.
184. Elyakim Rubinstein, Israel State Archives, May 5, 1994.
185. Meir Rosen, Menachem Begin Heritage Center, August 28, 2001.
186. Shlaim, *The Iron Wall*, 363.
187. Naor, *Begin in Power*, 180.
188. From the diary of Dan Patir; cited in Rahat, *13 Days in September*.
189. Comments of Sam Lewis at a seminar in the Menachem Begin Heritage Center, March 20, 2002.
190. Harry Horowitz, Israel State Archives, November 15, 1993.
191. Arie Naor, Menachem Begin Heritage Center, January 5, 2001.
192. Yechiel Kadishai, Menachem Begin Heritage Center, February 6, 2002.
193. The discussion and quotes in the next several paragraphs are from ibid.
194. Frois, *Begin in Power*, 60.
195. Yechiel Kadishai, Menachem Begin Heritage Center, February 6, 2002.
196. Yona Klimovitski, Israel State Archives, July 24, 1994.
197. Ibid.
198. *Haaretz*, December 11, 1978.
199. Yechiel Kadishai, Israel State Archives, February 23, 1993.
200. Ibid., April 15, 1993.
201. Yosef Burg, Israel State Archives, May 18, 1994.
202. Naor, *Begin in Power*, 195–196.
203. Quoted in ibid., 197.

CHAPTER 15. DETERIORATION

1. Tedi Frois, *Begin in Power* (Keter, 1984), 59.
2. "He had a huge conflict with himself." Yona Klimovitski, Israel State Archives, July 24, 1994.
3. "He's very fond of the Gush Emunim people due to their actions. He suffered very much from the meetings with them. . . . [Therefore] I would interrupt and say, 'Gentlemen, there is another meeting' because I saw the suffering they caused him was tremendous. My impression was, a psychological evaluation, that in fact he thought that if he were their age, he would have done the same. I had a feeling that he thought to himself: in fact they're right. He himself did not show it." Yechiel Kadishai, ibid., January 19, 1993.
4. Yosef Burg, ibid., May 8, 1994.
5. Yona Klimovitski, ibid., July 24, 1994.
6. *Haaretz*, July 21, 1979.
7. Ibid., September 18, 1979.
8. Ibid., July 24, 1979.
9. Ibid., July 22, 1979.
10. From author's conversation with Arie Naor, April 25, 2007.
11. "He had a heart attack and a stroke. Weizmann attacked him and said he was not functioning. But Begin continued as the utmost power who watched over the camp." Yosef Burg, Israel State Archives, May 8, 1994.
12. Avi Shlaim, *The Iron Wall* (Yediot Ahronot, 2005), 367.
13. Yechiel Kadishai, Menachem Begin Heritage Center, February 6, 2002.
14. Yitzhak Zamir, ibid., July 24, 2001.
15. Yechiel Kadishai, Israel State Archives, February 10, 1993.
16. Yosef Burg, ibid., May 8, 1994.
17. Naor, *Begin in Power*, 201.
18. Moshe Dayan, *Shall the Sword Devour Forever? Breakthrough: A Personal Account of the Egypt-Israel Peace Negotiations* (Yediot Ahronot, 1981), 242.
19. Akiva Eldar and Idit Zertal, *Lords of the Land* (Zmora Bitan-Dvir, 2004), 88.
20. Nir Chefetz and Gadi Bloom, *The Shepherd* (Yediot Ahronot, 2005), 310–320.
21. "Weizmann suggested serious alternative policies. For example, during the debate on the settlements that took place at the Ministerial Committee on Security Affairs . . . [he raised the issue of] whether to support a settlement policy of establishing five or six blocs of settlements surrounding the mountains that would be built toward the east, where there was no private and cultivated land, so that no private land would have to be expropriated for the settlements' construction (thus lessening the international pressure on Israel) or to establish a settlement wherever possible, pinhead settlements, without an economic infrastructure and a concentration of several small communities around a large center, as Israel had done up to then. The first approach was Weizmann's, the second Sharon's. The government adopted Sharon's. The assumption was that Sharon's policy would help prevent the division of the Land of Israel, as Begin put it, while Weizmann's approach would not necessarily prevent a division but could eventually lead to the

adoption of the borders according to the Allon Plan or the improved Allon Plan." Arie Naor, Menachem Begin Heritage Center, January 8, 2001.

22. Settlements in the Occupied Territories, the Supreme Court's position, a report by B'Tzelem, March 1997, 17.
23. Naor, *Begin in Power*, 204.
24. Dayan, *Shall The Sword Devour Forever?* 243–244.
25. Yechiel Kadishai, Israel State Archives, February 23, 1993.
26. Naor, *Begin in Power*, 205.
27. Yitzhak Shamir, *Summing Up: An Autobiography* (Yediot Ahronot, 1994), 137.
28. Halavi Project: The Decision-Making Process, State Auditor's Report, 1986.
29. "[Begin] was against the enactment of this law. He thought it was damaging and pointless. But once Geula Cohen brought this bill to the Knesset, Begin said, 'Well, what can I do? Can I resist this? How will I explain it to the world? That I am against the Jerusalem Law?" Arie Naor, Menachem Begin Heritage Center, January 8, 2001.
30. Noted in Resolution 478, adopted by the U.N. Security Council on August 20, 1980.
31. Frois, *Begin in Power*, 46–47.
32. Yona Klimovitski, Israel State Archives, July 24, 1994. Klimovitski pointed out, "[Begin] had two problems he was not familiar with—economics and security—and he paid the price."
33. Frois, *Begin in Power*, 55.
34. Ibid.
35. Tzohar, Central Bureau of Statistics, February 1999.
36. Frois, *Begin in Power*, 62.
37. "He believed with all his heart in the idea of social justice. He felt compelled to let people live with human dignity, with respect and so forth. He saw eradicating poverty as a holy cause. He also saw it as the fulfillment of his ideology, and the idea that he expressed several times, that the government must benefit the people was not only his election slogan but also his own philosophical belief. But the political negotiations swallowed up most of his time." Arie Naor, Menachem Begin Heritage Center, January 8, 2001.
38. From a lecture given by Yoram Aridor at the Menachem Begin Heritage Center, February 10, 2002, about a minimum-wage bill submitted on March 15, 1971.
39. Ibid.
40. Frois, *Begin in Power*, 46.
41. Ibid., 47.
42. Horowitz was a member of Hareshima Hamamlachtit, established by Rafi members who did not return to Haavoda after the split in Rafi; it joined the Likud on the basis of its support for a Greater Israel.
43. Naor, *Begin in Power*, 206.
44. Quoted in ibid.
45. From a lecture given by Yoram Aridor at the Menachem Begin Heritage Center, March 20, 2002.

46. "Already in Herut and then later in Gahal they talked about the slogan 'Not for the product, but for the needy'—that is, transfer money directly to those in need and do not subsidize particular products. But there were two products that Begin insisted must continue to be subsidized: bread and public transport. He saw bread as something symbolic and also the main dietary source for low-income families and public transport as something related mainly to those who could not afford a private car. So he insisted that the subsidies for these products, even if they were reduced here and there during general policy cuts, remain a significant percentage of the product prices. Also [this was a way] to pay his debt to those who had supported the Likud, even before the Herut movement, over the years. More than once he had arguments with his finance ministers on this issue, with two especially—with Ehrlich and then with Yigal Horowitz. With Yigal the arguments were more severe." Arie Naor, Begin Heritage Center, January 8, 2001.
47. Alexander Rafaeli, Begin's adviser, Israel State Archives, May 26, 1993.
48. Letter to the president of Egypt, August 1980, Israel State Archives.
49. "At the end of 1980, the public commission on the status of teachers, headed by Judge Etzioni, published its report. The commission was established when Ehrlich was finance minister. The report stated the need to raise teachers' salaries significantly and to invest more heavily in teacher education. The finance minister said, 'This is out of the question.' The education minister said it was out of the question for it not to happen; after all, the government had promised the teachers that it would accept the report's conclusions. Begin heard these arguments and said feebly, but in a determined manner, that it was unthinkable that a commission headed by a judge had been formed but that the government would not accept its conclusions. This resulted in the resignation of Yigal Horowitz. Yet another political calculation was part of the equation. Hammer put it very bluntly, almost as an ultimatum, that it was quite clear that accepting Yigal's position meant a crisis with the Mafdal. One must choose the lesser of two evils. So we don't have just an ideology here but also political considerations." Arie Naor, ibid., December 26, 2000.
50. Quoted in Frois, *Begin in Power*, 61.
51. *Ha'ooma*, no. 150 (November 2002): 141.
52. Harry Horowitz, Israel State Archives, November 15, 1993.
53. "There were two approaches: Begin's approach (of which David Levy was the main promoter) to designate the money for improving housing, adding living spaces, rooms, closed balconies, that sort of thing. The second approach was advocated by Katz, who convinced Yigael Yadin to engage also in social rehabilitation, mainly in these neighborhoods, to develop the residents' involvement in the community, etc. These are different perceptions of this issue. [Begin] saw the rehabilitation of the poor neighborhoods as a project with a double purpose. On one hand, [he saw it as] repaying his debt to the people who had supported him all along, certainly since 1955, when the residents of the immigration towns started voting for him. On the other hand, he saw this project as doing justice." Arie Naor, Menachem Begin Heritage Center, January 8, 2001.

54. Yechiel Kadishai, Israel State Archives, April 27, 1993.
55. Yona Klimovitski, ibid., July 24, 1994.
56. *Ha'ooma*, no. 150 (November 2002): 141.
57. From a lecture given by Eliezer Don Yihya at the Menachem Begin Heritage Center, March 20, 2002.
58. Frois, *Begin in Power*, 108.
59. Yechiel Kadishai, Israel State Archives, December 23, 1993.
60. "What stood at the background of Weizmann's resignation was a dispute between the defense minister and the finance minister about the defense budget. The real background, however, was Weizmann's attempt to bring about Begin's dismissal and to replace him. At that point Weizmann appeared to be Begin's natural replacement. There was a consensus over this idea. Therefore Weizmann believed that if he pressed for Begin's resignation, the leadership would fall into his hands. Weizmann took advantage of Begin's difficult visit to the United States; he was interviewed on television and criticized Begin sharply. He said that Begin was sowing despair among the people and that it was impossible to profit from the tremendous benefits of the peace treaty with Egypt through despair, and he advised [that the people] not think in yesterday's terms. Ever since then, Begin waited for Weizmann to resign. The conflict was an opportunity. Begin sided with the finance minister and left Weizmann no choice. But even Begin's supporters did not see Weizmann's departure favorably, for several reasons. First, it weakened the government. Second, it could have led to creating a coalition with Hamaarach. Third, it could have weakened the supporters of peace within the government vis-à-vis those opposed to this direction, led by the man perceived as Weizmann's ultimate successor—Ariel Sharon." Arie Naor, Menachem Begin Heritage Center, January 8, 2001.
61. Shlaim, *The Iron Wall*, 368.
62. Yona Klimovitski, Israel State Archives, July 24, 1994.
63. Naor, *Begin in Power*, 206.
64. Chefetz and Bloom, *The Shepherd*, 328.
65. Yona Klimovitski, Israel State Archives, July 24, 1994.
66. Yitzhak Shamir, ibid., February 6, 1995.
67. Arie Naor, Menachem Begin Heritage Center, January 8, 2001.
68. Quoted in Frois, *Begin in Power*, 66.
69. Ibid.
70. Chefetz and Bloom, *The Shepherd*, 327.
71. Yona Klimovitski, Israel State Archives, January 27, 1994.
72. "Before the election there was a clear majority in all surveys; the most obvious and solid public opinion was in favor of a Hamaarach government and against Begin's government. The election forecast was that Hamaarach, headed by Peres, would beat the Likud, headed by Begin, by a large margin. This was the type of thing that influenced Begin. Not only was he a bit ill at the time, but his mood was also affected by the data that continued to flow in his direction." Arie Naor, Begin Heritage Center, January 8, 2001.
73. Yona Klimovitski, Israel State Archives, July 24, 1994.

74. Ofer Grosbard, *Menachem Begin: A Portrait of a Leader—A Biography* (Resling, 2006), 246.
75. Yitzhak Zamir, Menachem Begin Heritage Center, July 24, 2001.
76. "The conclusions were not clear-cut; the suspects of Arlosoroff's murder were acquitted because there was insufficient evidence that they were the murderers. But the commission also found no evidence to point to someone else. The question of who murdered Arlosoroff still remains open." Yitzhak Zamir, ibid.
77. Quoted in Meron Isaacson, ed., *Begin* (Yediot Ahronot, 2003), 69.
78. Quoted in Naor, *Begin in Power*, 211.

CHAPTER 16. THE BEGIN DOCTRINE

1. "Shostak came to Begin and said, 'We now need a political minister of finance, and from all the people in the government, the most suitable for achieving our main purpose is Yoram Aridor.' Aridor is a lawyer and an economist. He also has a degree in political science. He's an educated, broad-minded man. The first minister of finance in the history of Israel with a degree in economics. Begin considered it for a while and accepted the suggestion." Arie Naor, Menachem Begin Heritage Center, January 8, 2001.
2. Arie Naor, *Begin in Power: A Personal Testimony* (Yediot Ahronot, 1993), 113.
3. Tedi Frois, *Begin in Power* (Keter 1984), 67.
4. "Aridor succeeded, by some administrative moves and by changes in the indirect tax policy on certain consumer products, to create a feeling among the public that the situation was getting better, that there was hope, and that they should think about prolonging the Begin government. It appears that demand for the products on which he lowered the taxes increased such that tax revenues increased as well. Despite the liberalization, inflation in the times of Ehrlich and Yigal Horowitz had been sky-high and kept rising and rocketing during the times of Shamir and Peres." Arie Naor, Menachem Begin Heritage Center, January 8, 2001.
5. Frois, *Begin in Power*, 64.
6. "The public mood changed after the Aridor policy. It became clear first of all in the election for the Histadrut. It turned out that the Likud got the same support it had had in 1977. Despite the rising inflation, support for the Likud among Histadrut members remained stable. It was like an adrenalin shot for Begin. The night the election results were published, he was motivated for battle and began his campaign. For the first time, he accepted help from an American election adviser brought by Yaakov Meridor." Arie Naor, Menachem Begin Heritage Center, January 8, 2001.
7. Naor, *Begin in Power*, 208–209.
8. Israeli Broadcasting Authority (IBA), April 19, 1981.
9. Yechiel Kadishai, Israel State Archives, January 5, 1993.
10. Yechiel Kadishai, Israel State Archives, January 5, 1993.
11. Quoted in Naor, *Begin in Power*, 212.
12. Ibid., 213.
13. Ibid., 214.

14. Quoted in Ofer Grosbard, *Menachem Begin: A Portrait of a Leader—A Biography* (Resling, 2006), 247.
15. Yechiel Kadishai, Israel State Archives, January 5, 1993.
16. The following discussion is from Naor, *Begin in Power*, 214–216.
17. "The historic Jewish tragedy was the deepest element in his personality." Sam Lewis, U.S. ambassador to Israel, Menachem Begin Heritage Center, March 20, 2002.
18. Naor, *Begin in Power*, 218–220; Shlomo Nakdimon, *Tamuz in Flames* (Yediot Ahronot, 1984), 87–91.
19. Comments of Sam Lewis at a seminar in the Menachem Begin Heritage Center, March 21, 2002.
20. Ibid., February 10, 2002.
21. Nakdimon, *Tamuz in Flames*, 168–177.
22. Quoted in Naor, *Begin in Power*, 212.
23. Shimon Peres, *Battling for Peace* (Weidenfeld and Nicolson, 1995), 210–212.
24. Arie Naor, Menachem Begin Heritage Center, January 8, 2001.
25. A note written by Begin about the meeting is kept by Professor Yaakov Bar Siman Tov.
26. "The elections for the Histadrut were the day prior to this meeting, and despite the poor Knesset election survey results for the Likud, the results for the Histadrut were that the Likud not only didn't lose but actually gained power, little as it may have been. For us it was a very important sign. I remember entering the Ministerial Committee for National Security Affairs the next morning, and I heard Begin, in the middle of one of the minister's talks, calling to me, 'Moshe,' with a hand gesture as if to say, 'Thank God we didn't fail.' From this day onward it was a different Begin. The known Begin, the leader, the aggressive, decisive man. All the weakness he used to have. . . . I remember some people from Haavoda talking badly about him, as if he were living on his pills and making his decisions according to the pills he was given, etc. Everything changed completely. The shining leader in Begin emerged from this day on." Moshe Nissim, Menachem Begin Heritage Center Archive, September 27, 2000.
27. Shimon Shiffer, *Snowball* (Yediot Ahronot, 1984), 41.
28. "I firmly supported the proposal but objected to the date suggested by Begin. That day, according to a decision accepted in the Ministerial Committee for National Security Affairs, we downed some Syrian helicopters that had attacked the Lebanese, the Christians. The same week we executed some more military actions with massive impact, and I, who supported Begin so much, told him I thought it was not the right timing the coming Sunday. We are allowed to do it. We should do it, but we are not a powerful country that can astound the world all at once with military actions. It's impossible to do that in three to four days. We should be more modest, even though we are strong. I offered to authorize the prime minister, the minister of defense (who was Begin himself as well), and the minister of foreign affairs to set the date, which would not be that coming Sunday. Begin listened to my reasoning, accepting it despite the enthusiasm of the more eager supporters of his original

proposal." Moshe Nissim, Menachem Begin Heritage Center Archive, September 27, 2000.
29. Quoted in Nakdimon, *Tamuz in Flames*, 175.
30. Arie Naor, Menachem Begin Heritage Center, January 8, 2001.
31. Ibid.
32. Yitzhak Chofi, Menachem Begin Heritage Center, January 11, 2002.
33. Told to me by Yonatan Ben Gal, November 24, 2006.
34. Arie Naor, Menachem Begin Heritage Center, January 8, 2001.
35. Naor, *Begin in Power*, 222–224.
36. Arie Naor, Menachem Begin Heritage Center, January 8, 2001.
37. Quoted in Nakdimon, *Tamuz in Flames*, 219.
38. Moshe Sasson, *Seven Years in the Land of the Egyptians* (Idanim, 1992), 148–149.
39. Ibid.
40. Yechiel Kadishai, Israel State Archives, April 15, 1993.
41. I am in possession of the telegram.

CHAPTER 17. KING OF ISRAEL

1. Quoted in Arie Naor, *Begin in Power: A Personal Testimony* (Yediot Ahronot, 1993), 224–225.
2. From author's conversation with Shaul Ben Gal (Yanush's son), September 8, 2006.
3. Naor, *Begin in Power*, 225.
4. Quoted in ibid., 217.
5. Israeli Broadcasting Authority (IBA), June 1981.
6. Quoted in Naor, *Begin in Power*, 227.
7. Israeli Broadcasting Authority (IBA), June 1981.
8. Ibid.
9. Ibid.
10. Ibid.
11. *Maariv*, June 26, 1981.
12. "It is a pleasure to see this crowd and a pleasure to see that there are no Chach'chachim destroying the election rallies.... The Chach'chachim are at Metzudat Ze'ev. They are barely Shin Gimelim [acronym for "battalion police"—low-cadre, usually problematic soldiers doing sentry duty at camp gates] if they even go into the army. The soldiers and commanders of the combat units are here [at the Hamaarach rally]." Dudu Topaz, Israeli Broadcasting Authority (IBA), June 27, 1981.
13. Yechiel Kadishai, Menachem Begin Heritage Center, February 6, 2002.
14. The full text of the speech, parts of which follow below, is on the Beitar Web site: http://www.betar.org.il/ideology/chachahim.htm.
15. Israeli Broadcasting Authority (IBA), July 1, 1981.
16. Dayan died of cancer shortly after the election. His party joined the coalition before he died, without him.
17. "Indirectly, in veiled speech, I think, Begin was saying to Sharon, 'You speak and act like a pig.'" Arie Naor, Menachem Begin Heritage Center, January 8, 2001.

18. Quoted in Naor, *Begin in Power*, 263.
19. Yona Klimovitski, Israel State Archives, July 24, 1994.
20. From author's conversation with Arie Naor, April 25, 2007.
21. *Maariv*, August 7, 1981.
22. Naor, *Begin in Power*, 265.
23. Sam Lewis, Menachem Begin Heritage Center, February 20, 2002.
24. Quoted in Naor, *Begin in Power*, 266.
25. From author's conversation with Yanush Ben Gal, April 14, 2005.
26. Ibid.
27. Yona Klimovitski, Israel State Archives, July 24, 1994.
28. Yechiel Kadishai, ibid., March 2, 1993.
29. Yosef Burg, ibid., May 18, 1994.
30. Yona Klimovitski, ibid., July 24, 1994.
31. Yosef Burg, ibid., May 18, 1994.
32. "Maybe the bath was slippery, and maybe the brain did not receive enough oxygen. You cannot say for sure what happened." Yosef Burg, ibid.
33. Ofer Grosbard, *Menachem Begin: A Portrait of a Leader—A Biography* (Resling, 2006), 262.
34. Yosef Burg, Israel State Archives, May 8, 1994.
35. "Begin was eager to pass this law. All day, from start to finish, he was in a state of euphoria ahead of enacting this law." Yitzhak Zamir, Menachem Begin Heritage Center, July 24, 2001.
36. Quoted in Naor, *Begin in Power*, 233.
37. Avi Shlaim, *The Iron Wall* (Yediot Ahronot, 2005), 376.
38. Quoted in Naor, *Begin in Power*, 234.

CHAPTER 18. "THERE WILL BE NOT A SINGLE KATYUSHA"

1. Quoted in Benny Morris, *Righteous Victims* (Am Oved, 2003), 463.
2. "The weakest link in the Arab coalition is Lebanon. The Muslim rule is artificial and easy to shake. A Christian state must be established, and its borders will be the Litani River. We shall make her our ally." David Ben Gurion, *War Diary* (Israel Ministry of Defense, 1982), 102.
3. Moshe Sharett, *A Personal Diary* (Maariv, 1978), 996.
4. The Black September events began after an attempted assassination of King Hussein while he was on his way to his plane in Amman on September 1, 1970. When he made sure that the United States and Israel would defend his regime against the Syrians, who supported the Palestinians in Jordan, Hussein ordered his army to suppress the Palestinians by force. According to the Jordanians, over 2,500 Palestinians were killed; Arafat estimated that the number of dead was 3,400, while the number of wounded stood at 10,000. Israeli intelligence sources estimated that there were twice as many wounded.
5. Morris, *Righteous Victims*, 472.
6. Shimon Shiffer, *Snowball* (Yediot Ahronot, 1984), 28.
7. Ibid., 61.
8. Syria's entrance into Lebanon in 1976, before the end of the civil war, resulted in an agreement between Syria and Israel limiting Syria's deployment up to the Litani River in Lebanon to avoid a clash between the armies.

9. Morris, *Righteous Victims*, 470.
10. Resolution 425 was accepted by the U.N. Security Council on March 19, 1978.
11. Arie Naor, *Begin in Power: A Personal Testimony* (Yediot Ahronot, 1993), 242–243.
12. The full text of the Chach'chachim speech is on the Beitar Web site: http://www.betar.org.il/ideology/chachahim.htm.
13. "He spoke about the Holocaust in the Lebanese context. Here we are, the Jews, and we will save the Christians. This blinded him from seeing what kind of Christians they were." Yona Klimovitski, Israel State Archives, July 24, 1994.
14. "The Mossad had contact with Christians in the north, in Beirut, and contact with the Christians in the army itself on the northern border. We gave them weapons. Yitzhak Rabin decided to give them Soviet weapons, spoils of war from 1967, which we had in abundance. The slogan was that we helped them to protect themselves. Begin saw it as beyond the expediency (let's call it that) of the State of Israel." Yitzhak Chofi, Menachem Begin Heritage Center, January 11, 2002.
15. Morris, *Righteous Victims*, 471–472.
16. Naor, *Begin in Power*, 240–241.
17. Arie Naor, Menachem Begin Heritage Center, January 8, 2001.
18. Between 1976 and June 1982 Israel provided the Lebanese Christians with weapons and training in the amount of $118.5 million. The IDF's intelligence services had reservations about the relationship and thought that it would not help Israel, but the Mossad, led by David Kimche, head of its foreign relations department, supported it; see Morris, *Righteous Victims*, 471–472.
19. *Yediot Ahronot*, April 17, 1981.
20. Protocols of the Knesset, vol. 24, June 3, 1981, 2885.
21. Quoted in Naor, *Begin in Power*, 240.
22. Morris, *Righteous Victims*, 474.
23. Arie Naor, Menachem Begin Heritage Center, January 8, 2001.
24. Quoted in Shiffer, *Snowball*, 56; Arie Naor, *Cabinet at War* (Yediot Ahronot, 1986), 18.
25. Naor, *Begin in Power*, 146.
26. Ibid., 26–27.
27. Quoted in Ze'ev Schiff and Ehud Yaari, *Israel's Lebanon War 1982* (Schocken, 1984), 94.
28. From author's conversation with Yanush Ben Gal, April 14, 2005.
29. Morris, *Righteous Victims*, 477–478.
30. From author's conversation with Yanush Ben Gal, April 14, 2005.
31. Naor, *Begin in Power*, 268.
32. Schiff and Yaari, *Israel's Lebanon War*, 96–98.
33. From author's conversation with Yanush Ben Gal, April 14, 2005.
34. Naor, *Begin in Power*, 269.
35. Morris, *Righteous Victims*, 479.
36. Naor, *Begin in Power*, 271.

37. "Begin debated [the operation] for a year and a quarter since [the time] he had told Ben Gal that the goal would be to enter the bunker in Beirut and get Arafat out of there. He sent officials to the Americans, and everyone concluded that if there were an internationally recognized provocation, he would be able to gain legitimacy for a defensive action designed to advance more or less to the range of the Katyusha rockets. Since then Begin was locked in on the small target, retreating from the idea he had shared with Ben Gal." Author's conversation with Arie Naor, April 25, 2007.
38. Ofer Grosbard, *Menachem Begin: A Portrait of a Leader—A Biography* (Resling, 2006), 267.
39. *Yediot Ahronot*, February 22, 2002.
40. Chaggai Segal, *Dear Brothers: History of the Jewish Underground* (Keter, 1987), 133.
41. Yitzhak Zamir, Menachem Begin Heritage Center, July 24, 2001.
42. Segal, *Dear Brothers*, 121.
43. Naor, *Begin in Power*, 273.
44. Schiff and Yaari, *Israel's Lebanon War*, 56–57.
45. Arie Naor, Menachem Begin Heritage Center, January 8, 2001.
46. Quoted in Naor, *Begin in Power*, 249.
47. Schiff and Yaari, *Israel's Lebanon War*, 89.
48. Naor, *Begin in Power*, 42.
49. "Eventually, the missions and the talks with American officials led to minimizing the goals of the war. Begin, in the summer of '81, thought that if the situation in Lebanon reached a flashpoint, then the goal should be to reach Arafat's bunker in Beirut. He even said something similar to Major General Ben Gal. But gradually, through the fall and winter, Begin began to understand that only if there were a provocation that was accepted as such by the world and the Israeli response was proportionate, defensive in nature, could they talk about an understanding. Because the range of rockets and artillery that the PLO in Lebanon had at the time reached about thirty-seven kilometers into Israel, the concept for a forty-kilometer range was conceived. Begin gradually fixated on this limited conception, on which Sharon also seemingly fixated, as the fact was that in the cabinet meeting that approved the war, Sharon was the one who suggested entering to a depth of forty kilometers." Arie Naor, Menachem Begin Heritage Center, January 8, 2001.
50. Avi Shlaim, *The Iron Wall* (Yediot Ahronot, 2005), 385.
51. Quoted in ibid., 386.
52. Arie Naor, Menachem Begin Heritage Center, January 8, 2001.
53. Naor, *Begin in Power*, 282.
54. Ibid., 280.
55. "We were with [Begin] at his home on Saturday. Defense officials presented a plan, including the occupation of Beirut, on that evening. The head of military intelligence, Major General Yehoshua Sagi, and I were opposed to the operation for all kinds of reasons. First of all, we said it was not a vacation, and to conquer a city was to conquer a city. This was a war in a built-up area, which also was not a vacation. There was a debate back and forth, and Begin decided

that there would be a limited operation, with the limit set at forty kilometers. The operation was to be called Operation Peace for Galilee. And indeed, they presented the small operation. When we left the meeting, cabinet secretary Dan Meridor and Uri Porat, the prime minister's media adviser asked, 'Well, are you satisfied?' They referred to the fact that I had objected to the large operation. I said, 'I'm pleased because it deals with terrorists and not beyond that.' But I told them that nevertheless, if the operation did not end as projected, as I know the people involved very well, then it would turn into the Likud's Yom Kippur. I used those words." Yitzhak Chofi, Menachem Begin Heritage Center, January 11, 2002.

56. Mapa (Secretariat of the High Command), M.N. 2792–341, March 12, 1982.
57. Ibid., M.N. 192–341, May 4, 1982.
58. "Begin did not believe Tsipori, who stood in front of the two [Rafael Eitan and Sharon]. He saw Tsipori's questions and attitude as a vendetta. Tsipori had wanted to be defense minister, and he had not been appointed. Begin did not treat him with the necessary seriousness." Arie Naor, Menachem Begin Heritage Center, January 8, 2001.
59. From author's conversation with Yanush Ben Gal, December 17, 2006.
60. Schiff and Yaari, *Israel's Lebanon War*, 16–20.
61. Arie Naor, Menachem Begin Heritage Center, January 8, 2001.
62. Quoted in Schiff and Yaari, *Israel's Lebanon War*, 389.
63. Naor, *Begin in Power*, 284–287.
64. *Maariv*, June 3, 1983.
65. "He called her from my room and said 'Alinka, I am going to the bunker for forty-eight hours; we are only pushing them back from the borders." Yona Klimovitski, Israel State Archives, July 27, 1994.
66. Azriel Nevo, Menachem Begin Heritage Center, August 28, 2000.
67. Schiff and Yaari, *Israel's Lebanon War*, 118–119.
68. Naor, *Cabinet at War*, 35.
69. From author's conversation with Yanush Ben Gal, December 17, 2006.
70. Quoted in Naor, *Cabinet at War*, 15.
71. Operations Branch, June 6, 14:30.
72. Mapa, M.N. 401–341, June 6, 1982.
73. Morris, *Righteous Victims*, 489.
74. Nir Chefetz and Gadi Bloom, *The Shepherd* (Yediot Ahronot, 2005), 354.
75. Quoted in Chanan Azran, *From Brisk to Jerusalem* (Israeli Broadcasting Authority [IBA], 1993).
76. Quoted in Schiff and Yaari, *Israel's Lebanon War*, 162.
77. Naor, *Cabinet at War*, 55.
78. Quoted in Naor, *Begin in Power*, 292–293.
79. Naor, *Cabinet at War*, 163.
80. Mapa, M.N. 417–341, June 7, 1982.
81. Protocols of the Knesset, vol. 10, June 8, 1982, 2747–2748.
82. Tubi was a Dash Knesset member.
83. Protocols of the Knesset, vol. 10, June 8, 1982, 2747–2848.
84. Schiff and Yaari, *Israel's Lebanon War*, 185.

85. Morris, *Righteous Victims*, 492.
86. Chefetz and Bloom, *The Shepherd*, 353.
87. See libel trial against Uzi Benziman and *Haaretz*, Tel Aviv 818/93, District Court, Tel Aviv, January 2, 1996.
88. Schiff and Yaari, *Israel's Lebanon War*, 191.
89. Naor, *Begin in Power*, 297.
90. *Haaretz*, April 11, 1981.
91. Schiff and Yaari, *Israel's Lebanon War*, 187.
92. Mapa, M.N. 341–431, June 9, 1982.
93. Morris, *Righteous Victims*, 494.
94. Ibid., 494.
95. Protocols of the Knesset, vol. 10, June 29, 1982, 2976–2977.
96. Schiff and Yaari, *Israel's Lebanon War*, 206.
97. Naor, *Begin in Power*, 297–300.
98. Morris, *Righteous Victims*, 492; Schiff and Yaari, *Israel's Lebanon War*, 206–222.
99. Naor, *Begin in Power*, 306–307.
100. Chefetz and Bloom, *The Shepherd*, 360.
101. Naor, *Begin in Power*, 307.
102. From author's conversation with Yanush Ben Gal, April 14, 2005.
103. "I know that Begin was not satisfied because of the lack of reporting; I do not want to go into details." Moshe Nissim, Menachem Begin Heritage Center, September 27, 2000.
104. *Moked*, Israeli Television, June 15, 1982.
105. From author's conversation with Arie Naor, May 24, 2007.
106. "I wrote Begin a letter on the seventh day of the war. I wrote him that we had reached the point at which we must stop because it was a point of no return, as after this point we might run into the Syrians. In a sense I wrote some sort of criticism, and Begin did not like the military to criticize the political echelon. He did not like it. He had scolded me several times. In this case he simply read the note and then tore it up. I was not smart enough to keep the pieces. Before that I had talked this over with Yechiel Kadishai, who was the closest man to whom I told this. He told me: write him a letter about it. My mistake was not keeping it." Azriel Nevo, Menachem Begin Heritage Center, August 28, 2000.
107. Morris, *Righteous Victims*, 496.
108. Quoted in *Operation Peace for Galilee: Information Items and Emphasis* (IDF booklet), June 21, 1982.
109. From author's conversation with Yanush Ben Gal, April 14, 2005.
110. Morris, *Righteous Victims*, 492.
111. Naor, *Cabinet at War*, 113.
112. Naor, *Begin in Power*, 312.
113. Morris, *Righteous Victims*, 497–498.
114. Quoted in Schiff and Yaari, *Israel's Lebanon War*, 226.
115. "Every time Sharon wanted to move forward another step, Begin said, 'Our soldiers are getting injured and we should avoid it.'" Yosef Burg, Israel State Archives, May 18, 1994.

116. Naor, *Cabinet at War*, 115.
117. Morris, *Righteous Victims*, 498.
118. Quoted in Tedi Frois, *Begin in Power* (Keter, 1984), 92.
119. See libel trial against Uzi Benziman and *Haaretz*, Tel Aviv 818/93, District Court, Tel Aviv, January 2, 1996.
120. Quoted in Naor, *Begin in Power*, 310.
121. "He decided to get rid of the terrorists. It was his goal. He decided and he agreed with the general program to start the war against the PLO. He did not think about entering Beirut, but he wanted to get the PLO out. I did not hear him say that he regretted the war with the PLO." Harry Horowitz, Israel State Archives, November 15, 1993.
122. Shiffer, *Snowball*, 104.
123. "They [Sharon and Eitan] had an ambivalent relationship. On the one hand, Arik appreciated his tactical ability, and vice versa; on the other hand, Raful was anxious about Arik.... I felt that Raful was opposed to the occupation of West Beirut and feared losing, but Arik pressured him." From author's conversation with Yanush Ben Gal, December 17, 2006.
124. Quoted in Schiff and Yaari, *Israel's Lebanon War*, 265.
125. Naor, *Begin in Power*, 291.
126. Yechiel Kadishai, Israel State Archives, April 20, 1993.
127. Protocols of the Knesset, vol. 10, June 29, 1982, 2978.
128. *Yediot Ahronot*, June 29, 1982.
129. From Menachem Begin's speech at the Mann Auditorium in 1959, during Jabotinsky's Memorial Day. See Efraim Even, ed., *Ze'ev Jabotinsky, My Teacher* (Menachem Begin Heritage Center, 2001), 121.
130. Protocols of the Knesset, vol. 10, June 29, 1982, 2977.
131. Ibid.
132. Telem was Moshe Dayan's party and had two Knesset seats. After Dayan's death Yigal Horowitz took his place. The Techiya party was founded by Geula Cohen after her retirement from the Likud because of her opposition to the Camp David Accords. It was headed by Yuval Ne'eman.
133. Protocols of the Knesset, vol. 10, July 26, 1982, 3367.
134. A meeting between Begin and the general staff officers, Kahan Commission Report, July 12, 1982.
135. *Yediot Ahronot*, June 25, 1982.
136. Azriel Nevo, Menachem Begin Heritage Center, August 28, 2000.
137. The discussion in the next several paragraphs is based on Naor, *Begin in Power*, 309, 321–322.
138. Yechiel Kadishai, Israel State Archives, January 19, 1993.
139. *Maariv*, August 20, 1982.
140. Protocols of the Knesset, March 24, 1954.
141. Morris, *Righteous Victims*, 503.
142. "For Begin, after the PLO left the Tripoli harbor, that was the end.... Why did we not leave Lebanon then? According to Begin, we could have pulled out. He said this: 'We have no desire, not to claim a grain of sand of the soil of Lebanon, and we have no desire to stay there. It does not interest us.' What

interested Begin was that the PLO would not be in Lebanon any more." Yechiel Kadishai, Israel State Archives, January 19, 1993.
143. Morris, *Righteous Victims*, 513.
144. Ibid., 503.
145. Quoted in Shlomo Nakdimon, *Tamuz in Flames* (Yediot Ahronot, 1984), 168.
146. Quotes in this paragraph are in Shiffer, *Snowball*, 119.
147. Yona Klimovitski, Israel State Archives, July 24, 1994.
148. Quoted in Shlaim, *The Iron Wall*, 396.
149. Schiff and Yaari, *Israel's Lebanon War*, 288–291.
150. Grosbard, *Menachem Begin*, 285.
151. Quoted in Shiffer, *Snowball*, 120.
152. "Much of the difficult entanglement was a result of an objective situation, things we did not know. Once Gemayel was elected, he no longer wanted to be an ally, and this was a serious blow to Begin. He avoided him, and since that time Begin was not the same man. It was a heavy blow to see that after the help he had received, he was not loyal to Begin." Yitzhak Shamir, Israel State Archives, February 6, 1995.
153. Quoted in Naor, *Begin in Power*, 328.
154. Quoted in Grosbard, *Menachem Begin*, 286.
155. "Phalange Activity in the Near Future," Kahan Commission Report, August 27, 1982.
156. Schiff and Yaari, *Israel's Lebanon War*, 300.
157. Thomas L. Friedman, *From Beirut to Jerusalem* (Maariv, 1990), 139.
158. Naor, *Begin in Power*, 151–152.
159. Schiff and Yaari, *Israel's Lebanon War*, 323.
160. Kahan Commission Report, 22–23.
161. Schiff and Yaari, *Israel's Lebanon War*, 330.
162. Kahan Commission Report, 32–33.
163. Schiff and Yaari, *Israel's Lebanon War*, 339–340.
164. Morris, *Righteous Victims*, 511.
165. *Maariv*, September 20, 1982.
166. Shiffer, *Snowball*, 129.
167. "He mainly talked; I hardly spoke. He said, 'The Jews are always to blame, the Jews are always to blame.'" Yehuda Lapidot, Menachem Begin Heritage Center, August 3, 2000.
168. See libel trial against Uzi Benziman and *Haaretz*, Tel Aviv 818/93, District Court, Tel Aviv, January 2, 1996.
169. From author's conversation with Shulamit Aloni, January 2007.
170. Protocols of the Knesset, vol. 10, September 22, 1982, 3716.
171. *Haaretz*, September 26, 1982.
172. Kahan Commission Report, 49.
173. "After Sabra and Shatila I asked to see him, Begin, and I told him you cannot let such a thing happen without checking it. We must establish a commission of inquiry. He said, 'If we establish a commission of inquiry, we accept that we are to blame.' I told him, 'On the contrary. The world has been saying we're guilty. The only way out of it and to refute it is to establish a committee.' Once

again he said he would think about it. He thought and said that we should place the issue in the hands of an IDF general to check it. I told him, 'Do not impose it on any general. Only on a judge. Otherwise his conclusions will not be trusted.' I called him and told him I was going to announce my position publicly, and I gave a statement on television and radio in support of establishing a legal inquiry. The Mafdal said it tipped the scales in favor of establishing the commission." Yitzhak Navon, Menachem Begin Heritage Center, December 18, 2000.

174. "The Kahan Commission humiliated him. The entire time he did not show one smile. He would sit in the office and showed no desire to meet with people. He was in a difficult state of mind." Yitzhak Shamir, Israel State Archives, February 6, 1995.
175. *Haaretz*, November 9, 1982.
176. Shlomo Frenkel and Shimshon Bichler, *The Privileged* (Kadim, 1984), 81–83.
177. Mordechai Tsipori, *In a Straight Line* (Yediot Ahronot, 1997), 81–83.

CHAPTER 19. THE DOWNFALL

1. Yosef Burg, Israel State Archives, May 8, 1994.
2. Quoted in Ofer Grosbard, *Menachem Begin: A Portrait of a Leader—A Biography* (Resling, 2006), 291.
3. Yosef Burg, Israel State Archives, May 8, 1994.
4. Ibid.
5. Yechiel Kadishai, ibid., May 5, 1993.
6. Ibid.
7. Chaim Corfu, Menachem Begin Heritage Center, June 21, 2000.
8. "I said comforting words to him. He came toward me, hugged me, and wept." Yitzhak Navon, ibid., December 18, 2000.
9. Sarah Doron, ibid., May 7, 2001.
10. Arie Naor, *Begin in Power: A Personal Testimony* (Yediot Ahronot, 1993), 331.
11. Yitzhak Shamir, Israel State Archives, February 6, 1995.
12. From author's conversation with Yanush Ben Gal, April 14, 2005.
13. Yosef Burg, Israel State Archives, May 8, 1994.
14. *Ha'ir*, September 14, 2000.
15. *Koteret Rashit*, no. 11, February 1983.
16. Kahan Commission Report, 66–67.
17. Naor, *Begin in Power*, 332.
18. Quoted in Ze'ev Schiff and Ehud Yaari, *Israel's Lebanon War 1982* (Schocken, 1984), 323.
19. "There was only one recommendation that was unclear, and that was the recommendation about Sharon. He was held responsible for not seeing what should have been expected; thus it was recommended that he should draw personal conclusions. It was the single recommendation that was unclear: what do "personal conclusions" mean? What should he conclude? Therefore this question was forwarded to the attorney general for his opinion. There were different opinions. The extreme opinion was that he had to resign from the government. I gave an opinion that making personal conclusions meant that

he must resign from his post as defense minister. He could stay as a minister but not as defense minister, and he accepted this. He resigned as defense minister and remained in the government as minister without portfolio. I think that it was clear to Sharon himself that he must accept responsibility." Yitzhak Zamir, Menachem Begin Heritage Center, July 24, 2001,

20. Quoted in Eric Silver, *Begin: The Haunted Prophet* (Random Housem 1984), 240.
21. Uri Dan, *Ariel Sharon: An Intimate Portrait* (Yediot Ahronot, 2006), 150–153.
22. Tedi Frois, *Begin in Power* (Keter, 1984), 170.
23. National Insurance Institute Report, January 1984.
24. Yosef Burg, Israel State Archives, May 8, 1994.
25. From a lecture by David Klein, former governor of the Bank of Israel, Kiryat Ono Academic College, September 11, 2003.
26. "It was terrible. We were afraid to go to him. I said to Nevo, 'You go.' He said, 'I am afraid to tell him.'" Yona Klimovitski, Israel State Archives, July 24, 1994.
27. "He took drugs for the heart. . . . The stroke affected his eyesight" (Yona Klimovitski, ibid.). "He suffered from sharp mood swings that were generally related to the successes or failures of public struggles. At one point, he was taking medication that sometimes slowed his pace, causing a kind of temporary fatigue" (author's conversation with Arie Naor, April 25, 2007).
28. From an interview with Dan Meridor, May 20, 2007.
29. Yosef Burg, Israel State Archives, May 18, 1994.
30. From author's conversation with Arie Naor, April 25, 2007.
31. Batya Eldad, Israel State Archives, January 9, 1994.
32. "When he didn't eat, it was also self-punishment." Yona Klimovitski, ibid., July 27, 1994.
33. "Burg went to him several times and asked that he remove the [protesters], but Begin said no. As if he were punishing himself for the tragedy." Yona Klimovitski, ibid.
34. Grosbard, *Menachem Begin*, 297.
35. Schiff and Yaari, *Israel's Lebanon War*, 363. Despite the approval of the agreement by Lebanon's parliament Gemayel dismissed it in the spring of 1984 on orders from Damascus.
36. From author's conversation with Arie Naor, April 25, 2007.
37. Naor, *Begin in Power*, 333.
38. *Haaretz*, July 8, 1983.
39. From an interview with Dan Meridor, May 9, 2007.
40. Harry Horowitz, Israel State Archives, November 15, 1993.
41. Quoted in Naor, *Begin in Power*, 318.
42. Ibid., 332.
43. David Danon, Israel State Archives, February 17, 1994.
44. Yitzhak Shamir, ibid., February 6, 1995.
45. Yona Klimovitski, ibid., July 24, 1994.
46. "I had a meeting with him before he retired. I felt the man was in a deep depression. He was passive, he was not witty, he did not make any jokes, and

he did not smile. I remember he told me, 'I cannot travel. I called the U.S. president and explained to him, and he understood.' That's what he said. It was then that I understood his crisis was so deep that he could not go to the United States." Yehuda Lapidot, Menachem Begin Heritage Center, August 3, 2000.

47. "Two and a half months before resigning, Begin retreated to his home. He asked that government meetings be conducted without him." Azriel Nevo, ibid., August 28, 2000.

48. "His voice was weaker. I heard it only sometimes. He also had some kind of rash. He was not healthy. . . . Not everything should be placed on the victims in Lebanon. No. It was physical. Aliza's death. He would come home alone. Though Leah lived there, there was no one to help him take off his shoes. He ate very little. I said once [that he needed help], perhaps I should have shouted it, but I did not have the brains or the courage. He is a man who never demanded or requested. There was no one to say, 'Gentlemen, not like that.'" Sarah Doron, ibid., May 7, 2001.

49. "The combination of the losses in Lebanon and the disillusionment, realizing that he had been tricked, broke him." Yona Klimovitski, Israel State Archives, July 24, 1994.

50. Yitzhak Shamir, ibid., January 3, 1995.

51. From an interview with Dan Meridor, May 9, 2007.

52. Yechiel Kadishai, Menachem Begin Heritage Center, February 6, 2002.

53. Yechiel Kadishai, Israel State Archives, May 5, 1993.

54. For further details, see Chaggai Segal, *Dear Brothers: History of the Jewish Underground* (Keter, 1987).

55. Yitzhak Zamir, Menachem Begin Heritage Center, July 24, 2001.

56. "He told me, 'I solved this problem.' Perhaps it affected the date of resignation." Harry Horowitz, ibid., August 15, 1993.

57. Yechiel Kadishai, ibid., May 5, 1993.

58. "On that day no one knew. Even Dan Meridor did not know. I think that Begin's family did not know. The hours passed, and he conducted the cabinet meeting as usual. His message did not come at the start of the meeting, not even in the middle, and then we heard at the end of the meeting Begin saying, 'Now I will ask the government permission to make a statement.' The meeting was on political and economic matters. It was not a special session." Moshe Nissim, Menachem Begin Heritage Center, September 27, 2000.

59. Quoted in Naor, *Begin in Power*, 339.

60. Ibid., 340.

61. National Photo Collection, August 28, 1983.

62. Yechiel Kadishai, Israel State Archives, May 5, 1993.

63. Yosef Burg, ibid., May 8, 1994.

64. Yechiel Kadishai, ibid., May 5, 1993.

65. Sarah Doron, Menachem Begin Heritage Center, July 5, 2001.

66. The discussion in this paragraph is based on Naor, *Begin in Power*, 341.

67. Ibid.

68. "It was a very difficult period because it was a time when he didn't want to deal with certain things, and so the problem arose: who will deal with them? He was prime minister; he was active; no one said he had ceased to be active. It was a huge dilemma. What to do and how to do it. There were no meetings; he did not see people; he did not [even] want to see Arens at his home.... Sometimes I needed to discuss practical matters, and then I would talk to him on the telephone.... In fact, we were doing all the work. We brought him things. Sometimes we decided what to do and how to do it." Azriel Nevo, Menachem Begin Heritage Center, August 28, 2000.

CHAPTER 20. SELF-FLAGELLATION

1. Arie Avnery, *Defeat* (Midot, 1993), 252.
2. Yona Klimovitski, Israel State Archives, July 27, 1994.
3. From author's conversation with Hasia Milo, May 10, 2007.
4. From author's conversation with Arie Naor, April 25, 2007.
5. "When he was depressed, he did not want to see anyone. On his birthday I called, and he was unable to talk. His daughter-in-law, Ruth Begin, asked me, 'Maybe you can convince him to get help; we can't.' He did not want it. He suffered much because he was very sensitive to the daily publications on Lebanon and to the number of casualties. He saw himself as having a monitoring role and was always ready to sacrifice himself. He was unable to make personal confessions, and therefore he could not go to therapy. He felt guilty over Lebanon." Batya Eldad, Israel State Archives, January 9, 1994.
6. "I called and he said 'I can't take it anymore,' without explaining." Yosef Burg, ibid., May 8, 1994.
7. "I said to him that he still had to play a big role regarding the settlements, and a smile came to his lips: 'I hear you, but some things are impossible.'" Geula Cohen, interview on Army Radio, March 9, 1992.
8. "Leah was not married, and Aliza was concerned and would say, 'What will become of her?'" Batya Eldad, Israel State Archives, January 9, 1994.
9. From author's conversation with Arie Naor, April 25, 2007.
10. Yona Klimovitski, Israel State Archives, July 27, 1994.
11. Yechiel Kadishai, ibid., January 5, 1993.
12. "He maintained the lifestyle of a bedridden man. He read a lot; every day there was a new book next to his bed. He rarely met with people." Chaim Corfu, Menachem Begin Heritage Center, July 21, 2000.
13. "He did not want to see people, so that they would not see him in his condition, even though I was friendly with him. He said a few laconic sentences to me on the phone. That's it. Chasia was very close to him and took care of him." Batya Eldad, Israel State Archives, January 9, 1994.
14. From author's conversation with Arie Naor, April 25, 2007.
15. "Aliza's death was difficult for him, but I do not think that's why [he withdrew]. Every Saturday I went to him. He did not talk to me about his own personal issues; why should I ask? His ability was gone. Why? That's his secret." Meir Kahn, Israel State Archives, September 14, 1993.

16. Harry Horowitz's assessment was somewhat different: "Seventy-five percent of the reason for his retirement was the death of Mrs. Begin. We were together when he got the news, and I told my wife immediately, 'This is the end; he is no longer the same man.' He started to say, 'Why did I leave her?' The other reasons were the conflicts—Lebanon and the fact that he himself was ill." Ibid., November 15, 1993.
17. *Yediot Ahronot*, February 22, 2002.
18. "Every Saturday night we talked about the entire world. He asked, 'What do you think about the developments in Russia? Mandela in South Africa?' About Israel we did not speak." Harry Horowitz, Israel State Archives, November 15, 1993.
19. From author's conversation with Arie Naor, April 25, 2007.
20. "For us, the next generation, Begin was a revered leader, the Etzel commander, the former prime minister. One could easily detect his mood swings, which were usually associated with successes or failures, and he did not hide them. But he was not one you could ask personal questions. Certainly not. We couldn't ask, 'Why are you depressed?'" Arie Naor, ibid.
21. Ibid.
22. Shabtai Tzvi (1626–1676) was a Jewish mystic who lived in the Ottoman Empire. He claimed to be the Messiah and managed to convince Jews around the world that they should follow him and immigrate to the land of Israel. Eventually, under pressure from Sultan Mehmed IV he converted to Islam. Modern research indicates that Shabtai Tzvi probably suffered from bipolar disorder. According to Israel Eldad, "Sometimes, during periods of stress—and you can talk about what happened in Vilnius as an example—he [Begin] would experience a drop in energy, and then he would retreat into himself. He would want to leave and retire. This was the basis for his comparison to Shabtai Tzvi." Israel Eldad, Israel State Archives, December 8, 1993.
23. Yechiel Kadishai, ibid., May 5, 1993.
24. "He was a man with an extraordinary sense of history. His scenario was peace with Egypt first and then with Lebanon. He always said, 'I'll finish, retire, and then write my memoirs.' But I knew he would not write them. Because it wasn't the happy ending he wanted." Yona Klimovitski, ibid., July 24, 1994.
25. Batya Eldad, ibid., January 9, 1994.
26. Ned Temko, *To Win or to Die* (William Morrow, 1987), 292.
27. Ibid., 293.
28. Yechiel Kadishai, Israel State Archives, January 5, 1993.
29. "Retirement was the result of his physical condition." Yochanan Bader, Israel State Archives, March 4, 1993.
30. Ofer Grosbard, *Menachem Begin: A Portrait of a Leader—A Biography* (Resling, 2006), 308.
31. "He felt guilty over Lebanon, and Aliza was no longer there to say, 'Do not cry over yourself; do things.'" Batya Eldad, Israel State Archives, January 9, 1994.
32. Azriel Nevo, Menachem Begin Heritage Center, August 28, 2000.

33. Yehuda Lapidot, ibid., August 3, 2000.
34. Menachem Porush, ibid., May 29, 2002.
35. Yitzhak Shamir, Israel State Archives, February 6, 1995.
36. *Yediot Ahronot*, February 22, 2002.
37. Ibid.
38. From author's conversation with Arie Naor, April 25, 2007.
39. Harry Horowitz, Israel State Archives, November 15, 1993.
40. *Yediot Ahronot*, February 22, 2002.
41. Chasia, the most extroverted of Begin's three children, married Matti Milo—brother of Ronnie, who was elected to the Knesset while Begin was serving as prime minister—and together they briefly managed a café they owned in Tel Aviv. Ayelet, their eldest child, participated in the Israeli beauty queen pageant and reached second place. She later married a young contractor named Sammy Levy. Begin was closest to his granddaughter Orit, who visited him often.
42. Batya Eldad, Israel State Archives, January 9, 1994.

CHAPTER 21. "SHARON WAS AFRAID OF ME"

1. Author's conversation with Dan Meridor, May 20, 2007.
2. Quoted in Ned Temko, *To Win or to Die* (William Morrow, 1987), 451.
3. From author's conversation with Arie Naor, April 25, 2007.
4. Uri Dan, *Ariel Sharon: An Intimate Portrait* (Yediot Ahronot, 2006), 194.
5. From Sharon's lecture at Tel Aviv University on August 12, 1987.
6. See libel trial against Uzi Benziman and *Haaretz*, Tel Aviv 818/93, District Court, Tel Aviv, February 28, 1996.
7. *Maariv*, August 28, 1987.
8. On May 17, 1991, *Haaretz* journalist Uzi Benziman relied on the facts Benny presented in an article he wrote, and he stated, "Begin was well aware that Sharon had deceived him." Of course, Sharon did not know about the conversations Begin had held with his son about the war, and he decided to sue *Haaretz*. Benny Begin agreed to testify on behalf of Benziman. In his ruling, Tel Aviv District Court judge Moshe Talgam said that although he did not "pretend to determine historical truth, the defendants had proved that the [Benziman article] was true." It was a heavy blow for Sharon, who filed an appeal with the Supreme Court. On February 18, 2002, while Sharon was serving as prime minister, the Supreme Court justices rejected the appeal and instructed Sharon to bear the trial's legal costs, but they criticized the Talgam ruling, saying that historical truth was the concern of historians and the District Court had erred in being tempted to decide on the issue. Benny wondered about the Supreme Court's verdict. Some thought that because Sharon was prime minister at the time, the ruling could have serious consequences for Israel's position and that Sharon's status affected the verdict.

   In this context, it is interesting to note the apparent disparity during the libel trial between the testimony of Kadishai, who insisted that Sharon had not deceived Begin, and that of Benny Begin. The difference between the two, who were both close to Begin, was that Benny, like his father, saw things at face value—one was lying and the other was telling the truth—and Kadis-

hai, who did not think that Begin was a man easily influenced, wished to preserve his image in history as an authoritarian leader.
9. *Chadashot*, August 2, 1991.
10. "The Etzel members went to him and asked him to sign [the recommendation to the president]. I felt his conscience tormented him because of my partial removal from the Etzel command." Author's conversation with Shlomo Lev Ami, May 24, 2007.
11. Yechiel Kadishai, Israel State Archives, May 5, 1993.
12. "He was able to say simple things such as 'Hello, how are you?' No more. I always called him to hear what he thought, and he would give a banal answer [such as] 'The situation is difficult; it will get better.' He had completely lost his ability to analyze. Arens said it was impossible to reach him. It's not that he didn't want to; he couldn't. His mental constitution was already unstable, and Lebanon continued to depress him." Shmuel Katz, ibid., August 20, 1993.
13. Elyakim Rubinstein, ibid., May 9, 1994.
14. *Yediot Ahronot*, February 22, 2002.
15. Yechiel Kadishai, Israel State Archives, January 19, 1993.
16. Israeli Broadcasting Authority (IBA), March 1991.
17. *Ha'ir*, April 4, 1991.
18. The Basic Law: Human Dignity and Liberty was intended to protect human rights in Israel. This law, as well as the Basic Law: Freedom of Occupation, was a constitutional revolution, as it gave the Israeli courts the authority to annul laws contradicting these basic laws. The law was initiated by the Likud government and was passed on March 17, 1992, when Dan Meridor was justice minister.
19. Menachem Begin, *On National Perspectives and Personal Perspectives* (Ba'sahar, 1952).
20. *Maariv*, May 31, 1991.
21. The following interview is from Galei Tzahal (Army Radio) Archives, July 10, 1991.
22. Shraga Alis, Menachem Begin Heritage Center, January 29, 2001.
23. Yechiel Kadishai, Israel State Archives, January 5, 1993.

BIBLIOGRAPHY

ARCHIVES

Menachem Begin Heritage Center Archives (Jerusalem)
Central Zionist Archives (Jerusalem)
Haganah Archives (Tel Aviv)
Institute of Contemporary Jewry
Israel Television Archives
Israel State Archives
Jabotinsky Institute Archives (Tel Aviv)
Protocols of the Knesset (Knesset Minutes)
Yad Vashem Archives (Jerusalem)
Yad Tabenkin Archives

INTERVIEWS

The interviews from the Menachem Begin Heritage Center were conducted by Iris Barletski; the interviews from the Israel State Archives were conducted by Nana Sagi.

Shraga Alis, Menachem Begin Heritage Center, 2001.
Betzalel Amitzur, Menachem Begin Heritage Center, 2000.
Avraham Appel, 2006.
Moshe Arens, Menachem Begin Heritage Center, 2002.
Moshe Aridor, Menachem Begin Heritage Center, 2003.
Yitzhak Avinoam, Menachem Begin Heritage Center, 2001.
Yehuda Avner, Menachem Begin Heritage Center, 2003.
Yochanan Bader, Israel State Archives, 1992.
Yaakov Banai, 2005.
Benny Begin, 2007.
Avigdor "Yanush" Ben Gal, 2005–2006.
Yosef Burg, Israel State Archives, 1994.
Avraham Caspi, Menachem Begin Heritage Center, 2004.
Yitzhak Chofi, Menachem Begin Heritage Center, 2002.
Geula Cohen, Israel State Archives, 1992.
Chaim Corfu, Menachem Begin Heritage Center, 2000.
David Danon, Israel State Archives, 1994.
Simcha Dinitz, Menachem Begin Heritage Center, 2002.
Sarah Doron, Menachem Begin Heritage Center, 2001.
Batya Eldad, Israel State Archives, 1994.
Israel Eldad, Israel State Archives, 1993.
Yitzhak Greenbaum, Institute of Contemporary Jewry, 1965.
Rachel Halperin, Menachem Begin Heritage Center, 2000.
Yehoshafat Halpert, Menachem Begin Heritage Center, 2004.
Yitzhak Hochman, Menachem Begin Heritage Center, 2002.

Harry Horowitz, Israel State Archives, 1993.
Yechiel Kadishai, Israel State Archives, 1993; Menachem Begin Heritage Center, 2002.
Meir Kahn, Israel State Archives, 1993.
Shmuel Katz, Israel State Archives, 1993.
Tzippora Kessel, Menachem Begin Heritage Center, 2000.
Yona Klimovitski, Israel State Archives, 1994.
Doris Lankin, Menachem Begin Heritage Center, 2001.
Yehuda Lapidot, Menachem Begin Heritage Center, 2000.
Shlomo Lev Ami, 2007.
Sam Lewis, Menachem Begin Heritage Center, 2002.
Dan Meridor, 2007.
Arie Naor, Menachem Begin Heritage Center, 2000; 2007.
Yitzhak Navon, Menachem Begin Heritage Center, 2000.
Azriel Nevo, Menachem Begin Heritage Center, 2000.
Moshe Nissim, Menachem Begin Heritage Center, 2000.
Amichai Paglin, Institute of Contemporary Jewry, 1970.
Menachem Porush, Menachem Begin Heritage Center, 2002.
Alexander Rafaeli, Israel State Archives, 1993.
Meir Rosen, Menachem Begin Heritage Center, 2001.
Elyakim Rubinstein, Israel State Archives, 1994.
Yitzhak Shamir, Israel State Archives, 1995.
Eli Shitrit, 2006.
Luca Wax, Menachem Begin Heritage Center, 2000.
Yitzhak Zamir, Menachem Begin Heritage Center, 2001.

LECTURES

Moshe Arens, Menachem Begin Heritage Center, March 21, 2002.
Yoram Aridor, Menachem Begin Heritage Center, October 2, 2002.
Motti Golani, Menachem Begin Heritage Center, March 21, 2002.
David Klein, IDC Herzliya Conference, Kiryat Ono, September 11, 2003.

REPORTS

Halavi Project: The Decision-Making Process (Proyect Halavi: Tahalich Kabalat Hahachlatot), State Auditor's Report, 1986.
Kahan Commission Report, Jerusalem, 1983.
National Insurance Institute (NII) Report, January 1984.
Review of state auditor's report, Dead Sea Canal Project, November 1984, Jerusalem.
Settlements in the Occupied Territories, Supreme Court position, report by B'Tzelem, March 1997.
Tal Committee report for the formulation of an appropriate arrangement regarding the recruitment of yeshiva students, vol. 1, April 2000.
Tzohar, Central Bureau of Statistics, February 1999.
West Bank Settlements (Hahitnachluyot Bashtachim), High Court position, report by B'Tzelem, March 1997.

BOOKS AND ARTICLES

Against Terrorist Groups (Neged Kvutzut Hateror). Pamphlet, Hashomer Hatzair Party Headquarters, June 1946.
Agassi, Yosef. *Between Faith and Nationality* (Bein Dat Veleom). Tel Aviv University, 1993.
Alfasi, Yitzhak. *The Etzel: A Collection of Sources and Documents* (Haetzel: Osef Mekorot Vemismachim), vol. 3. Jabotinsky Institute, 1990.
Allon, Yigal. "Israel: The Case for Defensible Borders." *Foreign Affairs*, 1976.
Amichal-Yavin, Ada. *Sambatyon* (Sambatyon). Beit El, 1995.
Amrami, Yaakov. *Things Are Greater Than We Are* (Hadvarim Gdolim Hem Meitanu). Hadar, 1994.
Ansky, Alex. *The Selling of the Likud* (Mechirat Halikud). Zmora Bitan–Modan, 1978.
Arian, Asher. *The Elections in Israel 1977* (Habchirot Beisrael 1977). Academic Press, 1980.
Assia, Ilan. *The Core of the Conflict: The Struggle for the Negev, 1947–1956* (Moked Hasichsuch: Hamaavak al Hanegev, 1947–1956). Yad Ben Tzvi, 1994.
Avnery, Arie. *Defeat* (Hatvusa). Midot, 1993.
Azran, Chanan. *From Brisk to Jerusalem* (Mibrisk Leyerushalayim). Israeli Broadcast Authority (IBA), 1993.
Bader, Yochanan. *The Knesset and I* (Haknesset Vaani). Yediot Ahronot, 1979.
———. *My Journey to Zion: 1901–1948* (Darki Letzion: 1901–1948). Jabotinsky Institute, 1999.
Banai, Yaakov. *Anonymous Soldiers* (Chayalim Almonim). Yair, 1958.
Bar-Yosef, Uri. *The Watchman Fell Asleep: The Surprise of the Yom Kippur War and Its Origins* (Hatzofe Shenirdam: Haftaat Yom Hakipurim Vemekoroteha). Zmora Bitan, 2001.
Barzel, Neima. "Israeli-Germany Relations, from Boycott Policy to Complex Relationships" (Yachasey Israel-Germanya, Mimediniyut Hacherem Leksharim Murchavim). In *The First Decade*, ed. Tzvi Tzameret and Hanna Yablonka. Yad Ben Tzvi, 1991.
Begin, Menachem. *On National Perspectives and Personal Perspectives* (Hashkafat Ha'im ve Hashkafa Leumit). Ba'sahar (Beitar publishing house), 1952.
———. "On the Living Teacher" (Al Hamore Hachai). *Haumma* 18 (September 1980).
———. *The Revolt* (Hamered). Achiasaf, 1956.
———. *White Nights: The Story of a Prisoner in Russia* (Leilot Levanim). Dvir, 1995.
———, ed. *In the Underground* (Bamachteret), vol. 1. Hadar, 1959.
Beitar Book, vol. 2. Ed. H. Ben Yeruham. Committee for Publishing Beitar Books, 1973.
Ben Gurion, David. *In the Battle* (Bamaaracha), vol. 2. Mapai, 1950.
———. *Path and Vision* (Chazon Vaderech), vol. 3. Mapai, 1953.
———. *The Renewed State of Israel* (Medinat Israel Hamitchadeshet), vol. 1. Am Oved, 1969.
———. *War Diary* (Yoman Milchama), vols. 1–2. Israel Ministry of Defense, 1982.

Benziman, Uzi. *Nothing but the Truth* (Emet Dibarty). Keter, 2002.

Bergman, Dubi. "The Herut Movement: From the Underground to Politics" (Tnuat Haherut: Meirgun Machteret Lemiflaga Politit). Master's thesis, Tel Aviv University, 1978.

Bernadotte, Folke. *To Jerusalem* (Leyerushalayim). Achiasaf, 1952.

Book of the Palmach, vol. 16. Ed. Zrobavel Gilad and Mati Meged. Hakibutz Hameuchad, 1956.

Brener, Uri. *Altalena* (Altalena). Hakibbutz Hameuchad, 1978.

Brosh, Tamar. *A Speech for Every Occasion/Against the Reparations Agreement* (Neum Lekhol Et/Dvarim Neged Heskem Hashilumim). Yediot Ahronot/Open University, 1993.

Carmel, Amos. *Everything Is Political* (Hakol Politi). Dvir, 1996.

Carpi, Daniel, ed. *Ze'ev Jabotinsky's Letters* (Ze'ev Jabotinsky: Igrot), vol. 5, *January 1926–December 1927*. Jabotinsky Institute, 2000.

Carter, Jimmy. *Keeping Faith: Memoirs of a President*. University of Arkansas Press, 1995.

Chefetz, Nir, and Gadi Bloom. *The Shepherd* (Haroe). Yediot Ahronot, 2005.

Chever, Chanan, Yehuda Shenhav, and Pnina Mutzafi-Haller, eds. *Mizrachim in Israel: A Critical Observation into Israel's Ethnicity* (Mizrachim Beisrael). Hakibbutz Hameuchad, 2002.

Cohen, Geula. *Historic Meeting: Haganah, Etzel and Lehi Chiefs around the Table* (Mifgash Histori: Mefakdey Hahagana, Etzel Velehi Misaviv Lasulchan Hameruba). Yair, 1986.

Cohen, Michael J. *Palestine: Retreat from the Mandate: The Making of British Policy 1936–45*. Holmes and Meier, 1978.

"Commanders' Platform" (Bamat Mefakdim). Etzel manual. April 1943.

Dacre, Daniel. "Defensible Borders: The Return of Repressed Strategy" (Gvulot Bney Hagana: Chazarata shel Estretegya Mudcheket). *Azure* 21 (Fall 2005).

Dan, Uri. *Ariel Sharon: An Intimate Portrait* (Besodo Shel Ariel Sharon). Yediot Ahronot, 2006.

Dayan, Moshe. *Shall the Sword Devour Forever? Breakthrough: A Personal Account of the Egypt-Israel Peace Negotiations* (Halanetzach Tochal Cherev). Yediot Ahronot, 1981.

Elam, Yigal. *Haganah, The Zionist Way to Power* (Hahaganah, Haderech Hatzionit El Hakoach). Zmora Bitan–Modan, 1979.

Encyclopedia of Exile. Ed. Eliezer Steinman. Encyclopedia of Exile Company, 1954.

Eldad, Israel. *First Tenth* (Maaser Rishon). Hadar, 1976.

Eldar, Akiva, and Idit Zertal. *Lords of the Land* (Adoney Haaretz). Zmora Bitan–Dvir, 2004.

Engel, David. "The Failed Alliance: The Revisionist Movement and the Polish Government-in-Exile, 1939–1945" (Habrit Hanikhzevet: Hatnua Harevisyonistit Vememshelet Polin Hagola). *Zionism* 11 (1986). (Hakibbutz Hameuchad, Tel-Aviv University.)

Etkes, Immanuel. *The Gaon of Vilna: The Man and His Image* (Yachid Bedoro). Zalman Shazar, 1998.

Even, Efraim. "The Underlying Ideology of the Etzel Revolt and Its Conflict with Reality" (Haidiologya Shebeyesod Hamered Shel Etzel Veimuta Im Hametziut). *Haumma* 2 (1974).

———, ed. *Ze'ev Jabotinsky, My Teacher* (Mori, Ze'ev Jabotinsky). Menachem Begin Heritage Center, 2001.

Evron, Yosef. *Gidi: The Jewish Insurgency against the British in Palestine* (Gidi Vehamaaracha Lepinui Habritim). Ministry of Defense, 2001.

Frenkel, Shlomo, and Shimshon Bichler. *The Privileged* (Hameyuchasim). Kadim, 1984.

Freundlich, Yehoshua. *From Destruction to Rebirth: The Zionist Policy after World War II and the Establishment of Israel* (Mechurban Letkuma: Hamediniyut Hatzionit Mitom Milchemet Haolam Hashniya Vead Hakamat Medinat Israel). Mifalim Universitaim, Tel Aviv, 1994

Friedman, Thomas L. *From Beirut to Jerusalem* (Mibeyrut Leyerushalayim). Maariv, 1990.

Frister, Roman. *Without Compromise* (Lelo Pshara). Zmora Bitan, 1987.

Frois, Tedi. *Begin in Power* (Begin Bashilton). Keter, 1984.

Gilad, Chaim. *In the Shadow of the Gallows* (Betzel Hagardom). Hadar, 1978.

Giladi, Dan. *Eshkol as a Leader* (Eshkol Kemanhig). Cathedra, Yad Ben Tzvi, 1985.

Golan, Aviezer, and Shlomo Nakdimon. *Begin* (Begin). Yediot Ahronot, 1978.

Golani, Motti. *There Will Be a War This Summer: Israel on the Road to the Sinai War 1955–1956*. Ministry of Defense, 1997.

Grosbard, Ofer. *Menachem Begin: A Portrait of a Leader—A Biography* (Menachem Begin: Dyukano Shel Manhig). Resling, 2006.

Guri, Haim. "On Hatred" (Al Hasin'ah). *Panim* 2 (1997).

Haber, Chanan, Yehuda Shenhav, and Pnina Mutzpi Haller, eds. *Mizrahim in Israel: A Critical Observation of Israel's Ethnicity*. Hakibbutz Hameuchad, 2002.

Haber, Eitan. *Today War Will Break Out* (Hayom Tifrotz Milchama). Yediot Ahronot, 1987.

Haber, Eitan, and Ze'ev Schiff. *Yom Kippur War Lexicon* (Lexicon Milchemet Yom Hakipurim). Dvir, 2003.

Harris, Ron. "The Israeli Law, the First Decade" (Hamishpat Haisraeli). In *The First Decade*, ed. Tzvi Tzameret and Hannah Yablonka. Yad Ben Tzvi, 1991.

"The Hebrew War of Independence" (Milchemet Hashichrur Haivrit). Etzel manual, n.d.

History Book of the Haganah (Sefer Toldot Hahaganah), vol. 3. Maarachot, 1973.

Hurewitz, Jacob Coleman. *The Struggle for Palestine*. Schocken Books, 1987.

Isaacson, Meron, ed. *Begin* (Begin). Yediot Ahronot, 2003.

Israeli, Chaim. *A Life Story* (Sipur Chaim). Yediot Ahronot, 2005.

Jabotinsky, Ze'ev. *Hadar* (Al Hahadar). Ari Jabotinsky, 1961.

Kafkafi, Eyal. *Lavon: Anti Messiah* (Navon: Anti Mashiach). Am Oved, 1998.

Karpin, Michael. *I Can't Take It Anymore* (Einy Yachol Od). Film, Channel 2, April 26, 2005.

Katz, Shmuel. *Day of Fire* (Yom Haesh). Karni, 1982.

———. *Jabo* (Jabo), vol. 2. Dvir, 1993.

———. *No Courage, No Glory* (Lo Oz Ve Lo Hadar). Dvir, 1981.
Katznelson, Kalman. *Israel after the Sinai Campaign* (Israel Leachar Mivtza Sinai). Hadar, 1957.
———. *Occupiers in Distress* (Kovshim Bemetzuka). Anach, 1983.
Kissinger, Henry. *Crisis: The Anatomy of Two Major Foreign Policy Crises* (Mashber: Nihul Mediniyut Hachutz Bemilchemet Yom Kippur Vebayetziya Mivietnam). Shalem, 2004.
Lankin, Eliyahu. *The Story of Altalena* (Sipuro Shel Mefaked Altalena). Hadar, 1974.
Lapidot, Yehuda. *In Flame of Revolt* (Belahav Hamered). Ministry of Defense, 1998.
———. *The Saison: The Hunting Down of Brothers* (Hasezon: Tzeid Achim). Jabotinsky Institute, 1994.
Lazar, Chaim. *Conquering Jaffa* (Kibush Yaffo). Shelach, 1971.
Lehi Writings (Lehi: Ktavim), vol. 1. Yair, 1959.
Lev Ami, Shlomo. "Etzel Headquarters during the Revolt" (Mifkedet Haetzel Bitkufat Hamered). Master's thesis, Bar-Ilan University, 1993.
———. *The Guilty Ones* (Haashemim). Friedman, 2000.
———. "Minutes of the Irgun Tzvai Leumi, July–November 1944" (Haprotokolim Shel Mifkedet Haetzel). *Zionism* 4 (1976): 391–442.
Levin, Dov. "The Crossroad in the Relations between the Lithuanians and the Jews in World War II" (Leparashat Hayachasim Bein Halitaim Layehudim Bemilchemet Haolam Hashniya). *Kivunim Chadashim, Journal of Judaism and Zionism*, 1975.
Lichtenstein, Yoram. "The Herut Movement, Internal Processes and Structure" (Tnuat Haherut, Mivne Vetahalichim Pnimiyim). Master's thesis, Hebrew University, 1974.
Livni, Eitan. *Hamaamad* (Hamaamad). Yediot Ahronot, 1987.
Markoviski, Yaakov. *The Irgun Lexicon* (Lexicon Etzel). Ministry of Defense, 2005.
Meridor, Yaakov. *A Long Road to Freedom* (Aruka Haderech Leherut). Achiasaf, 1978.
Milstein, Uri. *History of the War of Independence* (Toldot Milchemet Haatzmaut). Zmora Bitan, 1989.
Morgenthau, Henry. *United States Diplomacy on the Bosphorus: The Diaries of Ambassador Morgenthau 1913–1916*. Gomidas Institute, 2004.
Morris, Benny. *Righteous Victims* (Korbanot). Am Oved, 2003.
Nakdimon, Shlomo. *Altalena* (Altalena). Yediot Ahronot, 1978.
———. *Tamuz in Flames* (Tamuz Belehavot). Yediot Ahronot, 1984.
Naor, Arie. *Begin in Power: A Personal Testimony* (Begin Bashilton: Edut Ishit). Yediot Ahronot, 1993.
———. *Cabinet at War* (Memshala Bemilchama). Yediot Ahronot, 1986.
Niv, David. *Battle for Freedom: The Irgun Tzvai Leumi* (Maarachot Haetzel), vols. 1–6. Klausner Institute, 1973.
Oren, Michael B. *Six Days of War: June 1967 and the Making of the Modern Middle East* (Shisa Yamim Shel Milchama: Hamaaracha Shesinta Et Pney Hamizrach Hatichon). Dvir, 2007.

Oron, Israel. *Death, Immortality and Ideology* (Mavet, Almavet Veidiologia). Ministry of Defense, 2002.
Pa'il, Meir, and Pinchas Yorman. *The Test of the Zionist Movement, 1931–1948: The Political Leadership's Anger at the Dissidents* (Mivchan Hatnua Hatzyonit, 1931–1948: Mrut Hahahaga Hamedinit Mul Haporshim). Cherikover, 2002.
Peres, Shimon. *Battling for Peace*. Weidenfeld and Nicolson, 1995.
Peres, Yochanan. *Ethnic Relations in Israel* (Yachsey Edot Beisrael). Sifriat Hapoalim, 1976.
Perlmutter, Amos. *The Life and Times of Menachem Begin*. American University, Washington, D.C., 1987.
Picard, Avi. "The Beginning of Selective Immigration in the 1950s" (Reshita Shel Haaliya Haselektivit Beshnot Hachamishim). *Iyunim Bitkumat Israel* 9 (1999). (Ben Gurion University.)
Ratzabi, Shalom. "Jabotinsky and Religion" (Jabotinsky Vehadat). *Israel* 5 (2004). (Tel Aviv University.)
Recanati, David. *Deceitful Bridge* (Gesher Achzav). Hadar, 1977.
Rosenberg, Oren. "Begin and the Herut Movement, 1949–1952" (Begin Vetnuat Haherut, 1949–1952). Master's thesis, University of Haifa, 2002.
Sasson, Moshe. *Seven Years in the Land of the Egyptians* (Sheva Shanim Be'eretz Hamitzrim). Idanim, 1992.
Schechtman, Yosef. *The Life and Times of Vladimir Jabotinsky* (Ze'ev Jabotinsky Veparashat Chayav). Jabotinsky Institute, 1959.
Schiff, Ze'ev, and Ehud Yaari. *Israel's Lebanon War, 1982* (Milchemet Sholal). Schocken, 1984.
Segal, Chaggai. *Dear Brothers: History of the Jewish Underground* (Achim Yekarim). Keter, 1987.
Segev, Tom. *Israel in 1967* (1967). Keter, 2005.
Shaltiel, Eli. *Moshe Sneh: Life* (Tamid Bemeri), vol. 1, *1909–1948*. Am Oved, 2000.
Shamir, Moshe. *Yair* (Yair). Zmora Bitan, 2001.
Shamir, Yitzhak. *Summing Up: An Autobiography* (Besikumo Shel Davar). Yediot Ahronot, 1994.
Shapira, Anita. *The Army Controversy, 1948: Ben Gurion's Struggle for Control* (Mepiturey Harama Ad Peruk Hapalmach). Hakibbutz Hameuchad, 1985.
———. *Yigal Allon: The Spring of His Life* (Yigal Alon: Aviv Cheldo). Hakibbutz Hameuchad, 2004.
Shapira, Yonatan. *Chosen to Command* (Lashilton Bechartanu). Am Oved, 1989.
Sharett, Moshe. *A Personal Diary* (Yoman Ishi), vol. 4. Maariv, 1978.
Sharett, Yaakov, ed. *Moshe Sharett and the German Reparations Controversy*. Society to Commemorate Moshe Sharett, 2008.
Shavit, Yaakov. "Between Piłsudski and Mickiewicz: Policy and Messianism in the Zionist Revisionism" (Bein Pilsudsky Lemitzkeiviwtz: Mediniyut Vemeshichizm Barevisyunizm Hatzioni Beheksher Shel Hatarbut Hapolitit Hapolanit Vezikato Lepolin). *Zionism* 10 (1984). (Hakibbutz Hameuchad.)
———. *The Season of the Hunt* (Hasezon). Hadar, 1976.
Sherman, Arnold. *Ke'esh Beatzmotav* (Ke'esh Beatzmotav). Yediot Ahronot, 1986.
Shiffer, Shimon. *Snowball* (Kadur Sheleg). Yediot Ahronot, 1984.

Shlaim, Avi. *The Iron Wall* (Kir Habarzel). Yediot Ahronot, 2005.
Silver, Eric. *Begin: The Haunted Prophet*. Random House, 1984.
Stauber, Roni. "The Controversy in the Political Press over the Kastner Trial" (Havikuach Hapoliti Al Mishpat Kastner). *Zionism* 13 (1988). (Hakibbutz Hameuchad.)
Tabin, Eli. *The Second Front* (Hachazit Hashniya). Hadar, 1973.
Temko, Ned. *To Win or to Die*. William Morrow, 1987.
Tsipori, Mordechai. *In a Straight Line* (Bekav Yashar). Yediot Ahronot, 1997.
Tzur, Nadir. *The Rhetoric of Israeli Leaders in Stress Situations* (Retorika Politit). Hakibbutz Hameuchad, 2004.
Tzur, Yaron. *A Torn Community: The Jews of Morocco and Nationalism, 1943–1954* (Kehila Kruah). Am Oved, 2001.
Vassa, Pinchas. *The Mission: Procurement* (Hamsima Rechesh). Maarchot, 1967.
Vurembrand, Mordechai, and Betzalel S. Ruth. *The People of Israel: 4,000 Years* (Toldot Am Israel: 4,000 Shana). Massada, 1966.
Weitz, Yechiam. "The Alternative Flag: Israel's Ties with Germany in the Herut Movement" (Hadegel Hachilufi: Kishrey Israel Im Germanya Betnuat Haherut). *Zion* 16 (2001).
———. *From a Militant Underground to a Political Party* (Mimachteret Lochemet Lemiflaga Politit). Ben Gurion University, 2003.
———. *The Man Who Was Murdered Twice: The Life, Trial, and Death of Dr. Israel Kastner* (Ha'ish Shenirtzach Paamayim: Chayav, Mishpato Vemoto Shel Doctor Israel Kastner). Keter, 1995.
———. "The Turnover That Never Was" (Hamahapach Shelo Haya). *Panim* 9 (1999).
Ya'ar, Efraim, and Ze'ev Shavit, eds. *Trends in Israeli Society* (Megamot Bahevra Haisraelit). Open University, 2001.
Yosef, Dov. *Loyal City* (Kirya Neemana). Schocken, 1960.

INDEX

Abd-al-Majid, 332
Abdullah, king of Jordan, 108, 138, 146, 159
Abrushmy, Yona, 412
Abu Nidal, 374
Achdut Haavoda, 181–82, 190, 193, 208, 213
Achimeir, Abba, 138–39, 332
Achimeir, Yaakov, 351, 386, 442
Achituv, Avraham, 270
Acre Prison Break, 99, 100, 132, 182, 444
Adenauer, Konrad, 166–67, 174, 481n1
Admoni, Nachum, 402
Agnon, S. Y., 208
Agranat Commission, 241
Agudat Israel, 265–66, 279, 355
Alis, Shraga, 54, 94–95, 140, 198, 228–29
Alkachi, Mordechai, 94
Allon, Yigal, 71, 206, 211, 236, 243
Allon Plan, 211–12
Almog, Shmuel, 232
Aloni, Shulamit, 235, 269, 405
Altalena affair, 117–31, 133, 134, 148, 190, 196, 329–30, 430, 448
Alterman, Natan, 102, 167, 208
Altman, Arie, 49, 64, 158
Amit, Meir, 267, 314
Amitsur, Betzalel, 77, 81
Amper, Avraham, 25
Anders Army (Poland), 6, 39–42
Ansky, Alex, 253, 255
"Arab Events"/"Great Arab Revolt" (1936), 18, 50, 88, 99, 105
Arab League, 309–10, 396, 400
Arabs: guerrillas in border skirmishes, 175–77; Hebrew/"Eretz Israeli," 114, 159, 191, 244, 278, 290, 311, 317, 434; nationalism, 18, 84, 88; and nuclear energy, 339–47; peace negotiations with, 195, 215, 221, 244, 281–312, 314–15; PLO, *see* PLO; and the territories, 221, 293, 318–19; *see also* occupied territories; Zionism vs., 88, 276; *see also specific countries or wars*
Arafat, Yasser, 338; Begin's animosity toward, 223, 273, 349, 358, 396; evacuation from Beirut, 396–98; in Lebanon, 379, 392, 394, 395, 396; and Sadat, 284; *see also* PLO
Aran, Zalman, 145
Arbeli Almozlino, Shoshana, 253, 354
Arendt, Hannah, 142
Arens, Moshe, 252; as ambassador to U.S., 355–56, 373; and Begin government, 329, 355–56, 412–13, 422; and Lebanon, 373, 413, 416; and peace talks, 292, 293, 299, 309
Argov, Shlomo, 374, 378, 416
Aridor, Yoram, 252, 309, 324, 335–36, 356, 413–14
Arlosoroff, Chaim, 14, 120, 189–90, 249, 331–33, 406
Arnold, Fredericka, 23
Arnold, Herman Tzvi, 23
Assad, Hafaz al-, 349, 364, 368, 381–82, 384
Aswan Declaration, 295
Attlee, Clement, 84, 88
Avnery, Uri, 211, 443
Azar, Shmuel, 178

Bachmann, Avraham, 318
Bader, Yochanan, 40, 210, 445–46; and Begin in opposition, 225; and Begin's mood swings, 315; and Begin's resignation, 162, 163, 164; and elections, 141–42, 168, 170,

Bader, Yochanan (cont.)
172, 173, 194, 248; and Etzel, 46,
112, 141; and Herut, 112, 135,
157–58, 162, 168, 190, 199, 217, 220,
239, 244, 245; and Knesset, 141,
145, 148, 244, 245, 248; and Meir
government, 204, 216–17, 225;
retirement of, 248, 252, 260, 315;
and Six-Day War, 204, 225
Balfour Declaration, 88, 455n38
Banai, Yaakov, 26
Barak, Aharon, 406
Barak, Ehud, 376
Barazani, Moshe, 446
Bar-Kokhba, 263, 271
Bar Lev, Chaim, 319, 338, 378–79
Barnea, Nachum, 330, 411
Begin, Aliza Arnold (wife): at Camp
David, 300, 304; death of, 409–10,
418, 425, 426, 427, 429, 432, 435,
517n16; emigration to Palestine,
30, 36; health of, 24, 344, 408–9;
and her husband's health, 315; and
her husband's politics, 24, 29–30,
31, 45, 46, 97, 163, 198, 258, 300,
378; marriage of, 23–24; reunited
with her husband, 40–41; underground, 55, 74, 81–82; and vacation,
162–63
Begin, Binyamin Ze'ev (son), 257;
birth of, 42; at Camp David, 303,
304, 305, 306; and elections,
439–40, 446; and his father's
withdrawal, 426, 428, 431, 434,
438–39; and his mother's death,
409; and Lebanon war, 391–92,
438–40; and peace treaty, 317; and
underground, 46, 74, 81–82
Begin, Chasia (daughter): birth of,
82–83, 257; and her father, 358, 428,
442
Begin, Chasia Kossovski (mother), 1,
3, 5–6, 168
Begin, David-Eliezer (grandfather), 3
Begin, Herzl (brother), 1, 5, 7, 9
Begin, Leah (daughter), 409, 418, 427,
434, 442

Begin, Menachem: and *Altalena*
affair, 117–31, 133, 190, 196,
329–30, 430, 448; ambitions of, 9,
20, 44, 61, 95, 110, 113, 117, 163,
236, 276, 345; in Anders Army, 6,
39–42; arrest and imprisonment of,
17, 29–38; and Beitar, 10–12, 15–16,
18–19, 20–22, 27, 42, 61; and Ben
Gurion, *see* Ben Gurion, David;
birth and family background of, 1,
2–4, 6–8, 10–11; and Camp David,
299–312; changing politics of, 118,
130–32, 139–40, 150, 157–59, 172,
176–77, 186, 187–88, 200, 213–15,
225–26, 241, 252, 259, 274, 276, 286,
293–94, 298–99, 308, 338, 360,
449–50; childhood of, 7–10, 93;
clinging to the past, 190, 227, 241,
258, 266, 268; criticisms of, 21, 22,
24, 132, 142, 143–44, 150–51, 155,
162, 175, 195, 200, 220, 225, 273,
315; death of, 446, 447; as defense
minister, 329–30, 356; and destiny,
163, 260, 276, 431; details overlooked by, 20, 22, 45, 49, 52, 62, 87,
97, 107, 114, 157–58, 183, 239,
244–45, 282, 320, 322, 326, 366–67,
385, 392–94, 407, 411, 414, 448,
449, 451; education of, 7, 8–9,
10–11; and elections, *see* Israeli
elections; and Etzel, *see* Etzel; final
years of, 442–46; and fraternal war,
73, 76, 80, 118, 129–30, 172; and
German reparations, 167–73, 179,
194, 201, 241, 336, 337, 448, 449;
health of, 215–16, 250–51, 252, 254,
283, 297–98, 315–16, 331, 360–61,
369, 410, 415, 418, 432, 441–43,
444, 446; and Herut, *see* Herut;
impact of, 447–52; indecisiveness
under pressure, 30, 41, 45, 75, 79,
122, 128, 130; and Jabotinsky, *see*
Jabotinsky, Ze'ev; and Jaffa,
108–10, 148, 273; and Knesset, *see*
Knesset; lack of common sense,
45–46, 83, 148; marriage of, *see*
Begin, Aliza Arnold; and media, 56,

96, 99, 108, 111, 116, 122, 143, 206, 213, 231–32, 250, 266, 273, 284–85, 286, 351–52, 443; as minister without portfolio, 210, 212, 216; mood swings of, 27, 62–63, 82, 90, 95, 126, 150, 162, 164–65, 172, 269, 297, 315, 316, 330–31, 336, 410, 414–15, 416–18, 427, 430, 435; nationalism and law blended by, 12–13, 23, 73, 115, 275, 326, 448; national policy plans, 243–44; and Nobel Prize, 293, 310–11; as oppositionist, 147, 194–95, 214, 222–25, 227, 232, 259, 260, 294, 303, 348, 450; as outsider, 113, 147–48, 150, 177, 451; party politics vs. statesmanship, 222, 232; peace sought by, 272–312, 314–15, 317, 447–48, 450, 451; political reality denied by, 147, 148, 158, 244, 292; as prime minister, 12, 13, 140, 232, 257–58, 259–70, 278–80, 299, 309, 313, 330–31, 355–57, 406–7, 411–15, 450–51; and religion, 9, 115, 152–53, 154, 217, 265–67, 279; restraint shown by, 66–67, 71–73, 76–77, 80, 103; and retirement, 162–63, 196–97, 220–23, 231, 241, 242, 249, 336, 418–23, 424–28, 430, 434, 452; retreating under pressure, 162–64, 168, 197, 220, 293, 294, 307, 412, 414, 425–26, 449; rhetorical style of, 11, 13, 16–17, 21, 22, 28, 60, 76, 96, 111–12, 117, 129–30, 132, 133–35, 142–43, 146, 150, 159–61, 170–71, 173–75, 180–81, 182, 185–86, 196, 209–10, 214–15, 227, 236–37, 241–42, 247, 258, 262, 311, 348–54, 448, 451–52; rise to power, 256–58; on rituals, 13–14, 48, 97, 101–2, 139–40, 242; rumors about, 63–64; on "the sacred ballot," 131–32; on seizing land militarily, 176; travels of, 142, 162–64, 174, 177, 209, 226; underground, *see* Etzel; and U.S., 142, 177, 255, 276–79, 290–91, 296–97, 307, 322, 328, 357–58, 387–88, 408–9, 418; violence promoted by, 13; withdrawal of, 331, 411, 414–18, 420, 422, 423, 424–35, 438–39, 442, 445, 452; worldview of, 8, 61, 272; writings of, 31, 42, 60, 73, 83, 84, 94, 96, 101, 104–5, 111, 112–13, 164, 223–24, 430, 434

Begin, Rachel (sister), 1, 5–6, 7, 9, 97, 258, 269, 448

Begin, Ze'ev-Dov (father): birth and family background of, 2–4; and financial issues, 10–11; and his children, 1, 9; murder of, 5–6, 269, 448; in Poland, 2–3, 4–5, 9, 93; respect for German culture, 6, 448

Begin Doctrine, 345

Beitar, 10–16, 18–22, 25–27, 42, 61, 95, 152

Beit Zuri, Eliyahu, 68

Ben David (pseud.), 83

Ben Dov Halevi, Yerachmiel, 45

Ben Eliezer, Arie, 44, 203, 204; and Begin's resignations, 163, 164, 196; death of, 220, 260; and Etzel, 46, 49–50, 112; and foreign policy, 151; and German reparations, 167, 170; and Herut, 164, 167, 193; and Knesset, 141, 170; and Lavon Affair, 189

Ben Elissar, Eliyahu, 232, 261, 355

Ben Gal, Yanush, 349, 358, 370, 377, 382, 385, 387, 410

Ben Gurion, David, 199, 209, 239, 241, 260, 301, 327, 354, 443; and *Altalena* affair, 117–31, 134, 148, 329–30; ambitions of, 70, 273; and Begin, 53, 57, 58, 60–62, 70, 103, 117, 132, 134, 147–50, 174, 180, 184–87, 196, 203, 214, 245, 258, 329–30, 444–45, 449, 450, 451; and the British, 53, 57, 60, 61, 70, 96; death, anniversary of, 286–87; as defense minister, 178–79, 329, 367, 369; and elections, 134, 143, 144, 157, 158, 159, 160, 188, 189, 190;

Ben Gurion (cont.)
    and establishment of Israel, 47, 96, 103, 109, 111, 113, 148; and Etzel, 53, 54, 61, 63, 69–71, 80, 101, 102, 117, 118, 119, 120, 123–27, 129–31, 136, 137, 431; and first government, 138, 147–50, 151, 155–56, 180; and German reparations, 166–71, 174, 185; and Haganah, 88, 89–90; and independence, 111–12; influence of, 447; and Jabotinsky, 14–15, 178; and Jerusalem, 135, 136; and Jewish Resistance Movement, 84–85, 89–90; and Lebanon, 363–64; as Mapai leader, 179, 186, 191; and Operation Kadesh, 184–85; and Operation Nachshon, 106; as prime minister, 176, 259, 278, 338; and Rafi party, 191, 194, 195, 201, 238, 264; and religion, 178, 267; and Reshima Mamlachtit, 213; resignations of, 177, 189–90, 191, 231, 276, 428; and Saison, 71, 80, 186; and Six-Day War, 201, 202–4, 207, 444–45; and War of Independence, 106, 108, 121–22, 363
Ben Meir, Yehuda, 375
Ben Porat, Mordechai, 395
Ben Porat, Yishayahu (Shaike), 255
Ben Yosef, Shlomo, 18
Ben Ze'ef, M. (pseud.), 42
Bergman, Hugo, 70
Berman, Yitzhak, 377–78, 388, 406
Bernadotte, Count Folke, 121, 133, 136–37, 144
Bernstein, Peretz, 85, 186
Bethlehem, international trusteeship over, 104
Bett, Reuven, 441
Bevin, Ernest, 84, 89, 96, 98, 103
Bidault, Georges, 120
Biltmore Program (1942), 47, 460n46
Black Sabbath, 89, 92–93
Black September, 364, 506n4
Blum, Yehuda, 275
Bocwitz, Menachem, 42
Boutros-Ghali, Boutros, 291, 292, 303

Brest-Litovsk (Brisk), Poland: Begin family in, 2–3, 4–5, 6–7, 9, 337; Beitar group in, 13; Treaty of, 7
Brezhnev, Leonid, 383
Britain: Begin's opposition to, 28, 41, 44–45, 47, 84, 94, 104–5, 114, 120, 133, 177, 181, 190, 307, 448; and establishment of Jewish state, 20; Middle East policies of, 47, 88–89, 98; and peace talks, 291; post–World War II, 87–88, 98
Brit Hakanaim, 154–55
British Mandate: and Black Sabbath, 89, 92–93; borders of, 116, 147; declaration of rebellion against, 48–54; end of, 98–99, 103–5, 148–49; hanged sergeants affair, 99, 100–101, 102, 200, 226, 444; and Jewish Agency, 53–54, 57, 60, 64, 69–71, 84, 98; and Jewish immigration, 13, 84, 88, 89; and King David Hotel explosion, 90–92, 226; law of, 332–33; and Saison, 8, 70–80, 103; terrorist activities against, see Etzel
Brit Shalom, 70, 103
Brzezinki, Zbigniew, 296
Burg, Avraham, 412
Burg, Yosef, 171, 303, 408; and autonomy talks, 317–18; and Begin government, 320, 356, 359; and Begin's health, 315, 360, 361, 410; and Begin's withdrawal, 415, 421, 426; and Carter, 312, 415; and war in Lebanon, 370, 378, 389, 397; and withdrawal from Sinai, 314

Callaghan, James, 273, 291
Camp David talks, 299–312
Canaanites, 115
Carter, Jimmy, 269, 433, 440–41; Begin's meetings with, 276–78, 279, 280, 290, 296, 311–12, 415; and Camp David talks, 301–11; and Middle East peace, 276, 277–78, 284, 311, 358; and Nobel Prize, 310; and occupied territories, 275, 276,

277–78, 290; and Palestine self-determination, 295, 296
Ceausescu, Nicolae, 280–82
Chadad, Alon, 445
Chalutz, Dan, 347
Chamberlain, Neville, 307, 366
Chazit Hamoledet (Homeland Front), 136–37
Chmelnitski, Bogdan, 453n4
Chofi, Yitzhak, 270–72, 340, 376
Churchill, Winston, 47, 57, 68, 84, 434
Cohen, Chaim, 179
Cohen, David, 121
Cohen, Geula, 72, 169, 230, 252, 292, 309, 314, 320, 426, 434
Cohen, Yaakov, 103
Cohen families, 152
Cohen-Maguri, Chaim, 141
Cold War, 135, 151, 255, 281, 341, 358
Committee for the Jews of Poland, 30
Committee X, 85, 90
Corfu, Chaim, 265–66, 427, 445
Czechoslovakia, Beitar movement in, 16, 33

Daladier, Édouard, 366
Danon, David, 417
Darwish, Isa, 332
Dash party, 248, 256, 261, 265, 267, 269, 284, 314, 355
Dayan, David, 444
Dayan, Moshe, 72, 178, 213, 218, 241, 243, 250; and Begin's government, 261, 263–64, 267, 268, 274, 301, 357, 395; and elections, 194, 251, 355; health of, 318, 356; and Iraq, 340; and peace negotiations, 277, 280, 282, 289–92, 295, 296, 297–99, 304–6, 315, 317–19; resignation of, 320, 328, 329; and Six-Day War, 204, 205–6, 208; and Telem, 355; and territories, 211, 318–19; and underground, 56–58; and Yom Kippur War, 236
Deichs, Paula, 36

Deir Yassin, 106–8, 110, 119, 310, 406, 448
Dinitz, Simcha, 262, 303
Donevich, Natan, 241–42
Dori, Yaakov, 70
Dresner, Yechiel, 94
Drobles, Matityahu, 231
Drori, Amir, 380
Dunant, Jean Henry, 311

Eban, Abba, 207, 211, 213, 218, 254
Efrat, Yona, 406
Egypt: Arab infiltrators from, 175–76; and Arab League, 309–10; balance of power with, 184; and Camp David, 299–309; and cease-fires, 144, 215, 220–22, 233, 235; and Iraq, 341, 344; and Lavon Affair, 178, 189; and Operation Kadesh, 184–85; peace negotiations with, 244, 275, 277, 278, 280–81, 284–89, 291–92, 295–96, 298, 299–307, 317, 319, 340, 357, 359, 362, 434, 447, 451, 502n60; Sadat's assassination in, 358–60; Sinai return to, 200, 241, 286; and Six-Day War, 201–2, 205; and Yom Kippur War, 233–37
Ehrlich, Simcha, 256; and Begin government, 261, 268, 269, 282, 324–25, 356, 397; and Begin's mood swings, 269, 410; and the economy, 321, 322, 324–25; and Liberal Party, 248, 260; and Likud, 251, 260, 322; and war in Lebanon, 370, 371, 372, 377, 388, 397
Eichmann, Adolf, 76
Einstein, Albert, 142
Eitan, Rafael (Raful), 218, 319, 340, 349, 357, 370, 375, 385, 397, 403, 411
El-Al flights, 265–66
Elazar, David, 234, 236, 395
Eldad, Batya, 24, 27, 29, 81, 415, 432
Eldad, Israel, 27, 29, 30, 141, 162, 173, 175, 267; Begin criticized by, 21, 22, 24, 132; and Beitar, 21, 22; and Lehi, 42, 129, 137

INDEX 533

Eliyahu, Rabbi Mordechai, 154
Entebbe, Uganda, kidnapping, 245–47, 393
Epstein, Israel, 21, 42
Erem, Moshe, 119
Eshkol, Levi, 121, 123, 186, 190, 191, 192, 213, 245; and Six-Day War, 201, 202, 203–4, 205, 206, 207
Ethiopian Jews, 272, 432, 443
Etzel, 42–47, 48–80, 258, 431; and Acre Prison Break, 99, 100, 182, 444; and *Altalena* affair, 117–31, 134; anti-British activities, 8, 41, 42–47, 48–54, 56–57, 64–66, 68–70, 76, 85–87, 88, 90–94, 98–99, 114, 115; Begin as commander of, 42, 44–45, 47, 48, 49, 61, 66–67, 73, 75–79, 83–87, 97, 101, 110, 112, 114, 119, 126–27, 130, 131, 140, 163, 206, 225, 227, 273, 333, 444, 448; and Ben Gurion, *see* Ben Gurion, David; and Deir Yassin, 106–8, 110, 119; disbanding of, 112, 113, 117, 118–19, 131, 137, 144; fading influence of, 239; financial issues in, 79, 95, 102, 119, 121, 123, 245; founding of, 17–19; and hanged sergeants affair, 99, 100–101, 102, 444; and Herut, 116, 130, 132; and IDF, 111, 112, 118–19, 124–26, 130, 131, 135–36, 182; and independence, 111, 115, 144, 146; Irgun Tzvai Leumi, 8, 12; and Jaffa, 106, 108–10, 130, 148, 273, 397; in Jerusalem, 113, 115, 117, 119, 131, 133, 135–36, 137, 144; and Jewish Resistance Movement, 85–90, 102; and King David Hotel explosion, 90–92, 226; and Lehi, 67, 71, 94–95, 102; manifestos of, 60, 73, 84, 88; militancy of, 19, 50, 62, 78, 79, 83–84, 90, 102–3, 141, 444; and Operation Wall, 52–53, 75; political aspirations of, 63; protocols of, 48–49, 101–2; rebellion declared by, 48–54, 75; and Revisionist Party, 63, 64, 79, 116, 134; and Saison, 8, 70–80, 86, 93, 102–3, 110, 449; split within, 29; symbolic declarative acts of, 53; underground, 43–67, 69–80, 81–84, 86, 95–98, 104, 111, 117, 118–20, 175, 245, 449; U.S. office, 132; and War of Independence, 52, 88, 106–10, 111, 120–21, 124
Etzioni Commission, 325–26
Even, Dan, 125, 126

Fein, Monroe, 122, 124
Feinstein, Meir, 446
Feinstein, Rabbi Moshe, 279
Flumin, Yechezkel, 331
France: and *Altalena* affair, 121, 122, 123; and Iraq, 340, 342, 344
Friedman, Milton, 321, 322, 323, 324

Gahal, 199, 214, 215, 216; establishment of, 194, 450; and Liberal Party, 237; and Six-Day War, 202, 203, 204; and Weizmann, 217–18, 222, 224–25, 227, 229, 237
Galili, Israel, 69, 85, 87, 90–92, 118, 119, 121, 123–25, 206, 235
Garibaldi, Giuseppe, 13
Garth, David, 336
Gaza Strip, 185, 207, 256, 275, 277, 290, 293, 295, 298, 308, 318, 360, 447
Gazit, Shlomo, 61, 340
Gelblum, Arie, 150
Gemayel, Amin, 406, 415
Gemayel, Bachir, 364, 367–69, 384, 392, 399–402, 406, 416, 436
Geneva conference, 277, 278, 280, 282
Germany: ambassador to Israel, 194; and Baader-Meinhof Gang, 247; Begin's anti-German views, 6, 167–70, 172, 448, 449; and Entebbe kidnapping, 245–47; and Palestine, 337; Poland occupied by, 5; reparations for Holocaust, 165, 166–74, 179, 185, 186, 194, 201, 241, 336, 337, 449, 481n1
Geva, Eli, 390–91

Gibli, Binyamin, 178, 189
Giladi, Arie, 378
Giladi, Yoske, 191
Golan Heights, 206, 207, 210, 211, 243, 251, 256, 275, 276, 281, 360–62, 395
Goldmann, Nachum, 167
Golomb, Eliyahu, 15, 53, 64–66, 72, 79
Gonen, Shmuel (Gorodish), 234
Goren, Rabbi Shlomo, 246, 375
Gottesman, Marvin, 297
Greater Israel, 151–52, 181, 195, 208–9, 212, 238, 258
Great Reversal, 243, 257, 265, 267–68, 276, 282
Greenbaum, Yitzhak, 103, 126
Greenberg, Uri Tzvi, 42, 141, 145, 208
Grinzweig, Emil, 412
Gromyko, Andrei, 103
Groseberg, David, 77
Gross, Miriam, 416
Gruenwald, Malkiel, 179
Gur, Mordechai (Motta), 36, 206, 290, 319, 357, 440
Guri, Chaim, 174, 208
Gush Emunim, 56, 208, 270, 294, 314–15, 318, 319, 357, 371

Haavoda, 213, 215, 244, 262, 324, 447
Habib, Philip, 349, 368, 381
Hacohen, Rabbi Yisrael Meir, 266–67
Haddad, Saad, 365–66, 400
Haganah: and Black Sabbath, 89, 92–93; and the British, 76, 79, 87, 89, 93, 98; and Dayan, 57–58, 263; and defection, 41; and Etzel, 17, 49, 50, 53, 54, 64, 66–67, 69, 70, 85–87, 90, 92, 102–3, 118–19, 120, 121, 186; Haganah B, 17–18; *The History Book of the Haganah*, 79; and Jewish Resistance Movement, 85–90; and King David Hotel explosion, 91–92; Night of the Bridges, 89; and Palmach, 58, 70–72, 79; and Saison, 8, 70–80, 102–3; and War of Independence, 106, 108–10, 124, 138
Haig, Alexander, 342, 373, 374, 384, 388
Haile-Mariam, Mengistu, 272
Hakibbutz Hameuchad (United Kibbutz Movement), 69
Hakim, Eliyahu, 68
Halevi, Binyamin, 179, 242
Halevi, Yerachmiel Ben Dov, 45
Halikud Haleumi-Liberali, 238
Halperin, Immanuel, 345
Halperin, Rachel, *see* Begin, Rachel
Halpert, Dov, 157, 191
Hamaarach, 214–15, 238, 245; and autonomy plan, 295; and elections, 216, 240–41, 253–54, 256, 265, 338, 346–47, 348, 349–50, 351, 352, 355, 432; formation of, 193, 213, 237; and Labor Party, 293; and occupied territories, 361; and peace talks, 308
Hamaccabi, Yehudah, 214, 271
Hamerkaz Hachofshi, 198, 200, 228–29, 237, 284
Hammer, Zevulun, 265, 314, 326, 343, 390
hanged sergeants affair, 99, 100–101, 102, 200, 226, 444
Harel, Asa, 316
Harel, Isser, 137, 443
Harnik, Guni, 389
Harnik, Raya, 389
Harrison, Earl G., 84
Hashomer Hatzair, 69
Hassan, king of Morocco, 282
Hatechiya, 314
Hatzohar party, 14, 49–50, 134, 135, 144
Hebrew Committee for National Liberation, 112, 120
Herut, 131–34, 147, 164; Begin as party chairman, 15, 167–68, 199–201, 220; Begin as prime minister, 260–61, 263, 294, 298; conferences, 209–10, 243, 293;

Herut (cont.)
  dissent within, 114, 152, 175; and elections, 117, 134–35, 137–45, 146, 156–62, 181–82, 188–89, 190–91; and Etzel, 116, 130, 132; fading influence of, 239; finances of, 165, 244–45; and first government, 148, 149; founding of, 112–14, 118; and Gahal, 194, 450; and German reparations, 167; and Greater Israel, 208; ideology of, 237–38; Knesset list, 139–42, 145, 217; and Lamerchav, 155; and Land of Israel, 193–94; and Likud, 238; and Mapai, 133–34, 186; party platform of, 112–13, 114, 134; and Revisionists, 113, 116, 132, 134, 135, 152, 159, 450
Herzl, Theodor, 1, 4, 12, 137, 273, 311, 368, 454n38
Herzog, Chaim, 208, 417
Hezbollah, 401
Hillel, Shlomo, 253
Histadrut, 14, 15, 70, 135, 193, 214, 239, 324, 336
Hobeika, Eli, 402, 403–4
Hochman, Yitzhak, 40
Holocaust: Begin's references to, 54, 55, 62, 65, 84, 155, 167, 170–71, 218, 224, 247, 249, 269–70, 272, 273, 278, 337–38, 346, 366, 396, 398, 448, 451; German reparations for, 165, 166–74, 179, 185, 186, 194, 201, 241, 336, 337, 449, 481n1; memory of, 103, 207, 230, 292; refugees of, 47, 84, 89, 98; survivors of, 179; and Yad Vashem, 289
Horowitz, Harry, 429, 434
Horowitz, Yigal, 314, 325, 326, 335, 501n49
Hussein, king of Jordan, 209, 274, 280, 338, 364, 434, 506n4
Hussein, Saddam, 340, 441
Husseini, Abed al-Qader, 107

India-Pakistan War (1971), 233
Intifada, 434, 444

Iraq: Arabs in, 88; immigrants from, 160; and Iran, 340–41; Kuwait invaded by, 441; missiles fired at Israel, 441–42; nuclear reactor bombed (1981), 239, 339–48, 349, 352, 366, 442, 451
Islambouli, Khaled Ahmed Showky al-, 359
Israel: Arab guerrilla attacks on, 175–77; see also PLO; Austerity Regime, 156; as bi-national country, 69, 70, 88, 89, 98, 104; borders of, 116, 121, 143, 144, 146–47, 176, 221, 254, 275, 330, 365–66; economy of, 156, 158, 159, 174, 210–11, 239, 321–28, 335–36, 413–15; elections in, see Israeli elections; establishment of, 12, 18, 20, 22, 47, 61, 96, 99, 103–4, 109, 111–13, 117, 120, 148, 177, 258, 337, 464n89; and German reparations, 165, 166–74, 179, 185, 186, 194, 201, 241; Hebrew nation or Jewish people, 114–15, 132, 152, 177–78; immigration to, 112, 134, 156, 158, 161, 182–83, 186, 272, 332; independence of, 109, 110–12, 119, 121, 151, 167, 312; national identity of, 170, 177, 207, 327, 451; non-Jewish population in, 114; right to exist, 212, 269, 274, 285, 289; separation of religion and state in, 115, 152, 195, 279; West Jerusalem as capital of, 147; and worldwide Jewish communities, 177–78, 271–72
Israel Defense Forces (IDF): and *Altalena* affair, 125–31; and border clashes, 121; and Etzel, 111, 112, 118–19, 124–26, 130, 131, 135–36, 182; forming of, 111, 118; and Jerusalem, 135; and Lebanon, 365–68, 370, 372, 379–85, 387–90, 393–95, 399, 401, 402–7, 413, 415; and Six-Day War, 201–2, 207, 241; and Syria, 379–84; and War of Attrition, 221; and War of Indepen-

dence, 120, 121–22; and Yom
Kippur War, 234–37
Israeli Air Force (IAF): Iraq nuclear
reactor bombed by, 341–44, 366;
and Lavi fighter plane, 320; and
Lebanon, 342, 371, 372, 383, 390,
396–97; and Six-Day War, 205–7;
and Yom Kippur War, 233, 234
Israeli elections: first, 132, 133–34,
137–45, 256; second, 156–62, 256;
third, 180, 181–82; fourth, 187–89;
fifth, 190–91; sixth, 194–95;
seventh, 213–15; eighth, 230–31,
237, 240; in 1977, 248–58; in 1981,
330–31, 333, 336–39, 343, 348–55;
media coverage of, 250, 253–56, 350
Ivry, David, 340

Jabotinsky, Eri, 112, 132, 141, 152–55,
157, 192, 195, 200
Jabotinsky, Ze'ev: and Begin, 10,
19–21, 23–24, 27–29, 61, 131–32,
154, 182, 259, 279, 286; and Beitar,
10, 12, 14, 15, 16, 18–20, 61, 95; and
Ben Gurion, 14–15, 178; bones
transferred to Israel, 191–93; death
of, 27–28; and establishment of
Jewish state, 20, 258; and Etzel, 18,
19, 49, 95, 182; and Hatzohar,
454n38; ideas of, 12, 152, 154, 178,
188, 212, 244, 258, 263, 290, 299,
416; influence of, 28–29, 47, 57, 93,
94, 97, 101–2, 111, 116, 120, 134,
136, 137, 151, 152, 196, 200, 228,
230, 238, 249, 267, 273, 303, 332,
437, 443; "The Iron Wall," 88, 212,
244, 274–75, 285, 487–88n56; and
Revisionist Zionist Party, 472n39;
terrorism opposed by, 51, 92
Jaffa, Etzel, seizure of, 106, 108–10,
130, 148, 273, 397
Jarring, Gunnar, 220–21
Jerusalem: division of, 148, 149; Etzel
in, 113, 115, 117, 119, 131, 133,
135–36, 137, 144; international
trusteeship over, 104; Jewish right
to rule in, 303, 320–21; King David
Hotel explosion in, 90–92, 226;
military governor of, 135–36; and
peace talks, 299, 302; settlements
in, 210, 251; and Six-Day War, 206,
207, 208, 312
Jerusalem Law, 320–21
Jewish Agency, 115, 132; and Black
Sabbath, 89, 92–93; and British
Mandate, 53–54, 57, 60, 64, 69–71,
84, 98; and emigration to Palestine,
17, 84, 89; and Etzel, 50, 53–54, 58,
61–62, 63–64, 67, 70, 77, 92, 120;
and Haganah, 71, 92–93, 118; and
Jewish Brigade, 57–58, 60; and
U.N. debate, 99, 100, 111
Jewish Brigade, 57–58, 60
Jewish Councils conference, 225
Jewish Defense League, 225
Jewish Legion, 51
Jewish nationalism, 12–13, 18
Jewish Resistance Movement, 84–90,
92–93, 95, 102
Jewish Underground (terrorists), 419
Jews: Ashkenazim, 186, 188, 327, 450;
a country of their own, 103; in
Diaspora, 114, 150, 177, 179, 279,
321, 327, 451; Mizrahim, 134, 159,
160, 186, 188–89, 252–53, 328, 450;
new Jew, 177; persecution of, 4,
5–6, 7, 9, 93, 103, 226; *see also*
Holocaust; Sephardim, 158–59,
160–61, 188, 252–53, 327, 349,
353–54; in transition camps, 84, 89,
98, 156, 158, 160–61
Jibril, Ahmed, 416
Jordan: and Allon Plan, 211; Arab
infiltrators from, 176; Begin's
opposition to, 147; Hashemite
Kingdom of, 146, 274, 291, 399;
and London Agreement, 434;
negotiations with, 144, 280,
290–91, 317; and PLO, 364, 370;
and Six-Day War, 205
Jordan Rift Valley, 211, 251
Judea and Sumaria (West Bank): and
Allon Plan, 211; annexation of,
208–9; and autonomy plan, 211,

Judea and Sumaria (cont.)
317–18; Begin's unchanged position on, 241, 242, 268, 277, 281, 295, 361; Israeli sovereignty over, 243, 256, 290, 298, 308, 447; and Jabotinsky, 290; and Jordan, 211, 280, 290, 399; and Land of Israel, 447; proposed withdrawal from, 223, 275, 360, 399; and settlements, 260, 318, 360; Weizmann's stance on, 251

Kabbalah, 453n4
Kadishai, Yechiel, 54, 296, 337; and Begin's health, 417, 418, 441–42; as Begin's personal assistant, 191, 192, 223–24, 249–50, 261, 264, 268, 299, 301, 310, 409, 418–19, 427; and Begin's resignation, 419–21, 425, 427–29; and Begin's withdrawal, 431, 433, 443, 445–46; and Camp David, 301, 304; and Likud, 237–38; and war in Lebanon, 386, 391–92, 397
Kahan, Yitzhak, 406
Kahan Commission, 410–12, 416, 436
Kahane, Rabbi Meir, 225–26, 228, 239, 371
Kahn, Meir, 40, 43–45, 46, 83, 86, 429
Kamal, Ibrahim, 292, 297, 400
Kashani, Eliezer, 94
Kastner, Israel, 179–80, 181
Kastner Affair, 179–80, 181, 195
Katz, Shmuel, 130, 141, 149, 299; and neighborhood rehabilitation, 501n53; and peace talks, 274, 293–94, 440; and publications, 83, 103, 175; and Sinai, 243, 275
Katzir, Efraim, 268
Katznelson, Kalman, 113, 161, 190
Kazimierz, Prince Alexander, 2
Kelanter, Rachamim, 264
Kessel, Tzippora (Yael), 74, 82, 83
Kimchi, Binyamin, 93
King David Hotel, Jerusalem, explosion, 90–92, 226
Kital, Shalom, 296–97
Klarman, Yosef, 30

Klimovitski, Yona, 224, 261, 315, 417
Knesset: first, 146–51; second, 177, 178; third, 181–82; fourth, 187–89; fifth, 191, 193; sixth, 195; seventh, 213–15, 216–19; Begin's speeches in, 115, 147, 154, 173, 186, 187, 309, 422; function of, 151
Kohl, Helmut, 419
Kollek, Teddy, 71
Konigshofer, Jona (pseud.), 82
Konofnitzka, Maria, 16
Kook, Hillel, 18, 112, 245; and elections, 141, 157; and Hebrew nation vs. Jewish people, 114–15, 132; and Herut, 114, 155, 157, 159, 195, 200; retirement of, 157, 195; and Revisionists, 152
Kook, Rabbi Tzvi Yehudah Hacohen, 270, 309
Kotakhov, Pavel, 383
Krasner, Ephraim, 77
Kremerman, Rachel, 429, 441
Kremerman, Yosef, 244, 429
Kritzan, Max, 163

Labor Party, 147–50, 211, 243, 293, 336, 448
Landau, Chaim, 103, 140, 203, 292; and Begin government, 216–17, 218, 293, 294, 314; and Etzel, 77, 144; and Herut, 144, 194, 238; retirement of, 252, 260; and underground, 74, 77, 91–92, 96
Lankin, Doris, 139
Lankin, Eliyahu, 62–63, 71, 141; and *Altalena*, 118, 122–23, 127–28; and Etzel, 43, 49, 58–59, 64, 118, 120
Lapid, Yosef (Tommy), 331, 338
Lapidot, Yehuda, 355, 405
Lavon, Pinchas, 172, 178
Lavon Affair (Esek Habish), 178–79, 189, 191
Law for Free Education, 326
League of Nations, 116
Lebanon: Beaufort Castle battle, 380, 389; borders with Israel, 330, 365; Christians in, 366–68, 370, 372,

387, 390, 392, 399–407, 410, 413, 418; IAF action over, 342, 371, 372, 383, 390, 396–97; and Kahan Commission, 410–12, 416; negotiations with, 144, 415–16; PLO evacuation from, 395–400, 402; PLO in, 357, 358, 364–77, 379, 384–87, 392, 395, 451; siege of Beirut, 395–99, 438; and Syria, 349, 360, 364, 367–70, 376–84, 386, 388, 399, 400, 402, 413, 415–16, 506n8; war in, 363–407, 415, 427, 430, 437–39, 451

Lehi group: and Bernadotte, 136–37; against the British, 8, 42, 47, 54, 58, 93, 95; and Etzel, 67, 71, 94–95, 102; formation of, 43; and Halochamim, 144; and Jerusalem, 135; and Jewish Resistance Movement, 85–90, 102; Lochamei Herut Israel, 8; militancy of, 57, 62, 69, 81; and Moyne assassination, 67–68; as Stern Group, 63, 68; and War of Independence, 106–7

Leizerovich, Yosef, 73–74

Lenin, V. I., 129

Lev Ami, Shlomo, 44, 45, 49, 440

Levy, David, 325, 420, 423; and Begin government, 314, 356; and elections, 252, 446; and Mizrahim, 238, 252–53; and neighborhood rehabilitation, 326–27, 501n53; and war in Lebanon, 372, 388, 403

Levy, Israel, 91

Levy, Moshe, 389

Lewis, Samuel, 277, 283, 285, 304, 305, 333, 362, 385, 399, 418

Liberal Party, 197, 210, 227, 229, 260; creation of, 190; and elections, 248; and Gahal, 237; and Herut, 193–94, 200, 203, 450; and Land of Israel, 193–94; and Rogers Initiative, 222

Likud: and Arafat, 223; Begin as leader of, 240, 242, 254; and Begin as prime minister, 260–62, 265, 331; and Begin's resignation, 423; and the economy, 322–23; and elections, 143, 241, 248–49, 251–53, 254–55, 256, 260–62, 270, 336, 338, 346, 348, 350–52, 355, 432, 446; formation of, 237–39, 450; and peace treaty, 314; Shamir as leader of, 424–25, 431; and succession, 328

Limor, Micha, 232

Livneh, Eliezer, 58, 111

Livni, Eitan, 81–82, 262, 309; and elections, 252; and Etzel, 52, 54, 77, 78, 99, 195, 225; and Herut, 244; and Saison, 77; and underground, 54, 74, 79

Lloyd, Selwyn, 184

London Agreement, 434

Lotan, David, 42

MacDonald White Paper, 68, 104

MacMichael, Harold, 57

Mafdal, 190, 204, 208, 265, 314, 317, 320, 355

Magnes, Yehuda Leib, 103

Mahapach, *see* Great Reversal

Maki (Israeli Communist Party), 148, 167

Mandela, Nelson, 430

Mapai, 123, 136, 138, 141, 151, 162, 450; and Achdut Haavoda, 193, 213; Ben Gurion as leader of, 179, 186, 191; and the economy, 322; and elections, 143, 144, 145, 156–57, 161, 181, 188–90, 194, 199, 262, 270, 350; and German reparations, 167; and Herut, 133–34, 186; and Kastner Affair, 179, 181; and Labor Party, 293; and Six-Day War, 202, 204, 207–8

Mapam, 115, 116, 136, 167, 179, 181–82

Margalit, Dan, 228, 278

Martin, Clifford, 100

Marzouk, Moshe, 178

Maurois, Andre, 31

Mayski, Ivan, 39

Mazzini, Giuseppe, 28

Meir, Golda, 53, 102, 239, 262; as prime minister, 210, 213, 216–17,

Meir, Golda (cont.)
219, 221, 228, 229, 230, 236–37, 240, 241, 245, 274; and Six-Day War, 204, 207, 209; and Yom Kippur War, 236–37
Meridor, Dan, 180, 432, 440, 443; and Begin government, 372, 376; and Begin's withdrawal, 411, 415, 417, 418, 420, 422, 423, 425, 428–29
Meridor, Eliyahu, 260, 372, 440
Meridor, Yaakov, 43, 71–72, 159; and *Altalena*, 125, 126; and Begin's withdrawal, 420, 429; and elections, 141, 188, 424; resignation of, 220, 260, 431; and succession, 333–34; and war in Lebanon, 375, 407
Merlin, Shmuel, 112, 141, 152, 155, 161
Mitskevich, Adam, 11, 12
Mitterand, François, 342
Mitzna, Amram, 382, 389–90, 405
Mizrachi, Avraham, 94
Mizrachi, Eli, 250
Modai, Yitzhak, 314, 420
Mollet, Guy, 184
Morgenthau, Henry, 4
Morocco, immigrants from, 182–83
Morrison-Grady Plan, 98, 132
Mossad, 230, 270–72
Moyne, Lord, assassination of, 67–69
Mubarak, Hosni, 358–59, 360

Nakdimon, Shlomo, 284–85
Naor, Arie, 261–62, 264, 272, 283, 299, 330, 346, 369, 372
Nasser, Gamal Abdel, 184, 201, 233
National Labor Federation, 14, 193
Navon, Yitzhak, 171, 235, 253, 313, 406
Ne'eman, Yuval, 395
Neighborhood Rehabilitation Project, 326–28, 350, 501n53
Netzer, Shraga, 145
Neumark, Ben Zion, 3

Nevo, Azriel, 356, 386, 414, 423, 432–33
New Economic Reversal, 321–22
New Zionist Organization (NZO), 15, 16, 472n39
Nissim, Moshe, 342, 361, 385, 391, 420
Nixon, Richard M., 220
NKVD, 29, 30, 31
Nobel Peace Prize, 293, 310–11

occupied territories, 208, 215; Af Sha'al (Not an Inch), 447; and autonomy plan, 290–92, 294–95, 298–99, 311; proposed withdrawals from, 221, 242, 274–76, 280–81, 286, 292–94, 296, 298, 300, 303–10, 314, 357, 371–72, 450; settlements in, 210–12, 225, 240, 242–43, 244, 251, 261, 275–76, 295, 313, 315, 318–20, 499–500n21; and Six-Day War, 275–76, 301, 447; and Yom Kippur War, 235–36; *see also specific sites*
Olbrecht, Jan, king of Poland, 2
Olmert, Ehud, 194–95, 196, 309
Olmert, Mordechai, 194, 195, 225
Olympic Games, Munich (1972), 230
Operation Entebbe, 245–47, 393
Operation Kadesh, 184–85
Operation Litani, 365
Operation Moses, 432, 433
Operation Nachshon, 106
Operation Peace for Galilee, 378, 387, 389, 392, 395, 398, 425
Operation Wall, 52–53, 75
Oslo Accords (1993), 211, 447–48

Paget, Sir Bernard, 69
Paglin, Amichai (Gidi), 75–76, 173, 182, 195–96, 198, 270–71, 375; and Acre Prison Break, 99; and *Altalena*, 123–26; and elections, 139, 140, 217; and Etzel, 87, 91, 94, 98, 99, 100, 108–10, 135, 140; and hanged sergeants affair, 100; and Herut, 200, 245; and Jaffa, 108–10;

on turning against Arabs, 104–5, 228–29
Palestine: and Allon Plan, 211; Arab nationalism in, 18, 52, 88; Aswan Declaration, 295; Beitar in, 42; British evacuation of, 98–99; British in, *see* British Mandate; and Entebbe kidnapping, 245–47, 393; Jewish emigration to, 4, 13, 16, 17, 31, 32, 33, 39, 47, 68, 84, 87, 88, 89, 93, 98, 104; and Morrison-Grady Plan, 98; nationalism, 244; partition of, 69, 88, 104, 106, 108, 111, 118, 200, 272–73, 464n89; and peace negotiations, 276, 277, 290, 317, 447; refugees of, 211, 404; self-determination of, 276, 280, 289, 290, 291, 295, 296, 298, 315, 317, 349, 434, 447; and U.N., 88, 98–100, 103–4, 111, 118, 272; and War of Independence, 106–8, 120; Yishuv in, *see* Yishuv
Palestine Liberation Organization, *see* PLO
Palmach, 58, 62, 69–72, 79–80, 98, 106–7, 123, 128, 207, 271, 451
Peace Now movement, 296, 307, 411
Peres, Shimon, 443; and Begin's resignation, 420, 422; and elections, 194, 248, 250, 254–55, 267, 338–39, 349, 350–52, 355, 432; as foreign minister, 434; and Iraq, 342, 343, 344, 345, 346–47, 349; and Lebanon, 378, 393, 402; and peace talks, 281; and Six-Day War, 202, 204
Piłsudski, Józef, 4–5, 7, 12
PLO (Palestine Liberation Organization): and Arafat, 223, 273, 349, 358; establishment of, 488n8; evacuation from Beirut, 395–400, 402; in Lebanon, 357, 358, 364–77, 379, 384–87, 392, 395, 451; and peace talks, 280, 369, 447; and Syria, 364–77; terrorist attacks by, 277, 337, 357, 364–65, 368, 375

Poland: Anders Army of, 6, 39–42; anti-Semitism in, 4, 5–6, 7, 9, 93; Begin family in, 2–3, 4–5, 6–7, 9, 337; Begin's escape from, 25–27, 30; Begin's parents murdered in, 5–6; and World War II, 25
Polish national movement, 11–12, 13, 28
Poniatowski, Stanislaus, king of Poland, 2
Poran, Efraim, 283, 356
Porat, Chanan, 56, 208
Porat, Uri, 345
Porush, Menachem, 172, 265–66
Propes, Aaron, 15, 20–21, 36

Raanan, Mordechai, 106–8, 245
Rabin, Yitzhak: and *Altalena* affair, 128; and Dollar Account Affair, 250; and elections, 248, 251, 254, 339, 447; and Iraq, 339, 442; and Lebanon, 378–79, 393, 396; as prime minister, 241, 242, 245, 248, 256, 281, 367, 443; and settlements, 318; and Six-Day War, 201, 202, 204–5
Rafi party, 191, 194, 195, 201, 204, 213, 238, 264
Ramba, Isaac, 15, 16
Ratosh, Jonathan, 18
Ravid, Eliyahu, 72
Ravid, Miryam, 72
Raziel, David, 18, 29, 42, 67, 137, 262
Raziel-Naor, Esther, 141, 150–51, 196, 260, 262, 429
Reagan, Ronald, 342; Begin's meetings with, 357–58, 373, 387–88; and Begin's withdrawal, 415, 418, 421; and Lebanon, 373, 379, 383–84, 388, 391, 396, 400, 415, 439; and peace plan, 399–400, 401–2, 408; and U.S.–Israeli relations, 345–47, 368, 387
Recanati, Avraham, 141
Reshima Mamlachtit, 213, 237
Revisionist movement, 14, 17, 18–19, 28; and Arlosoroff murder, 332–33;

Revisionist movement (cont.)
  taking Begin to Israel, 40; underground, 49
Revisionist Party, 258; and elections, 134, 135, 162; and Etzel, 63, 64, 79, 116, 134; and first government, 108; and Herut, 113, 116, 132, 134, 135, 152, 159, 450; and Labor Party, 147–50, 193; returning to its roots, 250
Revisionist Zionist Party, 63, 116, 135, 472n39
"revolution" (1977), 215
Rhodes Armistice Agreement (1949), 146
Ribbentrop-Molotov Agreement, 235
Rimalt, Elimelech, 227, 248
Rogers, William, 220
Rogers Initiative, 220–22, 307
Rom, Yosef, 308
Romania, peace talks in, 280–81
Roosevelt, Franklin D., 47, 434
Rosen, Pinchas, 155
Rosenbaum, Shimshon, 199
Rosenblatt, Tzvi, 332
Rosenblum, Doron, 242
Rosenfeld, Shalom, 16, 52
Rubin, Yaakov, 167
Rubinstein, Amnon, 337
Rubinstein, Dov, 45

Sabras, 243, 271
Sadat, Anwar, 233, 326, 434; and Arab League, 310; assassination of, 358–60; and Camp David, 299–307, 308, 311–12; and Iraq, 344, 346, 349; and Nobel Prize, 310–11; and peace talks, 61, 278, 281, 288–89, 291–92, 295; and U.S., 291, 295; visit to Israel, 284–89, 292, 296, 440
Sadeh, Yitzhak, 79
Sagi, Yehoshua, 367, 381
Saison, 8, 70–80, 86, 93, 102–3, 110, 186, 360, 449
Samama, Dan, 244

Samet, Shimon, 181
Sandstroem, Emil, 100
Sapir, Pinchas, 212, 240
Sapir, Yosef, 193, 204, 211, 227
Sarid, Yossi, 253, 389, 443
Sarkis, Elias, 367, 385, 387–88
Sasover, Israel (pseud.), 54, 74
Sasson, Moshe, 346, 359
Schechter, Yaakov, 35
Scheinermann, Mordechai, 3
Schiff, Ze'ev, 352, 404
Schindler, Alexander, 279
Schmidt, Helmut, 337
Schwartzberg, Arie, 79
Sea-to-Sea Canal Project, 282
Second Reversal, 447
Serlin, Yosef, 171
Shabak (secret service), 270–71
Shach, Rabbi Eliezer Menachem, 266
Shahal, Moshe, 253
Shalom, Avraham, 374
Shaltiel, David, 107–8, 136
Shamgar, Meir, 141
Shamir, Moshe, 208, 309, 314
Shamir, Yitzhak, 11, 43, 95, 309; and Begin's government, 264, 320, 329, 356; and Begin's resignation, 420, 422, 423; and Begin's withdrawal, 410, 417; and Bernadotte murder, 137; and elections, 251, 252, 431, 446; and Iraq, 343; and Lebanon, 401, 404, 416; and Lehi, 42, 67, 137; and Likud, 424–25, 431; as prime minister, 431, 433
Shapira, Avraham, 417
Shapira, Chaim Moshe, 208
Shapira, Yaakov Shimshon, 206, 219
Sharett, Moshe, 77, 339, 367; and British Mandate, 89, 93; and elections, 182; and Etzel, 136, 144; and German reparations, 170, 174; and Jewish Agency, 70, 89; and Lavon Affair, 178–79; as prime minister, 177, 178–79, 364; and war in Lebanon, 364
Sharon, Ariel (Arik), 176, 218, 242, 301, 359, 450; and Begin's govern-

ment, 260, 261, 267, 274, 328, 329, 356–57; and Begin's retirement, 421, 422, 436–40; and elections, 248–49, 256, 260, 351, 446; and Iraq, 340, 343; and Lebanon, 367, 369–71, 372–74, 375–77, 379–92, 394–97, 400–405, 407, 411–12, 418, 437–39, 513n19; and Liberal Party, 237–39, 436; as minister without portfolio, 412; and Palestine, 290; and settlements, 282, 295, 299, 305–6, 308, 315, 318–19, 328, 338, 499n21; and Syria, 376–84; and Yom Kippur War, 234–35, 260, 354
Sheskin, Miron, 40
Shilansky, Dov, 309
Shin Bet, 137, 149–50, 158, 186, 219, 270
Shlomtzion party, 249, 256
Shmuelevitz, Matityahu, 355, 420
Shomer Hatzair, 9–10
Shostak, Eliezer, 158, 335, 420–21
Shultz, George, 388, 401, 415
Sikorski, Władysław, 39
Sinai Peninsula: cease-fire in, 220–21; demilitarization of, 309; Israeli control of, 185, 207, 256, 398; Israeli evacuation of, 360; not part of Land of Israel, 212, 275, 289, 293, 307; proposed withdrawal from, 212, 243, 251, 276, 281, 282, 288–90, 292, 293, 303, 306–9, 314, 317, 356–57; return to Egypt (1978), 200, 241, 286; settlements in, 210, 356, 357
Six-Day War, 201–7, 210, 241, 273, 312, 398, 440, 444–45; after the battles, 207–9, 214, 215, 225, 254; and occupied territories, 275–76, 301, 447; Waiting Period, 198, 201, 202–4, 207, 450
Sneh, Moshe, 25, 50, 58–66, 74, 77–78, 79, 85–86, 87, 89–91, 115, 186
Soloveitchik, Rabbi Chaim, 3, 4, 279
Soviet Union, 104, 116; Begin's imprisonment in, 30–38; and Cold War, 135, 151, 255, 281, 341, 358;

collapse of, 63, 84; and Iraq, 344; Jews emigrating from, 212, 271, 443; and PLO, 373; and Syria, 383
SS *Exodus*, 103
Stalin, Joseph, 84
Stavsky, Avraham, 120, 133, 332
Stern, Avraham (Yair), 18, 29, 43, 67, 71, 138, 456n85
Stern Group (Lehi), 63, 68
Straits of Tiran, 184, 185, 201
Suditi, Eliezer, 172
Suez Canal, 215, 233–34, 309
Sukenik, Eleazar, 30
Syria: Arab infiltrators from, 176; and Lebanon, 349, 360, 364, 367–70, 376–84, 386, 388, 399, 400, 402, 413, 415–16, 506n8; negotiations with, 144, 281; and PLO, 364–77; and Six-Day War, 201–2, 205; and Yom Kippur War, 233–37

Tabin, Eli, 232
Tabin, Miryam, 55
Tabin, Yaakov, 55, 58–59, 72
Tahori, David, 128
Tal, Israel, 413
Tamir, Avraham (Avrasha), 301, 312
Tamir, Shmuel, 141–42, 155, 179, 195–96, 198, 199–200, 228, 231, 238, 284
Tehomi, Avraham, 17–19
Telem party, 355, 395
Tevet, Shabtai, 248, 332
Tohami, Hassan, 281, 282, 305
Topaz, Dudu, 352–54
Transjordan, 274, 290
Truman, Harry S., 84, 99, 142
Trumpeldor, Yosef, 9–10
Tsipori, Mordechai, 330, 356, 367, 370, 376, 377–78, 388, 404, 407, 420
Tubi, Tufik, 381
Tzvi, Shabtai, 430

United Nations (U.N.): and Bernadotte assassination, 137; and Iraq, 345; and Israel, 121, 151, 185, 211,

United Nations (U.N.) (cont.)
221, 275, 345, 362, 379; and Jerusalem, 321; and Jewish state, 103; and Lebanon, 365, 379; and Palestine, 88, 98–100, 103–4, 111, 118, 272, 464n89; Resolution 242, 221, 222, 274–75, 277, 307; and Rogers Initiative, 220–21; and War of Independence, 121–22

United States: and Begin, 142, 177, 255, 276–79, 290–91, 296–97, 307, 322, 328, 357–58, 408–9, 418; and Cold War, 135, 151, 255; and establishment of Israel, 104; and Iraq, 341, 345–46; and Lebanon, 372–74, 399–400; and Middle East, 61, 295, 311–12; relations with, 116, 135, 292, 293, 345–47, 362, 368, 387–88, 401–2, 418

Vance, Cyrus, 297, 299, 301
Vilna, Lithuania: Begin's escape to, 25–27; Begin's interrogations in, 31–35; NKVD in, 29–30

War of Attrition, 221, 398
War of Independence, 52, 88, 106–10, 111, 120–22, 124, 138, 144, 157, 363, 398
Wax, Luca and Israel, 59, 62
Weinberger, Caspar, 373–74
Weizmann, Chaim, 60, 68, 89–90, 238, 254, 258, 454n38
Weizmann, Ezer, 287, 316, 355; and Begin government, 261, 267, 268, 280, 282, 290, 299, 320; conflicts with Begin, 220, 227–28, 230–31, 232, 237, 249, 252, 328–29, 359; and elections, 248, 251–52, 254, 257, 261, 348; and fighter planes, 320; and Gahal, 217–18, 222, 224–25, 227, 229, 237; and Iraq, 345; and Likud, 237, 238, 239, 249, 251–52, 450; and peace talks, 291, 301, 304, 305–6, 315; political ambition of, 229, 231, 249, 328, 502n60; resignation of, 242, 328–29;

502n60; and settlements, 295, 318–19, 320, 328, 499–500n21
West Bank, see Judea and Sumaria
White Paper, 67–68, 104
Witold, prince of Lithuania, 2
World Jewish Federation, 177–78
World War II, 5–6, 18; end of, 47, 60, 84; onset of, 25
World Zionist Organization (WZO), 10, 60, 119, 454–55n38

Yadin, Yigael, 30; and Begin government, 267, 284, 299, 320; and Dash, 248, 261, 284; and Iraq, 340, 341, 346; and neighborhood rehabilitation, 326–27, 501n53; and settlements, 290, 320; and war in Lebanon, 367
Yarmuk Army, 110
Yaron, Amos, 403, 406
Yavin, Chaim, 256, 257
Yellin Mor, Natan, 25, 36, 42, 68, 72, 85, 90, 95, 137, 353
Yemenite Association, 188
Yishuv, 46, 49, 134, 160, 179–80; and British Mandate, 47, 52, 57, 60–61, 65–66, 84, 95, 105; and establishment of the State of Israel, 111; and Etzel, 52, 53, 57–58, 61, 63, 65, 66, 68, 70, 71, 96, 101–2, 108; and hanged sergeants affair, 101; and Holocaust, 65, 103; and Jaffa, 108–10; and Jewish Agency, 57–58, 60, 89, 100; and Jewish refugees, 84, 89, 103; and Jewish Resistance Movement, 89, 93; and Palmach, 70, 71–72; and rebellion declared, 50–52, 75; and Saison, 71–73, 75, 77, 93; and underground, 57–63, 73, 77, 95–96
Yom Kippur War, 233–37, 260, 287, 354, 398; and Agranot Commission, 241; and elections, 238, 240, 257; failures of, 215, 241, 246, 248, 251, 257, 263; losses in, 236, 264; and revolution (1977), 215
Yoram, Shraga, 196

544
INDEX

Yosef, Dov, 186
Yosefovich, Michael, 2
Yotan, David, 21, 51, 197
Yunichman, Shimshon, 26–27, 30

Zak, Moshe, 40, 223
Zamir, Yitzhak, 332–33, 372
Zemer, Hannah, 264
Zionism: Acting Zionist Committee, 119; Arabs vs., 88, 276; and Begin family, 1–2, 3, 4, 9, 96, 102, 153; and Begin's rhetoric, 11, 13, 19, 51, 159; General Zionists, 85, 103, 136, 157, 158, 161, 167, 175, 181–82, 186, 190, 193; and Hamaarach, 193, 265; and Holocaust, 62, 451; idealism of, 368; and Jabotinsky, 10, 14, 15, 19, 28, 258; and Jewish refugees, 89; and Kastner Affair, 179; and Moyne assassination, 68; and nationalism, 9, 114–15, 258; NZO, 15, 16, 472n39; and occupied territories, 275, 450; post-Zionists, 115; practical vs. political, 19, 135–36; and Revisionists, 14, 28; Revisionist Zionist Party, 63, 116, 135, 472n39; and settlements, 318; and underground, 70, 89; WZO, 10, 60, 119, 454–55n38
Zionist Federation, 90

Lightning Source UK Ltd.
Milton Keynes UK
UKHW010200070223
416581UK00003B/108

9 780300 162356